THE PAPERS OF
BENJAMIN FRANKLIN

SPONSORED BY

*The American Philosophical Society
and Yale University*

Governor John Penn

THE PAPERS OF

Benjamin Franklin

VOLUME 11   *January 1 through December 31, 1764*

LEONARD W. LABAREE, *Editor*

Helen C. Boatfield and James H. Hutson, Assistant Editors

New Haven and London YALE UNIVERSITY PRESS, 1967

Designed by Alvin Eisenman and Walter Howe,
and printed in the United States of America
at The Lakeside Press,
R. R. Donnelley & Sons Company, Chicago, Illinois,
and Crawfordsville, Indiana.

Library of Congress catalogue number: 59—12697

Editor's Note

Helene H. Fineman, Assistant Editor, who had been a member of the editorial staff since 1956, resigned in 1966. The editor records his grateful appreciation of Mrs. Fineman's many and varied contributions to this undertaking during the ten years of her association with it.

L.W.L.

Henry R. Luce: In Memoriam

More than any other single individual, Henry R. Luce was responsible for making financially possible this edition of *The Papers of Benjamin Franklin*. On March 2, 1953, the late President A. Whitney Griswold of Yale University presented to Mr. Luce his hopes and those of colleagues and friends that funds might be procured to undertake the preparation of a comprehensive edition of Franklin's papers. Showing the quick imaginative grasp that was one of his outstanding characteristics, Mr. Luce expressed his warm interest in the proposal, and, after consulting his associates, he arranged that Time, Incorporated, should pledge to Yale, on behalf of *Life* Magazine, a gift of $400,000. With this support assured, President Griswold approached the late Justice Owen J. Roberts, President of the American Philosophical Society, which owns more than half of all surviving Franklin manuscripts, to suggest joint sponsorship of the project. An agreement soon followed, the Society pledging additional funds, and editorial work began in 1954. Mr. Luce maintained a continuing interest as the edition progressed; in 1964 he attended a luncheon given by the Yale University Press to celebrate both the tenth anniversary of the beginning of operations and the publication of a new edition of Franklin's *Autobiography*. In response to an invitation, Mr. Luce addressed the gathering briefly, speaking modestly but with obvious satisfaction about the part he had played in the launching of the enterprise.

Those of us who, like the writer of these words, knew Henry Luce when he was a boy, freshly arrived in America from his missionary home in China, recognized even then his keen and inquiring mind, the originality of his thought, and the broad range of his interests. In his later creative and distinguished career he more than fulfilled that early promise. The sponsors and editors of *The Papers of Benjamin Franklin* record here their gratitude for his support and encouragement and express their continued pride in his association with this undertaking.

LEONARD W. LABAREE

Contents

Henry R. Luce: In Memoriam   *vii*
List of Illustrations   *xv*
Contributors to Volume 11   *xix*
Method of Textual Reproduction   *xx*
Abbreviations and Short Titles   *xxiv*
Chronology   *xxviii*

1764

Post Office Commissions to Abraham Hunt, January 10
    (and October 13, 1775)   3
To Francis Bernard, January 11   6
Argument for Making the Bills of Credit Bear Interest,
    [January 13-14?]   7
To Richard Jackson, January 16   19
To Anthony Todd, January 16   20
From James Bowdoin, January 18   21
Pennsylvania Assembly: Reply to the Governor, January 20   22
From Francis Bernard, January 23   31
From Solomon Williams, January 25   32
From Richard Jackson, January 26   33
The Postmasters General to the Lords of the Treasury:
    Memorandum on the American Postal Service, January 28   36
A Narrative of the Late Massacres, [January 30?]   42
Pennsylvania Assembly: Reply to the Governor, February 11   69
To Richard Jackson, February 11   76
From Francis Bernard, February 13   78
To Catharine Greene, February 15   79
Pennsylvania Assembly Committee: Report, February 21   80
To Francis Bernard, February 21   87
To Jonathan Williams, February 24   88
From Francis Bernard, March 1   91
Pennsylvania Assembly Committee: Report, March 6   91

From George Price, March 7 93
To Richard Jackson, March 8 95
To John Canton, March 14 97
To John Fothergill, March 14 101
To Richard Jackson, March 14 105
To Mary Stevenson, March 14 110
Pennsylvania Assembly: Message to the Governor, March 22 111
Pennsylvania Assembly: Reply to the Governor, March 24 116
Pennsylvania Assembly: Resolves upon the Present Circum-
    stances, [March 24] 123
To Francis Bernard, March 28 133
Explanatory Remarks on the Assembly's Resolves,
    [March 29] 134
Petition of the Pennsylvania Freeholders and Inhabitants to
    the King, [March 29] 145
To Richard Jackson, March 29 148
To William Strahan, March 30 149
To Richard Jackson, March 31 150
From Francis Bernard, April 9 153
Cool Thoughts on the Present Situation of Our Public
    Affairs, April 12 153
To [Peter Collinson?], April 12 173
From Richard Jackson, [April 13] 175
To Francis Bernard, April 21 178
To Jonathan Williams, April 21 178
Smith, Wright & Gray Account Book, 1764–1774, [April 24] 179
To Peter Collinson, April 30 180
A Letter from a Gentleman in Crusoe's Island, [April?] 184
To Richard Jackson, May 1 185
To William Strahan, May 1 188
To Mary Stevenson, May 4 190
From Thomas Moffatt, May 12 191
Pennsylvania Assembly: Petition to the King, [May 23–26] 193
To Jonathan Williams, May 24 201
From Mary Stevenson, May 24 201
Pennsylvania Assembly: Reply to the Governor, [May 26] 203

Pennsylvania Assembly: Reply to the Governor, May 30 206
To Richard Jackson, June 1 214
Provincial Commissioners: Orders for Payment,
 June 4–October 20 221
Henry Bouquet to John Penn and the Provincial
 Commissioners, June 4 224
To Anthony Stickney, June 16 227
To William Strahan, June 17 228
To Richard Jackson, June 18 229
To Ezra Stiles, June 19 230
To George Whitefield, June 19 231
To John Ellicott, June 23 232
To Richard Jackson, June 25 234
To William Strahan, June 25 240
From Massachusetts House of Representatives Committee,
 June 25 242
From John Canton, June 29 244
From James Bowdoin, July 2 246
Edward Shippen to Benjamin Franklin and John Foxcroft,
 July 2 247
Post Office Accounts, [July 9] 248
Benjamin Franklin and John Foxcroft: Commission to
 James Parker, July 10 251
To Jane Mecom, July 10 253
To John Winthrop, July 10 254
To Richard Jackson, July 12 255
From John Mills, July 12 257
From James Habersham, July 14 259
Minutes of the Provincial Commissioners, July 20 260
To Jane Mecom, July 24 262
From ————, August 8 262
To Richard Jackson, August 9 263
From Thomas Becket, August 10 264
From Henry Bouquet, August 10 266
Preface to Joseph Galloway's Speech, [August 11] 267
From Richard Jackson, August 11 311

Philadelphia Linen Manufactory: Stock Certificate for Charles
    Thomson, August 13   314
To Henry Bouquet, August 16   316
James Pearson and Benjamin Franklin: Agreement for Sale,
    August 18   319
From Henry Bouquet (I), August 22   321
From Henry Bouquet (II), August 22   323
From Henry Bouquet, August 27   326
To Richard Jackson, September 1   326
To William Strahan, September 1   331
To [Peter Templeman], September 2   334
To Anthony Todd, September 2   335
Benjamin Franklin and John Foxcroft: Power of Attorney to
    Tuthill Hubbart, September 17   337
To Richard Jackson, September 20   339
Benjamin Franklin and John Foxcroft to Anthony Todd,
    September 21   341
Pennsylvania Assembly: Instructions to Richard Jackson,
    September 22   347
To Peter Collinson, September 24   352
To William Strahan, September 24   353
From Thomas Moffatt, September 24   356
To Richard Jackson, September 25   357
To the Freemen of Pennsylvania, September 28   360
To the Massachusetts House of Representatives Committee,
    September 28   365
To Henry Bouquet, September 30   366
Papers from the Election Campaign, [September]   369
Election Results in Philadelphia County, 1764, [October 1-3]   390
From Rhode Island Assembly Committee, [October 8]   395
To Richard Jackson, October 11   397
Outgoing Philadelphia Mail, 1764–1767, October 18   398
Inhabitants of Philadelphia: Remonstrance against the
    Appointment of Benjamin Franklin as Agent, [October 26]   402
Pennsylvania Assembly: Resolutions on the Appointment of
    Benjamin Franklin as Agent, [October 26]   407

John Dickinson and Others: Protest against the Appointment
   of Benjamin Franklin as Agent, October 26   408
From James Parker, October 27   413
From Lewis Jones, October 30   418
William Dunlap to Benjamin Franklin and John Foxcroft,
   [October?]   418
From William Dunlap, [October?]   420
Benjamin Franklin and John Foxcroft to William Dunlap,
   [October?]   421
From Pennsylvania Assembly Committee of Correspondence,
   November 1   422
Pennsylvania Assembly Committee of Correspondence to
   Richard Jackson, November 1   423
From John Smith, November 2   426
To Jonathan Williams, November 3   426
From Baynton and Wharton, November 3   427
To John Smith, November 4   429
Remarks on a Late Protest, November 5   429
Power of Attorney to James Parker, November 5   441
From Samuel Eckerling, November 5   443
From Edmund Quincy, Junior, November 5   444
To Anthony Todd, November 6   445
From Benjamin Humphreys: Bill and Receipt, November 6   446
To Richard Jackson, November 7   446
To Sarah Franklin, November 8   447
To Thomas Wharton, November 9   451
From James Bowdoin, November 12   451
Samuel Rhoads, Junior: Account Book, November 13   453
From Thomas Wharton, November 13   456
From Martin Howard, November 16   459
From Jonathan Williams, November 17   461
From Richard Jackson, November 18   462
From Joseph Galloway, November 23   465
From James Parker, November 23   469
From Samuel Wharton, November 23   471
From Samuel Johnson, [November?]   477

From Thomas Osborne, November 478
From Alexander Small, December 1 479
From Thomas Wharton, December 4 483
William Smith: An Answer to Mr. Franklin's Remarks,
    [December 7] 486
To Deborah Franklin, December 9 516
Journal, 1764–1776; Ledger, 1764–1776, December 10 518
To Mary Stevenson, [December 12–16] 521
From Charles Thomson, December 18 521
From Hannah Walker, December 18 524
From Samuel Wharton, December 19 525
From David Hall, December 20 529
From John Ross, December 20 531
From [Springett Penn], December 22 532
From Anthony Todd, December 24 534
To Deborah Franklin, December 27 534
Table of Revised Postal Rates, [1764] 535
To [Grey Cooper], [1764?–1775] 537
To Peter Franklin, [before 1765] 538
From Peter Collinson, [1764–1765] 543
From John Greenwood, [1764–1775] 544
From Alexander Small, [c.1764] 544

Index 547

List of Illustrations

Governor John Penn by Robert Edge Pine   *Frontispiece*

Oil painting by Robert Edge Pine (1730–1788). One of a family of
artists, Pine enjoyed a moderately successful career in England, chiefly
as a portrait painter, until he moved to Philadelphia in 1784. Although
he planned a series of historical paintings in America, he never carried
it through but again devoted himself mostly to portraiture. Among
his subjects were many of the leading figures of the American Revolution, including Franklin. *DAB, DNB*. Pine painted this portrait of John
Penn, proprietary lieutenant governor of Pennsylvania, 1763–71,
1773–76, in 1787, and Penn presented it, Dec. 18, 1787, to Edmund
Physick (1727–1804) in appreciation of his "probity and attachment"
to the Penn family. Physick had been agent for Thomas Penn and later
keeper of the great seal and receiver general. Surviving with the painting are Penn's autograph letter making the gift and Physick's grateful
response. The portrait is reproduced by courtesy of a private collector.

Post Office Commissions to Abraham Hunt   4

Acting at different times and under very different authorities, Franklin
signed these two commissions appointing Abraham Hunt postmaster
of Trenton, New Jersey. On the date of the first commission, January
10, 1764, he and John Foxcroft were joint deputy postmasters general
of North America under King George III; at the time of the second,
October 13, 1775, the United Colonies were in revolt against King
George, although they had not yet declared their independence, and
Franklin was postmaster general under appointment of the Continental
Congress. Reproduced by courtesy of the owner of the originals,
Theodore Sheldon, Chicago, Illinois.

A Micrometer for a Telescope   23

James Bowdoin of Boston sought Franklin's help in having a pedestal
and micrometer attached to his telescope by Edward Nairne, a London
instrument maker, under the supervision of Franklin's friend, John
Canton. To his letterbook copy of a letter on the subject, Bowdoin
appended this sketch of the attachment as he planned it. Canton reported later that Nairne was making a pedestal which would be an
"Improvement" on what Bowdoin had proposed, but that fitting the
micrometer would be "impracticable." Reproduced by courtesy of the
Massachusetts Historical Society.

Title Page of *A Narrative of the Late Massacres*   45

At a time when white settlers in the frontier areas of Pennsylvania were enraged by the depredations of hostile Indians and had retaliated violently upon a small and friendly group, Franklin addressed this pamphlet to the consciences and human sympathies of his fellow colonists in the hope of preventing further acts of vengeance on other Indians who had sought refuge and protection in Philadelphia. Reproduced by courtesy of the Yale University Library.

The March of the Paxton Men   70

The controversies in Pennsylvania during 1764 produced several widely circulated cartoons in which leading figures were caricatured. None of the artists—if that is the correct word—has been identified. What may be the earliest of the series was inspired by the march of the frontiersmen on Philadelphia, intent on dispatching the Indians sheltered there, and by the mobilization of citizens for the defense. A panel at the left depicts Israel Pemberton ("King Wampum"), friend of the Indians and hence detested by frontiersmen, and a squaw. According to current hostile rumor, she had rewarded his too friendly advances by stealing the watch from his pocket. In the center Joseph Fox, Quaker political leader and barrack master, is easily identifiable, while in the background are a squad of British soldiers and a group of armed men in Quaker hats emerging from the Meeting House (the "new Barrack") where, in fact, they had merely taken shelter from a shower. At the right Franklin cheers on his supporters while wearing dark glasses, presumably to shield from his eyes the light of truth. Below each segment of the cartoon are couplets appropriate to the caricature above. Reproduced by courtesy of the Library Company of Philadelphia.

Title Page of *Cool Thoughts*   155

After the Assembly had adjourned in March 1764 in order that its members might "consult their Constituents" about petitioning the King to take over the government of Pennsylvania, Franklin published this pamphlet in April to win support for the proposal. Opponents complained that this piece and another by Joseph Galloway "were distributed gratis by thousands" in Pennsylvania. Reproduced by courtesy of the Yale University Library.

Title Page of *The Speech of Joseph Galloway*   269

The climax of the Assembly debate on a proposal to seek royal government for Pennsylvania took place on May 24, 1764, when John Dickinson took the floor to attack the petition and Joseph Galloway followed him in its defense. When Dickinson's speech, with a long preface by William Smith, was published about a month later, Galloway put his reply into form for publication and Franklin contributed an even longer preface aimed primarily at the one Smith had written for Dickinson. The pamphlet by Galloway and Franklin appeared on August 11. Reproduced by courtesy of the American Philosophical Society.

Franklin and the Quakers   374

At the left of this cartoon the Quaker merchant Abel James is distributing tomahawks to a band of Indians from a barrel marked with the initials of Israel Pemberton. In the center a group of Quakers, with Joseph Fox at the left, express their fears over the rise of the "Paxton spirit" and the prospects of success of the "wicked Presbyterians." In the foreground Franklin eyes his Quaker friends, one hand clutching a bag containing the "Pensilvania Money" his mission to England had brought him, the other holding a letter to his influential scientific friend John Pringle. He is expressing his hope of becoming governor if the Crown takes over the colony. On the right Israel Pemberton and the Indian squaw appear in much the same postures as in the cartoon of the Paxton march. Reproduced by courtesy of the Historical Society of Pennsylvania.

William Smith, D.D.   486

Engraved by John Sartain (1808–1897) after the oil portrait by Benjamin West (1738–1820). Sartain's notation of Smith's age on the engraving, "Aet. 30," indicates that West painted the portrait about 1757. It is said to have been in some degree inspired by a painting of St. Ignatius by Murillo found on board a Spanish prize. Horace Wemyss Smith, *Life and Correspondence of the Rev. William Smith, D.D.* (Phil., 1880), I, 595. The original oil was presented to the Historical Society of Pennsylvania in 1870, but is no longer in a condition suitable for reproduction. John Sartain served his apprenticeship as an engraver in London and migrated to Philadelphia in 1830. Here he practiced his craft, "introduced pictorial illustration as a distinctive feature of American periodicals," and was himself proprietor and editor of a succession of noteworthy but unprofitable magazines. His general work as an engraver included some 1500 plates and won him distinction and honors both at home and abroad. *DAB.* He appears to have made this engraving about 1879. Reproduced by courtesy of the Historical Society of Pennsylvania.

Excerpts from Handel's "Judas Maccabeus"   540–2

Since the original manuscript of Franklin's letter to his brother Peter containing these brief passages is now lost, they are reproduced in facsimile from the text of the letter printed in *Experiments and Observations on Electricity,* 1769 edition, pp. 475–7, by courtesy of the Yale University Library.

Contributors to Volume 11

The ownership of each manuscript, or the location of the particular copy used by the editors of each contemporary pamphlet or similar printed work, is indicated where the document appears in the text. The sponsors and editors are deeply grateful to the following institutions and individuals for permission to print in the present volume manuscripts or other materials which they own:

INSTITUTIONS

American Philosophical Society
British Museum
Bureau of Land Records,
    Department of Internal Affairs,
    Harrisburg, Pennsylvania
Columbia University Library
General Post Office, London
Georgia Historical Society
Harvard College Library
Historical Society of
    Pennsylvania
Lehigh University Library
Library Company of
    Philadelphia
Library of Congress
The London Hospital

Lyme Historical Society—
    Florence Griswold Association,
    Inc., Old Lyme, Connecticut
Massachusetts Historical Society
New Hampshire Historical
    Society
New York Public Library
University of Pennsylvania
    Library
Pierpont Morgan Library
Princeton University Library
Public Record Office
The Royal Society
The Royal Society of Arts
Yale University Library

INDIVIDUALS

Richard B. Duane, Locust,
    New Jersey
Charles E. Feinberg, Detroit,
    Michigan
Frank Glenn, Kansas City,
    Missouri
The Hyde Collection, Mrs.
    Donald F. Hyde, Somerville,
    New Jersey

T. W. Schreiner, New York City
Theodore Sheldon, Chicago,
    Illinois
Drayton M. Smith, Philadelphia,
    Pennsylvania
Justin G. Turner, Los Angeles,
    California

Method of Textual Reproduction

An extended statement of the principles of selection, arrangement, form of presentation, and method of textual reproduction observed in this edition appears in the Introduction to the first volume, pp. xxxiv-xlvii. A condensation and revision of the portion relating to the method of reproducing the texts follows here.

Printed Material:

In general Franklin's writings printed under his direction should be regarded as his ultimate intention and should therefore be reproduced without change, except as modern typography requires. In fact, however, newspapers and pamphlets were often set by two or more journeymen with different notions of spelling, capitalization, and punctuation. Although the resulting inconsistencies and errors did not represent Franklin's intentions, they are not eliminated by the editors. Again, in cases where Franklin's writings were printed by another, they were sometimes carelessly or willfully revised without his consent. He once complained, for example, that an English printer had so corrected and excised one of his papers "that it can neither scratch nor bite. It seems only to paw and mumble."[1] What was thus printed was obviously not what Franklin wrote, but, in the absence of his manuscript, the editors have no alternative but to reprint it as it stands. Still other Franklin letters are known only in nineteenth-century printings, vigorously edited by William Temple Franklin, Duane, or Sparks. Here, too, the editors follow the texts as printed, only noting obvious misreadings.

In reproducing printed materials, the following general rules are observed:

1. The place and date of composition of letters are set at the top, regardless of their location in the original printing.

2. Proper nouns, including personal names, which were often printed in italics, are set in roman, except when the original was italicized for emphasis.

1. BF to William Franklin, Jan. 9, 1768.

3. Prefaces and other long passages, though italicized in the original, are set in roman. Long italicized quotations are set in roman within quotation marks.

4. Words in full capitals are set in small capitals, with initial letters in full capitals if required by Franklin's normal usage.

5. All signatures are set in capitals and small capitals.

6. Obvious typographical errors are silently corrected. An omitted parenthesis or quotation mark, for example, is inserted when the other of the pair was printed.

7. Every sentence is closed with a period or other appropriate mark of punctuation (usually a question mark).

8. Longhand insertions in the blanks of printed forms are set in italics, with space before and after.

Manuscript Material:

a. *Letters* are presented in the following form:

1. The place and date of composition are set at the top, regardless of their location in the original.

2. The complimentary close is set continuously with the text.

3. Addresses, endorsements, and docketing are so labeled and printed at the end of the letter.

b. *Spelling* of the original is retained. When, however, it is so abnormal as to obscure meaning, the correct form is supplied in brackets or footnote, as: "yf[wife]."

c. *Capitalization* has been retained as written, except that every sentence is made to begin with a capital. When there is doubt whether a letter is a capital, it is printed as like letters are in the same manuscript, or, that guide failing, as modern usage directs.

d. Words underlined once in the manuscript are printed in *italics;* words underlined twice or written in large letters or full capitals are printed in SMALL CAPITALS.

e. *Punctuation* has been retained as in the original, except:

1. Every sentence ends with a period or other appropriate mark (usually a question mark), unless it is not clear where the sentence ends, when the original punctuation (or lack of it) is preserved.

2. Dashes used in place of commas, semicolons, colons, or periods are replaced by the appropriate marks; and when a sentence ends with both a dash and a period, the dash is omitted.

3. Commas scattered meaninglessly through a manuscript are eliminated.

4. When a mark of punctuation is not clear or can be read as one of two marks, modern usage is followed.[2]

5. Some documents, especially those of a legal character, lack all punctuation. This is supplied with restraint, and the fact indicated in a footnote. In some other, inadequately punctuated documents, it is silently added when needed for clarity, as in a long series of names.

f. *Contractions and abbreviations* in general are expanded except in proper names. The ampersand is rendered as "and," except in the names of business firms, in the form "&c.," and in a few other cases. Letters represented by the thorn or tilde are printed. The tailed "p" is spelled out as per, pre, or pro. Symbols of weights, measures, and monetary values follow modern usage, as: £34. Superscript letters are lowered. Abbreviations in current use are retained, as: Col., Dr., N.Y., i.e.

g. *Omitted or illegible words or letters* are treated as follows:

1. If not more than four letters are missing, they are silently supplied when there is no doubt what they should be.

2. The omission of more than four letters or one or more words is supplied conjecturally within brackets. The addition of a question mark within the brackets indicates uncertainty as to the conjecture.

3. Other omissions are shown as follows: [*illegible*], [*torn*], [*remainder missing*], or the like.

4. Missing or illegible digits are indicated by suspension points in brackets, the number of points corresponding to the estimated number of missing figures.

5. Blank spaces are left as blanks.

2. The typescripts from which these papers are printed have been made from photocopies of the manuscripts, and marks of punctuation are sometimes blurred or lost in photography. It has often been impossible to consult the originals in these cases.

h. *Author's additions and corrections.*

1. Interlineations and brief marginal notes are brought into the text without comment. Longer notes are brought into the text with the notation [*in the margin*].

2. Author's footnotes are printed at the bottom of the appropriate pages between the text and any editorial footnotes.

3. Canceled words and phrases are in general omitted without notice; if significant, they are printed in footnotes. The canceled passages of important documents, such as drafts of treaties, are brought into the text enclosed in angle brackets *before* the words substituted.

4. When alternative words and phrases have been inserted in a manuscript but the original remains uncanceled, the alternatives are given in brackets, preceded by explanatory words in italics, as: "it is [*written above:* may be] true."

5. Variant readings of several versions are noted if important.

Abbreviations and Short Titles

Acts Privy Coun., Col.	W. L. Grant and James Munro, eds., *Acts of the Privy Council of England, Colonial Series, 1613–1783* (6 vols., London, 1908–12).
ADS	Autograph document signed.[1]
ALS	Autograph letter signed.
APS	American Philosophical Society.
Autobiog. (APS-Yale edit.)	Leonard W. Labaree, Ralph L. Ketcham, Helen C. Boatfield, Helene H. Fineman, eds., *The Autobiography of Benjamin Franklin* (New Haven, 1964).
BF	Benjamin Franklin
Bigelow, *Works*	John Bigelow, ed., *The Complete Works of Benjamin Franklin* . . . (10 vols., N.Y., 1887–88).
Board of Trade Journal	*Journal of the Commissioners for Trade and Plantations . . . April 1704 to . . . May 1782* (14 vols., London, 1920–38).
Cohen, *BF's Experiments*	I. Bernard Cohen, ed., *Benjamin Franklin's Experiments. A New Edition of Franklin's Experiments and Observations on Electricity* (Cambridge, Mass., 1941).
Colden Paps.	*The Letters and Papers of Cadwallader Colden.* New-York Historical Society *Collections* for 1917-23, 1934, 1935.
DAB	*Dictionary of American Biography.*
Darlington, *Memorials*	William Darlington, *Memorials of John Bartram and Humphrey Marshall* (Phila., 1849).
Dexter, *Biog. Sketches*	Franklin B. Dexter, *Biographical Sketches of the Graduates of Yale College* . . . (6 vols., N.Y. and New Haven, 1885–1912).
DF	Deborah Franklin

1. For definitions of this and other kinds of manuscripts, see above, I, xliv-xlvii.

xxiv

DNB	*Dictionary of National Biography.*
DS	Document signed.
Duane, *Works*	William Duane, ed., *The Works of Dr. Benjamin Franklin* ... (6 vols., Phila., 1808–18). Title varies in the several volumes.
Evans	Charles Evans, *American Bibliography* (14 vols., Chicago and Worcester, Mass., 1903–59). Surviving imprints are reproduced in full in microprint in Clifford K. Shipton, ed., *Early American Imprints, 1639–1800* (microprint, Worcester, Mass.).
Exper. and Obser.	*Experiments and Observations on Electricity, made at Philadelphia in America, by Mr. Benjamin Franklin,* ... (London, 1751). Revised and enlarged editions were published in 1754, 1760, 1769, and 1774 with slightly varying titles. In each case the edition cited will be indicated, e.g., *Exper. and Obser.,* 1751 edit.
Gipson, *British Empire*	Lawrence H. Gipson, *The British Empire before the American Revolution* (12 vols., to date: Vols. 1–3, Caldwell, Idaho, 1936; Vols. 4–12, N.Y., 1939–65; Vols. 1–3, revised edit., N.Y., 1958–60).
Lib. Co. Phila.	Library Company of Philadelphia.
LS	Letter signed.
Montgomery, *Hist. Univ. Pa.*	Thomas H. Montgomery, *A History of the University of Pennsylvania from Its Foundation to A.D. 1770* (Phila., 1900).
MS, MSS	Manuscript, manuscripts.
Namier and Brooke, *House of Commons*	Sir Lewis Namier and John Brooke, *The History of Parliament. The House of Commons 1754–1790* (3 vols., London and N.Y., 1964).
N.J. Arch.	William A. Whitehead and others, eds., *Archives of the State of New Jersey* (2 series, Newark and elsewhere, 1880–).

	Editors, subtitles, and places of publication vary.
N.Y. Col. Docs.	E. B. O'Callaghan, ed., *Documents relative to the Colonial History of the State of New York* (15 vols., Albany, 1853–87).
Pa. Arch.	Samuel Hazard and others, eds., *Pennsylvania Archives* (9 series, Phila. and Harrisburg, 1852-1935).
Pa. Col. Recs.	*Minutes of the Provincial Council of Pennsylvania* . . . (16 vols., Phila., 1838–53). Title changes with Volume 11 to *Supreme Executive Council.*
Pa. Gaʒ.	*The Pennsylvania Gaʒette.*
Pa. Jour.	*The Pennsylvania Journal.*
Phil. Trans.	The Royal Society, *Philosophical Transactions.*
PMHB	*Pennsylvania Magaʒine of History and Biography.*
Sibley's Harvard Graduates	John L. Sibley, *Biographical Sketches of Graduates of Harvard University* (Cambridge, Mass., 1873–). Continued from Volume 4 by Clifford K. Shipton.
Smyth, *Writings*	Albert H. Smyth, ed., *The Writings of Benjamin Franklin* . . . (10 vols., N.Y., 1905–07).
Sparks, *Works*	Jared Sparks, ed., *The Works of Benjamin Franklin* . . . (10 vols., Boston, 1836–40).
Statutes at Large, Pa.	*The Statutes at Large of Pennsylvania from 1682 to 1801, Compiled under the Authority of the Act of May 19, 1887 . . .* (Vols. 2–16, [Harrisburg], 1896–1911). Volume 1 was never published.
Van Doren, *Franklin*	Carl Van Doren, *Benjamin Franklin* (N.Y., 1938).
Van Doren, *Franklin-Mecom*	Carl Van Doren, ed., *The Letters of Benjamin Franklin & Jane Mecom* (Memoirs of the American Philosophical Society, XXVII, Princeton, 1950).

Votes	*Votes and Proceedings of the House of Representatives of the Province of Pennsylvania, Met at Philadelphia ... 1750, and continued by Adjournments* (Phila., 1751–). Each annual collection of the journals of separate sittings is designated by the year for which that House was elected, e.g., *Votes,* 1750–51.
WF	William Franklin
WTF, *Memoirs*	William Temple Franklin, ed., *Memoirs of the Life and Writings of Benjamin Franklin, LL.D., F.R.S., &c. ...* (3 vols., 4to, London, 1817–18).

Genealogical references. An editorial reference to one of Benjamin Franklin's relatives may be accompanied by a citation of the symbol assigned to that person in the genealogical tables and charts in volume I of this work, pp. xlix–lxxvii, as, for example: Thomas Franklin (A.5.2.1), Benjamin Mecom (C.17.3), or Benjamin Franklin Bache (D.3.1). These symbols begin with the letter A, B, C, or D. Similarly, a reference to one of Deborah Franklin's relatives may be accompanied by a symbol beginning with the letter E or F, as, for example, John Tiler (E.1.1.2), or Mary Leacock Hall (F.2.2.3). Such persons may be further identified by reference to the charts of the White and Cash families printed in VIII, 139–42.

Chronology

January 1 through December 31, 1764

1764

January 30?: BF publishes *A Narrative of the Late Massacres*, denouncing actions of the Paxton Boys at Conestoga Manor and Lancaster in December 1763.

February 3: Assembly and governor hastily pass a Riot Act to deal with threatened attack on Philadelphia.

February 5–8: The Paxton Boys march on the city; BF and other leading citizens join Governor Penn in organizing defenses; they meet with leaders of the rioters and persuade them to disperse after appointing spokesmen to present their grievances.

February 24–May 30: Assembly and Governor Penn wrangle over terms of a supply bill.

March 9: George Grenville proposes to House of Commons a colonial Stamp Act.

March 24: Assembly adopts a "Necklace of Resolves" outlining its case against proprietary rule and proposing a petition to the King for a change to royal government of Pennsylvania.

April 5: The parliamentary Sugar Act becomes law.

April 12: BF writes *Cool Thoughts* (published about two weeks later) in support of a change in government.

May 26: Isaac Norris resigns as speaker; BF elected to succeed him. Assembly adopts a petition to the King for change in government, drafted by BF, and he signs it as speaker.

May 30: Assembly finally submits to Governor Penn's basic demands concerning the supply bill and he enacts it. Assembly adjourns until September. On the same day the Proprietors' agent writes the governor from London instructing him to yield to the Assembly's position.

June 29: Publication of John Dickinson's May 24 speech to the Assembly opposing the petition for a change in government. An extended preface by William Smith defends the proprietary position regarding supply acts.

xxviii

August 11: Publication of Joseph Galloway's speech in the Assembly replying to Dickinson. A long preface by BF to refute Smith's preface reviews the protracted controversy and supports the Assembly position.

August 13: William Allen reaches Philadelphia from London bringing news of Proprietors' concession to Assembly position on supply bill, but Governor Penn and his supporters conceal this information until after the impending election.

August–September: The campaign for election of a new Assembly takes place between two well-defined parties, with many publications on each side attacking the leaders of the other in terms of unprecedented scurrility.

September 22: Assembly instructs Richard Jackson to try to prevent passage of Grenville's proposed Stamp Act and to seek modifications in the Sugar Act.

October 1–3: In the election BF is defeated as candidate from both the county and the city of Philadelphia. Galloway is also defeated, but their party retains a substantial majority in the new House. This is BF's only defeat for election during his political career.

October 20: Assembly refuses to recall petition for a change in government.

October 26: Assembly appoints BF as co-agent with Jackson. Minority members fail to get their protest entered in minutes but publish it six days later.

November 5: BF writes *Remarks on a Late Protest* defending his record; it is published two days later.

November 7: BF embarks for England. Three hundred friends and admirers accompany him to his ship at Chester.

November 9: BF's ship, *King of Prussia,* puts to sea from Delaware capes.

December 7: William Smith publishes anonymously *An Answer to Mr. Franklin's Remarks,* a long and bitter attack upon him personally and upon his official behavior.

December 9: BF arrives at the Isle of Wight after a fast but stormy passage.

December 10: BF reaches London and takes up residence at his old lodgings in Craven Street.

THE PAPERS OF
BENJAMIN FRANKLIN

VOLUME 11

January 1 through December 31, 1764

Post Office Commissions to Abraham Hunt[1]

Printed forms (two) with MS insertions in blanks: Theodore Sheldon, Chicago (1954)

The commission given by Franklin and William Hunter to Thomas Vernon as deputy postmaster at Newport, R.I., Dec. 24, 1754, is printed above, V, 451–2. With the text of that earliest known post-office commission signed by Franklin as deputy postmaster general appears a note listing five similar commissions known to the editors and stating that later these documents would not be printed individually in this edition at their respective dates. An unusual circumstance justifies an exception to that general statement.

Mr. Theodore Sheldon owns not only the original commission that Franklin and John Foxcroft, joint deputy postmasters general under the Crown, issued to Abraham Hunt as postmaster of Trenton, Jan. 10, 1764, but also the commission that Franklin, serving as postmaster general of the United Colonies, issued to Hunt, Oct. 13, 1775, after the beginning of the American Revolution.[2] It is as unusual as it is fortunate

1. Abraham Hunt was the principal merchant of Trenton. He was appointed barrack master, 1770; a member of the N.J. Committee of Correspondence, 1774; lieutenant colonel in the Hunterdon Co. militia the next year; and county commissioner, 1776–77. It was at Hunt's house that the Hessian Colonel Rall enjoyed, somewhat to excess, his Christmas revels the night before Washington's surprise attack in 1776, and Hunt's "hospitality" doubtless contributed to the success of the Americans. Hunt was later charged with high treason but was completely exonerated and continued in responsible service to the American cause. He was one of the founders of Trenton Academy, 1781; a charter member of the Board of Aldermen when the city of Trenton was incorporated, 1792; and a founder and director of the Trenton Banking Co., 1805. Trenton Historical Society, sponsor, *A History of Trenton 1679–1929 Two Hundred and Fifty Years of a Notable Town with Links in Four Centuries* (Princeton, 1929), pp. 113, 128, 132–4, 157–8, 354, 560, 710–11; William S. Stryker, *The Battles of Trenton and Princeton* (Boston and N.Y., 1898), pp. 122–5.

2. On May 29, 1775, the Continental Congress appointed a committee of six members, of whom BF was named first, "to consider the best means of establishing posts for conveying letters and intelligence through this continent." The committee reported on July 25 and, after considering the report the next day, Congress voted to appoint a postmaster general with power to name a secretary and comptroller and such deputies as he thought proper and necessary. It was also decided to establish a line of posts between Falmouth, Me., and Savannah, Ga., with a weekly service to Charleston, S.C. On the same day Congress elected BF postmaster general "for one year and until another is appointed by a future Congress." His son-in-law,

3

that two commissions, issued more than eleven years apart to the same individual for the same office and signed by the same postmaster general, but under the authority of two different governments, should survive approximately two centuries later in the same private collection. The editors greatly appreciate Mr. Sheldon's willingness to permit the reproduction of these documents together here.

Comparison of the texts of the two commissions to Hunt shows that the printed portions of the second are in most respects an almost *verbatim* repetition of the first. The differences, however, are significant. The headings reflect the contrasting governmental authorities under which they were issued. The commission of 1764 testified to Hunt's "Loyalty to His Majesty," while that of 1775 certifies instead his "public Spirit." Franklin and Foxcroft issued the first one jointly, but Franklin acted alone on the other; Foxcroft had become a Loyalist. By the terms of the earlier document Hunt was to hold office for three years "unless sooner removed by us"; the later commission, reflecting the unsettled political situation between the outbreak of hostilities and the Declaration of Independence, is less precise as to the method or authority for its possible termination. The dating at the end of the second commission also omits all reference to the British regnal year, although in October 1775 the United Colonies were still nearly nine months away from formally renouncing George III and proclaiming themselves the United States.

I

[January 10, 1764]

BENJAMIN FRANKLIN, and JOHN FOXCROFT, Esquires, POST-MASTERS-GENERAL of all His Majesty's Provinces and Dominions on the Continent of NORTH-AMERICA.

TO ALL to whom these Presents shall come, Greeting, KNOW YE, That We *the said Benjamin Franklin and John Foxcroft,* having received good Testimony of the Fidelity, and Loyalty to His Majesty, of *Abraham Hunt, of Trenton, in New-Jersey, Gent.* and reposing great Trust and Confidence in the Knowledge, Care, and Ability of the said *Abraham Hunt* to execute the Office and Duties required of a Deputy Post-Master, have Deputed, Constituted, Authorized, and Appointed, and by these Presents do Depute,

---

Richard Bache, comptroller of the Post Office, was elected to succeed him, Nov. 7, 1776, after his departure for France. *Journals of the Continental Congress, 1774–1789* (Washington, 1904–37), II, 71, 203, 208–9; VI, 931.

4

BENJAMIN FRANKLIN, and **JOHN FOXCROFT**, Esquires, Post-Masters-General of all His Majesty's Provinces and Dominions on the Continent of *NORTH-AMERICA.*

TO ALL to whom these Presents shall come, Greeting, KNOW YE, That We *he and Benjamin Franklin and John Foxcroft* — having received good Testimony of the Fidelity, and Loyalty to His Majesty, of *Abraham Hunt, of Trenton, in New Jersey, Gent* - and reposing great Trust and Confidence in the Knowledge, Care, and Ability of the said *Abraham Hunt,* - - - to execute the Office and Duties required of a Deputy Post-Master, have Deputed, Constituted, Authorized, and Appointed, and by these Presents do Depute, Constitute, Authorize, and Appoint the said *Abraham Hunt* - - - - to be our lawful and sufficient Deputy, to Execute the Office of Deputy Post-Master *at Trenton in New Jersey, aforesaid* - - - - - to have, hold, use, exercise and enjoy the said Office, with all and every the Rights, Privileges, Benefits and Advantages, to the same belonging, from the - - - - Day of *the Date hereof* - for the Term of three Years, unless sooner removed by us, under such Conditions, Provisoes, Payments, Orders and Instructions, to be faithfully observed, performed, and done, by the said Deputy, and Servants, as *he* - or they shall, from Time to Time, receive from Us, or by our Order. In Witness whereof, We the said *Benjamin Franklin,* and *John Foxcroft,* have hereunto set our Hands, and caused the Seal of our Office to be affixed: Dated the *Tenth* - - - Day of *January,* - 176*4,* in the *Fourth* - - - Year of HIS MAJESTY's Reign.

B. Franklin

John Foxcroft

By AUTHORITY *of the* CONGRESS.

BENJAMIN FRANKLIN, Esq;

Appointed Post-Master-General *of all the* United Colonies *on the* Continent *of* NORTH-AMERICA.

TO ALL to whom these Presents shall come, sends Greeting : KNOW YE, That I, the said Benjamin Franklin, having received good Testimony of the Fidelity and public Spirit of *Abraham Hunt, of Trenton, in New Jersey, Gent* and reposing great Trust and Confidence in the Knowledge, Care and Ability of the said *Abraham Hunt,* to execute the Office and Duties required of a Deputy Post-Master, have deputed, constituted, authorized and appointed, and by these Presents do depute, constitute, authorize and appoint the said *Abraham Hunt,* to be my lawful and sufficient Deputy, to execute the Office of Deputy Post-Master of *Trenton, in New Jersey,* to have, hold, use, exercise and enjoy the said Office, with all and every the Rights, Privileges, Benefits and Advantages, to the same belonging, from the *Thirteenth* Day of *October, Inst.* for the Term of three Years, or until he shall receive a new Commission, or until the present be superseded under such Conditions, Covenants, Provisoes, Payments, Orders and Instructions, to be faithfully observed, performed and done, by the said Deputy, and Servants, as *he* or they shall, from time to time, receive from me, or by my Order. In Witness whereof, I, the said Benjamin Franklin, have hereunto set my Hand, and caused the Seal of my Office to be affixed: Dated the *Thirteenth* Day of *October,* 1775. —

B. Franklin

Post Office Commissions to Abraham Hunt

Constitute, Authorize, and Appoint the said *Abraham Hunt,* to be our lawful and sufficient Deputy, to Execute the Office of Deputy Post-Master *at Trenton in New-Jersey, aforesaid,* to have, hold, use, exercise and enjoy the said Office, with all and every the Rights, Privileges, Benefits and Advantages, to the same belonging, from the Day of *the Date hereof* for the Term of three Years, unless sooner removed by us, under such Conditions, Covenants, Provisoes, Payments, Orders and Instructions, to be faithfully observed, performed, and done, by the said Deputy, and Servants, as *he* or they shall, from Time to Time, receive from Us, or by our Order. In Witness whereof, We the said Benjamin Franklin, and John Foxcroft, have hereunto set our Hands, and caused the Seal of our Office to be affixed: Dated the *Tenth* Day of *January,* 17 *64,* in the *Fourth* Year of HIS MAJESTY's Reign. B FRANKLIN

JOHN FOXCROFT

II

[October 13, 1775]

By AUTHORITY of the CONGRESS.

BENJAMIN FRANKLIN, ESQ;

Appointed POST-MASTER-GENERAL of all the UNITED COLONIES on the CONTINENT of NORTH-AMERICA.

TO ALL to whom these Presents shall come, sends GREETING: KNOW YE, That I, the said BENJAMIN FRANKLIN, having received good Testimony of the Fidelity and public Spirit of *Abraham Hunt, of Trenton, in New Jersey, Gent.* and reposing great Trust and Confidence in the Knowledge, Care and Ability of the said *Abraham Hunt,* to execute the Office and Duties required of a Deputy Post-Master, have deputed, constituted, authorized and appointed, and by these Presents do depute, constitute, authorize and appoint the said *Abraham Hunt,* to be my lawful and sufficient Deputy, to execute the Office of Deputy Post-Master of *Trenton, in New-Jersey,* to have, hold, use, exercise and enjoy the said Office, with all and every the Rights, Privileges, Benefits and Advantages, to the same belonging, from the *Thirteenth* Day of *October, Inst.* for the Term of three Years, or until he shall receive a new Commission, or until the present be superseded under

5

such Conditions, Covenants, Provisoes, Payments, Orders and Instructions, to be faithfully observed, performed and done, by the said Deputy, and Servants, as *he* or they shall, from time to time, receive from me, or by my Order. In Witness whereof, I, the said BENJAMIN FRANKLIN, have hereunto set my Hand, and caused the Seal of my Office to be affixed: Dated the *Thirteenth* Day of *October,* 177 5. B FRANKLIN

To Francis Bernard ALS: The British Museum

Sir Philada. Jan. 11. 1764
Having heard nothing from Virginia concerning your Son,[3] I have at length thought the best and surest Way of bringing him safely here, will be to send from hence a sober trusty Person to conduct him up, who will attend him on the Road, &c. I have accordingly this Day agreed with Mr. Ennis,[4] a very discreet Man, to make the Journey, who sets out to-morrow Morning. I shall send with him my own Horse for Mr. Bernard, and Money to bear his Expences; with a Letter to Mr. Johnson[5] engaging to pay any Account he may have against your Son, or any reasonable Debts he may have contracted there. I hope this will be agreable to you, and answer the End. I am, with sincerest Respect Your Excellency's most obedient and most humble Servant B FRANKLIN

Govr. Bernard

Endorsed: Mr Franklin r Jan 21. 1764

3. While in New England in the summer of 1763 BF promised Mrs. Francis Bernard that he would look after her eldest son, Francis, if he should reach the vicinity of Philadelphia during his travels in America. Young Bernard turned up in Alexandria, Va., in the fall of the year and was stranded there without money. As he had promised, BF assumed responsibility for getting the young man home to his parents. See above, x, 353–4, 373, 389–91, 410–11.
4. James Ennis, Sr., and James Ennis, Jr., were both couriers in the service of the government of Pa. *Autobiog.* (APS-Yale edit.), 251, 280; 8 *Pa. Arch.,* VI, 5054, 5065, 5151.
5. A lawyer of "Belvale," near Alexandria, with whom young Bernard was staying. See above, x, 410 n.

Argument for Making the Bills of Credit Bear Interest

MS:[6] American Philosophical Society

On Dec. 20, 1763, the day Franklin resumed his seat in the Assembly after his long trip to New England, Governor John Penn transmitted to it letters from General Amherst and his successor as commander-in-chief, General Thomas Gage,[7] demanding that the province raise and clothe one thousand men to act in concert with the regular troops against the Indians. In contrast to the negative reactions of the assemblies of New York, New Jersey, and Virginia to similar requisitions, the Pennsylvania House of Representatives promptly resolved, December 22, to provide the force required and, on January 6 after a holiday recess, voted to raise £50,000 to meet the costs involved. Franklin had written Richard Jackson on December 19 that the Assembly and the newly arrived governor, John Penn, seemed to be on good terms, but he added cautiously: "What Disputes may arise during the Session, I know not; but fear a Money Bill will revive the old ones."[8] His fear was soon fully justified.

On January 10 the Assembly began to consider ways and means of raising the £50,000 and continued the debate sporadically through the

6. This is the copy BF sent to Jackson with his letter of June 25, 1764; see below, p. 238. While the endorsement is in BF's hand, the text appears, curiously, to be in that of WF.

7. Thomas Gage (1721–1787), entered the British Army in 1741 and as a lieutenant colonel served gallantly in Braddock's disastrous campaign of 1754, during which he was wounded. He took an effective part in later campaigns and was promoted to brigadier general in 1759 and major general in 1761. After service as military governor of Montreal he succeeded Amherst as commander-in-chief of the British forces in North America in the autumn of 1763 with his headquarters in New York City. He was advanced to lieutenant general in 1770. While still holding his military command he replaced Thomas Hutchinson as governor of Massachusetts Bay in 1774 and occupied both posts at the outbreak of the Revolution. In October 1775, during the siege of Boston, he resigned his command and returned to England. Although promoted to full general in 1782, he never again occupied a major military post. *DAB; DNB;* Clarence E. Carter, ed., *The Correspondence of General Thomas Gage* (2 vols., New Haven, 1931–33); John R. Alden, *General Gage in America* (Baton Rouge, 1948).

8. *Votes,* 1763–64, pp. 11–14, 15, 18–23; above, X, 405 n, 408–9. The principal speakers in favor of the resolution were BF, John Hughes, Joseph Galloway, and John Dickinson; those opposed were George Ashbridge and William Smith. "Fragments of a Journal Kept by Samuel Foulke of Bucks County While a Member of the Colonial Assembly of Pennsylvania, 1762–3–4." *PMHB,* v (1881), 65.

rest of the month. On the 11th two members were sent to ask the governor for a copy of his instructions on supply bills, since the Assembly was "truly desirous to avoid every Occasion of Disagreement with his Honour in their intended Grant to the Crown." Penn complied the next day, sending down copies of his eleventh and twelfth instructions. These provided that he was to approve no measure that allowed any money to be left to the disposal of the Assembly alone, excluding the governor from a voice in the matter; that he do his best to keep the quantity of bills of credit in circulation at any one time as low as possible; that any act for bills of credit must conform to the agreement between the Proprietors and the provincial agents ratified by the Privy Council in 1760;[9] and that the bills of credit not be made legal tender for any quitrents "or other sterling Payments" due to the Proprietors, but that all such dues be payable in sterling exchange, unless an indemnity to the Proprietors be enacted to protect them from loss by the depreciation of the bills of credit.[1]

After receiving this information the Assembly spent virtually the whole of its sittings on January 13 and 14 debating ways and means of raising the supply.[2] It seems highly probable that Franklin delivered the speech printed below on one of those two days. It is true that before he sent this copy to Richard Jackson in the following June he endorsed it "December 1763," but the Assembly *Votes* give no indication that any discussion on the nature of a proposed supply bill took place during that month. The caustic reference in the fourth paragraph to the governor's instructions, "which we have seen," suggests strongly that he made the speech soon after those instructions were read to the Assembly on January 11. Probably by the next June he had forgotten the precise sequence of events during the long controversy over the supply bill.[3]

It seems clear from the record that by the end of the debate on January 14 the Assembly had informally agreed to raise the supply by an issue of paper currency to be financed chiefly by a general property tax, though the details of the measure and the procedures and rates of assessment remained to be determined. Much of the Assembly's time during the rest of the month was devoted to these problems of tax rates and property assessment in the several counties. Only on Jan-

9. See above, IX, 205–8.
1. *Votes*, 1763–64, pp. 26–7.
2. *Ibid.*, pp. 27–8.
3. Carl Van Doren first suggested that BF must have delivered this speech after January 12. *Letters and Papers of Benjamin Franklin and Richard Jackson 1753–1785* (Phila., 1947), pp. 125–6.

uary 31 did the House resume the general discussion of "ways and means."[4]

At the conclusion of the debate on that day three questions were put to vote: 1. Should the bills of credit be made legal tender "in all Payments whatsoever"? 2. Should they be made legal tender in all payments excepting "the Proprietary Quitrents, and their other Sterling Debts"? 3. Should the £50,000 "be struck in Provincial Notes, bearing Interest" (Franklin's proposal)? All three questions were voted in the negative.[5] Thus Franklin's speech, the longest in his lifetime of which the text survives, failed to persuade a majority of his fellow assemblymen to adopt his scheme.

On February 1 the House resumed the discussion, and this time a majority voted to issue bills of credit which would be legal tender "in all Payments, the Proprietaries Sterling Rents only excepted." A committee was appointed to prepare the bill; it was introduced on February 10 and, after an extended debate, was passed on the 24th and ordered to be delivered to the governor.[6]

It is unfortunate that the official journal of the Assembly is so barren of details on the debates that took place over this first supply bill of 1764. The deficiency is in some measure offset by a surviving fragment of a private journal kept by one of the members, Samuel Foulke, a Quaker assemblyman from Bucks County and obviously an admirer of Franklin.[7] His record for January 1764, written as a consecutive narrative, deals first with the problems created by the massacres of the Indians on Conestoga Manor and at Lancaster and then, without giving specific dates, describes the Assembly's deliberations after receiving copies of the proprietary instructions relating to supply bills.

The members, Foulke wrote, seeing that "it would be in vain to offer him [the governor] a Bill for raising money in the mode heretofore used in this Government, therefore, went into Consideration of new ways and Means for raising Money, which held the House Chiefly Employed for about four weeks, upon which Arose Very Serious and Arduous

4. *Votes,* 1763–64, pp. 30–8.
5. *Ibid.,* p. 39.
6. *Ibid.,* pp. 39, 42, 47–52.
7. Samuel Foulke (1718–1797) was the son of Hugh Foulke of Richland (Quakertown) in Bucks Co., and for about thirty-seven years he was clerk of the Richland Monthly Meeting. He was an assemblyman from Bucks Co., 1761–68. During the American Revolution he was "disowned" for too actively sympathizing with the colonial cause. His fragmentary journal, which covers parts of the Assembly sessions from September 1762 to February 1764, is printed in *PMHB,* v (1881), 60–73. The quotations reprinted here are from pp. 68–9.

debates, in which B. Franklin and John Dickinson[8] Greatly distinguished themselves; the first as a politician, the other as an Orator. The points Debated were whether we shou'd make Exceptions in Our Money bill in favour of the proprietaries, with a respect to their Quitrents, &c., Or Emit a new Species of bills of Credit, not to be Enforced as Legal Tender to any Man, but [which] to give them Credit, were to bear an Interest to the possessor, and by that means avoy'd any disputes with the proprietaries; the above-Named Gentlemen were for the latter. The Chief Speakers on the other side were Jos. Galloway, Jos. Fox, G. Ashbridge,[9] and tho' the first Named had to my appre[hen]sion much the advantage of the latter in reason and argument, yet to my great surprise, when the Question was put, it was Carried in favour of the propriet's; such was the unaccountable Attachment of a majority of the Members to the usual mode of raising money, and their Ill Judged fear of going out of the beaten track to try a new Method of making money, which probably would have Exempted them and their Constituents from the necessity of wearing that Servile piece of furniture Call'd a Neck-Yoke" until it should please the King to take the government into his own hands, "which I believe is the wish of every one who retains a Just sense of Freedom."

The adoption of Franklin's scheme for issuing interest-bearing notes instead of the familiar bills of credit might have settled the problem of legal tender, but that it could have prevented the controversy that did take place, as Foulke thought it would, is doubtful. Whether the £50,-000 needed for the troops took the form of bills of credit or of interest-bearing notes, provision had to be made for the future retirement of this

8. John Dickinson (1732–1808), born in Talbot Co., Md., moved with his family to Dover, Del., as a boy. He studied law at the Middle Temple, 1753–57, and then began what proved to be a most successful practice in Philadelphia. He was elected to the Assembly of the Lower Counties in 1760 and served in the Pa. Assembly, 1762–65 and 1770–76. He became a moderate supporter of the proprietary position and strongly opposed the movement for royal assumption of the government. Dickinson was a delegate to the Stamp Act Congress, 1765, and in 1767–68 wrote his influential *Letters from a Farmer in Pennsylvania to the Inhabitants of the British Colonies*. He was a member of the Continental Congress, 1774–76 and 1779–81, and president of the Supreme Executive Council of Delaware, 1781, and that of Pa., 1782–85. He represented Del. at the Federal Constitutional Convention of 1787. *DAB;* Charles J. Stillé, *The Life and Times of John Dickinson 1732–1808* (2 vols., Phila., 1891–95).

9. On Joseph Galloway, see above, VII, 29 n; and on Joseph Fox, above, VI, 284 n. George Ashbridge (1704–1773), of Goshen, Chester Co., usually a supporter of BF, had been a representative from that county since 1743.

paper money. Taxation, including a general property tax, was necessary in any case. And once a bill was passed and sent to the governor containing clauses taxing the proprietary estates along with all others, trouble was almost certain to follow. As the events of the next months were to show, the Assembly's bill set the stage for one of the most acrimonious disputes between a Pennsylvania Assembly and a proprietary governor, and their supporters, that ever confounded the politics of the province. Franklin's plan, however meritorious in other respects, would probably have produced the same result.

Sir   [January 13-14? 1764]
I have been long in this House, and have seldom seen Matters of more Importance under its Consideration; and never more Unanimity in sincere Desire of obtaining the Point in View, tho' we have not yet been so happy as to agree in the Mode of it.

During the Course of these weighty Debates I have been pleas'd to see some Members make use of Notes, who stood as little in need of such Helps in Speaking as any among us. It show'd they gave a serious Attention to the Business before us; and it appear'd rather respectful to the House, as they seem'd willing to offer us on this Occasion, not their hasty Thoughts, but They have thus afforded us some good Lights; and I could wish to see the Practice more frequent, since I think Notes would be useful to others besides myself, who have bad Memories, and particularly so to me who am but a very indifferent Speaker.

Three or four different Modes have been proposed of producing the Money we intend to give.

The first is, to strike the Sum, and make the Bills as heretofore a legal Tender to all, the Proprietaries not excepted. This I believe we are all pretty well satisfied is impracticable. We have seen the Instruction, and we know that whatever our Distresses are, the Proprietor has no Bowels; he never relents.

The second is, To make the Bills a legal Tender to all except the Proprietor—according to the Instruction. This we cannot do, because it is unequal and unjust.

The third is, To make the Proprietor a particular Compensation.[1] This is not only an unjust Preference given to one Possessor of

1. The indemnity provision mentioned in the governor's instructions; see the headnote. This method had been occasionally employed in earlier supply acts.

Property above another, but in the Proprietor's Case is of dangerous Example.

The fourth is, To make the Bills a legal Tender in all Cases, perpetual Contracts only excepted; which will take in the Cases of all others whose Contracts are in the same Circumstances with those of the Proprietors. I must own the Equality of this Proposition pleases me. I would only wish to have the Exception extended to all Specific Contracts, past, present, and to come; I mean Contracts in which the kind of Money, or other thing to be paid, is particularly express'd. All Contracts, Sir, are between two or more Parties, and intended by each for his own Advantage; the Parties are free Agents, they have their Eyes open and know what they do. If I want to purchase another Man's House, and he happens not to have sufficient Confidence in our Currency, but places his Affection upon Sterling, and will let me have the House at a Price I like, and afford me some Time for the Payment, provided I will oblige myself to pay in Sterling; If I like his Proposal, why should the Government interfere and say to the Seller take care what you do, I make such Contracts void by Law: The Seller then can have no Confidence in my Sterling Bond, if I should give it, and so the Bargain is broke off. Does the Government by such a Law think to favour me who was to have been the Debtor; I do not thank the Government. It has prevented me of a beneficial Bargain. It has hurt the Seller too, for his House sticks upon his Hands. If at length, to induce him to sell his House, and take the Risque which he thinks there is in the Currency, I agree to give him a greater Price than he would otherwise have required, the *over Price* I pay is so much Injury done me by the Government's officiously interfering in private Contracts. I do not mean to say, the Government has nothing to do with private Contracts; it ought undoubtedly to have a Power over them, but it is to enforce the Observance of them—that's all—unless the People were all Minors and Ideots. Again, If I sell a House to be delivered at some time hereafter, on a Contract to be paid in Sterling, and you come in with your Law in favour of my Debtor, that shall allow him if he pleases to pay me in Currency, at 33 and ⅓d. you, may with equal Justice, allow me, if I please, instead of a *House* to deliver him a *Hogstie.*

I am therefore for leaving all specific Contracts to be executed according to their Tenor; and that our Bills, if they must be made

12

a legal Tender, shall be such only in Common Dealings, where no specific Contract has been made.

I know it is objected, that this will make our Currency of less Use, and by Degrees of little or no Use at all; for People will gradually get into the Way of making all their Contracts in Sterling. I answer, they will not, unless they find by Experience they can fulfill 'em; and if they can where is the harm of it? If our Currency becomes of less and less Use, it will hardly be in a swifter Proportion than we are like to have less and less of it, if we sink it as the Laws direct. And what is there amiss in having the Occasion for a particular Currency diminish as the Currency itself diminishes?

But it will be said, we cannot in this Country do without a Paper Currency, we must always have one. I own, I am not clearly of that Opinion; but if it be true that we must always have a Paper Currency, then it is my Duty to advise, that it be an *honest One;* that the Bills have Advantages in themselves, which shall support their Value, and prevent their Depreciating as their Quantity increases. That which in all Dealings is to be the Measure of all other Values, ought itself to have as steady and fixt a Value, as human Wisdom can contrive. Were we about to order a true *Standard Yard* to be made for regulating Long Measure throughout the Country, and a true *Standard Peck* for other Measure, I imagine we should think of some Substance to make them of that would be firm enough to preserve the Dimension given; and that no Man in his Senses would propose the Yard to be made of a *knit Garter,* and the Peck of a *ribb'd Stocking.* At present every Bill that I receive tells me a Lie, and would cheat me too if I was not too well acquainted with it. Thirty Shillings in our Bills, according to the Account they give of themselves should be worth *five* Dollars; and we find them worth but *four:* They should be worth 22*s.* 6*d.* Sterling, and we find them worth scarce 17*s.* 2*d.* Sometimes indeed more or less as the Garter shrinks or stretches. When we sit here in Legislation, we have great Power, but we are not almighty. We cannot alter the Nature of Things. Values will be as they are valued or valuable, and not as we *call* them. We may stamp on a Piece of Paper, This is *Ten Shillings,* but if we do not make some other Provision that it shall always be really worth *Ten Shillings,* the *Say-so* of our Law will signify little. Experience in other Colonies as well as in ours, have demonstrated this. And indeed of what Force can it be to fix an arbitrary Value on the Bills, unless the Value of all Things to be purchased by the Bills could be fix'd by the same Law. I want to buy a Suit of Cloth, and am told by the Seller, that his Price is 20s. a Yard. Very well, says I, cut me off 5 Yards, and here are five 20s. Bills for you. I beg your Pardon, says he, the 20s. that I mean is 20s. lawful Money, according to such an Act of Parliament:[2] Your Paper Money is greatly depreciated of late; it is of no more than half its nominal Value, your 20s. is really worth but ten; so that if you pay me in those 20s. Bills you must give me ten of them for five Pounds. Don't talk so to me, says I, you are oblig'd by Act of Assembly to take these Bills at 20s. each. Very well, says he, if I *must* take them so I must; but as the Law sets no Price on my Goods, if you pay me with those Bills at 20s. each, my Cloth is 40s. a Yard, and so you must still give me ten of them; and pray then what becomes of your Law?

The true Way in my Opinion to preserve a Value in our Paper Bills nearly equal to the nominal Sums we stamp on them; is to consider 1st. on what we found them; 2dly. what real Value that Fund gives them; and how much less that real Value is than the nominal One we set on them; and 3dly. in what manner a Compensation may be made to every Possessor of them for the Difference. If we do these Things rightly, we then act with Wisdom, Justice and Honour; becoming the legislative Body of a reputable Country.

In the first Place then we propose to found the Credit of these Bills on a Tax to be raised, which is to sink them as I understand in Six Years at one Sixth Part per Annum, for the due and punctual Performance of which there is to be the Sanction of a Law. If this be the Case, and allowing the Security to be good, of which I make not the least Doubt, (tho' some Colonies have by subsequent Laws postpon'd the Payments they had engaged to make, for much longer Terms) I say, supposing the Law punctually executed, it is not difficult to come at the 2d. Point, which was to compute what real Value that Fund gives the Bills. When you pay them out, it is instead of so much *real Money* which you owe and

2. An Act for Ascertaining the Rates of Foreign Coins in Her Majesty's Plantations in America (1707), 6 Anne, c. 57.

ought to pay immediately, but not having the Money to pay, these are your Promisory Notes, obliging you to pay the whole Sum, not upon Demand, but in Six Years by annual Quotas; they are therefore in the nature of things, and between honest Men, really worth no more than the Sum that remains, when Interest for the Time is deducted; and allowing that publick Security is something better than private, I shall state that Interest at 5 per Cent only; then

The Interest of £50,000 for the first Year is	£2500: 0: 0
Do of 41,666: 13: 4	2d Year is	2083: 6: 8
Do of 33,333: 6: 8	3d Year is	1666: 13: 4
Do of 25,000: 0: 0	4th Year is	1250: 0: 0
Do of 16,666: 13: 4	5th Year is	833: 6: 8
Do of 8,333: 6 8	6th Year is	416: 13: 4
	Total of Interest	£8750: 0: 0

This Sum, £8750, taken from £50,000

8,750

leaves £41,250 for the *true Value* of the promisory Notes, or as we call them, Bills of Credit, which is almost 20 per Cent less than their nominal Value; and if People should compute the Interest at 6 per Cent instead of 5, and have withal any reason to doubt the Punctuality of the Government as to the Time of Payment, their Value would be proportionally lower.

We have thus considered the Fund of our intended Bills, the full real Value that Fund can give them, and how much less that real Value is than the nominal Value we mark upon them. We come now to consider, in what manner a Compensation may be made to every Possessor of them for the Difference. The Method I shall venture to propose, disgustful as it may be to my Brethren at first Sight, is plain easy and honest, and I am persuaded that the more they consider it, the more reasonable it will appear, and the less they will be averse to it. It is merely this, *Let the Bills bear an Interest of Five per Cent.* Some Gentlemen, whose Judgment I esteem, I know have already declar'd against this Method, and from very laudable Motives, a Concern for the Ease of the People they represent, already much burthen'd with Taxes; and an Apprehension that a Tax to pay this Interest would greatly aggravate that Burthen. I have already shown them, that the proposed Interest

15

will amount to much less than they conceiv'd it; for by a hasty Calculation, they call'd it 14 or £15,000 whereas it appears to be but £8750 for the Six Years, the Interest diminishing yearly as the Principal diminishes, which I suppose they did not advert to. I shall now endeavour to show, that the People *must and will* be tax'd that Sum, over and above the £50,000 whether a special Provision is made for it or not; whether the Bills express the Bearing of Interest or do not; in short a Sum equal to the Interest must and will be taken from the People, either in a way that is *honorable* to the Government, or in a Way that is *dishonorable*. And if I can make this appear, I think we shall not hesitate a Moment which to chuse.

Let us now suppose the Bills struck and made a legal Tender as heretofore, without bearing Interest; and as we can more easily conceive the Matter by a single Instance, let us suppose that the Government is to pay me £600 for Provisions the Produce of my Farm, for Cloathing, Arms, Ammunition, Carriages, or any other Thing I have supplied for the Army. The Government tenders me the nominal Value of £600 in Bills. I enquire on what they are founded, and when they are to be paid. The Government tells me that the Fund is this; I am to be tax'd £100 a Year for 6 Years, the Treasurer is order'd to receive these Bills in Payment of my Taxes, and so in 6 Years they are all to be taken off my Hands. But Mr. Government (I might humbly expostulate and say), by this taking from me Six Years Taxes at once, you really take more from me than Six hundred Pounds. That Sum you ought now to pay me, and no Tax will be due from me this 12-Month, and then but a 6th. Part of the Sum will be due, and the rest from Year to Year.

The Interest of £600 for the 1st. Year will be £30: 0: 0 which I lose.

The Interest of £500 for the 2d. Year will be 25: 0: 0
The Interest of £400 for the 3d. Year will be 20: 0: 0
The Interest of £300 for the 4th. Year will be 15: 0: 0
The Interest of £200 for the 5th. Year will be 10: 0: 0
and The Interest of £100 for the 6th. Year will be 5: 0: 0

In all £105: 0: 0

So that my real Tax for the Six Years is Seven hundred and five Pounds. Friend, says the Government you don't consider the whole of the Matter; I have made these Bills a *legal Tender;* you must take them, 'tis true; but then you may make any one else with whom you have Dealings take them again: So shuffle them off your Hands as fast as you can, let every body in their Turns have their Share of them, and so every one will lose his Share of the £105 you mention, in proportion to the Time that each Man keeps my Bills in his Hands. I thank you Mr. Government, I now understand you and am very much oblig'd to you; for I find, that instead of intending to cheat me alone you only intend to cheat every Body.

The House will readily perceive that the Case of every Sum and Parcel of Money the Government shall pay out till the £50,-000 is expended will finally be the same with that of this £600 which is only the Representative of the whole.

Gentlemen have said, This Paying Interest is a dear Way of coming at Money; we should get it upon the best Terms we can: We can save the Interest by our Law that shall make the Bills a legal Tender. Power to do a dishonest or dishonourable Action, and a Convenience obtain'd by doing it, if such a Thing could be, will not both together justify such an Action. But if we think we can by our Power save the Interest, and it is so good a Thing to avoid a Tax upon the People tho' it be to pay the People their just Due; let me propose an Improvement, by which we shall come at our Money on still better Terms. Why should not I be as desirous of easing the People as any Gentleman among us? It is only extending our Power then, one Step farther; and enacting that the Principal too shall never be paid any more than the Interest, but our Bills pass current for ever, and no Tax ever be laid to redeem them. I shall be told immediately that this would spoil their Credit and prevent their answering any End; they would lose all their Value. I am of the same Opinion, and I think too that they will lose a Proportion of their Value, if we do not pay the Interest; so that we shall really save Nothing by refusing it.

It has been objected that allowing the Bills to bear Interest would introduce the vile and mischievous Practice of Stock-Jobbing, I must own I do not see this, and that I cannot answer it because I do not understand it. Why should public Bills bearing Interest occasion Stock Jobbing any more than private Bonds? Such Bills have been and now are in Use in several of the Colonies, and I have never heard any Complaint or Mention of such Jobbing.

17

Other Gentlemen have express'd an Apprehension that such Bills would be refused and undervalued as no Law compelled the Taking of them. I own I have no such Apprehension. If the Bills are of convenient Denominations I think they will readily pass. Experience has shown it in other Governments. Interest is a powerful Motive; it will make Men break Laws, and do right without a Law.

Upon the whole the Method I have propos'd appears to me to have many Advantages. It will avoid that vile Dispute with the Proprietor, at the Time of all Times when we should be most careful to avoid it.[3] It will avoid the Necessity, and the dangerous Example of any partial and unjust Provision in his favour; It will give the Bills a steady and more equal Value which is necessary to make them a proper Measure of other Values: It will be a Conveniency to all who have Occasion to keep Money by them for future Purposes, and of course turn out into common Currency Money that would otherwise remain in their Chests; It will draw great Sums home that are now in the Funds in England; It will cost the people no more in reality than Bills without Interest, and will in my Opinion be a Measure in every respect prudent, just and honourable.

But I submit, as I ought to do, my Sentiments to the Wisdom of the House.

Endorsed: December 1763   Argument for making the Bills of Credit bear Interest   B.F.

3. BF seems to have had in mind the "vile Dispute with the Proprietor" which related to the payment of quitrents at less than sterling rates. He told Jackson when sending him the speech in June that "My View was partly, to avoid the Proprietary Dispute about legal Tender." He apparently did not foresee—perhaps he could not—that Governor Penn would insist on an interpretation of a very different point in the agreement embodied in the order in council of Sept. 2, 1760, an interpretation that the Assembly regarded as both erroneous and unjust. That difficulty would have beset the taxing sections of any bill based on Franklin's plan quite as much as it did those of the measures the Assembly actually sent to Penn.

To Richard Jackson

ALS: American Philosophical Society

Dear Sir   Philada. Jan. 16. 1764

I have just now receiv'd your Favour of Nov. 12.[4] and hear the Packet is to return directly from New York, while I have scarce time to write a Line before the Post goes.[5] The House have past a Bill to pay the other Colonies what was over-receiv'd by us; which Bill is now before the Governor.[6] We have lately had horrid Rioting on our Frontiers.[7] The Inhabitants came down armed into Lancaster County, and at two several times murdered 20 Innocent Indians, who had been settled on Conestogoe Mannor many Years, under the Protection of this Government. 140 converted Delawares, who refus'd to engage with their Nation in this War, and took Refuge in this Province, have been sent by the Governor into the Jerseys, he being apprehensive he should not be able to protect them from the Murderers who threatned them also. I hope, during your Session, to hear some true political News from you. The News papers only confound us. I am not much alarm'd about your Schemes of raising Money on us.[8] You will take care for your

4. See above, x, 368–72.

5. *Pa. Gaz.*, Feb. 2, 1764, printed a N.Y. dispatch of January 25 saying that the *Harriot* had sailed "yesterday" for Falmouth. *London Chron.*, Feb. 18–20, 1764, reported its arrival at Falmouth on February 16.

6. The parliamentary grant for 1760 was distributed in 1762 before General Amherst's return had been received showing what various colonies' contributions of troops had been in 1760. The agents had agreed that the money should be distributed in the same proportions as that for the campaign of 1759; if Amherst's return showed that any colony had been overpaid, then an adjustment would be made when the grant for the campaign of 1761 was received. It later developed that Conn. and Pa. had been overpaid, the latter colony owing £10,947 sterling. According to Amherst's return for 1761, however, Pa. was not entitled to any share of the grant for that year, and since its agents had transmitted to the colony the whole of what they had received for 1760, they had no way of making good the overpayment. The obligation was therefore transferred from London to Philadelphia. The Assembly passed a bill to pay the amounts due to six other colonies on Jan. 13, 1764, but the governor delayed approving it until March 23. *Pa. Col. Recs.*, IX, 47–52; *Votes*, 1763–64, pp. 22, 25–7, 68; *Statutes at Large, Pa.*, VI, 329–31.

7. For accounts of these matters relating to the Indians, see below, pp. 22–9, 42–55.

8. In his letter of November 12 Jackson had written of the proposed reduction in the duty on foreign molasses to make the law more effective, and

own sakes not to lay greater Burthens on us than we can bear; for you cannot hurt us without hurting your selves. All our Profits center with you, and the more you take from us, the less we can lay out with you. I had lodg'd some Money with Mr. Sargent to pay for my Part of the Carolana Purchase, if we had made it; but begin to think it will come to nothing.[9] I can now only add that I am, with sincerest Esteem and Respect, Dear Friend, Yours affectionately   B FRANKLIN

Addressed: To / Richard Jackson Esqr / Member of Parliament for Weymouth / London / Free to N York / B FRANKLIN

Endorsed: 16 Janry 1764 Benjn. Franklin Esqr

To Anthony Todd[1]   Extract:[2] Public Record Office

Sir   [Philadelphia, January 16, 1764]

In my last[3] I wrote you that Mr. Foxcroft, my Colleague, was gone to Virginia where and in Maryland some offices are yet unsettled. We are to meet again in April at Annapolis,[4] and then shall send you a full Account of our Doings. I will now only just mention, that we hope in the Spring to expedite the Communication between Boston and New York, as we have already that be-

---

had prophesied that Parliament would "infallibly" raise £200,000 annually on the colonies. BF's preoccupation with problems in Pa. at this time may have made him less concerned over this prospect than he might otherwise have been.

9. On this land scheme and the part BF and Jackson considered playing in it, see above, X, 208–9, 212–15, 254–5, 341–2, 369–71.

1. For Todd, secretary of the British Post Office, see above, X, 217 n.

2. This extract (C.O. 323: 17, f. 128) was sent by order of the postmaster general to John Pownall, secretary of the Board of Trade, "as it must be a great Satisfaction for them [the Board] to observe that the posts upon that extensive Continent are visible in a Course of Improvement." Todd to Pownall, March 3, 1764, P.R.O., C.O. 323: 17, f. 126. It was read before the Board on March 3d. *Board of Trade Journal*, Jan. 1764–Dec. 1767, p. 29.

3. Perhaps a letter, not found, written after BF returned to Philadelphia in November 1763 from his postal inspection trip to New England (see above, X, 276–9), or perhaps the "ample Report" on the American postal system which Todd on Jan. 28, 1764, said that he expected "by one of the two next Packet Boats"; see below, p. 38.

4. There is nothing in any of BF's surviving letters to indicate that this meeting took place.

tween New York and Philadelphia, by making the Mails travel by Night as well as by Day, which has never heretofore been done in America. It passes now between Philadelphia and New York, so quick that a Letter can be sent from one place to another, and an Answer received the Day following, which before took a week,[5] and when our Plan is executed between Boston and New York, Letters may be sent and answers received in four Days, which before took a fortnight; and between Philadelphia and Boston in Six days, which before required Three Weeks.[6] We think this expeditious Communication will greatly encrease the Number of Letters from Philadelphia and Boston by the Packets to Britain.

Endorsed: Plans Genl. Extract of a Letter from Benja. Franklin Esqr. Depy. Postmaster Genl. of No. America to the Secry of the Post Office dated Janry 16. 1764, respecting the Communicatn carried on between New York and other Colonies by Post.

Read March 3. 1764. R. 46.

From James Bowdoin

Letterbook copy: Massachusetts Historical Society

Sir   Boston, Janry: 18. 1764

I am very glad to hear you got home Safe with your Daughter and Mr. Foxcroft without any further accident; and hope your arm has recovered it's former Strength.[7]

I here enclose, open for your perusal, a Letter to Mr. Canton on the Subject I spoke to you about. If any thing should occur to you to improve the Telescope further than what is noticed in said Letter, I shall take it as a favor you would mention it to Mr. Can-

---

5. William Dunlap, postmaster at Philadelphia, advertised in *Pa. Gaz.*, Jan. 5, 1764, "By Order of the Post-master General," that mail for New York would be dispatched at 2 P.M. every Tuesday, Thursday, and Saturday and that mail from New York would be expected at 10 A.M. on the same days.

6. The dates of letters exchanged between BF and Francis Bernard printed in this volume do not suggest that the plan for improvement in the Boston-Philadelphia service had yet been put into effect by April of this year.

7. For BF's trip to New England in the summer of 1763, during which he twice fell and both times injured his shoulder, see above, x, 276–9.

21

ton; and that you'd be so good as to let my letter accompany your own.[8] I hope we shall soon have the pleasure of seeing you again. An annual tour this way would contribute much to your health. Please to make my Compliments to your good lady, to your daughter and Mr. Foxcroft and believe me to be with the utmost regard Dear Sir your most humble &c. Whenever Mr. Winthrop shall deliver me Æpinus, I will take care to send it to you.[9]

I would have a Micrometer of Dolland's Invention fixed to the Telescope.[1] I intirely forgot to mention it in my letter to Mr. Canton. I shall be obliged if you'll mention in your Letter to him. The micrometer to be taken off and put on at pleasure, if when on and not wanted, it would stand in the way.

This is the Figure which the Foregoing Letter to Mr. Canton refers to.

Benja. Franklin Esqr. in Philadelphia

Pennsylvania Assembly: Reply to the Governor

Printed in *Votes and Proceedings of the House of Representatives,* 1763–1764 (Philadelphia, 1764), pp. 33–4.

During the summer and early autumn of 1763 hostile Indians repeatedly attacked isolated settlements and farms on the Pennsylvania frontier, killing many whites, carrying others off into captivity, and driving the rest in terror from their homes to the relatively few garrisoned forts or the larger communities to the east. The small numbers of armed men authorized by the Assembly were quite inadequate to cope with the

8. BF enclosed this letter with his own to Canton of March 14, 1764; see above, x, 351 n, and below, p. 99.

9. Winthrop sent the Æpinus books to Ezra Stiles who returned them to BF; apparently Bowdoin was not able to see them. See above, x, 351–2 n, and below, p. 246.

1. Edward Nairne (above, x, 171 n), the English instrument maker who worked on Bowdoin's telescope, decided that the attachment of a micrometer was impractical; see above, x, 351 n, and below, p. 245. John Dollond (1706–1761), F.R.S., 1761, abandoned his trade of silk weaving in 1752 to devote himself to the study of optics. He won the Copley medal in 1758 for the invention of the achromatic telescope and in 1761 was appointed optician to the King. In 1753 and 1754 Dollond's papers describing the development of his "divided object-glass micrometers" were published in *Phil. Trans.*, from which Bowdoin probably learned about them. *DNB.*

22

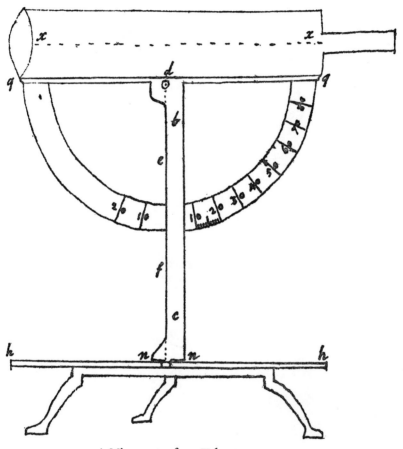

A Micrometer for a Telescope

raiding bands, and by the time cooler weather set in there were almost no settlers in the more exposed areas foolhardy enough to remain on their own lands.

The frontiersmen, both the refugees and those living in areas less vulnerable to attack, were vehemently critical of the seemingly do-nothing Assembly and violently hostile to the Indians—to all Indians, that is, not only those who had gone on the warpath but also the relatively small groups that had come sufficiently under the influence of white men, chiefly Quakers and Moravians, to settle down on nearby land and live as peaceable neighbors. Rumors spread around that some, at least, of these Indians were giving secret aid and comfort to more active tribesmen. It is impossible to say now how many of these reports, if any, were based on solid fact; the important point is that many white men believed them and concluded that the only sound policy was to remove all Indians from the areas under white control, either by evacuation or by death.

On October 21 the provincial commissioners reported to the Assembly that they believed the Moravians at Bethlehem had been secretly supplying a nearby body of Christianized Indians with arms and ammunition, which the Indians in turn had supposedly been bartering with "our Enemies on the Frontiers." These "Moravian Indians" were also believed to have been "principally concerned" in a series of murders in Northampton County.[2] The commissioners recommended that these Indians be removed to some place "where their Behaviour may be more closely observed." The House thereupon resolved that those who were "willing and desirous, from their Attachment to the Government, or regard for their own Safety," be invited to come down to some place the governor and Council should think "most safe and convenient for them," and that the government would pay for the expense of their removal and support.[3]

Some 127 Indians were thereupon moved to Philadelphia, arriving on November 11 in the company of a Moravian missionary, Rev. Bern-

2. These Christianized Indians had been living on a Moravian mission at Wechquetank on Head's Creek, beyond the Lehigh Gap and near the former mission at Gnadenhütten and Fort Allen, the locale of BF's military labors in January 1756. See above, VI, 290–382 *passim*, and map, p. 309. The Indians were moved to Nazareth on October 11. John W. Jordan, "Biographical Sketch of Rev. Bernhard Adam Grube," *PMHB*, XXV (1901), 15, 17.

3. *Votes*, 1763–64, pp. 8–9. On the day after the Assembly adopted this resolution, the governor approved a bill imposing a penalty of a £500 fine, thirty-nine lashes on the bare back, and imprisonment for twelve months on any one convicted of supplying arms or ammunition to an Indian without the prior consent of the governor or the commander-in-chief of the King's forces in the area. *Statutes at Large, Pa.,* VI, 319–20.

25

hard Adam Grube. They encountered great hostility in the city. The first plan was to place them in the barracks, but a group of soldiers and their wives living there would have none of them and took up arms to hold them out. After standing around for five hours enduring insults from the populace as well as the soldiery, the Indians were taken to Province Island in the Delaware at the mouth of the Schuylkill River, on which stood several buildings normally used as a pesthouse, or quarantine hospital.[4]

Since early in the century a small group of Indians had been living on the Penns' Conestoga Manor near the borough of Lancaster. During the autumn of 1763 rumors had been spreading that they had been harboring at least one hostile Indian. In the first part of December some men from Paxton, farther up the Susquehanna, investigated at Conestoga and returned home with the report that they had seen several armed Indians there. That news was enough; early in the morning of December 14 about fifty armed riders burst into the little village, murdered the six Indians they found there, and burned down the cabins. Fourteen other Indians who lived at Conestoga were saved for the time being because they were away from home the night of the raid. When the news of this massacre reached Lancaster, the authorities rounded up the fourteen survivors and placed them in the workhouse, the strongest building in the borough, for safety. But the men from Paxton, who asserted later that one of these Indians was a murderer, descended upon Lancaster on December 27, broke down the doors of the workhouse, and dispatched all fourteen Indians, men, women, and children alike.[5]

4. *PMHB*, xxv (1901), p. 17; Theodore G. Tappert and John W. Doberstein, eds., *The Journals of Henry Melchior Muhlenberg* (Phila., 1942), I, 703, 705.

5. Curiously enough, the Philadelphia newspapers carried no detailed reports of these two atrocities, though they printed in full the governor's proclamations for apprehending the men involved. For BF's moving account, see his *Narrative of the Late Massacres*, reprinted below, pp. 42–69. The way in which rumors could be exaggerated and distorted in such a period of tension is illustrated by an entry under date of December 29 in the journal of Henry Melchior Muhlenberg, a Lutheran minister in Philadelphia, who recorded that fifty persons had ridden into Lancaster, "stopped before the city prison, and shot fourteen imprisoned Indians. Some time previously six Indians were shot near where they lived, not far from Lancaster, by these very Indians who are our so-called Friends." *Muhlenberg Journals*, I, 728. Thus the fourteen later victims, placed in the workhouse for their protection, became in report fourteen murderers who had been imprisoned for killing their own relatives. These fourteen, regardless of age or sex, had presumably now met a just fate in punishment for their crimes against other Indians. Muhlenberg seems not to have known that among the self-appointed executioners were the actual murderers of the first group of Indians.

On December 21, two days after the Assembly had reconvened following an October adjournment, Governor Penn reported on a series of conferences he and his predecessor Hamilton had held with a group of friendly Indians living on the upper Susquehanna. They were "uneasy at their present Situation" and wished to come to live under the protection of the government. The Assembly would have to provide money, however, if it approved this proposal. In the same message Penn also reported on the massacre at Conestoga Manor on the 14th, done "without the least Reason or Provocation, in cool Blood," and he told the House of the orders he had given the magistrates of the western counties "to exert themselves, and endeavour, by all possible Means, to discover and secure the Principals concerned in this outrageous Act." He added that the survivors, then still lodged in the Lancaster workhouse, wanted to be transferred to Philadelphia or its neighborhood. The Assembly replied on the 24th with a brief message promising to provide funds to move both these groups of Indians to safety.[6]

When the assemblymen reconvened in January after a brief recess, they and the governor exchanged messages about the killing of the Indians in the Lancaster workhouse on December 27, and the Assembly unanimously resolved to provide funds for whatever additional force the governor and provincial commissioners might require "to frustrate the further wicked Designs of the lawless Rioters."[7] As early as November 22 rumors had begun to circulate that the country people, "becoming embittered because the authorities are taking no adequate measures for defense," were planning "to come to the city in droves and destroy everything in *revenge*."[8] Reports of a proposed march on the city increased, and after the events at Conestoga and Lancaster were known in Philadelphia it became clear that the major objective of such a march would be the killing of the Indians on Province Island. It seemed desirable, therefore, to get them away to some place of even greater safety.[9]

While the governor and Council were concentrating on this problem, the Assembly undertook to deal with another aspect of the general situation: the trial of the murderers at Conestoga and Lancaster, when and if they should be identified and caught. Granted the state of public opinion in Lancaster County, it seemed unlikely that any jury there would be likely to convict them, however strong the evidence might be. A committee of three, including Franklin, was therefore appointed to bring in a bill for the trial of capital offenses committed between white

6. *Votes*, 1763–64, pp. 15–16, 17; *Pa. Col. Recs.*, IX, 94–7.
7. *Votes*, 1763–64, pp. 19–20; *Pa. Col. Recs.*, IX, 108–10.
8. *Muhlenberg Journals*, I, 709.
9. *Pa. Col. Recs.*, IX, 100–1, 103.

men and women and Indians. The measure they introduced, January 4, provided that those accused of such crimes should be brought to Philadelphia and tried there. But this measure, so contrary to the principle of common law that a criminal trial should take place in the county where the crime was committed, "Occasion'd such a Clamour in the House and out-a-doors that the house thought proper to let it lye after the first reading untill the present unhappy Commotion and ferment should have time to subside."[1] The proposal was not revived.

The Indians on Province Island, alarmed for their own safety, petitioned the Assembly for a vessel large enough to take them all to England, but the governor and Council decided that a much more feasible plan was to send them to the protection of Sir William Johnson, superintendent of Indian affairs, on the Mohawk River in upper New York province. A detachment of Montgomery's Regiment of Highlanders, then in Philadelphia, was planning to set off early on the morning of January 5 for New York City, and its commander generously agreed to escort the Indians as far as that city. Letters were at once dispatched to Johnson and General Gage informing them of this action and also to Lieutenant Governor Cadwallader Colden of New York and Governor William Franklin of New Jersey asking permission to send the Indians through their provinces.[2]

William Franklin cooperated quickly, but when the Indians had reached Perth Amboy, January 11, ready to cross over to Staten Island and enter the province of New York, they were halted. Word came that when Colden consulted the New York Council, its members unanimously advised him to refuse permission for the Indians to travel through that jurisdiction. New Yorkers regarded the Indians living on the east side of the Susquehanna as "the most obnoxious" of any, Colden reported, "a Number of Rogues and Thieves, Runaways from the other Nations," and not to be trusted. General Gage wrote Penn that under the circumstances he would arrange for some companies of the Royal American Regiment, who were about to march to Philadelphia, to escort the Indians back there. And so this group of displaced men, women, and children, numbering about 140 by now, were forced to retrace their steps. They reached Philadelphia on January 24 and this time were quartered in the barracks under guard of British regulars.[3]

1. *Votes*, 1763–64, p. 21. A fragmentary journal of Samuel Foulke, assemblyman for Bucks Co., during parts of 1762–64, printed in *PMHB*, v (1881), 60–73, contains useful accounts of many events in the first part of 1764 from the point of view of a Quaker member; for this quotation, see pp. 67–8.
2. *Pa. Col. Recs.*, IX, 110–13.
3. *Pa. Col. Recs.*, IX, 119–22, 124–5; *PMHB*, XXV (1901), 17–18.

When Penn learned of Colden's refusal to permit the Indians to travel through New York, he laid the situation before his councilors on January 16. Acting on their recommendation, he sent a message to the Assembly the same day, reporting what had happened and asking its opinion and advice as to how the government could most effectually give the Indians "that Protection and Security which, under their Circumstances, they have an undoubted Right to expect and claim from us." The Assembly was prevented from conducting business from the afternoon of January 17 to the afternoon of the 19th by a "sudden Indisposition" of Speaker Norris, but when it did meet, a committee of four, including Franklin, was appointed to draft a reply. The message the committee prepared was sent to the governor on the 20th.[4]

May it please your HONOUR,   January 20, 1764.

We have taken into our Consideration your Honour's Message of the Sixteenth Instant, with the Letters therein referred to, and are pleased to find the Governor so heartily disposed to afford the Indians he mentions *"that Protection and Security which, under their Circumstances, they have an undoubted Right to expect and claim from us."* We should be very glad, if it was in our Power, *"to point out the Manner in which this can most effectually be done;"* but as our *"Opinion"* must be founded on the Information we have received, we can only mention such Measures as appear to us at present to be most reasonable; submitting our Sentiments to the Judgment your Honour may form from any Intelligence you have since received, or any Circumstances that may hereafter happen.

We observe, with particular Pleasure, *"the kind Part General Gage has taken in this Matter,"* in protecting these Indians, and directing the Escort, on their Arrival in this City, to receive *"such Orders as you shall judge proper to give them."*

As this humane and prudent Step of the General is equally calculated to secure these unhappy People, and preserve the internal Peace of this Province, while our own Troops are engaged in the Defence of our Frontiers, we shall be obliged to your Honour, if you will please to return his Excellency our Thanks for this generous and seasonable Act of Goodness.

The Indians, we apprehend, will be sufficiently protected by the Companies that compose this Escort, while they remain here. When these Companies march from hence, if there should appear to be

4. *Votes*, 1763–64, pp. 28–30, 31–33; *Pa. Col. Recs.*, IX, 122–4.

29

the same Danger of any Outrage being committed against these Indians, that there seems to be at present, we are of Opinion, that it will be adviseable for your Honour to lodge them in some Place where they can be most easily and conveniently guarded by an armed Force, to be raised by your Honour for that Purpose.

It will be with the utmost Regret we shall see your Honour reduced to the Necessity of pursuing these Measures; but with an Abhorrence altogether inexpressible we should behold *"these poor Creatures,"* who, desirous of living in Friendship with us, as Proofs of this Disposition quitting a Settlement that made them suspected, and surrendering their Arms, have delivered themselves, their Wives and Children, into our Power, on the Faith of this Province, barbarously butchered by a Sett of Ruffians, whose audacious Cruelty is checked by no Sentiment of Humanity, and by no Regard to the Laws of their Country.

Such a Massacre we have Reason to expect from the Persons who perpetrated such shocking Barbarities in Lancaster County, and their Abettors, unless they are deterred by a vigorous Exertion of Power, which never can be more properly employed than in vindicating the Honour and Dignity of a Government, enforcing an Obedience to the Laws, and repressing the dangerous Insolence of tumultuous Insurgents, who, guided by a blind Rage, undertake by open Force to controul the Conduct of the Administration, and counteract the best concerted Measures for the general Good.

It will therefore be agreeable to us, that your Honour would be pleased to order the Sheriff and Coroner of Lancaster County, and the Magistrates of that Borough, to come down, and give you the best Information that can be obtained of the Persons concerned in these Violences; that they being discovered and apprehended, due Punishment may be inflicted on such daring Disturbers of the public Peace.[5] *Signed by Order of the House,*

ISAAC NORRIS, Speaker.

5. When this message was read at the Council on January 23, "sundry difficulties" appeared to the members, "the same not being practicable," so the Council put off further consideration until February 2. The principal difficulty was in the Assembly's suggestion in the last paragraph that the officers in Lancaster be summoned to Philadelphia for an inquiry. This proposal may have seemed to imply that these proprietary appointees had failed in their duty of preventing the violence that had taken place and in apprehending the guilty. On February 2 the councilors unanimously agreed

From Francis Bernard
Letterbook copy: Harvard College Library

Sir   Boston, Jan 23. 1764

I am favoured with yours of the 11th inst.[6] and am much obliged to you for the trouble you have given yourself of sending a Messenger to Alexandria. I should have proposed this Measure long ago, if I had any Notion that the conveyance of letters to that Town had been so precarious: for tho' I have had sevral letters from him,[7] yet I cannot find that any of my letters (from Aug. 30, when I sent a letter to Mr. Dunlap[8] to be forwarded, to the present time,) have reached him. When he gets to Philadelphia, the easiest way of his return will be by Sea, if a good Vessell offers: but that I must leave to your Judgement.[9] But I am desirous in all things that your trouble should be lessened as much as possible.

I have less concern to trouble you with another business, because being intended for public Utility you will make it your own concern. I have a desire to endeavour to establish a Sturgeon fishery in the River Penobscot. And I have engaged a suitable Man for that purpose, who by means of the Garrison of the Fort there will have labour cheap:[1] all that We want is a good receipt. The

---

that such an open inquiry in Philadelphia "would be attended with many ill Consequences," and that it would be "more advisable" for the governor to instruct some justice or justices in Lancaster (also proprietary appointees), "in whose Prudence and discretion he can most confide," to examine the sheriff and coroner at the next court at Lancaster as to their knowledge of the "Authors and Perpetrators" of the murders "and to do this with all possible Secrecy." *Pa. Col. Recs.*, IX, 124, 128. On February 4 Penn wrote to three magistrates at Lancaster to call before them at the next court the sheriff, coroner, and anyone else who might have information and to learn all they could about the attacks on the Indians and the identity of the persons involved. He pledged that the names of informers would be kept secret to protect them from the "Resentment of the Rioters." 1 *Pa. Arch.*, IV, 160.

6. See above, p. 6.

7. Bernard's son Francis.

8. William Dunlap, postmaster at Philadelphia; see above, VII, 158.

9. Young Bernard traveled overland to N.Y. (riding BF's horse) and then sailed to Newport. Whether he continued to Boston by sea is unknown. See below, pp. 78-9.

1. On Nov. 12, 1764, Bernard and Col. Thomas Goldthwaite (1717–1779), the commander at Fort Pownall, 1763–70, bought "2,700 acres of land in the vicinity of what is now Fort Point, on the west bank of the Penobscot" and "were instrumental in settling 2400 able men" there, although

best pickled Sturgeon I ever eat, was cured at Trenton: and as your Neighbourhood to that Operator[2] must give you some acquaintance with him, I would trouble you to get his receipt in as precise Words as possible: and you may assure him in such case that Penobscot Sturgeon shall not be sent to Philadelphia or New York or any other Market, that he may call his.

I have a like desire to try the Pickling Salmon according to the New Castle Way. But I fear I shant be able to get a receipt from thence by the next Season: if you have one by you, I should be glad to be favoured with it. I am &c.

Benj Franklin Esqr.

From Solomon Williams[3]

Draft: Lyme Historical Society-Florence Griswold Association, Inc., Old Lyme, Conn.

Honored Sir   Leb: 25 Jany 1764.

You Will Pardon this Trouble and My Freedom In using your Name When I inform you that Mr. Webster[4] for Whom is the En-

---

it is not certain whether any of these settlers engaged in the sturgeon fishery. On Feb. 27, 1762, the Mass. General Court granted Bernard the island of Mount Desert, some miles east of Penobscot Bay, where the governor also intended to establish a fishery. William O. Sawtelle, "Sir Francis Bernard and his Grant of Mount Desert," Mass. Col. Soc. *Publications*, XXIV (1921), 199, 234–5 n.

2. Probably Edward Broadfield, who came to America from London in 1753, advertised pickled sturgeon at Bordentown, N.J., and moved to Trenton in 1754, where he continued to advertise his sturgeon until 1767. Broadfield boasted that he had received a premium from the Royal Society of Arts for his product. 1 *N.J. Arch.*, XIX, 268, 505; XXV, 146–8, 371–3, 459–60; XXVI, 169, 242. But for another possible producer, see below, p. 334 n.

3. Solomon Williams (1700–1776), A.B., Harvard, 1719; D.D., Yale, 1773, was the minister of the First Congregational Church at Lebanon, Conn., from 1722 to 1776. A moderate New Light who supported George Whitefield but opposed Jonathan Edwards, Williams founded the Lebanon town library and grammar school and was a trustee of Yale, 1749–76. *Sibley's Harvard Graduates*, VI, 352–61. His son William (1731–1811) was one of the signers of the Declaration of Independence.

4. Pelatiah Webster (1726–1795), B.A., Yale, 1746, was born in Lebanon, Conn. (hence his acquaintance with Williams) and was ordained to preach

32

closed Desired me thus to Make use of your Name to Carry a Letter to him with the Assurance that he had your Favorable permission for it. Since I have this Occasion to Speak to you Allow me sir in the Crowd of your Admirers to Return you My Sincere Thanks for your Eminent Services to the literary World by your Wonderful discoverys and Improvements In Electricity. I wish you Increasing and abundant Success and honor in All your Generous Endeavors to promote the Improvement and happiness of Mankind. I am Honored Sir with Great Respect your very humble Servant   S: W:

Copy of the Cover of my Letter to Mr. Webster to Mr. Franklin.[5]

Endorsed: Copy of My Lr to Mr Pelatiah Webster

From Richard Jackson   ALS: American Philosophical Society

Dear Sir   Inner Temple 26 Jany 1764

I have wrote to you by every Packet that has sailed and one that has not, I mean that of the present Month, which not being in England at the time, has been detained for the next, in the mean time, I write a line or two, by a Merchant Vessel that sails tomorrow or next day.[6]

I got pretty early intelligence of Major Barker's arrival in Eng-

---

at Greenwich, Mass., in 1749, but left the ministry six years later and went to Philadelphia where he became a merchant. During the Revolutionary War he wrote a series of essays on money and commerce which won him a considerable reputation as a political economist. He was an ardent advocate of a strong central government and wrote cogently in support of the adoption of the Federal Constitution. *DAB.*

5. The draft of Williams' letter to Webster is on the same sheet as the above. It chiefly concerns the disastrous circumstances of Webster's relatives in Lebanon. Because of their penury he suggested that Webster get BF to frank his and their letters back and forth—an example of what the deputy postmaster general might be expected to do for acquaintances. A new statute soon explicitly forbade such abuses of the franking privilege. See below, p. 39 n.

6. By May 1, 1764, BF had acknowledged receiving Jackson's letters of Nov. 12, 1763 (above, X, 368–72), Nov. 26, and Dec. 9, 1763 (neither has been found), Dec. 27, 1763 (above, X, 411–16), Jan. 14, 1764 (not found), and the present letter. See below, p. 185.

land,[7] but at the same time was informed of his Resolution to go to America, there to look after take Possesion of, and cultivate his Estate; I had long before discovered that this was the Gentleman you had in view; but thought it best to see him myself which I did an hour after I had wrote my last Letter, which however has not yet gone.

I found my Information well grounded and have no doubt he intends going to America in April. He is a sensible well-behaved man and as he has a great deal of military Merit, and is a friend of some Gentlemen of my Acquaintance who have long served in India, and who are too good Judges of Merit to bestow their friendship on one who did not deserve it, I think it is my Duty to recommend him to my friends in America and wish you would give him such Assistance as falls in your Way. Perhaps Mr. Hughes's Acquaintance with him may help him to the Purchase of any Part of Major Barker Estate that he may determine to sell, should he come to such a determination.

Measures are taken for bringing several American Questions before Parliament.[8] They are so numerous that I am quite at a loss where to begin, and I am so employd not only in attending the House, but in combating what I deem the most dangerous Errors in American Politicks in 100 Places, in many of which I am to begin with first Principles, that I am fit for little but sleep when I return home. Mr. Allen knows somewhat of my Assiduity on these Subjects.[9] I have Access to almost every Place any friends of the

7. For Major Robert Barker, from whom BF's friend John Hughes was trying to buy lands in western N.J., see above, X, 157 n. Contrary to Jackson's expectation stated in this letter, Barker did not go to America. He was knighted and returned to India and served the East India Co. with the rank of colonel. *DNB;* A. M. Davies, *Clive of Plassey* (London, 1939), p. 429.

8. The foremost American question confronting Parliament at this time was how money was to be raised from the colonies to pay for the British troops that were to remain in America to protect them. That a revenue was to be raised in America, Jackson had written BF on Dec. 27, 1763, was not "now to [be] argued against." The proposal to alter the duties on the colonial importation of foreign molasses, embodied in the Sugar Act of April 5, 1764, had already been discussed for some months by British politicians. See above, X, 371–2, 415.

9. William Allen, chief justice of Pa. (above, III, 296–7 n), visited England in the summer of 1763 and returned home in August 1764. Reports from London printed in *Pa. Gaz.,* May 10 and June 4, 1764, declared that Allen

Colony's would wish to have Access to[1] but I am not sensible of my making any Impression proportioned to my Endeavours, perhaps it is I, that am wrong.

I have long since given up all hopes of preventing some Parliamentary Tax to be imposed on N America as well as the W Indies for the maintenance of the Troops kept there, how far it is necessary to keep any considerable Number I will not say, but I have long argued that those kept there are for the most part maintained for the Intrests of G Britain only.

I am most averse to an Internal Tax, God knows how far such a precedent may be extended, and I have frequently asked, what internal Tax they will not lay.

Customs as well as Prohibitions on Trade, have been at all times, laid by England from the time of the long Parliament.[2] I wish this to be the Rule of Conduct on this Occasion.

There is a Bill in Embryo for restraining your Paper Currency and of all N america within the limits prescribed to the N England Governments by the Stat 24 Geo. 2d. I have not seen the Draught of it, if it be prepared. They will certainly carry it, if they are determined so to do.[3] My Compliments to my friends par-

---

had been "indefatigable" in opposing a stamp act and had used his "Acquaintance with the first Personages in the Kingdom, and the greatest Part of the House of Commons" to prevent the passage of such a measure that session.

1. Jackson was appointed secretary to the chancellor of the Exchequer, George Grenville, in 1763 and served until the fall of that administration in July 1765. He claimed to have a "good deal of access" to the chancellor. Namier and Brooke, *House of Commons*, II, 670, and above, X, 412–13.

2. The English Parliament which convened in 1640 was not technically dissolved until 1661, although Cromwell put a temporary end to its sessions in 1653. Cromwell's Navigation Act (or Ordinance) of 1651 and Charles II's first Navigation Act (1660) laid the foundation for the system of English control of colonial trade.

3. For the Board of Trade hearings and the parliamentary maneuverings that led to the passage of the Currency Act of April 19, 1764 (4 Geo. III, c. 34), which forbade further emission of legal-tender paper currency in the colonies south of New England, see Jack M. Sosin, "Imperial Regulation of Colonial Paper Money, 1764–1773," *PMHB*, LXXXVIII (1964), 174–98. For the repercussions of the act in the colonies, see Jack P. Greene and Richard M. Jellison, "The Currency Act of 1764 in Imperial-Colonial Relations, 1764–1776," 3 *William and Mary Quar.*, XVIII (1961), 485–518. See also Jackson's comments, below, pp. 176–7.

ticularly the Governor of N Jersey and his Lady. It is 11 at Night
and I have not dined. I am Dear sir your Affectionate humble Servant   RD JACKSON

The Postmasters General to the Lords of the Treasury: Memorandum on the American Postal Service

Letterbook copy: General Post Office, London[4]

This document is preceded in the letterbook by a letter of the same date
from Anthony Todd, secretary of the British Post Office, to Charles Jenkinson, secretary to the Treasury, indicating that the paper would be
given to George Grenville "the beginning of next Week" and that Jenkinson might "depend on a Copy of it."[5] Todd probably prepared at
least the draft of the memorandum, acting at the direction of the joint postmasters general, as an aid to the preparation of future legislation; much
of its contents reflects his correspondence with Franklin and Foxcroft in
America, and it clearly shows the influence of their suggestions for the
improvement of the colonial postal service.

28 Jany 1764
MEMORANDUM relating to some Improvements suggested to be
made in the Management of the Post Office in North America.

The beginning of last summer Mr. Franklin and Mr. Foxcroft,
Deputy PostMaster General for North-America, undertook a Survey, which was proposed to extend at least, through the whole
present Post Roads, in order to examine every where into the state
and Management of the several Post Offices; to make such new
Regulations as should appear to be necessary; and to observe what
Improvements, the Revenue might be capable of, in the different

4. In G.P.O., Treasury Letter Book, 1760–1771, pp. 95–105.
5. *Ibid.*, p. 94. On Todd, see above, X, 217 n. Charles Jenkinson (1729–
1808), was private secretary to Lord Holdernesse, 1758–61; under secretary
of state, 1761–62; private secretary to Lord Bute and treasurer of the Ord-
nance, 1762–63; and joint secretary to the Treasury, 1763–65. Thereafter he
held a succession of offices, none of major consequence, although as secretary
at war, 1778–82, he exercised considerable influence. He was regarded as an
able administrative manager and an expert on commerce and finance. He
was M.P., 1761–86, then was created Baron Hawkesbury, and was advanced
to the earldom of Liverpool, 1796. *DNB;* Namier and Brooke, *House of
Commons,* II, 674–8.

36

Colonies;[6] That they might be able, upon their return, to offer their Sentiments on the several points, which have been referred to them by the PostMaster General; particularly, That of rendering Correspondence in the vast Empire of America of the greatest utility to His Majesty's Subjects; at the same time keeping in View the Improvements of the Revenue itself; though the Postage cannot for a long while, be expected to exceed the charges of Management, because in the Colonies, settled in part only, where the Towns are situated at a great distance from each other, there is a continual necessity of erecting new Offices; it is however satisfactory to find, That many Offices in Virginia, and other Colonies, in the like situation, which were once a Burthen and Charge, have lately been brought to bear their own Expence and even afford a prospect of soon becoming profitable; as a Country increasing in Wealth and Commerce, and so speedily multiplying its Inhabitants, cannot fail to keep pace in an Increase of Correspondence, especially, since the Posts in America are under the Management of persons of acknowledged Abilities, who have been furnished, from hence with every Light, which could possibly be collected; And the more to excite in them a laudable Zeal, they have been given to understand, that they cannot exert themselves, on any subject which will do them greater honour, or their native Country of America more signal Service, than rendering the intercourse of Letters, every day more and more safe, expeditious and frequent to their fellow Subjects.[7]

They have already obeyed The PostMaster General, by remitting £494 4s. 8d. in full Payment of their Balance up to the 10th. of August 1761, and This is the first remittance ever made of the kind.[8]

6. On the 1763 journeys to Virginia and New England, see above, x, 252, 276–9.

7. The last part of this paragraph is copied almost *verbatim* from a letter of Todd to BF and Foxcroft of March 12, 1763; see above, x, 219.

8. This balance reflects the unprecedented accomplishments of the colonial postal service under the administration of BF and William Hunter. (The date given here may be slightly in error, for Hunter died on Aug. 12, 1761; *Pa. Gaz.*, Sept. 10, 1761.) While most of the credit for this favorable balance should go to the joint deputy postmasters general because of the expansion of the service and the more efficient procedures which they instituted, a share should doubtless be given to James Parker, the comptroller, who exer-

JANUARY 28, 1764

There is great reason to hope that the Packet Boats, which have been lately established between Falmouth and New York, as they are on no account to be interrupted in their regular Course, will contribute very materially to the Benefit of His Majesty's trading Subjects;[9] and may likewise, in a little Time, be aiding to the Revenue of the Posts; though at present Those Boats are, in appearance, some Burthen; as the Postage of Letters, to and from New York immediately, does not quite support the Charge of the Vessells; but, the Increase of The Inland Postage, in both Countries, occasioned thereby, tho' it cannot be exactly ascertained, may perhaps nearly amount to the remainder of the Expence.

As the Survey of the Deputy PostMaster General in America must have been finished at the End of this Summer, an ample Report is expected from them, by one of the two next Packet Boats, with Maps delineated and adapted to the Post Roads of America; particularly, such as relate to the Posts to and from the Chief-Office of New York, which is at present the only regular Center of this important and extensive Correspondence;[1] but, upon the establish-

cised immediate supervision while both BF and Hunter were in England. BF apparently submitted the account in April 1762; he sent two bills of exchange to cover the balance on June 1, 1763, after settling matters with Hunter's executors, and Todd acknowledged receiving £494 4s. 8d. on the following August 13. See above, X, 220, 270, 281, 322.

9. Todd had informed the deputy postmasters general, March 12, 1763, that the Post Office had made a change in the packet-boat system between Falmouth and New York, using smaller, more economical vessels than had been employed during the war, and providing more regular, dependable service, with a packet scheduled to leave each of the two ports "precisely on the second Saturday of every Month throughout the Year." BF and Foxcroft had replied pledging their cooperation in making the service a success. See above, X, 217–18, 280.

1. On Sept. 21, 1764, BF and Foxcroft told Todd that they had written him "pretty fully" on the 4th of that month, and in the next paragraph they apologized for their long delay in sending their "Account of the State of the Office." See below, p. 341. The communication of the 4th, not now found, was probably the overdue report. WF wrote Lord Halifax, Nov. 8, 1764, that there was no separate map of N.J., though one was in preparation; he added that BF and Foxcroft had sent the General Post Office in England "one of Evans's Maps of the Middle Provinces [above, III, 48 n, 392 n] with the Post Roads mark'd out thereon, which I saw, and thought very exact." 1 N.J. Arch., IX, 485. It is not known what other maps the deputy postmasters general may have sent.

ment of the Three New Packet Boats, about to take place, to and from the Southern Parts of the said Continent, including the late immense Acquisitions, the PostMaster General has Thoughts of erecting another Central Chief Office at Charles Town, from whence the Correspondence may be brancht out and extended as occasion shall require, thro' the Neighbouring Southern Colonies, as well as be properly connected with That already establisht in the Northern Ones.[2]

Amongst the many Injunctions relating to the American Posts, which the PostMaster General has sent to Their Deputies there; No one has been more strongly enforced, than not to permit or suffer, any Letter or Packet, under any pretence whatever not even on the Government's Service, to pass free of Postage; The Post-Master General, by the Post Act of the 9th. of Queen Anne, having no such dispensing Power; and the least Inovation of this kind might spread itself in such a Manner, as to prevent That Revenue from ever becoming advantageous; or perhaps even sufficient to support the Charges of maintaining a well established Post through That extensive Empire.[3]

The Law as it now stands with respect to Ship Letters seems only to have in View Letters coming by Shipping from parts beyond the Seas into the several Ports of Great Britain and Ireland, and not Letters going by Shipping to any of His Majesty's Islands, Colonies and Plantations in the West Indies, or America.[4]

2. Early in 1765 the British Post Office created a Southern Postal District, comprising the continental colonies from North Carolina through the Floridas and including the Bahama Islands. Benjamin Barons was named the first deputy postmaster general. A separate packet service to Charleston was part of the plan. Largely because settlement was so widely scattered in this region, the project was never very successful in the years before the American Revolution. For a brief account, see Ruth L. Butler, *Doctor Franklin Postmaster General* (N.Y., 1928), pp. 112–20.

3. While in London BF had reported his difficulty in persuading some governors that they must pay postage. Above, x, 283–4. An act of Parliament passed June 1, 1764 (4 Geo. III, c. 24), listed precisely which governmental bodies and officials in the British Isles and the colonies might receive or send letters without paying postage. In the colonies only the chief post office, the deputy postmasters general, and postal officers authorized by them (only for letters on the public business of their offices) received the franking privilege.

4. The act of 1710 (9 Anne, c. 10, sect. 15) did in fact require ship captains who brought letters to colonial ports, as well as those in Great Britain or

39

If a Clause to the purport of the Annext could be obtained obliging all Captains and other Officers of Ships, sailing to any of the
Islands, Colonies, or Plantations aforesaid, upon their Arrival, and
before they break Bulk, or are admitted to an Entry, to deliver
their Letters into the Post Office of such Port, These Ship Letters
would soon create a considerable Increase of the Post Office Revenue in That Country; And to encourage the Captains and others
to deliver their Letters at the first Post Office, The Deputy Post-
Master, to whom they are delivered, ought to be empowered to
pay a Penny for each Letter or Packet, as is now practiced in
Great Britain and Ireland.[5]

This Regulation would be of the greatest use to the Merchants
and Planters in all His Majesty's American Dominions; for at present their Correspondence is liable to very great Delays, by their
Letters being exposed to be embezzled, detained, or opened, by
the Persons, to whom the Ships, by which they send them, are con-
signed, particularly when such Persons happen to be in the same
Branches of Commerce.

These, amongst others, are the Reasons given in the Post Act
of the 9th. of Queen Anne, for the Clauses relating to Ship Letters
coming to Great Britain and Ireland; And there can be no Doubt
but the same Reasons are as well founded with respect to the Correspondence in the West Indies and America, and that after a very
short Experience of the safety, Regularity and Expedition of delivering, and conveying Ship Letters, by the Post, all the Merchants there will be as well pleased with this Method, as Those in

---

Ireland, to deliver them to the post office upon arrival, but the requirement
was loosely worded and was regularly ignored. BF and Foxcroft had proposed
that captains be made to take oath at the Customs House in the colonial port
before breaking bulk that they had delivered all letters to the post office, or,
alternatively, that British coffeehouses that collected letters for American-
bound ships should be required to bring them in bags to the local post office,
where the bags were to be sealed and addressed to the post office in the
colonial port before being given to the captains. See above, x, 280–1. As the
next paragraphs show, the postmasters general preferred the first suggestion.

5. BF later declared that the payment by the post office to the captain of a
penny for each letter delivered to it had been the practice as long as he could
remember, and that a second penny was charged to the addressee to compensate the local post office for its service. See below, p. 342. The first penny
was provided for in the act of 1710.

England are at present; and it is most certain That no Tax whatever is so chearfully paid here as the Postage upon Ship Letters.

The necessity of a regular Post between New York and Quebec, has been so strongly pressed by General Murray the Governor, and by such a Body of British Merchants residing there, as well as at Montreal, and other intermediate Places, that it has been undertaken about once a Month, on the Arrival of each Packet Boat at New York, except for a part of the Winter Season, at a much greater Charge than the Letters can be expected to produce;[6] especially on Account of the high rate of Postage, for the Governors Gage and Murray have both taken Notice of the legal Postage being so high on Account of the Distance; that in Canada, which is represented to be in a manner destitute of Cash, and in all places where Money is equally scarce, the people will forbear to correspond until they find Occasions, by Friends, Travellers and the like, to send their Letters, which makes it to be wished, the Legislature might also enact to the purport of the 2d. Clause annexed, That the Rate of Postage for the greatest Distances between one place and another upon the Continent of America may not exceed 1s. 6d. for a single Letter and so in proportion.[7]

6. On the establishment of a postal service between New York and the Canadian towns and on the complaints of the high postage charged, see above, x, 223–4, 279.

7. Here follow, to conclude the memorandum, drafts of two clauses of considerable length proposed for inclusion in future parliamentary legislation to implement the recommendations made above. Neither requires printing here. The proposed regulation on ship's letters was provided for in the Postal Act of 1765 (5 Geo. III, c. 25, sects. iii and iv) approximately as the postmasters general had recommended, though not in the words of their suggested clause. The act raised the penalty for violation from their proposed £5 to £20. The same statute (sect. ii) substantially reduced most of the postal rates in America from those set in the act of 1710. Thereafter the postage on a "single" letter was to be: for a distance not over 60 miles, 4d. sterling; 61–100 miles, 6d.; 101–200 miles, 8d.; and for every 100 miles or less above 200, an additional 2d. The cost of a letter from N.Y. to Montreal was thereby reduced from 2s. to 1s., and from N.Y. to Quebec from 3s. to 1s. 4d. "Double" and "triple" letters and packets were to pay proportionately. The proposal for a maximum charge of 1s. 6d. between any two places in America was not adopted. For some of the changes in rates resulting from the new law, see below, pp. 535–7.

A Narrative of the Late Massacres

A Narrative of the Late Massacres, in Lancaster County, of a Number of Indians, Friends of this Province, By Persons Unknown. With some Observations on the same. Printed in the Year M,DCC,LXIV.[8] (Yale University Library)

News of the massacre of six Indians at Conestoga Manor by men from Paxton and Donegal, two communities on the Susquehanna, on December 14, 1763, reached Governor Penn on the 16th. He laid the account before his Council three days later and informed the Assembly on the 21st.[9] The House was in recess when word came to Penn on the evening of December 28 that "upwards of a hundred men" had ridden into Lancaster the afternoon before and slaughtered the fourteen Conestoga Indians placed in the workhouse for their own protection.[1] The governor informed the Council the next day and on its advice wrote General Gage to ask that British troops at Carlisle be placed under Penn's orders "to support the Civil Authority in the execution of the Laws in case of need, and to give a check to these daring attacks on Government." He also wrote Sir William Johnson begging him to "take the properest

8. Hildeburn, 1992, indicates that the pamphlet was printed in Philadelphia by Anthony [Anton] Armbrüster. Later bibliographers have followed Hildeburn. Nothing has been found among BF's papers to indicate why the firm of Franklin & Hall was not the printer. David Hall printed very few of the controversial pamphlets of this year and seems to have avoided involvement as much as possible in the disputes.

9. Penn's first information came in a letter from Edward Shippen, a magistrate at Lancaster, written the evening of the attack on the manor. *Pa. Col. Recs.*, IX, 89–90; *Votes*, 1763–64, pp. 14–15. Additional particulars arrived later in the form of a report of a coroner's inquest held the same day as the attack and a letter from the Rev. John Elder, Presbyterian minister at Paxton and commander of a company of rangers. Elder wrote Penn, December 16, that he and a neighboring magistrate had unsuccessfully tried to dissuade the men who were organizing for the attack. 1 *Pa. Arch.*, IV, 147–9.

1. Edward Shippen's letter of December 27 also mentioned reports that the rioters planned to proceed to Philadelphia and kill the Indians lodged on Province Island. Other messages to Penn included a short, almost matter-of-fact report from the proprietary overseers of the Indian village at Conestoga and a letter from John Hay, sheriff of Lancaster. The latter had begun as a listing of the effects and papers belonging to the Indians which had been collected at Conestoga, and then continued as an account of the massacre at Lancaster, which had apparently taken place after he had begun to write. Hay listed the names of the Indians killed at each place and, like Shippen, reported the rumors of an intended attack on Province Island. *Pa. Col. Recs.*, IX, 100, 102–4; 1 *Pa. Arch.* IV, 151–2.

method" of telling the Six Nations the truth of the affair and of "removing any disadvantageous Impressions they may have received from an imperfect account of the matter."[2] After each of the attacks Penn issued a proclamation ordering all civil officers to use every possible means to identify the perpetrators. In the second proclamation he also offered a reward for the apprehension of the ringleaders.

By the time the Assembly convened again on January 2, the main facts of the attack on the Lancaster workhouse and the killing of the Indians there were common knowledge in Philadelphia. Not surprisingly, however, many conflicting reports of the details began to circulate both within and without the city:

The local officials in Lancaster, it was said, had done all they could to stop the attack; they had stood idly by, other rumors suggested, and it was even alleged that some officers had secretly abetted the rioters. There were British troops in Lancaster at the time, but their commander had refused to provide protection to the Indians; or, the troops were too scattered in billets around the town to be assembled in time to do anything before the rioters had galloped away; or, there were no British soldiers nearer than Carlisle, and they would have had no authority to interfere in any case. The Indians had been shot down quickly, they had been decently spared from the preliminary tortures red men usually inflicted on their white captives, and the bodies had been left untouched where they fell; or, the Indians had been hacked with knives and tomahawks and many of them scalped, and their bodies had been mutilated and then dragged into the street. For weeks after the affair at Lancaster these and other reports passed around, and many found their way into print in the pamphlets issued by sympathizers with the Paxton Boys or their opponents.[3]

Public opinion soon became sharply divided.[4] For once nearly all the

2. *Pa. Col. Recs.*, IX, 104–6.

3. Twenty-eight pamphlets, selected from some 63 dealing with either the massacres of the Conestoga Indians or the march of the Paxton Boys on Philadelphia, or both, are reprinted in John R. Dunbar, ed., *The Paxton Papers* (The Hague, 1957). While the selections are by no means wholly representative, as Paul A. W. Wallace has pointed out (*PMHB*, LXXXII, 227–9), they illustrate well the conflicting statements made at the time and the passionate feelings the events aroused.

4. The generalized statements in this and the next paragraph regarding the division of opinion and the groups supporting each side are necessarily much condensed. Many exceptions to the classifications could be cited, though in a broad sense the surviving evidence supports these groupings. As always happens, too, in time of controversy, there were many individuals who refused to become involved with either faction and sought to maintain a safe neutrality.

43

proprietary officials, with the more substantial among their adherents, and the members of the "Quaker Party," with their supporters both within and outside the Assembly, stood together in shocked and vigorous denunciation of the massacres. The ruthless slaughter of defenseless men, women, and children was both an attack on government, as Penn had called it when writing to General Gage, and an offense against all principles of justice and humanity, as the Quakers and many others maintained. Reports that the Indians sheltered on Province Island were to be the objects of similar annihilation led the advocates of peace and order to form a common front against the lawless men who threatened to alleviate the Indian menace by exterminating every tribesman within their possible reach.

On the other side stood many inhabitants of the western and northern counties and substantial numbers of the less well-to-do, and hence unenfranchised, residents of Philadelphia. More or less sympathetic, though not always so outspoken, were some adherents of religious bodies, notably Presbyterians and Lutherans, partly because of their long-standing denominational antagonism to the Quakers and Moravians, who had been known for years as the chief friends of the Indians. By no means all these people openly approved of the massacres, but many believed that the Paxton Boys had acted under great and perhaps ample provocation. They denounced the authorities for spending public funds to support and even coddle so-called "friendly," but actually dangerous, Indians while doing little to protect the settlers of exposed areas or alleviate the hardships and sufferings of those whites who had fled in terror from their ravaged homes.[5]

Throughout the month of January tensions continued to mount; more and more it became evident that if the men from Paxton and their allies should carry out their threats of coming to Philadelphia and, to use an expression of a later century, of "liquidating" the Indians sheltered there, they would find many sympathizers in the city, who certainly would do nothing to stop them and might even join them in their proposed attack.

5. According to the Lutheran pastor, Henry Melchior Muhlenberg, the "German citizens" felt that many of the Quakers and "Bethlehemites" (Moravians) "did not exhibit the least evidence of human sympathy, etc. when Germans and other settlers on the frontiers were massacred and destroyed in the most inhuman manner by the Indians. On the contrary, these Bethlehem Indians ... were brought to Philadelphia and maintained and supported at the expense of the inhabitants. Besides, the young male Indians had already escaped and were probably doing harm, while the old men and women and children were living off the fat of the land at the expense of the province." Theodore G. Tappert and John W. Doberstein, eds., *The Journals of Henry Melchior Muhlenberg* (Phila., 1945), II, 18.

A
NARRATIVE

OF THE LATE

MASSACRES,

IN

LANCASTER County,

OF A

Number of *INDIANS,*

FRIENDS of this Province,

By Persons Unknown.

With some *Observations* on the same.

Printed in the Year M,DCC,LXIV.

In this situation Franklin came forward with an effort to influence public opinion against such violence as had already occurred and threatened to occur again. Just when his *Narrative of the Late Massacres* appeared from the press is not certain; it was not advertised in either of the Philadelphia newspapers. His reference, near the close, to General Gage's orders to Captain Robertson to stay with the Moravian Indians and guard them until he was relieved by other British regulars, makes certain that Franklin did not finish the writing until after January 16, when Governor Penn laid Gage's letter containing that information before the Council and Assembly.[6] The pamphlet could hardly have been published much before the end of January because, as Franklin told Richard Jackson on February 11, they "had only time to circulate [it] in this City and Neighbourhood before we heard that the Insurgents were on their March from all Parts."[7] That news seems to have reached Penn by Thursday, February 2, when he appealed to the Assembly for the rapid passage of a riot act to deal with the impending situation.[8] It would seem, therefore, that Monday, January 30, would be at least an approximate date for the publication.

In one respect this pamphlet differs considerably from most of Franklin's efforts to influence the public with his pen. At this time of great excitement and emotional stress, he played much more directly than usual on the emotions of his readers, their religious principles, and their feelings of pride and superiority as Englishmen or as Christians. The tone of the pamphlet is quite different from that, for example, of *Plain Truth* of 1747, a call to arms and to self-defense, also addressed to his fellow Pennsylvanians,[9] or from that of the Canada Pamphlet of 1760, addressed to Englishmen in support of a proposed course of governmental action.[1] In comparison, those writings were cool and temperate proposals and arguments addressed to common sense and self-interest; the *Narrative* is a stirring evocation of humanitarian sentiments and impulses and of the principles of morality and justice. Seldom in his life did Franklin, the rationalist, appeal so little to the reader's head and so strongly and so warmly to his heart.

A NARRATIVE, &c. [January 30?, 1764]
These Indians were the Remains of a Tribe of the Six Nations, settled at Conestogoe, and thence called Conestogoe Indians. On

6. *Pa. Col. Recs.*, IX, 119–20; *Votes*, 1763–64, p. 30.
7. See below, p. 77.
8. *Pa. Col. Recs.*, IX, 129; *Votes*, 1763–64, p. 40.
9. Above, III, 180–204.
1. Above, IX, 47–100.

the first Arrival of the English in Pennsylvania, Messengers from this Tribe came to welcome them, with Presents of Venison, Corn and Skins; and the whole Tribe entered into a Treaty of Friendship with the first Proprietor, WILLIAM PENN, which was to last "as long as the Sun should shine, or the Waters run in the Rivers."[2]

This Treaty has been since frequently renewed, and the *Chain brightened,* as they express it, from time to time. It has never been violated, on their Part or ours, till now. As their Lands by Degrees were mostly purchased, and the Settlements of the White People began to surround them, the Proprietor assigned them Lands on the Manor of Conestogoe, which they might not part with; there they have lived many Years in Friendship with their White Neighbours, who loved them for their peaceable inoffensive Behaviour.

It has always been observed, that Indians, settled in the Neighbourhood of White People, do not increase, but diminish continually. This Tribe accordingly went on diminishing, till there remained in their Town on the Manor, but 20 Persons, *viz.* 7 Men, 5 Women, and 8 Children, Boys and Girls.[3]

Of these, Shehaes[4] was a very old Man, having assisted at the second Treaty held with them, by Mr. PENN, in 1701,[5] and ever

2. The tradition of such a treaty of friendship was of long standing, even at the time BF wrote, but if indeed it ever took place no documentary evidence of its phraseology survives. See Frederick D. Stone, "Penn's Treaty with the Indians. Did it take place in 1682 or 1683?," *PMHB*, VI (1882), 217–18. The quoted words, or variations of them, were often used in treaties between Indians and whites.

3. In the list of Indians killed at Conestoga and at Lancaster that Sheriff John Hay sent to Governor Penn, Dec. 27, 1763, the Indian names of all twenty are given and the English names of most of them. In some instances spellings differ from those BF used. *Pa. Col. Recs.,* IX, 105–6.

4. "Sheehays" according to Hay. He died at Conestoga. In 1758 BF's friend, James Wright of Hemphill, said that this Indian "has been intimate with me these many Years." *Ibid.,* VIII, 116.

5. Among the effects of the Indians found at Conestoga after the massacre there, Hays reported there was "A Writing in Parchment, purporting an Article of Agreement between William Penn, Proprietary, &ca., of Pennsylvania, and the King of the Indians inhabiting in or about the River Susquehannah, and other Indian Nations, dated the three and Twentieth day of the second month, called April, in the Year one thousand, seven hundred and one." *Ibid.,* IX, 102. The full text of this agreement, "never to be broken or Violated," was entered in the minutes of the Pa. Council the day it was signed. *Ibid.,* II, 15–18.

since continued a faithful and affectionate Friend to the English; he is said to have been an exceeding good Man, considering his Education, being naturally of a most kind benevolent Temper.

Peggy was Shehaes's Daughter; she worked for her aged Father, continuing to live with him, though married, and attended him with filial Duty and Tenderness.[6]

John was another good old Man; his Son Harry helped to support him.[7]

George and Will Soc were two Brothers, both young Men.[8]

John Smith, a valuable young Man, of the Cayuga Nation, who became acquainted with Peggy, Shehaes's Daughter, some few Years since, married her, and settled in that Family. They had one Child, about three Years old.[9]

Betty, a harmless old Woman; and her Son Peter, a likely young Lad.[1]

Sally, whose Indian Name was Wyanjoy, a Woman much esteemed by all that knew her, for her prudent and good Behaviour in some very trying Situations of Life. She was a truly good and an amiable Woman, had no Children of her own, but a distant Relation dying, she had taken a Child of that Relation's, to bring up as her own, and performed towards it all the Duties of an affectionate Parent.[2]

The Reader will observe, that many of their Names are English. It is common with the Indians that have an Affection for the English, to give themselves, and their Children, the Names of such English Persons as they particularly esteem.

6. Peggy (Chee-na-wan) and her husband, John Smith (Saquies-hat-tah), mentioned below, died at Lancaster. It was she who provided Hay with the list of names before the attack at Lancaster.

7. John, called "Captain John" (Kyunqueagoah) by Hay, died at Lancaster, his son Harry (Tee-Kau-ley) at Conestoga.

8. George (Wa-a-shen) died at Conestoga. Will Soc, more often called Bill Sock or Sack (Tenseedaagua), the most suspected among the Indians, died at Lancaster.

9. Which among the children taken to Lancaster this was Hay did not indicate.

1. Betty (Koweenasee) was the wife of Captain John. She and "little Peter, a Boy" (Hy-ye-naes), died at Lancaster with her husband.

2. "Sally, an Old Woman" (Tea-wonsha-i-ong), as Hay listed her, died at Conestoga. Which of the children killed at Lancaster was her adopted child is not indicated.

This little Society continued the Custom they had begun, when more numerous, of addressing every new Governor, and every Descendant of the first Proprietor, welcoming him to the Province, assuring him of their Fidelity, and praying a Continuance of that Favour and Protection they had hitherto experienced. They had accordingly sent up an Address of this Kind to our present Governor, on his Arrival; but the same was scarce delivered, when the unfortunate Catastrophe happened, which we are about to relate.[3]

On Wednesday, the 14th of December, 1763, Fifty-seven Men, from some of our Frontier Townships, who had projected the Destruction of this little Common-wealth, came, all well-mounted, and armed with Firelocks, Hangers and Hatchets, having travelled through the Country in the Night, to Conestogoe Manor. There they surrounded the small Village of Indian Huts, and just at Break of Day broke into them all at once. Only three Men, two Women, and a young Boy, were found at home, the rest being out among the neighbouring White People, some to sell the Baskets, Brooms and Bowls they manufactured, and others on other Occasions. These poor defenceless Creatures were immediately fired upon, stabbed and hatcheted to Death! The good Shehaes, among the rest, cut to Pieces in his Bed. All of them were scalped, and otherwise horribly mangled. Then their Huts were set on Fire, and most of them burnt down. When the Troop, pleased with their own Conduct and Bravery, but enraged that any of the poor Indians had escaped the Massacre, rode off, and in small Parties, by different Roads, went home.

The universal Concern of the neighbouring White People on hearing of this Event, and the Lamentations of the younger Indians, when they returned and saw the Desolation, and the butchered half-burnt Bodies of their murdered Parents, and other Relations, cannot well be expressed.

The Magistrates of Lancaster sent out to collect the remaining Indians, brought them into the Town for their better Security against

3. At the meeting of the Pa. Council, Dec. 19, 1763, Governor Penn first laid this address, dated November 30, before the members and then, somewhat dramatically perhaps, read them Edward Shippen's letter of December 14 reporting the massacre at Conestoga. *Pa. Col. Recs.*, IX, 88–90.

any further Attempt, and it is said condoled with them on the Misfortune that had happened, took them by the Hand, comforted and *promised them Protection*. They were all put into the Workhouse, a strong Building, as the Place of greatest Safety.

When the shocking News arrived in Town, a Proclamation was issued by the Governor, in the following Terms, *viz.*[4]

"WHEREAS I have received Information, That on Wednesday, the Fourteenth Day of this Month, a Number of People, armed, and mounted on Horseback, unlawfully assembled together, and went to the Indian Town in the Conestogoe Manor, in Lancaster County, and without the least Reason or Provocation, in cool Blood, barbarously killed six of the Indians settled there, and burnt and destroyed all their Houses and Effects: And whereas so cruel and inhuman an Act, committed in the Heart of this Province on the said Indians, who have lived peaceably and inoffensively among us, during all our late Troubles, and for many Years before, and were justly considered as under the Protection of this Government and its Laws, calls loudly for the vigorous Exertion of the civil Authority, to detect the Offenders, and bring them to condign Punishment; I have therefore, by and with the Advice and Consent of the Council, thought fit to issue this Proclamation, and do hereby strictly charge and enjoin all Judges, Justices, Sheriffs, Constables, Officers Civil and Military, and all other His Majesty's liege Subjects within this Province, to make diligent Search and Enquiry after the Authors and Perpetrators of the said Crime, their Abettors and Accomplices, and to use all possible Means to apprehend and secure them in some of the publick Goals of this Province, that they may be brought to their Trials, and be proceeded against according to Law.

"And whereas a Number of other Indians, who lately lived on or near the Frontiers of this Province, being willing and desirous to preserve and continue the ancient Friendship which heretofore subsisted between them and the good People of this Province, have, at their own earnest Request, been removed from their Habitations, and brought into the County of Philadelphia, and seated, for the present, for their better Security, on the Province-Island,

---

4. This proclamation was printed in the December 29 issues of both *Pa. Gaz.* and *Pa. Jour.*

and in other Places in the Neighbourhood of the City of Philadelphia, where Provision is made for them at the public Expence;[5]
I do therefore hereby strictly forbid all Persons whatsoever, to
molest or injure any of the said Indians, as they will answer the
contrary at their Peril.

> "Given *under my Hand, and the Great Seal of the said Province,
> at Philadelphia, the Twenty-second Day of December, Anno Domini
> One Thousand Seven Hundred and Sixty-three, and in the Fourth
> Year of His Majesty's Reign.* John Penn.
>
> "By *His Honour's Command,* Joseph Shippen, *jun. Secretary.*
> "God Save the King."

Notwithstanding this Proclamation, those cruel Men again assembled themselves, and hearing that the remaining fourteen Indians were in the Work-house at Lancaster, they suddenly appeared
in that Town, on the 27th of December. Fifty of them, armed as
before, dismounting, went directly to the Work-house, and by
Violence broke open the Door, and entered with the utmost Fury
in their Countenances. When the poor Wretches saw they had
no Protection nigh, nor could possibly escape, and being without
the least Weapon for Defence, they divided into their little Families, the Children clinging to the Parents; they fell on their Knees,
protested their Innocence, declared their Love to the English,
and that, in their whole Lives, they had never done them Injury;
and in this Posture they all received the Hatchet! Men, Women
and little Children—were every one inhumanly murdered!—in cold
Blood![6]

5. See above, pp. 25–30.
6. One of the later pamphlets, *The Conduct of the Paxton-Men, Impartially Represented: with some Remarks on the Narrative* (Phila., 1764), devoted
much of its attention to BF's pamphlet, defending the rioters against his
criticisms and countering his arguments and his general position, without
quite expressing approval of the massacres. Its author is believed to have
been Thomas Barton (1730–1780), an Anglican clergyman in Lancaster. In
one passage he quoted most of this paragraph and commented: "This was
cruel indeed, if it was so—But I would be glad to know who could give this
Gentleman so very particular an Account. I have been told that not a single
Circumstance happened which could have given rise to it; and that the above
Story was pick'd up from among a Parcel of old Papers in a Hop-Garden or
a Hempfield (I forget which) upon Susquehanna." These words were undoubtedly an allusion to BF's old friends (and Shehaes'), Susanna, James, and

The barbarous Men who committed the atrocious Fact, in Defiance of Government, of all Laws human and divine, and to the eternal Disgrace of their Country and Colour, then mounted their Horses, huzza'd in Triumph, as if they had gained a Victory, and rode off—*unmolested!*

The Bodies of the Murdered were then brought out and exposed in the Street, till a Hole could be made in the Earth, to receive and cover them.[7]

But the Wickedness cannot be covered, the Guilt will lie on the whole Land, till Justice is done on the Murderers. THE BLOOD OF THE INNOCENT WILL CRY TO HEAVEN FOR VENGEANCE.

It is said that Shehaes, being before told, that it was to be feared some English might come from the Frontier into the Country, and murder him and his People; he replied, "It is impossible: There are Indians, indeed, in the Woods, who would kill me and mine, if they could get at us, for my Friendship to the English; but the English will wrap me in their Matchcoat, and secure me from all Danger." How unfortunately was he mistaken!

Another Proclamation has been issued, offering a great Reward for apprehending the Murderers, in the following Terms, *viz.*[8]

John Wright of Hemphill, on the Susquehanna, about ten miles or so from Lancaster (see above, IV, 210–11 n, and indexes to vols. V–VIII). The writer pointed out that the whole attack had occupied not more than two minutes and that the only persons who saw the Indians were the men who killed them. These declared that "not one of them appeared in that Posture, nor spoke a Word." *Paxton Papers,* pp. 285–6.

7. The writer of *The Conduct of the Paxton-Men* denied, on what he said was excellent authority, that the bodies were removed from the workhouse and its yard "till they were brought out to be carried to their Graves." *Paxton Papers,* p. 286. It may be added here that the jailer, Felix Donnally, later submitted an itemized bill to the sheriff for food, maintenance, and firewood furnished the Indians during their stay in the workhouse, totaling £14 9s., and then added dispassionately one more entry for which he left blank the amount due: "To the Trouble and Expense of having the said Fourteen Indians carried to the grave and interred." Lottie M. Bausman, "Massacre of the Conestoga Indians, 1763. Incidents and Details," *Papers Read before the Lancaster County Hist. Soc.,* XVIII (1914), 179–80.

8. The proclamation was printed in the Jan. 5 and 12, 1764, issues of both *Pa. Gaz.* and *Pa. Jour.* At no time during December or January did either paper print any news of the two massacres in addition to what the governor's two proclamations contained.

"WHEREAS on the Twenty-second Day of December last, I issued a Proclamation for the apprehending and bringing to Justice, a Number of Persons, who, in Violation of the Public Faith; and in Defiance of all Law, had inhumanly killed six of the Indians, who had lived in Conestogoe Manor, for the Course of many Years, peaceably and inoffensively, under the Protection of this Government, on Lands assigned to them for their Habitation; notwithstanding which, I have received Information, that on the Twenty-seventh of the same Month, a large Party of armed Men again assembled and met together in a riotous and tumultuous Manner, in the County of Lancaster, and proceeded to the Town of Lancaster, where they violently broke open the Work-house, and butchered and put to Death fourteen of the said Conestogoe Indians, Men, Women and Children, who had been taken under the immediate Care and Protection of the Magistrates of the said County, and lodged for their better Security in the said Work-house, till they should be more effectually provided for by Order of the Government. And whereas common Justice loudly demands, and the Laws of the Land (upon the Preservation of which not only the Liberty and Security of every Individual, but the Being of the Government itself depend) require that the above Offenders should be brought to condign Punishment; I have therefore, by and with the Advice of the Council, published this Proclamation, and do hereby strictly charge and command all Judges, Justices, Sheriffs, Constables, Officers Civil and Military, and all other His Majesty's faithful and liege Subjects within this Province, to make diligent Search and Enquiry after the Authors and Perpetrators of the said last mentioned Offence, their Abettors and Accomplices, and that they use all possible Means to apprehend and secure them in some of the public Goals of this Province, to be dealt with according to Law.

"And I do hereby further promise and engage, that any Person or Persons, who shall apprehend and secure, or cause to be apprehended and secured, any Three of the Ringleaders of the said Party, and prosecute them to Conviction, shall have and receive for each, the public Reward of Two Hundred Pounds; and any Accomplice, not concerned in the immediate shedding the Blood of the said Indians, who shall make Discovery of any or either of the said Ringleaders, and apprehend and prosecute them to Conviction, shall, over and above the said Reward, have all the Weight and Influence of the Government, for obtaining His Majesty's Pardon for his Offence.

"GIVEN *under my Hand, and the Great Seal of the said Province, at Philadelphia, the Second Day of January, in the Fourth Year of His Majesty's Reign, and in the Year of our Lord One Thousand Seven Hundred and Sixty-four.* JOHN PENN.

"By His Honour's Command, JOSEPH SHIPPEN, *jun. Secretary.*
"GOD Save the KING."

These Proclamations have as yet produced no Discovery; the Murderers having given out such Threatenings against those that disapprove their Proceedings, that the whole County seems to be in Terror, and no one durst speak what he knows; even the Letters from thence are unsigned, in which any Dislike is expressed of the Rioters.

There are some (I am ashamed to hear it) who would extenuate the enormous Wickedness of these Actions, by saying, "The Inhabitants of the Frontiers are exasperated with the Murder of their Relations, by the Enemy Indians, in the present War." It is possible; but though this might justify their going out into the Woods, to seek for those Enemies, and avenge upon them those Murders; it can never justify their turning in to the Heart of the Country, to murder their Friends.

If an Indian injures me, does it follow that I may revenge that Injury on all Indians? It is well known that Indians are of different Tribes, Nations and Languages, as well as the White People. In Europe, if the French, who are White-People, should injure the Dutch, are they to revenge it on the English, because they too are White People? The only Crime of these poor Wretches seems to have been, that they had a reddish brown Skin, and black Hair; and some People of that Sort, it seems, had murdered some of our Relations. If it be right to kill Men for such a Reason, then, should any Man, with a freckled Face and red Hair, kill a Wife or Child of mine, it would be right for me to revenge it, by killing all the freckled red-haired Men, Women and Children, I could afterwards any where meet with.

But it seems these People think they have a better Justification; nothing less than the *Word of God.* With the Scriptures in their

55

Hands and Mouths, they can set at nought that express Command, *Thou shalt do no Murder;* and justify their Wickedness, by the Command given Joshua to destroy the Heathen. Horrid Perversion of Scripture and of Religion! to father the worst of Crimes on the God of Peace and Love! Even the Jews, to whom that particular Commission was directed, spared the Gibeonites, on Account of their Faith once given.[9] The Faith of this Government has been frequently given to those Indians; but that did not avail them with People who despise Government.

We pretend to be Christians, and, from the superior Light we enjoy, ought to exceed Heathens, Turks, Saracens, Moors, Negroes, and Indians, in the Knowledge and Practice of what is right. I will endeavour to show, by a few Examples from Books and History, the Sense those People have had of such Actions.

HOMER wrote his Poem, called the *Odyssey*, some Hundred Years before the Birth of Christ. He frequently speaks of what he calls not only *the Duties*, but *the sacred Rites of Hospitality*, (exercised towards Strangers, while in our House or Territory) as including, besides all the common Circumstances of Entertainment, full Safety and Protection of Person, from all Danger of Life, from all Injuries, and even Insults. The Rites of Hospitality were called *sacred*, because the Stranger, the Poor and the Weak, when they applied for Protection and Relief, were, from the Religion of those Times, supposed to be sent by the Deity to try the Goodness of Men, and that he would avenge the Injuries they might receive, where they ought to have been protected. These Sentiments therefore influenced the Manners of all Ranks of People, even the meanest; for we find that when Ulysses came, as a poor Stranger, to the Hut of Eumaeus, the Swineherd, and his great Dogs ran out to tear the ragged Man, Eumaeus drave them away with Stones; and

9. For Joshua's destruction by divine command of the cities of Jericho and Ai and their inhabitants, see Joshua, chaps. 6 and 8. For the preservation of the Gibeonites following a league with them entered into by the Jews, even though the Gibeonites had lied about their identity, see Joshua, chap. 9. The analogy of the Gibeonites also appeared in an anonymous anti-Paxton pamphlet which may have been published before BF's narrative: *A Dialogue between Andrew Trueman, and Thomas Zealot; About the killing the Indians at Cannestogoe and Lancaster* (Ephesus, [1764], reprinted in *Paxton Papers*, pp. 87–90).

Unhappy Stranger! (thus the faithful Swain
Began, with Accent gracious and humane)
What Sorrow had been mine, if at *my* Gate
Thy rev'rend Age had met a shameful Fate?
------But enter this my homely Roof, and see
Our Woods not void of Hospitality.
He said, and seconding the kind Request,
With friendly Step precedes the unknown Guest.
A shaggy Goat's soft Hide beneath him spread,
And with fresh Rushes heap'd an ample Bed.
Joy touch'd the Hero's tender Soul, to find
So *just* Reception from a Heart so kind:
And oh, ye Gods! with all your Blessings grace
(He thus broke forth) this Friend of human Race!
  The Swain reply'd. It never was our guise
To slight the Poor, or aught humane despise.
For Jove unfolds the hospitable Door,
Tis Jove that sends the Stranger and the Poor.[1]

These Heathen People thought, that after a Breach of the Rites of Hospitality, a Curse from Heaven would attend them in every thing they did, and even their honest Industry in their Callings would fail of Success. Thus when Ulysses tells Eumaeus, who doubted the Truth of what he related, *If I deceive you in this, I should deserve Death, and I consent that you should put me to Death;* Eumaeus rejects the Proposal as what would be attended with both Infamy and Misfortune, saying ironically,

Doubtless, oh Guest! great Laud and Praise were mine,
If, after social Rites and Gifts bestow'd,
I stain'd my Hospitable Hearth with Blood.
How would the Gods my righteous Toils succeed,
And bless the Hand that made a Stranger bleed?
No more.[2]——

Even an open Enemy, in the Heat of Battle, throwing down

1. This and later passages from *The Odyssey* are taken from Alexander Pope's translation. BF does not always indicate his omission of lines, and the capitalization and spelling are his own. This quotation is of Book XIV, lines 41–4, 53–4, 57–68.
2. Book XIV, lines 443, 445–9.

his Arms, submitting to his Foe, and asking Life and Protection, was supposed to acquire an immediate Right to that Protection. Thus one describes his being saved, when his Party was defeated.

> We turn'd to Flight; the gath'ring Vengeance spread
> On all Parts round, and Heaps on Heaps lie dead.
> ---The radiant Helmet from my Brows unlac'd,
> And lo on Earth my Shield and Jav'lin cast,
> I meet the Monarch with a Suppliant's Face,
> Approach his Chariat, and his Knees embrace.
> He heard, he sav'd he plac'd me at his Side;
> My State he pity'd, and my Tears he dry'd;
> Restrain'd the Rage the vengeful Foe express'd,
> And turn'd the deadly Weapons from my Breast.
> Pious *to guard the Hospitable Rite,*
> And *fearing Jove,* whom Mercy's Works delight.[3]

The Suitors of Penelope are by the same ancient Poet described as a Sett of Lawless Men, who were *regardless of the sacred Rites of Hospitality.* And therefore when the Queen was informed they were slain, and that by Ulysses, she, not believing that Ulysses was returned, says,

> Ah no! --- some God the Suitors Deaths decreed,
> Some God descends, and by his Hand they bleed:
> Blind, to contemn the Stranger's righteous Cause,
> *And violate all hospitable Laws!*
> ----------------The Powers they defy'd;
> But Heav'n is just, and by a God they dy'd.[4]

Thus much for the Sentiments of the ancient Heathens. As for the Turks,[5] it is recorded in the Life of Mahomet, the Founder of their Religion, That Khaled, one of his Captains, having divided a Number of Prisoners between himself and those that were with him, he commanded the Hands of his own Prisoners to be tied

3. Book XIV, lines 299–300, 305–15.
4. Book XXIII, lines 63–8. The omitted portion of line 67 reads "The good they hated, and."
5. Lib. Co. Phila. was well stocked with books on the Mohammedans and on the history of the Turks, Arabs, and Saracens, and it seems impossible to identify precisely the sources BF used for the incidents he describes here and in the following paragraph.

behind them, and then, in a most cruel and brutal Manner, put them to the Sword; but he could not prevail on his Men to massacre *their* Captives, because in Fight they had laid down their Arms, submitted, and demanded Protection. Mahomet, when the Account was brought to him, applauded the Men for their Humanity; but said to Khaled, with great Indignation, *Oh Khaled, thou Butcher, cease to molest me with thy Wickedness. If thou possessedst a Heap of Gold as large as Mount Obod, and shouldst expend it all in God's Cause, thy Merit would not efface the Guilt incurred by the Murder of the meanest of those poor Captives.*

Among the Arabs or Saracens, though it was lawful to put to Death a Prisoner taken in Battle, if he had made himself obnoxious by his former Wickedness, yet this could not be done after he had once eaten Bread, or drank Water, while in their Hands. Hence we read in the History of the Wars of the Holy Land, that when the Franks had suffered a great Defeat from Saladin, and among the Prisoners were the King of Jerusalem, and Arnold, a famous Christian Captain, who had been very cruel to the Saracens; these two being brought before the Soltan, he placed the King on his right Hand, and Arnold on his left; and then presented the King with a Cup of Water, who immediately drank to Arnold; but when Arnold was about to receive the Cup, the Soltan interrupted, saying, *I will not suffer this wicked Man to drink, as that, according to the laudable and generous Custom of the Arabs, would secure him his Life.*

That same laudable and generous Custom still prevails among the Mahometans, appears from the Account but last Year published of his Travels by Mr. Bell of Antermony,[6] who accompanied the Czar Peter the Great, in his Journey to Derbent through Daggestan. "The Religion of the Daggestans, says he, is generally Mahometan, some following the Sect of Osman, others that of Haly. Their Language for the most Part is Turkish, or rather a Dialect of the Arabic, though many of them speak also the Persian Language. One Article I cannot omit concerning their Laws of Hospitality, which is, if their greatest Enemy comes under their

6. The Pa. Proprietors had given Lib. Co. Phila. a set of John Bell of Antermony (1691–1780), *Travels from St. Petersburgh, in Russia, to divers Parts of Asia* (2 vols., Glasgow, 1763). See *The Charter, Laws, and Catalogue of Books, of the Library Company of Philadelphia* (Phila., 1764), p. 46.

Roof for Protection, the Landlord, of what Condition soever, is obliged to keep him safe, from all Manner of Harm or Violence, during his Abode with him, and even to conduct him safely through his Territories to a Place of Security."

From the Saracens this same Custom obtained among the Moors of Africa; was by them brought into Spain, and there long sacredly observed. The Spanish Historians record with Applause one famous Instance of it.[7] While the Moors governed there, and the Spaniards were mixed with them, a Spanish Cavalier, in a sudden Quarrel, slew a young Moorish Gentleman, and fled. His Pursuers soon lost Sight of him, for he had, unperceived, thrown himself over a Garden Wall. The Owner, a Moor, happening to be in his Garden, was addressed by the Spaniard on his Knees, who acquainted him with his Case, and implored Concealment. *Eat this,* said the Moor, giving him Half a Peach; *you now know that you may confide in my Protection.* He then locked him up in his Garden Apartment, telling him, that as soon as it was Night he would provide for his Escape to a Place of more Safety. The Moor then went into his House, where he had scarce seated himself, when a great Croud, with loud Lamentations, came to his Gate, bringing the Corps of his Son, that had just been killed by a Spaniard. When the first Shock of Surprize was a little over, he learnt, from the Description given, that the fatal Deed was done by the Person then in his Power. He mentioned this to no One; but as soon as it was dark, retired to his Garden Apartment, as if to grieve alone, giving Orders that none should follow him. There accosting the Spaniard, he said, *Christian, the Person you have killed, is my Son: His Body is now in my House. You ought to suffer; but you have eaten with me, and I have given you my Faith, which must not be broken. Follow me.* He then led the astonished Spaniard to his Stables, mounted him on one of his fleetest Horses, and said, *Fly far while the Night can cover you. You will be safe in the Morning. You are indeed guilty of my Son's Blood, but God is just and good, and I thank him that I am innocent of yours, and that my Faith given is preserved.*

The Spaniards caught from the Moors this *Punto* of Honour, the Effects of which remain, in a great Degree, to this Day. So that when there is Fear of a War about to break out between England and Spain, an English Merchant there, who apprehends the

7. BF's source for this story has not been identified.

Confiscation of his Goods as the Goods of an Enemy, thinks them safe, if he can get a Spaniard to take Charge of them; for the Spaniard secures them as his own, and faithfully redelivers them, or pays the Value, whenever the Englishman can safely demand it.

Justice to that Nation, though lately our Enemies, and hardly yet our cordial Friends, obliges me, on this Occasion, not to omit mentioning an Instance of Spanish Honour, which cannot but be still fresh in the Memory of many yet living.[8] In 1746, when we were in hot War with Spain, the *Elizabeth,* of London, Captain William Edwards, coming through the Gulph from Jamaica, richly laden, met with a most violent Storm, in which the Ship sprung a Leak, that obliged them, for the Saving of their Lives, to run her into the Havannah. The Captain went on Shore, directly waited on the Governor, told the Occasion of his putting in, and that he surrendered his Ship as a Prize, and himself and his Men as Prisoners of War, only requesting good Quarter. *No, Sir,* replied the Spanish Governor, *If we had taken you in fair War at Sea, or approaching our Coast with hostile Intentions, your Ship would then have been a Prize, and your People Prisoners. But when distressed by a Tempest, you come into our Ports for the Safety of your Lives, we, though Enemies, being Men, are bound as such, by the Laws of Humanity, to afford Relief to distressed Men, who ask it of us. We cannot, even against our Enemies, take Advantage of an Act of God. You have Leave therefore to unload your Ship, if that be necessary, to stop the Leak; you may refit here, and traffick so far as shall be necessary to pay the Charges; you may then depart, and I will give you a Pass, to be in Force till you are beyond Bermuda. If after that you are taken, you will then be a Prize, but now you are only a Stranger, and have a Stranger's Right to Safety and Protection.* The Ship accordingly departed, and arrived safe in London.

Will it be permitted me to adduce, on this Occasion, an Instance of the like Honour in a poor unenlightened African Negroe. I find it in Capt. Seagrave's Account of his Voyage to Guinea.[9] He relates that a New-England Sloop, trading there in 1752, left their second Mate, William Murray, sick on Shore, and sailed without him. Murray was at the House of a Black, named Cudjoe, with

8. BF may have derived this story from a newspaper account; if so, it has not been identified.
9. Not identified.

whom he had contracted an Acquaintance during their Trade. He recovered, and the Sloop being gone, he continued with his black Friend, till some other Opportunity should offer of his getting home. In the mean while, a Dutch Ship came into the Road, and some of the Blacks going on board her, were treacherously seized, and carried off as Slaves. Their Relations and Friends, transported with sudden Rage, ran to the House of Cudjoe to take Revenge, by killing Murray. Cudjoe stopt them at the Door, and demanded what they wanted? The White Men, said they, have carried away our Brothers and Sons, and we will kill all White Men; give us the White Man that you keep in your House, for we will kill him. *Nay,* said Cudjoe; *the White Men that carried away your Brothers are bad Men, kill them when you can catch them; but this White Man is a good Man, and you must not kill him.* But he is a White Man, they cried; the White Men are all bad; we will kill them all. *Nay,* says he, *you must not kill a Man, that had done no Harm, only for being white. This Man is my Friend, my House is his Fort, and I am his Soldier. I must fight for him. You must kill me, before you can kill him. What good Man will ever come again under my Roof, if I let my Floor be stained with a good Man's Blood!* The Negroes seeing his Resolution, and being convinced by his Discourse that they were wrong, went away ashamed. In a few Days Murray ventured abroad again with Cudjoe, when several of them took him by the Hand, and told him they were glad they had not killed him; for as he was a good (meaning an innocent) Man, *their God would have been angry, and would have spoiled their Fishing.* I relate this, says Captain Seagrave, to show, that some among these dark People have a strong Sense of Justice and Honour, and that even the most brutal among them are capable of feeling the Force of Reason, and of being influenced by a Fear of God (if the Knowledge of the true God could be introduced among them) since even the Fear of a false God, when their Rage subsided, was not without its good Effect.

Now I am about to mention something of Indians, I beg that I may not be understood as framing Apologies for *all* Indians. I am far from desiring to lessen the laudable Spirit of Resentment in my Countrymen against those now at War with us, so far as it is justified by their Perfidy and Inhumanity. I would only observe that the Six Nations, as a Body, have kept Faith with the English ever since we knew them, now near an Hundred Years; and that the governing Part of those People have had Notions of Honour, whatever may be the Case with the Rum-debauched, Trader-corrupted Vagabonds and Thieves on Sasquehannah and the Ohio, at present in Arms against us. As a Proof of that Honour, I shall only mention one well-known recent Fact. When six Catawba Deputies, under the Care of Colonel Bull, of Charlestown,[1] went by Permission into the Mohawks Country, to sue for and treat of Peace for their Nation, they soon found the Six Nations highly exasperated, and the Peace at that Time impracticable: They were therefore in Fear for their own Persons, and apprehended that they should be killed in their Way back to New-York; which being made known to the Mohawk Chiefs, by Colonel Bull, one of them, by Order of the Council, made this Speech to the Catawbas:

"*Strangers and Enemies,*

"While you are in this Country, blow away all Fear out of your Breasts; change the black Streak of Pain on your Cheek for a red One, and let your Faces shine with Bear's-Grease: You are safer here than if you were at home. The Six Nations will not defile their own Land with the Blood of Men that come unarmed to ask for Peace. We shall send a Guard with you, to see you safe out of our Territories. So far you shall have Peace, but no farther. Get home to your own Country, and there take Care of yourselves, for there we intend to come and kill you."

The Catawbas came away unhurt accordingly.[2]

It is also well known, that just before the late War broke out,

1. William Bull, the younger (1710–1791), active in So. Car. public affairs, lieutenant governor, 1759–75, and several times acting governor. In 1751, when the incident here described took place, he was a member of the Council. *DAB.*

2. The official record of this conference (*N.Y. Col. Docs.,* VI, 716–26) does not include any such speech as BF gives here. Conrad Weiser, who attended the conference as an unofficial observer, recorded that when the Catawba king asked if it would be safe for his delegation to go to the meeting, in case peace should not be concluded there, he answered that the Iroquois Council "will tell you to go home in peace and that they will Send after You and Kill you in your own Country." Weiser also recorded an Iroquois speech in 1737 to somewhat the same effect. Paul A. W. Wallace, *Conrad Weiser Friend of Colonist and Mohawk* (Phila., 1945), pp. 92, 324. BF may have had another record of the 1751 conference, or, having heard of the incident from Weiser, he may have himself composed in the Indian style the speech reported here.

63

when our Traders first went among the Piankeshaw Indians, a Tribe of the Twightwees, they found the Principle of *giving Protection to Strangers* in full Force; for the French coming with their Indians to the Piankeshaw Town, and demanding that those Traders and their Goods should be delivered up; the Piankeshaws replied, the English were come there upon their Invitation, and they could not do so base a Thing. But the French insisting on it, the Piankeshaws took Arms in Defence of their Guests, and a Number of them, with their old Chief, lost their Lives in the Cause; the French at last prevailing by superior Force only.[3]

I will not dissemble that numberless Stories have been raised and spread abroad, against not only the poor Wretches that are murdered, but also against the Hundred and Forty christianized Indians, still threatned to be murdered; all which Stories are well known, by those who know the Indians best, to be pure Inventions, contrived by bad People, either to excite each other to join in the Murder, or since it was committed, to justify it; and believed only by the Weak and Credulous.[4] I call thus publickly on the Makers and Venders of these Accusations to produce their Evidence. Let them satisfy the Public that even Will Soc, the most obnoxious of

3. This incident received considerable attention at the Treaty of Carlisle, at which BF was an official representative. See above, v, 95, 99–101, 104; *Pa. Col. Recs.*, v, 599–600, and Gipson, *British Empire*, IV, 221–3. The writer of *The Conduct of the Paxton-Men* ridiculed BF's illustrations of the observance of laws of hospitality by various peoples. To clinch his point he cited several instances to the contrary and quoted at length passages from accounts of two early Jewish heroines and the praise they received for their treacherous exploits: how Jael hid the fleeing Sisera, fed him, and after he had fallen asleep hammered a tent nail through his head (Judges 4:15–31; 5:23); and how Judith insinuated herself into the good graces of Holofernes, got him drunk, and then cut off his head with two well-aimed blows of his own sword (Judith 8:8; 11:17–19; 13:6–8, 18, 20). *Paxton Papers*, pp. 289–91.

4. See above, pp. 25–6. The Moravian Indians from Wechquetank and other mission stations were specifically charged with communicating with hostile Indians and supplying them with blankets, provisions, and ammunition. The smaller group of Delaware Indians from Wighalousin (Wyalusing) on the upper Susquehanna, some twenty miles from the present northern boundary of Pa., were under suspicion largely because numbers of their fellow tribesmen were actively hostile to the whites, and the frontiersmen were unable or unwilling to distinguish among them. Many of the contemporary documents, both official papers and controversial pamphlets, elaborate these charges or rebut them.

all that Tribe, was really guilty of those Offences against us which they lay to his Charge.[5] But if he was, ought he not to have been fairly tried? He lived under our Laws, and was subject to them; he was in our Hands, and might easily have been prosecuted; was it *English Justice* to condemn and execute him unheard? Conscious of his own Innocence, he did not endeavour to hide himself when the Door of the Work-house, his Sanctuary, was breaking open; *I will meet them*, says he, *for they are my Brothers*. These Brothers of his shot him down at the Door, while the Word Brothers was still between his Teeth! But if Will Soc was a bad Man, what had poor old Shehaes done? what could he or the other poor old Men and Women do? What had little Boys and Girls done; what could Children of a Year old, Babes at the Breast, what could they do, that they too must be shot and hatcheted? Horrid to relate! and in their Parents Arms! This is done by no civilized Nation in Europe. Do we come to America to learn and practise the Manners of *Barbarians?* But this, *Barbarians* as they are, they practise against their Enemies only, not against their Friends.

These poor People have been always our Friends. Their Fathers received ours, when Strangers here, with Kindness and Hospitality. Behold the Return we have made them! When we grew more numerous and powerful, they put themselves under our *Protection*. See, in the mangled Corpses of the last Remains of the Tribe, how effectually we have afforded it to them!

Unhappy People! to have lived in such Times, and by such Neighbours! We have seen, that they would have been safer among the ancient Heathens, with whom the Rites of Hospitality were *sacred*. They would have been considered as *Guests* of the Publick, and the Religion of the Country would have operated in their Favour. But our Frontier People call themselves Christians! They would have been safer, if they had submitted to the Turks; for ever since Mahomet's Reproof to Khaled, even the *cruel Turks*, never

5. Depositions charging Will Soc with threats to kill whites and with suspicious behavior, or reporting hearsay evidence of his bad character, were printed in some of the later pamphlets; for examples see *Paxton Papers*, pp. 196, 198–9. At least one eyewitness of the massacre, on the contrary, stated years later that Will Soc had been "practically [*sic*] well known and esteemed by the people of the town, on account of his placid and friendly conduct." *Papers Read before the Lancaster County Hist. Soc.*, XVIII (1914), 175–6.

kill Prisoners in cold Blood. These were not even Prisoners: But what is the Example of Turks to Scripture Christians? They would have been safer, though they had been taken in actual War against the Saracens, if they had once drank Water with them. These were not taken in War against us, and have drank with us, and we with them, for Fourscore Years. But shall we compare Saracens to Christians? They would have been safer among the Moors in Spain, though they had been *Murderers of Sons;* if Faith had once been pledged to them, and a Promise of Protection given. But these have had the Faith of the English given to them many Times by the Government, and, in Reliance on that Faith, they lived among us, and gave us the Opportunity of murdering them. However, what was honourable in Moors, may not be a Rule to us; for we are Christians! They would have been safer it seems among Popish Spaniards, even if Enemies, and delivered into their Hands by a Tempest. These were not Enemies; they were born among us, and yet we have killed them all. But shall we imitate *idolatrous Papists,* we that are *enlightened Protestants?* They would even have been safer among the Negroes of Africa, where at least one manly Soul would have been found, with Sense, Spirit and Humanity enough, to stand in their Defence: But shall *Whitemen* and *Christians* act like a *Pagan Negroe?* In short it appears, that they would have been safe in any Part of the known World, except in the Neighbourhood of the CHRISTIANS WHITE SAVAGES of Peckstang and Donegall![6]

O ye unhappy Perpetrators of this horrid Wickedness! Reflect a Moment on the Mischief ye have done, the Disgrace ye have brought on your Country, on your Religion, and your Bible, on your Families and Children! Think on the Destruction of your captivated Country-folks (now among the wild Indians) which probably may follow, in Resentment of your Barbarity! Think on the Wrath of the United Five Nations, hitherto our Friends, but now

6. The writer of *The Conduct of the Paxton-Men* quoted extensively from this paragraph, but changed it to suggest how much safer the *white frontiersmen* would have been if, while living in a Quaker government, they had been contending with the Turks, Saracens, and Spaniards BF had cited. He wound up with the final sentence, still in quotation marks, changed to read: "In short, it appears that they would have been safe in any Part of the known World—except in the Neighbourhood of the RELENTLESS and OBSTINATE QUAKERS of Pennsylvania!" *Paxton Papers,* p. 296.

66

provoked by your murdering one of their Tribes, in Danger of becoming our bitter Enemies. Think of the mild and good Government you have so audaciously insulted; the Laws of your King, your Country, and your GOD, that you have broken; the infamous Death that hangs over your Heads: For JUSTICE, though slow, will come at last. All good People every where detest your Actions. You have imbrued your Hands in innocent Blood; how will you make them clean? The dying Shrieks and Groans of the Murdered, will often sound in your Ears: Their Spectres will sometimes attend you, and affright even your innocent Children! Fly where you will, your Consciences will go with you: Talking in your Sleep shall betray you, in the Delirium of a Fever you yourselves shall make your own Wickedness known.

One Hundred and Forty peaceable Indians yet remain in this Government. They have, by Christian Missionaries, been brought over to a *Liking,* at least, of our Religion; some of them lately left their Nation which is now at War with us, because they did not chuse to join with them in their Depredations; and to shew their Confidence in us, and to give us an equal Confidence in them, they have brought and put into our Hands their Wives and Children. Others have lived long among us in Northampton County, and most of their Children have been born there. These are all now trembling for their Lives. They have been hurried from Place to Place for Safety, now concealed in Corners, then sent out of the Province, refused a Passage through a neighbouring Colony, and returned, not unkindly perhaps, but disgracefully, on our Hands. O Pennsylvania! once renowned for Kindness to Strangers, shall the Clamours of a few mean Niggards about the Expence of this *Publick Hospitality,* an Expence that will not cost the noisy Wretches *Sixpence* a Piece (and what is the Expence of the poor Maintenance we afford them, compared to the Expence they might occasion if in Arms against us) shall so senseless a Clamour, I say, force you to turn out of your Doors these unhappy Guests, who have offended their own Country-folks by their Affection for you, who, confiding in your Goodness, have put themselves under your Protection? Those whom you have disarmed to satisfy groundless Suspicions, will you leave them exposed to the armed Madmen of your Country? Unmanly Men! who are not ashamed to come with Weapons against the Unarmed, to use the Sword against Women,

67

and the Bayonet against young Children; and who have already given such bloody Proofs of their Inhumanity and Cruelty. Let us rouze ourselves, for Shame, and redeem the Honour of our Province from the Contempt of its Neighbours; let all good Men join heartily and unanimously in Support of the Laws, and in strengthening the Hands of Government; that JUSTICE may be done, the Wicked punished, and the Innocent protected; otherwise we can, as a People, expect no Blessing from Heaven, there will be no Security for our Persons or Properties; Anarchy and Confusion will prevail over all, and Violence, without Judgment, dispose of every Thing.

When I mention the Baseness of the Murderers, in the Use they made of Arms, I cannot, I ought not to forget, the very different Behaviour of *brave Men* and *true Soldiers,* of which this melancholy Occasion has afforded us fresh Instances. The Royal Highlanders have, in the Course of this War, suffered as much as any other Corps, and have frequently had their Ranks thinn'd by an Indian Enemy; yet they did not for this retain a brutal undistinguishing Resentment against *all* Indians, Friends as well as Foes. But a Company of them happening to be here, when the 140 poor Indians above mentioned were thought in too much Danger to stay longer in the Province, chearfully undertook to protect and escort them to New-York, which they executed (as far as that Government would permit the Indians to come) with Fidelity and Honour; and their Captain Robinson,[7] is justly applauded and honoured by all sensible and good People, for the Care, Tenderness and Humanity, with which he treated those unhappy Fugitives, during their March in this severe Season. General Gage, too, has approved of his Officer's Conduct, and, as I hear, ordered him to remain with the Indians at Amboy, and continue his Protection to them, till another Body of the King's Forces could be sent to relieve his Company, and escort their Charge back in Safety to Philadelphia, where his Excellency has had the Goodness to direct those Forces to remain for some Time, under the Orders of our Governor, for the Security of the Indians; the Troops of this Prov-

7. Capt. James Robertson (not Robinson) commanded the detachment of the 77th Regiment (Montgomery's) that escorted the Indians from Province Island to Perth Amboy on their attempted journey to the protection of Sir William Johnson. *Pa. Col. Recs.,* IX, 110–11, 119.

68

ince being at present necessarily posted on the Frontier.[8] Such just and generous Actions endear the Military to the Civil Power, and impress the Minds of all the Discerning with a still greater Respect for our national Government. I shall conclude with observing, that *Cowards* can handle Arms, can strike where they are sure to meet with no Return, can wound, mangle and murder; but it belongs to *brave* Men to spare, and to protect; for, as the Poet says,

Mercy still sways the Brave.

Pennsylvania Assembly: Reply to the Governor

Printed in *Votes and Proceedings of the House of Representatives*, 1763–1764 (Philadelphia, 1764), p. 43.

The plan of early January to send the Indians lodged on Province Island to Sir William Johnson for safety had failed because the New York authorities had refused to cooperate.[9] Governor Penn received a letter

8. Capt. J. Schlosser commanded the three companies of the Royal Americans that escorted the Indians back to Philadelphia and guarded them in the barracks there until danger of an attack by the Paxton Boys has passed. *Pa. Col. Recs.*, IX, 120, 127, 132; I *Pa. Arch.*, IV, 158, 160–2.

9. See above, pp. 28–9. The most satisfactory general account of the events dealt with in this headnote and their background is Brooke Hindle, "The March of the Paxton Boys," 3 *William and Mary Quar.*, III (1946), 461–86. Three useful contemporary accounts of the climactic incidents and occurrences are: a letter by an unidentified Quaker dated Feb. 29, 1764, in Samuel Hazard, ed., *Hazard's Register of Pennsylvania*, XII (1833–34), 9–13; Howard M. Jenkins, "Fragments of a Journal Kept by Samuel Foulke, of Bucks County, While a Member of the Colonial Assembly of Pennsylvania, 1762–3–4," *PMHB*, V (1881), 60–73, esp. 66–73; and Theodore G. Tappert and John W. Doberstein, eds., *The Journals of Henry Melchior Muhlenberg* (Phila., 1945), II, 18–24. The first two of these side emphatically with the administration and Assembly against the rioters. Muhlenberg presents the case of the Paxton men in detail and with considerable sympathy. He was confined to his house by illness during the most critical days, so his narrative is based chiefly on what he was told by friends. Although two of these accounts are in journal form, internal evidence establishes that they, like the letter, were written some days later, and the dates the writers assigned to specific incidents are not always clear or in agreement with each other. No certainly accurate reconstruction of the exact sequence of events seems possible two centuries later. The February 9 issues of *Pa. Gaz.* and *Pa. Jour.* contain, curiously enough, precisely identical accounts of the public events of February 4–8.

on Saturday, January 21, from Capt. J. Schlosser of the Royal American Regiment saying that he had brought them back as far as Trenton, and Penn directed him to resume the march to Philadelphia on Monday. He informed the Council, and that body advised him to place the Indians in the barracks in the city, since the military guard would have good quarters and would be "better able to secure and protect them from any Insults there than in any other place." They arrived on January 24.[1]

News of the return of these Indians to Philadelphia spread rapidly, and it soon became apparent that the Paxton Boys and their sympathizers did not intend to leave them at peace in the city. On Saturday, January 28, Benjamin Kendall, a Philadelphia merchant, appeared before the Council and reported a conversation he had held with a Robert Fulton of Lancaster, whom he had met while returning from that town to Philadelphia two days before. Fulton had told him, he said, that in ten days "fifteen hundred Men would come down in order to kill the said Indians, and that if Fifteen hundred were not enough, five thousand were ready to join them." Kendall tried to get Fulton to use his influence to stop the projected attack, but Fulton replied that "if Gabriel was to come down from Heaven" and tell them to stop they would not do so, "for they were of the same Spirit with the blood-ran, blood-thirsty Presbyterians, who cut off King Charles his Head." Fulton denied the rumor that the marchers intended to kill the Quakers of the city, as well as the Indians, but assured Kendall that they would kill any one who opposed them.[2]

The tempo of events now began to quicken. On Sunday, January 29, Penn wrote to Capt. William Murray, commander of the British troops at Carlisle, ordering him to move his forces to Lancaster.[3] On the Council's advice, he began to prepare instructions to Captain Schlosser at the Philadelphia barracks, directing him how to act in case of attack. On this matter Penn ran into legal technicalities, so on Thursday, February 2, he prepared a message to the Assembly asking for a "short Law" to extend the British Riot Act of 1715 to Pennsylvania. The Assembly received the message on the morning of the 3d, took it into immediate consideration, and appointed two men to draft the bill. They did so at once and the Assembly passed it through its three readings by special order and presented it to Penn by six o'clock of the same afternoon. Because of the speaker's illness the Assembly was meeting at the house of his brother, Charles Norris. Penn immediately went there; the speaker

1. 1 *Pa. Arch.*, IV, 158; *Pa. Col. Recs.*, IX, 124–5; *PMHB*, XXV (1901), 17–18.
2. *Pa. Col. Recs.*, IX, 125–7.
3. *Ibid.*, pp. 217–8.

An Indian Squaw King Wampum spies,
Which makes his lustful passions rise.
But while he doth a friendly Jobb.
She dives her Hand into his Fob.
And thence conveys as we are told.
His Watch whose Cases were of Gold.

When Danger's threaten
To talk of such a thing
To Arms to Arms with
The Sword of Quakers a
Fill Bumpers then of
We'll drink Success to

The March o

s mere Nonsense:	Fight Dog! fight Bear! you're all my Frien
Conscience:	By you I shall attain my Ends:
e Accord.	For I can never be content
t the Lord.	Till I have got the Government.
m or Arrach:	But if from this Attempt I fall,
e new Barrack.	Then let the Devil take you all.

e Paxton Men

broke with precedent and invited him into the room where the assembly-men were gathered, and Penn formally enacted the measure.[4]

On Saturday morning, February 4, the provincial commissioners told Penn and the Council that a letter from an assemblyman in Lancaster County had reported that "a very considerable number of the people living on the frontiers of that and other Counties, were actually as-sembling themselves" to march on Philadelphia and kill the Indians there, and that the next morning, Sunday, was "the time fixed on for the execution of their unlawful design." The Council thereupon advised Penn to give Captain Schlosser written instructions to defend the Indians with his troops after the Riot Act had been "first read by a proper Civil Officer."[5]

On the Council's advice Penn sent around notices of a general meeting of the inhabitants to take place at the State House at four o'clock that afternoon. The governor and Council, the members of the Assembly, the city magistrates, and a "Concourse" of inhabitants estimated at 3000 attended in spite of a pouring rain. Penn announced the impending approach of the frontiersmen, proclaimed the passage of the Riot Act, and called upon the citizens to take arms and join an Association for the defense of the city and the Indians. Some volunteers armed themselves

---

4. *Ibid.*, pp. 127, 129, 131–2; *Votes*, 1763–64, pp. 40–1. Penn was uncer-tain whether any orders he might give the troops would legally justify their using force against British subjects, "though riotously assembled," until the civil power had been called in and had "in vain endeavoured to suppress the Tumult." The Riot Act of 1 George I, stat. 2, c. 5, provided for a magistrate, justice of the peace, or other civil officer to order, "with a loud voice" and in the King's name, any assembly of twelve or more rioters to disperse. If they failed to do so in one hour, the civil authorities might then call on anyone to assist in breaking up the assembly and arresting its members, and no liability would attach to any such assistants who killed or injured rioters in the process. For the Pa. act of Feb. 3, 1764, which repeats *verbatim* most of the British act, see *Statutes at Large, Pa.*, VI, 325–8.

5. *Pa. Col. Recs.*, IX, 132. The "Rough Draft" of Penn's instructions to Schlosser, dated Feb. 4, 1764, does not mention the Riot Act, but directs that if armed men should approach the barracks, the officer on duty was to call out the troops and "with great Moderation and Civility" address the rioters, ask their intentions, and tell them he had orders to protect the In-dians. If they should indicate that they intended to kill the Indians or should make no reply but continue to advance, the officer was again to beg them to desist and warn them that he would open fire if they did not. Should they still persist, he was to "repel Force with Force" and take as many prisoners as possible, but his men were not to pursue them if he succeeded in routing them, in order "that there may not be more Bloodshed than shall be ab-solutely necessary." 1 *Pa. Arch.*, IV, 160–2.

at once and went to the barracks to support the regular troops; others, estimated at many hundreds, joined the Association and formed into six companies of foot and one of artillery and two troops of horse. According to Muhlenberg, many of the Germans in the city held back because of their sympathies with the frontiersmen, but others joined up, as did, surprisingly, a substantial number of Quakers in spite of the principles of their faith.[6]

Also on Saturday the governor and Council sent spies "up the different roads to observe the motions of the Rioters, and to bring intelligence of their Approach." The next morning the usual Sabbath calm was broken by the appearance at the barracks of a number of carpenters, hired by the governor, to build a "redoubt" and "several small fortresses or ramparts" under the direction of Captain Schlosser. Cannon were brought up and fixed in place and, so far as seemed possible, the barracks were placed in a posture of defense.[7]

Late Sunday night—Muhlenberg said it was about two o'clock Monday morning—the bells began to ring an alarm signaling that the Paxton men were coming. It was apparently during this night that, as Franklin put it later, the governor "did me the Honour, on an Alarm, to run to my House at Midnight, with his Counsellors at his Heels, for Advice, and made it his Head Quarters for some time."[8] Orders had gone out to bring all the ferryboats on the Schuylkill to the Philadelphia side. Had this been done the marchers would have had difficulty getting over because the river was in freshet, but about eleven on Monday morning it was realized that the crossing at Swede's Ford, some fifteen miles up from the city, had been forgotten. New orders came too late; the Paxton Boys, numbering perhaps 250 and saying that more were to follow, had already crossed the river and marched down through Chestnut Hill to Germantown. The governor and his advisers sent several clergymen to meet the insurgents and use what influence they might have to stop the approach. Among those who went were Gilbert Tennent, the evangelist and pastor of the Second Presbyterian Church, two Anglicans, a Presbyterian "professor from the Academy" (probably Francis Alison), and Paul Daniel Brycelius, a Swedish Lutheran from Raritan, N.J., then temporarily in Philadelphia. They told the marchers that the city was preparing for defense, and that an attack would certainly lead to

6. *Pa. Col. Recs.*, IX, 132–3; *Hazard's Register*, XII, 10–11; Foulke's journal, *PMHB*, V, 69; *Muhlenberg Journals*, II, 18–19. Muhlenberg, obviously writing up his journal at a later time, incorrectly dated this State House gathering on Wednesday, February 1, three days before it took place.

7. *Pa. Col. Recs.*, IX, 133; *Muhlenberg Journals*, II, 19; *Hazard's Register*, XII, 11.

8. See below, p. 103.

72

bloodshed. They underlined their warning to the astonished insurgents with the information that even many Quakers had taken up arms. The frontiersmen decided to pause at Germantown.[9]

Early Tuesday morning, February 7, the governor and Council sent a delegation of prominent citizens to talk with the rioters. The group included Attorney General Benjamin Chew and William Logan of the Council, Franklin and Joseph Galloway of the Assembly, Mayor Thomas Willing, Daniel Roberdeau, a leading Anglican merchant and former assemblyman, and Dr. Carl Wrangel, pastor of Gloria Dei (Old Swedes') Lutheran Church.[1] At Germantown they met the spokesmen of the insurgents, Matthew Smith and James Gibson.[2] The conference lasted for several hours; the Paxton men stated their grievances at length, by no means all of which related to the Indians under guard at the barracks; the men from the city convinced Smith and Gibson that the government, the British troops, and the volunteer defenders meant business and that any attempt to use force would lead to a heavy loss of life. It was finally agreed that the Paxton men would disperse and return to their homes, leaving Smith and Gibson to come into the city and draw up a formal paper stating the grievances of the men for whom they

9. *Hazard's Register,* XII, 11–12. Foulke's journal, *PMHB,* V, 70; *Muhlenberg Journals,* II, 20–2. On Tennent, see above, II, 313 n. This was one of his last services to the public; he died the following July 23. On Alison, see above, IV, 470 n. Brycelius, a former Moravian, had been converted to Lutheranism in 1760. He had gone out independently by order of Dr. Carl Magnus Wrangel, pastor of Gloria Dei (Old Swedes') Church in Philadelphia and provost of the Swedish Lutheran mission on the Delaware, to persuade the Lutherans of Germantown not to join the rioters and to give any Germans among the advancing party "an earnest and kindly admonition." Upon his return to Philadelphia he reported at length to Muhlenberg on his conversations with the insurgents. They had told him, according to Muhlenberg, that they did not intend to kill the Indians, "but only to conduct them out of the province," and that they were willing to put up a bond of £10,000 that such was their intention. What security they would have offered is not mentioned in Muhlenberg's account.

1. These are the names as given by Muhlenberg, but it is not certain that Wrangel was actually a member of the official delegation, though he did go out with the party and addressed the rioters. *Muhlenberg Journals,* II, 22–3. Foulke's journal mentions "4 members of the Assembly" (*PMHB*), V, 70, and the anonymous Quaker calls the party simply "a body of select patricians" (*Hazard's Register,* XII, 12).

2. Muhlenberg mentions a third Paxton spokesman simply by the name of Brown, but he adds that Col. John Armstrong (above, VII, 104 n), "perhaps the chief *agent* of the frontier inhabitants," was also present at the conference. *Muhlenberg Journals,* II, 23.

73

were acting. The governor and Assembly would then give these matters just consideration.[3]

When the official party returned to Philadelphia in the evening and reported to the governor, the volunteer "militiamen" were dismissed with a speech of thanks. The next morning, however, a fresh alarm took place when a small party of the Paxton men entered the city escorting their spokesmen, Smith and Gibson. Rumors quickly spread that the insurgents were advancing in force; shops were closed, and hundreds of defenders reassembled under arms. Fortunately, no violence followed, and some of the frontiersmen were allowed to look over the Indians at the barracks to see if they could recognize among them any reputed murderers or other enemies. They found none. Although charges and countercharges continued to fly back and forth for days, the city soon returned to its accustomed routine, if not to its theoretical condition of brotherly love.[4]

On Saturday, February 4, the day on which the mass meeting at the State House had organized the Association of volunteer defenders, Governor Penn had prepared and the Council had approved a message to the Assembly pointing out the difficulties under which he labored because

3. Muhlenberg states that the official delegates also agreed that BF and Mayor Willing would help Smith and Gibson "to get their *gravamina* on paper," but there is no other testimony to such a definite agreement and no evidence that either man helped the frontiersmen write their "Remonstrance." *Muhlenberg Journals*, II, 23. For a summary of its contents see below, pp. 81–2.

4. *Muhlenberg Journals*, II, 24; *Hazard's Register*, XII, 12–13; Foulke's journal, *PMHB*, V (1881), 71. After the fruitless inspection of the Indians, a boy came forward and swore that he and another lad had been hired one night by men dressed as Quakers to row four or five Indians away from the city to Province Island. These were presumably the guilty Indians who were being intentionally hidden. But when the authorities sought to question the boy again, he had disappeared and could not be found. The Quakers argued that the failure to identify any of the Indians proved the innocence of the group and that the boy's story had obviously been concocted to discredit the Quakers. Their opponents in the city, on the other hand, were quick to charge the Friends with deceit and with kidnapping the boy, thereby impugning his testimony. *Hazard's Register*, XII, 12–13; John R. Dunbar, ed., *The Paxton Papers* (The Hague, 1957), pp. 213, 227, 240. Surprisingly, Gov. John Penn sent no report on this entire affair to the Proprietors for more than five weeks. Then he compressed his whole account into one paragraph of 116 words. In it he omitted the names of any of the Philadelphians who had given him so much help during this grave crisis, whether clergymen, proprietary leaders, or members of the Assembly. John Penn to Thomas Penn, March 17, 1764, Penn Papers, Hist. Soc. Pa.

74

there was no act in force to provide an organized militia which could be called out in cases of emergency such as then existed. The situation was made especially precarious, he said, because the regular troops guarding the Indians would soon "be necessarily ordered on Duty elsewhere, and be employed against our open Enemies." He therefore asked the Assembly "to frame a Militia Law, in a manner as little Burthensome to the Inhabitants as possible, as the only natural and effectual means of preserving the publick Tranquility, and enabling the civil power to enforce the Laws and vindicate the Honour of the Government."[5]

The Assembly had adjourned that Saturday morning before Penn's message could be delivered; because of the activities and excitement resulting from the approach of the Paxton Boys, no quorum could be brought together until the following Thursday afternoon. On Friday morning, February 10, Secretary Richard Peters presented to the House the governor's message of the 4th. Upon its consideration, the Assembly appointed a committee of seven, including Franklin, to draft a reply. They brought it in on Saturday morning; it was approved at once, and was ordered to be delivered to Governor Penn.[6]

May it please your HONOUR,   February 11, 1764.
Your Honour's Message of the Fourth Instant we received Yesterday, and as we are of Opinion that it contains Matters of the utmost Importance to the Welfare of this Province, we shall take the same into our most serious Consideration, and as soon as possible acquaint you with the Result; and notwithstanding the Rioters, upon their Approach near this City, and a Discovery of the spirited Resolutions of the Citizens to oppose their barbarous and illegal Designs, are dispersed, your Honour may be assured that nothing in our Power, consistent with the Trust reposed in us, shall be wanting for the Security of the Government, and the Protection of the Inhabitants, against the future Violences of such licentious People, who disturb the publick Tranquility, and trample on all Laws divine and human.[7]   Signed by Order of the House,
                                                 ISAAC NORRIS, Speaker.

5. *Pa. Col. Recs.*, IX, 133–4.
6. *Votes*, 1763–64, pp. 41–3. Immediately after dispatching this message to Penn, the House resumed consideration of the matter and appointed a committee of eight—the same seven who had drafted the message and one other—to prepare and bring in a militia bill.
7. The committee brought in a militia bill on February 17; the Assembly debated it on the 21st, 22d, and 25th, and passed it on the 28th. Foulke re-

To Richard Jackson   <small>ALS: American Philosophical Society</small>

Dear Sir,   Philada. Feb. 11. 1764
    I have just received your Favour by the extra Packet of Nov.
26.[8] and am pleas'd to find a just Resentment so general in your
House against Mr. W.'s seditious Conduct,[9] and to hear that the
present Administration is like to continue.
    If Money *must* be raised from us to support 14 Batallions, as you
mention, I think your Plan the most advantageous to both the
Mother Country and Colonies of any I have seen. A moderate Duty
on Foreign Mellasses maybe collected; when a high one could not.[1]
The same on foreign Wines; and a Duty not only on Tea, but on
all East India Goods might perhaps not be amiss, as they are generally rather Luxuries than Necessaries; and many of your Manchester Manufactures might well supply their Places. The Duty
on Negroes I could wish large enough to obstruct their Importation, as they every where prevent the Increase of Whites.[2] But if
you lay such Duties as may destroy our Trade with the Foreign
Colonies, I think you will greatly hurt your own Interest as well
as ours. I need not explain this to you, who will readily see it. The
American Fishery, too, should be as little burthened as possible. It

---

ported that BF was one of the principal speakers for the bill during the debate
(he had been the author of the first Militia Act of Pa. in 1755 and obviously
felt strongly on the matter; see above, VI, 266–73). Penn and the Council
considered the bill on March 7 and returned it on the 12th with a series
of amendments unacceptable to the House. *Votes*, 1763–64, pp. 49, 51–3,
60, 61; *Pa. Col. Recs.*, IX, 150–1; *PMHB*, V (1881), 71–3. The governor's
proposed changes became one of the Assembly's major grievances, and the
failure of the bill was an issue in the election campaign of the summer and
fall. See below, pp. 122 n, 130–1, 141–2, 360–5.
    8. Jackson's "Favour" has not been found.
    9. On Nov. 15, 1763, the House of Commons voted, 273 to 111, that
John Wilkes's *North Briton*, no. 45, was "a false, scandalous, and seditious
libel" and on Jan. 19, 1764, expelled him from the House. See above, X, 366 n.
    1. For Jackson's proposal of a 1½d. per gallon duty on the importation
of foreign molasses into the American continental colonies, see above, X, 371.
    2. The Sugar Act of April 5, 1764 (4 Geo. III, c. 15), reduced the duty on
foreign molasses from 6d. to 3d. per gallon. It laid a duty of £7 a tun on
Madeira and other island wines imported directly into the colonies and also
laid duties on certain East India articles—silks, bengals, and calicoes. Tea
and Negroes were not taxed.

is to no purpose to enlarge on these Heads, as probably your Acts are pass'd before this can reach you.

In my last[3] I mention'd to you the Rioting on our Frontiers, in which 20 peaceable Indians were kill'd, who had long liv'd quietly among us.[4] The Spirit of killing all Indians, Friends and Foes, spread amazingly thro' the whole Country: The Action was almost universally approved of by the common People; and the Rioters thence receiv'd such Encouragement, that they projected coming down to this City, 1000 in Number, arm'd, to destroy 140 Moravian and Quaker Indians, under Protection of the Government.[5] To check this Spirit, and strengthen the Hands of the Government by changing the Sentiments of the Populace, I wrote the enclos'd Pamphlet,[6] which we had only time to circulate in this City and Neighbourhood, before we heard that the Insurgents were on their March from all Parts. It would perhaps be Vanity in me to imagine so slight a thing could have any extraordinary Effect. But however that may be, there was a sudden and very remarkable Change; and above 1000 of our Citizens took Arms to support the Government in the Protection of those poor Wretches. Near 500 of the Rioters had rendezvous'd at Germantown, and many more were expected; but the Fighting Face we put on made them more willing to hear Reason, and the Gentlemen sent out by the Governor and Council to discourse with them, found it no very difficult Matter to persuade them to disperse and go home quietly. They came from all Parts of our Frontier, and were armed with Rifle Guns and Tomhawks. You may judge what Hurry and Confusion we have been in for this Week past. I was up two Nights running, all Night, with our Governor; and my Rest so broken by Alarms on the other Nights, that the whole Week seems one confus'd Space of Time, without any such Distinction of Days, as that I can readily and certainly say, on such a Day such a thing happened. At present we are pretty quiet, and I hope that Quiet will continue. A Militia Bill is ordered by the House to be brought in, our Want of such a Law appearing on this Occasion to every-body; but whether we shall

3. That of Jan. 16, 1764; see above, pp. 19–20.
4. See above, pp. 42–55.
5. On the events described here, see the headnote to the document immediately above.
6. BF's *Narrative of the Late Massacres*.

77

be able to frame one that will pass, is a Question. The Jealousy of an Addition of Power to the Proprietary Government, which is universally dislik'd here, will prevail with the House not to leave the sole Appointment of the Militia Officers in the Hands of the Governor; and he, I suppose, will insist upon it, and so the Bill will probably fall through;[7] which perhaps is no great Matter, as your 14 Battallions will make all Militias in America needless, as well as put them out of Countenance.

The Bearer, Mr. Mifflin,[8] is a valuable young Man, Son of a Friend of mine, and one for whom I have a great Regard. I beg Leave to recommend him to your Civilities. With the sincerest Esteem, and Respect, I am, Dear Sir, Your most obedient and most humble Servant　　　　　　　　　　　　　　　　　　B FRANKLIN

R. Jackson Esqr.

Endorsed: 11 Febry 1764 Benjn. Franklin Esqr

From Francis Bernard　　Letterbook copy: Harvard College Library

Sir　　　　　　　　　　　　　　　　　　　Boston Feb 13. 1764

I am favoured with yours of Jan 27.[9] and have received one from my Son dated New York Feb 2 informing that being apprehensive of the badness of the Roads on the change of Weather, He had returned your Horse[1] and intended to take his passage in the New-

7. BF's prediction was correct; a militia bill, permitting the election of officers, was passed by the Assembly on Feb. 28, 1764, but was rejected by Governor Penn, who demanded that he himself be allowed to appoint officers and required other changes as well. See below, pp. 122 n, 130–1, 141–2, 360–5.

8. Thomas Mifflin (1744–1800), son of John Mifflin (above, I, 373 n), had been working for BF's old friend William Coleman (above, II, 406 n), and was going to Europe for a year of mercantile training, most of which was spent in France. An ardent patriot, Mifflin served in the First and Second Continental Congresses, was quartermaster general of the Continental Army, 1775–1778; president of Congress, 1783–84; president of the Supreme Executive Council, 1788–90; and governor of Pa., 1790–99. *DAB.*

9. Not found.

1. BF sent his horse to convey Bernard's son from Alexandria, Va., to Philadelphia, and the young man apparently rode it on to New York. See above, p. 6.

port packet boat with some other Gentlemen who were waiting for it. However He is not yet arrived.

I am extremely obliged to you for your Care in this business and shall be impatient till I have an opportunity to make some return. In regard to the charge, if it will be more convenient to you to have it paid at philadelphia, than to draw for it here, I shall soon have an opportunity of ordering it there. I shall wait your orders. I am

B Franklin Esq

To Catharine Greene   ALS: American Philosophical Society

Dear Friend,   Philada. Feb. 15. 1764

I have before me your most acceptable Favour of Dec. 24.[2] Publick Business and our public Confusions have so taken up my Attention, that I suspect I did not answer it when I receiv'd it, but am really not certain; so to make sure, I write this Line to acknowledge the Receiving it, and to thank you for it.

I condole with you on the Death of the good old Lady your Mother.[3] Separations of this kind from those we love, are grievous: But tis the Will of God that such should be the Nature of Things in this World; all that ever were born are either dead or must die. It becomes us to submit, and to comfort ourselves with the Hope of a better Life and more happy Meeting hereafter.

Sally kept to her Horse the greatest Part of the Journey, and was much pleas'd with the Tour.[4] She often remembers with Pleasure and Gratitude the Kindnesses she met with and receiv'd from our Friends every where, and particularly at your House. She talks of writing by this Post;[5] and my Dame sends her Love to you, and Thanks for the Care you took of her old Man, but having bad

2. Not found.
3. Caty's mother, Deborah Greene Ray, died Dec. 11, 1763. Louise B. Clarke, *The Greenes of Rhode Island* (N.Y., 1903), p. 101.
4. Sally Franklin accompanied BF on his trip to New England in the summer of 1763. See above, x, 276–9.
5. In a letter to Caty of June 14, 1764, at APS, Sally mentions having written her in February. The letter has not been found.

Spectacles, cannot write at present. Mr. Kent's[6] Compliment is a very extraordinary one, as he was oblig'd to kill himself and two others in order to make it: but being kill'd in Imagination only, they and he are all yet alive and Well, Thanks to God, and I hope will continue so as long as Dear Katy, Your affectionate Friend

B Franklin

My best Respects to Mr. Greene, and Love to the little dear Creatures.[7]

I believe the Instructions relating to the Post Office have been sent to Mr. Rufus Greene.[8]

Addressed: To | Mrs Catharine Greene | at | Warwick | Rhode-island Governmt | Free | B Franklin

Pennsylvania Assembly Committee: Report

Printed in *Votes and Proceedings of the House of Representatives,* 1763–1764 (Philadelphia, 1764), pp. 50–1.

When several clergymen and others went from Philadelphia to Germantown on Monday, February 6, to talk with the Paxton Boys,[9] they were given a "Declaration" of the frontiersmen's grievances, which they brought back to the city and delivered to Governor Penn.[1] Most of this

6. Benjamin Kent (1708–1788), A.B., Harvard, 1727, was ordained to preach at Marlborough, Mass., in 1733, but was dismissed two years later for professing unorthodox views and for being "offensively erratic." Kent then turned to the law, which he practiced successfully for the rest of his life. An ardent patriot, he served on many Boston committees during the Revolutionary War and made a fortune by owning and defending privateers. He migrated to Halifax, Nova Scotia, in 1785 to join his family and died there. *Sibley's Harvard Graduates,* VIII (1951), 220–30. The nature of his compliment is not known.

7. For Caty's children, see above, x, 191 n.

8. See above, x, 368 n.

9. See above, p. 72.

1. Printed soon afterwards together with the "Remonstrance" of Matthew Smith and James Gibson as an 18-page pamphlet entitled: *A Declaration and Remonstrance Of the distressed and bleeding Frontier Inhabitants Of the Province of Pennsylvania, Presented by them to the Honourable the Governor and Assembly of the Province, Shewing the Causes Of their late Discontent and Uneasiness and the Grievances Under which they have laboured, and which they humbly pray to have redress'd* ([Phila., William Bradford?], 1764).

paper is taken up with bitter complaints of the "excessive Regard manifested to Indians beyond his Majesty's loyal Subjects," with the citation of instances in which the consideration shown to the red men, including known enemies, contrasted with the indifference of the authorities to the protection of white settlers and the loss of life and property among them. Such was the "unhappy Situation" of the frontiersmen, "under the Villany, Infatuation and Influence of a certain Faction that have got the political Reigns [sic] in their Hand and tamely tyrannize over the other good Subjects of the Province! ... And must not all well disposed People entertain a charitable Sentiment of those, who at their own great Expence and Trouble, have attempted, or shall attempt rescuing a labouring Land from a Weight so oppressive, unreasonable and unjust? It is this we Design, it is this we are resolved to prosecute, tho' it is with great Reluctance we are obliged to adopt a Measure, not so agreeable as could be desired, and to which Extremity alone compels."[2]

At the negotiations on Tuesday, February 7, between the Paxton leaders and the delegation sent out by the governor, it was agreed that Matthew Smith and James Gibson should come into the city and prepare a paper setting forth explicitly the grievances of the frontiersmen. Their "Remonstrance," addressed to John Penn and the Assembly, is dated February 13; Penn laid it before the Council the next day and sent it to the Assembly, where it was read on the 15th.[3]

In the "Remonstrance" Smith and Gibson declared that they were speaking on behalf of the inhabitants of the five "Frontier Counties" of Lancaster, York, Cumberland, Berks, and Northampton, and they presented nine specific points of grievance: 1. Although these people were entitled to the same "Privileges and Immunities" as the residents of the counties of Philadelphia, Chester, and Bucks, the five counties were allowed to elect only ten members of the Assembly, while the three older ones and the city of Philadelphia elected a total of twenty-six. The remonstrants asked that their counties "may be no longer

Hildeburn, 1969; Evans, 9630. The "Declaration" is separately printed in *Votes*, 1763–64, pp. 47–9, and *Pa. Col. Recs.*, IX, 142–5. The pamphlet is reprinted in John R. Dunbar, ed., *The Paxton Papers* (The Hague, 1957), pp. 99–110. The date of the delivery of the "Declaration" is ascertained from *The Address of the People call'd Quakers, In the Province of Pennsylvania, To John Penn, Esquire, Lieutenant-Governor of the said Province, &c.* (Phila., John Steuart, 1764), reprinted in Dunbar, ed., *Paxton Papers*, pp. 131–8.

2. *Declaration and Remonstrance*, pp. 8–9.

3. *Pa. Col. Recs.*, IX, 138–42; *Votes*, 1763–64, pp. 44–46. It is printed in full in both places and also in the pamphlet mentioned in the second note above.

deprived of an equal Number" of representatives.[4] 2. A bill was pending in the Assembly for the trial in Philadelphia, Bucks, or Chester, of persons charged with killing Indians in Lancaster County. This measure would "deprive British Subjects of their known Privileges" and "contradict the well known Laws of the British Nation, in a point whereon Life, Liberty, and Security essentially depend, Namely, that of being tried by their Equals in the Neighbourhood."[5] 3. The frontier inhabitants who had "escaped from savage Fury" were "left destitute by the Public," but the Moravian and Wyalusing Indians, highly suspect individually and collectively, were protected and maintained in Philadelphia at public expense. 4. All Indians were "Perfidious," and to permit any of them to live within the inhabited parts of the province during an Indian war was "contrary to the Maxims of good Policy" and ought to be "remedied." 5. Frontier inhabitants wounded in the defense of the province were not now, but should be, cared for and cured at the cost of the public. 6. Rewards should be offered, as in the last war, for taking Indian scalps.[6] 7. No trade with the Indians should be permitted until "Numbers of our nearest and dearest Relatives," still in captivity in spite of promises, were all returned. 8. A "certain Society of People" (the Quakers) had been overly friendly to the Indians and one leader of the society had kept up relations with them "as if he had been our Governor." No private subject should be allowed

4. William Penn's Charter of Privileges provided that, in case the Three Lower Counties on Delaware should split off and form a separate Assembly (as they did in 1705), the three counties of Philadelphia, Chester, and Bucks should elect eight representatives each and the city of Philadelphia two. The charter said nothing about representation of new counties which might be formed later. When each of the five newer counties was created it had a relatively small population and was understandably allowed a lesser number of assemblymen: Lancaster, 4; Cumberland and York, 2 each; and Northampton and Berks, 1 each. No significant complaints of underrepresentation arose until the Indian incursions of 1763–64 led to a belief in the exposed counties that the Assembly was indifferent to the interests of those areas. By that time the combined population of the newer counties had grown to the point where it nearly equaled that of the three original counties including the city of Philadelphia. On the basis of population, then, the two sections should have had about equal representation, although the older region paid taxes in 1760 amounting to approximately half as much again as did the "back counties." Charles H. Lincoln, *The Revolutionary Movement in Pennsylvania 1760–1776* (Phila., 1901), pp. 45–8; Theodore Thayer, "The Quaker Party of Pennsylvania, 1755–1765," *PMHB*, LXXI (1947), 28–31.

5. See above, pp. 27–8.

6. For many references to the rewards offered and paid for Indian scalps during the Seven Years' War, see above, VI, index.

to "carry on a Correspondence with our Enemies."[7] 9. The garrison at Fort Augusta had given little assistance or protection to the nearby settlers.[8]

Two days after this "Remonstrance" was read in the Assembly, that body asked the governor for the "Declaration" previously given to him and for a conference with an Assembly committee on the "Remonstrance." Penn sent down the requested paper and proposed that the conference take place the next morning, Saturday, February 18. The Assembly thereupon named the nine men whose names appear at the end of the report printed below to serve as a conference committee.[9] Seven of the nine sat in the Assembly from one or another of the older counties or the city of Philadelphia; Lancaster and Northampton, alone among the five frontier counties, were represented on the committee by one member each. The results of the conference are stated in the committee report, which was presented to the Assembly the following Tuesday morning.

February 21, 1764.

We the Committee appointed, by Order of the House, to confer with and advise the Governor on the very extraordinary Remonstrance from Matthew Smith, and James Gibson, said to be in Behalf of the five Frontier Counties, complaining of certain supposed Grievances from the Government, and which his Honour had thought fit to send down to the House, do report, That we had a Conference accordingly on Saturday Morning with the Governor, attended by his Council, and did therein offer the following Proposition, *viz.* That as the present Ferment among the People of the Frontier Counties appeared to be a Distemper in the State, which

7. In the pamphlet printing of the "Remonstrance" the name of the Quaker leader is indicated only by blank lines, but in the copies entered in the minutes of the Council and in the Assembly *Votes* the initials "J. P." (*i.e.*, "I. P.") appear, standing for Israel Pemberton, founder of the "Friendly Association for Regaining and Preserving Peace with the Indians by Pacific Measures" (above, VII, 18 n). Pemberton knew how much he was hated by the frontiersmen because of his activities on behalf of the Indians, especially at the Easton Treaty of 1762, and when the Paxton Boys were approaching Philadelphia he prudently left town. Brooke Hindle, "The March of the Paxton Boys," 3 *William and Mary Quar.*, III (1946), 476.

8. The writers of the "Remonstrance" appended a note that they intended no reflection on the commander at Fort Augusta, their friend Col. John Armstrong.

9. *Votes*, 1763–64, pp. 47–9; *Pa. Col. Recs.*, IX, 142–5.

had already produced great Mischiefs, and was likely to be productive of more, and greater, if proper Means were not speedily applied for its Cure; and as it appeared from the Remonstrance, and the Declaration sent to the Governor by the same People, that their Discontents are founded on false or mistaken Facts, of which the Remonstrants and others might easily be convinced, if, at a public Hearing to be allowed them, in Support of their Remonstrance, proper Interrogatories were made them upon the several Articles thereof; and that the People being by this Means disabused, the Spreading of the Contagion would be prevented, and the Disturbances might more easily be quieted than by harsher Methods; therefore, and as the Governor was equally with the Assembly concerned in the Charges made against the Government, and it would give more Weight to the Proceeding, if all the Parts of the Government appeared unanimous therein, we did propose it for his Honour's Consideration, whether it would not be expedient to appoint such a public Hearing before his Honour, attended by his Council and the Assembly, previously framing such a Sett of Interrogatories as would naturally, by their Answers, show that the several Matters contained in those Papers, respecting the Conduct both of the executive and legislative Powers of Government, were unjust, and without Foundation, and by that Means make it unnecessary to enter into any Argument with the Remonstrants on the Subject of their Complaints, which it was objected, by one of the Council, might seem unbecoming the Honour and Dignity of the Government?[1]

After some Time spent in Conference on this Proposition, which seemed to be approved by several of the Council, the Committee were acquainted that the Governor inclined to confer with his Council thereupon in private, on which we immediately withdrew, and returned to the House.

The same Day the Secretary came down with a verbal Message

---

1. The Council minutes do not state so baldly the scheme of preparing in advance a series of "loaded" questions to put to Smith and Gibson. In this connection the minutes simply record the proposal that the governor and Assembly act in concert in publicly interrogating the representatives of the frontiersmen, "and convincing them that the several matters set forth respecting the Conduct of the Executive and Legislative Powers of Government, are unjust and without foundation." *Pa. Col. Recs.,* IX, 146.

from his Honour, that it being a Matter of Importance, he would consider further of it till Monday.

And on Monday Evening the Secretary delivered to one of the Committee the following Paper from the Governor, *viz.*[2]

"The Governor's Answer to the Proposal made him by a Committee of Assembly, in a Conference with them on Saturday last; which was, that he would act in Concert with the House in sending for Matthew Smith, and James Gibson, who lately presented to the Governor and Assembly a Remonstrance or Petition, in Behalf of themselves and the five Frontier Counties of this Province, praying a Redress of certain supposed Grievances; and in interrogating them in public, and shewing that the several Matters and Things therein contained, respecting the Conduct both of the executive and legislative Powers of Government, are unjust, and without Foundation.

"The Governor would, with great Pleasure, take every legal and constitutional Measure, which had a Tendency to promote the public Peace and Harmony, and quiet the Minds of such of His Majesty's Subjects in this Province as are discontented, and remove any Errors or Mistakes they lie under; but he cannot accede to the Method proposed by the Assembly on this Occasion, for the following Reasons:

"*First,* Because it would, in his Opinion, be not only unbecoming the Honour and Dignity of the Government, which he shall always think it his Duty to support, but tacitly giving up the indubitable Rights of both Branches of the Legislature, to enter into any Argument or Justification with the Petitioners, on the Subject Matter of their Complaints. Whether any Article in the Remonstrance or Petition is, or is not, a real Grievance, or requires Redress, is proper for the Consideration of the Representative Body of the People only, in the first Instance; after which the Governor is to exercise his Judgment on any Bill which may be prepared for that Purpose; whatever may be ultimately determined on by both Branches of

2. The Council spent most of its meeting on Monday, February 20, in discussing the Assembly's proposal of a joint public hearing and in preparing the answer which follows here. The minutes do not show whether the Council was unanimous in its judgment. *Ibid.,* pp. 146–8. According to BF, "the moderate Part of the Council" approved the Assembly's proposal. See below, p. 107.

85

the Legislature, will be final and binding upon the People; and the Governor conceives that he cannot concur with the Measure proposed, without inverting the Order of Government, and departing from the Rights the legislative Body is vested with by the Constitution.

"*Secondly,* The legislative and executive Powers of Government are independent of one another, and are lodged in different Hands; and though the Petitioners have, in this Case, very injudiciously blended together Matters which regard both, yet that can be no Reason why the Governor and Assembly should follow their Example.

"The Governor doubts not but the House will take into Consideration such Parts of the Remonstrance as are proper for their Cognizance, and do therein what in their Wisdom and Justice they think right, as he will, with regard to such other Parts as relate to the executive Branch of Government.

"February 20, 1764.   JOHN PENN."

Which Answer from the Governor seeming to preclude any farther Conference on the Subject, the Committee do accordingly close their Report, submitting the same to the Consideration of the House.

JOSEPH FOX,	WILLIAM RODMAN,
JOSEPH GALLOWAY,	JOHN MORTON,
BENJAMIN FRANKLIN,	JOHN DOUGLAS,
SAMUEL RHOADS,	JOHN TOOL.
JOHN HUGHES,[3]	

3. Upon receiving this report and hearing that Smith and Gibson were anxious to go home, the Assembly told them that the House would consider the parts of the "Remonstrance" within its cognizance when it had finished the King's business then before it. *Votes,* 1763–64, p. 51. On March 23 a long petition from Cumberland Co. was presented, repeating some of the same grievances discussed in the "Remonstrance" and adding others; somewhat similar petitions from several other counties and communities came in later. On May 24 all these and the "Remonstrance" were referred to a committee of eight. *Ibid.,* pp. 66–7, 76–7, 82–3, 84, 94. BF was named a member of this group, but long before it reported, September 20, he had become speaker, and there is no evidence that he shared in its deliberations. By September, too, the Indian war was essentially over and many of the grievances had ceased to be important. The committee, therefore, reported on only two matters. On the question of underrepresentation of the newer counties it merely "submitted to the Consideration of the House" whether

86

To Francis Bernard   ALS: Historical Society of Pennsylvania

Sir   Philada. Feb. 21. 1764
    I ought sooner to have answered yours of the 23d past,[4] but the
dangerous Riots and Tumults we have lately had here,[5] took up all
our Attention.
    I hope Mr. Bernard is well with you before this Time.[6] As our
Navigation was stopt by the Ice, and it was uncertain when our
River would be open, and a good Vessel offer for Boston, I thought
it might be best for him to proceed by Land, especially as he could
have Col. Elliot's[7] Company so great a Part of the Journey. They
parted, however, at New York, Mr. Bernard meeting there with
Company going in the Packet to Rhodeisland.
    I have no Receipts for Pickling either Sturgeon or Salmon, but
will endeavour to procure you one for Sturgeon. In my Opinion a
great deal depends on the kind of Salt to be used. For this I would

this complaint was well founded. The Cumberland petition had pointed out
that the Supreme Court held sessions only in Philadelphia and that for the
convenience of litigants and others the judges of that court ought to ride
circuit at least once a year; the committee agreed that this situation "loudly
calls for speedy redress by a suitable Law." Time did not permit any action
before the coming election, however, so the House referred the report to
the next Assembly. *Ibid.*, pp. 101, 104. That body passed no remedial legislation on either of the matters mentioned in the report.
    The Indians in the Philadelphia barracks remained there until March 20,
1765. Then, reduced in numbers from 140 to 83 by dysentery and smallpox,
they set forth under the leadership of David Zeisberger, a Moravian missionary. After a slow and painful journey they reached Wyalusing on the
upper Susquehanna on May 9. They built a village which their Moravian
friends named Friedenshütten (Tents of Peace), and there they were allowed
to live quietly. For an account of their migration and settlement, see Edmund
de Schweinitz, *The Life and Times of David Zeisberger The Western Pioneer
and Apostle of the Indians* (Phila., 1870), pp. 306–18. Accounts submitted to
the Assembly show that the cost to the province of bringing the Indians to
Philadelphia, feeding and caring for them there for about sixteen months,
and escorting them to Wyalusing, amounted to a little over £2200. 8 *Pa.
Arch.*, VIII, 5913–21 *passim.*
    4. See above, pp. 31–2.
    5. See above, pp. 69–75.
    6. For Francis Bernard, Jr.'s trip from Philadelphia to N.Y. and from
there to Newport, see above, pp. 78–9.
    7. Probably Col. Aaron Eliot of New London, Conn.; see above, VI, 173 n;
X, 205 n.

refer you to Brownrigg's Book[8] where you may find what Salt the Dutch use for their Herrings. There is an alcaline corrosive Quality in common coarse Salt, which must be corrected by some Acid, in the Boiling or Refining of it. The Dutch use Buttermilk, I think, for that purpose. I am, with great Respect, Your Excellency's most obedient and most humble Servant   B FRANKLIN

P.S. I send the Account of my Disbursements, which if you please may be paid to Mr. Jonathan Williams, Mercht. Boston, for my Account.[9]

Governor Bernard

Endorsed: Dr Franklin Feb. 1764[1]

To Jonathan Williams   ALS: American Philosophical Society

Loving Cousin   Philada. Feb. 24. 1764
I have taken the Liberty to trouble you with a Box put this Day on board the Sloop William Capt. Ephraim Jones, directed for you.[2] In it is a Portmantle and Mail Pillon belonging to Mr. Bernard, your Governor's Son, which please to send to the Governor's as soon as it gets to hand:[3] Also a Parcel for Sister Mecom; and some Books on Inoculation,[4] which I should be glad you could conveniently distribute in your Country gratis.

8. William Brownrigg (1711–1800), physician and chemist, F.R.S., 1741, published *On the Art of Making Common Salt* (London, 1748). BF sent a copy of this book to James Bowdoin in 1753, and there is a copy of it in APS with BF's marginal notes. See above, V, 79, 110. Edward H. Davidson, "Franklin and Brownrigg," *American Literature*, XXIII (1951), 38–56.
9. In his account with BF (see above, X, 359) Jonathan Williams, Sr., recorded the receipt of £24 1s. 1½d. sterling from Governor Bernard on Feb. 28, 1764.
1. Added in another hand: "Sent me by Mr. O. Rich from London in 1832—It was addressed to Governor Bernard of Massachusetts. R. GILMOR." Robert Gilmor, Jr. (1774–1848) was an autograph collector of Baltimore.
2. *Pa. Gaz.*, March 1, 1764, reported the clearance of the *William*.
3. For BF's efforts to get Francis Bernard, Jr., from Alexandria, Va., to Boston, see above, p. 6, and the document immediately above. Portmantle: an archaic or dialect form of "portmanteau," a traveling bag or case.
4. Dr. William Heberden's *Some Account of the Success of Inoculation for the Small-Pox in England and America,* for which BF had written an introduction; see above, VIII, 281–6.

Just before I left London, a Gentleman requested I would sit for a Picture to be drawn of me for him by a Painter of his choosing. I did so, and the Pourtrait was reckon'd a very fine one.[5] Since I came away, the Painter has had a Print done from it, of which he has sent a Parcel here for Sale.[6] I have taken a Dozen of them to send to Boston and it being the only way in which I am now likely ever to visit my Friends there, I hope a long Visit in this Shape will not be disagreable to them. Be so good then, to take the Trouble of distributing them among such of my Friends as think them worth Accepting.[7]

The Box, with perhaps a little Alteration, may serve to send the 10 Folio Volumes of Bayle's Dictionary in, of which I saw one or two at your House, the rest are at Cousin Hubbard's I suppose. I should be glad to have them the first Opportunity.[8]

My Wife and Sally join in Love to you and yours and your Children, with Your affectionate Uncle   B FRANKLIN

P.S. Perhaps the Prints might be acceptable to some of the following Persons—*viz*.

Revd. Dr. Mayhew[9]

5. For the portrait by Mason Chamberlain, commissioned by Col. Philip Ludwell, and the mezzotint print by Edward Fisher, see above, x, frontispiece and illustration note.

6. WF had agreed to take 100 of the prints, possibly hoping to sell them for a profit. Charles C. Sellers, *Benjamin Franklin in Portraiture* (New Haven, 1962), pp. 58, 221.

7. Mather Byles (see below) received one of the prints on March 15, 1764, the earliest record of their arrival in Boston. *Ibid.*, p. 221.

8. BF must have been referring to the translation by John Peter Bernard, Thomas Birch, and John Lockman of Pierre Bayle's *A General Dictionary, historical, and critical* . . . (10 vols., London, 1734–41). The set may have been owned by BF's brother John (C.8) who died leaving an "unusually extensive library." Soon after John Franklin's death in 1756, his stepdaughter Elizabeth Hubbart sent BF a catalogue of his library and extended an offer from her mother to let him have whatever books he pleased before they were offered for sale. BF may have indicated a preference for Bayle's *Dictionary* at the time, but may have been unable to make arrangements to have it sent to Philadelphia. See above, VI, 402–3. Williams and Tuthill Hubbart, John Franklin's stepson, were executors of his estate.

9. Jonathan Mayhew (1720–1766), A.B., Harvard, 1744, pastor of the West Church, Boston, from 1747 to his death, was one of the leading theological liberals of his day and has often been called the founder of American Unitarianism. He was a virulent opponent of the Church of England and

Revd. Mr. Cooper[1]
Revd. Mr. Byles[2]
Mr. Bowdoin[3]
Mr. Winthrop of Cambridge[4]
Mr. B. Kent[5]
Miss Betsey Hubbard
Cousin Rogers[6]
Cousin Griffitts[7]
Cousin Williams[8]
And my Sister will possibly like to have one for herself, and one for her Doctor Perkins.[9]

Addressed: To / Mr Jonathan Williams / Mercht / Boston / per the William / Capt. E. Jones. / With a Box[1]

Endorsed: Feby 24 1764 F

------

his attacks on Anglican proselytizing in New England embroiled him in heated controversy. He was greatly admired by Whigs in Massachusetts and England, but he appears to have taken little part in politics until shortly before his death. *DAB; Sibley's Harvard Graduates,* XI, 440–72.

1. Samuel Cooper; minister of Brattle Square Church, Boston. See above, IV, 69–70 n.
2. Mather Byles (1701–1788), A.B., Harvard, 1725, grandson of Increase Mather and nephew of Cotton Mather, was minister of the Hollis Street Congregational Church for most of his life. In an undated letter of 1765 to BF, Byles spoke of being a "long Acquaintance" and thanked BF for helping him get the S.T.D. degree at the University of Aberdeen. Byles became a Tory during the Revolutionary War. A poet, humorist, and noted punster, he once called an American sentry, standing guard over him, his "Observe-a-Tory." *DAB; Sibley's Harvard Graduates,* VII, 464–93.
3. James Bowdoin; see above, IV, 69 n. He acknowledged the gift, July 2, 1764; see below, p. 247.
4. John Winthrop, Hollis professor of Mathematics at Harvard. BF had known him personally since 1754; above, V, 267.
5. Benjamin Kent, see above, p. 80 n.
6. Presumably BF's niece Mary Davenport Rogers (C.12.3).
7. Presumably BF's niece Abiah Davenport Griffith (C.12.5).
8. Probably Jonathan Williams himself.
9. John Perkins, the Boston physician and scientist; see above, IV, 267 n.
1. In APS there is an undated sheet on which BF wrote a memorandum, probably at about the same time as this letter, of articles he wanted to send to Boston and to Ezra Stiles in Newport. The same list of names that appears in the postscript of this letter is set down, though not in precisely the same order, and with "Yrself" substituted for "Cousin Williams." Above this list

From Francis Bernard Letterbook copy: Harvard College Library

Sir   Boston Mar 1 1764
I am favoured with yours[2] and shall immediately order the sum
of £40 1*s*. 10*d*. (which I suppose is at 7*s*. 6*d*. per dollar) to be paid
to Mr. Williams. There is still wanting the charge at Annapolis. I
have heard that there has been a Dutch trading Ship seized at
Anchor at Sandy hook. As the forfeiture arises from importing &c.
Is it not worth consideration whether the Governor's Share does
not belong to the Governor of New Jersey? as Sandy hook is in that
province and within the port of Amboy.[3] I am &c.

See 15 Car 2[4]

B Franklin Esq

Pennsylvania Assembly Committee: Report

Printed in *Votes and Proceedings of the House of Representatives*, 1763–
1764 (Philadelphia, 1764), pp. 57–8.

On Feb. 25, 1764, a petition was read before the Assembly from a
"Number" of inhabitants of Philadelphia, praying that debates in the
House be henceforth open to the public and asking the House to adopt
"a standing Order, that the Freemen of the Province shall have free

---

appear the following notes: "One [*torn*] Books for R Draper / Rec[eipt?
torn] Sturgeon for Govr. Bernard / Send by next Post Narratives to / Dr.
Mayhew Dr. Perkins / Mr. Cooper / Mr. Stiles / Mr. Bowdoin / And Prints
to Sister Jane." The illegible words between "One" and "Books" may have
been "lot of Heberden's," referring to the account of inoculation mentioned
in this letter. Draper was probably Richard Draper (1727–1774), printer and
publisher of the *Massachusetts Gazette and Boston News Letter*. The "Narratives" must have been copies of BF's pamphlet, *A Narrative of the Late
Massacres*.
    2. BF's of Feb. 21, 1764; see above, pp. 87–8.
    3. BF passed this suggestion along to his son William, but it is not known
whether anything ever came of it. See below, p. 178.
    4. An Act for the Encouragement of Trade, 1663, the so-called Staple Act,
15 Car. II, c. 7, sec. 6, forbade the importation of any European goods (with
certain exceptions) into the colonies except when laded in England, Wales,
or Berwick-on-Tweed, and carried in British or colonial ships. In case of
violation the ship and cargo were to be forfeited, one third going each to the
Crown, the governor of the colony, and the informer.

Access, at all seasonable Times in future, to inform themselves" about matters before the House, "as is the Custom of the Honourable House of Commons in Great Britain, and elsewhere in his Majesty's Dominions."[5] The petition was laid on the table, but on February 29, a committee of eight, including Franklin, was appointed "to examine the Journals of the House of Commons, and the Usage and Practice thereof, in respect to the Privelege petitioned for by the said Inhabitants; and to enquire likewise what the Practice is in the other American Colonies."[6] After receiving this report on March 6 the Assembly dropped the matter.

March 6, 1764.

In Obedience to the Order of the House, we have examined the Journals of the House of Commons, and do find, that respecting the Practice and Usage mentioned in the Petition of divers Inhabitants of the City of Philadelphia, the standing Orders of that House have, for some Years past, been as follow, *viz*.

Ordered,
"That the Sergeant at Arms attending this House do, from time to time, take into his Custody any Stranger or Strangers that he shall see, or be informed of to be, in the House or Gallery, while the House, or any Committee of the House, is sitting; and that no Person, so taken into Custody, be discharged out of Custody, without the special Order of the House."

Ordered,
"That no Member of this House do presume to bring any Stranger or Strangers into the House, or Gallery thereof, while the House is sitting."

And we are informed that, in Pursuance of these Orders, the Doors are kept, and no Stranger admitted, for whom Leave has not been expresly asked and given by the House.

With Regard to the Practice in the Colonies, we have not been able to obtain perfect Information concerning all of them; but we

5. *Votes,* 1763–64, p. 52. It is not certain what group or faction in Philadelphia was responsible for this petition. It seems probable, however, that the march of the Paxton Boys and the possibility of Assembly debates over the "Remonstrance" of Smith and Gibson had created a strong desire on the part of some citizens to attend the sessions and hear what the legislators had to say on the controversial matters before them.

6. *Ibid.,* p. 54.

understand, that in the Provinces of Maryland and Virginia the Assembly Doors are left open, and Persons are permitted to stand without, so as to hear the Debates; but that in the neighbouring Provinces of New-Jersey and New-York the Practice is, as hitherto it has been in this Province, to keep the Doors shut, except at Hearings on contested Elections, or the like, which are usually public. *Submitted to the House, by*

JOHN HUGHES,	JOHN DOUGLASS,
BENJAMIN FRANKLIN,	JOHN BLACKBURN,
WILLIAM SMITH,	JOHN MONTGOMERY,
GEORGE ASHBRIDGE,	JOHN TOOL.

From George Price[7]   ALS: American Philosophical Society

Sir   Fort Prince George[8] March the 7th: 1764
    I would be wanting in Gratitude if I did not make some Acknowledgement for the honour of your Letters to Messrs: Timothy and Lemprie:[9] My Name barely mentiond in them by you would have been sufficient but the Additional Compliment on my behaviour makes me as much at a loss how to Thank you as to restrain my Vanity.
    Mr: Timothy receiv'd me very kindly, but I had not once an opportunity of seeing Captain Lemprie in Town or of going to see

7. George Price was commissioned an ensign in the Royal American (60th) Regiment on Feb. 18, 1761, and served on the Pa. frontier under Col. Henry Bouquet. He commanded at Fort LeBoeuf, 1762–3, but was forced to retire to Fort Pitt on the outbreak of Pontiac's uprising. Ordered to South Carolina at the end of 1763, he commanded at Fort Prince George from January 1764 until February 1767. John R. Alden, *John Stuart and the Southern Colonial Frontier* (Ann Arbor, 1944), p. 215 n.
    8. A fort on the Keowee River in South Carolina built by Gov. James Glen in the fall of 1753. *Ibid.*, pp. 36–7.
    9. These letters, probably introducing Price, have not been found. Peter Timothy (above, v, 341 n) was editor of the *South Carolina Gazette* and postmaster at Charleston. "Lemprie" was probably Capt. Clement Lempriere (d. 1778), a sea captain from the isle of Jersey, who appears to have settled in South Carolina about 1743. Lempriere was a privateersman during King George's War and served in the South Carolina navy, 1775–76. He died in a shipwreck in 1778, *South Carolina Hist. and Geneal. Mag.*, I (1900), 66–7; XXI (1920), 14; XXV (1924), 10–11; LIX (1958), 1–10.

him at his Place[1] being in hourly expectation of my Marching Orders many days before I got them and then I had no time. So I forwarded the Letter to him with my excuses.

That I might send you something more worthy your Notice than a Letter of Compliment I defer'd paying my Respects to you till now, but dare not flatter myself the following will answer that purpose.

Fort Prince George is built of Stockades, has four regular Bastions and a Ditch round it but the Works, originally slight, are a good deal out of Repair as are the Carriages for six Iron and two brass Guns. Its situation is upon a Branch of the River which divides the two Provinces of South Carolina and Georgia near where a Cherokee Town, call'd Keowee formerly stood, and surrounded with Hills, from some of which there has been Men kill'd and Wounded in the Fort by random Shots.

It has been beseig'd more than once[2] but the Enemy could never do more than harass the Men by continual Alarms and keep them in the Fort thinking to starve them into a surrender and had once near accomplish'd it owing to the backwardness of the People below, who though they were acquainted in January of the Attack, yet their succours did not arrive till June.

There are a number of Indian Towns from within one to fifty Miles of the Fort, exclusive of what are beyond the Hills, all Cherokee: The number of Men Women and Children in each I have not been able to learn; however I have been told that there are above two thousand Warriors in the Nation who seem inclin'd to Peace with us, having felt all the severitys of extreme Want in the losses they sustain'd of Corn &ca: which Coll: Montgomerys Army destroy'd for them and to this Day the Effects keep it recent in their Memories,[3] blameing the Creeks for having drawn them into that War and then leaving them at our Mercy: Usage they fain would retort, and have said, are ready to put in execution if we

1. Lempriere seems to have lived at Hobcaw, So. Car.
2. Especially during the first months of the "Cherokee War," Jan. 1760–Sept. 1761. Alden, *John Stuart*, pp. 101–3.
3. From late May until early July 1760 Col. Archibald Montgomery with 1200 regulars drawn from the 1st and 77th Regiments ranged through Cherokee country around Fort Prince George burning Indian villages, destroying supplies, and fighting several small actions. Montgomery then returned to New York to join Gen. Jeffery Amherst. *Ibid.*, pp. 106–13.

will join them. How a Message they sent down to the superintendant to that effect is look'd upon or whether any notice will be taken of it I cant say but the Creeks having between th[ree] and four thousand fighting Men are too many for the Cherokees alone and this consideration may, if they are left to themselves repress their Ardour till a more favourable opportunity, tho' they threaten if the Creeks do kill the Traders coming to their Towns that they will kill them in turn.

A Report prevails that the Creeks refuse giving up the late Murderers as demanded by the Governor or any satisfaction; and the Indians here tell us they will do more Mischief by and by.[4]

I hope you are recover'd of your Hurt and that your good Lady and Miss Sally are both well. I resquest them to accept of my kindest Compliments and am, Sir, Your most Obedient and most Humble Servant   G Price

(Benjn: Franklin Esqr.)

To Richard Jackson   ALS: American Philosophical Society

Dear Sir,   Philada. March 8. 1764
I hear our Money Bill is to come down this Day from the Governor with a Negative.[5] It comply'd with four of the Stipulations made at the Council Board, viz. 1. The Proprietaries unappropriated Lands are explicitly exempted from Taxation. 2. Provincial Commissioners of Appeal are appointed. 3. The Paper Currency is made no legal Tender to the Proprietaries. 4. The Money is not to be dispos'd of without the Governor's Consent. But the other Two, That the best of the Proprietor's located uncultivated Lands should be taxed no higher than the worst of the People's; and, That his

4. In the early months of 1764 war appeared imminent between South Carolina and the Creek nation because of the Creeks' refusal to comply with Indian Superintendent John Stuart's demand that they execute the murderers of fourteen white settlers at the Long Canes area of upper South Carolina, Dec. 24, 1763. In March 1764 Stuart secured a promise from the Cherokees that they would assist the English in case hostilities began with the Creeks, but war was wisely averted. *Ibid.*, pp. 186–91.

5. For Governor John Penn's rejection of the Assembly's £50,000 supply bill of Feb. 24, 1764, see below, p. 111.

Town Lots should be exempted from all Tax;[6] these the House thought too unjust to be comply'd with. So the Bill will be damn'd, and the King's Service depriv'd of £50,000, to save the Proprietaries a trifling Tax: unless the House should comply and alter their Bill, which is very uncertain.

Virginia has refus'd to comply in the least with the General's Requisition;[7] as you will see by the enclos'd Papers.

Chief Justice Morris is dead, and another of the Jersey Judges, Mr. Nevil, being disabled by a Palsey, there seem'd to be a Necessity of an immediate new Appointment.[8] The Governor, by the

6. Technically, at least, BF's words here (repeated in later correspondence) misstate the governor's position regarding the taxation of proprietary town lots. John Penn never seems to have demanded the total exemption of the Proprietors' ungranted lands in cities and boroughs from taxation, but rather, as the order in council of Sept. 2, 1760, specified, that they should "be deemed located and uncultivated Lands and rated accordingly and not as Lots." See above, IX, 206. As a practical matter, however, the application of this principle in combination with the stipulation that located, uncultivated lands in general belonging to the Proprietors should not be assessed higher than the lowest rate applied to located, uncultivated lands of the inhabitants, would result in merely nominal taxation of proprietary town lots. The Assembly's supply bill provided that the lowest rate of assessment for the inhabitants' located, uncultivated lands was to be £5 per hundred acres. On this basis, a proprietary town lot would be assessed at one shilling per acre. Since the tax rate was to be 18d. per pound of assessed valuation, the Proprietors would therefore be required to pay only nine-tenths of a penny tax per acre for such a town lot, however valuable it might be. Similar town lots of the inhabitants, on the other hand, were to "be rated at the value which they do or may rent for on short leases" and taxed accordingly.

7. In November 1763 Gen. Jeffery Amherst requested Virginia and Pa. to raise 1500 men to be ready by March 1, 1764, to take the offensive against "Delawares, Shawanese, and other Tribes" which had committed atrocities in the Ohio Valley. Pa. promptly complied with the general's request, but the Virginia House of Burgesses rejected it in January 1764 on the grounds that the colony could not afford the expense. See above, x, 405 n, and this volume, p. 7.

8. Robert Hunter Morris (see above, v, 527–8 n; IX, 161 n), formerly governor of Pa., and chief justice of N.J., 1738–64, died on Jan. 27, 1764, while dancing at a ball. Samuel Nevill (c.1698–1764) came to New Jersey from England in 1736 as heir through his sister's marriage to Peter Sonmans, one of the East New Jersey Proprietors. He served in the N.J. Assembly, 1743–44, 1749–54, was mayor of Perth Amboy and judge of the Court of Common Pleas, and from 1749 to 1764 was second judge of the Supreme Court. He died in October 1764. William A. Whitehead, *Contributions to the Early History of Perth Amboy* (N.Y., 1856), pp. 120–4.

Advice of his Council has accordingly appointed Charles Read, Esqr. (who was second Judge) to be Chief Justice, and Mr. Berrien to be Second in his Place. As these are Persons of good Character, and acquainted with the Law, I could wish to hear that the Appointment is confirm'd at home. A Word from you, properly plac'd, may do the Business.[9]

Sometime last Spring I sent you a Catalogue of a large Collection of Ores, Minerals, and other Fossils of these Parts of America, which Collection is now in our Library; and I requested you would show it to our Friend Tissington.[1] I never heard of your receiving it. I sent also Copies of sundry Schemes then on foot here for settling new Colonies.[2]

I shall write farther by a Ship that sails for London next Sunday. This viâ Bristol, from, Dear Sir, Your most obedient humble Servant   B Franklin

R. Jackson, Esqr

Endorsed: 8 Mar. 1764 Benjn Franklin Esq

To John Canton   ALS: The Royal Society

Dear Sir,   Philada. Mar. 14. 1764
    When I left London, I promis'd myself the pleasure of a regular Correspondence with you and some others of the ingenious Gen-

---

9. Charles Read (1715–1774), the author of a well-known letter on agriculture to Jared Eliot, long ascribed to BF (see above, III, 436), was secretary of the province of New Jersey, 1744–67, member of the Assembly, 1751–58, member of the Council, 1758–73, and justice of Supreme Court, 1749–54, 1762–64. William Alexander, Lord Stirling, had recommended that Read be appointed chief justice. WF complied with the recommendation and Read took the oaths of office on Feb. 20, 1764. In July, however, the Board of Trade sent notice that Frederick Smyth had been made chief justice, and when Smyth took office in November, Read was relegated to associate justice. John Berrien (1711–1772) was a merchant of Somerset County and a trustee of the College of New Jersey, 1763–72. For Charles Read's career, see Carl R. Woodward, *Ploughs and Politicks: Charles Read of New Jersey* (New Brunswick, 1941). On Berrien, see I *N.J. Arch.*, XXVI, 208–9 n.
    1. See above, X, 273 n.
    2. See above, X, 208–9, 212–15, 225, 231, 254–7, 286.

tlemen that compos'd our Club.[3] But after so long an Absence from my Family and Affairs, I found, as you will easily conceive, so much Occupation, that philosophical Matters could not be attended to; and my last Summer was almost wholly taken up in long Journeys.[4] I am now a little better settled, and take the Liberty of Beginning that Commerce of Letters with you, in which I am sure to be the Gainer.

I have little that is new at present to offer you. I have made no Experiments myself. Mr. Kinnersley has shewn me one, that I think is mention'd in a Letter of his to me, which I left in London, and it is a beautiful one to see.[5] By a Stroke from his Case of Bottles pass'd thro' a fine Iron Wire, the Wire appears first red hot, and then falls in Drops, which burn themselves into the Surface of the Table or Floor. The Drops cool round like very small Shot. I enclose some of them.[6] This proves that the Fusion of Iron by a Stroke of Lightning may be a hot and not a cold Fusion as we formerly suppos'd, and is agreable to the Acct. publish'd some Years since in the Transactions, of the Effects of Lightning on a Bell Wire in Southwark.[7]

Mr. Kinnersley told me of a much stranger Experiment, to wit, that when he had sometimes electrify'd the Air in his Room, he open'd the Windows and Doors, and suffer'd the Wind to blow through, which made no Alteration in the electric State of the Room, tho' the whole Air must have been changed; That he had even try'd the same abroad in the open Air on a windy Day, and found the Electricity remain'd long after the Operation, tho' the

3. The so-called Club of Honest Whigs, formed by Canton and composed chiefly of writers, dissenting clergymen, and men of scientific interests. Richard Price, James Burgh, and William Rose, mentioned later in this letter, were members. It met fortnightly on Thursday evenings at St. Paul's Coffeehouse and after 1772 at the London Coffeehouse. For a thoroughgoing treatment of this informal organization, often alluded to but never before examined in detail, see Verner W. Crane, "The Club of Honest Whigs: Friends of Science and Liberty," 3 *William and Mary Quar.*, XXIII (1966), 210–33.

4. To Virginia and New England, see above, X, 252, 276–9.

5. See above, IX, 282–93, esp. 290.

6. Canton described this experiment in a note to an article on lightning rods by William Watson, published in *Phil. Trans.*, LIV (1764), 201–7.

7. See "An Account of some extraordinary Effects of Lightning, in a Letter to Dr. Gowin Knight: by Mr. William Mountaine, F.R.S.," *Phil. Trans.*, LI (1759), 286–94, and Dr. Knight's "Remarks" on the letter, *ibid.*, 294–9.

Air first electrify'd must have been all driven away. This surpris'd me, as it seem'd to indicate that some fix'd Medium subsisted between the Particles of Air, thro' which Medium they might pass as Sand can thro' Water; and that such fix'd Medium was capable of Electrisation. I went to see it, but had however my Doubts that there might be some Deception in the Experiment; and tho' at first it seem'd to succeed astonishingly, I afterwards found what I thought might occasion the Deception. As your little Balls, which were us'd to discover the Electricity by their Separation, would be too much disturb'd by the Wind when it blow'd fresh, Mr. Kinnersley had put them into a Phial, suspended from the Bottom of the Cork. They were as easily affected there, by any Electricity in the outward Air as if they had not been enclos'd; but I suspect that the Glass receives some Degree of Electricity from the electris'd Air, and so kept the Balls separated after the electris'd Air was blown away. I think Mr. Kinnersley was not quite satisfy'd with that Solution of the Phenomenon. I wish you would try it when you have Leisure, and let me know the Result.[8]

An ingenious Gentleman in Boston, who is a Friend of mine,[9] desired me when there last Summer, to recommend a good Instrumentmaker to him, to make a Pedestal of a new Construction for his Reflecting Telescope. I accordingly recommended our Friend Nairne; but as it was a new Thing to Mr. Nairne, it might be well, for preventing Mistakes, to get some Gentleman accustomed to the Use of Telescopes in Astronomical Observations, to inspect the Execution; and I took the Liberty to mention you, as one who would be good enough to take that Trouble if he requested it. I find he has accordingly wrote to you, and sent his Telescope. If it may not be too much Trouble, I hope you will oblige him in it, and I shall take it as a Favour to me. I send you enclos'd a second Letter of his.[1] The Charge of Postage that you pay, should be put into his Account. I have no Improvement to propose. The whole is submitted to you.

Please to present my respectful Compliments to Lord Charles

8. Canton "entirely" agreed with BF's explanation of Kinnersley's experiment; see below, p. 244.

9. James Bowdoin; for BF's assistance in the construction of his telescope, see above, X, 351 n, and this volume, pp. 21–2.

1. Presumably that of Jan. 18, 1764, cited immediately above.

Cavendish and Mr. Cavendish,[2] when you see them, to whom I am much oblig'd for their Civilities to me when I was in England. Also to Mr. Price,[3] Mr. Burgh,[4] Mr. Rose,[5] and the rest of that happy Company with whom I pass'd so many agreable Evenings, that I shall always think of with Pleasure. My best Respects to Mrs. Canton, and believe me, with sincere Regard, Dear Sir, Your most obedient and most humble Servant   B FRANKLIN

Mr. Canton

Addressed: To / Mr John Canton / Spital Square / Bishopsgate Street / London

2. For the Cavendishes, see above, X, 41 n.

3. Richard Price (1723–1791), D.D., Aberdeen, 1767, LL.D., Yale, 1783, was one of the most famous dissenting clergymen of his day and a respected writer on morals and political economy. His *Appeal to the Public on the Subject of the National Debt,* published first in 1771, had a great impact and is said to have influenced the younger Pitt to re-establish the sinking fund in 1786. Price was an ardent sympathizer with the cause of American independence, and his pamphlet supporting the colonies, *Observations on the Nature of Civil Liberty, the Principles of Government, and the Justice and Policy of the War with America,* published in 1776, enjoyed a tremendous vogue and was partly responsible for Congress' invitation in 1778 that he come to America and help regulate its finances. Price was also a strong supporter of the French Revolution. *DNB.*

4. James Burgh (1714–1775), an intimate friend of Dr. Price and a first cousin of the historian William Robertson, kept an academy at Stoke Newington, 1747–71, and wrote what was "perhaps the most important political treatise which appeared in England in the first half of the reign of George III," *Political Disquisitions* (2 vols., 1774, a 3rd vol., 1775). BF had used his "Hymn to the Creator" in the 1753 and 1754 editions of *Poor Richard* (see above, IV, 404–5 n) and also received Burgh's assistance in the preparation of the "Colonist's Advocate" series in 1770. *DNB.* Caroline Robbins, *The Eighteenth-Century Commonwealthman* (Cambridge, Mass., 1959), pp. 364–8; Verner W. Crane, *Benjamin Franklin's Letters to the Press* (Chapel Hill, 1950), pp. 285–7.

5. William Rose (*c.*1719–1786) of Chiswick was a schoolmaster and co-editor of the *Monthly Review.* He was also the friend and executor of the estate of BF's old companion James Ralph. See *DNB* under Ralph, and above, IX, 404 n.

To John Fothergill   ALS: Yale University Library

Dear Doctor,   Philada. March 14. 1764.
    I received your Favour of the 10th. of Decemr.[6] It was a great
deal for one to write, whose Time is so little his own. By the way,
When do you intend to live? i.e. to enjoy Life. When will you retire
to your Villa,[7] give your self Repose, delight in Viewing the Operations of Nature in the vegetable Creation, assist her in her
Works, get your ingenious Friends at times about you, make them
happy with your Conversation, and enjoy theirs; or, if alone, amuse
yourself with your Books and elegant Collections? To be hurried
about perpetually from one sick Chamber to another, is not Living.
Do you please yourself with the Fancy that you are doing Good?
You are mistaken. Half the Lives you save are not worth saving,
as being useless; and almost the other Half ought not to be sav'd,
as being mischievous. Does your Conscience never hint to you
the Impiety of being in constant Warfare against the Plans of Providence? Disease was intended as the Punishment of Intemperance,
Sloth, and other Vices; and the Example of that Punishment was
intended to promote and strengthen the opposite Virtues. But here
you step in officiously with your Art, disappoint those wise Intentions of Nature, and make Men safe in their Excesses. Whereby
you seem to me to be of just the same Service to Society as some
favourite first Minister, who out of the great Benevolence of his
Heart should procure Pardons for all Criminals that apply'd to
him. Only think of the Consequences!
    You tell me the Quakers are charged on your side the Water
with being by their Aggressions the Cause of this War.[8] Would
you believe it, that they are charg'd here, not with offending the
Indians, and thereby provoking the War, but with gaining their

6. Not found.
7. In August 1762 Fothergill bought an estate at Upton, Essex, where he
established a botanical garden, but he "could seldom visit it except on Satur-
days, owing to the press of his other work." Richard Hingston Fox, *Dr.
John Fothergill and his Friends* (London, 1919), pp. 22, 184–201.
8. See, for example, "An Authentic Account of the Cause of the Indian
War" in the supplement to *Gent. Mag.*, XXXIII (1763), 640, in which the
author alleged that the Quakers caused the Pontiac Uprising by settling on
lands "on the river Ohio" in violation of treaties confining settlements to
the east of the Alleghenies.

Friendship by Presents, supplying them privately with Arms and Ammunition, and engaging them to fall upon and murder the poor white People on the Frontiers?[9] Would you think it possible that Thousands even here should be made to believe this, and many Hundreds of them be raised in Arms, not only to kill some converted Indians supposed to be under the Quakers Protection, but to punish the Quakers who were supposed to give that Protection?[1] Would you think these People audacious enough to avow such Designs in a public Declaration sent to the Governor?[2] Would you imagine that innocent Quakers, Men of Fortune and Character, should think it necessary to fly for Safety out of Philadelphia into the Jersies, fearing the Violence of such armed Mobs, and confiding little in the Power *or Inclination* of the Government to protect them?[3] And would you imagine that strong Suspicions now

9. This charge was made in *A Declaration and Remonstrance of the distressed and bleeding Frontier Inhabitants*, dated Feb. 13, 1764, but its plainest presentation is in Hugh Williamson's *Plain Dealer*, no. III, dated May 12, 1764, and hence not the foundation for BF's present statement. Williamson stated that "many a thousand pounds have been distributed in support of Indians, his Majesty's enemies: that they have been aided and encouraged in plundering and murthering the frontier inhabitants, are propositions that can hardly be disputed; but least they should, I shall offer a few Proofs of them out of a great Number that I am provided with. Very early in the War the Quakers persuaded the Indians that the Proprietor and the Traders had cheated them, and therefore they ought to scourge the white people who live on the frontiers. In other words, plunder, tomahawk and burn them; and they faithfully adhered to the advice." John R. Dunbar, ed., *The Paxton Papers* (The Hague, 1957), pp. 104, 109, 375–6. A committee of Quakers prepared a defense addressed to the governor, dated Feb. 25, 1764, which was printed in *Pa. Jour.*, March 1, 1764, and also separately by Andrew Steuart. It is reprinted in *Paxton Papers*, pp. 131–8.

1. For the Paxton Boys' march on Philadelphia with the alleged intention of massacring the 140-odd Indians quartered in the capital for their own protection, see above, pp. 69–75.

2. BF probably referred to the passage in the Remonstrance of the frontier inhabitants, Feb. 13, 1764, that reads: "the Indians now at Philadelphia, are His Majesty's perfidious Enemies, and therefore to protect and maintain them at the public Expence, while our suffering Brethren on the Frontiers are almost destitute of the Necessaries of Life and are neglected by the Public, is sufficient to make us mad with Rage, and tempt us to do what nothing but the most violent Necessity can vindicate." *Paxton Papers*, p. 108.

3. Israel Pemberton, the particular object of the Paxton Boys' wrath, fled Philadelphia on the advice of friends. Theodore Thayer, *Israel Pemberton King of the Quakers* (Phila., 1943), p. 189.

prevail, that those Mobs, after committing 20 barbarous Murders,[4] hitherto unpunish'd, are privately tamper'd with to be made Instruments of Government, to awe the Assembly into Proprietary Measures?[5] And yet all this has happen'd within a few Weeks past!

More Wonders! You know I don't love the Proprietary, and that he does not love me. Our totally different Tempers forbid it. You might therefore expect, that the late new Appointment of one of his Family, would find me ready for Opposition. And yet when his Nephew arriv'd our Governor, I consider'd Government as Government, paid him all Respect, gave him on all Occasions my best Advice, promoted in the Assembly a ready Compliance with everything he propos'd or recommended;[6] and when those daring Rioters, encourag'd by the general Approbation of the Populace, treated his Proclamations with Contempt,[7] I drew my Pen in the Cause, wrote a Pamphlet[8] (that I have sent you) to render the Rioters unpopular; promoted an Association to support the Authority of the Government and defend the Governor by taking Arms, sign'd it first myself, and was followed by several Hundreds, who took Arms accordingly;[9] the Governor offer'd me the Command of them, but I chose to carry a Musket, and strengthen his Authority by setting an Example of Obedience to his Orders. And, would you think it, this Proprietary Governor did me the Honour, on an Alarm, to run to my House at Midnight,[1] with his Counsellors at his Heels, for Advice, and made it his Head Quarters for some time: And within four and twenty Hours, your old Friend was

4. See above, pp. 42–55.

5. See the document immediately below.

6. For John Penn's arrival in Philadelphia, Oct. 30, 1763, and for BF's civilities toward him, see above, x, 375–6, 401. Fothergill apparently showed this letter to Thomas Penn, or at least told him of it, for the Proprietor, writing to John Penn, June 8, 1764, referred to this passage, citing BF's resolve "to act a very quiet part." Thomas Penn asked for immediate information on the present (mentioned in the next paragraph of the present letter) which he supposed the Assembly had given the governor. Penn Papers, Hist. Soc. Pa.

7. For Penn's proclamations, Dec. 22, 1763, and Jan. 2, 1764, issued in response to the news of the murder of the Conestogas, see above, pp. 51, 54.

8. *A Narrative of the Late Massacres;* see above, pp. 42–69.

9. For the measures taken to defend Philadelphia against the Paxton Boys, see above, pp. 69–75.

1. About two o'clock in the morning, Monday, February 6.

103

a common Soldier, a Counsellor, a kind of Dictator, an Ambassador to the Country Mob, and on their Returning home, *Nobody*, again. All this has happened in a few Weeks!

More Wonders! The Assembly receiv'd a Governor of the Proprietary Family with open Arms, address'd him with sincere Expressions of Kindness and Respect,[2] open'd their Purses to him, and presented him with Six Hundred Pounds;[3] made a Riot Act[4] and prepar'd a Militia Bill[5] immediately at his Instance; granted Supplies[6] and did every thing that he requested, and promis'd themselves great Happiness under his Administration. But suddenly, his dropping all Enquiry after the Murderers, and his answering the Deputies of the Rioters privately and refusing the Presence of the Assembly who were equally concern'd in the Matters contain'd in their Remonstrance,[7] brings him under Suspicion; his Insulting the Assembly without the least Provocation, by charging them with Disloyalty and with making *an Infringement on the King's Prerogatives*, only because they had presumed to name in a Bill offered for his Assent, a trifling Officer (somewhat like one of your Toll-Gatherers at a Turn pike) without consulting him;[8] and his refusing several of their Bills, or proposing Amendments needlessly disgusting;[9] these Things bring him and his Government into sudden Contempt; all Regard for him in the Assembly is lost; all Hopes of Happiness under a Proprietary Government are at an End; it has now scarce Authority enough left to keep the common Peace;

2. See "The Address of the Representatives of the Freemen" to Governor Penn, Dec. 24, 1763, in *Votes*, 1763–64, pp. 16–17.

3. On Dec. 24, 1763; *ibid.*, pp. 17–18.

4. See above, pp. 70–1.

5. See above, pp. 74–5.

6. See above, pp. 7–9.

7. See above, pp. 80–6.

8. On March 12, 1764, Governor Penn returned a bill entitled "A Supplement to the Act, intituled, An Act for erecting a Light-house at the Mouth of the Bay of Delaware" with a message that he had no other objection to it, other "than that the House have, by inserting the Officer's Name for collecting the Duties thereby imposed, without even consulting him in the Appointment or Nomination of such Officer, made an Infringement on the Prerogatives of the Crown, with which he is entrusted; and that he cannot therefore pass it in its present Form." *Votes*, 1763–64, p. 60.

9. Those concerning the assessment of the Proprietors' located, unimproved lands are obviously meant. See below, pp. 118–21.

and was another Mob to come against him, I question whether, tho' a Dozen Men were sufficient, one could find so many in Philadelphia, willing to rescue him or his Attorney-General,[1] I won't say from Hanging, but from any common Insult. All this, too, has happened in a few Weeks!

In fine, every thing seems in this Country, once the Land of Peace and Order, to be running fast into Anarchy and Confusion. Our only Hopes are, that the Crown will see the Necessity of taking the Government into its own Hands, without which we shall soon have no Government at all.

Your civil Dissensions at home give us here great Concern. But we hope there is Virtue enough in your great Nation to support a good Prince in the Execution of Good Government, and the Exercise of his just Prerogatives, against all the Attempts of Unreasonable Faction.

I have been already too long. Adieu, my dear Friend, and believe me ever Yours affectionately   B FRANKLIN

Dr. Fothergill

Endorsed: B Franklin

To Richard Jackson

ALS: American Philosophical Society

Dear Sir,   Philada. March 14. 1764

I wrote to you on the 8th Instant,[2] intending that Letter via Bristol, but it goes with this.

The Bill I mention'd is since come down with an absolute Refusal,[3] as the Proprietary Instructions were not comply'd with, to have his Town Lots exempted, and his best located unimprov'd Lands rated no higher than the lowest of the People's. The House, extreamly desirous to grant the Money to the Crown, as they approve highly of the General's Plan,[4] will break thro' all their Rules,

1. Benjamin Chew.
2. See above, pp. 95–7.
3. For Gov. John Penn's message of March 7, 1764, rejecting the Assembly's £50,000 supply bill of Feb. 24, 1764, see below, p. 111.
4. Gen. Jeffery Amherst's plan, espoused by his successor, Gen. Thomas Gage, to raise 1500 troops from Pa. and Va. to launch an offensive against the Ohio Valley Indians in the spring of 1764; see above, pp. 7, 96 n.

and send up a new Bill complying with every Demand, and making every Amendment;[5] but as they esteem those I have mention'd to be contrary to common Justice and common Sense, tho' supported by the old Order in Council, they are highly provok'd at the Governor's insisting on them.[6] I wish some good Angel would forever whisper in the Ears of your great Men, that Dominion is founded in Opinion, and that if you would preserve your Authority among us, you must preserve the Opinion we us'd to have of your Justice. That Decision was certainly unequal. A Lot the Proprietor lately sold to Mr. Stamper here, pays now, as they tell me, near £7 Tax, which in the Proprietor's Hands would not (being to be rated as unimprov'd Land) pay more than 7 pence half penny. And this not owing to any Improvement, but merely the Change of Owner. Some other of the Amendments to that and the Militia Bill[7] (which is likewise return'd) are very disgusting, appearing to be calculated for that purpose, and I foresee an immediate Breach; tho' the House had a sincere Desire to continue on good Terms with the Governor, and have accordingly treated him with the utmost Respect ever since his Arrival, shewing on all Occasions the greatest Regard to every thing he recommended to them. But the Proprietary Aversion to the People here appears now to be hereditary and inveterate, and the People's old Dislike to them and their Government will of course be revived. As yet nothing unkind has proceeded from the House; but yesterday another little Bill for collecting a small Tonnage to support a Lighthouse, came down refused, with a Message, that it was for no other Reason, than that the House had nam'd the Officer in the Bill, and thereby *made an Infringement of his Majesty's Prerogatives, which were intrusted to his the Governor's Care.*[8] The House had put in the Name because it was

5. For the Assembly's new £55,000 supply bill, passed and sent to Gov. John Penn on March 14, 1764, see below, pp. 111–12. Penn did not think that it had complied with his amendments and therefore returned it unsigned on March 19; see *ibid.*

6. BF seems to be admitting privately here that Governor Penn's interpretation of the order in council of Sept. 2, 1760, was technically justified. For the order in council of Sept. 2, 1760, and the hearings which led up to it, see above, IX, 196–211.

7. For Penn's amendments to the Assembly's militia bill, passed Feb. 28, 1764, see below, pp. 130–1, 131 n.

8. See the document immediately above.

not proper to send the Bill up with a Blank; and had the Governor by way of Amendment, propos'd another Officer, they would have made no Objection, having no particular Attachment to the Person, and the Office a Trifle;[9] but they observe this first Occasion is readily snatch'd at, to charge them with Disloyalty, tho' the King's Prerogative of appointing a Toll-gatherer at a Turnpike was what they had never heard of before, and this is no more. Violent Suspicions, too, now begin to prevail, that the armed Mob in the Country, tho' not at first promoted, has since been privately encourag'd by the Governor's Party, to awe the Assembly, and compell them to make such a Militia Law as the Governors have long aim'd at. What increases that Suspicion is, that the Assembly's Proposal of joining with the Governor in giving Answer to the Remonstrance presented by the Deputies of that Mob, was rejected, tho' intended merely to add Weight to that Answer, by showing that the Government was unanimous.[1] The Proposal was approved by the moderate Part of the Governor's Council. He chose, however, to give his Answer separately, and what it was is a Secret;[2] we only learn that they went home extreamly well satisfy'd with the Governor, and are soon expected down again. To encrease our Confusions, a bitter Enmity has arisen between the Presbyterians and Quakers; abusive Pamphlets are every Day coming out on both sides,[3] and I think there is some Danger of Mischief between them. All Parties begin now to wish for a King's Government. The Mobs strike a general Terror, and many talk of Removing into other Provinces, as thinking both their Persons and Properties insecure.

I receiv'd duly your Favours of Nov. 12. and 26. and of Decemr. 9.[4] I have been so busy lately, that I could not attend to the Affair

9. The name of the collector included in this bill is not known. In the September session an Assembly committee conferred with Penn and proposed the name of Thomas Coombe (c.1721–1799). Penn concurred and a new bill became law Sept. 22, 1764. Coombe was the father of the Rev. Thomas Coombe (1747–1822), who figures in BF's later letters. *Pa. Col. Recs.,* IX, 197; *Statutes at Large, Pa.,* VI, 372–9.

1. See above, pp. 80–6.

2. It still is, no record of the governor's answer having survived.

3. John R. Dunbar has collected many of these in *The Paxton Papers* (The Hague, 1957).

4. For Jackson's letter of Nov. 12, 1763, see above, X, 368–72. Those of Nov. 26 and Dec. 9, 1763, have not been found.

with Mr.Coxe, and have not talk'd with him as I intended on the Subject of his Proposal, but shall soon, in order to have it clear and explicit.[5] The Assembly think themselves much misrepresented and very ill used by General Amherst, but will not give the Treasury any Trouble about the Inequality of Division, and have pass'd a Bill to refund the other Colonies.[6] The rigorous Execution of the Sugar Act,[7] occasions much Commotion among our Merchants in North America; and the Difficulty foreseen of making Returns to England for Goods, if the Trade is stopt with the Foreign Islands, begins to produce Schemes of Industry and greater Frugality among the People, which many suppose will be more advantageous to us than that Trade if it were quite open.

The Maryland People are no happier under their Proprietary Government than we are under ours. You will see this by a Pamphlet I send you that is lately publish'd there.[8] The Gentlemen of that Country have no Agent or Patron in London,[9] and have begg'd me to recommend them and their Affairs to your Protection. I think 'tis likely that at their next Session the Assembly will petition the Crown to take the Government, making the Proprietaries

5. In his letter of Nov. 12, 1763, Jackson wrote at length of the terms of his and BF's participation with the heirs of Dr. Daniel Coxe in a scheme to obtain royal confirmation of the grant of "Carolana."

6. See above, p. 19 n.

7. That is, the stricter enforcement of the Molasses Act of 1733 in which the British Navy, empowered by an act of April 1763 to help enforce the laws of trade, played a major role. See Bernhard Knollenberg, *Origin of the American Revolution* (N. Y., 1960), pp. 138–49. The Sugar Act of 1764 was not passed until April 5.

8. This was almost certainly *Remarks upon a Message sent by the Upper to the Lower House of Assembly of Maryland, 1762 ... By a Friend to Maryland.* It has been variously attributed to Thomas Ringgold, Edward Tilghman, and James Tilghman; Gov. Horatio Sharpe of Md. thought BF himself may have had a hand in its preparation, and John Penn told his uncle, Oct. 20, 1764, that the Md. leaders were "governed by Franklin," adding that "it is extraordinary that this man cannot be contented with what he is doing in this Province." Penn Papers, Hist. Soc. Pa. Although BF states here that the pamphlet was "publish'd" in Md., it was printed in Philadelphia by Franklin & Hall, as the firm's workbook shows. George S. Eddy, ed., *A Work-Book of the Printing House of Benjamin Franklin & David Hall* (N.Y., 1930), pp. 13–14.

9. This was a long-standing complaint of the popular party in Maryland, see BF's "Queries," Sept. 19, 1758, above, VIII, 163–8.

a Compensation.[1] They have no Publick Money to defray the Charges of prosecuting such a Petition, but will raise a handsome Sum by Subscription. If you should think that Pamphlet can do them any Service, they send a Score of them, requesting you would cause them to be distributed so as to come into proper Hands, in which you need not appear, your Bookseller can send them.

There is a worthy Friend of mine, Mr. Joseph Chew,[2] of New London, who writes me, that the Collectorship of the Customs there is vacant, and that he has apply'd to be appointed. I should be glad he might succeed, and could wish, if not inconvenient, that you would speak a good Word for him. I am, with the greatest Regard, Dear Sir, Your most obedient humble Servant

B FRANKLIN

P.S. Just as the London Ship was on the Point of Sailing, some Reasons occur'd against sending my Letters in her. This therefore goes viâ Bristol. But the Parcel of Pamphlets above mention'd are gone in the London Ship.

R. Jackson, Esqr.

Endorsed: 14th Mar 1764 Benjn. Franklin Esq

1. Because of continued prorogations by Gov. Horatio Sharpe, the Assembly did not meet between Nov. 26, 1763, and Sept. 23, 1765, when it was called to consider Massachusetts' invitation to send representatives to the Stamp Act Congress. J. Hall Pleasants, ed., *Archives of Maryland,* LIX (Baltimore, 1942), xvii.

2. Joseph Chew (1720–1799?) was born in Spotsylvania Co., Virginia, fought under William Johnson in New York in 1747 and by 1750 settled as a merchant in New London, Conn., where he was subsequently appointed postmaster, assistant collector of the port, and marshal of the vice-admiralty court. In 1774 Sir William Johnson appointed him secretary of Indian affairs, and as a result he moved to Tryon Co., N.Y. A Loyalist, he continued as secretary of Indian affairs in Canada under Guy Johnson and Sir John Johnson until his death.

To Mary Stevenson   ALS: American Philosophical Society

Dear Polly   Philada. Mar. 14. 1764
I have received your kind Letters of Augt. 30.[3] and Nov. 16.[4]
Please to return my Thanks with those of my Friend, to Mr. Stanley for his Favour in the Musick, which gives great Satisfaction.[5]
I am glad to hear of the Welfare of the Blunt Family, and the Additions it has lately received; and particularly that your Dolly's
Health is mended. Present my best Respects to them, and to the
good Dr. and Mrs. Hawkesworth[6] when you see them. I believe
you were right in dissuading your good Mother from coming hither.
The Proposal was a hasty Thought of mine, in which I consider'd
only some Profit she might make by the Adventure, and the Pleasure to me and my Family from the Visit; but forgot poor Polly,
and what her Feelings must be on the Occasion; and perhaps did
not sufficiently reflect, that the Inconveniencies of such a Voyage
to a Person of her Years and Sex, must be more than the Advantages could compensate.
    I am sincerely concern'd to hear of Mrs. Rooke's[7] long con-
tinu'd Affliction with that cruel Gout. My best Wishes attend her,
and good Mrs. Tickell. Let me hear from you as often as you can
afford it: You can scarce conceive the Pleasure your Letters give
me. Blessings on his Soul that first invented Writing, without which
I should, at this Distance, be as effectually cut off from my Friends
in England, as the Dead are from the Living. But I write so little,
that I can have no Claim to much from you as Business, public and
private, devours all my Time. I must return to England for Repose.
With such Thoughts I flatter my-self, and need some kind Friend
to put me often in mind that *old Trees cannot safely be transplanted.*

3. See above, x, 333–5. Many of the people—the Blunts, Polly's mother,
Polly's aunts Mrs. Rooke and Mrs. Tickell—and the affairs mentioned in
the present letter are discussed more fully there.
    4. Not found.
    5. John Stanley, the blind British composer, had provided a score for a
poem written by Francis Hopkinson, the friend BF refers to here. See above,
x, 333 n.
    6. For the Hawkesworths, proprietors of a school for young ladies at
Bromley, Kent, see above, ix, 265–6 n.
    7. Polly's aunt, with whom and another aunt, Mrs. Tickell, Polly lived,
first at Wanstead and now at Kensington.

Adieu, my amiable Friend, and believe me ever Yours most affectionately　　　　　　　　　　　　　　　　　　　B FRANKLIN

Miss Stevenson

Endorsed: Phil Mar 14 64

Pennsylvania Assembly: Message to the Governor

Printed in *Votes and Proceedings of the House of Representatives*, 1763–1764 (Philadelphia, 1764), pp. 64–5.

The Assembly passed its £50,000 supply bill on February 24 and delivered it to Governor Penn.[8] He held it until March 7 when he sent it back with a message of rejection. It was expressly contrary to the decree of the Privy Council of Sept. 2, 1760,[9] he said, particularly in the following points: 1. In the manner of taxing the Proprietors' located, uncultivated lands in the country and their lots in cities and boroughs. 2. In subjecting part of the money to be raised to payment on drafts and certificates issued by order of the Assembly only, without the governor's consent or prior knowledge. 3. In its mutually contradictory statements stipulating how many commissioners of appeals were needed to settle cases of alleged overassessment brought before them.[1]

On March 10, "after a considerable Debate," the House appointed a committee to bring in a new supply bill, this time for £55,000. With unprecedented speed the committee reported the bill on the same morning. After two days' debate the Assembly passed and sent it to Penn on March 14.[2] No copy of the original £50,000 bill has been found, but the short time the committee devoted to preparing its successor indicates that they could have made few changes to meet the governor's objections. A surviving copy of the very long bill passed by the House on March 14, certified by Charles Moore, clerk of the Assembly, is in the American Philosophical Society Library and provides a basis for understanding Penn's chief objection to both bills.

The critical issue was the assessment of the Proprietors' located but uncultivated lands. The £55,000 bill (and clearly also the rejected £50,-

8. See above, pp. 7–9.
9. See above, IX, 205–8.
1. *Votes*, 1763–64, pp. 58–9; *Pa. Col. Recs.*, IX, 149–50. Only the first of these objections persisted throughout the dispute. The Assembly appears to have met the other two by changes in the £55,000 bill presented to Penn on March 14.
2. *Votes*, 1763–64, pp. 59–60.

ooo bill) provided that such lands should not be assessed "higher than the lowest Rate at which any located uncultivated Lands belonging to the Inhabitants thereof, *under the same Circumstances of Situation, Kind and Quality* [italics added], shall be assessed"; and that ungranted land of the Proprietors lying in boroughs and towns should be deemed located, uncultivated lands and assessed accordingly. The words printed in italics above were the crux of the problem. They do not appear in the corresponding passage of the stipulations incorporated into the order in council of Sept. 2, 1760.[3] The question was: did the Privy Council intend that the Proprietors' located, uncultivated lands should be assessed at the same rates as *comparable* lands of the inhabitants, or that even the *best* of such proprietary country lands and town lots should be assessed at only the same rate as the *worst* country lands of other taxpayers? In the protracted dispute the Assembly contended for the first interpretation as the only just one, while the governor insisted that the literal second interpretation represented the true intention of the Privy Council.

Penn returned the £55,000 bill to the Assembly, March 19, with a verbal message stating that it was liable to the same objection as its predecessor on this matter of the proprietary lands. The Assembly immediately sent two members to the governor to ask what he took to be the intention of the stipulation in the order in council. He replied the next day, quoting the pertinent clauses of the order and adding that the words were "so express and certain as to admit no Doubt or Ambiguity." He asked the House "to insert in the Bill the above Clauses in the very Words of the Decree." The Assembly immediately tried to pin him down to a direct assertion "that the best and most valuable of the Proprietaries Lands and Lots should be taxed no higher than the worst and least valuable of the Lands or Lots belonging to the People." He shrewdly refused to use any such words and declined to enter into any dispute "about the Intent or Meaning of the Agents in the Stipulation they made" (Franklin, one of those agents, was there in the Assembly), but Penn insisted that the lords of the committee of the Privy Council "most certainly understood the Force of the Words they made use of to convey their Ideas," and that "the English Language does not afford Words more forcible, clear and explicit" than those contained in the disputed stipulation.[4]

Thereupon the Assembly resolved without dissent on the morning of March 21 to adhere to the bill as it stood, and appointed a committee of eight members, including Franklin, to prepare a message to the

3. See above, IX, p. 206.
4. *Votes*, 1763–64, pp. 60–4; *Pa. Col. Recs.*, IX, 152–5.

governor. The committee presented its draft message the same after-noon, and "after some Alterations" it was agreed to and ordered tran-scribed. On the morning of the 22d the message was again read, was signed by the speaker, and sent to Governor Penn.[5]

May it please your HONOUR,   March 22, 1764.

The House, upon Review of the Messages that have passed be-tween your Honour and them, concerning the Money Bill, beg Leave to declare, that they had the sincerest Desire to comply with the Requisitions of His Majesty's General, and therefore immedi-ately, at your Honour's Instance, voted the Number of Men re-quired, and the Sum necessary to raise, cloathe and pay them; and are sorry they should be obliged to say, that the Delays and Difficulties they have met with in compleating a Bill to carry that Vote into Execution, have arisen wholly from the Interven-ing of Proprietary Interests and Instructions, which your Honour, who are *"no Stranger to the long Disputes and Differences that un-happily subsisted, for many Years, between the two Branches of the Legislature, on Bills of the like Nature,"*[6] must know were ever the great and sole Obstruction to His Majesty's Service in this Province.

To prevent a Revival of those Disputes, the House have, in the present Bill, complied, to the best of their Understanding, with the Opinion of the Lords of the Committee, approved by His late Maj-esty, respecting our Supply Bills, and therefore had the greatest Reason to hope that no Objection could now arise to its Passage.

But your Honour is pleased to refuse your Assent to the Bill, unless in two of the six Alterations proposed by their Lordships, the *very Terms* by them made use of in theirReport are inserted in the Bill, alledging that you cannot in Duty deviate from them.

Such a Reason for not passing this Bill appears the more extraor-dinary to us, as the six Articles in that Report are evidently Heads only of proposed Amendments, and do not appear to be ever in-tended as formed Clauses, the very Words of which were to be inserted in our future Supply Bills.

5. *Votes,* 1763–64, p. 64.
6. A quotation from John Penn's message of March 7 (omitting a few words). He had attended the hearings in England in 1760 on the Supply Act of 1759 and other acts of the Assembly.

For Instance, one is, *"That the real Estates to be taxed be defined with Precision, so as not to include the unsurveyed waste Lands belonging to the Proprietaries."* Can it be thought that these Words ought to make a Part of the Bill? Another is, *"That the Governor's Consent and Approbation be made necessary to every Issue and Application of the Money to be raised by Virtue of such Act."* Another, *"That Provincial Commissioners be named to hear and determine Appeals brought on the Part of the Inhabitants, as well as of the Proprietaries."* Another, *"That the Payments by the Tenants to the Proprietaries of their Rents, shall be according to the Terms of their respective Grants, as if such Acts had never been passed."* All these appeared to us to be merely Heads of Provisions to be made in the Bill, and the Provisions are accordingly made, though in very different Words, but such as fully and particularly express the same Meaning: Thus the last, *"That the Payments by the Tenants to the Proprietaries of their Rents, shall be according to the Terms of their respective Grants, as if such Act had never been passed,"* is provided for in the Clause that makes the Paper Money a legal Tender in all Payments whatsoever, by adding these Words, *"the Sterling Rents due, or to become due, to the Proprietaries of this Province only excepted;"* which Words we conceived would effectually answer that Purpose. And these Changes your Honour has not disapproved. If the *"very Terms"* of the Order in Council are so sacred that they must be made use of, and no other, and your Honour cannot in Duty deviate from them, the House are at a Loss to account for your agreeing to all those Alterations, and particularly to the latter, without the least Objection.

Their Lordships Words, relating to the Points now under Consideration, are these:

"That the located uncultivated Lands belonging to the Proprietaries, shall not be assessed higher than the lowest Rate at which any located uncultivated Lands belonging to the Inhabitants shall be assessed." And, *"That all Lands not granted by the Proprietaries within Boroughs and Towns, be deemed located uncultivated Lands, and rated accordingly, and not as Lots."*

Those Provisions in our Bill are thus expressed, *viz.*

And be it further enacted and provided nevertheless, that the located uncultivated Lands belonging to the Proprietaries of this Province shall not, by Virtue of this Act, be assessed higher than the lowest Rate at which any located uncultivated Lands belonging to the Inhabitants thereof, under the same Circumstances of Situation, Kind and Quality, shall be assessed; and that all Lands not granted by the Proprietaries within Boroughs and Towns, be deemed located and uncultivated Lands, and rated accordingly, any Thing in this Act to the contrary thereof in any wise notwithstanding.

We thought, may it please your Honour, that we had herein expressed the true Intention of those two Articles; but you have been pleased to let us know that you think otherwise, and that, in your Opinion, *"the Words made use of in those Articles convey a meaning very different from the Provisions made respecting these Matters in the present Bill."* We then, by a Message, requested your Honour would be pleased to acquaint us, what Meaning you conceive they do convey. This you have refused. We then endeavoured to conjecture, from the former Tenor of Proprietary Measures, what Sense your Honour might possibly be willing to understand them in; and by another Message, after setting forth, that as your Honour and the House differed in their Opinion of the Meaning of those Articles, it was very probable the Commissioners and Assessors of the several Counties, who were to execute the Act, might, if the same Terms only were used, differ likewise in their Opinion, and thence differ in the Modes of Taxation, we requested you would be pleased to acquaint us, whether you understood the Meaning to be, that the *best* and *most valuable* of the Proprietaries Lands and Lots, should be taxed no higher than the *worst* and *least valuable* of the Lands belonging to the People? This your Honour has been pleased neither to own nor deny; but continue to insist, that the Words of those Articles are so clear and explicit, that any Additions to them will rather tend to perplex than explain them; and therefore urge us again to put them, and no others, in the Bill.

We beg your Honour would be pleased to reflect for a Moment, how absurd it would be for the two Branches of the Legislature to agree to pass an Act in Terms which both of them have, in public Messages, declared beforehand that they understand very differently; and particularly, how extremely wrong in the Assembly, when the other Branch, the Executive, will not declare what it understands by those Terms, but reserves that till the Law shall come to be executed.

MARCH 22, 1764

Under these Circumstances it is impossible for us to use, in this Bill, the Terms unexplained, which your Honour insists upon.

We do therefore unanimously adhere to our Bill, and once more earnestly request your Honour would be pleased to pass the same without further Delay, as His Majesty's Service, and the present deplorable Circumstances of the Frontiers, require its being carried into immediate Execution. *Signed by Order of the House,*

ISAAC NORRIS, Speaker.

Pennsylvania Assembly: Reply to the Governor

Printed in *Votes and Proceedings of the House of Representatives,* 1763–1764 (Philadelphia, 1764), pp. 69–72.

Governor Penn apparently spent most of the morning of March 23 composing a reply to the Assembly's message of the 22d (see immediately above). He signed it in the afternoon and sent it to the Assembly. In it he expressed his deep concern that in the critical military situation the supply bill must be lost unless the Assembly should insert the clauses of the Privy Council report, but he insisted that the failure of the supply would not be his fault. He reviewed the dispute up to date and then for the first time stated flatly what he believed the disputed stipulations to mean: "The only Construction I can put upon them or that they can bear, without torturing is, that if Five, Ten, or Fifteen Pounds, is the lowest at which *any* such Lands of the Inhabitants are assessed, *none* of the located uncultivated Lands of the Proprietors shall be assessed higher."[7] If, as the Assembly had asserted in their previous verbal messages, the wording of the Privy Council's stipulations was so ambiguous as probably to cause varying interpretations among the local assessors,

7. The bill provided that "All located and unimproved Tracts of Land, shall be rated in Manner following, to wit, the best of such Lands considering the Situation thereof at Fifteen Pounds per Hundred Acres; and the worst, at Five Pounds per Hundred Acres; and the same Kind of Land of any intermediate Value, in a just and comparative Proportion to the above Rates and Valuations." Another clause provided that "All unimproved Lots in or near any City Borough or Town or the District of Southwark (the Lots granted by the Charter of the City of Philadelphia for the use of the said City only excepted) shall be rated at the Value, which they do or may rent for on short Leases." A later section, quoted in part in the headnote to the document immediately above, provided for assessment of located, uncultivated proprietary lands and lots at the same rates as land of the inhabitants of similar "Situation, Kind and Quality."

116

he explained, the provincial Board of Appeals provided for in the bill would quickly bring about uniformity of assessment.[8]

Upon hearing this message the Assembly voted, again without dissent, to adhere to the bill as it stood, and appointed a new committee of eight, including Franklin, to prepare a response to the governor. The committee presented its draft on the 24th; "some Alterations" were made; it was agreed to, transcribed, signed by the speaker, and sent to Penn the same day.[9]

The rising temper of the Assembly can be readily detected in the phraseology of the final paragraphs of this message.

May it please your HONOUR,   March 24, 1764.

We have considered your Honour's Message of Yesterday Afternoon, sent down to us with our Supply Bill, and are extremely concerned to find, that notwithstanding His Majesty's Service, and the present Situation of our Affairs, which you well describe in the first Lines of the Message, do so plainly mark the Utility and Necessity of passing that Bill, yet it must, you are pleased to say, be rejected.

We are sensible that your Honour did make to a former Bill the Objection you mention, concerning the incidental Charges;[1] but as the House long since dropt that Bill, and, out of Zeal for the Service, broke through their Rules, and in the same Sitting prepared and presented another Bill, free from that Objection, we cannot conceive why it is repeated here, unless to swell, in Appearance, the Number of supposed Faults in the present Bill, with which it has nothing to do.

It obliges us now, however, to explain that Matter. The incidental Charges of the current Year are well known, and cannot be, as your Honour unkindly says, "every Thing that the Assembly shall please to certify to be such." The Sum they may amount to, is not indeed so certain, varying a little in different Years; but was always, and must be small, compared to the Sum granted in the Bill. The Course relating to them, even since the Order of Council, has been, for the Governor to request an Estimate of the Particulars, and for the House to give it, as near as they could; and his

8. *Votes*, 1763–64, pp. 68–69; *Pa. Col. Recs.*, IX, 158–60.
9. *Votes*, 1763–64, p. 69. Of the eight members of this committee, four, including BF, had been on the committee to draft the message of March 22.
1. See the headnote to the document immediately above.

passing the Bill, after receiving such Estimate, was understood, both by him and the House, to be his Consent to that Application, and those Issues. The Clause was inserted in Compliance with that Practice, and your Honour might, and would, have had the Estimate as soon as it could be prepared, on the least Intimation; but it seems you were better pleased with the Opportunity you supposed it gave you, of making some Charge against us, as contravening the fourth Article in the Order of Council, *viz.* "That the Governor's Consent and Approbation be made necessary in every Issue and Application of the public Money." It was a Matter of so small Consequence, that we did not think it worth a Word of "Controversy," at such a Time, and therefore, in the new Bill, totally dropt the Clause, leaving those incidental Charges to be provided for in some other Way we might afterwards agree upon; but your Honour chuses to repeat the Accusation, though now so evidently out of Time.

You are pleased to say, "you know of no other certain Rule of judging of the Intentions of another, than by the plain Import of the Words made use of to convey them." We beg Leave to point out to your Honour another Rule, and, we think, a better. Laws and Ordinances, though composed by the wisest Men, in Councils and Parliaments, practiced in using the greatest Clearness and Precision, are sometimes found to contain Obscurities and Uncertainties, which those who are to execute them, find difficult to clear and settle: It is no Reflection on such Bodies, to say this: Every Thing human is subject to Imperfection: But where the Words are, by Construction, capable of two opposite Meanings, the one manifestly *unjust* and *unequal,* and the other perfectly consistent with *Justice* and *Equity,* we conceive it a good Rule to judge that the Intention is with the latter. Respect to the Body forming such Law requires it. Common Candour demands it. Now, in the present Case, the Intention of the Lords of the Council, in certain Words by them made use of, is to be judged of by your Honour and the Assembly, in order to form a Law agreeable to them. The House, in the Bill, put a Construction on them, conformable to common Justice and Equity; your Honour was pleased to tell us, that the Words have a very different Meaning, but for some Time refused to say what you conceived that different Meaning to be, insisting on our using the *very Words,* without Explanation. It was not till after three Messages, requesting your Honour's Judgment of that Meaning, and several Days spent in our Endeavours, that we have been able to obtain it; and now that we have it, and consider it, we do not wonder it should be so long refused. It is at length this, "That if *Five, Ten,* or *Fifteen Pounds,* is the *lowest* at which *any* such [*i.e.* located uncultivated]² Lands of the Inhabitants are assessed, none of the located uncultivated Lands of the Proprietaries shall be assessed higher." Had we been fortunate enough to have used these Words in our Bill, we now have Reason to believe your Honour would not have referred us back to the *very Terms* of the Report, and insisted, that any Amendments or Additions of ours would rather tend to perplex than explain those Terms. But your Honour must know, that many of the located uncultivated Lands belonging to the Inhabitants cannot, from the Nature of them, be, in Justice, assessed higher than *Five Pounds per* Hundred Acres, while the best of their Lands must by the Law be assessed at *Fifteen Pounds*. And can your Honour think it just, that because the *worst, and least valuable* of the Peoples Lands are rated at *Five Pounds,* the *best, and most valuable* of the Proprietaries Lands should be assessed no higher, when it is well known they select and locate the best in every new Purchase, before the People are allowed to take up any? Your Honour will not say this, because it is inconsistent with all our Notions of common Honesty. The same Modesty which so long prevented your Honour's confessing to us your Opinion of the Meaning of those Words in the Order of Council, will prevent your insisting on that Meaning as a *just One*. And for our Parts, we dare not put so iniquitous a Construction on their Lordships Words. Respect and Decency forbid it.

Your Honour tells us, that you cannot, "consistent with your Duty," pass this Bill. If Duty to the Crown is meant, can your Honour seriously attempt to persuade us, that the Crown will be offended with a Proprietary Governor, for giving up an unjust Proprietary Claim to Partiality in Assessments in Favour of Proprietaries private Estate, where no Point of Government, or Prerogative of the Crown, is concerned? But perhaps your Honour means Duty to the Proprietaries, as your honoured Father and Uncle; if so, we must allow *that Duty* well supported, and enforced by your own private Interest; for such a Partiality in Favour of Proprietary Estates,

2. Brackets in the original.

must not only be extremely agreeable to the present Possessors, (from our Acquaintance with them for some Years past we speak it) but, if it can be established, will be highly advantageous to their Posterity.

Your immediate Predecessor, Governor Hamilton, assured a former Assembly, that "nothing was further from his Thoughts, than to desire that the Proprietaries Estate should be exempted from paying a proportionable Part of the Supplies for the current Service." And, "that it was of the Essence of free Governments, that the Money raised for public Services should be assessed equally upon all *Ranks and Conditions* of Men, otherwise the highest Injustice may be committed under the Sanction of Law."[3] There seems now some Reason to apprehend, that these equitable Sentiments of that Gentleman might possibly have a Share in occasioning his Removal; and we shall not wonder if your Honour, from a nearer Connection with the Proprietaries, has imbibed others extreamly different.

The Inconvenience we mentioned that might arise from the Assessors of different Counties differing in their Opinion of the Meaning of the Terms you require in the Bill, your Honour apprehends will be removed by Means of the Provincial Commissioners of Appeal; which we own we do not see. The Assessors of different Counties may not only fall on different Modes of Taxation, as they differently understand those unexplained Terms, but should Half the Assessors in one County understand them one Way, and the other Half the other, no Tax can be laid, or Money raised in that County, till they agree. The Provincial Commissioners of Appeal too, being nine, and five of them a Board, three of which can determine, may, being of different Opinions, give different Judgments at different Sittings, as often as three, the Majority of a Board, happen to be taken from those who are of one or the other Opinion; besides, though the Assessors below should, from a right Understanding of the unexplained Words, act rightly, if the Provincial Commissioners, for Want of Explanation, understand the Words in the wrong Sense, they may, on Appeals, overthrow every right Assessment in the Province. In short, we conceive that much Confusion must arise from the using of Terms in a Law, that the Gov-

3. In a message to the Assembly, April 2, 1760, relating to the supply bill of that year. 8 *Pa. Arch.*, VI, 5123, 5124.

ernor and the Assembly both declare they understand so differently. We may both be separately clear in our Conceptions of their Meaning, but our differing so widely in those Conceptions, seems to indicate at least some Ambiguity or Obscurity in the Terms; and we believe this is the first Time that ever the Enacting an Obscurity in a Law was insisted upon, in Hopes that some who were to execute it, might possibly see more clearly through it than the Legislators themselves.

Your Honour is pleased to profess great Concern for the "Safety and Security of the Province, and for the Blood of His Majesty's brave Subjects, which may be spilt on the Frontiers, for Want of a Law to provide for their Protection," and yet refuse to pass this Bill, unless gross Partiality in taxing is established by it in Favour of the Proprietary Estates. You have twice told us, that "you are not unacquainted with the long and various Contests on this Subject that have been agitated between the legislative Branches here, nor with the Evils and Miseries which were entailed on the Frontier Inhabitants by those Disputes:" As you must then know that those Contests arose solely from Proprietary Injustice, you cannot be ignorant to whom all those Evils and Miseries ought to be imputed. And, on a little further Reflection, will find that you do really "flatter yourself," as you well express it, when you imagine, that "none of the ill Consequences which may ensue from the Failure of this Bill can justly be imputed to" You. Your Honour has refused to pass it at present, and our Affairs lay us under a Necessity of making an Adjournment; but we now acquaint you, that the Bill continues to lie ready for your Assent, and that we shall chearfully return on your Summons, whenever, upon more mature Consideration, you shall find yourself willing to enact it into a Law. In the mean Time, if any ill Consequences ensue from the Delay, they will undoubtedly add to that Load of Obloquy and Guilt the Proprietary Family is already burdened with, and bring their Government (a Government which is always meanly making Use of public Distress, to extort something from the People for its own private Advantage) into (if possible) still greater Contempt.

For our own Parts, we consider the Artifices now using, and the Steps taking to enflame the Minds of unthinking People, and excite Tumults against the Assembly, as concerted with a View to awe us into Proprietary Measures: But as these Seats were given us from no Solicitations of ours, and as we have no private Interest to serve by retaining them, nor any Pleasure in the Possession of them, we are very willing to quit them, whenever our Constituents think proper to relieve us, by chusing other Representatives, which our annual Elections give them frequent Opportunities of doing. And for the present Safety of the Persons and Properties of the good People of this Province, since the Governor will not pass the equal Militia Bill we offered him, but upon Terms of great Addition to Proprietary Power,[4] which we hope, and are persuaded, no future Assembly will agree to, we must for the present depend on ourselves and our Friends, and on such Protection as the King's Troops can afford us, which we hope, by the Blessing of God, will be sufficient to defend us, till His Majesty shall graciously think fit to take this distracted Province under His immediate Care and Protection.   Signed by Order of the House,

ISAAC NORRIS, Speaker.[5]

4. As the result of the disturbances caused by the march of the Paxton Boys, Governor Penn recommended to the Assembly on February 4, 1764, the passage of a militia act. BF was a member of the committee thereupon appointed to prepare a bill. It was introduced February 17, debated at various sittings, and passed by the Assembly on the 28th. Penn returned it March 12 "with a Sheet of Amendments." The most important of his objections was to the provision for the election of militia officers, as had been the rule under previous militia laws as far back as BF's first act of 1755; see above, VI, 266–73. Penn felt that he should have the right to appoint the officers, but Assembly members regarded this and other proposals as tending to increase dangerously the proprietary authority. They debated the matter on March 17 but took no further action. *Votes*, 1763–64, pp. 43, 44, 49, 51–3, 60, 61; *Pa. Col. Recs.*, IX, 133–5, 151. See also the document immediately below, and BF's defense of the Assembly's bill, Sept. 28, 1764, below, pp. 360–5.

5. The assemblymen appointed to carry this message to Governor Penn were instructed to tell him that the Assembly proposed to adjourn to May 14 if he had no objections, "to which he was pleased to answer, it was very well." *Votes*, 1763–64, p. 72. Consequently he had no opportunity to reply for more than seven weeks. For the next documents in this exchange see below, pp. 203–13.

Pennsylvania Assembly: Resolves upon the Present Circumstances

Printed in *Votes and Proceedings of the House of Representatives*, 1763–1764 (Philadelphia, 1764), pp. 72–4.

As soon as the Assembly had considered on March 10 the governor's message of the 7th rejecting the £50,000 supply bill and had appointed a committee to bring in a new £55,000 bill,[6] it named a second committee of eight members, including Franklin, "to draw up and bring in certain Resolves upon the present Circumstances of this Province, and the Aggrievances of the Inhabitants thereof."[7] The committee reported on March 24 immediately after the Assembly had approved the reply to the governor of that date (see immediately above). The House "deliberately considered" the draft resolutions and "after some Alterations" adopted them, in each case, according to the record, without a dissenting voice. Soon afterwards the Assembly adjourned to May 14.

This "Necklace of Resolves," as Franklin called it to his friend William Strahan a few days after its adoption,[8] encompassed virtually all the major complaints of the Assembly against the proprietary government. Some of the grievances were of long standing, others of more recent origin; some were solidly grounded in frustrating experience, others were trivial or perhaps unjustified on the basis of any impartial examination of the circumstances. Taken together, however, they summarize the case which the party dominant in the elective body proposed to make against proprietary authority in the existing system of government of Pennsylvania. To use a modern analogy, they constituted a platform for the Assembly election of 1764.

That this dominant party did not necessarily represent the views of a majority of the inhabitants is obvious from any examination of the distribution of seats in the Assembly. The city of Philadelphia with two seats, and the three counties of Philadelphia, Bucks, and Chester with eight each, together held twenty-six of the thirty-six seats in the House of Representatives, although they included only a little more than half the taxable inhabitants of the colony in 1760.[9] That such a

6. See above, p. 111.

7. *Votes*, 1763–64, p. 60. Six men were named to both committees appointed this day; BF and one other were on only the committee on resolves.

8. See below, p. 149. John Penn, by contrast, called the document "this dirty piece of Scurrility." To Thomas Penn, May 5, 1764, Penn Papers, Hist. Soc. Pa.

9. Charles H. Lincoln used the number of taxable inhabitants in each county in 1760 (the best available evidence of total population) to prepare a

distribution of seats, however fair it had once been, was no longer equitable in a truly democratic sense after the five newer counties had attained substantial populations, can hardly be debated. It may be remarked in passing, however, that equality of representation was far from being a generally accepted principle at this time in the English-speaking world. Pennsylvania's system was at least as fair at this period as were the systems of several other rapidly growing colonies, and its basis of representation was much more equitable than that of the British House of Commons before 1832.[1]

At the same time, an objective analysis of the political system in Pennsylvania leads to the conclusion that control of the executive branch of government by a private (and nonresident) family which was also vested with extensive rights to the soil as a source of personal income was no longer an appropriate basis of operation in the 1760s, however useful it had been for the first settlement of the colony eighty years before. Conflict of public and private interest on the part of the Penns was virtually inescapable. In this respect the Assembly's position was fundamentally sound.[2]

---

reapportionment table for the Assembly. With Philadelphia County's eight seats taken as a standard, the city of Philadelphia and the three oldest counties would, according to this table, have been entitled to a combined representation of 23; the five newer counties to a fraction under the same number. *The Revolutionary Movement in Pennsylvania, 1760–1776* (Phila., 1901), p. 47. The assumption that the proprietary party would have controlled the Assembly if the counties had been represented on this basis of population is, however, not necessarily true. Using Lincoln's figures, Theodore Thayer recomputed the results of the bitterly contested election of 1764, when, if ever during this time, the proprietary party might have been expected to win. He allowed each of the two parties the same proportion of each county's new number of seats that it actually won under the existing apportionment and found that the so-called Quaker party would still have held approximately 60 percent of the seats in the House. "The Quaker Party of Pennsylvania, 1755–1765," *PMHB*, LXXI (1947), 30–1.

1. And after the under-represented Pennsylvanians launched their attack on the Assembly in 1764 nearly two centuries went by before the United States Supreme Court established the "one-man-one-vote" principle as the only valid basis for representation in American state legislatures. It is always dangerous to apply too rigidly the standards of one age to the conditions of an earlier time.

2. Thomas Penn and some of his supporters in England and America contended, and a recent writer seems to agree with their contentions, that the proprietary family was useful to Pennsylvania in that it offered a "buffer" between the colony and "the Ministry's plans for reform." William S. Hanna, *Benjamin Franklin and Pennsylvania Politics* (Stanford, Calif., 1964), pp.

These two undesirable conditions, both long in development, reached crisis proportions simultaneously in 1764, largely as the result in both cases of the Indian uprising that demanded active measures of defense and consequent expenditures of money. A paradoxical alignment of political forces ensued. The "democratic" inhabitants of the more exposed counties rose up against the dominant group whose chief political strength lay in the old eastern counties. They accused the Assembly and its leaders of a selfish indifference to the needs of the frontier areas, and in consequence formed a political alliance with the supporters of the essentially obsolete and undemocratic proprietary regime. The dominant party in the east, believing itself to be the champion of the "people's" rights against the "self-interested" proprietary family, saw the colony in danger of losing the gains the party had so long struggled to obtain, and the party itself in danger of losing its position of political leadership.[3]

The apparent solution, from the Assembly party's point of view, however naive it may seem in retrospect, was to seek the elimination of the Proprietors from the scene and the assumption of governmental control directly by the Crown. This idea had been privately discussed among the leaders, including Franklin, for about six years.[4] With substantial experience in London, Franklin may not have been as optimistic as some of his fellow assemblymen that royal government would bring Utopia to Pennsylvania. He apparently believed, however, that his colony suffered under special disadvantages experienced nowhere else except in Maryland and that the removal of the Proprietors from a share in the government of Pennsylvania would be a permanent advantage to its people, placing them for the first time in a position of equality with the inhabitants of a majority of the English colonies. In his opinion, we may conclude from his writings of this period, the matter of the claims

---

162, 163–4. An over-all view of the relations between the American colonies and the British government between 1763 and the Revolution provides little or no evidence that Pennsylvania, the Delaware counties, or Maryland, the surviving proprietorships, received either better or worse treatment from the ministry and Parliament than did the other colonies as a result of having such "buffers" in England.

3. A division along religious lines further complicated these political alignments. While there were many individual exceptions, the Quakers in the old counties and members of the German pietistic sects generally supported the party that controlled the Assembly; Anglicans and Presbyterians (including many of the Scotch-Irish in the interior counties) formed a large part of the opposition.

4. See for example, above, VIII, 6–7, 20–1, 157–8, 228, 236, 299–300.

of the western settlers to political equality with the east was a secondary issue that could be ignored while the more pressing question was being resolved.[5]

[March 24, 1764]

Resolved, N.C.D.

1. That it is the Opinion of this House, that the Proprietaries of this Province, after having delegated their Powers of Government, can be justly or legally considered in no other Light than as private Owners of Property, without the least Share or constitutional Power of Legislation whatever.[6]

Resolved, N.C.D.

2. That the Obstructions and Delays the Measures of the Crown

5. In connection with the resolves that follow, reference should be had to the "Explanatory Remarks" printed below, pp. 134–44.

6. In his "Explanatory Remarks" BF called this the "most important" of the resolves, but its legal and historical bases are highly questionable. The contention here is that, if the Proprietors did not reside in the colony and exercise in person the powers of government conferred by the charter, but delegated authority to a lieutenant governor, they should have nothing to say about the government of the colony. The lieutenant governor, by the terms of the royal charter and by the nature of his office, became empowered to act in legislative matters according to his own discretion. Thirty-nine years earlier David Lloyd, leader of the opposition to proprietary authority, had published a small pamphlet asserting this principle: *A Vindication of the Legislative Power, Submitted to the Representatives of All the Free-men of the Province of Pennsylvania, now sitting in Assembly* (Phila., 1725). From time to time thereafter assemblies of Pa. had tried to establish the principle, but without success. William R. Shepherd, *History of Proprietary Government in Pennsylvania* (N.Y., 1896), pp. 474–94; above, VII, 251; VIII, 181. The history of proprietary government in the American colonies in the seventeenth and eighteenth centuries shows no instance of a successful challenge of the right of nonresident proprietors to direct their deputies in the carrying out of the political authority delegated to them, except at various times in Pa., Md., So. Car., and the Bahamas, when for one reason or another the Crown itself had assumed the powers of government. The British officials certainly regarded the Proprietors of Pa. as still holding the rights and responsibilities granted to William Penn. This attitude is shown in the Board of Trade report of June 24, 1760, which severely criticized the Penns because "they seem to have Consider'd themselves only in the narrow and Contracted view of Landholders in the Province, and to have been regardless of their Prerogatives as long as their Property remained secure." Above, IX, 171. The present Assembly resolve completely reverses that basis for criticizing the Proprietors.

have so repeatedly met with in this Province, during the late War, were solely owing to Proprietary Instructions, respecting the private Interest of the Proprietaries.[7]

Resolved, N.C.D.

3. That all the Mischiefs to the Province, which the Governor mentions in his late Messages, as occasioned by those Obstructions, are therefore chargeable wholly to the Proprietaries.

Resolved, N.C.D.

4. That it is high Presumption in any Subject to interfere between the Crown and the People; and by his private Instructions to a Deputy Governor, enforced by penal Bonds,[8] prevent the Crown's receiving, and the Peoples granting, the Supplies required, and necessary for the Defence of His Majesty's Province.

Resolved, N.C.D.

5. That it has appeared fully to the Assemblies of this Province, on due Enquiry made, that no Injustice has been done the Proprietaries in the Taxation of their Estates, and that not the least Cause has been given them to apprehend any such Injustice.[9]

Resolved, N.C.D.

6. That the Assemblies of Pennsylvania have, in many Instances, and for a long Course of Years, shewn their affectionate Regard for the Proprietary Family; that Family and its Deputies having received from the mere Benevolence of the People, within these last Forty Years, near Four-score Thousand Pounds.[1]

Resolved, N.C.D.

7. That in return for this Goodness of the People of Pennsylvania, the present Proprietaries have, ever since their Accession,

7. Many documents and references in previous volumes relate to the disputes over supply bills "during the late War" that had been proposed to support the military operations planned by the British government.

8. On the effort of the Assembly to protect Governor Denny from forfeiture of his bond for violation of his proprietary instructions, see above, IX, 136–7, 137 n, 226 n.

9. On the proprietary officials' complaints of injustice in the assessments in Cumberland Co. in 1759–60, and the Assembly's inquiry, see Shepherd, *Proprietary Government,* pp. 465–8, and above, IX, 192–3 n, 233–4, 238.

1. This figure seems to have been calculated on the basis that lieutenant governors had received on the average about £2000 a year in salary and perquisites. See above, V, 57. On the arrangement by which Gov. George Thomas had agreed with the Penns in 1736–38 to turn over to them secretly part of his receipts, see Shepherd, *Proprietary Government,* pp. 206–8.

been endeavouring to diminish and annihilate the Privileges granted by their Honourable Father, to encourage the Settlement of the Province.[2]

Resolved, N.C.D.

8. That from an Attachment to Proprietary Interest, and to increase the Revenue of their Deputies arising from Licences, the Benevolence of the People in granting the same has been grosly abused, and publick Houses and Dram-shops have been encreased to an enormous Degree, to the great Corruption of Morals in the Populace, and Scandal of the Government; and that, from the same Causes, reasonable Bills presented to Proprietary Governors, for restraining or preventing this Evil, have been from time to time refused.[3]

Resolved, N.C.D.

9. That after Indian Purchases made by the Proprietaries, their causing to be located and surveyed the best Tracts of Land for themselves and their Dependants, to lie waste in great Quantities for a future Market, is the Cause that our Frontiers are so thinly and scatteringly settled, whereby the poor Inhabitants there have been rendered less able to defend themselves, and become a more easy Prey to the small skulking Parties of the Enemy.[4]

Resolved, N.C.D.

10. That the Proprietaries having a Monopoly of the Lands of this Province, has enabled them to hold up the vacant unlocated Lands at exorbitant Prices, and the more, as they pay no Quit-rent, but a small Acknowledgment only to the Crown, pay no

2. See above, VII, 360–2, 363–4 n.

3. Licenses of various sorts, and especially those of public houses, were perquisites of government, usually assigned to the lieutenant governor as part of his income. The selection of men to receive such licenses and the number to be issued were subjects of repeated dispute. In 1763 Thomas Penn contended that efforts to limit them were intended as much "to distress a governor as to preserve the morals of the people," but he acknowledged two years later that these and other perquisites had become so large as to be sufficient to support the governor without any salary from the Assembly. *Pa. Col. Recs.*, II, 159–60; Shepherd, *Proprietary Government*, pp. 77, 80–1, 294, 377–8.

4. Charges in this and the following resolve that the Proprietors reserved for themselves or for future sale at an advanced price the best tracts in any purchase from the Indians were often made and as often denied.

Taxes for those Lands, and are under no Obligation of settling them in any limited Time.[5]

Resolved, N.C.D.

11. That their exorbitant Demands in the Price of Lands, have driven many Thousands of Families out of this Province into Maryland, Virginia, North and South-Carolina, where Lands are to be had reasonably; the Frontiers of all those Provinces being chiefly settled with People from Pennsylvania, who likewise carried away with them great Sums of Money, and thereby this Province has been doubly weakened, in the Loss of People to defend it, and of Substance and Improvements taxable towards its Defence.[6]

Resolved, N.C.D.

12. That it was therefore the more unreasonable in the Proprietaries to contend as they have done, first, that they should not be taxed at all; then that their Quit-rents should not be taxed; then that their located uncultivated Lands should be exempted; and put the Province to great Expence, in getting those Points decided against them at Home;[7] while their Estate was equally to be defended with others, and the Province, on whom they would throw the Burden, was at the same Time so greatly weakened by Proprietary Avarice only.

Resolved, N.C.D.

13. That the present Proprietary Demand, of having the *best and*

5. William Penn's charter from Charles II provided that as an acknowledgment of the grant he, his heirs, and successors, should deliver annually at Windsor Castle two beaver skins and should also turn over to the Crown one-fifth of all gold and silver ore found in Pa. No occasion for the second form of payment ever arose. The agreement of Sept. 2, 1760, stipulated that the Proprietors' "unsurveyed waste land" should not be taxed.

6. This charge was entirely valid. The standard purchase price in Pa. of £15 10s., currency, per 100 acres compares with £5 sterling in Md. and with grants requiring fees but no purchase price in the colonies farther south. The Pa. quitrent, normally 1d., sterling, per acre (8s. 4d. per 100 acres) annually in the older counties and varying from ½d. (4s. 2d. per 100 acres) to 1d. in the newer ones, compares with quitrents farther south which ranged generally from 2s. to 4s. 2d., sterling, per 100 acres. In consequence of these disparities there was a great migration from Pa. through the Great Valley to the western sections of the southern colonies. To combat this trend the Penns reduced the purchase price to £5 sterling per 100 acres in 1765. Shepherd, *Proprietary Government*, pp. 34–5; Beverley W. Bond, Jr., *The Quit-Rent System in the American Colonies* (New Haven, 1919), *passim*.

7. See above, IX, 199–200.

most valuable of their located uncultivated Lands, rated and assessed no *higher* than the *worst and least valuable* of the located uncultivated Lands belonging to the Inhabitants, is equally unreasonable and unjust with any of their former Claims.[8]

Resolved, N.C.D.

14. That the Proprietaries taking Advantage of Times of public Calamity to extort Privileges from the People, or enforce Claims against them, with the Knife of Savages at their Throat, not permitting them to raise Money for their Defence, unless the Proprietary arbitrary Will and Pleasure is complied with, is a Practice dishonourable, unjust, tyrannical and inhuman.

Resolved, N.C.D.

15. That the Proprietaries contending for the Power of appointing Judges during *their Pleasure,* who are to determine in all Causes between the Proprietaries and their Tenants, the Inhabitants of the Province, is unjust, renders the Liberties and Properties of the Subject precarious, and dependant on the Proprietary Will and Pleasure, and is by no Colour of Reason supportable.[9]

Resolved, N.C.D.

16. That the bad Light this Province unhappily stands in with our gracious Sovereign and His Ministers, has been owing to Proprietary Misrepresentations and Calumnies.

Resolved, N.C.D.

17. That it is the Opinion of this House, that the late Militia Bill offered to the Governor was equal and just, with regard to the Freemen of the Province, and sufficient for all good Purposes. And that the sole Appointment of the Officers, insisted on by the Gover-

---

8. See above, pp. 111–12, 114–15, 116–17, 118–21.

9. However meritorious this complaint might seem to the members of the committee that drafted it (and to people in other colonies as well as Pa.), BF, at least, was in a position to know how futile it was. The Board of Trade had discussed the issue of judicial tenure at length in its report of June 24, 1760, and had recommended the disallowance of a Pa. act of 1759 because it provided for tenure during good behavior. The Privy Council had followed that recommendation. See above, IX, 160–2, 204–5. Writing to David Barclay & Sons, Sept. 24, 1764, Chief Justice William Allen expressed great resentment at the implication that the judges had ever shown, or even had occasion to show, partiality to the Proprietors in cases before them. Lewis B. Walker, ed., *The Burd Papers. Extracts from Chief Justice William Allen's Letter Book* ([Pottsville, Pa.], 1897), p. 57.

nor, however willing the House might be to comply with the same under a Royal Government, would be an Addition to the Proprietary Power, that by no Means can be safely trusted by the People in their Hands.[1]

Resolved, N.C.D.

18. That the Fines proposed by the Governor, for Offences in the Militia, are enormously high, and calculated to enslave the good People of this Province.

Resolved, N.C.D.

19. That the Power insisted on by the Governor, of marching any Number of the Militia to any Part of the Province, and keeping them there during any Time, at Pleasure, without the Advice and Consent of the Commissioners, who are to pay them, is a Power that may be used so as greatly and unnecessarily to harrass the Freemen of the Province, and cannot safely be trusted in the Hands of a Proprietary Governor.

Resolved, N.C.D.

20. That Courts-martial proposed in the Governor's Amendments to the Militia Bill, to be held by Officers of the sole Appointment of a Proprietary Governor, with the Power of Life and Death over the Inhabitants of the Province, may be used greatly to their Prejudice, as a destructive Engine of Proprietary Power.

Resolved, N.C.D.

21. That the House, in the present Supply Bill, from a dutiful Respect to the Judgment of their Lordships of the Privy Council, and an earnest Desire of promoting His Majesty's Measures, wisely concerted for the Protection of this Province, have fully complied with the same: And that the Sense in which some of the Articles

---

1. On this militia bill and the issue of the appointment of officers, see above, pp. 74–5, 122, and below, pp. 360–5. Resolves 18, 19, and 20 below relate to the other principal objections the governor and his Council found to the bill: "2dly. That the Governor shall not have the power of ordering a part of the Militia to do duty on the Frontiers, for the defence of the Province, while the Provincial Troops were employed elsewhere, without the advice and consent of the Provincial Commissioners. 3dly. The several Fines to be imposed on the Officers and Soldiers for neglect of Duty, in every instance are too small, and by no means sufficient to answer the pur-- poses intended by them. 4thly. No provision is made for holding Courts Martial, for punishing Capital Crimes, such as Mutiny, &ca., in time of actual Service." *Pa. Col. Recs.*, IX, 151.

of their Lordships Report is understood and explained by the Governor, is inconsistent with Reason and Justice, and what therefore their Lordships cannot be supposed ever to have meant or intended.[2]

Resolved, N.C.D.

22. That it is the Opinion of this House, that the Governor's rejecting the said Bill does not arise from its not being conformable to that Report, but because it is not formed agreeable to Proprietary Instructions.

Resolved, N.C.D.

23. That the House having fully complied with their Duty to His Majesty, and the good People of this Province, in offering an equitable Supply Bill to the Governor for his Assent, all the Distresses and Mischiefs that shall happen on the Failure of the said Bill, are justly imputable to an undue Influence of the Proprietary Interest and Instructions on the Governor.

Resolved, N.C.D.

24. That the sole executive Powers of Government being in the Hands of the Proprietaries, together with the very extensive and growing Power arising naturally from their vast and daily increasing Property, must in future Times, according to the natural Course of human Affairs, render them absolute, and become as dangerous to the Prerogatives of the Crown as to the Liberties of the People.

Resolved, N.C.D.

25. That it is therefore the Opinion of this House, that the powers of Government ought, in all good Policy, to be separated from the Power attending that immense Property, and lodged, where only it can be properly and safely lodged, in the Hands of the Crown.

And as all Hope of any Degree of Happiness, under the Proprietary Government, is, in our Opinion, now at an End,

Resolved, N.C.D.

26. That this House will adjourn, in order to consult their Constituents, whether an humble Address should be drawn up, and transmitted to His Majesty, praying that he would be graciously pleased to take the People of this Province under His immediate Protection and Government, by compleating the Agreement heretofore made with the first Proprietor for the Sale of the Govern-

2. On this and the next two resolves see above, pp. 7–9, 111–16, 116–22.

ment to the Crown, or otherwise, as to His Wisdom and Goodness shall seem meet.[3]
Ordered,
That the foregoing Resolves be made public.[4]

To Francis Bernard

Photostat of ALS: Historical Society of Pennsylvania

Sir   Philada. March 28. 1764
I am favour'd with yours of the 17th.[5] with the Letters return'd concerning Sturgeon.[6] I lately sent you a good Receipt for Pickling, which I hope got to hand.[7] I shall forward your Son's Letter to Mr. Johnston.[8] Enclos'd is one I received a few Days since from that Gentleman.[9] I paid his Order, as you will see by the Receipt. Please to pay the Sum, £12 12s. 0d. Pensilva Money to Mr. Jonathan Williams, who has acknowledg'd the Receipt of the former.[1]
At our College here, they have not yet got into the Collegiate Way of living that was intended in the new Building,[2] so that our

3. See below, pp. 145–7, 193–200.
4. *Pa. Gaz.*, March 29, 1764, printed in full the verbal messages between Penn and the Assembly of March 19, 20, and 21, their written messages of March 22, 23, and 24, and these resolves. *Pa. Jour.* did not print these documents. Under date of April 12, 1764, the MS Franklin & Hall workbook contains a charge to the province of £6 5s. for 3000 copies of "the Assembly's Proceedings on the Supply Bill." George Simpson Eddy, *A Work-Book of The Printing House of Benjamin Franklin & David Hall 1759–1776* (N.Y., 1930), p. 8. While no copy of this broadside has been located, it almost certainly consisted of a reprinting of all this material, intended for wide distribution throughout Pa.
5. Not found.
6. It is not clear what these letters were. For BF and Bernard's correspondence about a method of pickling sturgeon, see above, pp. 31–2, 87–8.
7. Not found.
8. George Johnston, a lawyer at whose estate of "Belvale" near Alexandria, Va., Bernard's son, Francis, stayed during December 1763; see above, x, 410 n.
9. Not found.
1. Williams acknowledged receiving £7 11s. 2¼d. sterling from Bernard on April 10, 1764; on Feb. 28, 1764, he had acknowledged receiving £24 1s. 1½d. from the governor. See above, x, 359–60, and this volume, p. 88 n.
2. The "New Building" of the College of Philadelphia, erected with funds

Scholars still lodge and board in private Houses; the Expence I understand is about £40 per Ann, for Diet, Lodging, Washing, Mending, and Tuition. I know not when the other Method will be entred upon, nor can the Expence yet be ascertain'd. My Respectful Compliments to Mrs. Bernard, in which my Daughter joins, and to your Son. With great Respect, I am, Your Excellency's most obedient humble Servant   B FRANKLIN

Governor Barnard

Explanatory Remarks on the Assembly's Resolves

Broadside: Library Company of Philadelphia

On March 30, 1764, the day after the *Pennsylvania Gazette* printed the recent messages between the governor and the Assembly and the twenty-six Assembly "Resolves upon the Present Circumstances," Joseph Galloway wrote to William Franklin enclosing "a Copy of your worthy Father's Remarks on our Assembly Resolves. No answer has yet been attempted by the Proprietary Faction, who seem much depressed."[3] Under date of April 12, 1764, the firm of Franklin & Hall charged the province £8 for printing 3000 copies of the "Explanatory Remarks of the Assembly's Resolves,"[4] a folio of two pages. It is undated, but someone wrote in ink on the present copy "March 29, 1764," just below the "No. 1840" of the heading. Perhaps this writer intended merely to indicate the date of this issue of the *Gazette*, in which the Resolves were printed, yet the fact that Galloway was able to send a copy of the

---

procured by William Smith on his tour abroad, was fitted up in part for the accommodation of students during the latter part of 1764 and was opened for occupancy that winter with Ebenezer Kinnersley (above, IV, 192 n) in charge. Montgomery, *Hist. Univ. Pa.*, pp. 443–7.

3. Quoted by Paul L. Ford in "Franklin's 'Explanatory Remarks,' " *The Nation*, LIX (July 26, Aug. 2, 1894), 60–1, 76–7. Ford printed in parallel columns the full texts of eight of the most important Assembly Resolves and the corresponding passages of the "Explanatory Remarks." He interspersed these quotations with commentary of his own, which shows that his sympathies lay almost completely with the Assembly's position.

4. George Simpson Eddy, *A Work-Book of The Printing House of Benjamin Franklin & David Hall 1759–1766* (N.Y., 1930), p. 8. This entry accompanies the charge to the province for printing 3000 copies of the documents relating to the Supply Bill with the text of the Resolves. Apparently the Assembly leaders intended to distribute the two broadsides together.

Remarks to the governor of New Jersey on the 30th makes clear that Franklin had written them before that date.

These Explanatory Remarks must, of course, be read in conjunction with the Resolves to which they refer (above, pp. 126-33), and which, as the introductory paragraph makes clear, they were intended to amplify and explain. This paper is one of many examples of the importance Franklin attached throughout his career to informing the public on issues for which he wanted support.

[March 29, 1764]

EXPLANATORY REMARKS on the ASSEMBLY's RESOLVES,
published in the *Pennsylvania Gazette*, No. 1840.

RESOLVES of ASSEMBLY being short Resolutions, formed after Debate and full Consideration of any particular Matter, they are generally very concise, and seldom contain the Reasons at large upon which they are founded; and although they are always so full and expressive, as to be clearly understood by those who have attended to the Subject, yet, to enable others rightly to comprehend their Meaning, an explanatory Account of the Facts seems necessary. It is with this View the following Remarks are submitted to the Consideration of the Publick.

Remarks on Resolve the First. As this Resolve is the first in Order, so it is the most important, and is intended to point out the deepest Wound which has been made, by an undue Attachment to Proprietary Interest, in the original Constitution of this Government. By the Royal Grant, *"free, full* and *absolute* Power," is given to the Proprietary "Lieutenants" and Governors, "to ordain, make, and enact Laws, for the Raising of Money, &c. according to their *best Discretion,* with the Advice, Consent and Approbation of the Freemen of the Country, or of their Delegates and Deputies."[5] The

5. BF's quotation from the royal charter is incomplete and perhaps disingenuous. Charles II had granted the legislative power both to William Penn and his heirs and "to his and their Deputies and Lieutenants." The "their" in the charter phrase "according to their best Discretion" clearly refers to the first Proprietor and his heirs as well as to the lieutenant governors. BF's phraseology suggests, incorrectly, that the charter conferred "Power" and "Discretion" in legislative matters solely upon the lieutenant governor, when there was such an officer, to the exclusion of William Penn and his heirs. From this premise followed BF's conclusion in the following sentences that the Proprietors had no constitutional right "to give Instructions to their Governors" or in any way limit these deputies' discretion.

Powers of Legislature being thus fully granted by the Crown, to the Governor for the Time being, and the Peoples Representatives, 'tis evident the Proprietaries can have no Constitutional Share in Legislation, or Right to give Instructions to their Governor, whereby his "Discretion" must be totally destroyed. And therefore all such Instructions are a manifest Violation of the Royal Favour to the good People of this Province, and a most dangerous Invasion on the Rights of the Subject. They not only destroy the Exercise of Judgment in the Governor, but render the Representative Body of the People mere Cyphers in the Constitution. And vain is it for the People to send their Delegates to the Seat of Representation, as all they can do when met, is to give up their Freedom and Exercise of Judgment, betray those very Rights they were sent to preserve, and servilely submit to Proprietary Will and Pleasure. Much better will it be for the Inhabitants of Pennsylvania to invest the Proprietaries with absolute Power at once, permit them to ordain and enact Laws at Three Thousand Miles Distance, and only transmit them here for Publication and *Execution.* For whose Interest they will in that Case be calculated, and of what Spirit they will partake, modern Measures have fully demonstrated.

Remark on the Second and Third Resolves. The first Attempt to enforce this mischievous Claim, happened about Fifty Years past, when William Penn, in Governor Evans's Commission, inserted a Clause, reserving "to himself and his Heirs, their final Assent to the Laws" which should be passed; and thus assumed the Royal Power, which by the original Charter was reserved to the Crown. How evidently does this demonstrate, that Men of the fairest Characters are not to be trusted, when under the Influence of private Interest. A virtuous Opposition, however, both in the *Proprietary Council,* and Assembly, repelled this Invasion of their Rights, and the Reservation was declared illegal and void.[6] And from this Time

6. This incident occurred in May 1704, about two months after John Evans had assumed office as lieutenant governor. The Assembly took notice of a clause in William Penn's commission to Evans under which measures passed by the Assembly and assented to by the governor would, as the Assembly put it, "be of no use till sent to England, where they were either to be passed or rejected" by the Proprietor. The House contended that the royal charter "would allow of no such Reserve." After conferences between the Assembly and Council, ten members of the Council, including William

136

Proprietary Instructions never appeared, till in the Beginning of the late War.[7] A Time when the Frontiers were bleeding in every Quarter, and the unhappy Inhabitants reduced to every Kind of Misery and Distress that the deepest Want, and the most relentless Barbarities of a savage Enemy could devise and inflict. This it seems was thought the most convenient Time to enforce those Claims, and reduce the People to a Subjection to them. And certainly a Time like this was necessary to their Success. For, upon their being laid before the Assembly, they plainly appeared to be formed solely with a View to increase the immense Wealth of the Proprietaries, and to oblige the People to bear their Burthens; and were found equally regardless of the Orders of the Crown, as of the Good and Safety of the distressed Inhabitants.[8]

Influenced by these illegal Instructions, what unjust Claims have the Governors of this Province made in Favour of their Principals! They first insisted that the Proprietaries should not be taxed at all, although their Property was to receive equal Protection from it; then that their Quitrents should not be rated; next that their located and uncultivated Lands should be exempted; and lastly, that the Bills of Credit, issued as well for the Protection of their Property as that of the Inhabitants, should not be a Tender in the Payment of their Rents, contrary to all Justice and good Conscience. The Assembly, consistent with that Duty they indispensably owed to

---

Penn, Jr., then in the province, signed a paper at the Assembly's request agreeing that this reserve clause was "void in it self," but declaring that this fact did not invalidate the rest of Evans' commission. They stated that "those Bills, which the present Lieut. Govr. shall think Fitt to pass into Laws, and cause the said Propr[ietor]s great Seal to be affixed, cannot afterwards be vacated or annull'd by the Proprietor without assent of the assembly of this Province." William Penn was forced to yield on his reservation of a veto on legislation after it had received his deputy's approval. *Pa. Col. Recs.*, II, 144–7; William R. Shepherd, *History of Proprietary Government in Pennsylvania* (N.Y., 1896), pp. 483–5.

7. This statement is incorrect. William Penn and his successors continued to give instructions regularly to their governors, although in 1724 Sir William Keith, anxious to curry favor with the Assembly, agreed that he was not bound by them. In consequence he was removed from office two years later. *Ibid.*, pp. 485–7.

8. For documents relating to the matters summarized here and in the next paragraph, see the indexes to earlier volumes in this series, especially vols. V–VII, under "Instructions, proprietary."

their Constituents, could not agree to these unjust Demands. This created Disputes; those Disputes created Delays, which greatly obstructed His Majesty's Measures; and whether the Proprietary Pretensions, or the Assembly's Opposition, were most just and well founded, is submitted to the Candid and Impartial.

Resolve the Fourth. It is certainly an high Presumption in the Proprietaries, to give Instructions inconsistent with the Royal Grant; to take Bonds to enforce a strict Execution of them, and to adhere to them without the least Abatement, when His Majesty's Subjects are in the greatest Danger and Distress from the Incursions of a savage Enemy; and especially, by those Instructions, to delay and prevent those Aids His Majesty demands of this Province, for the Preservation of his Colonies, and the Safety of his People.

Resolve the Fifth. In the Year One Thousand Seven Hundred and Sixty-one, an Enquiry was made, by Order of Assembly, into the State of the Provincial Taxes. And it appeared that the Proprietaries whole Estate paid no more than Five Hundred Sixty-six Pounds, Four Shillings and Ten-pence, when the Tax of one of the Members amounted to more than One Third of that Sum, though not possessed of a One-fiftieth Part of the Property owned by *them;* although it was asserted before the Privy Council, in a Debate on *that very Bill* by which the Tax was laid, that the Proprietaries would be obliged to pay more than all the People of Pennsylvania together.[9]

Resolve the Sixth. By Contract with the first Adventurers, the Quitrents were settled, as the certain Support of the Government, as is the Case in those Colonies immediately under the King.[1] On this Income the Governor was supported many Years. When the

9. The figures on the total proprietary tax under the Supply Act of 1759 are taken from the report of an investigative committee of the Assembly, which reported March 12, 1761. The Committee also reported that the total tax paid by the inhabitants amounted to £27,103 12s. 8d. 8 *Pa. Arch.*, VI, 5216. No details are recorded of the debate in the Privy Council, Aug. 27–28, 1760, at which the Supply Act of 1759 was considered and which led to the order in council of Sept. 2, 1760; above, IX, 196–211.

1. As early as the first years of the century the Assembly had asserted that Penn intended the quitrents to be used for the support of government and that such an arrangement had been a contract between him and the early purchasers of land. Governor Evans denied that any such compact existed

Proprietor returned to England, he had Occasion for those Rents to support his Family there; to which Purpose, and to distress the Province, they have been ever since carefully applied. Upon this Misapplication of the first Revenues of the Government, the Assembly were at that Time, by the most artful Management, and undue Influence, prevailed on to grant the Monies arising by Tavern Licences to support his Deputy. The Monies received from this Source, and the Sums given to the Governors for Forty Years past, will amount to more than the Sum mentioned in the Resolve.

Resolve the Seventh, appears to be just, from many of the other Resolves.

Resolve the Eighth. It is notorious, the Number of Taverns, Alehouses and Dram-shops, have encreased beyond all Measure or Necessity. That they are placed so near to each other, that they ruin one another; and Two Thirds of them are not merely useless, but are become a Pest to Society. There are very few of them that are able to provide the necessary Conveniences for entertaining Travellers, or accommodating the People either in Country or City; and this is entirely owing to that weak Policy in a former Assembly, of making it the Interest of a Governor to encourage and promote Immorality and Vice among the People. Many Bills have been presented to the late Governors, to lessen the Number, and to regulate those Nurseries of Idleness and Debauchery, but without Success. From whence it seems evident, that so long as the Proprietaries are interested in our Ruin, ruined we must be: For no Deputy will dare to regulate this Mischief, because it will lessen the Revenue; nor accept a Compensation *for this Revenue,* as it will

---

and declared that quitrents and government were completely unrelated. *Pa. Col. Recs.,* II, 416, 418. The tradition persisted, however, and was reasserted from time to time, as, for example, in Richard Jackson's *An Historical Review of the Constitution and Government of Pensylvania* (London, 1759), p. 14, where it was stated, undoubtedly on a suggestion by BF, that Penn had justified the imposition of quitrents on the ground that "by this Expedient they [the inhabitants] would be exempt from other Taxes." William R. Shepherd, a leading authority, states flatly that "the claim of the assembly is not substantiated by any law, instrument, or act which was sanctioned by Penn or his successors." *Proprietary Government,* p. 68. Quitrents were indeed used, as BF states, as a source of salaries for governors of several of the royal colonies in the South, although inefficient collection in the Carolinas caused difficulties for the governors.

affect his Successor; nor even accept a greater Annuity, because it may, in Time, encrease to an higher Sum.

Resolve the Ninth. The purchasing or taking up large Tracts of Land on the Frontiers, to lay by for a future Market, must prevent a compact Settlement of the People, render them less defensible, and of Course encrease the Taxes necessary for their Protection.

Resolve Tenth and Eleventh. In Virginia and Carolina the People pay no Purchase Money for their Lands, and in the former only Two Shillings, and in the latter Four Shillings and Two-pence Sterling Quit-rent *per* Hundred Acres. In Pennsylvania the Proprietaries Waste Lands are sold for Fifteen Pounds Ten Shillings *per* Hundred Acres; their Manor Lands from Fifty to Sixty times that Value, with an annual Quit-rent reserved of Four Shillings and Two-pence Sterling *per* Hundred Acres. This exorbitant Price, with the great Difficulty of obtaining Justice at the Land Office,[2] and the continued public Disputes, occasioned by Proprietary Exactions and Instructions, have driven a great Number of wealthy Settlers into the Southern Colonies.

Resolves Twelve, Thirteen, Fourteen and Fifteen [12, 13, 14],[3] being fully explained by what is said before, and in the Assembly's Messages, they can need no further Explanation.

Resolve the Sixteenth [15]. The People of our Mother Country, under the immediate Government of a Sovereign who had little private Interest in the Kingdom to influence him, have thought that they had no Security in their Lives, Liberties and Properties, while the Judges of the several Courts held their Commissions *during the Pleasure of the Crown.* If they were right, how much more precarious and insecure are those invaluable Blessings in this Province,

2. For an illustration of such alleged injustice, see above, VIII, 374–9, for the "genuine Account" of John Fisher's experience in 1747, when he received a patent for two pieces of land and was charged £91 11*s.*: 4¾*d.* more than the "legally" correct total of £120 12*s.* 2¼*d.*

3. As printed in the Assembly *Votes,* the resolves are numbered consecutively from 1 to 26, but the *Gazette* printing omits this numbering. Here and again a little later BF slipped, and the numbering of his remaining remarks fails to correspond with that of the resolves to which they refer. Bracketed numbers have therefore been inserted at this and similar points throughout the rest of this document to indicate the resolves to which BF's paragraphs actually relate.

where so great and unjust an Attachment to the Interest of the Proprietaries is discovered, *who* are not only consulted in the Nomination of the Judges, but can, and often have, from Reasons of Policy *only*, removed them at their Pleasure? The Time may come, when the People of Pennsylvania may experience the arbitrary Policy of a Richard the Second, and a James the Second, and the unjust and cruel Determinations of the servile Belknap, and the blood-thirsty Jeffries.[4]

Resolve the Seventeenth [16]. Nothing was too unjust, nothing too dishonest and false to be alledged against the Assembly and People of Pennsylvania, in the late Pleadings before their Lordships of the Privy Council, and we all know by whom the Pleaders were instructed. The Pleadings themselves having been taken in Short Hand, will soon be published, and fully demonstrate the Truth of this Resolve.

Resolve the Nineteenth [17]. However safe it may be to entrust an immediate Governor under the Crown with the Nomination of Militia Officers, who has no private Interest or Schemes of his own to promote, it certainly never can be safe to commit that Power into the Hands of a Deputy of the Proprietaries, bound by penal Obligations to obey Instructions wholly calculated to promote their private Interest. If we may judge from what we have seen, they would, no doubt, commission none but those who would implicitly obey their Orders, and pursue their Schemes for enslaving the People. This would create a vast Number of New Relations and Dependencies in the Government, all under the Controul of the

4. Sir Robert de Bealknap, or Belknap (d. 1400?), chief justice of the Common Pleas, was one of the judges who, acting under threats of death, as they later alleged, upheld Richard II in his contest with opposing peers in 1387. When the King's antagonists gained the upper hand these judges were arrested, imprisoned by order of Parliament, and sentenced to death, but the bishops interceded and their punishment was commuted to banishment to Ireland and the forfeiture of their properties. Bealknap was recalled to England in 1397, but died without having his attainder removed. *DNB*. George, Baron Jeffreys of Wem (1648–1689), lord chief justice, notorious for his prejudicial conduct of politically motivated trials, presided at the "Bloody Assizes" following the Monmouth Rebellion, 1685, and was rewarded by James II by promotion to lord chancellor. During the "Glorious Revolution" he tried to escape, but was captured and died while imprisoned in the Tower of London. *DNB*.

Proprietaries and their Governors, who holding their Offices during their Pleasure, would no doubt conform to *that Pleasure*. The Officers would influence the private Men, and the whole would influence our Elections in Favour of the Proprietary System, and by these Means render their Will the sole Rule, in both the Executive and Legislative Parts of Government.

Resolve Twenty, Twenty-one and Twenty-two [18, 19, 20]. These Resolves on the proposed Amendments to the Militia Bill, are so full and easily understood, that they carry Conviction with them, upon the least Attention.

Resolve the Twenty-third [21] is fully explained by the Messages between the Governor and Assembly, lately published.[5]

Resolve the Twenty-fourth [22, 23].[6] No sooner did the Proprietaries obtain the Opinion of our Superiors, that the Bills of Credit should not be a Tender in the Payment of their Rents, than they laid a new Scheme for putting their Purchase Money, and other Contracts, under the same Circumstances, that thereby they might not, in common with the People of this Province, suffer by a Depreciation, in case it should happen, though in common with the People they reaped all the Advantages of those Bills, and though the Protection of their Estates, in common with the Peoples, rendered the emitting them necessary. They accordingly gave Orders to their Commissioners of Property, to make their future Contracts for the Sale of Lands *in Sterling;* and by their Instructions to their Governor, positively forbid him to pass any Supply Bill, unless those Contracts are also exempted from being discharged by the said Bills. This seems, in the Opinion of the House, to have been one of the Causes of the Failure of the *Supply Bill*.[7] To which

5. In the same issue of the *Gazette* in which the Resolves appeared.
6. While BF cites only one resolve here, his comment seems to apply in general to both Resolves 22 and 23.
7. The sixth stipulation embodied in the order in council of Sept. 2, 1760, provided "That the Payments by the Tenants to the Proprietaries of their Rents, shall be according to the terms of their respective Grants, as if such Act had never been passed." Above, IX, 206. John Penn's twelfth instruction, which he sent to the Assembly, Jan. 12, 1764, directed him to take care that bills of credit authorized in the future should "not be capable of being made a Tender, or any satisfaction, or discharge for any Quitrents, *or other sterling Payments* [italics added], due to or to become due to us." Above, p.

may be added, that by the Bill, had it passed, the Proprietary Agents would be obliged to give an *honest* Account of their Estates, under a Penalty of Four-fold the Tax for all Property by them wittingly concealed.[8] And when we consider the many Instances of the most unjust Claims of Exemption from Taxes by the Proprietaries, this alone will appear an Objection likely to be strong enough with their Deputy to reject the Bill, the House having complied fully with the Stipulations their Agents had entered into before the Council.

Resolve the Twenty fifth [24]. Power, when separate from great Property, and properly restrained by salutary Laws, is so far from being prejudicial to Society, that it cannot well exist or continue without it. But Power united with great Wealth, is all that is neces-

---

8. While the order in council had forbidden the Assembly to make bills of credit legal tender only in the case of quitrents, the words in the proprietary instruction italicized above expanded the prohibition to include any other payments which the Proprietors might require to be made in sterling. This expansion appears to have been intended primarily as a safeguard for directions to the commissioners of property, who were charged with the sale of proprietary land, ordering them to specify in all future contracts for land sales that payment of the purchase price (usually £15 10s. per 100 acres) be made in sterling rather than in currency, as had certainly been the previous practice (see for example, above, VIII, 374–9; also Shepherd, *Proprietary Government*, p. 34). On the basis of the 1764 rate of exchange, the effect of this new requirement would be a sudden jump of about 75 percent in the already excessive cost to the buyer of Pa. land. The Assembly ignored the phraseology of Governor Penn's instruction and worded the £55,000 supply bill to conform to that of the order in council by stipulating that the bills of credit should be legal tender for all purposes, including contracts, "the sterling Rents due, or to become due to the Proprietaries of this Province only excepted." It may be observed that, although Penn demanded in his message of March 19 that the Assembly insert in the bill the clauses regarding the Proprietors' located, uncultivated lands and town lots "in the very Words of the Decree" (above, p. 112), he very wisely (from his point of view) never directed them to do the same with the clause regarding payments to the Proprietors.

8. The £55,000 supply bill required every property owner to list in detail on a printed form all his taxable property and to deliver this paper to the assessors. Failure to do so subjected him to a penalty of double the normal rate of the tax due, and failure to make "a just and true Account and Report" would result in a penalty of quadruple the tax on any concealed property. This provision remained in the bill as finally enacted on May 30. *Statutes at Large, Pa.*, VI, 348.

sary to render its Possessor absolute, and every thing, under him, at his own Disposal. Great Riches alone, says a late Writer, in a private Person, are as dangerous to the Prerogatives of the Crown as to the Rights of the Subject.[9] It enables him to form a great Number of Dependants, much greater than is consistent with the Safety of either. They place the Subject too near a Level with his Sovereign. They form in the Mind ambitious Designs, and not only give the Hope, but create the Power, of carrying them into Execution. And if this be the Case of great Wealth alone, how much more must the Addition of all the Powers of Government in the same Persons (Three Thousand Miles distant from the Eye of the Sovereign) render the Rights of the Crown and the Privileges of the People precarious, and at the Disposal of the Proprietaries? Look through all History, and the Experience of Ages will demonstrate this Truth.

Resolve the Twenty sixth [25]. The Reason of this Resolve is fully shewn in the Explanation of the last.

Resolve the last [26]. By this Resolve it appears all Hopes of serving the People, or the least Degree of Happiness, under a Proprietary Government, are wholly given up by the Assembly. And that, in their Opinion, no Asylum from arbitrary Power and its mischievous Effects remains, but that of a Change of Government. And nothing is now left for the People to determine, but to inform their Representatives, whether they had rather submit to the most unjust Proprietary Instructions, subversive, and indeed effectually destructive, of their essential Privileges, and of Course become Slaves to the usurped and arbitrary Power of private Subjects; or implore the immediate Protection of a Sovereign, justly celebrated for his tender Regard to the constitutional Rights of Englishmen.

9. While the author to whom BF refers here has not been certainly identified, some of the ideas expressed in this and the following sentences are very close to those in a passage in one of David Hume's *Essays Moral and Political,* first published in 1741 and conveniently reprinted in T. H. Green and T. H. Grose, eds., *Essays Moral, Political and Literary by David Hume* (London, 1898), I, 123.

Petition of the Pennsylvania Freeholders and
Inhabitants to the King   Draft: American Philosophical Society

When the Assembly adjourned on Saturday, March 24, it gave its members a recess of seven weeks "in order to consult their Constituents, whether an humble Address should be drawn up, and transmitted to His Majesty, praying that he would be graciously pleased to take the People of this Province under his immediate Protection and Government."[1] It is clear that the Assembly leaders planned to use this time to procure the widest possible expression of public sentiment in favor of the proposed change in government. To this end Franklin prepared the draft of a petition to the King which was to be printed, circulated through the province, and signed by as many "Freeholders and Inhabitants" as could be induced to do so. Writing to Richard Jackson on the following Thursday, March 29, he enclosed a copy of this draft of what he thought would be "pretty nearly the Petition, that you may see the Tenor of it."[2] This draft, which Jackson preserved among his papers, is printed here, assigned to the date of the letter to Jackson.

Two days later the firm of Franklin & Hall printed "100 copies of a Petition to his Majesty, on fine Writing Paper" and provided both blue and brown paper within which the petitions were stitched, charging Franklin personally £1 14s. 6d. for the job.[3] In addition to some alterations in punctuation, this printed version contains a few minor verbal changes from Franklin's draft; though none of the latter affect the meaning, all are indicated in footnotes to the text as printed here from the draft. A German translation was also printed, probably by Anton Armbrüster; and apparently at about the same time another English petition, differently worded but for the same purpose, was printed for circulation among the Quakers. The latter document omits Franklin's generalizations about proprietary governments but contains, as Franklin's text does not, a strong plea for the "Continuation and Confirma-

1. See above, p. 132.
2. See the next document.
3. George Simpson Eddy, *A Work-Book of The Printing House of Benjamin Franklin & David Hall 1759–1766* (N.Y., 1930), pp. 8–12. A second order for 200 copies of "a Petition to his Majesty" costing £2 9s. was charged to BF on April 18. Whether this order was for additional copies of the same petition or represented the printing of the Quaker petition, described later in the above paragraph, has not been determined. Eddy's account of the various anti-proprietary petitions submitted in 1764, reinforced by facsimile reproductions of three of them, is most useful. It avoids the errors and confusions into which most writers, both before and since, have fallen.

tion" of the "inestimable Religious and Civil Liberties" which had encouraged the first settlement of the colony, "now become a very valuable Part of the King's extensive American Dominions." The author of this document has not been identified.

The Assembly reconvened on May 14. Four days later a petition (Franklin's printed text in what appears to have been several copies) "signed by upwards of Fifteen Hundred Inhabitants of this Province, was presented to the House, with a verbal Request by the Member who brought them in, that the same be transmitted by their Representatives to the Crown." Immediately afterwards the Quaker petition was also presented. The texts of both documents appear in full in the *Votes and Proceedings*.[4] On May 23 members from Bucks, Lancaster, and Northampton Counties presented petitions signed in their constituencies, and on the next day similar papers were offered from Philadelphia and Chester Counties.[5] All these documents were ultimately submitted to the Privy Council, among the papers of which they still remain. They include 23 examples of the English petition originally written by Franklin, 2 of its German translation, and 8 of the Quaker petition.[6]

The actions that the Assembly took in consequence of these petitions are described below, pp. 193-200.

[March 29, 1764]
To the King's most excellent Majesty in Council.

The Petition of the Freeholders and Inhabitants
of the Province of Pensilvania

Most humbly sheweth.

That great Obstructions to your Majesty's Service, and Mischiefs to the said Province, have during the two last Wars been occasion'd by a continual Disagreement between the Proprietaries

4. *Votes*, 1763–64, pp. 80–1.
5. *Ibid.*, pp. 82, 83.
6. These figures are taken from Eddy, *Work-Book*, p. 11. In preparing this headnote the editors have used both the texts of the two English petitions as printed in *Votes* and photocopies of single examples of each of the three printed petitions, all of originals in the Public Record Office, London. The example of the English petition based on BF's draft that has been used contains 207 signatures. Most of the easily recognized names are those of Philadelphians, including a substantial number of Quakers. The petition in German used here contains 62 names, and the Quaker document, 127.

of the Province, who are Governors of the same, and the Assemblies annually chosen[7] by the People.

That the like Disagreements between the Proprietaries and People in all the other Colonies of America settled under Proprietary Governments and like Mischiefs attending those Disagreements, have in most of the said Colonies occasioned a Surrender of the Powers of Government,[8] or a Resumption of the same by your Majesty's Predecessors, only two Proprietary Governments now remaining in America.

That your Petitioners humbly conceive such mischievous Disagreements to proceed from the very Nature of Proprietary Governments; the Multitude of Disputes arising between the Proprietaries and private Persons concerning Matters of Property, naturally occasioning mutual Opinions of Injustice, and thence in the Proprietaries a Dislike of the People; and in the People[9] Want of Respect to the Proprietary Government; while the Proprietaries Power as Governors of appointing Judges during their Pleasure to judge in their own as well as all other Causes subjects them to Suspicion, and their making Use of their Powers of Government, especially in Times of Publick Distress, to enforce Claims of private Interest, renders their Government Odious.

The Petitioners therefore, desirous of enjoying the Privileges granted them by your Majesty's Royal[1] Predecessors, freed from the Inconveniencies which they conceive incident to Proprietary Governments, and which they have long laboured under; and earnestly wishing to partake of that Happiness and Security which they see all those Colonies around them enjoy, who are under your Majesty's immediate Government, do humbly pray, that your Majesty would be graciously pleased to take the Government of this Province likewise into your own Royal Hands, making the Proprietaries such equitable Compensation for the same, as to your Majesty's Wisdom and Goodness shall seem meet.

And your[2] Petitioners, as in Duty bound, shall ever pray, &c.

7. The printed petition reads: "chosen annually."
8. The printed petition adds: "to the Crown."
9. The printed petition adds: "a."
1. The printed petition omits: "Royal."
2. The printed petition reads: "the."

To Richard Jackson

ALS: American Philosophical Society

Dear Sir   Philada. March 29. 1764

In my last[3] I inform'd you that the Agreement between the Governor and Assembly was not likely long to continue. The enclos'd Paper[4] will show you that the Breach is wider now than ever. And 'tis thought there will be a general Petition from the Inhabitants to the Crown, to take us under its immediate Government. I send you this early Notice of what is intended that you may prepare Minds for it, as they fall in your Way. If I can have time I will send you a Copy of the Bill we last sent up,[5] and which was refused. But if it goes not by this Vessel, we shall send it via Lisbon in one that sails in a few Days.

Be assured, that we all think it impossible to go on any longer under a Proprietary Government. By the Resolves you will see, that never was greater Unanimity in any Assembly. Enclos'd I send you a Draft of what I think will be pretty nearly the Petition, that you may see the Tenor of it.[6] Note, There was an Agreement between the First Proprietor W. Penn, and the Crown, for the Sale of the Government at £11,000 of which £2,000 was paid him.[7] Note also, that the Crown has a great Sum in the Proprietaries Hands, half the Quitrents of the Lower Counties belonging to the Crown, of which the Proprietaries are Receivers, and I believe have never render'd any Account.

You will endear yourself to us forever, if you can get this Change of Government compleated.

I write in great haste; but am Dear Friend, Yours most affectionately   B FRANKLIN

3. That of March 14, 1764; see above, pp. 105–9.

4. Almost certainly *Pa. Gaz.*, March 29, 1764, which printed the messages that had passed between the governor and the Assembly between March 14 and 24 on the £55,000 Supply Bill. Among the documents printed were the Assembly's messages to the governor, March 22 and 24, 1764, and its Resolves of the 24th, for all of which, see above, pp. 111–33.

5. The £55,000 Supply Bill of March 14, 1764; see above, pp. 111–12.

6. See immediately above.

7. In 1712 William Penn and the Board of Trade agreed to the sale of the government of Pennsylvania for £12,000, but although Penn received £1000, the contract was never formally executed. William R. Shepherd, *History of Proprietary Government in Pennsylvania* (N.Y., 1896), pp. 540–4. See also below, p. 151.

p.s. Besides the general Petitions of the Inhabitants the Assembly will present an Address to the same Purpose.[8]

Endorsed: 29 Mar 1764 Benjn Franklin Esq

To William Strahan   ALS: University of Pennsylvania Library

Dear Friend,   Philada. March 30. 1764

I begin to think it long since I had the Pleasure of hearing from you.[9]

Enclos'd is one of our last Gazettes,[1] in which you will see that our Dissensions are broke out again; more violently than ever. Such a Necklace of Resolves! and all Nemine contradicente, I believe you have seldom seen. If you can find Room for them and our Messages in the Chronicle, (but perhaps 'tis too much to ask) I should be glad to have them there; as it may prepare the Minds of those in Power for an Application that I believe will shortly be made from this Province to the Crown, to take the Government into its own Hands.[2] They talk of sending me over with it; but it will be too soon for me. At least I think so at present. Adieu, my dear Friend, and believe me ever Yours affectionately

B FRANKLIN

p.s. My Love to my young Wife,[3] and to Mrs. Strahan, Rachey, Billey, &c. &c. In your next tell me how you all do, and don't oblige me to come and see, before I am quite ready.

Mr Strahan

8. See below, p. 193–200.
9. The last letter from Strahan to BF that has been found is that of Aug. 18, 1763; see above, X, 324–31.
1. Undoubtedly *Pa. Gaz.*, March 29, 1764, which printed the messages that had passed between the governor and Assembly, March 14–24, concerning the passage of the £55,000 Supply Bill, and the Assembly Resolves of March 24. For the more important of these documents see above, pp. 111–33, Strahan reprinted them in *London Chron.*, June 12–14, 14–16, 1764.
2. See the document immediately above.
3. Strahan's youngest daughter, Margaret Penelope; for brief sketches of the Strahan children, see above, X, 169 n.

To Richard Jackson   ALS: American Philosophical Society

Dear Sir,   Philada. March 31. 1764

I wrote to you pretty largely on the 14th Instant,[4] and yesterday a small Letter[5] enclosing a Newspaper, with the late Proceedings of the House. In the former I acquainted you, that our first Money Bill was rejected by the Governor, and that the House would prepare another, which they accordingly did, and herewith you have a Copy of it. By that, and by the Messages, you will see why it did not pass. We are now in the utmost Confusion, Tumults threatned and daily expected, no Money to pay the Troops that have been some time raised, nor any likelihood of obtaining any; violent Animosities between the Presbyterians and Quakers, and nothing in which we seem generally to agree but the Wish for a King's Government.[6] I enclose you a Copy of the Petition, that is now handing about, and 'tis said will be pretty generally sign'd throughout the Province;[7] tho' some Pains are taken to prevent it, by frightning the Presbyterians and Quakers with the Bugbears of Bishops and Tythes as if they were necessary Consequences of a Royal Government.[8] For my own Part, I think it impossible to go on longer with the Proprietary Government; the Treatment given by the Governor to the House in return for their most respectful Behaviour towards him, showing the rooted Dislike of that Family to the People; and the sudden Flame in which they (the Assembly) broke out again, showing that the old Coals were only covered, and that the Ill-will is as fix'd as it is mutual: Whence continual Jarrs must arise, and of course Obstructions to all necessary Business. I there-

4. See above, pp. 105–9.
5. BF probably meant that he mailed his letter of March 29 "yesterday," March 30. See above, pp. 148–9.
6. Writing to Thomas Penn, March 17, 1764, Governor Penn reported that "there appears to be a greater spirit of opposition than ever, and I am persuaded they would go to any lengths to satisfy their inveterate malice, which seems to be more violent than ever against the Proprietary family." After mentioning the "scheme" of BF and his associates for a change of government, the governor added that "some of the members [of the Assembly] the other day were for pulling down the Arms over the Speakers Chair and putting up the King's in their Place." Penn Papers, Hist. Soc. Pa.
7. See above, pp. 145–7.
8. BF addressed himself to these "Bugbears" in his pamphlet *Cool Thoughts,* see below, pp. 162–9.

fore wish most devoutly for a Change, and join with our other Friends of the Assembly in requesting all your Endeavours and Interest in bringing it about. We confide in the Opinion you once gave on the Case stated, that our Privileges could not, on such a Change, be taken from us, but by Act of Parliament;[9] and we hope there will be no Necessity of Applying to Parliament on this Occasion, as an unfulfill'd Agreement still subsists, (if we are rightly inform'd) between the Crown and the Proprietary for the Sale of the Government for 11, or £12,000 (See W. Penn's Will[1]) of which £2000 has been paid; and much more than the Remainder must be in the Proprietaries Hands; as Half the Quit-Rents of the three Lower Counties belong to the Crown, and the Proprietaries are Collectors of the same for the Crown, and have never, as I have heard, accounted or paid anything:[2] So that the Agreement may easily be compleated. Tho' perhaps the Crown may, on Enquiry, find that the present Proprietaries have not the Right of Selling, as being the youngest Branch of the Penn Family; if so, Mr. Life[3] can probably tell where young Springet may be found, who no doubt would willingly surrender to the Crown for such a Sum; as he seems not able to contend for his Right. You will observe in the Resolves[4] the great Unanimity of the House. When they meet again in May, if the Petitions are generally sign'd, they will be sent to you accompanied by one from the House,[5] together with

9. For Jackson's opinion, April 24, 1758, see above, VIII, 19–21.

1. By a will, dated April 6, 1712, Penn devised the "Government of my Province of Pennsilvania and Territories thereunto belonging and all powers relateing thereunto" to three trustees "to dispose thereof to the Queen or any other person to the best advantage they can," the proceeds to be given as he directed further on in the will. This instrument gave rise to a prolonged and exceedingly complicated legal battle between Penn's heirs, one of the points at issue being whether the will did not invalidate a contract for the sale of the province which Penn had entered into with the Queen earlier in the year. The will of 1712 is printed in *PMHB*, XXI (1897), 151–3. See also William R. Shepherd, *History of Proprietary Government in Pennsylvania* (N.Y., 1896), pp. 198–201, and this volume, above, p. 148 n 7, and below, p. 172 n 5.

2. See below, p. 172 n 6.

3. For Thomas Life, a lawyer whom BF employed in a manner not yet clear to prove the title of Springett Penn to the government of Pa., see above, X, 369 n. For BF's dealings with Springett and his mother, Mrs. Ann Penn, see above, IX, 260–2, 315–17.

4. Those of March 24, 1764; see above, pp. 126–33.

5. See below, pp. 193–200.

some Cash. You can never, I am persuaded, do us any Service more acceptable, than procuring for us the desired Success to those Petitions.

I this day saw Mr. Daniel Coxe, and mention'd to him your Doubt of the Intention of their Proposals which he immediately explain'd as I understood it; and said that he should in a few Days see his Uncle (William Coxe) now in the Country, would mention the Matter to him, and they would write jointly and explicitly to you upon it.[6]

By the London Ship I sent you 20 of the Maryland Pamphlets.[7] Since the Ship sail'd, I receiv'd the enclos'd from Mr. Ringold, with some Errata, which they wish might be corrected with a Pen. Your Clerk can easily do it, if they are not distributed before this comes to hand. I send you their Supply-Bill also,[8] and the Messages relating to it. The Maryland Assembly will at their next Sitting, as I am told, agree to a Petition for a King's Government,[9] and I believe the Transacting that Matter will come into your Hands likewise. I mention this, that you may, if you think proper, be occasionally preparing Minds for both. Please to present my best Respects to the Speaker;[1] and believe me ever, with the greatest Esteem, Dear Sir, Your most obedient and most humble Servant   B Franklin

R. Jackson Esqr

Endorsed: 31st. Mar 1764 B: Franklin Esqr

6. See above, x, 370–1, and this volume, below, p. 185, for the confusion about the terms on which BF and Jackson were to participate in attempting to obtain royal confirmation for the Coxe family grant of "Carolana."

7. See above, p. 108 n.

8. A bill to grant £45,000 for military purposes, passed by the Maryland Lower House on April 9, 1762, but rejected by the Upper House. This bill provoked an exchange of bitter messages between the two bodies which occasioned the pamphlet referred to above.

9. Governor Sharpe's repeated prorogations of the Md. Assembly until Sept. 23, 1765, after the Stamp Act crisis had arisen, prevented action on such a petition.

1. Speaker of the House of Commons, Sir John Cust; above, x, 32 n.

From Francis Bernard   Letterbook copy: Harvard College Library

Sir   Boston, Ap 9. 1764
    I am favoured with yours of the 28th of March[2] and have or-
dered £12 12s. philadelphia currency to be paid to Mr. Williams
for which I am obliged to you. The present state of the College
here makes it more expedient to send my Son to philadelphia: but
I am desirous he may be boarded where he may be under a proper
restraint. I have heard that Dr. Ellison[3] takes boarders: I should
like to have him with the Doctor for whom I have a great regard:
I should be obliged to you if you would speak to him if it is proper,
and let me know his answer. Give me leave to trouble you to send
the inclosed by the first Vessel bound for Madeira.[4] I am &c.

B Franklin Esqr.

Cool Thoughts on the Present Situation
of Our Public Affairs

*Cool Thoughts on the Present Situation of Our Public Affairs. In a Letter
to a Friend in the Country.* Philadelphia: Printed by W. Dunlap. MDCCLXIV[5]
(Yale University Library).

The Resolves of March 24 and the assemblymen's immediate adjournment for seven weeks "in order to consult their Constituents" (above,
pp. 123-33) brought forcefully to public attention the project for a
formal appeal to the King to assume direct control of the government
of Pennsylvania. A vigorous campaign for support of the scheme began
almost at once, as did a similar campaign in opposition to it. Each side

2. See above, pp. 133-4.
3. For Francis Alison, vice-provost of the College of Philadelphia, see
above, IV, 470 n.
4. Apparently a letter to a mercantile house at Madeira; see below, p. 178.
5. The text also appeared with the same title in a supplement to the April
26, 1764, issue of *Pa. Jour.*, occupying a page and a half of a single sheet, the
remainder of which contained advertising. While the precise date of publication of the Dunlap pamphlet has not been determined, Hildeburn (1990) is
authority for the statement that the appearance in *Pa. Jour.* was the first
publication. Andrew Steuart of Philadelphia also published the piece in
pamphlet form in 1764 (Hildeburn 1991; Evans 9664). It is placed at this
point in the present volume because of the date line at the start of the text.

produced a series of articles and pamphlets in defense of its position and in attack upon its opponents' writings. Franklin's broadside *Explanatory Remarks on the Assembly's Resolves* (above, pp. 134-44), five days after the adjournment, seems to have opened the debate on behalf of the anti-proprietary party. At about the same time, or very soon afterwards, an anonymous pamphlet generally attributed to Hugh Williamson, called *The Plain Dealer, No. I,* appeared in support of the existing system of government and in strong attack on the Quakers.[6] It asserted, and undertook to show, that this faction was responsible for "almost all the contentions, and all the miseries under which we have so long struggled." A reply soon followed in the form of *An Address to the Freeholders and Inhabitants of the Province of Pennsylvania,* attributed to Joseph Galloway.[7] It pointed out that the Assembly had voted "upwards of £500,000" for defense during recent years, with a resulting annual tax on the inhabitants of 1s. 6d. per pound (7.5 percent) on the yearly value of their property; if there was a failure of defense, it was the fault of the governor, who had appointed the provincial military officers and had exercised general control of the actions of the troops.

Franklin re-entered the lists with his *Cool Thoughts.* This "Letter to a Friend in the Country" attempted both to explain the advantages Pennsylvania would attain by direct royal government and, more importantly perhaps, to convince doubters that the change would not deprive the inhabitants, especially those of non-Anglican religious affiliation, of any rights or privileges they already enjoyed under the existing system. To these ends Franklin cited the experiences of other colonies which had undergone somewhat similar changes from proprietary to royal government, and of Massachusetts, where the charter of 1691 had greatly increased the direct authority of the Crown.

Franklin's party gave this pamphlet and Galloway's *Address* wide circulation. Copies of *Cool Thoughts* were "thrown into the Houses of the several Inhabitants of the City" and both pamphlets "were distrib-

6. *The Plain Dealer: Or, A few Remarks upon Quaker-Politicks, And their Attempts to Change the Government Of Pennsylvania. With Some Observations on the false and abusive Papers which they have lately publish'd. Numb. I. To be continued.* Philadelphia: Printed Anno MDCCLXIV. (Hildeburn 2087; Evans 9875.) On Hugh Williamson, at this time professor of mathematics at the College of Philadelphia, see above, x, 266–7 n.

7. *An Address to the Freeholders and Inhabitants of the Province of Pennsylvania. In Answer to a Paper called The Plain Dealer.* Philadelphia: Printed and sold by Anthony Armbrüster, at the German and English Printing-Office; in Moravian-Alley, 1764. (Hildeburn 1942; Evans 9561.) Attacks in *Plain Dealer, No. III* (mentioned below) on the lawyer who wrote the *Address* point unmistakably to Galloway.

Cool Thoughts

ON THE

PRESENT SITUATION

OF OUR

PUBLIC AFFAIRS.

In a Letter to a Friend in the Country.

PHILADELPHIA:

PRINTED BY W. DUNLAP. M,DCC,LXIV.

uted gratis by thousands," according to critics. Two further issues of
The Plain Dealer undertook to respond.[8] *Plain Dealer, No. II,* carrying
a date line of May 7, 1764, probably written by someone other than
Williamson,[9] is a comparatively feeble effort, picking minor flaws in
Franklin's presentation and contributing little to the discussion of the
primary questions in the dispute. *Plain Dealer, No. III,* dated May 12,
certainly by the same author as *No. I,* is a much stronger piece. It presents a vigorous attack on the "Quaker Assemblymen" and other Quaker
leaders, guardedly but unmistakably identifying individuals and casti-
gating their actions, and it pointedly criticizes some of Franklin's arguments and his attempts to draw historical parallels. In order to present
as fairly as possible both sides of the dispute, so far as it had developed
by the middle of May, footnotes at appropriate points in Franklin's text
will give the gist of the principal replies to his argument.

A LETTER To A FRIEND In the COUNTRY.

Sir,   Philadelphia, April 12, 1764.

Your Apology was unnecessary. It will be no *Trouble,* but a *Pleasure,* if I can give you the Satisfaction you desire. I shall therefore
immediately communicate to you my Motives for approving the
Proposal of endeavouring to obtain a *Royal Government,* in Exchange for this of the Proprietaries; with such Answers to the Objections you mention, as, in my Opinion, fully obviate them.

8. *The Plain Dealer: Numb. II. being a Tickler, For the Leisure Hour's
Amusement of the Author of Cool Thoughts. Wherein the Force of his several
Arguments in Favour of a Change of Government is stated in a clear Light and
accommodated to the Comprehension of Readers of every Capacity. By X. Y. Z.
Gentleman. To be continued.* Philadelphia: Printed in Second-street, where
Numb. I. may be had. 1764. (Evans 9877.) *The Plain Dealer: or, Remarks on
Quaker Politicks in Pennsylvania. Numb. III. To be continued. By W. D.
Author of No. I.* Philadelphia: Printed Anno MDCCLXIV. (Evans 9878.)
Hildeburn cites both pamphlets at no. 2087, but without locating copies or
assigning separate identifying numbers. The first and third numbers of
Plain Dealer are reprinted in John R. Dunbar, ed., *The Paxton Papers* (The
Hague, 1957), pp. 339–51, 365–86, but the second is omitted. The quotations
in the sentence of the headnote immediately preceding the one to which this
note is attached are taken from *Plain Dealer, No. II* and *No. III* respectively.
9. An "Advertisement" at the front of *Plain Dealer, No. III,* thanks the
author of *No. II,* "As his E[n]deavours to prevent the Public from being
deceived by the Chicane of a Faction, prove him to be a Friend to the oppress'd Inhabitants of this Province." The first and third numbers are each
signed at the end "W.D."; the second was by "X.Y.Z."

I do not purpose entering into the Merits of the Disputes between the Proprietaries and the People: I only observe it as a Fact known to us all, that such Disputes there are, and that they have long subsisted, greatly to the Prejudice of the Province, clogging and embarrassing all the Wheels of Government, and exceedingly obstructing the publick Defence, and the Measures wisely concerted by our Gracious Sovereign, for the common Security of the Colonies. I may add it as another Fact, that *we are all heartily tired of these Disputes.*[1]

It is very remarkable, that Disputes of the same Kind have arisen in ALL Proprietary Governments, and subsisted till their Dissolution; All were made unhappy by them, and found no Relief but in recurring finally to the immediate Government of the Crown. Pennsylvania and Maryland, are the only Two of the Kind remaining and both at this Instant agitated by the same Contentions between Proprietary Interest and Power, and Popular Liberty.[2] Thro' these Contentions the good People of that Province are rendered equally unhappy with our selves, and their Proprietary, perhaps, more so than our's; for he has no Quakers in his Assembly to saddle with the Blame of those Contentions, nor can he justify himself with the Pretence, that turning to the Church has made his People his Enemies.

Pennsylvania had scarce been settled Twenty Years, when these Disputes began between the first Proprietor and the original Settlers; they continued, with some Intermissions, during his whole Life; his Widow took them up, and continued them after his Death. Her Sons resum'd them very early, (a) and they still sub-

(a) See their Message to the Assembly, in which the Right of sitting on their own Adjournments is denied.[3]

1. See below, p. 181, for BF's confession to Collinson of his weariness with the political disputes in Pa. *Plain Dealer, No. II,* commented acidly that if the writer was so tired, it seemed strange that he should write this piece, which was not designed to calm the minds of the people but rather to exasperate them against each other to such a further point of weariness that they would accept any remedy. The critic cited as an example of BF's inflammatory purpose his reference, at the end of the next paragraph, to Thomas Penn's abandonment of Quakerism in favor of the Church of England.

2. On BF's interest in the political controversies in Maryland and his willingness to assist the anti-proprietary party there, see above, VIII, 157–8, 162–8; IX, 386–91.

3. The particular message from the Proprietors to the Assembly referred

sist. Mischievous and distressing as they have been found to both Proprietors and People, it does not appear that there is any Prospect of their being extinguish'd, till either the Proprietary Purse is unable to support them, or the Spirit of the People so broken, that they shall be willing to submit to any Thing, rather than continue them. The first is not very likely to happen, as that immense Estate goes on increasing.[4]

Considering all Circumstances, I am at length inclin'd to think, that the Cause of these miserable Contentions is not to be sought for merely in the Depravity and Selfishness of human Minds. For tho' it is not unlikely that in these, as well as in other Disputes, there are *Faults on both Sides,* every glowing Coal being apt to inflame its Opposite; yet I see no Reason to suppose that all Proprietary Rulers are worse Men than other Rulers, nor that all People in Proprietary Governments are worse People than those in other Governments. I suspect therefore, that the Cause is radical, interwoven in the Constitution, and so become of the very Nature, of Proprietary Governments; and will therefore produce its Effects, as long as such Governments continue. And, as some Physicians say, every Animal Body brings into the World among its original Stamina, the Seeds of that Disease that shall finally produce its Dissolution; so the Political Body of a Proprietary Government, contains those convulsive Principles that will at length destroy it.[5]

---

to here has not been identified. William Penn's Charter of Privileges, 1701, gave the Assembly power to sit upon its own adjournments. A dispute over this power began in 1704 under Gov. John Evans and continued sporadically for many years, in spite of the fact that Penn had bound himself, his heirs and assigns, never to infringe or break any provision of the charter. William R. Shepherd, *History of Proprietary Government in Pennsylvania* (N.Y., 1896), pp. 295–6 n, 297–300, 312.

4. For the estimate of the proprietary estate and BF's remarks on it, printed in Richard Jackson's *Historical Review of the Constitution and Government of Pensylvania* in 1759, see above, VIII, 360–79. In commenting on this passage in *Cool Thoughts,* the author of *Plain Dealer, No. III,* asked: "Was it pardonable in him [BF] to represent the Proprietors estate ten, fifteen or perhaps twenty times as great as it really was, for it was said that he was the original author of this computation, which has since been published in the newspapers, in order to make the nation jealous of the Proprietors wealth."

5. *Plain Dealer, No. II,* wanted to know whether this analogy applied only to *proprietary* governments.

I may not be Philosopher enough to develop those Principles, nor would this Letter afford me Room, if I had Abilities, for such a discussion. The *Fact* seems sufficient for our Purpose, and the *Fact* is notorious, that such Contentions have been in all Proprietary Governments, and have brought, or are now bringing, them all to a Conclusion. I will only mention one Particular common to them all. Proprietaries must have a Multitude of private Accounts and Dealings with almost all the People of their Provinces, either for Purchase-money or Quit-rents. Dealings often occasion Differences, and Differences produce mutual Opinions of Injustice. If Proprietaries do not insist on small Rights, they must on the Whole lose large Sums; and if they do insist on small Rights, they seem to descend, their Dignity suffers in the Opinion of the People, and with it the Respect necessary to keep up the Authority of Government. The People, who think themselves injured in Point of Property, are discontented with the Government, and grow turbulent; and the Proprietaries using their Powers of Government to procure for themselves what they think Justice in their Points of Property, renders those Powers odious. I suspect this has had no small Share in producing the Confusions incident to those Governments. They appear, however, to be, *of all others,* the most unhappy.

At present we are in a wretched Situation.[6] The Government that ought to keep all in Order, is itself weak, and has scarce Authority enough to keep the common Peace. Mobs assemble and kill (we scarce dare say *murder*) Numbers of innocent People in cold Blood, who were under the Protection of the Government. Proclamations are issued to bring the Rioters to Justice. Those Proclamations are treated with the utmost Indignity and Contempt. Not a Magistrate dares wag a Finger towards discovering or apprehending the *Delinquents,* (we must not call them *Murderers*). They assemble again, and with Arms in their Hands, approach the Capital. The Government truckles, condescends to cajole them, and drops all Prosecution of their Crimes; whilst honest Citizens, threatened in their Lives and Fortunes, flie the Province, as having no Confidence in the Publick Protection. We are daily threatened with more of these Tumults; and the Government, which in its

6. For some account of the events referred to here—the massacres of the Conestoga Indians and the march of the Paxton Boys on Philadelphia—and documents relating thereto, see above, pp. 22–30, 42–75.

Distress call'd aloud on the sober Inhabitants to come with Arms to its Assistance, now sees those who afforded that Assistance daily libell'd, abus'd, and menac'd by its Partizans for so doing; whence it has little Reason to expect such Assistance on another Occasion: In this Situation, what is to be done? By what Means is that Harmony between the two Branches of Government to be obtain'd, without which the internal Peace of the Province can not be well secured? One Project is, to turn all Quakers out of the Assembly; or, by obtaining more Members for the Back Counties, to get a Majority in, who are not Quakers. This, perhaps, is not very difficult to do; and more Members for those Counties may, on other Accounts, be proper; but I much question if it would answer this End, as I see among the Members, that those who are not Quakers, and even those from the Back Counties, are as hearty and unanimous in opposing what they think Proprietary Injustice, as the Quakers themselves, if not more so.[7] Religion has happily nothing to do with our present Differences, tho' great Pains is taken to lug it into the Squabble.[8] And even were the Quakers extirpated, I doubt whether the Proprietaries, while they pursue the same Measures, would be a Whit more at their Ease. Another Project is, to chuse none for Assembly-men but such as are Friends to the Proprietaries. The Number of Members is not so great, but that I believe this Scheme may be practicable, if you look for Repre-

7. Of the three assemblymen who asked to have their reasons for voting against the petition for royal government recorded in the minutes on May 28 (see below, p. 198), two were from "Back Counties": Isaac Saunders from Lancaster and John Montgomery from Cumberland; the third was John Dickinson from Philadelphia Co., who became the foremost spokesman for the opponents of a change in the government. While the names of the individuals who voted for the petition ("a great Majority") are not recorded and some other "Back County" members may have abstained from voting, it may be observed that none of the eight others from those areas protested against the petition.

8. While believing that the disputes were fundamentally political, not religious, BF was perfectly aware that religious affiliations were important factors in the party alignments and that many inhabitants were fearful that a change to royal government would endanger the complete liberty of conscience and worship solemnly and perpetually guaranteed by William Penn in the Charter of Privileges of 1701. Hence, in spite of his disclaimer that religion played a part in "our present Differences," BF devoted a large part of this pamphlet to a discussion of religious matters.

sentatives among Proprietary Officers and Dependants. Undoubtedly it would produce great Harmony between Governor and
Assembly: But how would both of them agree with the People?
Their Principles and Conduct must greatly change, if they would
be elected a second Year. But that might be needless. Six Parts in
Seven agreeing with the Governor, could make the House per-
petual.[9] This, however, would not probably establish Peace in the
Province. The Quarrel the People now have with the Proprie-
taries, would then be with both the Proprietaries and Assembly.
There seems to remain then but one Remedy for our Evils, a
Remedy approved by Experience, and which has been tried with
Success by other Provinces; I mean that of an immediate ROYAL
GOVERNMENT, without the Intervention of Proprietary Powers,
which, like unnecessary Springs and Movements in a Machine,
are so apt to produce Disorder.

It is not to be expected that the Proposal of a Change like this,
should meet with no Objections. Those you have mention'd to me
concerning Liberty of Conscience and the Privileges of Dissenters,
are, however, not difficult to answer; as they seem to arise merely
from want of Information, or Acquaintance with the State of other
Colonies, before and after such Changes had been made in their
Government. Carolina and the Jerseys, were formerly Proprietary
Governments, but now immediately under the Crown; and their
Cases had many Circumstances similar to ours. Of the First we
are told,

"There was a natural Infirmity in the Policy of their Charter,
which was the Source of many of the Misfortunes of the Colony,
without any Imputation on the noble Families concern'd. For the
Grantees, [the Proprietors][1] being eight in Number, and not incorporated, and no Provision being made to conclude the whole
Number by the Voices of the Majority, there could not be timely
Measures always agreed on, which were proper or necessary for
the good Government of the Plantation. In the mean Time the
Inhabitants grew unruly and quarrelled about Religion and Poli-

9. The Charter of Privileges provided that no change might be made in
any of its provisions except by the consent of the governor "and *Six* Parts of
Seven of the Assembly met." It went on to prohibit completely any alteration
in the guarantee of liberty of conscience, even by this method of amendment.

1. Brackets are BF's.

ticks; and while there was a mere Anarchy among them, they were expos'd to the Attacks and Insults of their Spanish and Indian Neighbours, whom they had imprudently provok'd and injur'd; and as if they had conspir'd against the Growth of the Colony, they repealed their Laws for Liberty of Conscience, though the Majority of the People were Dissenters, and had resorted thither under the publick Faith for a compleat Indulgence, which they considered as Part of their *Magna Charta*. Within these four Years an End was put to their Sorrows; for about that Time, the Lords Proprietors and the Planters, (who had long been heartily tir'd of each other) were, by the Interposition of the Legislature, fairly divorced for ever, and the Property of the Whole vested in the Crown."* And the above-mention'd injudicious and unjust Act, against the Privileges of Dissenters, was repeal'd by the King in Council.[3]

Another Historian tells us, "Their intestine Distractions, and their foreign Wars, kept the Colony so low, that an Act of Parliament, if possible to prevent the last ruinous Consequences of these

New and accurate Account of Carolina, p. 14. Printed at London, 1733.[2]

2. *A New and Accurate Account of the Provinces of South-Carolina and Georgia* (London, 1733). The quotation is from pp. 14–16 of the 1733 edition. Authorship has been attributed both to General James Oglethorpe and to Benjamin Martyn; for a discussion see Verner W. Crane, "The Promotion Literature of Georgia," *Bibliographical Essays A Tribute to Wilberforce Eames* (n.p., 1924), pp. 288–91. The "four Years" mentioned near the end of the quotation were to be reckoned backward from the writing of the pamphlet on Carolina, making the date in question 1729, when the proprietorship was terminated.

3. In 1704, at a time of violent religious animosities in So. Car., the Assembly passed two laws: one specified that only communicants of the Church of England be eligible for membership in that body, and the other established the Church of England, laid out parishes, and created a lay commission of twenty members with power to remove from his rectorship "any immoral or imprudent clergyman." The dissenters sent an agent to England, and he applied to the Proprietors, who were headed by an ardent Tory, for repeal of these laws. Getting no satisfaction, he appealed to the strongly Whig House of Lords, which thereupon addressed Queen Anne against the acts, and she directed the Proprietors to order the repeal. The Assembly obeyed in 1706. The affair is described in considerable detail in Edward McCrady, *The History of South Carolina under the Proprietary Government 1670–1719* (N.Y., 1897), pp. 402–51.

Divisions, put the Province under the immediate Care and Inspection of the Crown."†

And Governor JOHNSON,[5] at his first meeting the Assembly there, after the Change, tells them, "His Majesty, out of his great Goodness and Fatherly Care of you, and at the earnest Request and Solicitation of your selves, has been graciously pleased, at a great Expence, to purchase seven Eights of the late Lords Proprietaries Charter, whereby you are become under his immediate Government; a BLESSING and SECURITY we have been *long praying for,* and solicitous of; the *good Effects* of which we *daily experience* by the *Safety* we enjoy, as well in our Trade, by the Protection of his Ships of War, as by Land, by an Independant Company maintain'd purely for our Safety and Encouragement. The taking off the Enumeration of Rice, is a peculiar Favour, &c."‡

By these Accounts we learn, that the People of that Province, far from losing by the Change, obtain'd internal Security and external Protection, both by Sea and Land; the Dissenters a Restoration and Establishment of their Privileges, which the Proprietary Government attempted to deprive them of; and the whole Province, Favours in point of Trade with respect to their grand Staple Commodity, which from that Time they were allowed to carry directly to foreign Ports, without being oblig'd, as before, to enter in England.[7]

†*Account of the British Settlements in America.* Page 233 *concerning Carolina.*[4]

‡HISTORICAL REGISTER, No. 63, for 1731.[6]

4. *An Account of the European Settlements in America* (2 vols., London, 1757), II, 233. The author is believed to have been William Burke (1729–1798), for whom see above, IX, 53 n.

5. Robert Johnson (*c.*1676–1735), proprietary governor of the Carolinas, 1717–19, and royal governor of South Carolina, 1730–35. He was the son of Sir Nathaniel Johnson, the governor under whom the obnoxious acts of 1704 had been passed. *DAB.*

6. *The Historical Register, Containing An Impartial Relation of all Transactions, Foreign and Domestick,* XVI (For the Year 1731), no. 63, p. 179. Rice, an enumerated commodity, was allowed in 1730 (3. Geo. II, c. 29) to be exported from Carolina directly to European ports south of Cape Finisterre, paying a duty equal to the import duty in England less the drawback allowable on reexportation.

7. Both *Plain Dealer, No. II* and *No. III* denied that the South Carolina case was relevant to the situation in Pennsylvania. The former pointed out

With regard to the neighbouring Province of New-Jersey, we find, in a Representation from the Board of Trade to the Crown, dated Whitehall, Oct. 2, 1701, the following Account of it, *viz.* "That the Inhabitants in a Petition to his Majesty the last Year, complained of several Grievances they lay under by the Neglect or Mismanagement of the Proprietors of that Province, or their Agents; . . . unto which they also added, that during the whole Time the said Proprietors have govern'd, or pretended to govern, that Province, they have never taken care to preserve or defend the same from the Indians, or other Enemies, by *sending* or *providing* any Arms, Ammunition or Stores, *as they ought to have done;* and the said Inhabitants thereupon humbly prayed, his Majesty would be pleased to commissionate some fit Person, to be Governor over them. That it has been represented to us by several Letters, Memorials and other Papers, as well from the Inhabitants as Proprietors; that they are at present in *Confusion* and *Anarchy,* and that it is much to be apprehended, lest by the Heats of the Parties that are amongst them, they should fall into such Violences, as may endanger the Lives of many Persons; and destroy the Colony."(*b*)

(*b*) *Grants* and *Concessions,* and *original Constitutions* of *New-Jersey,* printed at Philadelphia by W. Bradford. p. 606.[8]

---

that an essential weakness in the Carolina situation had been that the eight Proprietors were always quarreling among themselves, while Thomas and Richard Penn were always in agreement. The writer of *No. III* explained that "The Government of Carolina was changed because there was *a natural Infirmity in the Policy of their Charter.* But the philosopher has not discovered any such infirmity in our charter, and yet he sayd the cases are similar." BF's point, of course, was primarily that the British government had firmly opposed an attempt to deprive dissenters of their privileges, as well as that the colony as a whole had benefited from the change in government.

8. Aaron Leaming and Jacob Spicer, *The Grants, Concessions, and Original Constitutions Of the Province of New Jersey* (Phila., [1752]). The full text of this rather long representation recommending assumption of the government by the Crown is also printed in 1 *N.J. Arch.,* II, 420–7; the passage quoted here is on pp. 423–4. Besides some minor omissions of phrases and changes in spelling, capitalization, etc., BF failed to indicate in the first sentence quoted that the petition summarized was from the inhabitants of East New Jersey only, not from both parts of the area. More importantly, he omitted several lines complaining of the Proprietors' complete neglect during time of war, 1689–92, so that there was neither adequate civil government nor military leadership for defense. He indicated this omission by a series of hyphens, here replaced by the ellipsis.

In Consequence of these Disorders, and Petitions from the People, the Proprietors were oblig'd to surrender that Government to the Crown; Queen Anne then reigning; who of all our Crowned Heads since the Revolution, was by far the least favourable to Dissenters; yet her Instructions to Lord Cornbury, her first Governor, were express and full in their Favour,[9] *viz.* INSTR. 51."You are to permit a Liberty of Conscience to all Persons, (except Papists) so that they may be contented with a quiet and peaceable Enjoyment of the same, not giving Offence or Scandal to the Government."[1]

INSTR. 52. "And whereas we have been informed that divers of our good Subjects inhabiting those Parts, do make a religious Scruple of Swearing, and by reason of their refusing to take an Oath in any Court of Justice and other Places, are or may be liable to many Inconveniencies, our Will and Pleasure is, that in Order to their Ease in what they conceive to be Matter of Conscience, so far as may be consistent with good Order and Government, you take Care that an Act be passed in the General Assembly of our said Province, to the like Effect as that passed here in the Seventh and Eighth Years of his late Majesty's Reign, entitled, *An* ACT *that the solemn Affirmation and Declaration of the People called Quakers,*[2] *shall be accepted instead of an Oath in the usual Form;* and that the same be transmitted to us, and to our Commissioners for Trade and Plantations, as before directed."[3]

INSTR. 53. "And whereas we have been farther informed, that in the Settlement of the Government of our said Province, it may so

9. The complete set of instructions issued to Lord Cornbury and dated Nov. 16, 1702, is printed in 1 *N.J. Arch.,* II, 506–36. The three printed below are on pp. 522–3.

1. This is the standard form of the instruction on liberty of conscience given regularly to the royal governors of nearly all colonies from about 1680 on, although the words "except Papists" were always omitted during the reign of James II and in Maryland until 1703. Other instructions, however, granting tolerance to Roman Catholics were given to governors of colonies taken from France or Spain in the eighteenth century. Leonard W. Labaree, ed., *Royal Instructions to British Colonial Governors 1670–1776* (N.Y., [1935]), II, 494–502. There is no reason to suppose that there would have been any deviation from the standard form had Pa. come under the Crown.

2. 7 and 8 William III, c. 34.

3. This instruction was repeated unchanged to N.J. governors until 1732, when it was dropped, laws covering this matter having recently been enacted.

happen, that the Number of Inhabitants fitly qualified to serve in our Council, in the General Assembly, and in other Places of Trust and Profit there, will be but small; it is therefore our Will and Pleasure, that such of the said People called Quakers, as shall be found capable of any of those Places and Employments, and accordingly be elected or appointed to serve therein, may, upon their taking and signing the Declaration of Allegiance to us, in the Form used by the same People here in England, together with a solemn Declaration for the true Discharge of their respective Trusts, be admitted by you into any of the said Places or Employments &c.*"(c)*

And the same Privileges have been, and still are, fully enjoy'd in that Province by Dissenters of all Kinds; the Council, Assembly, and Magistracy, being fill'd with Episcopalians, Presbyterians and Quakers, promiscuously, without the least Distinction or Exclusion of any.[5] We may farther remark, on the above Report of the Board of Trade, That the Defence of a Proprietary Province was originally look'd upon as *the Duty of the Proprietaries,* who receiv'd the Quit-rents, and had the Emoluments of Government; whence it was, that in former Wars, when Arms, Ammunition, Cannon, and Military Stores of all Kinds, have been sent by the Crown to all the Colonies under its immediate Government, whose Situation and Circumstances requir'd it; nothing of the Kind has been sent to Proprietary Governments. And to this Day, neither Pennsylvania nor Maryland have receiv'd any such Assistance from the Crown; nor did Carolina, till it became a King's Government.

Massachusetts-Bay, in New-England, lost its Charter in the latter End of King CHARLES's Reign, when the Charters of London, and all the Corporations in England, were seized. At the Revolution the Crown gave them a better Constitution, which they enjoy to this Day: No Advantages were taken against the Privileges of

(c) Grants and Concessions, &c. page 633.[4]

4. This instruction was repeated virtually unchanged to N.J. governors until 1758, when it was dropped, presumably because it was obsolete and its subject matter already covered by law.

5. *Plain Dealer, No. III,* summarily dismissed BF's use of the N.J. example, commenting that "When the New-Jersey Government was changed, Queen Ann favoured Dissenters and allowed them to hold places of trust in the Government. But she did this because there were not other people enough to fill those places, which is not the present case with Pennsylvania."

the People, tho' then universally *Dissenters*. The same Privileges are enjoy'd by the Dissenters in New-Hampshire, which has been a Royal Government ever since 1679, when the Freeholders and Inhabitants petition'd to be taken under the immediate Protection of the Crown.[6] Nor is there existing in any of the American Colonies, any *Test* imposed by Great-Britain, to exclude *Dissenters* from Offices. In some Colonies, indeed, where the Episcopalians and in others, the Dissenters, have been predominant, they have made partial Laws in favour of their respective Sects, and lay'd some Difficulties on the others; but those Laws have been, generally, on Complaint, repealed at home.

It is farther objected, you tell me, that *if we have a Royal Government, we must have with it a Bishop, and a Spiritual Court, and must pay Tythes to support an Episcopal Clergy*. A Bishop for America has been long talk'd of in England, and probably from the apparent Necessity of the Thing, will sooner or later be appointed; because a Voyage to England for Ordination is extreamly inconvenient and expensive to the young Clergy educated in America; and the Episcopal Churches and Clergy in these Colonies cannot so conveniently be governed and regulated by a Bishop residing in England, as by one residing among these committed to his Care. But this Event will happen neither sooner nor later for our being, or not being, under a Royal Government. And the Spiritual Court, if the Bishop should hold one, can have Authority only with his own People, if with them, since it is not likely that any Law of this

6. This is, of course, an extremely simplified account of the transition to royal participation in the government of both these New England colonies. In Mass. the charter of 1691 guaranteed liberty of conscience to all Christians, except Papists. The New Hamp. governors' instructions from 1692 on and those of Mass. governors from 1701 followed the identical form as No. 51 to Cornbury of N.J., quoted above. The Crown did not interfere with Mass. laws requiring tax support of the "orthodox" (Congregational) churches; over a period of years, however, these were gradually relaxed to permit members of other religious bodies to divert their taxes to support their own ministers. The last vestiges of an established church in Mass. disappeared only in 1833. *Plain Dealer, No. III*, commented that Mass. lost its charter "because all charters were then taken away, and they obtained a new one of course; and for our great comfort we are informed that in their new charter no advantages were taken, nor tests imposed on them. Is not this drol enough: How in the name of sense, could tests have been imposed on a people who were every one Dissenters?"

Province will ever be made to submit the Inhabitants to it, or oblige them to pay Tithes; and without such Law, Tithes can no more be demanded here than they are in any other Colony; and there is not a single Instance of *Tithes* demanded or paid in any Part of America. A Maintenance has, indeed, been established in some Colonies, for the Episcopal Clergy; as in Virginia, a Royal Government; and in Maryland, a Proprietary Government: But this was done by Acts of their own, which they were not oblig'd to make if they did not chuse it.[7]

That *we shall have a standing Army to maintain,* is another Bugbear rais'd to terrify us from endeavouring to obtain a King's Government. It is very possible that the Crown may think it necessary to keep Troops in America henceforward, to maintain its Conquests, and defend the Colonies; and that the Parliament may establish some Revenue arising out of the American Trade to be apply'd towards supporting those Troops.[8] It is possible too, that we may, after a few Years Experience, be generally very well satisfy'd with that Measure, from the steady Protection it will afford us against Foreign Enemies, and the Security of internal Peace among ourselves without the Expence or Trouble of a Militia. But assure yourself, my Friend, that whether we like it or not, our

7. Proposals for the appointment of one or more Anglican bishops in the colonies had appeared sporadically for many years. After a period of dormancy, active discussion revived in the early 1760s and rumors, some much exaggerated, began to spread. Increased activity among missionaries of the Society for the Propagation of the Gospel and the indiscretions and militancy of some of these men gave credence to the reports and aroused the antagonism of many ministers and laymen of other faiths. Fears, largely unjustified, grew that the prospective bishops would promote the formal establishment of the Anglican Church in colonies where it held no such position, that the bishops would receive support from public funds, and that they would attempt to exercise some degree of ecclesiastical jurisdiction over other ministers as well as over their own clergymen. This agitation, which persisted through several years, added to the tensions between the colonies and the British government that the Stamp Act and later legislation produced. For treatment of this subject, see Arthur L. Cross, *The Anglican Episcopate and the American Colonies* (N.Y., 1902), pp. 139–262; and more recently, Carl Bridenbaugh, *Mitre and Sceptre Transatlantic Faiths, Ideas, Personalities, and Politics 1689–1775* (N.Y., 1962), esp. pp. 207–59.

8. Richard Jackson had twice assured BF during the winter that a parliamentary tax of some sort would be levied on the colonies to support the British troops there. See above, X, 415, and this volume, p. 35.

continuing under a Proprietary Government will not prevent it, nor our coming under a Royal Government promote and forward it, any more than they would prevent or procure Rain or Sunshine.[9]

The other Objections you have communicated to me, are, that *in case of a Change of Proprietary for Royal Government, our Judges and other Officers will be appointed and sent us from England, we must have a Legislative Council; our Assembly will lose the Right of Sitting on their own Adjournments; we shall lose the Right of chusing Sheriffs, and annual Assemblies, and of voting by Ballot.* I shall not enter into the Question, whether Judges from England would probably be of Advantage or Disadvantage to our Law Proceedings. It is needless, as the Power of appointing them is given to the Governor here, by a Law that has receiv'd the Royal Assent, the *Act for establishing Courts.* The King's Governor only comes in Place of a Proprietary Governor; he must (if the Change is made) take the Government as he finds it. He can alter nothing. The same Answer serves for all the subsequent Objections.[1] A Legislative Council under proper Regulations might perhaps be an Amendment of our Constitution, but it cannot take Place without our Consent, as our Constitution is otherwise establish'd; nor can our Assembly lose the *Right of Sitting on their own Adjournments;* nor the People that of *chusing Sheriffs, and annual Assemblies,* or of *Voting by Ballot.* These Rights being all confirm'd by Acts of Assembly assented to by the Crown. I mean the Acts entitled *An Act to ascertain the Number of Members of Assembly and to regulate the Elections;* and *An Act for Regulating the Elections of Sheriffs and Coroners;* both past in the 4th of Queen Anne. I know it has been asserted, to intimidate us, that those Acts, so far from being approved by the Crown, were never presented. But I can assure you, from good Authority, that they, with forty-eight others (all pass'd at the same Time by Governor Evans,) were duly laid before the

9. BF was, of course, perfectly correct on this point. The Stamp Act of 1765 and the Townshend duties of 1767 applied equally to all American colonies, whether royal or proprietary, or completely self-governing as were R.I. and Conn.

1. In giving such a categorical assurance, BF undoubtedly relied on the legal opinion Richard Jackson had delivered to him, April 24, 1758, on the effect royal assumption of government might have on the constitution of Pa. Jackson had declared that only "by an Act of Parliament and by no other Authority in Great Britain" could any of these alterations be made. Above, VIII, 20–1.

Queen in Council; who on the 28th of April 1709 referred the same to the Board of Trade. The Board on the 8th of September 1709, reported upon the said Fifty Acts, that they had considered the same, and had taken the Opinion of the Attorney General upon several of them in point of Law; and they represented against Six of them, as unfit to be continued in force; but as to the other forty-four, the Titles of which are given at large, and among them the two *material Acts* above mentioned, they had *no Objection* to the same. Whereupon there issued two Orders of the Queen in Council both dated at the Court at Windsor, the 24th of October 1709, one repealing the Six Laws objected to; and the other, approving the remaining Forty-four. This is a Fact that you may depend upon.[2] There is therefore nothing now that can deprive us of those Privileges but an Act of Parliament; and we may rely on the united Justice of King, Lords, and Commons, that no such Act will ever pass, while we continue loyal and dutiful Subjects. An Act of Assembly, indeed may give them up; but I trust, urgent as they are for Admission, we shall never see Proprietary Friends enow in the House, to make that detestable Sacrifice.[3]

In fine, it does not appear to me, that this *Change of Government* can possibly hurt us; and I see many Advantages that may flow from it. The expression, *Change of Government,* seems, indeed, to be too extensive; and is apt to give the Idea of a general and total Change of our Laws and Constitution. It is rather and only a *Change of Governor,* that is, instead of self-interested Proprietaries, a gracious King! His Majesty who has no Views but for the Good of the People will thenceforth appoint the Governor, who, unshackled by Proprietary Instructions, will be at Liberty to join with the Assembly in enacting wholesome Laws. At present, when

2. See above, VIII, 15, 62 n, 400–1. BF had reported to Isaac Norris that WF had found these laws duly entered in the books of the Board of Trade and certified by Governor Evans and Secretary Logan.

3. Neither issue of *Plain Dealer* commented specifically on matters BF discussed in this and the two paragraphs immediately preceding; *No. III* dismissed BF's answers to all the objections he discussed by asserting without further argument: "But whatever precedents the Philosopher has quoted, and whatever evasive answers he has given to some small objections, yet he is most firmly assured that if our Government should now be changed we must loose a great many valuable privileges." Much of the rest of *No. III* was devoted to answering assertions made in the Galloway pamphlet.

the King requires Supplies of his faithful Subjects, and they are willing and desirous to grant them, the Proprietaries intervene and say, *unless our private Interests in certain Particulars are served,* NOTH-ING SHALL BE DONE. This insolent Tribunitial VETO,[4] has long encumbered all our Publick Affairs, and been productive of many Mischiefs. By the Measure proposed, not even the Proprietaries can justly complain of any Injury. The being oblig'd to fulfill a fair Contract is no Injury. The Crown will be under no Difficulty in compleating the old Contract made with their Father,[5] as there needs no Application to Parliament for the necessary Sum, since half the Quit-Rents of the Lower Counties belongs to the King, and the many Years Arrears in the Proprietaries Hands, who are the Collectors, must vastly exceed what they have a Right to demand, or any Reason to expect.*

On the whole, I cannot but think, the more the Proposal is considered, of *an humble Petition to the* KING, *to take this Province under his Majesty's immediate Protection and Government,* the more unanimously we shall go into it. We are chiefly People of *three Countries:* British Spirits can no longer bear the Treatment they have received,

*In 1722 the Arrears then in their Hands were computed at £18,000 *Sterling.*[6]

4. In the Roman republic the two tribunes had the right to exercise an absolute veto over legislation passed by the Senate.

5. William Penn offered to surrender the government to the Crown in 1703, but agreement on terms proved difficult, and sporadic negotiations continued until 1712. A deed of surrender was then drawn up according to which Penn received £1000 of a promised total of £12,000. But Penn suffered a stroke which rendered him nearly helpless, financial differences with holders of a mortgage on the property occurred, and the agreement had not been completely executed at the time of his death in 1718. His heirs later decided to drop the entire proposal. Shepherd, *Proprietary Government in Pennsylvania,* pp. 540–4; Louise P. Kellogg, "The American Colonial Charter," Amer. Hist. Assn. *Annual Report* for 1903, I, 240–4; Winfred T. Root, *The Relations of Pennsylvania with the British Government, 1696–1766* (N.Y., 1912), pp. 354–64.

6. The legal status of Penn's claim to the Delaware counties was never fully resolved and the right to the quitrents remained equally unclear. *Plain Dealer, No. III,* was scornful of BF's estimate that £18,000 arrears in quitrents were in the Proprietors' hands in 1722: "I conceive it may be prov'd, for reasons well known, that the Proprietor has never received £5000 quit rents from all the Lower counties. And the half of 5 is not quite 18. But to oblige the Philosopher, I shall grant that it is 20. Yet I am certain the Philosopher knows very well that the Government will never be purchased for twice that sum."

nor will they put on the Chains prepared for them by a Fellow Subject. And the Irish and Germans have felt too severely the Oppressions of *hard-hearted Landlords* and *arbitrary Princes,* to wish to see, in the Proprietaries of Pennsylvania, both the one and the other united.

I am, with much Respect, Sir, Your most obedient humble Servant.

A.B.[7]

To [Peter Collinson?][8]

ALS: Charles E. Feinberg, Detroit, Michigan (1960)

Dear Sir   Philada. April 12. 1764

We have just now receiv'd the following Advice from Northampton County, viz.

One David Owens, a Soldier belonging to the Regulars, but

7. Writing to Thomas Penn, May 5, a few weeks after the publication of this pamphlet, Gov. John Penn paid his respects to BF: "Mr: Franklin may be consider'd as the chief Cause of this faction being carried to it's present height, for it is observ'd by every body that while he was in England there was at least an appearance of Peace and Quietness, but Since his return, the old Sparks are again blown up and at present the flame rages with more violence than ever. I really believe there never will be any prospect of ease or happiness here, while that Villain has the liberty of Spreading about the poison of that inveterate Malice and ill Nature, which is so deeply implanted in his own black heart. He certainly looks upon Mischief, in the light other people do upon Virtue, as carrying with it its own reward. This is the best way I can account for his present Politicks." Penn Papers, Hist. Soc. Pa.

8. The recipient is so identified because the notes following BF's signature are certainly in Collinson's handwriting. The "A Pedagoge," which appears in the lower left-hand corner of the first page, where the name of the person addressed was often placed in eighteenth-century letters, including BF's, is highly puzzling. It is not in BF's hand, and only possibly in Collinson's; no person of that or a similar name is known among BF's correspondents, nor can any schoolmaster be suggested to whom this letter might have been sent. Against the identification of Collinson as the intended recipient of this letter are its formality of address, close, and general tone, as compared, for example, with BF's letter of April 30, 1764 (below, pp. 180–3), and the fact that the later communication makes no reference to the earlier one or its subject matter. Perhaps someone else in England received this letter and passed it along to Collinson, who then added the notes at the end. Alternatively, the final sentence of this letter suggests the possibility that BF, writing as one of the provincial commissioners, was addressing one of the governmental officials in Pa., but this suggestion leaves unanswered the question of how the letter got to Collinson.

deserted sometime since to the Indians, came in last Week to Capt. Carns's Post and deliver'd himself up.[9] He brought with him a white Boy that had been taken Prisoner by the Indians last Fall, when they kill'd the People in the Flat upon Delaware; and also five fresh Indian Scalps. The Account given by him and the Boy is, that they were with a Party of nine Indians to wit, 5 Men, 2 Women, and 2 Children, coming down Sasquehanah to fetch Corn from their last Year's Planting Place; that they went ashore and encamp'd at Night, and made a Fire by which they slept; that in the Night Owens made the white Boy get up from among the Indians, and go to the other side of the Fire; and then taking up the Indians Guns, he shot two of the Men immediately, and with his Hatchet dispatch'd another Man together with the Women and Children. Two Men only made their Escape. Owens scalp'd the 5 grown Persons, and bid the white Boy scalp the Children; but he declin'd it; so they were left. He reports that the Indians were assembling in great Numbers when he left them. I am, Sir, Your most obedient Servant   B FRANKLIN

A Pedagoge

22d: Sent Henton Brown the Gazett   June 2: 1764[1]

The Above Bloody Scheme of D: Owen to Atone for His Desertion is very Shocking. What must the Five Indian Nations Think of the White Men Who Vie with them in Cruelties.[2]

9. Owens' story, confirmed by Sir William Johnson, was that he had been a corporal in Capt. McClean's independent company in N.Y., had deserted and been captured, and lived among the Indians on the Susquehanna for four years. Governor Penn sent him to Col. Henry Bouquet on April 26, 1764. Bouquet and Sir William Johnson later used him as an interpreter. Sylvester K. Stevens and Donald H. Kent, eds., *The Papers of Col. Henry Bouquet,* XV (Harrisburg, 1942), 114, 116; *Johnson Papers,* IV, 586, 620; XI, 224–5, 241, 439, 451, 460; *Pa. Col. Recs.,* IX, 188–92, 215–22, 228.

1. The "22d" at the beginning of this line may mean that Collinson sent one or more issues of *Pa. Gaȝ.* to Brown on the 22d of some unspecified month. Henton Brown and his son James were BF's London bankers; see above, IX, 218 n. Since there was no issue of *Pa. Gaȝ.* on June 2, 1764, this date probably indicates when Collinson wrote his notes.

2. While the Iroquois may have been displeased at Owens' behavior, the Delaware and Shawnee Indians concerned were not their responsibility, and they would hardly have been shocked by his actions. For a report of a later murder of an Indian attributed to Owens, see below, p. 528.

174

From Richard Jackson

AL (incomplete): American Philosophical Society

[April 13, 1764][3]

[*First part missing*] K.William. I send you a List of Papers I found entered in Books in 1699 besides these there is a long Memorial of Dr. Coxes in 1719[4] I suppose just before his Death, to the B of T pressing much to have his claim insisted on at the Court of France by the Commisssary then going there on the Subject of Ste Lucie &c. This Memorial contains much the same Matter as his former Paper and his printed Book and as it says not a Word of K. Williams Grant it is impossible to suppose such a grant exists. No Instruction was given to the Commissarys on this Head. I then looked over the Instruction.

I do not however quite give up the Claim, whatever may become of our Project, but as I am satisfied that after the length of Time elapsed since the grant to Sir Robert Heath, and the Settlement of the Carolinas in the Country granted, it is too hazardous (especially since the Determination of the Council on Lord Cadigans Claim to St. Lucie and St. Vincent) to venture a Petition on the meer Rights.[5] I think it most Advisable to put the Claim on foot in

3. On June 18, 1764, BF acknowledged the receipt of Jackson's letter of April 13, 1764, and it seems almost certain that the present fragment is a part of that letter. It was certainly written later than March 26, 1764, because it mentions the Privy Council's decision on Lord Cardigan's claim, which was handed down on that date. Supporting the assumption that the fragment was written in April is Jackson's statement that he returned to his seat in Parliament about "a fortnight before the House was to rise," its date of adjournment being April 19, 1764, and found a bill forbidding the American colonies to issue legal-tender paper currency lying before the House (at least this is what one strongly infers to have been his meaning). Such a bill was introduced in Parliament on April 4 and passed on April 19, 1764. See Lewis B. Namier, "Charles Garth," *English Historical Review*, LIV (1939), 640.

4. For Jackson's efforts to confirm the claim of the descendants of Dr. Daniel Coxe to "Carolana," a venture in which BF was also involved, see above, X, 368–70.

5. The application of the Earl of Egmont for a grant of the island of St. John (Prince Edward Island) in the Gulf of St. Lawrence and the petition of the Earl of Cardigan for recognition of claims to St. Lucia and St. Vincent (above, X, 414) provoked a brief controversy in *London Chron.*, Feb. 11–14, 14–16, 1764, on the desirability of colonial proprietorships in general, with the Penn family and its alleged great estate prominently mentioned. Perhaps

Conversation, where it may never reach those who have laid down Principles inconsistent with Mr. Coxe's Claim and if we can but remove (which I Hope I see a prospect of) the Prepossessions against Settlements on the Mississippi and in what is called the back Country, I hope a Project for a Settlement on that River may be approved and the Title of Messrs. Coxes, may be at least considered as a Title to favour, being till then kept on [*torn*] as an Obstacle to any Designs the Crown might entertain of ma[king Co]lonies in that part of America.

I have had 2 or 3 interviews with Sir Matthew Featherstone on this Subject as well as with Mr. Sargent.[6] We dined at Sir Matthews House a Week ago, however I expect little from either of them at present.

A Project for putting all the Colonies in America on an equal footing with respect to Paper Currency has been on foot at the Board of Trade most part of this Winter,[7] you know my Sentiments on that Subject, I have been always inclined against a Paper Currency, I mean a legal Tender Paper Currency and though I conceive Difficultys occurring for want of it at times, I am satisfied

---

Jackson felt that his position as agent for the Pa. Assembly would make it unwise for him to press publicly the Coxe claims, which were based on a grant somewhat similar to that held by the Penns.

6. BF had been concerned with Sir Matthew Fetherstonhaugh (above, X, 214 n) and John Sargent (above, VII, 322 n, IX, 359 n) in an abortive scheme to obtain a land grant in America and recommended these gentlemen to Jackson as worthy participants in the Coxe grant. See above, X, 214 n.

7. As a result of the depreciation of paper money in Virginia and North Carolina the Board of Trade conducted hearings in December 1763 on the currency problem in Virginia and the next month held broader hearings on the paper-money problem in all of the continental American colonies. The hearings lasted well into February with the Board on February 9 signing a representation calling for the prohibition of future issues of legal-tender paper money in the colonies and for the retirement by given dates of the legal-tender paper then circulating. What happened then is obscure but from "the correspondence of the agents, it seems clear that as late as March 24, the Commissioners of Trade dropped the idea of bringing a bill into Parliament that year." On March 29, however, Anthony Bacon, a No. Car. merchant and M.P. for Aylesbury, "unexpectedly revived" the proposal in the Commons, and on April 19 the Currency Act of 1764 was passed. *Board of Trade Journal*, 1759–63, p. 418; 1764–67, pp. 3, 4, 6, 11, 14, 15, 18–20; *Acts Privy Coun., Col.*, IV, 630–1; Jack M. Sosin, "Imperial Regulation of Colonial Paper Money, 1764–1773," *PMHB*, LXXXVIII (1964), 174–98.

they are to be removed by a Bank, subject to none of the Objections made to a P. C. and (if insurmountable Objections should arise in the Way of a Publick Bank, I wish it were a Provincial one) by private Bankers on a sufficient Foundation.

However when there was a Meeting at the Board of Trade of the Lords, the former Governor of Provinces, Commanders of Forces &c. at which I was present,[8] I gave my Opinion flatly against any Bill in Parliament this Session, founded chiefly on this, that I thought it one thing to prevent an Evil, another to cure it, and that no Provision could be made by way of Remedy, but might produce great Mischiefs for want of our knowing the exact state of the Paper Currency, in every Province, as well as the Objections that might be against the Bill. Besides which I urged that I judged it rather an Indecorum to make Laws respecting People so remote without their even knowing what we were about. Mr. Penn was of the same Opinion on this Point. Nobody else said much on the Subject against a Bill, except that both Monckton and [Sir Charles Hardy?][9] agreed that they had seen the good Effects and even Necessity of Paper Money. The Board seemed to have dropped their Project for this year, it was [under]stood the Treasury would not support a Bill in the House. About a fortnight before the House was to rise, upon my Return from Norfolk where I went to support the Election of the Sollicitor Generals Brother,[1] I found a Bill [remainder missing].

8. This meeting took place on Feb. 2, 1764. Among others, Thomas Penn and William Allen were present. *Board of Trade Journal*, 1764–7, p. 15.

9. Robert Monckton was the governor of New York; above, x, 290 n. Hardy had been governor of the same province, 1755–57; above, VI, 450 n.

1. Thomas de Grey of Merton, Norfolk. He was elected on April 11, 1764, and served until 1774. *London Chron.*, April 10–12, 1764; Namier and Brooke, *House of Commons*, II, 306–7. For his brother, William de Grey, see above, x, 23 n.

To Francis Bernard

ALS: The Hyde Collection, Mrs. Donald F. Hyde, Somerville, N.J. (1955)

Sir   Philada. April 21. 1764

Mr. Williams has acknowledg'd the Receipt of the £12 12s. 0d.[2]

Dr. Allison is out of Town, and not expected home these 10 Days. As soon as he returns I will speak to him, and write you his Answer.

I communicated your Favour of the 1st. ult.[3] to my Son, who desired me to return his grateful Acknowledgements for your kind Intimation relating to the Seizure made within his Government, concerning which he is now, I believe, taking some Steps to obtain what may be his Right.

Mr Hall, one of the House at Madeira, being here, I sent your Letter to him.[4] With sincere Respect, I am, Your Excellency's most obedient humble Servant   B FRANKLIN

Govr. Bernard

To Jonathan Williams   ALS: Richard B. Duane, Locust, N.J. (1955)

Loving Kinsman   Philada. April 21. 1764

I have received yours of the 12th Inst.[5] As to the Mistake I mention'd, I find on Revisal that it was not in your Account but in my Eyes, which mistook one Figure for another.

I wrote to you from Burlington that I should pay your Order in favour of Robinson as soon as I return'd to Town, which I accordingly did. The Sum £47 15s. 4d.[6]

---

2. For this and other matters mentioned in this letter, see above, p. 153.

3. See above, p. 91.

4. A letter Bernard had asked BF to forward to Madeira by the first available vessel.

5. Not found; probably in answer to an earlier letter from BF (also not found) explaining that Governor Bernard would repay to Williams the sums BF had spent in behalf of Bernard's son. See above, pp. 133, 153.

6. In the Jonathan Williams account, 1763–1774 (above, X, 359), is an entry dated Feb. 27, 1764, in which Williams acknowledged owing BF £38 4s. 3d., in Mass. "lawful money" (the equivalent of £47 15s. 4d. in Pa. currency) for "an Order in Favr. Robbins." BF's Memorandum Book, 1757–1776, p. 16, contains an undated entry of the payment of this order in Pa. currency "in favr. of Tho' Robinson."

I should be glad to know what Sum your Government has paid for the Bounty on Wheat last Year, if you can get at it easily.[7]

It grieves me that the Glasses are not yet come for the Armonica.[8] How does Cousin Josiah[9] go on with his Spinnet? But I make no doubt he improves very fast.

We all join in Love to you and all yours. I am Your affectionate Uncle   B FRANKLIN

Addressed: To / Mr Jonathan Williams / Mercht / Boston / Free / B FRANKLIN

Endorsed: April 21 1764 F Franklins letter

Smith, Wright & Gray Account Book, 1764-1774

MS account book: American Philosophical Society

[April 24, 1764]

In the spring of 1764 Franklin opened an account with the London banking firm of Smith, Wright & Gray;[1] he kept it at least moderately

---

7. In 1754 the Mass. legislature laid a duty of 9*d.* per hundred on flour, 10*d.* on ship's bread and on other bread in proportion, to be paid out as a bounty to growers of wheat. In 1763 the bounty on wheat was increased. William B. Weeden, *Economic and Social History of New England 1620–1789* (Boston, 1890), II, 690, 735. The reason for BF's inquiry has not been determined; there seems to have been no proposal in the Pa. Assembly for a similar measure at this time.

8. BF had an armonica with him in Boston during his trip in 1763 (above, X, 383–4) and had probably given Jonathan Williams' blind son, the musically gifted Josiah, some instructions in playing it. He had apparently promised to have an armonica made for the 14-year-old boy, the case to be built in Philadelphia and the glasses sent over from England. On Nov. 3, 1764, just before sailing, he wrote the father that, although the case and spindle were finished, it would be better to send a complete armonica from England after he arrived there. See below, pp. 426–7.

9. A note on the MS, keyed to "Josiah" identifies the boy. It is initialed "SB" for Sarah Bache, BF's daughter. Other notes, written on or attached to the MS, trace its ownership through five later generations of the Bache and Duane families to 1913.

1. This firm was established about 1758 under the name of Smith Wright & Co., with an office on Lombard Street, London. In 1763 its name was changed to Smith, Wright & Gray, the partners then being Thomas Smith, John Wright, and Henry Gray, all prominent Quakers. F. G. Hilton Price,

179

active until the summer of 1774. A record of this account, separate from his other financial books and records, survives among his papers in the form of a comparatively small volume, of which 24 pages have been used. His deposits are entered on the left-hand pages, his withdrawals and drafts, and some other charges against the account, are listed on the right-hand pages. The earliest entry credits him with a bill of exchange for £1000 sterling received by the bankers on April 24, 1764; the last entry records a cash withdrawal of £21 on Aug. 24, 1774. Between these dates a balance was struck on six occasions. The first of these shows that he was overdrawn in June 1767 to the extent of £86, but all the other balances are in his favor, the amount reaching as high as £1283 7s. 6d. in July 1770. The last recorded withdrawal left 10s. 3d. still deposited to his credit. Comparison of this account book with his Memorandum Book, 1757-1776, for the period before he left Philadelphia in November 1764, and with the Journal and Ledger he maintained while on his second mission to England, shows that all but a very few transactions found in the Smith, Wright & Gray account are also entered in one form or another in those more generalized records. When the annotation of documents belonging to the period covered requires reference to this record it will be cited as Smith, Wright & Gray Account Book, 1764-1774.

To Peter Collinson   ALS: The British Museum

Dear Friend,   Philada. April 30. 1764
    I have before me your kind Notices of Feb. 3. and Feb. 10.[2] Those you enclos'd for our Friend Bartram,[3] were carefully deliver'd.
    I have not yet seen the Squib you mention against your People, in the Supplement to the Magazine;[4] but I think it impossible they should be worse us'd there than they have lately been here; where

---

A Handbook of London Bankers (London, 1876), p. 125. John Wright continued as a personal friend and occasional correspondent of BF until almost the end of BF's life.

2. Neither of these letters has been found.

3. John Bartram, the eminent Quaker botanist. See above, II, 378 n.

4. The squib was "An Authentic Account of the Cause of the Indian War," which appeared in the supplement to *Gent. Mag.*, XXXIII (1763), 640. The piece charged the Quakers with instigating Pontiac's Uprising by settling on Indian lands "on the river Ohio."

sundry inflammatory Pamphlets[5] are printed and spread about to excite a mad armed Mob to massacre them. And it is my Opinion they are still in some Danger, more than they themselves seem to apprehend, as our Government has neither Goodwill nor Authority enough to protect them.

By the enclos'd Papers[6] you will see that we are all to pieces again; and the general Wish seems to be a King's Government. If that is not to be obtain'd, many talk of quitting the Province, and among them your old Friend, who is tired of these Contentions, and longs for philosophic Ease and Leisure.

I suppose by this Time the Wisdom of your Parliament has determin'd in the Points you mention, of Trade, Duties, Troops and Fortifications in America.[7] Our Opinions or Inclinations, if they had been known, would perhaps have weigh'd but little among you. We are in your Hands as Clay in the Hands of the Potter; and so in one more Particular than is generally consider'd: for as the Potter cannot waste or spoil his Clay without injuring himself; so I think there is scarce anything you can do that may be hurtful to us, but what will be as much or more so to you. This must be our chief Security; for Interest with you we have but little: The West Indians vastly outweigh us of the Northern Colonies. What we get above a Subsistence, we lay out with you for your Manufactures. Therefore what you get from us in Taxes you must lose in Trade. The Cat can yield but her Skin. And as you must have the whole Hide, if you first cut Thongs out of it, 'tis at your own Expence. The same in regard to our Trade with the

5. Many of which are reprinted in John R. Dunbar, ed., *The Paxton Papers* (The Hague, 1957).

6. One of which may possibly have been the March 29 issue of *Pa. Gaz.*, which printed the messages that had passed between the Assembly and the governor concerning the passage of the £55,000 supply bill of March 14, 1764 (above, p. 148 n). One of the documents printed was the Assembly's Resolves of March 24, 1764, which Collinson in a letter to Bartram of June 1, 1764, praised as being "able" and "spirited." Darlington, *Memorials*, p. 264. BF probably also sent Collinson a copy of the petition for royal government and a copy of *Cool Thoughts*. See above, pp. 145–7, 153–73.

7. Collinson's letters of Feb. 3 and Feb. 10, 1764, had probably discussed the intention of the British ministry to raise a revenue in America to support the fourteen battalions of regular troops that were proposed to be stationed there. The revenue measure finally resolved upon was, of course, the Sugar Act, signed by George III on April 5, 1764.

foreign West India Islands: If you restrain it in any Degree,[8] you restrain in the same Proportion our Power of making Remittances to you, and of course our Demand for your Goods; for you will not clothe us out of Charity, tho' to receive 100 per Cent for it, in Heaven. In time perhaps Mankind may be wise enough to let Trade take its own Course, find its own Channels, and regulate its own Proportions, &c. At present, most of the Edicts of Princes, Placaerts [Placets], Laws and Ordinances of Kingdoms and States, for that purpose, prove political Blunders. The Advantages they produce not being *general* for the Commonwealth; but *particular*, to private Persons or Bodies in the State who procur'd them, and *at the Expence of the rest of the People*. Does no body see, that if you confine us in America to your own Sugar Islands for that Commodity, it must raise the Price of it upon you in England? Just so much as the Price advances, so much is every Englishman tax'd to the West Indians. Apropos. Now we are on the Subject of Trade and Manufactures, let me tell you a Piece of News, that though it might displease a very respectable Body among you, the Button-makers, will be agreable to yourself as a Virtuoso: It is, that we have discover'd a Beach in a Bay several Miles round, the Pebbles of which are all in the Form of Buttons, whence it is called *Button-mold Bay;* where thousands of Tons may be had for fetching; and as the Sea washes down the slaty Cliff, more are continually manufacturing out of the Fragments by the Surge. I send you a Specimen of Coat, Wastecoat and Sleeve Buttons; just as Nature has turn'd them.[9] But I think I must not mention the Place, lest some Englishman get a Patent for this *Button-mine*, as one did for the *Coal mine* at Louisburgh, and by neither suffering others to work it, nor working it himself, deprive us of the Advantage God and Nature seem to have intended us.[1] As we have now got Buttons, 'tis some-

8. The Sugar Act lowered the duty on molasses imported into the continental American colonies from the foreign West Indies from the prohibitively high figure of 6d. per gallon to 3d. per gallon. This lowered duty was expected to yield greater revenue, however, because it was to be more strictly collected, and the cost of legal importation would be only a little higher than that involved in smuggling with its attendant bribery and other special expenses.

9. This is perhaps one of BF's tall stories, which he was fond of spinning to illustrate some moral, though he apparently did send some samples of these stone or fossil "Buttons."

1. BF appears to have been misinformed about the status of the coal mines

182

thing towards our Cloathing; and who knows but in time we may find out where to get Cloth? for as to our being always supply'd by you, 'tis a Folly to expect it. Only consider *the Rate of our Increase,* and tell me if you can increase your Wooll in that Proportion, and where, in your little Island you can feed the Sheep. Nature has put Bounds to your Abilities, tho' none to your Desires. Britain would, if she could, manufacture and trade for all the World; England for all Britain; London for all England; and every Londoner for all London. So selfish is the human Mind! But 'tis well there is One above that rules these Matters with a more equal Hand. He that is pleas'd to feed the Ravens, will undoubtedly take care to prevent a Monopoly of the Carrion. Adieu, my dear Friend, and believe me ever Yours most affectionately   B FRANKLIN

Mr. Collinson

Extract From Doctor Gale of Conecticut   May 10: 17[64][2]
If the report of what your Parliament has done |*illegible*| be complyed with, wee must then Drink Wine of our own Makeing or none at all.[3]
The More Duties Wee pay, the less Brittis[h] Manufactures wee shall be able to Import.

---

in the vicinity of Louisburgh. When that fortress fell to the British in 1758, exploitation of the mines was reserved for the garrison stationed there, a regulation which was still in force in 1764, despite numerous efforts of entrepreneurs to have the mines turned over to private individuals. See D. C. Harvey, ed., *Holland's Description of Cape Breton Island and other Documents* (Halifax, 1935), pp. 22–3, 27, 93; *Board of Trade Journal,* 1759–63, pp. 50, 52, 62, 347; 1766–68, pp. 97, 391. *Acts Privy Coun., Col.,* IV, 659–61.

2. This extract of Gale's letter to Collinson is in Collinson's hand; he apparently copied and filed it with BF's letter because of the similarity in subject matter. Benjamin Gale (1715–1790), M.A., Yale, 1733, studied medicine with Jared Eliot (above, III, 147–8 n), married Eliot's daughter, and eventually took over his practice in Killingworth, Conn. Gale was a man of wide interests, writing papers on smallpox inoculation, on the cultivation of Smyrna wheat, on Connecticut politics (he was an ardent Whig), and on Biblical prophecy. He also carried on a number of interesting agricultural experiments and in 1783 was awarded a medal by the Society of Arts for improving the drill plow. *DAB;* George C. Groce, "Benjamin Gale," *New England Quarterly,* X (1935), 697–716.

3. The Sugar Act of April 5, 1764, laid a duty of £7 a tun on all wines imported into America from Spain or Portugal or their possessions. Madeira wine, the great favorite in the colonies, was of course subject to the new duty.

And the More Wee must be Obliged to Manufacture both Woolen and Linnen you may Easily foresee the Consequences if you by Severe Laws, for[c]e us to It. For so fond is the Generallity of our People of Noveltys, they had rather have Goods Manufactur'd from you, than Do It themselves but Necessity will force them.

A Letter from a Gentleman in Crusoe's Island

Draft (unfinished): Library of Congress

This fragment of a projected pamphlet or newspaper article in Franklin's hand, apparently never finished, is dated at the end of April 1764 because of its statement that John Penn, "young Cruso," arrived in Pennsylvania with a commission as governor six months ago—Penn arrived on October 30, 1763.[4] Though Franklin not infrequently employed the allegorical or analogical form in pamphlets, the approach in the present fragment may have been suggested to him by a pamphlet published in Boston in 1720, entitled *New News from Robinson Cruso's Island, in a Letter to a Gentleman at Portsmouth.*

[April 1764?]

A Letter from a Gentleman in Crusoe's Island to his Friend in Pennsylvania.

Dear Sir,

You desire a particular Account of the present State of our Public Affairs, which I shall endeavour to give you.

Young Cruso Grandson to honest old Robinson our first Proprietor arriv'd about 6 Months since, with a Commission to be Governor of the Island. He was received with universal Joy, and welcom'd by all Ranks and Orders of People with the greatest Cordiality.[5] For our old Disputes with the Proprietary Family had slept some time, and were almost forgotten. The young Gentleman was known to us, having visited the Island formerly.[6]

4. See above, X, 375.
5. For BF's own reception of "young" Penn (now 34) see above, X, 401.
6. John Penn was in Pennsylvania from 1752 to 1755, serving as a member of the Council and a commissioner at the Albany Conference; see above, IV, 458 n.

To Richard Jackson ALS: American Philosophical Society

Dear Sir   Philada. May 1. 1764
 I have receiv'd your Favours of Dec. 27. Jan. 14. Jan. 26. and
Feb. 11.[7]
 I wrote to you Dec. 24. Jan. 16. Feb. 11. March 8. 14. and 31.[8]
I could wish your Letters would from time to time mention which
of mine come to hand.
 Since my last I have had a Conversation with Mr. William Coxe,
on the Subject of our being at any or no Expence in the Pursuit
of their Right.[9] And he tells me, that their Proposal was, to be at
all Expence themselves as far as £500 Sterling would go; and if
the Expence should exceed that Sum, such Excess to be equally
divided between them and us. He thinks his Letter to you very
clear in that respect.
 We continue in great Disorder here; Reports frequently spreading that the Frontier People are assembling to come down again;
and 'tis thought they will certainly be here when the Assembly sit,
the Middle of this Month.[1] Petitions to the King are handing about,
and signing in most parts of the Province for a Change of Government.[2] I have written the enclos'd Pamphlet[3] to promote it, as I

7. Only those of Dec. 27, 1763, and Jan. 26, 1764, have been found; see
above, x, 411–16, and this volume, pp. 33–6.
 8. See above, x, 408–10, and this volume, pp. 19–20, 76–8, 95–7, 105–9,
150–2. BF forgot his March 29 letter, above, pp. 148–9.
 9. See above, x, 214, 341–2, 370–1, and this volume, p. 152, for the confusion about the terms on which BF and Jackson were to assist the heirs of Dr.
Daniel Coxe in obtaining royal confirmation for the "Carolana" land grant.
 1. Having adjourned on March 24, 1764, the House reconvened on May 14
and sat until May 30, 1764. No frontiersmen disturbed their deliberations,
although several petitions were presented from inhabitants in the frontier
counties, praying for the redress of their grievances, including their unequal
representation. *Votes*, 1763–64, pp. 75, 76, 82. Muhlenberg recorded in his
journal, March 29, 1764, however, a visit from a frontiersman from beyond
Easton, who opposed the Assembly petition for a change in government as a
"Quaker invention" to avoid doing anything to protect the frontiers. If the
Indians resumed their attacks during the planting season, he said, "the frontier
settlers from four counties would flock to Philadelphia by the thousands and
speak to the government." Theodore G. Tappert and John W. Doberstein,
eds., *The Journals of Henry Melchior Muhlenberg*, II (Phila., 1945), 54–5.
 2. See above, pp. 145–7.
 3. *Cool Thoughts;* see above, pp. 153–73.

see no Prospect or Probability of any Agreement with the Proprietaries, and, in the Way we are in, publick Business cannot go on, nor the internal Peace of the Province be preserved. I enclose you also a little Piece of Mr. Galloway's.[4] The Rhodeisland People, too, are tired of their Charter Government, as you will see by one of their late Papers, which I send you.[5]

You have in some of your late Letters mention'd a Post you hold under the Prime Minister, but do not say what it is.[6]

I long to hear what has been done in Parliament relative to America. Your Objection to internal Taxes is undoubtedly just and solid.[7] Two distinct Jurisdictions or Powers of Taxing cannot well subsist together in the same Country. They will confound and obstruct each other. When any Tax for America is propos'd in your Parliament, how are you to know that we are not already tax'd as much as we can bear? If a Tax is propos'd with us, how dare we venture to lay it, as the next Ship perhaps may bring us an Account of some heavy Tax impos'd by you. If you chuse to tax us, give us Members in your Legislature, and let us be one People.

You mention that you could interest me in a Grant in Nova Scotia. I wish then that you would do it if in any Part likely for Settlement.[8] As I have some Money to spare, I know not how bet-

4. Perhaps the piece entitled *An Address to the Freeholders and Inhabitants of the Province of Pennsylvania*, attributed to Galloway; see above, p. 154.

5. BF probably sent Jackson the April 23, 1764, issue of the *Newport Mercury*, which contained a letter by "Z. Y.," supposed to be either Martin Howard, Jr., or Dr. Thomas Moffatt (see below, p. 191 n), both of whom were BF's friends and correspondents, advocating the revocation of the Rhode Island charter of 1663 and the establishment of royal government in the colony. For Howard, Moffatt, and their group of Rhode Island conservatives, see Edmund S. and Helen M. Morgan, *The Stamp Act Crisis* (Chapel Hill, [1953]), pp. 47–52.

6. In his letter to BF of Dec. 27, 1763 (see above, X, 412–13) Jackson spoke of having "received a very considerable Mark" of Prime Minister George Grenville's "good will and Esteem"; he was referring to his appointment as secretary to Grenville in his capacity as chancellor of the Exchequer, a post which Jackson held until sometime in 1765. Namier and Brooke, *House of Commons*, II, 670.

7. See Jackson's letters of Nov. 12, Dec. 27, 1763, and Jan. 26, 1764; above, X, 371, 415, and this volume, pp. 33–6.

8. BF's Nova Scotia land dealings are clouded in obscurity. What is known is that in either the winter of 1764 or the spring of 1765 he and a number of unidentified associates, presumably from Philadelphia, applied to Governor

ter to dispose of it for the Advantage of my Children. And since there is no Likelihood of my being engag'd in any Project of a new Government, the Popular Character I have in America may at least be of Use in procuring Settlers for some Part under an old one. St. John's Island, I see by the Papers, is granted to Lord Egmont.[9] The Nantucket Whalers, who are mostly my Relations, wanted a Settlement there, their own Island being too full. At their Request I drew a Petition for them last Year, to General Amherst;[1] but he had no Power to settle them any where. They are desirous of being somewhere in or near the Bay of St. Lawrence, where the Whale—as well as other—Fishing is excellent.

This brings me to mention another Affair of the same kind. There are in the Government of Quebec, two Tracts of vacant Land, the Right of which is at present in the Crown. Inclos'd you have a short Account of their Situation. They were discover'd by two Friends of mine, Mr. John Baynton, and Mr. Samuel Wharton, Merchants of this Place,[2] who desire to obtain a Grant of them, in which

---

Montague Wilmot for a grant of 200,000 acres and that in October 1765, in connection with Alexander McNutt and several other people, he was granted 100,000 acres on the north side of the Saint John River. W. O. Raymond, "Colonel Alexander McNutt and the Pre-Loyalist Settlements of Nova Scotia," Royal Society of Canada *Proc. and Trans.*, 3d ser., V (1911), section II, 86–7, 91–2; William O. Sawtelle, "Acadia: The Pre-Loyalist Migration and the Philadelphia Plantation," *PMHB*, LI (1927), 269–85.

9. For John Perceval, 2d Earl of Egmont, at this time first lord of the Admiralty, see above, X, 286 n. *Pa. Gaz.*, April 26, 1764, mentioned the certainty of St. John Island being granted to him, but his plan came to nothing.

1. See above, X, 429–31.

2. John Baynton (1726–1773) and Samuel Wharton (1732–1800) were partners in a mercantile firm bearing their names (after 1763 the firm became Baynton, Wharton & Morgan) which specialized in the Indian trade. The company suffered heavily during Pontiac's Uprising, and for several years thereafter Wharton attempted to reimburse these losses by obtaining a grant of land from the Indians. He succeeded at Fort Stanwix in 1768, receiving the cession of a large tract in what is now West Virginia from the Six Nations. Wharton was sent to England in 1769 to procure royal confirmation for this grant, but he soon was involved in a much larger land speculating venture, the Walpole Company, of which BF was also a member. BF and Wharton's relations were very close for several years thereafter. Wharton, an incorrigible land speculator, visited BF in Paris in 1779 to discuss a project to get Congressional recognition for the Vandalia claim. A letter from

they would be glad to have me joined. Can you obtain such a Grant for us, and will you share my Third with me? If it be practicable and you like the Proposal, the sooner 'tis push'd the better; as 'tis fear'd that Governor Murray, when he receives his Commission may otherwise grant the Land away.[3] That Tract in Bay Chaleur[4] may probably suit my Nantucket Friends extreamly well.

Three of your Convicts are to be executed here next Week for Burglaries, one of them suspected of a Murder committed on the Highway.[5] When will you cease plaguing us with them?

Your Complaints of that old Fever on your Spirits, give me real Concern. Take care of yourself for the sake of your Friends, among whom none can interest themselves more cordially in whatever relates to your Welfare and Happiness, than, Dear Sir, Your affectionate and most obedient humble Servant   B FRANKLIN

R. Jackson, Esq.

Endorsed: Philada. May 1st. 1764 Benjn. Franklin Esqr

To William Strahan   ALS: Yale University Library

Dear Straney   Philada. May 1. 1764

I receiv'd your Favour of Decemr. 20.[6] You cannot conceive the Satisfaction and Pleasure you give your Friends here by your political Letters. Your Accounts are so clear, circumstantial and com-

---

Baynton and Wharton to BF, Nov. 3, 1764 (below, pp. 427–8) gives some particulars of the Canadian tracts in which they were interested; the letter of March 11, 1764, from which they then quoted may have been the "short Account" BF sent to Jackson with the present proposal.

3. Gen. James Murray (see above, x, 223 n), governor of the town of Quebec since 1760, was appointed governor of the whole province on Nov. 21, 1763, serving until 1766.

4. A bay in the Gulf of St. Lawrence at the present boundary between New Brunswick and Quebec.

5. Dr. Friedrich Wilhelm Autenried (Autenrieth, Handenried), John Williams (alias John Hines), and John Brinckloe (alias John Benson) were convicted of burglary in April. The first two were hanged, May 12, 1764, but Brinckloe was told at the foot of the gallows that he had been reprieved. *Pa. Col. Recs.*, IX, 172–4; *Muhlenberg Journals*, II, 43–72 passim, 76–7; *Pa. Gaz.*, May 17, 1764.

6. Not found.

pleat, that tho' there is nothing too much, nothing is wanting to give us, as I imagine, a more perfect Knowledge of your Publick Affairs than most People have that live among you. The Characters of your Speakers and Actors, are so admirably sketch'd, and their Views so plainly open'd, that we see and know every body; they all become of our Acquaintance.[7] So excellent a Manner of Writing, seems to me a superfluous Gift to a mere Printer. If you do not commence Author for the Benefit of Mankind, you will certainly be found guilty hereafter, of burying your Talent. It is true that it will puzzle the Devil himself to find anything else to accuse you of, but remember that he may make a great deal of that. If I were King (which may God, in Mercy to us all, prevent) I should certainly make you the Historiographer of my Reign. There could be but one Objection. I suspect you might be a little partial in my Favour. But your other Qualifications for an Historian being duly consider'd, I believe we might get over that.

Our petty publick Affairs here are in the greatest Confusion, and will never, in my Opinion, be compos'd, while the Proprietary Government subsists. I have wrote a little Piece[8] (which I send enclos'd) to persuade a Change. People talk of sending me to England to negociate it, But I grow very indolent. Bustling is for younger Men.

Mrs. Franklin, Sally, and my Son and Daughter of the Jerseys, with whom I lately spent a Week, all join in best Wishes of Prosperity to you and all yours, with Dear Sir, Your affectionate humble Servant   B FRANKLIN

P.S. I will do every thing in my Power to recommend the Work Mr. Griffith[9] mentions, having the same Sentiments of it that you express. But I conceive many more of them come to America than he imagines. Our Booksellers perhaps write for but few; but the

7. WF's opinion of Strahan's political reporting was similarly enthusiastic; writing to him on May 1, WF said that the now missing letter "made me imagine myself present at the debates." Charles H. Hart, ed., "Letters from William Franklin to William Strahan," *PMHB*, XXXV (1911), 437.

8. *Cool Thoughts;* see above, pp. 153–73.

9. Almost certainly Ralph Griffiths (1720–1803), publisher of *The Monthly Review* for which Strahan was the printer. Apparently Griffiths and Strahan were trying to enlist BF's assistance in increasing the *Review's* circulation in America.

Reason is, that a Multitude of our People trade more or less to London; and all that are bookishly dispos'd receive the Reviews singly from their Correspondents as they come out.

Mr. Strahan

To Mary Stevenson

ALS: American Philosophical Society

Dear Polly   Philada. May 4. 1764

Since making up my Packet for your good Mother,[1] I have receiv'd your Favour of the 1st. of March;[2] and have only time now to acknowledge it, the Bearer Mrs. Empson[3] being just going to the Ship; but purpose writing to you fully per next Week's Packet. I beg Leave to reccommend her to your Friendly Advice and Civilities, as she is a Daughter of one of my good Friends and Neighbours, and will be quite a Stranger in London. I am, my dear Friend, Yours affectionately   B FRANKLIN

The Verses on Vanity extreamly pretty.[4]

Miss Stevenson

Endorsed: Phila May 4 - 64

1. The contents of this packet have not been determined; they may have included a copy of *Cool Thoughts,* though how much that pamphlet would have interested Mrs. Stevenson is uncertain. Earlier BF had sent Polly a copy of *A Narrative of the Late Massacres.* See below, p. 202. On May 1 BF drew on Smith, Wright & Gray for £35 in favor of Mrs. Stevenson. Memorandum Book, 1757–1776, p. 17; Smith, Wright & Gray Account Book, 1764–1774.
    2. Not found.
    3. Elizabeth Soumaine, the daughter of the Franklins' neighbor Samuel Soumaine, silversmith (above, X, 135 n), married Thomas Empson, May 5, 1763. 2 *Pa. Arch.,* VIII, 191. Daniel Fisher, whom BF employed as a clerk for a time in 1755 (above, VI, 67 n, 113), lodged with Soumaine and recorded that he had a daughter then aged thirteen. Mrs. Conway R. Howard, "Extracts from the Diary of Daniel Fisher, 1755," *PMHB,* XVII (1893), 271. Members of this family are mentioned several times in later correspondence.
    4. Probably verses of Polly's composition.

From Thomas Moffatt[5]   ALS: American Philosophical Society

Sir   Newport Rhode Island May 12th 1764
    Three days ago on my return from an excursion of pleasure I
was favourd with Yours of Aprill 7th.[6] Some years are past since
I kept a register of the Barometer, Thermometer &c. and from
it I find that on Decr. 31st 1751 Fahreenheits thermometer fell two
lines below Cypher and next day or Janr. 1st in the morning the
mercury was at the same station but before evening rose up three
lines above blank and next morning eight. This was the greatest
degree and continuance of cold I ever knew at Newport. I do not
remember that ever the mercury mounted up to Eighty four in
Summer but once in Agust 21st 1759. I should be fond of knowing
the extent or utmost heat you have observd in summer at Philadelphia.[7]
    I never saw any fever like unto that describd as the yellow or
bilious fever though I have often heard of it but on visiting the
persons I always found the characters or type of that distemper
wanting. That fever being the confessd offspring of heat and mois-
ture may be brought into Philadelphia in your hot season and may
even be communicated to others but will I suppose be much milder
than in the Climate proper to generate and produce it and therefore will decline or dysappear with the first temperate and cool

5. Thomas Moffatt (c. 1702–1787), Scottish-born physician, studied at Edinburgh and Leyden, and followed his uncle John Smibert, the painter, to
Newport in 1729. There he practiced medicine, collected art, and became
librarian and director of the Redwood Library. He established a snuff mill
and brought Gilbert Stuart, father of the painter, from Scotland to manage it.
A member of a club of Newport conservatives, Moffatt strongly supported
the strengthening of royal authority in the colonies, as this letter shows.
During the Stamp Act disturbances he was hanged in effigy, his house was
sacked, and his paintings, books, and scientific instruments destroyed. The
British government compensated him by appointment as collector of customs
at New London. In 1775 he took refuge in Boston with the army and then
went to England, where he lived out his life on a pension of £200. Henry
Wilder Foote, *John Smibert, Painter* (Cambridge, Mass., 1950), esp. pp. 34,
46–7; Edmund S. and Helen M. Morgan, *The Stamp Act Crisis Prologue to
Revolution* (Chapel Hill, [1953]), pp. 47–52, 145–8, 301.
    6. Not found.
    7. This would probably have been on Sunday, June 18, 1749, when the
temperature in Philadelphia reached 100° F. See above, IV, 336; VIII, 110.

weather.[8] Violent exercise in some habits or constitution may induce fevers of the greatest rapidity with other circumstances attending the yellow fever but [I] suppose the difference would be very conspicuous in many points at least it appears so to me.

I do not think our College will ever be executed in any respect otherwise I would have sent you the Act and Charter.[9] It would perhaps have been better if all foundations of this sort in America had been united or conjoind to the first as they are all too narrow and poor at bottom to produce the liberal fruits of art and knowledge.[1]

We are agitated here with imperfect rumours from home about our Charter. The (few) Friends to regular and good government are wishing for a deprivation while the Herd deplore it as a Calamity.[2] I salute you with the greatest esteem and respect and am Sir Your most Obedient Humble Servant   THOMAS MOFFATT

8. For Dr. John Mitchell's writings on yellow fever, see above, III, 17–21, 41–4; and for the Philadelphia epidemic of 1747, above III, 179, 228, 276.

9. The charter of the College of Rhode Island (now Brown University) was voted by the two houses of the General Assembly, March 2 and 3, 1764, although the governor did not affix his signature until Oct. 24, 1765. An organizational meeting took place Sept. 5, 1764. Considerable controversy occurred because of rivalries between the denominations, chiefly the Baptists and Congregationalists, over control of the institution. William C. Bronson, *The History of Brown University, 1764–1914* (Providence, 1914), pp. 34–5, 501.

1. In May 1759 Francis Alison of the College of Philadelphia had passed on to Ezra Stiles a suggestion from Thomas Clap of Yale for a somewhat more limited association among the colonial colleges. It would have called for uniformity on plan of education and college laws and refusal by any college to admit a student expelled by another without prior consultation. Franklin B. Dexter, ed., *Extracts from the Itineraries and other Miscellanies of Ezra Stiles, D.D., LL.D. 1755–1794 with a Selection from his Correspondence* (New Haven, 1916), p. 423.

2. At this time Rhode Island politics were inflamed by a personal feud between two leaders, Samuel Ward (above, v, 504 n) and Stephen Hopkins. Moffatt and his conservative friends, particularly Martin Howard, Jr., disgusted by what seemed an excess of democracy, started a campaign in the spring of 1764 for the revocation of the charter of 1663 and the establishment of royal government in the colony. E. S. and H. M. Morgan, *Stamp Act Crisis*, pp. 47–50. Their newspaper articles are discussed with quotations in Bernard Bailyn, ed., *Pamphlets of the American Revolution 1750–1776*, I (Cambridge, Mass., 1965), 524–7.

Pennsylvania Assembly: Petition to the King

I. Draft: Library of Congress. II. DS: Public Record Office[3]

When on the morning of May 23 the Assembly received and read the second group of the inhabitants' petitions to the King asking him to assume the government of Pennsylvania, that body voted "by a great Majority"[4] that a committee be appointed "to prepare and bring in the Draft of a Petition to the King from this House, to accompany the afore-mentioned Petitions to His Majesty." Eight men were named: Joseph Galloway (Philadelphia County), Benjamin Franklin (City of Philadel-phia), Abraham Chapman (Bucks), Isaac Pearson (Chester), John Doug-lass (Lancaster), John Montgomery (Cumberland), John Ross (Berks), and John Tool (Northampton). The only constituency unrepresented was York County. Immediately after this action the Assembly adjourned for the mid-day recess.[5]

As soon as the House reconvened in the afternoon the committee reported that it "had made an Essay" of a petition. This paper was then read and ordered "to lie on the Table for the Perusal of the Members."[6] The speed with which the committee acted suggests strongly that at least one member had prepared himself in advance of the committee's appointment. It is not surprising, therefore, to discover among Frank-

---

3. The draft, including all its emendations, is in BF's hand. The DS is on a large sheet; all but the "B Franklin Speaker" and the endorsements is in the hand of a professional scrivener.
4. The vote was 27 to 3 according to the (unpaged) "Advertisement" in *The Speech Of Joseph Galloway, Esq; . . . Delivered in the House of Assembly . . . May 24, 1764* (Phila., 1764). See below, p. 308.
5. *Votes*, 1763–64, p. 82. The order in which these names appear in the record has no significance as to any intended chairman and, as usual, none was specifically named. It was standard practice in listing members of com-mittees in the Pa. Assembly to name first the member or members from Philadelphia Co., followed in sequence by those from the city, the other original counties of Bucks and Chester, and then those from the newer counties in the order of their erection: Lancaster, York, Cumberland, Berks, and Northampton. Since BF represented the city of Philadelphia throughout his legislative career, his name in the listing of a committee membership was almost always preceded at least by that of one member from the county, whatever their relative importance on the committee may have been. Of the group named here, Galloway, BF, Pearson, and Ross are known to have supported the petition, while Montgomery opposed it. The positions of Chapman, Douglass, and Tool are not certainly known, though it would appear that all three favored the petition.
6. *Votes*, 1763–64, p. 82.

lin's papers a document in his handwriting that is clearly an early draft of what ultimately became the Assembly's petition to the King. It is printed below as Number I.

This draft contains numerous cancellations and revisions. Although some of them could have been inserted later, others were clearly made during the course of composition. It is probable, therefore, that this paper represents Franklin's first draft of the petition. Whether he made any further revisions not appearing on this paper before he showed it to the committee, and whether that group made any additional changes before presenting it to the whole House, cannot now be determined, for no other complete manuscript draft seems to have survived, and the text of the paper which the committee presented to the Assembly has not been found.[7]

On the afternoon of May 24, after receiving further petitions for a change in government from the inhabitants and after transacting other business, the Assembly resumed consideration of the petition and engaged in "a considerable Debate thereon" before adjourning to the next day.[8] One of the highlights of this debate was a speech by John Dickinson opposing the petition. He freely admitted the "inconveniences" of the system of proprietary instructions which controlled the governor and the "distinct and partial mode of taxation" John Penn had demanded for the proprietary lands, but he argued forcefully that this was "neither the *proper season,* nor the *proper method,* for obtaining a change in our government." In exchanging proprietary for royal government the colony would "run the *risque* of *suffering* great *losses*" of privileges, religious and political, which it currently enjoyed.[9] To this speech Galloway replied, apparently attacking with vigor Dickinson's statements of alleged fact as well as his arguments.[1] The debate was undoubtedly spirited.

7. Among the Franklin Papers in Lib. Cong. there is a one-page MS in a hand other than BF's containing the headings and the first paragraph of his draft and incorporating his revisions of that paragraph. Since this passage underwent considerable further amendment before the final approval of the whole, the paper appears to be part of a copy of the entire petition at some intermediate stage between BF's first draft and the final transcribed and signed petition.

8. *Votes,* 1763–64, p. 83.

9. *A Speech, Delivered in the House of Assembly of the Province of Pennsylvania, May 24th, 1764. By John Dickinson, Esq; One of the Members for the County of Philadelphia. On Occasion of a Petition, drawn up by Order, and then under consideration, of the House; praying his Majesty for a Change of the Government of this Province. With a Preface* (Phila., 1764). The quotations are from pp. 2 and 29. The speech, with a preface by the Rev. William Smith, was published as a pamphlet on June 29, 1764.

1. Galloway's speech was delivered extemporaneously, since he had time

When the motion was made the next morning to resume consideration of the petition, the speaker, Isaac Norris, found himself in trouble. He had long been an opponent of the proprietary party and had for several years been involved in the discussions of a possible change to royal government. Yet, now that the proposal was clearly about to shift from the discussion stage to one of formal action, he had serious qualms. Almost certainly he was afraid, as were other influential Quakers, that a change to royal government would jeopardize the special religious privileges that the colony as a whole, and the Friends in particular, enjoyed and the political and constitutional advantages the Assembly exercised by grant of William Penn. If the petition to the King, now under debate, should be adopted by the Assembly, Norris would have to sign the document as speaker even though he could not approve its substance.

Consequently, he now addressed the Assembly, pointing out that his position "had hitherto prevented him from giving his Opinion on the Subject of the said Petition, and requesting, if his Duty as Speaker should require his Signing the same, that he might, previous thereto, be indulged with the Privilege of speaking his Sentiments thereon, and entering them upon the Minutes." Such a request was probably quite unprecedented in the Assembly, but out of respect for the man who had been their speaker for most of the past fourteen years the members agreed. Thereupon the petition was read the second time "by Paragraphs, which being fully considered and debated, was, after some Alterations, agreed to by a great Majority, and ordered to be transcribed." The Assembly then adjourned for the day.[2]

Overnight, Norris concluded that he could not face the ordeal before him. When the Assembly convened on the morning of Saturday, May

---

to prepare no more than "short Notes" while Dickinson held the floor. On August 11 a carefully written version of what this speech was said to have been, "taken from his short Notes, and put in Order," with a long preface by BF (below, pp. 267–311), was published as *The Speech of Joseph Galloway, Esq; One of the Members for Philadelphia County: In Answer To the Speech of John Dickinson, Esq; Delivered in the House of Assembly, of the Province of Pennsylvania, May 24, 1764. On Occasion of a Petition drawn up by Order, and then under the Consideration of the House; praying his Majesty for a Royal, in lieu of a Proprietary Government* (Philadelphia, 1764). On September 17 Dickinson published a reply in which he called the Galloway pamphlet "*a pretended speech,* of which he never spoke one sentence in the House," while Dickinson's own printed speech, he said, was exactly as delivered except for a few corrections and "some slight alterations in a few places." John Dickinson, *A Reply To a Piece called the Speech of Joseph Galloway, Esquire* (Phila., 1764), esp. pp. 2, 44.

2. *Votes,* 1763–64, p. 84.

26, the clerk produced a letter just received from the speaker in which Norris wrote that his attendance during this and the previous week had "proved too much for my Constitution, and particularly the long Sitting of Yesterday and the bad Night I have had in Consequence of it." It was impossible, he said, for him to attend this day and he could not predict when his condition would mend sufficiently. Hence he asked the House to choose a new Speaker.[3] The assemblymen concluded that the "important Business" before them could not be indefinitely delayed for Norris' recovery, so those present "proceeded to the Choice of another Speaker, when Benjamin Franklin, Esq; was unanimously chosen Speaker, and accordingly placed in the Chair." A committee at once notified the governor of these events, and in the afternoon John Penn formally confirmed Franklin's election.[4]

When the assemblymen had returned to their chamber from the ceremony of confirmation they adopted a unanimous vote of thanks to Norris for his services and then dealt with the governor's most recent message on the pending supply bill.[5] Then the transcribed petition to the King was read once more and the question was put whether the speaker should sign it "in order that the same be transmitted to the Crown." The House formally "Resolved in the Affirmative, by a great

3. *Ibid.*, p. 84. It is uncertain how much Norris' incapacity was due to genuine illness and how much to the uncomfortable position he was in regarding the pending petition to the King. Probably both circumstances were involved. In January 1758 a convenient illness had enabled him to escape from the speaker's chair in the same way when the Assembly's controversial "trial" of William Smith was about to take place. Above, VII, 385; VIII, 60 n, 96. On the other hand, he had certainly experienced other bouts of ill health in recent years, including one in February 1764, when he was unable to go to the State House and the Assembly had met for some weeks at his brother's house where he was lodging (above, p. 70), and another on May 14, when the Assembly reconvened after the spring recess. On the latter occasion a committee of assemblymen had prevailed upon him to make the effort to attend and occupy the speaker's chair. *Votes*, 1763–64, pp. 75–6. Now, twelve days later, he was able to plead his bad health rather convincingly.

4. *Votes*, 1763–64, pp. 84–5; *Pa. Col. Recs.*, IX, 181–2. The immediate presentation of a newly elected speaker to the governor for approval was a necessary procedure in all royal and proprietary colonies in imitation of that in the House of Commons. The governor gave his approval almost automatically; for Penn to have denied approval of BF's election, however much he disliked the choice, would have been construed as a serious breach of the Assembly's privileges and would certainly have brought all legislative activity to a complete halt.

5. See below, pp. 205–6.

Majority," and Speaker Franklin signed the document accordingly.[6]
This final version is printed below as Number II.

Comparison of these two versions of the petition shows that the final text as voted and signed is about two-thirds again as long as Franklin's rough draft. Every idea and nearly every word and phrase in his draft reappear in the signed petition. Most of the individual changes consist of added words and phrases expanding and sometimes clarifying his statements in minor respects. A majority of the assemblymen doubtless considered them to be desirable additions; with his fondness for concise expression Franklin may have privately considered some of them superfluous, but he was not one to insist on his own shorter phraseology when near unanimity of approval was important.

The most notable addition, as well as the longest, however, was one of substance, appearing in the last paragraph. Franklin had proposed very briefly to ask the King to preserve merely "the Privileges that have been granted" to his subjects in Pennsylvania by his royal predecessors. The final text specified more definitely "those Civil and Religious Privileges" that had been instrumental in encouraging the first settlement "of this Wilderness Country, to the Extension of the British Dominions and Commerce," and had been and still continued to be important in drawing "many Thousands of Foreigners" to settle in Pennsylvania and become his Majesty's subjects. The earlier form of this passage is not found in anything Franklin had written but rather in the petition the Quakers had prepared and circulated for signature among members of their Society.[7] Its purpose was twofold: to emphasize, as Franklin had not done, the petitioners' desire to keep the special privileges that the colony enjoyed, and to point out that the existence of these privileges had been and still was an important factor in the "Extension of the British Dominions and Commerce" and hence was advantageous to the mother country as well as to the colony. The threat to the preservation of these privileges that a change to royal government posed was by far the strongest deterrent to general local support of the petition. Franklin would doubtless agree that these additions constituted a tactical improvement on his draft.

On May 28 some members of the Assembly asked to have their reasons for voting against the petition entered on the minutes "by way of Protestation." By a vote of 24 to 3 the House denied permission. The

6. *Votes,* 1763–64, p. 86. The text of the petition was not printed in the minutes, perhaps, as its opponents seemed to think, to prevent their getting a copy to use in countering its effect in England. William Smith's preface to Dickinson's *Speech,* p. xii.
7. See above, pp. 145–6.

names of those voting in the majority were not listed in the *Votes and Proceedings,* but the three in the minority had at least the consolation of having their names recorded for posterity. They were John Dickinson of Philadelphia County, Isaac Saunders of Lancaster, and John Montgomery of Cumberland. These were apparently the only assemblymen who had opposed the petition on the final vote of May 26.[8] They formed the small band that William Smith later called "a NOBLE FEW, a PATRIOT MINORITY."[9]

The added emphasis given in the final text of the petition to the preservation of the colony's privileges had not set the minds of the members entirely at rest. Before the Assembly adjourned on May 28 it directed that, in sending the Assembly's petition and those of the inhabitants to Richard Jackson, the agent in London, the Committee of Correspondence should instruct him "particularly" to proceed "with the utmost Caution" in dealing with them to secure for the people "all those Privileges, civil and religious, which, by their Charters and Laws, they have a Right to enjoy under the present Constitution." If upon "the most careful Enquiry, and mature Deliberation and Advice" he had reason to believe there was danger that these privileges might be lost, he was to suspend action until he had reported to the Assembly and received further directions.[1] Thus the Assembly made clear to Jackson —and to Franklin who was later associated with him in responsibility— that the change in government, however greatly desired, was less important than the preservation of the privileges that William Penn had conferred on the colony many years before.

8. *Votes,* 1763–64, p. 86. BF told Jackson, June 1, that the petition had "pass'd thro' the House with great Unanimity, only 3 Negatives." Below, p. 218.

9. William Smith's preface to Dickinson's *Speech,* p. v. Smith stated (p. vi) that Joseph Richardson of Philadelphia Co. had joined these three in voting, May 25, against having the petition transcribed. If BF's statement to Jackson is to be believed, however, Richardson either voted for the petition on the 26th or stayed away when that final and critical vote was taken. In either case, he did not support the request of the other three on the 28th to have their objections to the petition entered on the minutes.

1. *Votes,* 1763–64, p. 87. The one remaining problem before the Assembly had finished its action on the petition was how to finance its prosecution in England. On May 29 the Committee of Correspondence was authorized to draw on the provincial treasurer for the remaining balance in his hands from the proceeds of the old excise and the rent of Province Island (where the friendly Indians had first been lodged) and to apply these funds to the prosecution of the petition before the Privy Council. *Ibid.,* p. 88.

198

I

[May 23, 1764]

To the King's most excellent Majesty, in Council

The Petition of the Representatives of the Freemen of the Province of Pennsylvania, in General Assembly met.

Most humbly sheweth

That the Government of this Province by Proprietaries, has by long Experience been found inconvenient, attended with many Difficulties, and Obstructions to your Majesty's Service, arising from the Intervention of Proprietary private Interests in publick Affairs, and Disputes concerning those Interests.

That the said Proprietary Government is weak, unable to support its own Authority, and maintain the common internal Peace, of the Province, great Riots having lately arisen therein, armed Mobs marching from Place to Place, and committing violent Outrages, and Insults on the Government with Impunity, to the great Terror of your Majesty's Subjects. And these Evils [are] not likely to receive any Rem[edy] here, the continual Disputes be[tween] the Proprietaries and People, and the mutual Jealousies and Dislikes [pre]venting.

We do therefore most humbly pray, that Your Majesty would be graciously pleased to resume the Government of this Province, making such Compensation to the Proprietaries for the same as to your Majesty's Wisdom and Goodness shall appear just and equitable, and permitting your dutiful Subjects therein to enjoy under your Majesty's more immediate Care and Protection, the Privileges that have been granted to them, by and under your Royal Predecessors.   Signed by Order of the House

II

[May 26, 1764]

To the KINGS most excellent MAJESTY in Council,

The PETITION of the REPRESENTATIVES of the Freemen of the Province of PENNSYLVANIA in General Assembly met.

Most humbly Sheweth.

THAT the Government of a Province by Proprietaries has here as well as elsewhere, been by long Experience found inconvenient and attended with many Difficulties and Obstructions to the Service of the Crown and the Welfare of the People, arising from the Intervention of Proprietary private Interests in Public Affairs, and Disputes concerning those Interests, and Proprietary Instructions for enforcing them.

THAT hence, the Proprietary Government here, not being attended with that Respect in the Minds of the common People, which usually accompanies a Royal Government, is weak, unable to support its own Authority in a Degree sufficient to maintain the common internal Peace of the Province. Great Riots having lately arisen therein, armed Mobs marching from Place to Place, and committing voilent [sic] Outrages and Insults on the Government with Impunity to the great Terror of your Majesty's Subjects. And these Evils are not like to receive any Remedy here, during the Continuance of the Proprietary Government, the continual Disputes between the Proprietaries and People, and their mutual Jealouses and Distrusts preventing.

WE do therefore (in Concurrence with great Numbers of the Freeholders and other reputable Inhabitants of the Province, whose Petitions to the same Purpose will be herewith presented) most humbly pray, that your Majesty would be graciously pleased to resume the Government of this Province; making such Compensation to the Proprietaries for the same, as to your Majesty's Wisdom and Goodness shall appear just and equitable, and permitting your dutiful Subjects therein to enjoy, under your Majesty's more immediate Government and Protection, those Civil and Religious Priviledges, which to encourage the Settlement of the Province, have been granted and confirmed to them by your Royal Predecessors; by the Influence whereof, our Fathers were induced to undertake the Cultivation of this then Wilderness Country, to the Extention of the British Dominions and Commerce, and many Thousands of Foreigners have been, and still are drawn here to become your Majesty's Subjects.

SIGNED by order of the HOUSE   B FRANKLIN
Speaker

In Assembly May   1764.

Endorsed: Petition of the Assembly of Pensilvania Rx. 4th Novr. 1765 22d. Do. Ordered to be postponed.

To Jonathan Williams

MS not found; reprinted from [Jared Sparks, ed.,] *Familiar Letters and Miscellaneous Papers of Benjamin Franklin; Now for the First Time Published* (Boston, 1833), p. 93.

Dear Kinsman,   Philadelphia, 24 May 1764.
The bearer is the Reverend Mr. Rothenbuler,[2] minister of a new Calvinist German Church, lately erected in this city. The congregation is but poor at present, being many of them new comers, and, (like other builders) deceived in their previous calculations, they have distressed themselves by the expense of their building; but as they are an industrious, sober people, they will be able in time to afford that assistance to others, which they now humbly crave for themselves.

His business in Boston is to petition the generous and charitable among his Presbyterian brethren for their kind benefactions. As he will be a stranger in New England, and I know you are ready to do every good work, I take the freedom to recommend him and his business to you, for your friendly advice and countenance. The civilities you show him shall be acknowledged as done to Your affectionate uncle,   B. FRANKLIN.

From Mary Stevenson   Draft: American Philosophical Society

My dear Sir   Kensington May 24. 1764
Your Indulgence to me gives you a Claim to as much as you can desire from me, therefore don't think I am so unreasonable

2. Frederick Rothenbuehler (1726–1766), German Reformed (Calvinist) minister, was born in Bern, Switzerland, educated at the University of Bern, and ordained in 1752. After a year in the Netherlands, he served a German Reformed church in London, migrated to New York in 1761, and became pastor of the newly organized St. George's Church in Philadelphia in 1762. This church, the second of its denomination in the city, ran heavily into debt, and four years after Rothenbuehler's death the building was sold to a Methodist organization. Frederick L. Weis, "The Colonial Clergy of the Middle Colonies," Amer. Antiq. Soc. *Proc.*, LXVI (1956–57), 303; J. Thomas Scharf and Thompson Westcott, *History of Philadelphia. 1609–1884* (Phila., 1884), II, 1413; J. H. Dobbs, "The Reformed Church in Philadelphia," Pa. German Soc. *Proc. and Addresses,* XI (1902), 168.

to expect an answer to every Letter I write, I am sufficiently paid
by the assurance that you receive mine with Pleasure, and when
you have leisure to write me one I hope you are sensible I receive
the favour with Gratitude. I was with my Mother when your Letter of March 14. arriv'd.[3] Were I no otherwise interested in it than
the part I take in what gives you pain I should be sorry to give you
an account of her bad state of health. She has had a return of the
disorder in her Head, and applied again to Dr. James, from whose
prescription she found relief,[4] and I hope she is in that respect
better, but she is under the hands of good Mr. Small[5] from a hurt
she receiv'd in her Leg by a fall, and I fear the confinement will
retard the Recovery of her Health: However let us hope that ere
you receive this account she will be well; I don't love to spread
dejection. My Aunt is well, and so is my Aunt Rooke, excepting
her Lameness.[6] They are much oblig'd by your kind Remembrance, and send their good Wishes in return. I have seen Miss
Blunts[7] since I receiv'd your last favour, and let them know the
obliging notice you took of their family. My Dolly is better upon
the whole than she was last year, but she is far from well. I often
say I know very few that are good for anything who enjoy Health:
I hope you will ever be one exception.

I thank you, my dear, Sir for the Narrative[8] you sent me, which

3. See above, pp. 110–11.
4. For Mrs. Stevenson's "disorder in her Head," see above, x, 428. Robert
James (1705–1776), B.A., St. John's College, Oxford, 1726; M.D., Cambridge, 1728, was a neighbor of the Stevensons on Craven St. In 1746 he
patented a powder and pill for use in fevers and inflammatory pain; it caused
some controversy but enjoyed considerable vogue and was prescribed for
George III early in his mental illness in 1788. *DNB*.
5. Probably Alexander Small, Scottish army surgeon and a friend of BF. See
above, IX, 110 n.
6. Mrs. Tickell and Mrs. Rooke, with whom Polly lived.
7. Polly's friends, Catherine and Dorothea (Dolly) Blunt. The latter had
been ill during 1763. See above, IX, 327 n; X, 334.
8. *A Narrative of the Late Massacres;* above, pp. 42–69. It was reprinted
in *Gent. Mag.*, XXXIV, 173–8, the April 1764 issue, published in early May. In an
introductory note to the publisher written from Bromley in Kent and signed
"J.H.," Dr. John Hawkesworth, warm friend of BF and Polly Stevenson, identified the author of the pamphlet he was sending and commented that "It is,
indeed, so strongly marked, that by those who know him it could not be mistaken; it has all the Plainness and Force, all the Quietness and Philanthropy of
the Author's Mind and Manner, which equally characterise and recommend it."

has afforded me the pleasure of attending to the just applause that
has been given you by those who had the happiness of knowing
you were the amiable man who ever breath'd such sentiments,
and likewise of those who knew you only by name. You cannot
imagine how proud I was upon this occasion to have you call'd *my*
Friend. Why will you not come to seek Repose in this Island.
Don't let them tell you "old trees cannot safely be transplanted,"[9]
I have lately seen some fine tall firs remov'd from Kensington to
the Queen's Palace without injury, and Why should not the valuable
North American plants flourish here? I am, my dear, my ever-
honour'd Friend, with the highest gratitude most affectionately
yours   M.S.

Pennsylvania Assembly: Reply to the Governor

Printed in *Votes and Proceedings of the House of Representatives*, 1763–
1764 (Philadelphia, 1764), p. 85.

The Assembly had reconvened on May 14 after a seven-week recess,
and on the 17th Governor Penn sent down a long message in reply to
that of the House on March 24 concerning the £55,000 supply bill.[1]
He reviewed the circumstances leading to the order in council of Sept.
2, 1760,[2] and argued that, if the wording of the stipulation regarding
assessment of the Proprietors' located but uncultivated lands was as
ambiguous as the Assembly now alleged, their agents and counsel should
have demanded a clarification at that time. He would not now discuss
"the Equity and Justice of the Decree," he said; to do so would subject
him "to the Charge of offering the highest Affront to, and flying in the
Face of, that supream and august Judicatory who pronounced it." The
Assembly's argument that a sound rule for interpreting "the Intention
of another," when two opposite meanings were possible, was to apply
the one which was "perfectly consistent with Justice and Equity" Penn
found quite "extraordinary" and an attempt to "shift the Question, and
state a different Case" than the one before them. The "Abuse and
Obliquy" the Assembly had bestowed on the Proprietors "with so lavish
a Hand" in the last message and the censure passed on the governor for
doing his duty were groundless and he would "pass over them with the
silent Disregard they deserve." Penn concluded by urging once more

9. So BF had remarked in his letter of March 14.
1. Above, pp. 116–22.
2. Above, IX, 196–211.

the revision of the bill so that the military forces could be kept up and the large arrears be paid to the troops employed in the defense of the frontier.[3]

After this message had been read, the Assembly appointed a committee of seven, including Franklin, to prepare a reply, and voted "by a great Majority" to send the bill back to the governor unaltered. Penn returned it promptly the next morning, May 18, by the secretary, who was instructed to say that the governor found the same objections to it as before and hence "could not agree to pass it." The Assemblymen, faced with this "final Negative," recognized their defeat. Since "the Demands of His Majesty's General cannot be complied with by the Province, but upon such unequal Terms as his Honour is pleased to prescribe," a majority voted that a committee previously appointed to draft a reply to the message of the 17th should now bring in a new bill "conformable to the Amendments proposed by the Governor on the former Bill." Immediately afterwards two petitions to the King were read asking him to take the province under his immediate government; one of these was "signed by upwards of Fifteen Hundred Inhabitants" and the other "by the Society in this Province called Quakers."[4]

The committee presented the new bill on May 19, and the Assembly passed and sent it to Penn on the 22d. In the paragraph dealing with the assessment of the Proprietors' located but uncultivated lands—the major subject of controversy—the offending words "under the same Circumstances of Situation, Kind and Quality" had been struck out, so that the bill now used the precise language of the order in council and provided that the best located uncultivated lands of the Proprietors were to be assessed at no higher rate than were the worst such lands of the inhabitants.

Governor Penn thus won a major victory but, as events showed, he was not content with this achievement. When he laid the bill before the Council his advisers pointed out that, although Franklin and Charles had promised the Privy Council in 1760 that the Assembly would amend the supply acts of 1759 and 1760 in accordance with the stipulations then laid down, no such amendments had ever been enacted and the present bill failed to include them. Furthermore, the receivers general, Richard Hockley and Edmund Physick, now complained that the bill required them to file a detailed account of all proprietary property and of all quitrents due the Proprietors, arranged by townships and counties, within fifteen days of receiving the necessary forms from the assessors. Repeated changes in the boundaries of townships, districts, and counties, they said, and frequent resales of lands on which quitrents were due

3. *Votes*, 1763–64, pp. 77–9; *Pa. Col. Recs.*, IX, 174–7.
4. *Votes*, 1763–64, pp. 79–81; *Pa. Col. Recs.*, IX, 177–8. On these petitions and others relating to the same subject, see above, pp. 145–7.

made accurate reports in such a short time impossible. The receivers general asked that they be given more time and that they be not held liable for "mistakes and inadvertencies." Governor Penn therefore returned the bill to the Assembly, May 25, with a message asking for inclusion of the specific amendment of the earlier supply acts and for the changes which the receivers general considered necessary.[5]

The assemblymen, who thought they had complied fully with the governor's terms, were naturally infuriated by these fresh demands. Without taking time to appoint a committee, they prepared "at the Table" a curt reply pointing out that in all his previous messages the governor had insisted that they make the bill conformable to words of the order in council, "after which you would readily pass it into a Law." They had "strictly complied" with this demand, they said, but Penn had now "been pleased to start two Objections, both of them new, notwithstanding the Parts of the Bill objected to have been repeatedly and long before you." They asked him to assent to the bill and sent it back to him for the purpose.[6]

Before any further action by the Assembly on this issue was possible, Isaac Norris had resigned as speaker and Franklin had been elected in his place.[7] When the assemblymen returned to their quarters after the ceremony in which Penn had confirmed their choice of Franklin and were prepared to resume business, they received a written message from the governor demanding "a speedy and explicit Answer" whether they "would or would not amend the present Supply Bill, or frame a separate One, in compliance with the Stipulations of your Agents, so often mentioned and recommended," but which they had ignored in their message of the day before. It was "absolutely necessary," Penn said, to have their answer before he could decide about the bill before him. The House took this message into consideration at once, and "after some Time spent therein," prepared an answer "at the Table," and agreed to it. Then for the first time in his capacity as speaker Franklin signed a message to the governor.[8]

May it please your HONOUR,   [May 26, 1764]

In Answer to your Message of this Day, we beg Leave to observe, that in Compliance with the General's Requisition, we have

5. *Votes*, 1763–64, pp. 81–3; *Pa. Col. Recs.*, IX, 178–80.
6. *Votes*, 1763–64, pp. 83–4; *Pa. Col. Recs.*, IX, 180–1.
7. See above, pp. 195–6.
8. *Votes*, 1763–64, p. 85. Penn dropped his request for the changes asked for by the receivers general, and the matter was not raised again during the controversy.

voted the Number of Men demanded for the Service of the Crown, and have prepared a Bill for their Support, strictly conformable to the Stipulations entered into by the Agents of this Province, which Bill is now before you, and we again request your Honour would, without Delay, give your Assent thereto, it being so immediately necessary for His Majesty's Service, and the Defence of His Colonies.

As to the Amendments you require of the Acts of 1759 and 1760, we do not conceive how that Matter can be *"absolutely necessary"* to your Determination on the Supply Bill now before you: Those Amendments have been repeatedly required of former Assemblies, who, after full Enquiry, were of Opinion, that no Injustice had ever been done to the Proprietaries in the Execution of those Acts; however, should your Honour hereafter make the contrary appear to this House, we shall chearfully take the Matter proposed under our Consideration, and do the Proprietaries all the Justice that can be reasonably desired. Signed by Order of the House, BENJAMIN FRANKLIN, Speaker.

Pennsylvania Assembly: Reply to the Governor

Printed in *Votes and Proceedings of the House of Representatives*, 1763–1764 (Philadelphia, 1764), pp. 89–91.

The Assembly's message of May 26 (immediately above) had made clear to Governor Penn and his Council that the assemblymen had no intention of including in the supply bill any formal amendment of the acts of 1759 and 1760. It did include references to the Supply Act of 1760, however, and in the opinion of the councilors these had the effect of reenacting it. Consequently Penn sent the bill back again on May 29 with a message "earnestly" desiring the Assembly to "free it from this Objection, by striking out the exceptionable Clause." If it did so Penn would "no longer with-hold my Assent" to the bill.[9] After considering this message the same day, the House formally *"Resolved,* That the Necessity of raising Money for His Majesty's Service, and the Defence of this Province, is so great and pressing, that the House will, in this Instance, as they have done in some preceding Instances during their present Session, wave their important Parliamentary Rights relating to Money Bills, and agree to the Alteration of the present Bill as proposed

9. *Pa. Col. Recs.,* IX, 183–4; *Votes,* 1763–64, p. 87.

by the Governor; protesting at the same time against the Violence done to the Constitution, and declaring that the same ought never, never to be drawn into Precedent."

Thereupon the assemblymen made one last retreat and amended the bill by striking out all reference, direct or indirect, to the Supply Act of 1760 and substituting new phraseology where necessary. They sent the bill to the governor at once and Penn enacted it on the morning of May 30, nearly five months after the Assembly had first voted to raise £50,000 for the military expenses of the year.[1]

The Assembly did not now—and never did thereafter—formally amend the acts of 1759 and 1760, yet they had clearly suffered a major defeat over the central issue in the controversy: the basis for assessing the Proprietors' located but uncultivated lands and ungranted town lots. The actions of the Paxton Boys, the complaints of inhabitants of the interior counties that they were underrepresented, and the requirements of colonial defense against the Indians had combined to create pressures too strong to resist. And John Penn had absolutely refused to yield on this central issue. Such firmness was unusual among governors of either proprietary or royal provinces. Again and again in times of war or other danger the executives, usually with a more acute realization of the needs of the moment than their assemblies showed, had given way to the demands of the legislatures that were made effective by the control over appropriations. In Pennsylvania in 1764, however, the outcome was reversed. The Assembly surrendered under heavy fire and the governor held the field.

Each party to the dispute was doubtless sincere in thinking that right was on its side. What made the Assembly's defeat even more galling to its members was the belief that Penn was holding out, not from some abstract principle of government at large or some general interest of the public, but simply to protect a personal and financial interest of his father and uncle, the two Proprietors of the colony, whose taxes would be somewhat lowered if his interpretation of the disputed words in the order in council of 1760 were to prevail. This belief and the bitterness it engendered were responsible for the decision, long discussed but formally reached only at this session, to petition the King to remove the Proprietors from any share in the government. This feeling also led the Assembly to deliver one final blast against the governor before adjourning for the summer.

On May 17, after reading Penn's long message of that day, the Assembly had appointed a committee of seven, including Franklin, to prepare a reply. On the 28th, with Franklin now officiating as speaker,

1. *Votes*, 1763–64, pp. 87–8.

the committee reported its draft. The Assembly debated it paragraph by paragraph, agreed to it, and ordered it to be transcribed. Then on May 30, after all remaining business was finished, the transcription was brought forward, "compared at the Table," and signed. Two members were directed to present it to the governor with the information that the House proposed to adjourn to September 10. To this adjournment Penn replied that "he had no Objection."[2]

May it please your HONOUR,   May 30, 1764.

The professed Intention of your Honour's Message of the Seventeenth Instant being to vindicate the Character of the Proprietaries, and give a fairer State of the Dispute between us than we had done, it would have pleased us, could either of those Purposes have been executed. We apprehend your Honour has failed in both.

The long Recapitulation of what passed at the Council Board in 1760, and from thence to the present Time, answers no End, as we conceive, but to insinuate that we have been contending against a Determination of the King in Council, while the Fact really is otherwise, we having made the late Bill conformable, in our Opinion, to every Article of that Determination. And the Dispute between us relates merely to the Meaning of one of those Articles, which we understand to intend an equal Taxation of the Proprietary Lands with those of the People, and which your Honour will have to mean, a partial and unequal Taxation in the Proprietaries Favour. And as you thought the Words alone of that Article would best bear the unjust Meaning you were pleased to put on them, you contended against our using any others with them, that might explain them in an equitable Sense. This was our sole Dispute; and though we think it extreamly inconvenient and improper to use in an Act Words of whose Meaning the two Branches of the Legislature have previously declared they have such different and contrary Conceptions, yet rather than His Majesty's Service should

2. *Votes*, 1763–64, pp. 77–9, 86, 89, 91, and above, p. 204. It is uncertain whether BF participated with the others on the committee in the drafting of this message after he became speaker. The long paragraph dealing with the hearing before the Privy Council Committee and defending the Assembly agents and their counsel on the matter of ambiguity in phraseology must at least have been based on his comments to the other members of the Assembly committee.

be longer obstructed, we have given up the Point, and, in a new Bill, inserted the very Words; confiding, that the Sense of natural Justice in the Assessors and Commissioners, who are to execute the Act, will determine them to do what is right.

Thus the Matter might have rested; but as your Honour, with a View of placing our Conduct in an unfavourable Light, is pleased to ask us a Number of Questions, we are obliged to give them Answers, which, though short, we hope will be clear and satisfactory. "Were not learned Counsel," you ask, "employed, and fully instructed by the Agents, on the Part of the Assembly, to advocate the Supply Bill of the Year 1759?" We answer, yes. "Were not those Counsel twice fully heard, both before the Lords of Trade and the King in Council, antecedent to the Decree?" They were fully heard before the Lords of Trade, and a Committee of the Council.[3] "Did not the Agents understand the Force and Meaning of the second and third Articles, previous to their signing the Stipulation?" Undoubtedly; and as we have no Dispute about the Meaning of the third, we scarce know why it is mentioned.[4] "If they entertained a Notion that they were ambiguous, why did they not then object to them, when they might have had their Doubts removed upon the Spot?" It seems they entertained no such Notion, nor had any Doubts to be removed. It appears, by the Pleadings of the Proprietaries Counsel, of which we have a Copy taken first in Short-hand,[5] that they there made no such Claim of a partial and unequal Taxation of their located uncultivated Lands, as is now made for them. They only pretended Fears that the People would tax them *unequally,* and desired no more than that such Provision should be made, as might secure for them an *equal* Taxation. The Doubts you mentioned, if there are any, have arisen in Pennsylvania. Your Honour makes it a Crime in us, to suppose any

3. For those hearings and the reports based on them, see above, IX, 125–73, 196–211.
4. Interpretation of the third article, which stipulated that the Proprietors' ungranted lands in boroughs and towns should be rated as if they were located uncultivated lands, depended almost entirely on the interpretation of the second article, which dealt with such lands in general.
5. The Assembly agents' solicitor engaged a Mr. Cooke to take shorthand notes of the proceedings before the Privy Council Committee and paid him ten guineas for his services. Above, IX, 24, 197. BF apparently delivered a transcript of these notes to the Assembly but it cannot now be found.

Ambiguity or Obscurity in the Words of a Report of a Committee of Council, though that Supposition arose merely on the Observation of your differing so widely from us in the Construction of them. This was our Remark; "We may both be separately clear in our Conceptions of their Meaning, but our differing so widely in those Conceptions, seems to indicate at least some Ambiguity or Obscurity in the Terms." If your Honour had not differed from us in the Meaning of these Words of the Report, there would have been no Doubts about it, for we made none. And our Observation, that Laws, composed by the wisest Men, are sometimes found to contain Obscurities and Uncertainties, which those who are to execute them find difficult to clear and settle: And that, when any Words of such Laws are capable of two Meanings, one unjust and unequal, and the other consistent with Justice and Equity, we conceived it a good Rule to judge that the Intention is with the latter, arose originally upon your differing with us in that Construction. But this you candidly call a "contending that the controverted Articles of the Decree require Additions and Explanations to be made to them by us, to reconcile them to common Justice and Honesty." For our Parts, we cannot yet perceive any Thing indecent or "immodest" in our Observation, that Laws made by the wisest Bodies of Men (by King, Lords and Commons, for Instance) do sometimes contain Obscurities and Uncertainties. Subsequent Laws frequently made by the same august Legislators, to explain the preceding, are Proofs of it. We therefore added justly, that it was no Reflection on such Bodies to say this. But as your Honour purposed to make us appear guilty of a Reflection on them, you thought fit to mutilate the Sentence in your Quotation of it from our Message, and leave those Words intirely out. But to return to your Honour's Questions. "Why were not the Objections lately made against those Parts of the Decree, pointed out and urged to Mr. Hamilton, as Reasons for not coming into the Measure, when he repeatedly solicited you to comply with the Stipulations of your Agents?" Answer, The Objections in Question are against an unjust Construction that, in our Opinion, your Honour put on certain Words, which being used in the Stipulations of the Agents, you contended should be inserted, without Explanation, in the Bill. As this Construction was never put on those Words by Governor Hamilton, we could not point out and urge to him those Objections against it. "Why have these Objections been treasured up, and kept in Reserve till this critical Period?" Objections not in Being could not be "treasured up;" and Objections of no Kind can exist, previous to a Supposition of the Thing objected to. Your Honour will please to reflect that your Construction, which these Objections relate to, was as new and strange, as it is unjust and unequal, and so glaringly unjust and unequal, that you was yourself unwilling to own it, and could not, till after three Messages, urging an Explanation from you, prevail with yourself openly to avow it.[6]

You are pleased to add, "as to the Equity and Justice of the Decree, I should think I justly subjected myself to the Charge of offering the highest Affront to, and flying in the Face of, that supreme and august Judicatory who pronounced it, were I to enter into any Arguments with you in Support of it." Will your Honour give us Leave once more to put you in Mind, that it is not the Equity and Justice of a Decree that we are disputing, but your *unequal* and *unjust* Construction of it, *viz.* that the *best and most valuable* of the Proprietaries Lands shall be taxed no higher than the *worst* of the Peoples. Your total Inability of supporting this Construction by the least Colour of Argument or Reason, is what you would fain conceal under that extravagant Pretence of Respect to the Judicatory who, you say, pronounced it. Could you, by any Arguments, have shewn the Equity and Justice of such a Taxation, we should not now have heard, for the first Time, this extraordinary Position, that demonstrating the Equity and Justice of a Decree, would be flying in the Face of Authority. Wise, learned and pious Men, have in all Ages thought themselves well employed in convincing Mankind of the Reasonableness, Equity and Justice of Laws, human and divine; and never once dreamt that, by so doing, they were "offering the highest Affront to, and flying in the Face of, the supreme and august Judicatories who pronounced them."

Your Honour charges us with bestowing much *Abuse* on the Proprietaries. Stating plain public Facts, where necessary, we do not conceive to be *Abuse,* though done in plain Terms: But the misrepresenting a loyal and dutiful People to their Sovereign, as the Proprietaries, to cloak their own Avarice, have done the People

6. The Assembly's verbal messages of March 19 and 20 and written message of March 22; Penn's verbal messages of March 20 and 21 and written message of March 23; above, pp. 112–17.

of this Province for many Years past, is, in our Opinion, *Abuse*, though it were delivered in the politest Language. It was in this Part of your Honour's Message that we expected that Vindication of the Proprietaries, which in the first Paragraph seemed to be proposed: But now you chuse to pass all over with a "silent Disregard," reflecting probably on the Maxim you had before advanced, that "Facts are stubborn Things," and despairing, it seems, by any "Colouring" to "disguise the Truth."

Your Honour's "Resolution to discharge the Station you fill, with Fidelity and Justice to the good People of this Province," is highly laudable; but may we be permitted to ask a Question or two in our Turn? Is it consistent with *Justice* to the good People of this Province, to insist on taxing the *best* and *most valuable* of the Proprietaries Lands no higher than the *worst and least valuable* of the Peoples Lands, in a common Tax to be levied for the Defence of the whole? And farther, when the Requisition was made to your Honour, by the General, of raising a Number of Men for His Majesty's Service in your Province, were not the three lower Counties understood to be included?[7] Your Honour has since met, and exchanged Compliments with the Assembly of those Counties, without making (as far as we have heard) the least Demand of them. Is it "Justice to the good People of this Province," to saddle them with all the Expence of defending that Government, with all the Proprietary Property contained in it, and not call upon it for the least Assistance, while we are, and shall so long be, loaded with the heavy Debt the Wars have occasioned? The Troops raised here will perhaps all be marched to the Westward, in His Majesty's Service: In which Case, at least, we cannot but think it reasonable to have expected a Proportion of Forces from that Government, to assist in the Protection of our Frontier.

Your Honour's Message concludes with recommending to us (as if we had hitherto neglected it) the raising Supplies for the

7. Sir Jeffery Amherst's letter to Governor Hamilton of Nov. 5, 1763, which Penn laid before the Assembly on December 20, said in one paragraph: "I must apply to the Province of Pennsylvania, and Colony of Virginia, for their Assistance on the Occasion," and in the next paragraph: "The Proportion I must demand from your Province is One Thousand Men, exclusive of Commissioned Officers." *Votes*, 1763–64, p. 13. The Delaware counties with their separate Assembly are not specifically mentioned in the letter, nor is the colony of Maryland, parts of which were even more exposed.

King's Service, the Defence of the Frontiers, and Discharge of the public Debt. Which obliges us to remark, that within a few Months we have sent up to your Honour three Bills for those Purposes,[8] two of which have been rejected, because they required a fair and equal Taxation of the Proprietary with other Estates, for their common Defence. And we may add that, in our Zeal for the publick Service, we have departed from the ancient Forms of Parliamentary Proceeding, and waved very important Rights, which, under a more equitable Government, we should not have been constrained to; and such a Government we now hope is not far distant, and that an End will thereby be put to these disagreeable and mischievous Proprietary Contentions, and the People of this much injured Province restored to their Privileges, which they have long been deprived of; Proprietary Will and Pleasure, expressed in their Instructions, being now our only Law, which, through public Necessities, and the Distresses of War, we have been and are compelled to obey.   Signed by Order of the House,
BENJAMIN FRANKLIN, Speaker.[9]

8. A £50,000 bill on February 24, a first £55,000 bill on March 14, and a second £55,000 bill on May 22. The last of these, amended on May 29, was the one Penn finally accepted on the 30th. *Votes*, 1763–64, pp. 52, 60, 81, 88.

9. The controversy over the Supply Act had a strange sequel. On May 30, 1764, the very day it became law, Henry Wilmot, the Proprietors' solicitor, wrote Governor Penn that he, Wilmot, had advised the Proprietors to yield the disputed point of the taxation of their uncultivated, located lands. He believed, he said, that the governor's interpretation was the one originally intended, but he was "not certain that after this length of time, when matters are cool, at least in this country, if this act alone were now to be debated, unaccompanied with any other flagrant acts of the assembly, that the construction might not be put upon [the stipulation in the order in council of Sept. 2, 1760] contended for by the assembly." The Proprietors had agreed with him; if the act had already passed in the form the governor had demanded, Penn was to direct that it was to be executed according to the Assembly's construction of the original stipulation. *Statutes at Large, Pa.*, VI, 585–8. Thomas and Richard Penn enclosed this letter with one of their own to the governor, June 1, 1764, confirming the decision, since the matter was one "that regards our own property only." They added that they supposed "the dispute on the mode of taxation must now be entirely settled." In subsequent letters to the governor and other supporters in Pa. during the summer and fall, Thomas Penn emphasized that he and his brother had given in, not through fear of an application to the Crown for a change in government, but because "there does appear some equity" in the Assembly's argument. He admitted to William Smith in October that "at this distance of time, no Person here that considers

213

To Richard Jackson

ALS: American Philosophical Society

Dear Sir   Philada. June 1. 1764

My last to you was of the 1st. of May,[1] since which I am favour'd with yours of the 13th. of February and 10th. March.[2]

[the stipulation] looks upon it in any other light than that the Assembly contended for." Thomas and Richard Penn to John Penn, June 1; Thomas Penn to John Penn, June 8; to Benjamin Chew, June 8; to James Hamilton, June 13; to William Smith, Oct. 12, 1764, Penn Papers, Hist. Soc. Pa.

Governor Penn must have received notice of the Proprietors' decision at least by August 13, when William Allen arrived from England, and he acknowledged his new orders on September 1. He expressed regret that they had not come before he passed the bill, "as I might have had it in my power to have prevented the flame that has since broke out." Yet, with what must be recognized as political shrewdness but something less than candor to the public, he did nothing to quench the fire during the last month of the election campaign. As he explained to his uncle, he could not "help thinking it would be of bad consequence to let the Contents [of the letters from Wilmot and the Proprietors] be known before the new Assembly is chosen. Mr. Chew and Mr. Hamilton are of the same opinion." To Thomas Penn, Sept. 1, 1764, Penn Papers, Hist. Soc. Pa. So the bitter campaign was fought out with no hint from the governor that his superiors in England had reversed his position on the issue that had precipitated the crisis. Although word of the decision in England became known in October, Governor Penn preserved official silence until Jan. 17, 1765, when he addressed a circular letter to the commissioners of appeal informing them of the Proprietors' decision and asking them and the county commissioners and local assessors to interpret the Supply Act in the way the Assembly had wanted from the start. On January 26, the commissioners and assessors for Philadelphia Co. reported to him that they were bound by the express terms of the law as passed and could not comply with Penn's request without the passage of a special act for the purpose. Thereupon the governor was forced to the mortifying procedure of sending the Assembly a formal message, Jan. 30, 1765, announcing the Proprietors' reversal of his steadfastly held position of the previous year and proposing a supplemental bill to amend the Supply Act accordingly. *Pa. Col. Recs.*, IX, 237, 240–1; 8 *Pa. Arch.*, VII, 5730. The Assembly passed the proposed bill February 7; Penn returned it with an amendment relating in an unspecified way to the taxation of the Proprietors' town lots; neither side would yield to the other; and the bill failed of passage. *Pa. Col. Recs.*, IX, 244–5; 8 *Pa. Arch.*, VII, 5731, 5735, 5738, 5739, 5741–2. Twice thereafter, in September 1766 and January 1774, the Supply Act of 1764 was successfully amended in other particulars, but never in the controversial matter of the assessment and taxation of proprietary lands.

1. See above, pp. 185–8.
2. Neither of these letters has been found.

We are oblig'd to you for deferring the propos'd Stamp Act.[3]
I hope, for Reasons heretofore mention'd, it will never take Place.
We see in the Papers that an Act is pass'd for granting certain
Duties on Goods in the British Colonies, &c. but are not yet acquainted with its Contents.[4] The Men of War station'd in our several Ports are very active in their new Employment of Custom
house Officers;[5] a Portmanteau cannot go between here and New
York without being search'd: Every Boat stopt and examin'd, and
much Incumbrance by that means brought upon all Business. Undoubtedly the illicit Trade ought to be stopt; and if all this Strictness is necessary to that end, I have the less Objection to it. But
they tell me a Ship from Lisbon is seizable for a Chest of Lemons.
Methinks such Trifles are not proper Objects of Laws. Lemons are
no Produce of Britain: In our hot Summers they are necessary to
our Health: Why may we not be indulg'd with them? To carry
them first to England and then bring them here is the Way to have

3. For the fullest treatment of this complicated affair, see Edmund S.
Morgan, "The Postponement of the Stamp Act," 3 *William and Mary
Quar.*, VII (July 1950), 353–92. But for a substantial disagreement with part,
at least, of Morgan's interpretation, see Jack M. Sosin, *Agents and Merchants
British Colonial Policy and the Origins of the American Revolution, 1763–
1775* (Lincoln, Neb., 1965), pp. 50–3. On hearing that the Americans credited
him with securing the postponement of the act, Jackson denied it, saying
that he had "very little Weight or Influence" in Great Britain. See below,
pp. 313–14.
4. *Pa. Gaz.*, May 31, 1764, printed the news (under a Boston, May 17, date
line) of the passage by the House of Commons on March 22 of the "Bill for
laying a Duty of Three Pence Sterling per Gallon on foreign Molasses," a
prolix description of the Sugar Act (which was actually passed on April 5,
1764). The May 24 issue of *Pa. Gaz.* had carried a list of some of the duties
which were supposed to be laid under this act.
5. "In April, 1763, Parliament passed an act laying the basis for the use of
the British Navy in time of peace as an arm of the British customs service to
enforce the British acts of trade and customs throughout the empire. Eight
warships and twelve armed sloops were assigned to service in North American
waters, whose commanders were deputed by the Commissioners of Customs
. . . 'to seize and proceed to condemnation of all such Ships and Vessels as
you shall find offending against the said Laws [of trade].' " Bernhard Knollenberg, *Origin of the American Revolution: 1759–1766* (New York, 1960), p.
142. For complaints about the Navy's overzealous enforcement of the laws
of trade, see E. S. and H. M. Morgan, *The Stamp Act Crisis* (Chapel Hill,
1953), pp. 29–30.

them spoilt.[6] Thus People reason here; perhaps too partially to themselves.

This Use of Lemons brings to my Mind a Passage I once read in an old Journal of an East India Voyage, I think it was in Purchas's Pilgrim.[7] Three Ships sail'd from England in Company, and being long delay'd by Calms in the hot Latitudes, two of them grew very sickly, so that when they came to Saldanha, there were not well Men enow on board to bring them properly to anchor; but the other which had been very healthy, spar'd them Hands for that purpose. The Health of the other Ship is ascrib'd to the Captain's obliging each Man of his Crew to drink a Glass of Lemon Juice fasting every Morning during the Voyage, having brought with him a Quantity for that purpose.[8] This was printed 150 Years ago, and yet it is not become a Practice.

I saw in the Chronicle a Line of Notice, that after the Christmas Hollidays would be published *The Administration of the Colonies.* I imagin'd it might be the Title of your intended Work, and hop'd to have had it here by this time.[9]

Our Assembly met on the 4th. ulto. and rose the 30th. From the Time of their preceding Adjournment was about Six Weeks, during

6. The Navigation Act of 1663, the so-called Staple Act, stipulated that all European goods imported into the colonies, with the exception of salt, horses, servants, and provisions from Scotland and Ireland, and wines from Madeira and the Azores, had to be first brought to England, unloaded, and taxed, on pain of forfeiture of the ship.

7. Samuel Purchas, *Hakluytus Posthumus, or Purchas his Pilgrimes, contayning a History of the World in Sea Voyages and Land-Trauells by Englishmen and others* (4 vols., London, 1625). This work is listed in the Lib. Co. Phila. Catalogue for 1764, p. 26. The most convenient edition is the Hakluyt Soc. reprint, Extra Series, 20 vols., in which the passage here referred to appears in II (Glasgow, 1905), 395–6.

8. This voyage was taken in 1600–1 by Capt. James Lancaster in command of the first East India Company fleet of four vessels, not three. For Lancaster, see *DNB.*

9. *London Chron.* March 1–3, 1764, advertised that *The Administration of the Colonies* (by BF's old friend Thomas Pownall, above, v, 339–40 n) would be "Speedily" published, and the March 29–31 issue of the paper printed an extract from the work; BF's mention of "Christmas Hollidays" was apparently a slip of the pen for Easter. Jackson had written BF, April 4, 1763 (see above, x, 242), that he had completed "the Skeleton of my work," and by Dec. 27, 1763 (see above, x, 413), he wrote that he had "begun to print" it, but whatever the piece was, it was apparently never published.

and middle Values mentioned in our Laws, viz. Lands rated at £5 at £10 and at £15 per hundred Acres; and suppose A possesses 100 Acres of the first Sort; B 100 Acres of the second Sort, and C 100 Acres of the third Sort. Now, according to our present Laws, to raise from these Lands a Tax of Thirty Pounds in five Years, at 4s. (suppose) in the Pound:

A's Land, worth and rated at £ 5 would pay 20s., which for 5 Years is £ 5:0. 0
B's Land, worth and rated at £10 would pay 40s., which for 5 Years is £10:0. 0
C's Land, worth and rated at £15 would pay 60s., which for 5 Years is £15:0. 0

Total of the Tax in 5 Years is £30:0. 0

But suppose all reduc'd to £5 Value in the Rating, and the Tax to be continu'd till the £30 is rais'd, then there will be only 20s. a Year paid by each, which producing only £3 per Annum, the Tax must continue Ten Years to compleat the Sum, in which time each Man will pay £10 towards it; and tho' thereby the middling kind, B's Tract, pay neither more nor less than before, yet £5 is taken from C's Tax, and added to A's, by which the Tax of A is doubled, and the Burthen taken off the best Lands to be laid on the worst. The Proprietaries Lands we say are generally good, as he has the best Opportunities of choosing them; but not desiring to do them any Injustice, we us'd Words to this purpose, "that their Lands should not be tax'd higher than the lowest of the People's under the same Circumstances of Situation, Kind and Quality:" and this we thought fully answer'd the Intention of preventing any unjust Burthens being laid on the Proprietaries. So much by way of Justification of our Conduct, which others must judge of.

I am, Dear Sir, with sincerest Esteem and Respect, Your most obedient and most humble Servant   B FRANKLIN

Richard Jackson Esqr.

Endorsed: 1 June 1764 Benjn. Franklin Esqr

Provincial Commissioners: Orders for Payment

DS: Historical Society of Pennsylvania

As in previous supply acts, the measure passed on May 30, 1764, after so much controversy, named seven men—two councilors and five assemblymen—as provincial commissioners, a majority of whom "with the consent and approbation of the governor or commander in chief of this province for the time being, and not otherwise," were empowered to expend the £55,000 appropriated. The men appointed were the same seven, including Franklin, who had served during the previous autumn under the terms of the £24,000 Supply Act of Oct. 22, 1763.[6]

On June 4 the commissioners issued their first order for payment after the passage of the new act, and they continued to sign similar orders from time to time through the summer and fall and until after Franklin had sailed for England in November. As has been done in previous volumes of this series, a list of all located orders for payment issued during the period when Franklin was present in Philadelphia is given here, showing the date, name of the payee, purpose for which payment was made, and the amount of each.[7] As before, any order that Franklin failed to sign personally—usually because he was absent from the meeting at the time the order was drawn and signed—is indicated by an asterisk (*) following the date.

It will be seen that several entries relate, not to general military activities, but to expenses connected with the march of the Paxton Boys on Philadelphia in February or the maintenance of the Moravian Indians at the barracks there. Payments totaling £1145 18s. 7d. made during the period covered by this list can be clearly identified as relating directly to these matters.

Date	Payee	Purpose	Amount		
June			£	s.	d.
4	James Young	To be applied to recruiting service	500	0	0
27*	John Galbreath	9 muskets delivered during Feb. disturbance	11	5	0
27	Thomas Robinson	Express services during Feb. disturbances	8	2	3
27	James Young	To be applied to recruiting service	500	0	0
27	James Young	To pay arrears due troops	8500	0	0

6. See above, X, 363 n.

7. See above, VI, 392–6, 437–40; VII, 3–5, 25–8; X, 362–4. All the pay orders listed here are also recorded in the accounts of the trustees of the Loan Office submitted to and approved by an auditing committee of the Assembly, Sept. 18, 1766. These accounts also show further payments from the proceeds of the Supply Act of May 30, 1764, made on order of the commissioners after BF's departure but before May 8, 1765, when the unexpended balance stood at £156 15s. 6d. 8 Pa. Arch., VII, 5915–21. One pay order for a small sum which BF did not sign is included in the file and recorded in the Loan Office account as paid from the £55,000 Supply Act, although it was dated May 15, 1764, and paid the next day, two weeks before the act was passed, probably from a remaining balance of the £24,000 act of the previous October. The Loan Office account also includes one payment in July of £500 for which no original pay order has been located. Neither is included in the present list.

Date	Payee	Purpose	Amount		
July			£	s.	d.
3	Joseph Fox	To purchase clothing etc. for troops	5000	0	0
4*	Robert Levers	Provisions for troops	1000	0	0
6	John Nelson	To repay cash borrowed by Col. Bouquet	500	0	0
16	Baynton & Wharton	Sundries delivered during late Riot	158	4	0
17	David Deshler	Medicines and attendance to 2 wounded children of Hans Sneider killed by Indians	19	15	2
17	James Young	Recruiting service	1300	0	0
17	James Young	Arrears and advance of pay for troops and officers	14,500	0	0
19	Isaac Howell and John Howard	Support of sick and disabled French Neutrals	143	9	7
20	Job Chillaway	Services under Col. Clayton	13	16	0
20	Joseph Fox	Expences of clothing etc.	1000	0	0
20	Robert Levers	Victualing troops, account settled	618	2	7
20	Joseph Shippen, Jr.	Balance of account	8	1	0
27	Balsar Geerh	Armourer at Ft. Augusta	75	0	0
27	Joseph Shippen, Jr.	Premium for 4 scalps taken last fall	100	0	0
August					
14*	William Dunwick	Repairing arms	80	0	0
14	James Ennis	Victualing Pa. troops	200	0	0
14	Jacob Weiss	Pasturage of Indian horses and cows	18	4	3
16	David Scott	Pay and subsistence of 27 Cumberland Co. Rangers	169	0	0
16	Leonard Stoneburner	Carrying stores to Harris's Ferry and Reading	11	16	0
23*	Robert Callender	Provisions	1637	10	10
23*	Joseph Fox	Expenses for clothing etc.	400	0	0
23*	Robert Levers	Victualing troops	629	19	9
23*	Wm. Norton and Th. Masterman	Provisions for soldiers at barracks	27	18	7
23*	Christian Voght	Attendance on Cornelius Atkinson, wounded volunteer	15	0	0
23*	James Webb	Disbursements for Lancaster barracks	259	11	3
28	Col. James Burd	Disbursements at Ft. Augusta	58	8	7
28	William Dunwick	In full, repairing arms	110	7	4
28	Andrew McNair	Delivering notices and attending 123 meetings of Commissioners, Jan. 16, 1761, to July 20, 1764	9	4	6
31*	George Dods	For wounds received at Munsey Hill fighting Indians	25	0	0
31	Reuben Haines	Victualing Indians	85	10	0
September					
6*	John Hill	Coffins for French Neutrals	3	15	0
18	Thomas Apty	Services as an express	2	8	0

223

Date	Payee	Purpose	Amount £	s.	d
September					
18	Joseph Fox	Cloathing and Carriage account settled	561	13	2
18	Joseph Fox[8]	Provisions for Indians at barracks	781	13	9
18	John Hughes	Expenses at Easton Treaty	4	6	4
18	John Little	Entertainment of Paxton volunteers and Capt. Hoffman's troops	36	5	10
18	John Montgomery	To relieve Thos. McMurray, wounded by Indians	20	0	0
18	Richard Swan	Collecting and caring for provincial arms	20	0	0
26	Jacob Weiss	Medicine and attendance of sick Indians at barracks	46	13	6
October					
11*	Robert Levers	Provisions for troops	400	0	0
20*	James Cogly	Subsistence and 2 horses to Indians going to the last Treaty	10	0	0

Henry Bouquet[9] to John Penn and the Provincial Commissioners

Copy: British Museum[1]

Gentlemen   Philadelphia 4th. June 1764

There being too few of His Majesty's Regular Troops in this Department to act offensively against the Enemy, till they are joined by the Thousand Men granted by this Government, I re-

8. Joseph Fox had been appointed barrackmaster when the Philadelphia barracks were built in 1758; he was therefore the officer responsible for feeding the Indians housed there.

9. On Col. Henry Bouquet, see above, VII, 63 n. At the time of this letter he was in command of one of two prospective expeditions planned by General Amherst and carried forward by Gage to march westward and compel the submission of the hostile Indian tribes. Col. John Bradstreet (above VIII, 344 n) was to lead one force through the Lake region to Detroit; Bouquet, with parts of the 42d and 60th Regiments and the Pa. provincial regiment of 1000 men authorized the previous December (above, X, 405 n, 408), was to move westward to Fort Pitt and from there advance into the Ohio Country against the Delaware and Shawnee. Bouquet had been in Carlisle and Philadelphia since the latter part of April, making preparations and fuming at the delay caused by the failure of the Pa. Assembly and Governor Penn to agree on a supply act to finance the colony's contingent of Bouquet's army. Sylvester K. Stevens, Donald H. Kent, and Leo J. Roland, eds., *The Papers of Col. Henry Bouquet*, II (Harrisburg, 1940), 279–96.

1. Printed here from a photostat in Lib. Cong.

quest that you will please to give the necessary orders to compleat, arm, and Cloathe these Troops as soon as possible.[2]

The king's Arms formerly lent to this Province having not been returned, There must be a sufficient quantity for present use, when put in repair.

I would also recommend to provide each man with a good Hatchet made in the form of a common Axe, in lieu of a Bayonet.

The difficulty of Supplying the Troops with shoes out of the Settlements, obliges me to mention that Two Pairs will be necessary for Each man besides the Two Pairs he is to have with him; Carriages will be furnished for those Spare Shoes, and the men must pay for it.[3]

In the Campaign of 1758, This Province granted to General Forbes, Two Troops of Light Horse, which were found of good service, and as I am of opinion that we might employ Horses with success against the savages, I request that you will grant me and equip one Troop; and in case that additional Expence Should be an objection, rather than to be deprived of the Service I expect from them, I would be satisfied to have Fifty men less, whose Pay for the Campaign would amount nearly to the Expence of Horses &c.[4]

I think the Horses would be fitted for that Service, if bought on the Frontiers of Virginia where they are commonly bred in the Woods.

I can not omit to Submit to your Consideration the use that might be made of Dogs against our Savage Enemies; It would be needless to expect that our Foot Soldiers can overtake an Indian in the Woods, and their audacious attempts in attacking our Troops and settlements may, in a great Measure, be ascribed to the certainty of evading our Pursuit by their flight: a few Instances of Indians Seized and worried by Dogs, would, I presume, deter them

2. A memorandum in Bouquet's hand of about the same date as this letter indicates that his available force, other than the Pa. regiment, consisted of 1050 men: 400 of the 42d Regiment, 250 Royal Americans (the 60th), 200 friendly Indians, and 200 drivers. *Bouquet Papers*, XV, 147.

3. Bouquet ordered that 2,000 pairs of spare shoes be procured for the Pa. troops, 1 *Pa. Arch.*, IV, 179.

4. Bouquet's marching orders, Sept. 15, 1764, indicate that his force included two troops of light horse, but how many of the men were Pa. provincials is not indicated. *Bouquet Papers*, II, 319.

more effectualy from a War with us, than all the Troops we could raise, and as we have not in this Country the Species of those animals, which would best answer this Purpose, I beg leave to recommend it to you, to have Fifty Couples of proper Hounds imported from Great Britain, with People who understand to train and manage them.[5]

They might be kept on the Frontiers, and a few given to Every Scouting Party, to discover the Ambushes of the Enemy, and direct the Pursuit: This requires that the men intended to follow the Dogs should be well mounted.

As soon as the Troops (which I must suppose inlisted to the End of December next) are compleated; Equipped, and ready to take the Field: I beg that they may have orders to assemble at Fort Loudoun, where they are to join the Regulars, and from that time they will be supplied with Provisions at the Charge of the Crown.[6] I have the honor to be with great Respect Gentlemen Your most obedient, and most Humble Servant   HENRY BOUQUET

NB. All the Articles mentioned in the above Letter have been agreed to by the Governor and the Commissioners the 4th. of June 1764.
                                                                H. B.

To the Governor and Commissioners

Endorsed: Copy of Coll. Bouquet's Letter to Govr. Penn and the Commissioners at Pensilvania 4th June 1764

5. For BF's suggested use of dogs in campaigning against Indians, as early as November 1755, see above, VI, 235. Bouquet's proposal that dogs be imported from Great Britain came rather late for use in connection with the campaign he was planning for that summer and fall. Governor Penn and the commissioners, however, offered 3s. per month to soldiers, not exceeding ten to a company, who would procure strong dogs to take with them on this service. 1 *Pa. Arch.,* IV, 180–1.

6. The troops were very slow in assembling; they left Carlisle about August 10, reached Fort Loudoun (14 miles west of Chambersburg) on the 13th, and Fort Pitt on September 17. [William Smith], *An Historical Account of the Expedition against the Ohio Indians in the Year MDCCLXIV, under the Command of Henry Bouquet, Esq.* (Phila., 1766), pp. 3–4.

To Anthony Stickney[7]

ALS: Justin G. Turner, Los Angeles (1959); Transcript: Harvard College Library (Sparks)

Loving Kinsman   Philada. June 16. 1764

I received yours of the 16th May,[8] and am glad to hear that you and your Family are well, and that your Wife is safely delivered of another Daughter, which I hope will prove a Blessing to you both.[9] I got home without any farther Accident, but have not yet recovered fully the former Strength of my Arm.[1] Your Brother Josiah Davenport[2] is still at Pitsburg, near 400 Miles west of this Place, where he has the Care of the Provincial Store, that was establish'd there during the Peace, for the Indian Trade; and since the War broke out again, there has been no good Opportunity of bringing off the Goods, so he is oblig'd to remain with them. His Wife and Children are here; and she seems to be in a bad State of Health, but the Children are well.[3] My Wife and Daughter thank you for your good Wishes, and return theirs for you and yours. Present my best Respects to Mr. and Mrs. Lowell,[4] and my

---

7. Anthony Stickney (1727–1774) was the husband of BF's niece, Dorcas Davenport (C.12.2), whose mother was BF's next elder sister, Sarah. Stickney was a chairmaker and lived in Newburyport, Mass. BF had visited the family on his journey between Boston and Portsmouth, N.H., in the summer of 1763. Stickney had the reputation among his wife's relatives of being "a lazy fellow." Van Doren, *Franklin-Mecom*, p. 290.

8. Not found.

9. *Vital Records of Newbury Massachusetts to the End of the Year 1849* (Salem, 1911), I, 491–7, lists the births of six children of Anthony Stickney, the youngest of whom was Dorcas, born Sept. 5, 1763. Her birth must have been almost daily expected when BF visited the Sticknes in late August or early September of 1763.

1. On the Boston-Portsmouth journey during the previous summer BF had fallen and dislocated his shoulder. See above, X, 278, 338.

2. Josiah [Franklin] Davenport (C.12.4), younger brother of Stickney's wife; see above, VII, 203 n. He is mentioned several times in the journal of his fellow storekeeper at Pittsburgh, James Kenny, 1761–63. *PMHB*, XXXVII (1913), 18, 19, 23, 170, 195, 201.

3. Davenport had four children by his second wife, the former Ann Annis; the youngest, Franklin Davenport (C.12.4.4; 1755–1832), became a U.S. senator from N.J., 1798–99, and a member of the House of Representatives, 1799.

4. John Lowell (1704–1767), A.B., Harvard, 1721; M.A., 1724. He was

Love to your Wife and Children. Remember me too, to your Brother Davenport[5] and his Family. I am, Your affectionate Uncle

B FRANKLIN

To William Strahan

ALS: Lehigh University Library[6]

Dear Mr. Strahan   Philada. June 17. 1764

I receiv'd your Favour per Capt. Walker,[7] which I shall answer fully per Hammet,[8] who sails in about ten Days. I think I am slighted lately per Mr. Becket.[9] Pray enquire and tell me the Reason, that if I have been in fault I may amend.

I left some Receipts with you for Subscription Monies to Books. I wish you to enquire about them, particularly Stewart's Athens.[1]

---

ordained in 1726 pastor of the Third Church of Newbury, later known as the First Church of Newburyport. *Sibley's Harvard Graduates,* VI, 496–501.

5. William Davenport (1717–1773), son of James Davenport (Stickney's father-in-law) by his first wife, and therefore a half-brother of Stickney's wife. He had settled in Newbury about 1738; served as captain of a company in the Quebec campaign of 1759; and in 1762 opened the Wolfe Tavern in Newbury, known also as Davenport's Inn. *New Eng. Hist. and Geneal. Register,* XXXIII (1879), 31–2; John J. Currier, *"Ould Newbury"; Hist. and Biog. Sketches* (Boston, 1896), pp. 492–501.

6. Plans for the publication of this edition of *The Papers of Benjamin Franklin* were announced in the newspapers of Sunday, January 17, 1954 (BF's 248th birthday). The next morning Mr. James D. Mack, Librarian of Lehigh University, mailed to the editor a photostat of this previously unpublished letter. The editorial staff gratefully and happily recorded it as Accession No. 1.

7. Strahan's letter has not been found; *Pa. Gaz.,* June 14, 1764, reported the arrival of the *Friendship,* Capt. J. Walker.

8. See below, pp. 240–2; *Pa. Gaz.,* June 28, 1764, reported the clearance of the *Dragon,* Capt. Francis Hammett. *London Chron.,* Aug. 2–4, 1764, reported its arrival off Tor Bay.

9. Thomas Becket of Tully's Head in the Strand, the publisher of BF's *The Interest of Great Britain Considered;* see above, IX, 274 n. BF had ordered some books from Becket on Dec. 17, 1763, and apparently felt that his order had not been filled quickly enough; see above, X, 393–5, and below, pp. 264–5.

1. James Stuart and Nicholas Revett, *The Antiquities of Athens* (London, 1762). Stuart, known as "Athenian Stuart," died in 1788. Additional volumes of this work were published in 1789, 1795, 1814, and 1830. Stuart was a member of a Club of Thirteen formed by BF and David Williams (1738–1816) about 1773 for philosophical discussion. David Williams, "More Light

228

My Love to Mrs. Strahan and your Family. I am, Dear Friend,
Yours affectionately   B FRANKLIN
We are all well, and as happy as other Folks for the present.
Addressed: To / Mr Wm. Strahan / Newstreet / Shoe Lane / London

To Richard Jackson   ALS: American Philosophical Society

Dear Sir   Philada. June 18. 1764
I received yours of the 13th. April,[2] which I shall answer fully
per Hammet, who is to sail in about 10 Days.[3] By that Ship you
will also receive a Letter from the Committee[4] with the Petitions
to the King,[5] mention'd in my former Letters. I wrote you a long
one via Bristol, of the 1st Instant,[6] to which I refer, and beg you
would per first Opportunity be very particular as to any Necessity
or Use of my being with you in the Prosecution of those Petitions,
my going over, or not, depending on the Opinion you may give
on that Head. I am, as ever, Yours most sincerely   B FRANKLIN

P.S. Our Provincials, 1000 Men under Col. Bouquet, are preparing
to march to the Westward.[7]
Great Mischiefs done lately on the Virginia Frontier.[8] People
wonder at your prohibiting our Carrying Staves directly to Ireland.[9]

Addressed: To / Richard Jackson Esqr / Inner Temple / London
Endorsed: Philad. June 18th. 1764 Benjn. Franklin

---

on Franklin's Religious Ideas," *Amer. Hist. Rev.,* XLIII (1937–38), 803–12,
esp. p. 810.
2. See above, pp. 175–7.
3. See the document immediately above for Captain Hammett's departure.
4. That is, a letter from the Assembly's Committee of Correspondence.
Such a letter has not been found, but for an indication of its probable contents, see above, pp. 198, 219–20 n.
5. See above, pp. 145–7, 199–200.
6. See above, pp. 214–21.
7. See above, p. 217.
8. *Pa. Gaz.,* June 14, 1764, carried an extract from a letter from Virginia,
dated June 4, which reported that the Indians had recently killed "upwards
of forty Persons . . . at the Pastures, on the Frontiers of Augusta County."
9. See below, p. 235.

To Ezra Stiles

ALS: Yale University Library

Reverend and dear Sir,   Philada. June 19. 1764

I sent you some time last Fall a Set of Chinese Prints, or rather Prints taken from Chinese Pictures, relating to the Culture of Silk in that Country.[1] I hope they got to hand, tho' I have not heard of your Receiving them.

My Brother brought me from you, Æpinus's Pieces.[2] I thank you for your Care in returning them. He tells me you would like to have one of the new Prints of your Friend.[3] As there are a few others in your Government, who do me the Honour to have some regard for me, and who perhaps I may never again have the Pleasure of visiting in any other Manner, I have taken the Liberty to trouble you with the Care of six of those Prints to be distributed agreable to the enclos'd List, as you have convenient Opportunity. They are said, in Point of Execution, to be extreamly well done. As to Likeness, there are different Opinions, as usual in such Cases. I send them roll'd in a Tin Case, as folding might damage them. With the sincerest Esteem, I am, Dear Sir, Your most obedient humble Servant   B FRANKLIN

Revd. Mr. Stiles.

Endorsed: Recd June 1764 Ansd July 17 1764[4]

List[5]

Rev. Mr Stiles

Govr Ward

1. See above, x, 389.

2. Peter Franklin (C.9), formerly of Newport, moved to Philadelphia in the spring or early summer of 1764 with his wife (below, p. 253) and assumed charge of the local post office in the following October. BF's copies of Aepinus' writings on magnetism had been lent to interested friends in New England. See above, x, 351–2, 389, and this volume, above, p. 254, and below, pp. 246, 254.

3. In May 1763 BF had no print available of either of his recent portraits, those by Benjamin Wilson and Mason Chamberlain, but on Feb. 24, 1764, he was able to send a number of Edward Fisher's mezzotint prints of the Chamberlain portrait to Jonathan Williams for distribution. See above, x, 266, and this volume, pp. 89–90.

4. Not found.

5. In addition to Stiles himself, the persons in R.I. to receive copies of the Fisher mezzotint were: Gov. Samuel Ward (above, v, 504 n); Catharine Ray

Mrs. Cath. Greene of Warwick
Dr. Babcock
Capt. Buckmaster
Mr. Lendall als[?] Lyndon

To George Whitefield[6]   Draft: American Philosophical Society

Dear Friend   Philada. June 19. 1764
   I received your Favour of the 21st past, and of the 3d. Instant and immediately sent the inclos'd as directed.[7]
   Your frequently repeated Wishes and Prayers for my Eternal as well as temporal Happiness are very obliging. I can only thank you for them, and offer you mine in return. I have my self no Doubts that I shall enjoy as much of both as is proper for me. That Being who gave me Existence, and thro' almost threescore Years has been continually showering his Favours upon me, whose very Chastisements have been Blessings to me, can I doubt that he loves me? And if he loves me, can I doubt that he will go on to take

---

Greene (above, v, 502 n); Joshua Babcock of Westerly (above, vi, 174 n); probably George Buckmaster, whose first wife had been BF's niece Abiah Franklin (C.11.1; above, viii, 93 n); and probably also Josias Lyndon (1704–1778), of Newport, clerk of the R.I. Assembly, trustee of the newly founded College of R.I., governor, 1768–69. According to Stiles, Lyndon was "a Gentleman of an amiable and respectable reputation, of Politeness and of a good Estate." Edmund S. and Helen M. Morgan, *The Stamp Act Crisis Prologue to Revolution* (Chapel Hill, [1953]), p. 185; David S. Lovejoy, *Rhode Island Politics and the American Revolution, 1760–1776* (Providence, 1958), pp. 136–40; *Biographical Cyclopedia of Representative Men of Rhode Island* (Providence, 1881), pp. 97–8.
   6. Whitefield had been in Philadelphia when BF returned from his New England journey in Nov. 1763, but they had missed seeing each other then. See above, x, 383. The preacher had gone on to New York City and then to New England. He traveled north as far as Portsmouth, then went to Boston in April 1764, moved southward in June, and spent the summer in New York City and Long Island, declining to go to Philadelphia until the middle of September because of the heat. On October 22 he set out for Georgia. Luke Tyerman, *The Life of the Rev. George Whitefield, B.A., of Pembroke College, Oxford* (London, 1876–77), ii, 469–78. These travels can be followed in some detail in the pages of *Pa. Gaz.*, which reported on them frequently.
   7. Neither of these letters has been found, and the enclosure referred to has not been identified.

care of me not only here but hereafter? This to some may seem Presumption; to me it appears the best grounded Hope; Hope of the Future; built on Experience of the Past.

By the Accounts I have of your late Labours, I conclude your Health is mended by your Journey, which gives me Pleasure. Mrs. Franklin presents her cordial Respects, with those of Dear Sir, Your affectionate humble Servant   B FRANKLIN

PS. We hope you will not be deterred from visiting your Friends here by the Bugbear Boston Accounts of the Unhealthiness of Philadelphia.[8]

Mr Whitefield

To John Ellicott

ALS: The London Hospital

Sir   Philada. June 23. 1764
Since the Receipt of your Letter of Jany. 8th. 1763.[9] I have been twice at New York, and at York in Virginia; at both which Places I made all the Enquiry I could, in the time I was there; after the Elizabeth Holland mention'd in Capt. Holland's Will; but not learning any thing, I desir'd Mr. Colden, Postmaster of New York, and Col. Hunter of Virginia,[1] to make farther Enquiry as they had Opportunity, which likewise produc'd no Information. At length I put Advertisements in the Gazettes of both those Provinces, as you will see by the inclos'd; and they were continu'd in the Papers for several Weeks successively.[2] I also engag'd a Gentleman, Mr.

8. Perhaps a sly dig at Boston, where Whitefield had been dissuaded from preaching for about a month, earlier this spring, because of a smallpox epidemic there. *Pa. Gaz.*, March 15, 1764.

9. Not found. It undoubtedly dealt with the same subject as correspondence of the previous year. Ellicott, a leading clockmaker of London and a strong supporter of the London Hospital, had asked BF to locate an Elizabeth Holland, mentioned in the will of her brother, Capt. William Holland. Ellicott seems to have believed that she lived in New York, but the will mentioned that the Hollands' father was "of James River," and so would have placed him in Virginia. BF had promised to have inquiries made in both colonies. See above, X, 248–50.

1. Alexander Colden, eldest son of Lieut. Gov. Cadwallader Colden (above, VI, 113 n), and Col. John Hunter of Hampton, Va. (above, VI, 223 n).

2. Eleven issues of *The Virginia Gazette* and one of *The New-York Gazette;*

Foxcroft, my Brother Postmaster General, who lives in Virginia to make what Enquiry he could at the General Court there, in April last, when the Gentlemen assemble from all Parts of that Province at Williamsburg. He did so accordingly, and informs me, that he could hear of none of the Name there, but those mention'd in the enclos'd Memorandum,[3] viz. one Richard Holland and Rebecca his Wife, who have a Daughter Lucy which is all the Information my Advertisement and his Enquiry has produc'd from thence, and amounts to nothing. From New York came a Person to me, in behalf of one Elizabeth Waldron, whose maiden Name was Holland. I told him, that in order to intitle her to the Claim, she must send me authenticated Certificates of her Father and Mother's Names, what Children they had, and other material Circumstances relating to the Family, that might evince her being the Person enquir'd after. On which I receiv'd from her the enclos'd Letter,[4] by which I think it appears that she cannot be the Person, for she seems to know nothing of a Brother Capt. William Holland. However I send it, that you and the Gentlemen concern'd may judge of it. It is all the Light I have been able to obtain by the Steps taken. And if you would have any thing farther done in the Affair, I shall readily obey your Commands.

The Reason of my making Enquiries in Virginia, was, that James River is in Virginia, and there is a York not far from it; and I apprehended that the New York might be a Mistake for that Virginia York.

I hope Mrs. Ellicot and your valuable Son and Daughters con-

---

or, Weekly Post-Boy were preserved at the London Hospital until 1936, when they were presented to the city of Williamsburg, Va. They were probably either the ones BF sent to Ellicott with this letter or copies he procured in 1771 and 1772 with affidavits that the advertisements had not succeeded in locating the missing woman. BF to Alexander Colden, BF to John Dixon, both dated Oct. 7, 1772. Lib. Cong. The advertisement printed in *N.-Y. Gaz.*, April 26, 1764, reads as follows: "If Elizabeth, Daughter of William Holland and Agnes his Wife, formerly of James River, and, as it is said, lately of New-York, be living, she may, by Inquiry of B. Franklin of Philadelphia, hear of something greatly to her advantage. And if the said Elizabeth is deceased, and hath, or hath not left Issue, those who are acquainted with such Circumstances are requested to give Information thereof to the said B. Franklin."

3. Not found.
4. Not found.

tinue well. Please to present my Respects to them, and to the Gentlemen at the George and Vulture in whose Company I spent so many agreable Hours.[5] With great Esteem, I am, Sir, Your most obedient Servant   B FRANKLIN
Mr. Ellicot

To Richard Jackson   ALS: American Philosophical Society

Dear Sir,   Philada. June 25. 1764
We here esteem ourselves greatly oblig'd to you for your un-wearied Endeavours in and out of Parliament to prevent Measures hurtful both to the Colonies and to the Mother Country. Several Letters from People at home to their American Friends, have been printed in the Papers of the different Provinces, mentioning in the strongest Terms your Zeal for the Welfare of the Colonies, and the Success attending it; so that your Name is now generally known and honour'd throughout North America.[6]
The Act of Parliament, which is now published here,[7] makes a great Stir among our Merchants, and much is said of the ill Effects that must attend it. My Opinion is, that more is apprehended than will happen; and that Experience only will inform us clearly, how short it will fall of procuring on one hand the Good, and producing

5. On the Monday Club at the George and Vulture Tavern, see above, x, 250 n.
6. *Pa. Jour.*, April 5, 1764, printed the following extract from a letter from a gentleman in London to a friend in New York, dated Feb. 7, 1764: "There is a Gentleman, who is a Member of Parliament, and Agent for Connecticut and Pennsylvania, by the Recommendation of Mr. Ingerson [Ingersoll] and Mr. Franklin, that has great weight with all the Ministry, and whose honesty will prompt him to stand in our Interest: He has been often to the Board of Trade, and has succeeded so well, as to gain them over to our interest, and the Lords of Trade will have great Influence over the House." The same paper, May 10, 1764, carried the following news from New York, May 7: "Mr. Jackson, agent for Connecticut, (a member of the house) exerted him-self nobly, and that it was chiefly owing to him that the stamp act did not take place, likewise that Mr. Allen of Philadelphia, was indefatigable in remon-strating to many of the members, with whom he was acquainted, on the illegality of an internal tax, and had considerable influence in preventing it."
7. *Pa. Gaz.*, June 14, printed the "heads" of the Sugar Act, 4 Geo. III, c. 15. *Pa. Jour.*, June 14, 21, printed the complete act.

234

on the other hand the Evil, that People engag'd in different Interests expect from it. If it is not finally found to hurt us, we shall
grow contented with it; and as it will, if it hurts us, hurt you also,
you will feel the Hurt and remedy it. The Thing in it I least understand the Policy of, is your forbidding us to carry Iron and Lumber
directly to Ireland.[8] Flaxseed we carry thither in great Quantities,
and Staves us'd to be pack'd between the Casks, with some Pig
Iron at the Bottom for Ballast. The Staves are a trifling Commodity,
and the Quantity small in such a Cargo; and it cannot be worth
while for the sake of carrying them, to enter first and unload in
England; and we do not see how that Trade could hurt or affect
any Interest of Britain. As to the foreign Linnens, I do not wonder
that our Merchants and your Hamborough Merchants contended
against the Reduction of the Drawback,[9] for it might have lessen'd
their Trade by so much as the Linen Branch amounted to: But I
am not clear that it would not have prov'd an Advantage to us, as
we have in the Nature of our Country every kind of Ability to
provide ourselves with Linnen, in Plenty, if Dearness should once
compel us into the more general Practice and Habit of making it.
The Duties on the India Goods I hear little objected to.[1] That on
foreign Mellasses is still thought too high;[2] and that on foreign
Sugar is likewise complain'd of.[3] But I believe the Demand for the
former will lessen by Degrees, from some Circumstances I may

8. Section 28 of the Sugar Act "enumerated" iron and lumber, stipulating
that neither commodity could be carried directly from "any British Colony
or Plantation in America" to "any part of Europe except Great Britain." An
act passed in 1765, 5 Geo. III, c. 45, sect. 22, repealed these restrictions as far
as importation into Ireland was concerned.

9. Section 13 of the Sugar Act withdrew the drawback on East Indian and
Western European fabrics imported into America from Britain (exceptions
were made for white calicos and muslins).

1. Section 1 of the Sugar Act laid a duty of 2s. per pound on "Wrought
Silks, Bengals, and Stuffs, mixed with Silk or Herba, of the Manufacture of
Persia, China, or East India" imported into the colonies from Great Britain
and a duty of 2s. 6d. on "every Piece of Callico painted, died, printed, or
stained in Persia, China, or East India" and imported into the colonies.

2. The Sugar Act reduced the duty on "foreign Mellasses" from 6d. per
gallon to 3d. per gallon.

3. The duty on foreign white and clayed sugars was raised £1 ss. on every
hundredweight avoirdupois "over and above all other Duties imposed by
any former Act of Parliament."

hereafter mention. And the less we get of foreign Sugar the more we must consume of that made in our own Islands, which will, I think, proportionably raise the Price on you; for they cannot easily encrease the Quantity in Proportion as our Demand must increase by the Increase of our People: Unless Plantations are admitted on the Mosquito Shore, where I am told there is plenty of suitable Land; and Numbers ready to go and plant there, if the Crown will allow it and protect them. The Indians there do not admit that the Spaniards have any Right to that Country, as they never conquer'd it, and it was never surrender'd to them. They love the English, look upon them as their Protectors from the Spaniards, and are willing to have them establish'd there. How stands that Matter between us and Spain?[4] This is a Digression; for I was going to say, that when you find the high Duties on foreign Sugars to us, raises the Price of English Sugars upon you, you will probably think of abating those Duties.

I note what you say of the Colonies applying for a Stamp Act.[5]

4. The respective pretensions of Britain and Spain to control over the Mosquito Indians exacerbated relations between the two countries throughout the eighteenth century. The merits of the dispute are as complicated as they are obscure. Britain claimed to exercise a protectorate over the Indians who lived in what is now Nicaragua and also exerted from Jamaica loose control over a settlement of logwood cutters on the coast of present-day British Honduras. Her objective was to expand her influence in both areas; Spain's of course was to constrict it and, if possible, drive the British out of Central America completely. In his letter of August 11 (below, p. 313) Jackson promised to mention the matter of the Mosquito Coast and reported British hopes that sugar might be raised in recently acquired Florida.

5. When George Grenville presented his budget to the House of Commons, March 9, 1764, he indicated his intention to impose a stamp tax upon the colonies, but he deferred action for a year. Just how he explained this delay is uncertain, for the text of his speech has not been preserved. The reports that reached America cited varying reasons: the colonies were to be given time to present their objections to this particular tax, to suggest a more satisfactory form of parliamentary taxation, or to agree among themselves and then propose a method of raising by self-taxation "a sum adequate to the expense of their defence." Precisely what Richard Jackson told BF about this speech cannot be definitely established, because his letter of March 10, in which he apparently reported what Grenville had said, is now lost (see above, p. 214), and his letter of April 13, in which he may also have discussed the matter, has survived only in part (see above, pp. 175–7). To judge by BF's response in the present paragraph, however, it is probable that Jackson had given him to understand that the colonies were to be allowed to propose

JUNE 25, 1764

In my Opinion there is not only no Likelihood that they will generally agree in such an Application, but even that any one Colony will propose it to the others. Tho' if a gross Sum were generally requir'd of all the Colonies, and they were left to settle the Mode of raising it at some general Congress, I think it not unlikely that instead of settling Quotas, they would fall on some such general Tax, as a Stamp Act, or an Excise on Rum, &c. or both; because Quota's would be difficult to settle at first with Equality, and would, if they could be made equal at first, soon become unequal, and never would be satisfactory; whereas these kind of Taxes would nearly find their own Proportions. And yet I think I could propose a better Mode by far, both for us and for you, if we were together to talk it over; but a Letter will not suit the Discussion of it. And for my own Part, I begin, as I grow old, to be more willing than I us'd to be, that the World should take its own Course, without my officiously intermeddling with its Affairs.[6]

some method, perhaps by stamp duties, of raising the required funds through their own legislation.

The colonial agents in London, in some doubt about what was expected of their constituents, asked for and secured a conference with Grenville, May 17. Again there is uncertainty as to just what Grenville said, but the surviving accounts concur in establishing that at least by May 17, if not before, Grenville had decided that agreement among all the colonies on any method of self-taxation was not to be expected, and that a parliamentary act modeled on the British system of stamp duties was the best available method, although prior consultation with, and assent by, the assemblies was desirable. BF certainly had not heard of this conference when he wrote the present paragraph; no ship leaving England after May 17 reached America until later than June 25. This entire episode is shrouded in uncertainty and has led to controversy among historians. The fullest and best discussion is Edmund S. Morgan, "The Postponement of the Stamp Act," 3 *William and Mary Quar.*, VII, 353–92; but Jack M. Sosin takes exception to some of Morgan's interpretations in *Agents and Merchants British Colonial Policy and the Origins of the American Revolution* (Lincoln, Neb., 1965), pp. 49–54.

6. This paragraph shows how little BF had as yet thought through the issues presented by the impending act, or perhaps how little he then realized what form the measure would actually take. For one solution of the problem of a revenue he harked back to his scheme at the Albany Congress of 1754, whereby "some general Congress" would raise a common fund, either by a quota system or by some equitable "general Tax" imposed by the colonists' own representatives. Clearly, the underlying constitutional issue that eventually developed had not yet appeared in his thinking. As the final sentence suggests, he was a tired man, worn by the domestic political struggle of the

I could wish you to write a Letter now and then to Messrs. Coxe. I communicate to them what you say to me on their Affair;[7] but yet I think they would like to have Letters themselves. By the way, on what Principles was Lord Cardigan's Claim to St. Lucia set aside? You have in several Letters mention'd the Fact, but not the Reasons.[8]

The Paper Currency Act,[9] I suppose is pass'd in the Shape, or near it, of the Sketch you sent me. It occasions much Talk here; but if we may still make Money bearing Interest, I do not, in my private Opinion, apprehend much Inconvenience from that Currency's being no legal Tender. The chief will be the Hoarding it; but we may make enough for that and all other Purposes. There will indeed be some Trouble in computing Interest on every Bill, but those are much less Mischiefs than a Depreciation. In our last Winters Session, I took some Pains to bring our Assembly to strike in that way the Sum then about to be rais'd; as you will see by my Argument inclos'd;[1] and I miss'd it by no great Majority; tho' the Proposal was new, and not easily understood: It appear'd too, very strange to an Assembly to pay Interest on Paper Money, who had been us'd to receive Interest for Paper that cost them nothing; and so was not agreed to. My View was partly, to avoid the Proprietary Dispute about legal Tender.

past six months. The "better Mode" of raising a revenue he had in mind was probably a scheme which he suggested unsuccessfully to Grenville the following winter and which Thomas Pownall published in somewhat modified form in the 1768 edition of *The Administration of the Colonies*, pp. 240–3. It called for Parliament to authorize a legal-tender colonial paper currency. Loan offices in all the colonies would lend these bills of credit to borrowers at 6 percent interest on the security of real-estate mortgages. There were provisions for systematic repayment of the loans and safeguards to prevent depreciation and inflation of the currency. The net proceeds of the interest, which would be considerable, would go to the Crown as a fund to serve in lieu of any direct taxation of the colonies. BF's autograph draft of a part of the scheme is printed with a commentary in Verner W. Crane, ed., *Benjamin Franklin's Letters to the Press 1758–1775* (Chapel Hill, [1950]), pp. 25–30.

7. For the efforts to confirm the claim of the descendants of Dr. Daniel Coxe to "Carolana," in which both BF and Jackson were deeply interested, see above, pp. 175–6.

8. See above, X, 414 n.

9. This act, passed by Parliament on April 19, 1764, prohibited further issues of legal-tender paper currency in the colonies. See above, p. 176 n.

1. See above, pp. 7–18.

You justly remark on the inhuman Acts of our Mobs,[2] that it is more easy to excuse the Mob than such as justify them or their Actions. And I am sorry to tell you, that the Mob being Presbyterians, the whole Posse of that Sect, Priests and People, have foolishly thought themselves under a Necessity of justifying as well as they could their mad and bloody Brethren;[3] and the most violent Parties, and cruel Animosities have hence arisen, that I have ever seen in any Country. So that I doubt the Year will scarce pass over without some civil Bloodshed.

I hope your domestic Feuds[4] begin to subside, and that John Bull is come a little to his Senses.

By this Ship you will receive the Petitions to the King,[5] mention'd in my former Letters, with a Letter from the Committee of Correspondence relating to them,[6] so that I need say the less on that head. I only wish to see a Government here that we can respect. Your Observations of the Justice of the Proprietary's paying Taxes not only for his located Lands, but for every other Part of his Property,[7] are founded in Reason and natural Equity; but who can convince him of such Truths?

I am afraid our Indian War will become perpetual (as they begin to find they can, by Plunder, make a Living of it) without we can effectually Scourge them, and speedily. We have at length concluded to send for 50 Couple of true Bloodhounds to assist in hunting them.[8] If any Gentleman of your Acquaintance has such,

2. The reference is, of course, to the Paxton Boys; see above, pp. 42–75.

3. A sampling of pro-Paxton, pro-Presbyterian pamphlets is printed in John R. Dunbar, ed., *The Paxton Papers* (The Hague, 1957.)

4. An allusion to the troubles swirling about John Wilkes, the publisher of the *North Briton:* see above, x, 366 n.

5. See above, pp. 145–7, 193–200.

6. This letter has not been found, but its substance can be inferred from instructions that the Assembly gave the committee on May 28, 1764; see above, p. 198.

7. In formulating the conditions on which the Assembly's £100,000 Supply Act of April 17, 1759 (and by extension all future Assembly supply acts), might be allowed to stand, the Privy Council on August 28, 1760, ruled that the Proprietors' unlocated, unoccupied lands should be exempt from taxation. Jackson apparently disagreed with this ruling. See above, ix, 205–6.

8. This was apparently done on the recommendation of Col. Henry Bouquet (vii, 63 n), who had proposed the same idea to the provincial commissioners on June 4; see above, pp. 235–6. For BF's approving comments on

I wish you would persuade them to spare 'em to us. Mr. Neate,[9] a Merchant of London, I think, is apply'd to, to collect them. With unchangeable Esteem, I am, Dear Friend, Yours affectionately
B FRANKLIN

R. Jackson Esqr

Endorsed: 25 June 1764 Benj Franklin Esqr.

To William Strahan

ALS: Pierpont Morgan Library

Dear Sir, Philada. June 25. 1764

I wrote a few Lines to go to you via Liverpool; but they were too late for the Ship, and now accompany this.[1]

I gave Mr. Parker[2] a Power of Attorney to act for you and myself, with respect to Mecom's Affairs, who has, under Oath, surrendred all he possess'd into his Hands, to be divided proportionably between us and his other Creditors, which are chiefly Rivington and Fletcher, and Hamilton and Balfour.[3] The Effects consist

---

hunting the Indians with dogs, made almost a decade earlier, see above, VI, 235. *London Chron.*, April 2–4, 1765, reported from Bristol that 48 couple of bloodhounds had been shipped to N.Y., "where the breed of these useful animals are to be kept up for the benefit of the province." Whether this usefulness was thought to be in Indian warfare, the capture of escaped criminals, servants, and slaves, or mere sport is undetermined.

9. Probably William Neate, who had previously performed various mercantile commissions for BF. See above, VIII, 306, 324, 423.

1. The "few Lines" must have been BF's letter of June 17 (above, pp. 228–9); he probably meant to send them by the brig *Polly*, Capt. P. Long, whose clearance for Liverpool *Pa. Gaz.*, June 14, 1764, recorded.

2. For James Parker, New Jersey printer and comptroller of the North American Post Office, see above, II, 341 n.

3. Benjamin Mecom, whose failure to make a go of the *New-York Pacquet* in the summer of 1763 was only the latest in a long series of business failures, was described by BF on Dec. 19, 1763, as being "dejected and spiritless"; he was also very bankrupt. See above, X, 153 n, 406 n. Rivington and Fletcher, a bookselling firm in St. Paul's Churchyard, London, had become bankrupt in 1760. James Rivington (1724–1802) then migrated to America and set up in business in Philadelphia and later New York. William Strahan warned David Hall against him. In 1773 Rivington started a newspaper in New York which soon led to his being regarded as one of the most obnoxious Tories in the city. *DAB; DNB;* Septimus Rivington, *The Publishing Family of Riving-*

of a Printing Press, some tolerably good Letter, and some Books and Stationary. He has render'd particular and exact Accounts, but his All will fall vastly short of Payment. I suppose it will scarce amount to 4s. in the Pound.[4] Parker thinks him honest, and has let him have a small Printing-House at Newhaven in Connecticut, where he is now at work;[5] but having a Wife and a Number of small Children, I doubt it will be long ere he gets anything beforehand, so as to lessen much of his old Debt. I think it would be well for each of his Creditors to take again what remains unsold of their respective Goods, of which there are separate Accounts, and join in impowering Mr. Parker to sell the Remainder, to be divided among us.[6] Tho,' on second Thoughts, perhaps the fairest Way, is to sell and divide the whole. You can obtain their Sentiments, and send me your own. As to what Parker owes you, it is very safe, and you must have Interest.[7]

I hope the Bath will fully re-establish good Mrs. Strahan's Health.[8] I enjoy the Pleasure with which you speak of your Children.[9] God has been very good to you, from whence I think you may be *assured* that he loves you, and that he will take at least as good Care of your future Happiness as he has done of your present. What Assurance of the *Future* can be better founded, than that which is built on Experience of the *Past?*[1] Thank me for giving you this Hint, by the Help of which you may die as chearfully as you live. If you had Christian Faith, quantum suff[icit]. This might not be necessary: But as Matters are, it may be of Use.

---

ton (London, 1919), pp. 41–6. Hamilton and Balfour were booksellers in Edinburgh; see above, IX, 295 n.

4. See below, p. 332, for Parker's account of Mecom's effects.

5. At New Haven Mecom revived Parker's *Connecticut Gazette*, but this paper failed in 1768. Mecom was appointed postmaster of New Haven in 1765. The press was the one BF had bought in 1753; see above, V, 82–3.

6. Parker sold Mecom's effects at public auction in New York in 1770. Parker to BF, Feb. 2, April 23, 1770, APS.

7. BF assumed this debt when he returned to England, paying Strahan £163 13s. 7d. on Feb. 1, 1765. See above, X, 406 n, and below, pp. 414, 470–1.

8. Mrs. Strahan suffered from a "bilious, cholicy disorder" and frequently sought relief in the waters at Bath. J. A. Cochrane, *Dr. Johnson's Printer The Life of William Strahan* (Cambridge, Mass., 1964), p. 96.

9. For Strahan's children, see above, X, 169 n.

1. For an almost identical expression of these sentiments, see above, p. 231.

241

Your Political Letters are Oracles here. I beseech you to continue them. With unfeigned Esteem, I am, as ever, Dear Friend, Yours affectionately   B FRANKLIN

Mr. Strahan

Addressed: To / Mr William Strahan / Printer, Newstreet Square, / Shoe Lane / London / per Capt. Hammet[2]

From Massachusetts House of Representatives Committee
LS: Library of Congress

Sir,   Boston June 25th. 1764.

The House of Representatives of his Majesty's Province of the Massachusetts Bay at the Session of the General Assembly in May last, being informed of the late Act of Parliament relating to the Sugar Trade with the foreign Colonies, and the Resolutions of the House of Commons relating to the Stamp Duties and other Taxes proposed to be laid on the British Colonies, were humbly of Opinion, that those Measures have a Tendency to deprive the Colonists of some of their most essential Rights as British Subjects, and as Men; particularly the Right of assessing their own Taxes and being free from any Impositions but such as they consent to by themselves or Representatives.

Our Agent informs us, that in a Conference he had with Mr. Greenville on these Subjects, he was told that the Ministry were desirous of consulting the Ease, the Quiet and Goodwill of the Colonies.[3]

Such Expressions induce us to hope that there is Nothing punitive in these Measures, and that humble dutiful Remonstrances may yet have their Effect. But if while these Things are thus pub-

2. *Pa. Gaz.*, June 28, 1764, reported the clearance of the *Dragon*, Capt. Francis Hammett. *London Chron.*, Aug. 2–4, 1764, reported its arrival off Tor Bay.

3. The Massachusetts agent, Jasper Mauduit, wrote the House of Representatives, March 13, 1764, informing it that the Stamp Act was "deferr'd till next Year. I mean the actual laying it: Mr. Grenville being willing to give to the Provinces their option to raise that or some equivalent tax, Desirous as he express'd himself to consult the Ease, the Quiet, and the Good will of the Colonies." Quoted in Edmund S. Morgan, "The Postponement of the Stamp Act," 3 *William and Mary Quar.*, VII (1950), 357.

242

lickly handled, no Claim is made, no Remonstrance preferred on the Part of the Colonies, such Silence must be interpreted a tacit Cession of their Rights, and an humble Acquiescence under all these Burdens.

The House have wrote fully upon this Subject to the Agent of this Province, and directed him to remonstrate against these Measures, and to endeavour a Repeal of said Act, and if possible to prevent the Imposition of any further Duties and Taxes on the Colonies. For this Purpose they were desirous of the united Assistance of the several Colonies in a Petition against such formidable Attacks upon what they conceive to be the inseparable Rights of British Subjects; and that the Agents of the several Colonies might be directed by the Representatives of the People on the Continent of North America to unite in the most serious Remonstrance against Measures so destructive of the Liberty, the Commerce and Property of the Colonists, and in their Tendency so pernicious to the real Interest of Great Britain.[4]

The House have done us the Honour to appoint us a Committee in the Recess of the General Court to inform the several Houses of Representatives of this Continent of their Desires; and we do our selves the Honour to subscribe ourselves, Your most, Humble Servants,[5]

JAMES OTIS.
THOMAS CUSHING
OXENBRIDGE THACHER
THOMAS GRAY
EDW SHEAFFE

4. On June 13, 1764, the Mass. House of Representatives appointed the present committee "to write to the other Governments, to acquaint them with the Instructions this Day voted to be sent to the Agent of this Province, directing him to use his Endeavours to obtain a Repeal of the Sugar Act, and to exert himself to prevent a Stamp-Act, or any other Impositions and Taxes upon this and the other American Provinces: and that the said Committee, in the Name and Behalf of this House, desire the several Assemblies on this Continent to join with them in the same Measure." Quoted in *Jasper Mauduit Agent in London for the Province of the Massachusetts-Bay 1762–1765* (Mass. Hist. Soc. *Coll.*, vol. 74, [Boston], 1918), p. 164 n.

5. BF received this letter in his capacity of speaker of the Pa. Assembly during its summer recess. His personal views regarding a possible Stamp Act were certainly not yet clarified, as is shown in his comments to Jackson written on the same day as this letter from Mass. See above, p. 237. He laid the letter before the Assembly on Sept. 12 after it had convened; for its action, see below, pp. 347–51, 365–6.

From John Canton

ALS: American Philosophical Society

Dear Sir,   London 29 June 1764

Your Favour of the 14th of March[6] came to my Hands the 15th of May last, and gave me great pleasure. The first Experiment of Mr. Kinnersley's which you mention, is, as you observe, a beautiful one to see; and I think, fully proves that the Fusion of Metals by Lightning is not a cold Fusion. I have myself, several times, melted small brass Wire by a Stroke from your Case of Bottles, which left a Mark where it lay upon the Table, and some Balls of twice or three times its Diameter near the Mark but no part of the Wire could be found. At the time of the Stroke, a great Number of Sparks, like those from a Flint and Steel, fly upward and laterally from the place where the Wire was laid, and lose their Light in the daytime, at the Distance of about two or three Inches. The Diameter of a piece of Mr. Kinnersley's Wire, which you was so kind as to send me with the Balls, I found to be one part in 182 of an Inch; mine was but one part in 330.

The second of Mr. Kinnersley's Experiments which you relate, and which seems to be a very extraordinary one, I have several times endeavour'd to make, but without Success. The Air with you must certainly be much drier than in England: For I have never observ'd the inclos'd pith Balls to separate by the electris'd Air of a Room, without having first heated the Phial; notwithstanding which, they always came together in the Phial, before the outward Air had lost its Electricity, as appears by their separating again when taken out of it. I once electrified the Air of my largest Room to a considerable degree, and by opening the Windows and Doors suffer'd the Wind to blow through for about five Minutes; I then shut them, and examin'd the Air in the Room, but found no Sign of Electricity remaining. This Air I electrified to about the same degree as before, and leaving it confin'd, it retain'd a sensible degree of its Electricity for more than three quarters of an hour. Hence I entirely agree with you, that the Glass in Mr. Kinnersley's Experiment receiv'd some degree of Electricity from the electrised Air, and so kept the Balls separated after that Air was blown away.

I have put your ingenious Friend Mr. Bowdoin's Telescope into Mr. Nairn's Hands, who is making a Pedestal for it, which I think

6. See above, pp. 97–100.

will be an Improvement of that which Mr. Bowdoin has describ'd in his last Letter to me, which you saw. You may depend on my taking all possible Care to get it well executed, and soon. I find the fitting Dollond's Micrometer to the Telescope is impracticable.[7]

Since the publication of a short Paper in the Transactions, which contains an account of Experiments to prove that Water is not incompressible,[8] I have discover'd a remarkable property belonging to that Fluid, which is new to me, though perhaps it may not be so to you. The Property I mean is, It's being less compressible in Summer than in Winter.[9] This is contrary to what I find in Spirit of Wine, and Oil of Olives; which are (as one would expect Water to be) more compressible when expanded by Heat, and less so when contracted by Cold. For when Fahrenheit's Thermometer is at 34 Degrees, and the Barometer at 29½ I[nches], Water is compress'd by the Weight of the Atmosphere 49 parts in a Million of its whole Bulk, and Spirit of Wine 60 of the same parts; When the Thermometer is at 50 degrees, Water is compressed 46 parts, and Spirit of Wine 66 parts in a Million, by the same Weight; and when the Thermometer is at 64 degrees, this Weight will compress Water no more than 44 parts in a Million, but it will compress Spirit of Wine 71 of these parts.

As I am not able, at present, to account for this Difference in the Compressibility of Water myself, I should be very glad to have your Thoughts upon it.

The Compression by the Weight of the Atmosphere, and the specific Gravity of the following Fluids; (which are all that I have

7. For matters mentioned in this paragraph, see above, x, 351 n, and this volume, pp. 21–2, 99.

8. Canton's short paper, "Experiments to prove that Water is not incompressible," was read before the Royal Society on Dec. 16, 1762, and published in *Phil. Trans.*, LII, Part II (1761–62), 640–3. *The Monthly Review*, XXIX (1763), 142–3, criticized the performance of the experiments as inadequate to prove Canton's thesis.

9. The remainder of this letter was read, in some parts in the identical words, to the Royal Society, Nov. 8, 1764, and it was published in *Phil. Trans.*, LIV (1764), 261–2, as "Experiments and Observations on the Compressibility of Water and some other Fluids." *The Monthly Review*, XXXIII (1765), 455–6, again criticized the adequacy of Canton's methodology. Because of the criticism that Canton's experiments evoked, the Council of the Royal Society in the summer of 1765 appointed a committee, of which BF was a member, to repeat and verify them. See Emanuel da Costa to BF, July 20, Aug. 25, 1765, Hist. Soc. Pa.; also da Costa to the Earl of Morton, Aug. 1, 1765, APS.

yet try'd) are set down as they were found in a temperate Degree of Heat, and when the Barometer was at a mean Height.

	Millionth parts.	Specific Gravity
Compression of Spirit of Wine	66	846
Oil of Olives	48	918
Rain Water	46	1000
Sea-Water	40	1028
Mercury	3	13595

You will easily perceive that the Compressions of these Fluids by the same Weight, are not in the inverse Ratio of their Densities, or specific Gravities, as might be expected. The Compression of Spirit of Wine, for instance, being compar'd with that of Rain-Water, is *greater* than in this proportion it ought to be, and the Compression of Sea-Water is *less*.

Mr. Price, Mr. Rose, Mr. Cooper and the rest of the Club[1] desire their most respectful Compliments to you, and very much regret, as I do myself, your leaving England. I am, with the most sincere Regard, Dear Sir Your most obliged and most humble Servant

JNO. CANTON.

From James Bowdoin

Letterbook copy: Massachusetts Historical Society

Sir   Boston, July 2–1764

Your last favor[2] informed me that you had sent my Letter to Mr. Canton inclosed in one of your own per the Packet:[3] for which I am much obliged.

When I last saw Mr. Winthrop, I inquired of him after Æpinus: he told me he sent it to Mr. Stiles of Newport, who would convey it to you.[4] I thank you for your Pamphlet relative to the Massacre of the Indians.[5] You have given in it a very entertaining account

1. The Club of Honest Whigs; see above, p. 98 n.
2. The last letter from BF to Bowdoin which has been found is that of Oct. 11, 1763, written while in Boston; see above, x, 351–2. Judging from several statements which Bowdoin makes in the present letter, BF must have written him one and possibly two letters after January 1764 which have not been found.
3. See above, p. 99.
4. Stiles conveyed Aepinus' writings through BF's brother Peter. BF acknowledged their receipt in a letter to Stiles of June 19, 1764; see above, p. 230.
5. For BF's *Narrative of the Late Massacres*, see above, pp. 42–69.

of the hospitality practised even by Barbarians towards their enemies; and such as must touch the souls (if they have any) of the Perpetrators of so horrid a deed. Horrid, if it had been comitted on enemies under the circumstances of the Sufferers; and ten fold more so, as on persons that were friends. Such Diabolism (one would think) could be comitted only in the infernal regions.

The measures your Assembly have taken to rid the Province of Proprietary influence will probably occasion the establishment of such a Government among you, as will have sufficient Strength to prevent the like Outrage in future, or exemplarily to punish the authors of it, if it should happen. The Pamphlet published among you previous to the Spirited Resolves of the Assembly fully obviates the Objections to a change of Government;[6] and is well calculated to procure a change. The Proprietaries I dare say will not think themselves very greatly obliged to the author: especially as he has pointed out such an easy way for the Crown to Satisfy any demand they may have on account of their present right of Jurisdiction.

I am much obliged to you for the Metzotinto-Print of yourself, which I received by Mr. Williams.[7] I esteem it a valuable Present, as it exhibits so good a Likeness of a Gentleman, for whom I have a Sincere regard. My Compliments to your good Family. I am with great respect. Yours   JB.

Benjamin Franklin Esqr in Philadelphia

Edward Shippen[8] to Benjamin Franklin and John Foxcroft

Letterbook copy: American Philosophical Society

Lancaster 2d July 1764

I Received your Favour of the 29th Ulto.[9] and had the perusal of

6. The pamphlet to which Bowdoin is referring seems to be BF's *Cool Thoughts*, published toward the end of April 1764; see above, pp. 153–73. The "Spirited resolves" were the "Necklace" of 26 resolves adopted by the Assembly on March 24, 1764; see above, pp. 123–33. Bowdoin obviously has his chronology confused.

7. See above, pp. 89–90.

8. For Edward Shippen, mayor of Philadelphia in 1749 and a resident of Lancaster after 1752, see above, v, 195 n.

9. Not found.

yours to Mr: George Ross[1] of the same Date which we answered
this Morning jointly.[2] Francis Campbel Esqr: and Mr: John Piper
of Shippensburg I think I could Take the Liberty to Recommend as
Honest Men and very proper Persons to under Take the Management of a Post office in that Town.[3] Colonel Bouquet[4] is acquainted
with them both and if the former should not Chuse to accept of
the Commission perhaps the Latter may. I wish I could write with
greater Certainty about this and as to a proper person at Carlisle
I must Refer you to the Colonel, who I think, is better acquainted
with the People there Than I am. I am Sorry I can Say nothing
Concerning the weekly Post which you intend to Carry on from
Lancaster through York and Baltimore to Annopolies.[5] I am Sirs
Your most obedient Humble Servand   EDWD: SHIPPEN

To Messieurs Franklin and Foxcraft
Postmasters General

Post Office Accounts   AD: American Philosophical Society

Among Franklin's miscellaneous post-office records is a folio sheet
containing a memorandum of amounts due to him and his colleague
John Foxcroft for traveling expenses while on official business and a

1. George Ross (1730–1779), a Lancaster lawyer, was a member of the
Pa. Assembly, 1768–75, a member of the First and Second Continental
Congresses, and a signer of the Declaration of Independence. *DAB*.
2. Neither the letter from BF and Foxcroft to Ross nor the joint answer
from Ross and Shippen has been found.
3. BF and Foxcroft had apparently decided to establish a postal route from
Philadelphia to Shippensburg and were looking for personnel to man the
offices. On July 18 William Dunlap, postmaster at Philadelphia, announced
the establishment of a regular post from the capital to Shippensburg, leaving
the Philadelphia post office every Thursday afternoon at 3 o'clock and passing
through Lancaster, York, and Carlisle. *Pa. Gaz.*, July 26, 1764. Francis
Campbell (d. 1790?) was an Indian trader, storekeeper, and minor officeholder
at Shippensburg. Charles H. Browning, "Francis Campbell," *PMHB*, XXVIII
(1904), 62–70. A Col. John Piper of Bedford Co. served on the Pa. Executive
Council in 1781 and is mentioned occasionally in the documents of the period.
Whether this is the same man as the one mentioned here is not certain.
4. Col. Henry Bouquet (above, VII, 63 n) was at this time in Philadelphia
organizing an expedition against the Delaware and Shawnee towns in the
Ohio Valley.
5. Nothing is known of plans to establish at this time a direct postal service

balance sheet of his account with the General Post Office with entries dated between July 9, 1764, and March 20, 1765. Both are in Franklin's hand. Parts of two pages contain various monetary calculations, but with a single unexplained exception, none of the amounts appearing in these calculations matches any of the entries in the memorandum or balance sheet, hence they are not reproduced here.

[July 9, 1764]
G.P.O. Dr. to B.F.

| His Allowance for travelling Expences thro' all the Colonies from Virginia to New Hampshire to visit and regulate the Offices establish new ones, &c. 79 Days at 21s.[6] | 82. 19. 0 |

G.P.O. Dr. to J.F.

| His Allowance &c. 93 Days at 21s.[7] | 97. 13. 0 |

G.P.O. Dr. to J.F.

| His Allowance &c. to Annapolis 18 Days at 21s.[8] | 18 18 0 |

G.P.O. Dr. to J.F.

| His Allowance to Lancaster and York 9 Days at 21.[9] | 9. 9 |

See his Letter from March 16. 1765

southward from Lancaster and York, although the Record of Outgoing Philadelphia Mail, 1764–1767 (below, pp. 398–402), indicates the probability that such a route had been set up by the autumn of 1764.

6. The journeys represented here were those of 1763 to Virginia in April-May and to New England in June-November. Above, x, 252, 276–9. The charge for 79 days, however, is puzzling. BF was away from Philadelphia on the Virginia trip for about 29 days and on the New England trip for 151. He probably took credit, at one guinea sterling per day, only for the days actually spent in travel, omitting the time spent in Williamsburg, New York, Boston (where he was laid up for several weeks with his injured shoulder), and other places at which he spent a few days with friends or relatives. Although many details of the New England trip are known, none is recorded for the earlier journey to Virginia, and it is impossible now to determine the exact basis BF used for this calculation.

7. As two entries in the balance sheet show, the 93 days for which Foxcroft was entitled to a *per diem* travel allowance were made up of one journey of 79 days and one of 14 days to Portsmouth. The longer of these matched BF's travels in distance but in a different sequence of places: BF's itinerary was Philadelphia–Williamsburg–Philadelphia–New England–Philadelphia; Foxcroft's was Williamsburg–Philadelphia–New England–Philadelphia–Williamsburg. Foxcroft's additional credit for 14 days to Portsmouth (specifically shown on the balance sheet), however, presents another puzzle. If BF's accident occurred soon after the two men left Boston for Portsmouth in

[Notes 7, 8, and 9 continued on next page]

Dr   General Post Office[1]

			£		
1764 July	12. To B Franklin for Bills remitted R. Trevor Esqr.[2]	£1500:	0:	0
Aug.	9. To Do. Do.	550:	0:	0
	To Do. for Fees paid Lawyers[3]	4.	13.	11
Oct.	2. To Do. for One Years Salary	300:	0.	0
	To J.F. for One Years Salary	300:	0:	0
	To Fr. and Foxt. Comptrollers Salary and [Int. paid?]	105:	0:	
1765 Mar.	15. To J.F. for Ballance of Williamsburg Office			
	paid J Royle	46.	15:	5
	To B F. travelling Expences 79 Days at 21	82.	19	—
	To J F. Do.	82.	19	—
	To J F. Journey to Portsmouth 14 Days	14.	14	—
	To J F. Do. to Annapolis 18 Days	18.	18	—
	To J F. Do. to Lancaster 9 Days	9:	9:	—
		3015:	8:	4
	Ballance	428:	15:	9
		£ 44:	4:	1

August 1763, he may have turned back, allowing Foxcroft to make that trip alone, and claiming no travel time for himself for that part of the entire expedition. But in two letters of early September, BF wrote very definitely of his return to Boston "from Portsmouth" (above, x, 337, 338), and he later told Peter Collinson that his journey had taken him "to the easternmost Part of New England" (above, x, 400), an expression which a native of Boston would hardly have used had he gone only a few miles beyond that town. It is possible, though not likely, that Foxcroft made a second trip to Portsmouth in September or early October while BF was recuperating in Boston. It seems even less likely that a journey from Williamsburg to Portsmouth, Va., was meant; there was no post office in that place at the time, and its residents were doubtless served by the office in nearby Norfolk.

8. The date of this trip is not recorded.

9. Foxcroft undoubtedly made this inspection trip during one of his stays in Philadelphia: either after they had both come up from Virginia together in May 1763; or after their return from New England in November (he did not leave for Virginia until at least the end of that month (see above, x, 384); or sometime in 1764, perhaps in September (see below, pp. 341–6). BF would probably have been too deeply involved in Assembly business to have made the trip with Foxcroft at any of these times.

1. None of the transactions entered in this balance sheet appears to have been recorded in either BF's Memorandum Book, 1757–1776, or the Journal and Ledger he kept while in England on his second mission.

2. Receiver general of the revenue of the Post Office.

3. On Dec. 19, 1763, BF had paid Jared Ingersoll 30s. as a fee for attaching property of John Holt, former New Haven postmaster, to secure a debt due the Post Office. See above, x, 402–3. The rest of this £4 13s. 11d. may represent fees to lawyers for similar services in connection with other delinquent postmasters.

Cr

Sterling.

July	9.	1764.	By Ballance of Account to this Day	£2070.	12.	3¼
	25		By B F. Cash received of J.P. Tower hill Office⁴	3.	11.	3
	28.		By B F. received of Do. N York Office £500 Currency	266.	13.	4
Sept.	5.		By B F. received of Philadelphia Office	805.	10.	6
Oct.	5.		By B F. received of Philadelphia Office	68:	16:	7¼
			By J. F. received of Annapolis Office	17.	18.	3¼
	22.		By Do. received of York Office Virginia	2:	12.	1½
Nov.	2.		By Do. received of W. Dunlap per Hunter's Executors	51:	9:	2½
March	5: 1765.		By Do. received of Do. per Mr. Royle⁵	77:	6.	5
	15.		By Do. received of York Office Virginia Omitted above	6:	2.	3¼
Aug.	2. 1764.		By B F. received of J P. from Tower Hill Office 32s. 6d. York	–	17.	0
			By J F. received of Do. [Ballance of Lottery Account £36: 5. 0]⁶ Pennsylvania Money	21.	0.	0
March	18. 1765.		By B F. received of J P. £82. 4: 0 Pennsylvania Money	45.	0.	0
	20.		By B F. received of Do. 11: 16. 0 Do.	6.	14.	10
				3444:	4:	1

Query. Whether the two last Articles of this Account were not paid by Mr. Parker as part of his private Debt to B F.?

Benjamin Franklin and John Foxcroft: Commission to James Parker⁷

DS: University of Pennsylvania Library

[July 10, 1764]

BENJAMIN FRANKLIN and JOHN FOXCROFT ESQUIRES His Majesty's Deputy Postmaster General of all his Majesty's Dominions on the Continent of North America.

4. "J.P." was James Parker, comptroller of the colonial postal service. Tower Hill was the landing place for Newport vessels on the west shore of Narragansett Bay.

5. Joseph Royle (d. 1766), brother-in-law of BF's former colleague in the Post Office, William Hunter. After Hunter's death Royle conducted the Williamsburg printing office and published the *Virginia Gazette* for the benefit of Hunter's estate and his young son and heir.

6. Brackets in the original.

7. For Parker, the New Jersey printer, see above, II, 341 n. On April 22, 1757, BF and William Hunter commissioned Parker comptroller of the North

To all to whom these Presents shall come: Greeting. Know ye That we the said Benjamin Franklin and John Fox-croft reposing special Trust and Confidence in James Parker of Woodbridge in New Jersey, Gentleman, and having received good Testimony of his Fidelity and Loyalty to his Majesty and of his Ability and Sufficiency to execute the Office and Duties required of a Secretary, Comptroller, Accomptant, and Receiver General of the General Post Office do by these presents nominate and appoint him our Secretary Comptroller, Accomptant and Receiver General, with full power to demand, receive, examine, correct and allow, the Monthly Bills call'd Comptrollers Bills, and the Quarterly and General Accounts of the several Deputy Postmasters in every Province relating to the Postage of Letters; and to demand recover and receive for us, the Ballance from such Accounts arising and proper Discharges thereupon to give and generally to do and perform every other Matter and Thing that to the Office and Duty of Secretary, Comptroller, Accomptant and Receiver General of the General Post-Office doth or may Appertain, under such Instructions Restrictions and Orders as he shall from time to time receive from us: And we do hereby authorize the said James Parker to have, hold, exercise and enjoy the said Offices, with all the Powers Privileges Benefits and Advantages thereunto belonging, from the Day of the Date hereof, for and during the Term of three Years, or till he receive a new Commission from us, or till this present Commission be superseded; Hereby strictly charging and requiring all Officers and others employ'd in and about the Posts already settled or to be settled in any part of his Majesty's said Provinces and Dominions in North America, or in Relation to the Revenue arising by the Post of Letters therein; from time to time to render their Accounts regularly and duly according to their Instructions to the said James Parker, and to pay unto him the Ballances thereof, and to observe and obey his Orders and Directions relating to their Accompts and Remittances. And we do also hereby give and grant unto him the said James Parker, for his Care, Pains and Trouble in the Execution of the Offices and Trust hereby granted and committed unto him, the Yearly

American Post Office; his commission is printed above, VII, 192–4. The present commission merely differs in giving Parker the additional titles of secretary, "Accomptant," and receiver general.

Salary of Eighty Pounds Sterling to commence from the Date hereof, which Salary he is to receive or be allowed in his Accounts. And we do hereby revoke and make null and void from the Day of the Date hereof all and every other Constitution and Appointment to the same Office made given or granted by us, or any former Deputy Postmaster General, to the said James Parker, or to any other Person or Persons whatsoever, IN WITNESS whereof, we the said Benjamin Franklin and John Foxcroft, have hereunto set our Hands, and caused the Seal of our Office to be Affixed this tenth Day of July One thousand seven Hundred and Sixty four in the fourth Year of his Majesty's Reign.   B FRANKLIN
                                                    J. FOXCROFT

Endorsed: Commission to Mr Parker

To Jane Mecom   ALS: Yale University Library

Dear Sister   Philada. July 10. 1764
  We all condole with you most sincerely on the Death of your Daughter.[8] She always appear'd to me of a sweet and amiable Temper, and to have many other good Qualities that must make the Loss of her more grievous for Brother and you to bear. Our only Comfort under such Afflictions is, that God knows what is best for us, and can bring Good out of what appears Evil. She is doubtless happy: which none of us are while in this Life.
  Brother Peter and Sister are well.[9] Their Maid which they brought with them, and a young Girl, have been both inoculated, and have got finely over the small Pox. They join with my Mrs. Franklin[1] Sally and myself in Love to you and yours: But do not write; as no Letters can now go free in America but mine, Mr. Foxcroft's

8. Jane Mecom's daughter Sarah (1737–1764; C.17.5), who had married William Flagg of Boston in 1756, died June 12, 1764. She had given birth to four children within a period of six years. The youngest daughter, Sarah, died the following November 9 and the next youngest, Mary (Polly), died in March 1765. Van Doren, *Franklin-Mecom*, p. 101.
  9. Peter Franklin (C.9), BF's only surviving brother, had recently moved from Newport to Philadelphia. He had become postmaster of the city by October 1764, replacing BF's relative William Dunlap. Above, x, 183 n, 392 n. His wife was the former Mary Harman.
  1. BF's wife, Deborah, as distinguished from Peter's wife.

and our Secretary's; the latter only Business of the Office. The Act of Parliament forbidding.[2] I am, Your ever affectionate Brother

B FRANKLIN

Addressed: To / Mrs. Jane Mecom / Boston / Free / B FRANKLIN

To John Winthrop

ALS: Harvard College Library

Sir   Philada. July 10. 1764

I received your Favour of the 12th. past,[3] and congratulate you on the Recovery of Mrs. Winthrop and your Children from the Small Pox.[4]

Mr. Stiles return'd Æpinus to me sometime since.[5] I must confess I am pleas'd with his Theory of Magnetism. Perhaps I receive it the more readily on Account of the Relation he has given it to mine of Electricity. But there is one Difficulty I cannot solve by it quite to my Satisfaction, which is that if a Steel Ring be made magnetical by passing Magnets properly round it, and afterwards broken into two Semicircles, each of them will have strong N. and S. Poles, in whatever Part the Ring is broken. I have not try'd this, but have been assur'd 'tis so: and I know that a magnetic Bar broken has after Breaking 4 Poles, i.e. it becomes two compleat Bars. I think with him that Impermeability to the El. Fluid, is the Property of all El[ectric]s per se; or that, if they permit it to pass at all, it is with Difficulty, greater or less in different El[ectric]s per se. Glass hot permits it to pass freely; and in the different degrees between hot and cold may permit it to pass more or less freely.

I shall think of the Affair of your unfortunate College, and try

2. On the new restrictions on the franking privilege, which became law June 1, 1764, see above, p. 39 n. The secretary of the North American Post Office was James Parker, for whose new commission see the document immediately above.

3. Not found.

4. Boston experienced a smallpox epidemic in 1764 after inoculation had been prohibited because it spread infection. The town lifted the ban in February 1764. John Duffy, *Epidemics in Colonial America* (Baton Rouge, [1953]), pp. 64–6.

5. On BF's lending of a volume of Aepinus' writings to friends in New England and its return, see above, x, 267, 351, 389; and this volume, pp. 230, 246. For a summary of Aepinus' theories of magnetism and electricity, see I. Bernard Cohen, *Franklin and Newton* (Phila., 1956), pp. 538–43.

if I can be of any Service in procuring some Assistance towards restoring your Library.[6] Please to present my respectful Compliments to Dr. Chauncy, Mr. Elliot and Mr. Cooper;[7] and believe me with sincere Esteem, Sir Your most obedient humble Servant
B FRANKLIN

My Respects to the President, and to Mr. Danforth.[8]

J. Winthrop Esqr

Endorsed: Dr Franklin 10 July 1764 [*and on another page:*] Recd July 23.

To Richard Jackson   ALS: American Philosophical Society

Dear Sir,   Philada. July 12. 1764
By Capt. Hammet, who lately sail'd from hence, the Committee wrote to you, and sent you the Petition to the King.[9] By this Con-

6. On the night of Jan. 24, 1764, during a snowstorm, Harvard Hall, then being used by the Mass. General Court because of the smallpox in Boston, was destroyed by fire and the library and philosophical apparatus in it were completely lost. The members of the General Court, joined actively by Governor Bernard, assisted in saving the nearby college buildings. The General Court voted two days later to rebuild the hall, and the authorities hoped that the contents would be replaced by private generosity. *Pa. Gaz.*, Feb. 23, 1764, had printed an account of the catastrophe. See also F. Apthorp Foster, "The Burning of Harvard Hall, 1764, and Its Consequences," Col. Soc. Mass. *Publications,* XIV (1911–13), 2–43.

7. These friends were: Charles Chauncy (1705–1787), minister of the First Church in Boston, an outspoken opponent of the emotionalism of the Great Awakening and later a leader in the movement towards Unitarianism *(DAB);* probably Andrew Eliot (1718–1778), pastor of the New North Church in Boston, who took an active part in seeking replacement of the books and apparatus lost in the Harvard fire, and for whom BF later tried to get a Scottish honorary degree (*Sibley's Harvard Graduates,* X, 128–61); and Samuel Cooper (1725–1783), minister of the Brattle Square Church (above, IV, 69–70 n; *DAB*).

8. Edward Holyoke (1689–1769) was president of Harvard College, 1737–69 (*Sibley's Harvard Graduates,* V, 265–78); and Samuel Danforth (1696–1777), an early advocate of inoculation, was a judge and member of the Mass. Council, 1739–74. In 1773 BF called him a friend of half a century's standing (*ibid.,* VI, 80–6; BF to Danforth, July 25, 1773, Lib. Cong.).

9. *Pa. Gaz.*, June 28, 1764, reported that the *Dragon,* Captain Hammett, had cleared for London. *London Chron.,* Aug. 2–4, 1764, recorded its arrival

veyance they send you some other Papers. The Proprietary Party are endeavouring to stir up the Presbyterians to join in a Petition against a Change of Government: what that [Endea]vour will produce I cannot say.[1]

I hope soon to receive your Sentiments on this Affair, which will probably enable me to determine, whether I shall stay here, or retire to some other Colony, or England, to spend the Remainder of my Days.[2]

Col. Bouquet sets out in a short time with the 1000 Men, rais'd, cloath'd and paid by this Province, against the Indians on the Ohio.[3] Our Heats have lately been so excessive, that many have died, chiefly after drinking cold Water while warm with Exercise.[4] How

off Tor Bay, Devonshire. For the Assembly's petition to the King for a change in government, see above, pp. 193–200. The "other Papers" being sent to Jackson, mentioned in the next sentence, have not been identified.

1. Among the Franklin Papers, Lib. Cong., fo. 41, is a longhand petition to the King, with spaces for signatures, asking that he disregard the Assembly's petition for a change in government. Paul L. Ford identified the author as John Dickinson and reprinted the text from a printed broadside, stating that a German translation was also issued. *The Writings of John Dickinson,* I, *Political Writings 1764–1774* (Phila., 1895), 61–7. BF quoted extensively from this petition in his preface to Galloway's speech and commented sarcastically on its statements. See below, pp. 300–7.

2. For Jackson's somewhat reserved comments when he had received the Assembly's petition, see below, pp. 312–13. He did not refer to BF's possible going to England.

3. Bouquet probably left Philadelphia during the last week of July; he had reached Lancaster by July 30. Sylvester K. Stevens, Donald H. Kent, and Leo J. Roland, eds., *The Papers of Col. Henry Bouquet,* II (Harrisburg, 1940), 309.

4. *Pa. Gaz.,* July 12, 1764, printed a warning and advice, marked for special attention by a pointing hand: "As several Persons, during this very hot Weather, have lost their Lives, by indiscreetly drinking cold Water, while they were warm, and sweating, we think it our Duty to acquaint the Publick therewith; and to request that every One, before he drinks, will mix a little Spirit with his Water, which should stand some Time after taken from the Pump, as the Consequence, without doing so, seems to be immediate Death. —— It is said to be a good Way to keep the Water in the Mouth some Time, before it is swallowed." In the issue of August 2 "A Citizen" wrote suggesting that before drinking water a person heated by exercise should "wet the fore Part of his Wrists, by sprinkling or pouring some on them." He did not wish to detract from the *Gazette's* advice, he wrote, but offered his method because "Rum or Spirit is not always in the Possession of every One."

much more happy is your temperate Climate? I am, dear Sir, Your most obedient humble Servant   B FRANKLIN

P.S. Inclos'd is a Duplicate of the Petition.

For large Pacquets I suppose you pay Postage, which should be charg'd to the Province.[5]

R. Jackson Esqr

Addressed: To / Richard Jackson, Esquire / Member of Parliament for Weymouth, / Inner Temple / London / via New York / per Packet

Endorsed: 12 July 64 Bn Franklin Esqr

From John Mills[6]   ALS: American Philosophical Society

Sir,   London, July 12th, 1764

I am greatly indebted to you for your most obliging favour of the 10th of March,[7] which was safely delivered to me by Mr. Shadwell,[8] whose channel (directing to him at the Secretary of State's Office) will always be a sure conveyance.

I thank you, Sir, most heartily, for your kindness to me in presenting to Colonel Elliot the first volume of my Husbandry.[9] I

5. The Post Office Act of 1764 allowed the franking privilege to members of Parliament for letters they received (Jackson was M.P. for Weymouth) but said nothing about packets sent to them. In his Memorandum Book, 1757–1776, p. 19, BF recorded under date of Oct. 31, 1764, a charge against the province for £3 8s. 9d. "for Postage of Pacquet from the Committee of Correspondence to N York for England." This may represent a belated entry of the charges by the American post for the packet sent Jackson containing "some other Papers" mentioned in the first paragraph of this letter.

6. For John Mills, British writer on agriculture, and for some of the matters mentioned in this letter, see above, X, 205–6.

7. Not found.

8. Richard Shadwell, "formerly chief clerk in the Secretary of State's office," died at Bath, June 1, 1785. *Gent. Mag.,* LV (1785), pt. 1, 490.

9. Mills had sent a copy of the first volume of his *A New and Complete System of Husbandry* to BF in March 1763 to be forwarded to Jared Eliot in Conn. But Eliot died April 22, 1763, so BF apparently sent the book to Eliot's son Aaron (1718–1783), the only one in his family described as "colonel." He was a deacon in his church and a physician, and he had been associated with his father and others in the production of steel at Salisbury, Conn. Above, VI, 173 n; William H. Eliot, Jr., *Genealogy of the Eliot Family* (New Haven, 1853), pp. 160–2.

wish I had known there was such a descendant of that worthy Gentleman, the Doctor, that I might e'er this have requested his acceptance of the rest of what has been published of that work, as a mark of my sincere veneration for the memory of his Father. I expect the 2d., 3d. and 4th volumes of my work hourly from my bookseller, whom I have ordered to get them bound up for the Colonel: but such is the negligence of those gentry in all affairs which are not their own immediate concern, or attended with lucre to them, that I fear I shall not yet be able to get them in time for the ship by which Mr. Small[1] will be so kind as to send this letter, with my fourth volume, for you, Sir, whose acceptance of it I request, as of a feeble mark of my respect for you.

I am greatly obliged to you for the list of American booksellers,[2] and shall make use of it in the proportions and manner you direct, as soon as my fifth volume is finished at the press: for as that will complete my task, and as it is now printing, I apprehend that it may be best to send the whole work together: at least my bookseller, Mr. Johnson,[3] is clearly of that opinion.

I should esteem it a singular happiness to be able to prove the esteem and regard with which I am, Sir, Your most obedient and most humble servant JOHN MILLS

I am just now sending to the Society of Agriculture Arts and Commerce established by the States of Britany at Rennes, a small parcel of your American Orchard grass Seeds, with which Mr. Small has kindly favoured me:[4] and I likewise send to the same Society (at their desire) an hundred weight of Mr. Roque's Burnet seed.[5]

Dr. Benj. Franklin

1. On Alexander Small, Scots army surgeon living in London, see above, IX, 110–11 n.
2. BF had apparently sent Mills such a list with his letter of March 10, 1764.
3. Probably Joseph Johnson (1738–1809), first of Fish Street Hill, then of Paternoster Row, and finally of St. Paul's Churchyard. During his last years he was regarded as "the father of the book trade." *DNB*.
4. Perhaps procured from Jared Eliot before his death.
5. For Small's laudatory description of burnet, see above, X, 306–7.

From James Habersham[6]   Copy:[7] Georgia Historical Society

Savannah in Georgia the 14th July 1764

Last Fall I made my two Sons at New Jersey College a Visit[8] and at the Same time embraced the opportunity of paying my Respects to my Friends in Philadelphia, among whom I waited on Mrs. Franklin, but was deprived the Pleasure of seeing you, as she informed me, you were on your Way from Boston, and had met with an unlucky accident, which I hope you are perfectly recovered from.[9] My Brother in Law Mr. Robert Bolton is the Bearer of this.[1] He goes to visit his Native Place and his relations, after being settled here near 20 years. He has some Thoughts of setting up a Post between this and Charlestown, which, if he can meet with suitable Encouragement, must be of public Utility. To this End, He tells me, He has been advised by our Worthy Governor to get an appointment from the Post Master General, and as I suppose it may be in your Power to Constitute him Post Master of this Province, your doing it would lay me, and him under great obligations. I am sensible, I have no Pretensions to ask this Favour from the

6. For James Habersham, cofounder and first superintendent of George Whitefield's Bethesda Orphanage in Georgia, planter, merchant, and public official, see above, III, 72 n, and *DAB*.

7. Copied, probably during the 1840s, from the original Habersham Papers (now presumed lost), by William Bacon Stevens, a founder and later librarian of the Georgia Historical Society and subsequently an Episcopal clergyman and Bishop of Pennsylvania. *DAB*. The copy is headed "Book No. I page 16. To Benjamin Franklin Esq. in Philadelphia."

8. At that time Habersham's two elder sons, James and Joseph, were students at the College of New Jersey (Princeton), though neither one seems to have continued there until graduation. Ga. Hist. Soc. *Colls.*, VI (Savannah, 1904), 26–7, 51, 67.

9. For BF's two falls during his New England journey in 1763, see above, X, 278, 338.

1. Robert Bolton (1722–1789), was the son of Robert Bolton (1688–1742), an emigrant to Philadelphia from Yorkshire. The younger man was the dancing-master whose assemblies in the Philadelphia Concert Room had been stopped by followers of George Whitefield in 1740. Above, II, 257–9, 284. Later in the same year Bolton moved to Georgia, probably after his sister Mary (1724–1763) had married James Habersham. He became a follower and personal friend of Whitefield; during his life he held various minor public offices in Georgia. J. G. B. Bulloch, *A History and Genealogy of the Habersham Family* (Columbia, S.C., 1901), pp. 75, 78–9.

slender Acquaintance I have with you, but I will Venture to say from many Years experience, that if you should be pleased to Confer any Trust in Mr. Bolton, you will find him an honest, prudent and punctual Man. He has lately buried an excellent wife, and is left with Seven fine Children, who he has hitherto supported and brought up reputably, and as his trade has lately slackened, any additional Means of getting a little Money must greatly assist him.[2] I need say nothing of his family connections in Pennsylvania, as they must be better Known to you than to me. You will please to excuse the Freedom, I have taken, and if in my power, I shall be pleased with an opportunity of shewing that I am with great Truth, Sir Your most obedient humble Servant   JAMES HABERSHAM

Please to make my respects acceptable to Mrs. Franklin.

Minutes of the Provincial Commissioners

MS: Massachusetts Historical Society

The provincial commissioners named in the Supply Act of May 30, 1764, assumed their duties almost at once. Their activities in directing the recruitment, maintenance, and disposition of the troops authorized by the provincial government are reflected in part by the pay orders they approved (above, pp. 221–4) and by the commissions and orders Governor Penn issued as commander-in-chief to various officers.[3] But

2. BF and Foxcroft seem to have acted favorably on this request. On Jan. 21, 1765, Bolton petitioned the Ga. General Assembly, stating that "His Majesty's Post Masters General of North America" had lately given him a commission "impowering him to establish a Post Office for the safe and speedy conveyance of Letters to and throughout the different parts of this Province," and believing that a regular mail service at 10-day intervals to and from So. Car. "would be of Immediate Importance and Advantage to the commercial Interest and general Conveniency of the Inhabitants of this Colony," he asked the House for assistance. His petition was laid on the table and nothing further was heard of it. Allen D. Candler, ed., *The Colonial Records of the State of Georgia*, XIV (Atlanta, 1907), 185–6. This silence may be explained by the fact that the postmasters general in England had issued a commission, Jan. 5, 1765, to Benjamin Barons, appointing him deputy postmaster general of a newly erected Southern District comprising the two Carolinas, Georgia, the Floridas, and the Bahamas, and any appointment within that region by BF and Foxcroft would automatically lapse.

3. Some of the documents of this sort issued by Penn in the summer of

the formal records of meetings of the governor and commissioners at which decisions were reached seem for the most part to have disappeared. Minutes of actions taken on July 20 alone seem to have survived among those of the numerous sessions that certainly took place during the summer of 1764. These minutes are printed here to illustrate some of the decisions on military matters in which Franklin participated as one of the commissioners.

July 20th 1764
Present.
The Governor

Benja. Franklin   Lynford Lardner

}Esqrs.[4]

Joseph Fox   Joseph Galloway

John Baynton

The Board taking under their consideration the disposition of the Troops for the Defence of the Frontiers.[5]

Agreed.

That four companies be stationed and range between the River Delaware and Susquehanna, including thirty men to Garrison Fort Augusta, and that the two remaining companies of the Provincials be stationed and range on the Frontiers westwards of the Susquehanna, and that one commanding Officer be appointed for these companies.

Agreed.

That Robert Callender be the victualler for the three western Companies save those in Fort Augusta who are victualled by the Crown, and that Robert Levers victual the other three companies to the eastward.[6]

1764 are printed in 1 *Pa. Arch.*, IV, 176–81, 193–200. On this general subject see also below, pp. 316–7.

4. Provincial commissioners named in the act of May 30, 1764; absent from this meeting were Thomas Cadwalader and John Hughes.

5. Since a provincial regiment of two battalions was about to accompany Colonel Bouquet on his march to the Ohio Country, it was necessary to decide on the assignments of the units remaining behind to guard the frontier settlements of Pa. itself.

6. Robert Callender (d. *c.*1775) of Carlisle, one of the leading Indian traders of Pa., had at one time been associated with Croghan & Trent. Robert Levers (d. 1788) had been a clerk in Richard Peters' office before going to Northampton Co. He kept a store and inn at Easton and became prothonotary of the county. William J. Heller, *Historic Easton* (Easton, 1911), pp. 7, 9–10.

Agreed.

That the above mentioned Troops be supplied with Arms from the Public Armory and with Amunition Blankets Sheetes Haversacks and Tomahawks.

To Jane Mecom

ALS: American Philosophical Society

Dear Sister   Philada. July 24. 1764

It is not in my Power to dispense with an Act of Parliament. To attempt it would hazard my Place. The Privilege of Franking my own Letters is indulg'd to me by the Act;[7] but I have been given to understand that 'tis a Trust, which tis expected I will not violate by covering the Letters of others. Mr. Flag[8] must therefore pay for the Letters you send him; and I think he should also pay the Letters he sends to you. Your Sister[9] has just now paid 2*s.* 6*d.* for a Letter to herself from New York. She would have wrote to condole with you on your late Loss, and so would Brother Peter, but that they would not put you to Charge. We all join in Love to you and yours. Your affectionate Brother   B FRANKLIN

Addressed: To | Mrs Jane Mecom | Boston | Free | B FRANKLIN

From ———[1]

AL (mutilated): American Philosophical Society

Sir   Philada. 8th. Augt. 1764.

[I am] returning you my kind thanks for your favour in lending me the Perusal of Mr. Pringles account of the Meteor seen in England[2] &c. some time agone, which I herewith return.

7. For the act of Parliament passed June 1, 1764, which regulated franking privileges in North America, see above, p. 39 n.

8. Van Doren suggests that this person is less likely to have been William Flagg, the husband of Jane Mecom's recently deceased daughter Sarah, than one of Flagg's relatives, perhaps an uncle. Van Doren, *Franklin-Mecom,* p. 81. For Sarah Mecom Flagg's death, June 12, 1764, see above, p. 253 n.

9. Either DF, or BF's brother Peter's wife, Mary Harman Franklin.

1. The editors have no clue as to who BF's correspondent was. No part of the signature remains.

2. Almost certainly a paper read by Pringle before the Royal Society in 1759 and published in *Phil. Trans.* of that year; see above, IX, 300 n.

I have been at some Pains in geting the account of this that appear'd here the 20th Ulto. in the Evening,[3] but a Great Deal Appears from what has been said to be Imperfect unless there were more than one.

However from the Perusal of the whole, I shall at Present desist, and have for my own part to say, that with proper Instruments I have taken the Altitude, and Course from my Standing Place, and with the help of two Young Men of Account, where the Meteor Pass'd directly in their Zenith, which is taken with a Land Compass, the Intersection of the two Lines undoubtedly will be Perpendicular to the place it broke. As everybody seems silent in so curious an Affair, makes me doubt that a more ungenerous a Spirit Subsists, than that, that wou'd be becoming [to a] Soul, Springing from an Eternal Spirit, which [has no] beginning nor end. The Lord Preserve Sir your [Life?] for abundance has been said, what end [torn] I am at a Stand. I have been buisy, or [torn] d[raw]n the Cut, together with the Lin[torn] own get so much in favour [torn].

To B. Franklin

To Richard Jackson   ALS: American Philosophical Society

Dear Sir   Philada. Augt. 9. 1764

Two Packets successively are arriv'd without my having a Line from you: So I suppose you have been in the Country, or perhaps have wrote by the Ship Mr. Allen comes in, which is not yet arriv'd.[4] I never more wanted to hear from you, as you must long

3. *Pa. Gaz.* and *Pa. Jour.*, July 26, 1764, printed an identical letter to the publisher dated Philadelphia, July 21, and signed "T.T.," describing a fireball that passed about 2½ miles southwest of the city at 7:40 P.M. the previous evening, taking a course "near North-west." Considerably larger than the sun, "it appeared like large flaming Sheets of Fire, inclining together, like that of a new blown Rose." When it touched a small cloud "it broke into Thousands of Pieces, like that of springing a Mine." The report of the explosion came about 30 seconds later and lasted about "one full Minute." An identical note appended to the letter in each paper asked for other accounts of the meteor, its position and course in the sky, and the length of time that elapsed between the visible explosion and the arrival of its sound.

4. The *Philadelphia Packet*, Capt. Richard Budden, with William Allen aboard, left Deal on June 11, but was held by contrary winds at Cowes

since have heard of our Convulsions. I can now only acquaint you, that Counter Petitions to the Crown are going about, against a Change of Government,[5] on a Suggestion of the Proprietary Party, that all our Privileges will be demolish'd by the Change. They boast of great Numbers. The next Election will show where the Strength lies. I am, as ever, with sincerest Esteem, Dear Sir, Your most obedient humble Servant   B FRANKLIN

R. Jackson Esqr.

Endorsed: 9 Augst. 1764 Benjn. Franklin Esqr

From Thomas Becket[6]   ALS: American Philosophical Society

Sir   London Aug. 10. 1764

I am just favour'd with yours of the 17th. June with a Copy of yours of the 3d, (I never Received the first).[7] Inclosing also a Bill on Mr. Brown for Twelve Pounds which is paid.[8]

It is impossible for me to express the concern I am in at receiving such a Letter from you who has been so remarkably my friend; and that I have given cause for it I cannot deny—but this I can aver, that it was not wilful. It must seem almost an absurdity to pretend to vindicate myself, but yet I must beg your patience for one minute.

---

until June 20 and arrived in Philadelphia only on August 13, 1764. *London Chron.*, June 9–12, 21–23, 1764; *Pa. Jour.*, Aug. 16, 1764. Allen brought with him Jackson's letter to BF of June 14, 1764 (not found); see below, p. 327. At about this same time BF received from some other hand Jackson's letter of June 4 (also not found).

5. See below, p. 300.

6. For this London bookseller, see above, IX, 274 n; X, 261 n.

7. BF's letters of June 3 and 17 have not been found. It is clear from what follows here and from BF's letter to Strahan of June 17 (above, pp. 228–9) that one or both of these missing letters had scolded Becket for not filling BF's book order of Dec. 17, 1763 (above, X, 393–5).

8. Two of the last pages of BF's Memorandum Book, 1757–1776, record his account with Henton Brown & Son for 1764, in which he entered an undated draft on these bankers for £12 in favor of Becket and another dated September 24 for £10. Becket's present draft apparently represents his repayment of the first of those from BF, since he had not filled the December order on time. BF's second draft may have been in partial payment of Becket's account as stated in the present letter.

I received your last favour[9] the begining of Feby, and thought that by staying about 2 Mo. I should be able to send you a few New Articles that the course of that time might produce and well might be agreeable to you. I also was in expectation of receiving some more Numbers of the *Arts et Metiers* from Paris which you particularly desird, and did not receive any till May, which was the *Art de Refiner le Sucre*.[1] There was then no Ships going till June, and I sent every thing you wrote for with some additional articles by the Mary and Elizabeth Capt. Spark, and wrote you at the same time, with a state of the Account, by which there was a ballance due me of £16 13s. 6d.[2]

It is true that I ought to have sent by the first Ship such articles as you wrote for without waiting for other things—I now see the absurdity of my Conduct—and feel your just resentment. To say any more, would be superfluous—and as I know you to be the best of Men, I trust you will forgive this disapointment I have laid you under. Depend upon it, good Sir, I shall be ever watchful for the future to obey your commands with the stricktest punctuality being Sir Your greatly Obliged and Most Obedient Humble servant

T BECKET

I herewith send in 2 packets the Reviews, Magazines, and 4 New pamphlets.[3]

To Benjamin Franklyn Esqr.

9. BF's letter of Dec. 17, 1763, with its accompanying order for books.

1. This volume of *Descriptions des Arts et Métiers* was H. L. Duhamel du Monceau, *Art de refiner le sucre* (n.p., 1764).

2. The departure of the *Mary and Elizabeth* from Deal for Philadelphia is not recorded until July 9 (*London Chron.*, July 7–10, 1764), although Richard Budden's *Philadelphia Packet* had gone down the Thames and sailed from Deal on June 11 (*ibid.*, June 9–12, 1764). The arrival of the *Mary and Elizabeth* at Philadelphia is reported in *Pa. Gaz.*, Sept. 13, 1764. Becket's letter to BF, mentioned in this sentence, has not been found.

3. The publications Becket sent at this time cannot be identified.

From Henry Bouquet

ALS and copy:[4] American Philosophical Society

Dear Sir   Carlisle. August 10th. 1764

I am sorry that the first Letter I have the Pleasure to write you, must be upon a disagreeable Subject.[5] The Desertion has already reduced your Two Battalions to about 750 Men, and I have too much cause to expect they will lose many more before they reach Fort Loudoun.

I can not spare so considerable a Number from the diminutive Force I was to have, and am obliged to apply to the Governor and Commissioners to enable me to compleat these Troops, and to send by a proper Person the money necessary allowing the same Terms as before, viz. The Three Pounds in advance to be afterwards deducted from their Pay and the 20s. for Every Recruit to the officers.[6]

This will be no additional Expence to the Public and only the

4. The MS described as a "copy" is followed on the same folio by the text of the first of Bouquet's two letters to BF of Aug. 22, 1764. The contemporary writing on this folio is entirely in BF's hand. He labeled it at the top "Copies" and endorsed the fourth page: "Copies of Col Bouquet's Letters of Augt. 10 & 22. 1764 Originals sent to Secy Todd Genl Post Office." In a letter of July 26, 1770, he also told Lord Le Despencer, then joint postmaster general, that he was enclosing "original Letters to me from Gen. Bouquet, who commanded the British Troops in Pensilvania in 1764." APS. The rest of the passage makes clear that BF was referring to Bouquet's letters of Aug. 10 and 22, 1764. Despite these two statements, ALS versions of both letters copied on this folio are now among the Franklin Papers, APS.

5. That is, Bouquet's first letter to BF after leaving Philadelphia about the end of July in command of the expedition against the Indians in the Ohio Valley. The Pa. troops in his force were supposed to number 1000 men. BF was both one of the provincial commissioners named in the Supply Act of May 30, 1764, to handle expenses for military defense, and a personal friend of Bouquet of several years' standing and had helped him before. See above, VII, 62 n, 63–5, 181–4. Bouquet wrote to Governor Penn on the same day about the subject of this letter (1 *Pa. Arch.*, IV, 199–200; Sylvester K. Stevens and Donald H. Kent, eds., *The Papers of Col. Henry Bouquet*, XVI [Harrisburg, 1943], 59), yet it was natural that he should also communicate with his friend in hopes of a sympathetic presentation of his problem to the other provincial commissioners.

6. In his letter to Penn mentioned in the preceding note Bouquet said that he planned to raise the additional recruits in Va., "as I don't expect to be able to raise them in this Province."

application of the whole money voted for that Service, Except the 20 shs. to raise again the men who have deserted, an Article too inconsiderable to form an objection.

As I realy apprehend some Risk in proceeding on this Expedition with so few Troops, I beg you will use your Interest with the Board to obtain me that favour, and prevent a delay, which in the Circumstances would be equal to a denial.[7]

We are hitherto perfectly quiet here, being neither disturbed by our active Enemy, nor assisted by our Indolent and mean Spirited Frontier Friends.[8] I am with great Regard Dear Sir Your most obedient and Humble Servant HENRY BOUQUET

Benjamin Franklin Esqr.

Endorsed: Col. Bouquet Augt. 10. 64 requesting Money to compleat the Troops. 1st. Letter after his Departure.

Preface to Joseph Galloway's Speech

The Speech of Joseph Galloway, Esq; One of the Members for Philadelphia County; In Answer To the Speech of John Dickinson, Esq; Delivered in the House of Assembly, of the Province of Pennsylvania, May 24, 1764. On Occasion of a Petition drawn up by Order, and then under the Consideration of the House; praying his Majesty for a Royal, in lieu of a Proprietary Government. (Philadelphia: Printed and sold by W. Dunlap, in Market street. 1764.) Pp. iii–xxxv, [xxxvii–xxxix]. (Yale University Library.)

When the debate on the petition to the King for a change in government reached its climax in the Assembly on May 24, John Dickinson rose and delivered a long written speech opposing the proposal (see above, pp. 194–5). Joseph Galloway responded in favor of the petition, talking from "short Notes" jotted down while his opponent was speaking. Dickinson's speech was published by William Bradford on June 29 with a substantial preface generally believed to have been written by the Rev. William Smith.[9] This preface reviewed briefly the

7. For BF's support of Bouquet's application when it came before the commissioners and for the colonel's gratitude to his friend, see below, pp. 316, 322, 323.

8. Here and elsewhere Bouquet expressed scorn for the apathy of the frontiersmen, the very persons who earlier had so vigorously criticized the Assembly for neglecting their defense and the prosecution of the war against the Indians.

9. *A Speech, Delivered in the House of Assembly of the Province of Pennsyl-*

267

Supply Act of 1759, attributing its passage to the bribery of Governor William Denny, and summarized the action of the Privy Council and Assembly agents in agreeing to certain stipulations for its approval (above, IX, 196–211). The "Prefacer" then described the controversy over the Supply Bill of 1764, the Assembly's decision to seek public support for a change in government, and the debates over the petition to the King, all of which have been dealt with at length in earlier pages of this volume. He then cited several expressions of gratitude to William Penn and his descendants, offered by assemblies over the years, for the privileges which the colony enjoyed, and complained that no copy of the recent petition had been made available to the public and particularly to those who wanted to answer its accusations.

During the next weeks Galloway wrote up in full form his speech in reply to Dickinson of May 24, "taken from his short Notes, and put into Order." Franklin contributed the preface, and the pamphlet was printed by William Dunlap and published on August 11.[1] Dickinson was unwilling to allow Galloway the last word; although, as he explained, he was very busy attending court sessions in the Lower Counties and in Chester and Philadelphia Counties in Pennsylvania, he found time to prepare a *Reply*, dating the foreword September 4. Bradford rushed it into print.[2]

Franklin's preface to the Galloway speech is one of his major con-

---

vania, May 24th, 1764. By John Dickinson, Esq; One of the Members for the County of Philadelphia. On Occasion of a Petition, drawn up by Order, and then under Consideration, of the House; praying his Majesty for a Change of the Government of this Province. With a Preface (Phila., 1764). Pa. Gaz. and Pa. Jour., June 28, 1764, both announced that the pamphlet was to be published "To Morrow." Almost all modern writers on the subject ascribe the preface to Smith, though it was suggested at the time that the man responsible was one of the other clergymen associated with the proprietary party. In the foreword to his *Reply* to Galloway, Dickinson professed not to know, "but by common report," who had written the preface and "never was made acquainted with its contents, till it was published." On Dickinson's speech itself (not Smith's preface) and his attitude towards the Proprietors, see David L. Jacobson, "John Dickinson's Fight against Royal Government, 1764," 3 *William and Mary Quar.*, XIX (1962), 64-85.

1. Pa. Gaz., and Pa. Jour., Aug. 9, 1764, announced that it would be published "On Saturday next." In his *Reply* Dickinson confirmed that the Galloway pamphlet had been "published on Saturday the 11th of August."

2. A Reply to a Piece called the Speech Of Joseph Galloway, Esquire; by John Dickinson (Phila., 1764). Bradford's Pa. Jour., Sept. 13, 1764, announced that it would be published "on Monday next," September 17; Pa. Gaz. carried no advertisement of this pamphlet until the issue of September 20, when it was described as "Just published."

THE
SPEECH

Of

Joseph Galloway, Efq;

One of the MEMBERS for PHILADELPHIA COUNTY :

IN ANSWER

To the SPEECH of *John Dickinfon*, Efq;

Delivered in the Houfe of ASSEMBLY, of the
PROVINCE of PENNSYLVANIA, May 24, 1764.

On Occafion of a Petition drawn up by Order, and
then under the Confideration of the HOUSE ;
praying his MAJESTY for a ROYAL, in lieu of
a PROPRIETARY GOVERNMENT.

Audi et alteram Partem.

PHILADELPHIA :
Printed and fold by W. DUNLAP, in *Market-ftreet.*
MDCCLXIV.

tributions to the controversy over the petition to the King and to the political campaign leading to the election of a new Assembly set for October 1. It is an unusually long preface, exceeding by several hundred words the speech which it introduces. Franklin addressed himself very little to the arguments Dickinson had used in his speech (leaving that task to Galloway), but almost wholly to Smith's preface to Dickinson's speech, and to the counter-petition to the King drawn up and circulated for signatures by the proprietary leaders. As an attempt to refute the highly partisan statement of the other party's case, as presented in the earlier preface and the counter-petition, it is at least equally partisan. Franklin's jibes at Thomas Penn and his colonial adherents clearly reflect the bitterness that the controversy had produced in Pennsylvania.

Between Franklin's preface and the text of Galloway's speech as they appear in the pamphlet appears an "Advertisement," something more than two pages long in the original. It is not wholly clear whether Franklin or Galloway wrote this piece—it refers to Galloway in the third person—but it is included here with the preface because of the possibility that Franklin was the author and because it gives an account, from the Assembly leaders' point of view, of some of the events connected with the speeches of Dickinson and Galloway presented in the opposing pamphlets.

PREFACE.

It is not merely because Mr. Dickinson's Speech was usher'd into the World by a Preface, that one is made to this of Mr. Galloway. But as in that Preface, a Number of Aspersions were thrown on our Assemblies, and their Proceedings grossly misrepresented, it was thought necessary to wipe those Aspersions off, by some proper Animadversions; and by a true State of Facts, to rectify those Misrepresentations.

The Preface begins with saying, that "Governor Denny, whose Administration will never be mentioned but with Disgrace, in the Annals of this Province, was induced by *Considerations* to which the World is *now* no Stranger, to pass sundry Acts," &c. thus insinuating, that by some unusual base Bargain secretly made, but afterwards discover'd, he was induc'd to pass them.[3] It is fit, therefore, without undertaking to justify all that Governor's Administra-

3. For Denny's acquiescence in bills presented by the Assembly and for the sums the Assembly gave him, see above, VIII, 327 n, 419–20 ns. The italics in the quotation are BF's.

tion, to shew what those Considerations were. Ever since the Revenue of the Quit-rents first, and after that the Revenue of Tavern Licences, were settled irrevocably on our Proprietaries and Governors,[4] they have look'd on those Incomes as their proper Estate, for which they were under no Obligations to the People: And when they afterwards concurr'd in passing any useful Laws, they considered them as so many Jobbs, for which they ought to be particularly paid. Hence arose the Custom of Presents twice a Year to the Governors, at the close of each Session in which Laws were past, given at the Time of Passing. They usually amounted to a Thousand Pounds per Annum. But when the Governors and Assemblies disagreed, so that Laws were not pass'd, the Presents were with-held. When a Disposition to agree ensu'd, there sometimes still remain'd some Diffidence. The Governors would not pass the Laws that were wanted, without being sure of the Money, even all that they call'd their Arrears; nor the Assemblies give the Money without being sure of the Laws. Thence the Necessity of some private Conference, in which, mutual Assurances of good Faith might be receiv'd and given, that the Transactions should go hand in hand. What Name the impartial Reader will give to this Kind of Commerce, I cannot say: To me it appears, an Extortion of more Money from the People, for that to which they had before an undoubted Right, both by the Constitution, and by Purchase: But there was no other Shop they could go to for the Commodity they wanted, and they were oblig'd to comply. Time establish'd the Custom, and made it seem honest; so that our Governors, even those of the most undoubted Honor, have practis'd it. Governor Thomas, after a long Misunderstanding with the Assembly, went more openly to work with them in managing this Commerce and they with him. The Fact is curious, as it stands recorded in the Votes of 1742-3, Sundry Bills sent up to the Governor for his Assent,

4. From as early as 1705, Assemblies had often contended that the quitrents due to the Proprietors for lands held under their grants were intended by compact for the support of government. Governors had as often denied the contention, and there seems to be no evidence to uphold the Assembly's contention. William R. Shepherd, *History of Proprietary Government in Pennsylvania* (N.Y., 1896), pp. 67–8, 90–1. Fees for tavern licenses were certainly a perquisite of the governor and were regarded as part of his income. *Ibid.*, p. 377. BF's linking of the Proprietors and their governors here blurs the distinction between them as recipients of revenues arising in the province.

had lain long in his Hands without any Answer.[5] Jan. 4. The House "Ordered, That Thomas Leech, and Edward Warner, wait upon the Governor, and acquaint him, that the House had long waited for his Result on the Bills that lie before him, and desire to know when they may expect it. The Gentlemen return and report, that they waited upon the Governor, and delivered the Message of the House according to Order, and that the Governor was pleased to say, He had had the Bills long under Consideration, and *waited the Result* of the House." The House well understood this Hint; and immediately resolv'd into a Committee of the whole House, to take what was called *the Governor's Support* into Consideration, in which they made, the Minutes say, *some Progress;* and the next Morning it appears, that that *Progress,* whatever it was, had been communicated to him; for he sent them down this Message by his Secretary; "Mr. Speaker, The Governor commands me to acquaint you, that as he has received Assurances of a *good Disposition* in the House, he thinks it incumbent on him to shew *the like* on his Part; and therefore sends down the Bills which lay before him, without any Amendment." As this Message only *shew'd a good Disposition,* but contain'd no Promise to pass the Bills; the House seem to have had their Doubts; and therefore, February 2, when they came to resolve, on the Report of the Grand Committee, to give the Money, they guarded their Resolves very cautiously, *viz.* "Resolved, That *on the Passage* of such Bills as now lie before the Governor, the Naturalization Bill, and such other Bills as may be presented to him, during this Sitting, there be PAID him the Sum of Five Hundred Pounds. Resolved also, That *on the Passage* of such Bills as now lie before the Governor, the Naturalization Bill, and such other Bills as may be presented to him this Sitting, there be PAID to the Governor, the further Sum of One Thousand Pounds, for the current Year's Support; and that Orders be drawn on the Treasurer and Trustees of the Loan Office, pursuant to these Resolves." The Orders were accordingly drawn, with which being acquainted, he appointed a Time to pass the Bills, which was done with one Hand, while he received the Orders in the other; and

5. The transactions between the Assembly and Governor George Thomas described here are recorded in full in *Votes*, 1742–43, pp. 38–9, 47–9, but the date of the House's first order is there given as January 14, not 4. The italics in the quotations were added by BF.

then with the utmost politeness, thank'd the House for the Fifteen Hundred Pounds, as if it had been a *pure Free Gift,* and a mere mark of their Respect and Affection. "I *thank you,* Gentlemen, (says he) for this *Instance* of *your Regard;* which I am the more pleased with, as it gives an agreeable Prospect of *future Harmony* between me and the Representatives of the People." This, Reader, is an exact Counterpart of the Transaction with Governor Denny; except that Denny sent Word to the House, that he would pass the Bills before they voted the *Support.* And yet, here was no Proprietary Clamour about Bribery, &c. And why so? Why, at that Time, the Proprietary Family, by Virtue of a secret Bond they had obtained of the Governor at his Appointment, were to share with him the Sums so obtained of the People!⁶

This Reservation of the Proprietaries they were at that Time a little asham'd of, and therefore such Bonds were then to be Secrets. But as in every Kind of Sinning, frequent Repetition lessens Shame, and increases Boldness, we find the Proprietaries ten Years afterwards, openly insisting on these Advantages to themselves, over and above what was *paid* to their Deputy:⁷ "Wherefore, (say they,) on this Occasion, it is necessary, that we should inform the People, through yourselves, their Representatives, that as, by the Constitution, OUR CONSENT is NECESSARY to their LAWS, at the same Time that they have an *undoubted Right* to such as are necessary for the Defence and real Service of the Country; so it will tend the better to *facilitate* the several Matters which *must* be transacted with us, for their Representatives to shew a *Regard* to us and our INTEREST." This was in their Answer to the Representation of the Assembly, [*Votes,* December, 1754, Page 48]⁸ on the Justice

6. According to this secret agreement Thomas was to turn over to the Penns annually either £500 sterling or one half the profits of his office, whichever he preferred. Shepherd, *Proprietary Government in Pa.,* pp. 205–9, discusses this affair in detail.

7. The Assembly's address to Thomas and Richard Penn, Aug. 23, 1751, which elicited the response quoted in part here, asked the Proprietors to contribute towards the cost of Indian treaties. It is printed in full above, IV, 188–91. The Penns' answer was laid before the House, May 24, 1753, and an Assembly committee, of which BF was a member, reported on it Sept. 11, 1753. The quotations from the Proprietors' answer and the committee's comment which BF gives here may be found above, V, 47, 48. BF supplied the emphasis in the quotation from the Penns' answer.

8. Brackets in the original.

of their contributing to Indian Expences, which they had refused. And on this Clause, the Committee make the following Remark; "They tell us, their Consent is *necessary* to our *Laws,* and that it will tend the better to *facilitate* the Matters which *must* be transacted with them, for the Representatives to shew a Regard to their INTEREST: That, is, as we understand it, though the Proprietaries have a Deputy here, supported by the Province, who is, or ought to be, fully impower'd to pass all Laws *necessary for the Service of the Country;* yet, before we can obtain such Laws, we must *facilitate their Passage,* by paying Money for the Proprietaries which they ought to pay, or in some Shape make it their *particular* INTEREST to pass them. We hope, however, that if this Practice has ever been *begun,* it will never be *continued* in this Province; and that, since, as this very Paragraph allows, we have an *undoubted Right* to such Laws, we shall always be able to obtain them from the Goodness of our Sovereign, without going to Market for them to a Subject." Time has shewn that those Hopes were vain; they have been oblig'd to go to that Market ever since, directly, or indirectly, or go without their Laws. The Practice has continued, and will continue, as long as the Proprietary Government subsists, intervening between the Crown and the People.

Do not, my courteous Reader, take Pet at our Proprietary Constitution, for these our Bargain and Sale Proceedings in Legislation. 'Tis a happy Country where Justice, and what was your own before, can be had for Ready Money. 'Tis another Addition to the Value of Money, and of Course another Spur to Industry. Every Land is not so bless'd. There are Countries where the princely Proprietor claims to be Lord of all Property; where what is your own shall not only be wrested from you, but the Money you give to have it restor'd, shall be kept with it, and your offering so much, being a Sign of your being too rich, you shall be plunder'd of every Thing that remain'd. These Times are not come here yet: Your present Proprietors have never been more unreasonable hitherto, than barely to insist on your Fighting in Defence of their Property, and paying the Expence yourselves; or if their Estates must, (ah! *must*) be tax'd towards it, that the *best* of their Lands shall be tax'd no higher than the *worst* of yours.[9]

9. The issue of the taxation of the Proprietors' located but uncultivated lands, which had for so long held up the passage of a supply act earlier this year.

Pardon this Digression, and I return to Governor Denny; but first let me do Governor Hamilton the Justice to observe, that whether from the Uprightness of his own Disposition, or from the odious Light the Practice had been set in on Denny's Account, or from both, he did not attempt these Bargains, but pass'd such Laws as he thought fit to pass, without any previous Stipulation of *Pay* for them.[1] But then, when he saw the Assembly tardy in the Payment he expected, and yet calling upon him still to pass *more Laws,* he openly put them in Mind of the Money, as a *Debt* due to him from Custom. "In the Course of the present Year, (says he, in his Message of July 8. 1763) a great Deal of public Business hath been transacted by me; and I believe, as many useful *Laws enacted,* as by any of my Predecessors in the same Space of Time; yet I have not understood, that any *Allowance* hath hitherto been made to me for my Support, as *hath been customary* in this Province." The House having then some Bills in hand, took the Matter into immediate Consideration, and voted him five Hundred Pounds; for which an Order or Certificate was accordingly drawn; and on the same Day the Speaker, after the House had been with the Governor, reported, "That his Honor had been pleased to give his Assent to the Bills, by *enacting the same into Laws;* and Mr. Speaker farther reported, that he had *then,* in behalf of the House, presented their Certificate of Five Hundred Pounds to the Governor, who was pleased to say, he was obliged to the House for the same."[2] Thus we see the Practice of purchasing and paying for Laws, is interwoven with our *Proprietary* Constitution, us'd in the best Times, and under the best Governors. And yet, alas poor Assembly! How will you steer your brittle Bark between these Rocks? If you pay ready Money for your Laws, and those Laws are not lik'd by the Proprietaries, you are charg'd with Bribery and Corruption: If you wait a While before you pay, you are accus'd of detaining the Governor's customary Right, and dun'd as a negligent or dishonest Debtor, that refuses to discharge a just Debt!

But Governor Denny's Case, I shall be told, differs from all

1. This tribute to James Hamilton may have been due to the belief that he favored the change to royal government. See William Allen to D. Barclay & Sons, Nov. 20, 1764, Lewis Burd Walker, ed., *The Burd Papers. Extracts from Chief Justice William Allen's Letter Book* ([Pottsville, Pa.], 1897), p. 64.

2. *Votes,* 1762–63, p. 48.

these, for the Acts he was induced to pass, were, as the Prefacer tells us, "contrary to his Duty, and to every Tie of Honor and Justice."[3] Such is the Imperfection of our Language, and perhaps of all other Languages, that notwithstanding we are furnish'd with Dictionaries innumerable, we cannot precisely know the import of Words, unless we know of what Party the Man is that uses them. In the Mouth of an Assembly-man, or true Pennsylvanian, *Contrary to his Duty, and to every Tie of Honor and Justice,* would mean, the Governor's long Refusal to pass Laws, however just and necessary, for taxing the Proprietary Estate; a Refusal contrary to the Trust reposed in the Lieutenant Governor, by the Royal Charter, to the Rights of the People, whose Welfare it was his Duty to promote, and to the Nature of the Contract, made between the Governor and the Governed, when the Quit-rents and Licence Fees were estab-lish'd, which confirm'd what the Proprietaries call our *undoubted Right* to necessary Laws. But in the Mouth of the Proprietaries, or their Creatures, *contrary to his Duty, and to every Tie of Justice and Honor,* means, his Passing Laws, contrary to *Proprietary Instructions;* and contrary to the *Bonds* he had previously given to observe those Instructions: Instructions however, that were unjust and uncon-stitutional, and Bonds that were illegal and void from the beginning.

Much has been said of the Wickedness of Governor Denny in Passing, and of the Assembly in prevailing with him to pass those Acts. By the Prefacer's Account of them, you would think the Laws so obtain'd were *all* bad, for he speaks of but seven, of which, six he says were repeal'd, and the seventh reported to be "fundamentally WRONG and UNJUST," and "ought to be repealed unless six certain Amendments were made therein."[*4] Whereas in fact there were *nineteen* of them; and several of those must have been good Laws, for even the *Proprietaries* did not object to them. Of the eleven that they oppos'd, only six were repeal'd;[5] so that

*This Act is intitled, An Act for granting to his Majesty, the Sum of One Hundred Thousand Pounds, striking the same in Bills of Credit, and sinking the Bills by a Tax on all Estates real and personal.

3. Preface to Dickinson's *Speech,* p. iii.
4. Preface to Dickinson's *Speech,* p. iii, quoting in part the order in council of Sept. 2, 1760, above, IX, 205.
5. For the titles of the 19 acts and the final disposition of each, see above, IX, 204-5, 208-10.

it seems these good Gentlemen may themselves be sometimes as *wrong* in opposing, as the Assembly in enacting Laws. But the Words *fundamentally* WRONG and UNJUST are the great Fund of Triumph to the *Proprietaries* and their Partizans. These their subsequent Governors have unmercifully dinn'd in the Ears of the Assembly on all occasions ever since, for they make a Part of near a Dozen of their Messages. They have rung the Changes on those Words, till they work'd them up to say that the Law was *fundamentally wrong and unjust* in SIX several Articles. [Governor's Message, May 17th, 1764.] instead of "ought to be repealed unless six Alterations or Amendments could be made therein."[6] A Law unjust in six several Articles, must be an unjust Law indeed; Let us therefore once for all, examine this unjust Law, Article by Article, in order to see whether our Assemblies have been such Villains as they are represented.

The first Particular in which their Lordships propos'd the Act should be amended, was, "That the real Estates to be tax'd, be *defined with Precision,* so as not to include the unsurveyed waste Land belonging to the Proprietaries." This was at most, but an *Obscurity* to be cleared up. And tho' the Law might well appear to their Lordships incertain in that Particular; with us, who better know our own Customs, and that the Proprietaries waste unsurveyed Land, was never here considered among Estates real, subject to Taxation, there was not the least Doubt or Supposition, that such Lands were included in the Words, "all Estates real and personal." The Agents therefore, knowing that the Assembly had no Intention to tax those Lands, might well suppose they would readily agree to remove the Obscurity.

Before we go farther, let it be observ'd, That the main Design of the Proprietaries, in opposing this Act, was, to prevent their Estates being tax'd at all. But as they knew that the Doctrine of *Proprietary Exemption,* which they had endeavoured to enforce here, could not be supported there, they bent their whole Strength

6. Governors Hamilton and Penn had directly quoted the words "fundamentally wrong and unjust" in five messages during 1763 and 1764 (*Votes,* 1762–63, pp. 10, 32, 60; 1763–64, pp. 58, 77), besides referring to the point on several other occasions. In the last of the direct quotations Penn had introduced the distortion of the Privy Council's statement of which BF here complained.

against the Act on other Principles to procure its Repeal, pretending great willingness to submit to an equitable Tax; but that the Assembly, out of mere Malice, because they had conscienciously quitted Quakerism for the Church![7] were wickedly determin'd to ruin them, to tax all their unsurvey'd Wilderness Lands, and at the highest Rates, and by that Means exempt themselves and the People, and throw the whole Burden of the War on the Proprietary Family. How foreign these Charges were from the Truth, need not be told to any Man in Pennsylvania. And as the Proprietors knew, that the Hundred Thousand Pounds of Paper Money, struck for the Defence of their enormous Estates, with others, was actually issued, spread thro' the Country, and in the Hands of Thousands of poor People, who had given their Labor for it; how base, cruel, and inhuman it was, to endeavour, by a Repeal of the Act, to strike the Money dead in those Hands at one Blow, and reduce it all to Waste Paper, to the utter Confusion of all Trade and Dealings, and the Ruin of Multitudes, merely to avoid paying their own just Tax! Words may be wanting to express, but Minds will easily conceive, and never without Abhorrence!

The second Amendment propos'd by their Lordships was, "That the located uncultivated Lands belonging to the Proprietaries shall not be assessed higher than the lowest Rate, at which any located uncultivated Lands belonging to the Inhabitants shall be assessed." Had there been any Provision in the Act, that the Proprietaries Lands, and those of the People, of the same Value, should be taxed differently, the one high, and the other low, the Act might well have been call'd in this Particular, *fundamentally wrong and unjust.* But as there is no such Clause, this cannot be one of the Particulars on which the Charge is founded; but, like the first, is merely a Requisition to make the Act clear, by express Directions therein, that the Proprietaries Estate should not be, as they pretended to believe it would be, tax'd higher in proportion to its Value, than the

7. Thomas Penn seems to have drifted gradually away from the Society of Friends, though he retained friendships among its members. His wife, the former Lady Juliana Fermor, daughter of Thomas, first Earl of Pomfret, was certainly an Anglican, and after his marriage in 1751 he attended church regularly. Though it was said in 1771 that he had never received the Sacraments, he was not "looked upon as a Protestant Dissenter." *PMHB*, xxi (1897), 339, 343. His brother Richard appears to have become an Anglican communicant.

Estates of others.[8] As to their present Claim, founded on that Article, "that the *best and most valuable* of their Lands, should be tax'd no higher than the *worst* and *least valuable* of the People's," it was not then thought of; they made no such Demand, nor did any one dream, that so iniquitous a Claim would ever be made by Men who had the least Pretence to the Characters of *Honorable* or *Honest.*

The third Particular was, "That all Lands not granted by the Proprietaries within Boroughs and Towns, be deemed located uncultivated Lands, and rated accordingly, and not as Lots." The Clause in the Act that this relates to, is, "And whereas many valuable *Lots* of Ground within the City of Philadelphia, and the several Boroughs and Towns within this Province, remain unimproved; Be it enacted, &c. That *all* such unimproved *Lots* of Ground, within the City and Boroughs aforesaid, shall be rated and assessed, according to their Situation and Value, for and towards raising the Money hereby granted." The Reader will observe, that the Word is *all* unimproved Lots, and that *all* comprehends the Lots belonging to the People, as well as those of the Proprietary. There were many of the former, and a Number belonging even to Members of the then Assembly; and considering the Value, the Tax must be proportionably as grievous to them, as the Proprietary's to him. Is there among us a single Man, even a Proprietary Relation, Officer, or Dependant, so insensible of the Differences of Right and Wrong, and so confus'd in his Notions of just and unjust, as to think and say, that the Act in this Particular, was fundamentally *wrong* and *unjust?* I believe not one. What then could their Lordships mean by the propos'd Amendment? Their Meaning is easily explain'd. The Proprietaries have considerable Tracts of *Land* within the Bounds of Boroughs and Towns, that have not yet been divided into Lots: They pretended to believe, that by Virtue of this Clause, an imaginary Division would be made of those Lands into Lots, and an extravagant Value set on such imaginary Lots, greatly to their Prejudice: It was answered, that no such Thing was intended by the Act; and that by *Lots,* was meant only such Ground

8. Though BF did not know it, Thomas Penn had admitted early in June that the stipulation in the order in council "would bear the Construction the Assembly put upon it." Penn to Benjamin Chew, June 8, 1764, Penn Papers, Hist. Soc. Pa. Chew and the other proprietary leaders kept this admission to themselves.

as had been surveyed and divided into Lots, and not the open un-divided Lands. If this only is intended, say their Lordships, then let the Act be amended, so as clearly to express what is intended. This is the full Amount of the third Particular.[9] How the Act was understood here, is well known by the Execution of it, before the Dispute came on in England; and therefore before their Lordships Opinion on the Point could be given; of which full Proof shall presently be made. In the mean Time it appears, that the Act was not *on this* Account, *fundamentally wrong and unjust.*

The fourth Particular is, "That the Governor's Consent and Approbation be made necessary to every Issue and Application of the Money to be raised by Virtue of such Act." The Assembly intended this, and tho't they had done it in the Act. The Words of the Clause being, "That [the Commissioners named] or the major Part of them, or of the Survivors of them, *with the Consent* and *Approbation* of the Governor or Commander in Chief of this Province, for the Time being, shall order and appoint the Disposition of the Monies arising by Virtue of this Act, for and towards paying and cloathing two Thousand seven Hundred effective Men, &c." It was understood here, that as the Power of disposing, was expressly to be *with* the Consent and Approbation of the Governor, the Commissioners had no Power to dispose of the Money *without* that Approbation: But their Lordships, jealous (as their Station requires) of this Prerogative of the Crown, and being better acquainted with the Force and Weakness of Law Expression, did not think the Clause explicit enough, unless the Words, *and not otherwise,* were added, or some other Words equivalent. This Particular therefore was no more, than another Requisition of greater Clearness and Precision; and by no Means a Foundation for the Charge of *fundamentally wrong and unjust.*

9. BF draws a distinction here between what we should today call "building lots" and larger tracts of land within municipalities but not yet marked off for subdivision into such "building lots." The phraseology of the stipulation to which he had agreed in 1760 would seem to justify such a distinction, one which, at any rate, is commonly recognized in the assessment for tax purposes of vacant land in twentieth-century communities. Governor Penn's interpretation would mean that an empty houselot in the heart of Philadelphia or Lancaster belonging to one of his relatives would be taxed at the same low acreage rate as a piece of swampland or barren hillside somewhere in the country belonging to an inhabitant.

281

The fifth Particular was, "That Provincial Commissioners be named to hear and determine Appeals, brought on the Part of the Inhabitants as well as the Proprietaries." There was already subsisting a Provision for the Appointment of County Commissioners of Appeal, by whom the Act might be, and actually has been, as we shall presently shew, justly and impartially executed, with Regard to the Proprietaries; but Provincial Commissioners, appointed in the Act, it was thought might be of Use, in regulating and equalizing the Modes of Assessment of different Counties, where they were unequal; and, by affording a second Appeal, tend more to the Satisfaction both of the Proprietaries and the People. This Particular was therefore a mere proposed Improvement of the Act, which could not be, and was not, in that respect, denominated *fundamentally wrong and unjust.*

We have now gone thro' five of the six proposed Amendments, without discovering any Thing on which that Censure could be founded; but the sixth remains, which points at a Part of the Act, wherein we must candidly acknowlege there is something, that in their Lordships View of it, must justify their Judgment: The Words of the 6th Article are, "That the Payments by the Tenants to the Proprietaries of their Rents, shall be according to the Terms of their respective Grants, as if such Act had never been passed." This relates to that Clause of the Act, by which the Paper Money was made a legal Tender in "Discharge of all Manner of Debts, Rents, Sum and of Sums of Money whatsoever, &c. at the Rates ascertained in the Act of Parliament, made in the sixth of Queen Anne." From the great Injustice frequently done to Creditors, and complain'd of from the Colonies, by the vast Depreciation of Paper Bills, it was become a general fixed Principle with the Ministry, that such Bills, whose Value, tho' fixed *in* the Act, could not be kept fixed *by* the Act, ought not to be made a legal Tender in any Colony, at those Rates. The Parliament had before passed an Act to take that Tender away in the four New-England Colonies, and have since made the Act general.[1] This was what their Lordships would therefore have proposed for the Amendment. But it being represented, That the chief Support of the Credit of the Bills, was the legal Tender, and that without it they would become of no Value; it was allowed generally to remain, with an Exception to the

1. See above, p. 176 n.

Proprietaries Rents, where there was a special Contract for Payment in another Coin.[2] It cannot be denied, but that this was doing Justice to the Proprietaries, and that had the Requisition been in favour of all other Creditors also, the Justice had been equal, as being general. We do not therefore presume to impeach their Lordship's Judgment, that the Act, as it enforced the Acceptance of Bills for Money, at a Value which they had only nominally and not really, was in that Respect *fundamentally wrong and unjust.* And yet we believe the Reader will not think the Assembly so much to blame, when he considers, That the making Paper Bills a legal Tender, had been the universal Mode in America for more than threescore Years. That there was scarce a Colony that had not practised that Mode, more or less. That it had always been thought absolutely necessary in order to give the Bills a Credit, and thereby obtain from them the Uses of Money. That the Inconveniencies were therefore submitted to, for the Sake of the greater Conveniencies. That Acts innumerable of the like Kind had been approved by the Crown. And, that if the Assembly made the Bills a legal Tender at those Rates to the Proprietaries, they made them also a legal Tender to themselves, and all their Constituents, many of whom might suffer in their Rents, &c. as much, in proportion to their Estates, as the Proprietaries. But if he cannot on these Considerations, quite excuse the Assembly, what will he think of those *Honourable* Proprietaries, who when Paper Money was issued in their Colony, for the common Defence of their vast Estates, with those of the People, and who must therefore reap, at least, equal Advantages from those Bills with the People, could nevertheless *wish* to be exempted from their Share of the unavoidable Disadvantages. Is there upon Earth a Man besides, with any Conception of what is honest, with any Notion of Honor, with the least Tincture in his Veins of the Gentleman, but would have blush'd at the Thought; but would have rejected with Disdain such undue Pref-

2. The Supply Bill passed March 14, 1764 (MS, APS), and probably the bill of February 24 also, had included a clause making the bills of credit legal tender for all payments, "the sterling Rents due, or to become due to the Proprietaries of this Province only excepted." Dickinson had opposed this concession, offered as a compromise, calling it "fundamentally unjust" and "a precedent of proprietary prerogative." Jacobson, 3 *William and Mary Quar.,* XIX (1962), 68.

erence, if it had been offered him? Much less would he have struggled for it, mov'd Heaven and Earth to obtain it, resolv'd to ruin
Thousands of his Tenants by a Repeal of the Act rather than miss
of it;* and enforce it afterwards by an audaciously wicked Instruction, forbidding Aids to his King, and exposing the Province
to Destruction, unless it was complied with.⁴ And yet, These are
HONOURABLE Men.†

Here then we have had a full View of the Assembly's Injustice;
about which there has been so much insolent Triumph! But let the
Proprietaries and their discreet Deputies hereafter recollect and
remember; that the same august Tribunal, which censured some
of the Modes and Circumstances of that Act, did at the same Time

*This would have been done, and the Money all sunk in the Hands
of the People, if the Agents, Benjamin Franklin and Robert Charles,
had not interposed, and voluntarily, without Authority from the Assembly so to do, but at their own Risque, undertaken that those Amendments should be made, or that they themselves would indemnify the
Proprietaries from any Damages they might sustain for want thereof.
An Action, which, as the Prefacer says in another Case, "Posterity
perhaps, may find a Name for."³

†It is not easy to guess from what Source our Proprietaries have
drawn their Principles. Those who study Law and Justice as a Science,
have establish'd it a Maxim in Equity. *Qui sentit commodum, sentire
debet et onus.*⁵ And so consistent is this with the *common* Sense of Mankind, that even our lowest untaught Coblers and Porters feel the Force
of it in their own Maxim, (which *they* are *honest enough* never to dispute) *Touch Pot, touch Penny.*

3. The Preface to Dickinson's *Speech,* p. vii, had pointed out that "as one
of his first acts" after becoming speaker, BF had signed the petition to the
King, "an act which * * * but posterity will best be able to give it a name!"
4. The stipulation agreed to and incorporated in the order in council,
Sept. 2, 1760, had required payment "according to the terms of their respective Grants" (i.e., in sterling) only for the *rents* due the Proprietors. Above,
IX, 206. The 12th article of the Instructions to Governor John Penn upon
his appointment had directed him to require that "any Quitrents *or other
Sterling Payments* due, or to become due to us" (italics added), be paid in
sterling or at the rate of sterling exchange. *Votes,* 1763–64, p. 27. The additional words are explained by the fact that subsequent to the order in council
the Proprietors had directed that future land purchases should also require
sterling payments of the purchase money.
5. He who enjoys the gain should feel the burden.

establish and confirm the Grand Principle of the Act, viz. That the Proprietary Estate ought, with other Estates, to be taxed: And thereby did in Effect determine and pronounce, that the Opposition so long made in various Shapes, to that just Principle, by the Proprietaries, was *fundamentally* WRONG *and* UNJUST. An Injustice, they were not, like the Assembly, under any Necessity of committing for the public Good; or any other Necessity but what was impos'd on them by those base Passions that act the Tyrant in bad Minds, their *Selfishness,* their *Pride,* and their *Avarice.*

I have frequently mentioned the equitable Intentions of the House, in those Parts of the Act that were suppos'd obscure, and how they were understood here. A clear Proof thereof is found, as I have already said, in the actual Execution of the Act; in the Execution of it before the Contest about it in England, and therefore before their Lordships Objections to it had a Being. When the Report came over, and was laid before the House, one Year's Tax had been levied; and the Assembly, conscious that no Injustice had been intended to the Proprietaries, and willing to rectify it if any should appear, appointed a Committee of Members from the several Counties, to examine into the State of the Proprietaries Taxes thro' the Province, and nominated on that Committee, a Gentleman of known Attachment to the Proprietaries, and their Chief Justice, Mr. Allen, to the end that the strictest Enquiry might be made. Their Report was as follows:[6]

"We the Committee appointed to enquire into, and consider the State of the Proprietary Taxation thro' the several Counties, and report the same to the House, have, in pursuance of the said Appointment, carefully examined the Returns of Property, and compared them with the respective Assessments thereon made through the whole Province: and find,

"FIRST, That no Part of the unsurveyed waste Lands, belonging to the Proprietaries, have, in any Instance, been included in the Estates taxed.

"SECONDLY, That some of the located uncultivated Lands, belonging to the Proprietaries in several Counties, remain unassessed,

6. Presented to the House March 12, 1761, and also incorporated in a message to the governor (without the signatures) two days later. 8 *Pa. Arch.,* VI, 5216, 5220–1.

and are not, in any County, assessed higher than the Lands under like Circumstances, belonging to the Inhabitants.

"THIRDLY, That all Lands, not granted by the Proprietaries, within Boroughs and Towns, remain untaxed, excepting in a few Instances, and in those they are rated as low as the Lands which are granted in the said Boroughs and Towns.

"The whole of the Proprietary Tax of eighteen Pence in the Pound, amounts to - - - - - - - - - - - - - - - - - £. 566 4 10

"And the Sum of the Tax on the Inhabitants for the same Year, amounts, thro' the several Counties, to } 27,103 12 8

"And it is the Opinion of your Committee, that there has not been *any Injustice* done to the Proprietaries, or *Attempts made* to rate or assess *any Part* of their Estates, *higher* than the Estates of the like Kind belonging to the Inhabitants, are rated and assessed; but on the contrary, we find, that their Estates are rated, in *many* instances *below* others.

THOMAS LEECH,	GEORGE ASHBRIDGE.
JOSEPH FOX.	EMANUEL CARPENTER.
SAMUEL RHOADS.	JOHN BLACKBURN.
ABRAHAM CHAPMAN.	WILLIAM ALLEN."

The House communicated this Report to Governor Hamilton, when he afterwards press'd them to make the stipulated Act of Amendment; acquainting him at the same Time, that as in the Execution of the Act, no Injustice had hitherto been done to the Proprietary, so, by a Yearly Inspection of the Assessments, they would take Care that none should be done him; for that if any should appear, or the Governor could at any Time point out to them any that had been done, they would immediately rectify it; and therefore, as the Act was shortly to expire, they did not think the Amendments necessary. Thus that Matter ended during that Administration. And had his Successor, Governor PENN, permitted it still to sleep, we are of Opinion it had been more to the Honor of the Family, and of his own Discretion. But he was pleas'd to found upon it a Claim manifestly unjust, and which he was totally destitute of Reason to support. A Claim, that the Proprietaries *best* and *most valuable* located uncultivated Lands should be taxed *no higher* than the *worst* and *least valuable* of those belonging to the Inhabitants:

286

To enforce which, as he thought the Words of one of the Stipulations seem'd to give some Countenance to it, he insisted on using those very Words as sacred, from which he could "neither in *Decency* or *in Duty*," deviate, tho' he had agreed to deviate from Words of the same Report, and therefore equally sacred, in every other Instance. A Conduct which will, as the Prefacer says in Governor Denny's Case, forever disgrace the Annals of his Administration.*

Never did any Administration open with a more *promising* Prospect.[7] He assur'd the People, in his first Speeches, of the Proprietaries paternal Regard for them, and their sincere Dispositions to do every Thing that might promote their Happiness. As the Proprietaries had been pleased to appoint a Son of the Family to the Government, it was thought not unlikely that there might be something in these Professions; for that they would probably chuse to have his Administration made easy and agreeable, and to that End might think it prudent to withdraw those harsh, disagreeable and unjust Instructions, with which most of his Predecessors had been hamper'd: The Assembly therefore believ'd fully, and rejoic'd sincerely. They show'd the new Governor every Mark of Respect and Regard that was in their Power. They readily and chearfully went into every Thing he recommended to them. And when he and his Authority were insulted and indanger'd by a lawless murdering Mob, they and their Friends, took Arms at his Call, and form'd themselves round him for his Defence, and the Support of his Government. But when it was found that those mischievous Instructions still subsisted, and were even farther extended; when the Governor began, unprovok'd, to send the House affronting Messages, seizing every imaginary Occasion of reflecting on their Conduct; when every other Symptom appear'd of fixt deep-rooted Family Malice, which could but a little while bear the unnatural Covering that had been thrown over it, what Wonder is it, if all the old Wounds broke out and bled afresh, if all the old Grievances, still unredress'd, were recollected; if Despair succeeded of any Peace with a Family, that could make *such Returns* to all their Overtures of Kindness? And when, in the very Proprietary Coun-

*For a fuller Account of this Dispute, the Reader is re[ferred] to the News-Papers and Votes of Assembly.

7. For one of the many addresses of welcome presented to John Penn following his arrival, see above, x, 375–6.

cil, compos'd of stanch Friends of the Family, and chosen for their Attachment to it, 'twas observ'd, that the *old Men,* (I. Kings, Chap. 12.) withdrew themselves, finding their Opinion slighted,[8] and that all Measures were taken by the Advice of two or three *young Men,* (one of whom too denies his Share in them) is it any Wonder, since like Causes produce like Effects, if the Assembly, notwithstanding all their Veneration for the first Proprietor, should say, with the Children of Israel under the same Circumstances, *What Portion have we in* DAVID, *or Inheritance in the Son of* JESSE: *To your Tents, O Israel!*[9]

Under these Circumstances, and a Conviction that while so many natural Sources of Difference subsisted between Proprietaries and People, no Harmony in Government could long subsist; without which, neither the Commands of the Crown could be executed, nor the public Good promoted; the House resum'd the Consideration of a Measure that had often been propos'd in former

---

8. Richard Peters, now aged 60, and James Hamilton, 54, were no longer as active in political affairs as formerly, and William Allen, 60, miffed at Penn's failure to consult him on appointments, was threatening to withdraw. Benjamin Chew, 42; Edward Shippen, Jr., 35; Joseph Shippen III, 32; and Richard Penn, 29, were now among the most influential advisors of Governor John Penn, 35. William S. Hanna, *Benjamin Franklin and Pennsylvania Politics* (Stanford, 1964), p. 162, discusses these changes.

9. A sympathetic reader would have found BF's Biblical analogy especially striking: "And king Rehoboam consulted with the old men, that stood before Solomon his father while he yet lived, and said, How do ye advise that I may answer this people? And they spake unto him, saying, If thou wilt be a servant unto this people this day, and wilt serve them, and answer them, and speak good words to them, then they will be thy servants for ever. But he forsook the counsel of the old men, which they had given him, and consulted with the young men that were grown up with him, and which stood before him: And he said unto them, What counsel give ye that we may answer this people, who have spoken to me, saying, Make the yoke which thy father did put upon us lighter? And the young men that were grown up with him spake unto him, saying, Thus shalt thou speak unto this people that spake unto thee . . . My little finger shall be thicker than my father's loins. And now whereas my father did lade you with a heavy yoke, I will add to your yoke: my father hath chastised you with whips, but I will chastise you with scorpions. . . . So when all Israel saw that the king hearkened not unto them, the people answered the king, saying, What portion have we in David? neither have we inheritance in the son of Jesse: to your tents, O Israel: now see to thine own house, David. So Israel departed unto their tents." I Kings, 12:6–11, 16. An Assembly committee, of which BF was a member, had used the Rehoboam story against the Proprietors in 1753. See above, V, 57.

Assemblies; a Measure that every Proprietary Province in America had, from the same Causes, found themselves oblig'd to take, and had actually taken or were about to take; and a Measure that had happily succeeded, wherever it was taken; I mean the Recourse to an immediate Royal Government.

They therefore, after a thorough Debate, and making no less than twenty-five unanimous Resolves,[1] expressing the many Grievances this Province had long laboured under, thro' the Proprietary Government; came to the following Resolution, viz.

RESOLVED, *Nemine contradicente,*
"That this House will adjourn, in order to consult their Constituents, whether an humble Address should be drawn up, and transmitted to his Majesty, praying, that he would be graciously pleased to take the People of this Province under his immediate Protection and Government, by compleating the Agreement heretofore made with the first Proprietary for the Sale of the Government to the Crown, or otherwise as to his Wisdom and Goodness shall seem meet."*

This they ordered to be made public, and it was published accordingly, in all the News Papers;[3] the House then adjourn'd for no less then seven Weeks, to give their Constituents Time to consider the Matter, and themselves an Opportunity of taking their Opinion and Advice. Could any thing be more deliberate, more fair and open, or more respectful to the People that chose them? During this Recess, the People in many Places, held little Meetings with each other, the Result of which was, that they would mani-

*These Words, "by completing the Agreement," &c. are omitted by the honest Prefacer, in his Account of the Resolve, that they might not interfere with his Insinuation of the Measure's being impracticable, "Have the Proprietors, by any Act of theirs, forfeited the least tittle of what was granted them by his Majesty's Royal Ancestors? Or can they be *deprived* of their Charter Rights without their Consent?" &c. Sensible, that these Questions are impertinent, if those Rights are already sold.[2]

1. For the full text of these Resolves, see above, pp. 126–33.
2. The preface to Dickinson's *Speech*, p. iv, quotes this Resolve ending with the words "protection and government &c." BF took the questions he quoted in this note from the preface, p. xi, and added the italics. He omitted the word "own" before "Consent" in the second question.
3. The entire series of Resolves was printed in *Pa. Gaʒ.*, March 29, 1764, but *Pa. Jour.* printed none of them.

fest their Sentiments to their Representatives, by petitioning the Crown directly of themselves, and requesting the Assembly to transmit and support those Petitions. At the next Meeting, many of these Petitions were delivered to the House with that Request; they were signed by a very great* Number of the most substantial

*The Prefacer, with great Art, endeavours to represent this Number as insignificant. He says the Petitioners were but 3500, and that the Province contains near THREE HUNDRED THOUSAND SOULS! His Reader is to imagine that TWO HUNDRED AND NINETY-SIX THOUSAND FIVE HUNDRED of them were apply'd to and refus'd to sign it.[4] The Truth is, that his Number of Souls is vastly exaggerated. The Dwelling Houses in the Province in 1752 did not exceed 20,000. Political Arithmeticians reckon generally but 5 Souls to a House, one House with another; and therefore, allowing for Houses since built, there are not probably more than an Hundred and ten Thousand Souls in the Province: That of these scarce 22,000 could with any Propriety be Petitioners.[5] And considering the scatter'd Settlement of the Province, the general Inattention of Mankind, especially in new Countries, to public Affairs; and the indefatigable Pains taken by the Proprietors new Allies, the Presbyterian Clergy of Philadelphia, (who wrote circular Letters to every Congregation in the County, to deter them from petitioning, by dutiful Intimations, that if we were *reduc'd* to a Royal Government it would be the "Ruin of the Province,")[6] 'tis a Wonder the Number (near a sixth Part) was so great as it was. But if there had been no such Petitions, it would not have been material to the Point. The Assembly went upon another Foundation. They had adjourned to consult their Constituents, they return'd satisfy'd that the Measure was agreeable to them, and nothing appear'd to the contrary.

4. Preface to Dickinson's *Speech*, p. iv. BF seems to have accepted this total number of signers of the petition, though he disputed the inference Smith drew from it.

5. BF's estimate of the total population of Pa. at this time seems low. In his examination before the House of Commons in 1766 he said the total white population "may be about 160,000." Smyth, *Writings*, IV, 415. Other suggested figures for the 1760s range from 180,000 to 400,000 or 500,000, with a median of all estimates, including BF's, of 250,000 men, women, and children, white and Negro. Evarts B. Greene and Virginia D. Harrington, *American Population before the Federal Census of 1790* (N.Y., 1932), pp. 115–16. BF's figure of 22,000 potential signers obviously refers to heads of households only; relatively few others had the right to vote.

6. Sparks, *Works*, VII, 281–2 n, prints a circular letter to this effect, dated March 30, 1764, and signed by Gilbert Tennent, Francis Alison, and John Ewing.

Inhabitants, and not the least Intimation was receiv'd by the Assembly from any other of their Constituents, that the Measure was disapproved, except in a Petition from an obscure Township in Lancaster County, to which there were about forty Names indeed, but all evidently signed by three Hands only.[7] What could the Assembly infer from this express'd Willingness of a Part, and Silence of the Rest; but that the Measure was universally agreeable? They accordingly resum'd the Consideration of it, and tho' a small, very small Opposition then appear'd to it in the House,[8] yet as even that was founded, not on the Impropriety of the Thing, but on the suppos'd unsuitableness of the Time, or the Manner; and a Majority of nine tenths being still for it, a Petition was drawn agreeable to the former Resolve, and order'd to be transmitted to his Majesty.

But the Prefacer tells us, that these Petitioners for a Change were a "Number of *rash, ignorant,* and *inconsiderate* People," and generally of a *low Rank.*[9] To be sure they were not of the Proprietary Officers, Dependants, or Expectants, and those are chiefly the People of *high Rank* among us; but they were otherwise generally Men of the best Estates in the Province, and Men of Reputation. The Assembly who come from all Parts of the Country, and therefore may be suppos'd to know them at least as well as the Prefacer, have given that Testimony of them. But what is the Testimony of the Assembly, who in his Opinion, are equally *rash, ignorant,* and *inconsiderate* with the Petitioners? And if his Judgment is right, how *imprudently* and contrary to their *Charter* have his THREE HUNDRED THOUSAND SOULS acted in their Elections of Assemblymen these twenty Years past; for the Charter requires them to chuse Men of *most Note* for *Virtue, Wisdom,* and *Ability!*

7. While the petition to the King was pending in the House, that body received (mostly through the governor) a number of petitions from western counties praying for the redress of grievances. None of these was entered in full in the *Votes.* One of them may have included objections to the proposed petition, but the *Votes* include no mention of such objections in any of its brief descriptions of the petitions.

8. Only four assemblymen are known to have voted against the petition on any of the motions relating to it: John Dickinson and Joseph Richardson of Philadelphia Co., Isaac Saunders of Lancaster Co., and John Montgomery of Cumberland Co. The largest vote in support of the petition for which figures are given totaled 27.

9. Preface to Dickinson's *Speech,* p. iv.

But these are Qualities engross'd, it seems, by the Proprietary Party. For they say, "the WISER and BETTER Part of the Province had far different Notions of this Measure. They *considered,* that the Moment they put their Hands to these Petitions, they might be surrendering up their Birthright."[1] I felicitate them on the *Honor* they have thus bestow'd upon themselves, on the *sincere* Compliments thus given and accepted, and on their having with such noble Freedom, discarded the sniveling Pretence to Modesty, couch'd in that thread-bare Form of Words *Though we say it that should not say it.* But is it not surprising, that during the seven Week Recess of the Assembly, expressly to consult their Constituents on the Expediency of this Measure, and during the fourteen Days the House sat deliberating on it, after they met again; these their *Wisdoms* and *Betternesses* should never be so kind as to communicate the least Scrap of their *Prudence,* their *Knowledge,* or their *Consideration,* to their *rash, ignorant,* and *inconsiderate* Representatives? Wisdom in the Mind is not, like Money in the Purse, diminish'd by Communication to others. They might have lighted up our farthing Candles for us, without lessening the Blaze of their own Flambeaux. But they suffer'd our Representatives to go on in the Dark, till the fatal Deed was done, and the Petition sent to the King, praying him to take the Government of this Province into his immediate Care, whereby, if it succeeds, "our glorious Plan of public Liberty, and Charter Privileges is to be barter'd away,"[2] and we are to be made Slaves forever! Cruel Parsimony! to refuse the Charity of a little *Understanding,* when GOD had given you so much, and the Assembly begg'd it as an Alms! O that you had but for once remember'd and observ'd the Counsel of that wise Poet, Pope, where he says,

"*Be* Niggards *of* Advice *on no Pretence;*
For the worst Avarice *is that of* Sense."[3]

In the Constitution of our Government, and in that of one more, there still remains a Particular Thing that none of the other Amer-

1. *Ibid.,* pp. iv–v.
2. According to *ibid.,* p. v, to approve the petition would be "to barter away that glorious plan of public liberty and charter privileges, under which this Province has risen to the highest degree of prosperity, with a rapidity almost unparallelled in history."
3. Pope, *Essay on Criticism,* Pt. III, lines 19–20.

ican Governments have, *to wit,* the Appointment of a Governor by the Proprietors, instead of an Appointment by the Crown.[4] This Particular in Government, has been found inconvenient, attended with Contentions and Confusions where-ever it existed, and has therefore been gradually taken away from Colony after Colony, and every where greatly to the Satisfaction and Happiness of the People. Our wise first Proprietor and Founder, was fully sensible of this, and being desirous of leaving his People happy, and preventing the Mischiefs that he foresaw must in time arise from that Circumstance, if it was continued, he determined to take it away, if possible, during his own Life-time. They accordingly entred into a Contract, for the Sale of the Proprietary Right of Government to the Crown, and actually received a Sum in Part of the Consideration. As he found himself likely to die, before that Contract (and with it his Plan for the Happiness of his People) could be compleated; he carefully made it a Part of his last Will and Testament, devising the Right of the Government to two Noble Lords, in Trust that they should release it to the Crown.[5] Unfortunately for us, this has never yet been done. And this is merely what the Assembly now desire to have done. Surely he that form'd our Constitution, must have understood it. If he had imagin'd that all our Privileges depended on the Proprietary Government, will any one suppose that he would himself have meditated the Change, that he would have taken such effectual Measures, as he thought them, to bring it about speedily, whether he should live or die? Will any of those who now extol him so highly, charge him at the same time with the Baseness of endeavouring thus to defraud his

4. BF seems momentarily to have forgotten Maryland, where the governor was still appointed by Lord Baltimore.

5. In William Penn's will, April 6, 1712, he granted the government of Pa. in trust to Robert Harley, Earl of Oxford and Mortimer, and John Poulett, Earl Poulett, with instructions to dispose of it to the Queen or a private person if they could make an advantageous arrangement. His serious financial difficulties were at least fully as responsible as his problems of government for inducing him to negotiate with the Crown on a surrender of political rights. He had begun these negotiations as early as 1703, but they remained incomplete at the time of his death in 1718. On these exceedingly tangled affairs, see Shepherd, *Proprietary Government in Pa.,* pp. 183–201, 540–4; Winfred T. Root, *The Relations of Pennsylvania with the British Government* (N.Y., 1912), pp. 354–64.

People of all the Liberties and Privileges he had promised them, and be the most solemn Charters and Grants assur'd to them, when he engag'd them to assist him in the Settlement of his Province? Surely none can be so inconsistent! And yet this Proprietary Right of Governing or appointing a Governor, has, all of a sudden, chang'd its Nature; and the Preservation of it, become of so much Importance to the Welfare of the Province, that the Assembly's only Petitioning to have their venerable Founder's Will executed, and the Contract he entered into for the Good of his People completed, is stil'd an "Attempt to violate the Constitution for which our Fathers planted a Wilderness; to barter away our glorious Plan of public Liberty and Charter Privileges; a risquing of the whole Constitution; an offering up our whole Charter Rights; a wanton sporting with Things sacred," &c.[6]

Pleasant, surely it is, to hear the Proprietary Partizans, of all Men, bawling for the Constitution, and affecting a terrible concern for our Liberties and Privileges. They who have been, these twenty Years, cursing our Constitution, declaring that it was no Constitution, or worse than none, and that Things could never be well with us, 'till it was new-modell'd, and made exactly conformable to the British Constitution. They who have treated our distinguishing Privileges as so many Illegalities and Absurdities; who have solemnly declared in Print, that though such Privileges might be proper in the Infancy of a Colony, to encourage its Settlement, they became *unfit for it* in its grown State, and *ought to be taken away:*[7] They, who by numberless Falshoods, propagated with infinite Industry, in the Mother Country, attempted to procure an Act of Parliament for the actual depriving a very great Part of the People of their Privileges: They too who have already depriv'd the whole People, of some of their most important Rights, and are daily endeavouring to deprive them of the rest![8] Are these become

6. The passage within quotation marks is a composite of several phrases brought together and rearranged from the preface to Dickinson's *Speech*, pp. v, vi, vii, xi.

7. This sentence reflects passages in William Smith's *A Brief State of the Province of Pennsylvania* (London, 1755), pp. 6–7. On this pamphlet see above, VI, 52 n.

8. Smith had advocated (*Brief State,* pp. 39–43) an act of Parliament that would have had the effect of barring Quakers from the Pa. Assembly, depriving Germans of the right to vote until they had acquired "a sufficient

Patriots, and Advocates for our Constitution? Wonderful Change! Astonishing Conversion! Will the Wolves then protect the Sheep, if they can but persuade 'em to give up their Dogs? Yes; The Assembly would destroy all their own Rights, and those of the People; and the Proprietary Partizans are become the Champions for Liberty! Let those who have *Faith,* now make Use of it: For if 'tis rightly defin'd, *the Evidence of Things not seen,*[9] certainly never was there more Occasion for such Evidence, the Case being totally destitute of all other.

It has been long observ'd, that Men are, with that Party, Angels or Demons, just as they happen to concur with or oppose their Measures. And I mention it for the Comfort of old Sinners, that in Politics, as well as in Religion, Repentance and Amendment, tho' late, shall obtain Forgiveness and procure Favour. Witness the late Speaker, Mr. Norris, a steady and constant Opposer of all the Proprietary Encroachments, and who, for thirty Years past, they have been therefore continually abusing, allowing him no one Virtue or good Quality whatsoever; but now, as he show'd some Unwillingness to engage in this present Application to the Crown, he is become all at once the *faithful Servant*—but let me look at the Text, to avoid Mistakes—and indeed I was mistaken. I thought it had been *faithful Servant of the Public;* but I find 'tis only—*of the House.*[1] Well chosen, that Expression, and prudently guarded. The former, from a Proprietary Pen, would have been Praise too much, only for disapproving the *Time* of the Application. Could you, much respected Sir, go but a little farther; and disapprove the

---

Knowledge of our Language and Constitution," and requiring that all newspapers, almanacs, and legal documents in the province be written in English. Others in the proprietary faction were talking in 1755 about a similar law; above, VI, 249 n.

9. "Now faith is the substance of things hoped for, the evidence of things not seen." Hebrews 11:1.

1. On Norris' resignation as speaker, see above, pp. 295–6. The preface to Dickinson's *Speech,* pp. vi–vii, quoted Norris' request to have his sentiments on the petition recorded in the minutes, and used phraseology which implied that the speaker agreed with Dickinson's position. It then concluded the account with: "Thus this aged member and faithful servant of the House, as if foreseeing troubles to come, chose to retire, and leave them to those whose temper they better suited." Writing to Thomas Penn, June 4, 1764, William Peters had expressed doubts as to Norris' sincerity in opposing the petition. Penn Papers, Hist. Soc. Pa.

Application itself; could you but say, the Proprietary Government is a good one, and ought to be continued; then might all your political Offences be done away, and your scarlet Sins become as Snow and Wool; then might you end your Course with (Proprietary) Honor. P——should preach your funeral Sermon, and S—— the Poisoner of other Characters, embalm your Memory. But those Honors you will never receive; for with returning Health and Strength, you will be found in your old Post, firm for your Country.

There is Encouragement too for young Sinners. Mr. Dickenson, whose Speech our Prefacer has introduc'd to the World, tho' long hated by some, and disregarded by the rest of the Proprietary Faction, is at once, for the same Reason as in Mr. Norris's Case, become a *Sage* in the Law, and an *Oracle* in Matters relating to our Constitution.[2] I shall not end[e]avour to pluck so much as a Leaf from these the young Gentleman's Laurels. I would only advise him carefully to preserve the Panegyrics with which they have adorn'd him: In time they may serve to console him, by balancing the Calumny they shall load him with, when he does not go *through* with them in all their Measures: He will not probably do the one, and they will then assuredly do the other. There are Mouths that can blow hot as well as cold, and blast on your Brows the Bays their Hands have plac'd there. *Experto crede Roberto.*[3] Let but the Moon of Proprietary Favor, withdraw its Shine for a Moment, and that *"great Number* of the *principal Gentlemen* of Philadelphia," who apply'd to you for the Copy of your Speech, shall immediately despise and desert you.

Those *principal Gentlemen!* What a Pity it is that their Names were not given us in the Preface, together with their admirable Letter![4] We should then have known where to run for Advice, on

2. "Having devoted to a severe course of study those years which too many give to dissipation and pleasure, he shewed himself, at his first entrance on public life, possessed of a knowledge of the laws and constitution of his country, which seldom falls to the share even of grey hairs." Preface to Dickinson's *Speech*, pp. v–vi.

3. Believe one who has borne (or experienced) it. Vergil, *Aeneid*, XI, 283. The source of the *"Roberto"* is uncertain.

4. The letter of these *"principal Gentlemen,"* applying for a copy of Dickinson's speech, is dated June 6, 1764. It is printed in the preface to Dickinson's *Speech*, p. viii, but without the signatures. The quotations which follow here (except the first) are taken from the letter. A second letter, printed on

all Occasions. We should have known who to chuse for our future Representatives. For undoubtedly, these were they that are elsewhere called, "the WISER and BETTER Part of the Province." None but their *Wisdoms,* could have known beforehand, that a Speech which they never heard, and a Copy of which they had never seen, but were then requesting to see, was "a *Spirited Defence,*" and "of our Charter Privileges;" and that "the Publication of it would be of great Utility, and give general Satisfaction." No inferior Sagacity could discover, that the Appointment of a Governor by the Proprietor, was one of our "Charter Privileges;" and that those who oppos'd the Application for a Royal Government, were therefore *Patriot Members,* appearing *on the Side* of our Privileges and our Charter!

Utterly to confound the Assembly, and shew the Excellence of Proprietary Government, the Prefacer has extracted from their own Votes, the Praises they have from Time to Time bestow'd on the first Proprietor, in their Addresses to his Sons. And tho' Addresses are not generally the best Repositories of Historical Truth, we must not in this Instance, deny their Authority.[5] That these Encomiums on the Father, tho' sincere, have occur'd so frequently, was owing, however, to two Causes; First, a vain Hope the Assemblies entertain'd, that the Father's Example, and the Honors done his Character, might influence the Conduct of the Sons. Secondly, for that in attempting to compliment the Sons on their own Merits, there was always found an extreme Scarcity of Matter. Hence, *the Father, the honored and honorable Father,* was so often repeated that the Sons themselves grew sick of it; and have been heard to say to each other with Disgust, when told that A. B. and C. were come to wait upon them with Addresses on some public Occasion, *"Then I suppose we shall hear more about our Father."* So that, let me tell the Prefacer, who perhaps was unacquainted with this Anecdote, that if he hop'd to curry more Favor with the Family, by the Inscription he has fram'd for that great Man's Monu-

---

the same page of the preface, expressed the wish of Isaac Saunders and John Montgomery to have it known publicly "how heartily we have concurred with you in the same sentiments" that Dickinson had expressed.

5. The preface to Dickinson's *Speech,* p. ix, gives extracts from three Assembly documents between 1730 and 1764 in praise of William Penn and the privileges he had granted.

ment,[6] he may find himself mistaken;—for—there is too much in it of *our Father*.

If therefore, he would erect a Monument to the Sons, the Votes of Assembly, which are of such Credit with him, will furnish him with ample Materials for his Inscription.

To save him Trouble, I will essay a Sketch for him, in the Lapidary Stile, tho' mostly in the Expressions, and every where in the Sense and Spirit of the Assembly's Resolves and Messages.

Be this a Memorial
Of T—— and R—— P——,
P—— of P——[7]
Who with Estates immense,
Almost beyond Computation,
When their own Province,
And the whole British Empire
Were engag'd in a bloody and most expensive War,
Begun for the Defence of those Estates,
Could yet meanly desire
To have those very Estates
Totally or Partially
Exempted from Taxation,
While their Fellow-Subjects all around them,

6. The preface (pp. ix–x) offers a panegyric on William Penn in the form of an epitaph composed of phrases from other Assembly documents, 1719–56, all identified by footnotes. This composition, with the divisions between lines indicated here by diagonals, reads as follows: "WILLIAM PENN, / A man of principles truely humane, / an Advocate for / RELIGION and LIBERTY / *Possessing* a noble spirit / That exerted itself / For the good of mankind, / WAS / The great and worthy founder / Of / PENNSYLVANIA. / To its Inhabitants, by CHARTER, / He granted and confirmed / Many singular PRIVILEGES and IMMUNITIES, / CIVIL and RELIGIOUS / Which he continually studied / to preserve and defend for them, / *Nobly declaring* / That they had not followed him so far / To lose a single tittle / Of the GREAT CHARTER / To which all *Englishmen* were born! / *For these Services*, / Great have been the acknowlegements / Deservedly paid to his MERIT; / And his MEMORY / Is dear to his people, / *Who have repeatedly confessed* / That / Next to divine Providence, / Their Happiness, Prosperity and Increase / Are owing / To his wise conduct and singular goodness / Which deserve ever to be remembered / With / GRATITUDE and AFFECTION / By PENNSYLVANIANS."

7. That is, "Of Thomas and Richard Penn, / Proprietaries of Pennsylvania."

Groan'd
Under the universal Burthen.
To gain this Point,
They refus'd the necessary Laws
For the Defence of their People,
And suffer'd their Colony to welter in its Blood,
Rather than abate in the least
Of these their dishonest Pretentions.
The Privileges granted by their Father
Wisely and benevolently
To encourage the first Settlers of the Province.
They,
Foolishly and cruelly,
Taking Advantage of public Distress,
Have extorted from the Posterity of those Settlers;
And are daily endeavouring to reduce them
To the most abject Slavery:
Tho' to the Virtue and Industry of those People
In improving their Country,
They owe all that they possess and enjoy.
A striking Instance
Of human Depravity and Ingratitude;
And an irrefragable Proof,
That Wisdom and Goodness
Do not descend with an Inheritance;
But that ineffable Meanness
May be connected with unbounded Fortune.*

What then avails it to the Honor of the present Proprietors, that our Founder, and their Father, gave us Privileges, if they, the Sons, will not permit us the Use of them, or forcibly rend them from us? David may have been a Man after GOD's own Heart, and Solomon the wisest of Proprietors and Governors; but if Rehoboam will be a Tyrant and a——,⁸ who can secure him the Affections of the

*Votes and Proceedings of the House of Representatives, 1754, *passim.* 1755, 1756, 1757, *passim.* 1758, 1759, 1760, 1761, 1762, 1763, 1764, *passim.*

8. BF left the reader to make his own choice of epithets here.

People! The Virtue and Merit of his Ancestors may be very great, but his Presumption in depending on those *alone,* may be much greater.

I lamented a few Pages ago, that we were not acquainted with the Names of those *principal* Gentlemen the *wiser* and *better* Part of the Province: I now rejoice that we are likely some time or other to know them; for a Copy of a Petition to the King is now before me, which, from its similarity with their Letter, must be of their inditing, and will probably be recommended to the People, by their leading up the Signing.[9]

On this Petition I shall take the Liberty of making a few Remarks, as they will save me the Necessity of following farther the Preface, the Sentiments of this and that being nearly the same.

It begins with a formal Quotation from the Petition, which they own they have not seen, and of Words that are not in it,[1] and after relating very imperfectly and unfairly; the Fact relating to their Application for a Copy of it, which is of no great Importance;[2] proceeds to set forth, "That—As we, and all your American Subjects must be governed by Persons authorized and approved by your Majesty, on the best Recommendation that can be obtained of them, we *cannot perceive* our Condition in this Respect to be *different* from our Fellow-Subjects around us, or that we are thereby less under your Majesty's particular Care and Protection, than they are, since there can be no Governors of this Province, without your Majesty's *immediate Approbation* and Authority." Such a Declara-

9. On this counter-petition, of which a copy survives in Franklin Papers, Lib. Cong., fo. 41, see above, p. 256 n. This may have been the copy BF had before him when he wrote. The first two passages from the counter-petition which he quotes in the next paragraphs are surrounded in the MS by quotation marks clearly added by someone other than the person who prepared this copy. The text of the counter-petition is printed from a broadside copy in Paul Leicester Ford, ed., *The Writings of John Dickinson,* 1 (Phila., 1895), 65–7.

1. The spurious quotation speaks of the "Mischievous disagreements" in the province and the "Spirit of violence Riot and Confusion" among the people, which "cannot be controuled by the present powers of Government and renders a change in the same necessary." The Assembly's petition contains no such passage, though the idea is expressed in other language. See above, pp. 199–200.

2. A rather light dismissal of the fact that the text of the Assembly's petition was withheld from the people of the province.

tion from the *wiser* Part of the Province, is really a little surprizing. What! When Disputes concerning Matters of Property are daily arising between you and your Proprietaries, cannot your Wisdoms *perceive* the least *Difference,* between having the Judges of those Disputes appointed by a Royal Governor, who has no Interest in the Cause; and having them appointed by the Proprietaries them-selves, the principal Parties against you, and *during their Pleasure* too? When Supplies are necessary to be rais'd for your Defence, can you perceive no Difference, between having a Royal Gover-nor, free to promote his Majesty's Service, by a ready Assent to your Laws, and a Proprietary Governor, shackled by Instructions, forbidding him to give that Assent, unless some private Advantage is obtain'd, some Profit got, or unequal Exemption gain'd for their Estate, or some Privilege wrested from you? When Prerogative, that in other Governments is only used for the Good of the People, is here strained to the extreme, and used to their Prejudice, and the Proprietaries Benefit, can you *perceive* no *Difference?* When the direct and immediate Rays of Majesty, benignly and mildly shine on all around us, but are transmitted and thrown upon us thro' the Burning Glass of Proprietary Government, can your Sensibilities feel no Difference? Shelter'd perhaps, in Proprietary Offices, or benum'd with Expectations, it may be you cannot. But surely you might have known better than to tell his Majesty, "that there *can be* no Governors of this Province without his *immediate* Approba-tion." Don't you know, who know so much, that by our blessed Constitution, the Proprietors themselves, whenever they please, may govern us in Person, without such Approbation?

The Petition proceeds to tell his Majesty, "That the particular Mode of Government, which we enjoy under your Majesty—is held in the highest Estimation by Good Men of all Denominations among us, and hath brought Multitudes of industrious People from various Parts of the World," &c. Really! Can this be from Pro-prietary Partizans? That Constitution which they were forever censuring, as defective in a Legislative Council, defective in Gov-ernment Powers, too popular in many of its Modes; is it now be-come so excellent? Perhaps as they have been tinkering it these Twenty Years, till they have stript it of some of its most valuable Privileges, and almost spoilt it, they now begin to like it. But then, it is not surely, this *present Constitution* that brought hither those

Multitudes. They came before. At least, it was not that Particular in our Constitution, the Proprietary Power of Appointing a Governor, which attracted them; that single Particular which alone is now in question; which our venerable Founder first, and now the Assembly, are endeavouring to change. As to the remaining valuable Part of our Constitution, the Assembly have been equally full and strong in expressing their Regard for it, and perhaps stronger and fuller; for their Petition in that respect, is in the Nature of a *Petition of Right,* it lays Claim, tho' modestly and humbly, to those Privileges, on the Foundation of Royal Grants, on Laws confirmed by the Crown, and on *Justice* and *Equity;* as the Grants were the Consideration offer'd to induce them to settle, and which they have in a Manner purchas'd and paid for, by executing that Settlement without putting the Crown to any Expence.

Whoever would know what our Constitution was, when it was so much admir'd, let him peruse that elegant farewell Speech of Mr. Hamilton, Father of our late Governor, when as Speaker he took his Leave of the House, and of public Business, in 1739, and then let him compare that Constitution with the present.[3] The Power of appointing public Officers by the Representatives of the People, which he so much extols: *Where is it now?* Even the bare naming to the Governor in a Bill, a trivial Officer to receive a Light-house Duty, which could be consider'd as no more than a mere Recommendation, is, in a late Message, stil'd, "An Encroachment on the Prerogative of the Crown!"[4] The sole Power of raising and disposing of the Public Money, which, he says, was then lodged in the Assembly, that inestimable Privilege, *What is become of it?* Inch by Inch they have been wrested from us, in Times of public Distress, and the rest are going the same Way. I remember to have seen, when Governor Hamilton was engag'd in a Dispute with the Assembly, on some of those Points, a Copy of that Speech, which then was intended to be reprinted, with a Dedication to that honor-

3. When Andrew Hamilton, father of the later governor, was about to retire from the speakership, he delivered a long address to the Assembly, Aug. 6, 1739, which so moved the members that they asked for a copy and had it inserted in the minutes. *Votes and Proceedings of the House of Representatives,* Franklin & Hall edit., III (Phila., 1754), 349–50. For an earlier reference to this speech in a message to Governor Morris, Aug. 19, 1755, see above, v, 155.
4. See above, p. 104 n.

able Gentleman, and this Motto from John Rogers's Verses in the Primer.[5]

> We send you here a little Book,
> For you to look upon;
> That you may see your Father's Face,
> Now he is dead and gone.[6]

Many a such *little Book* has been sent by our Assemblies to the present Proprietaries. But they don't like to see their *Father's Face;* it puts their own *out of Countenance.*

The Petition proceeds to say, "That such Disagreements as have arisen in this Province, we have beheld with Sorrow, but as others around us are not exempted from the like Misfortunes, *we can by no Means conceive them incident to the Nature of our Government,*[7] which hath *often* been adminstred with remarkable Harmony: And your Majesty, before whom our late Disputes have been laid, can be at no Loss, in your great Wisdom, to discover whether they proceed from the above Cause, or should be ascribed to some others." The disagreements in question, are Proprietary Disagreements in Government, relating to Proprietary private Interests. And are not the Royal Governments around us, exempt from these Misfortunes? Can you, really, Gentlemen, *by no Means conceive,* that Proprietary Government Disagreements, *are incident to the Nature of* Proprietary Governments? Can they in Nature be incident to any other Governments? If your *Wisdoms* are so hard to

5. The Rev. John Rogers (1500?–1555) was burned at the stake during the reign of Queen Mary for heresy in persistently denying the Real Presence in the Sacrament. A large crowd, including his wife and children, attended the execution and loudly cheered his fortitude. The verses, which BF quotes only in small part, though composed by Robert Smith, another victim of the Marian persecution, were attributed to Rogers and were printed in John Foxe's *Book of Martyrs* (7th edit., 1632). They were reprinted, with a woodcut of the burning, through many editions of *The New-England Primer* by numerous booksellers. Between 1749 and 1766 Franklin & Hall printed and sold 37,100 copies of the *Primer*. Paul L. Ford, *The New-England Primer* (N.Y., 1897), pp. 19, 20, 32–7, 250, 313. A copy of the *Primer*, complete with woodcut and verses, printed by Franklin & Hall in 1764 (the year BF quoted from it), is in Yale Univ. Lib.

6. In the original the first line begins "I leave you," and the fourth, "When he is."

7. BF's italics.

conceive, I am afraid they will never bring forth. But then our Government "hath *often* been adminstred with remarkable Harmony." Very true; as *often* as the Assembly have been able and willing to purchase that Harmony, and pay for it, the Mode of which has already been shewn. And yet that Word *often* seems a little unluckily chosen: The Flame that is *often* put out, must be *as often* lit; If our Government hath *often* been administred with remarkable Harmony, it hath as *often* been administred with remarkable Discord. One *often* is as numerous as the other. And his "Majesty," if he should take the Trouble of looking over our Disputes, to which the Petitioners, (to save themselves a little Pains, modestly and decently refer him) where will he, for twenty Years past, find any but Proprietary Disputes concerning Proprietary Interests, or Disputes that have been connected with, and arose from them?

The Petition proceeds to assure his Majesty, "That this Province (except from the Indian Ravages) enjoys the *most perfect internal Tranquility!*" Amazing! What! *the most perfect Tranquility!* When there have been three atrocious Riots within a few Months![8] When in two of them horrid Murthers were committed on twenty innocent Persons, and in the third, no less than one Hundred and forty like Murthers were meditated, and declar'd to be intended, with as many more as should be occasion'd by any Opposition. When we know that these Rioters and Murderers, have none of them been punish'd, have never been prosecuted, have not even been apprehended! When we are frequently told, that they intend still to execute their Purposes, as soon as the Protection of the King's Forces is withdrawn—Is our Tranquility more perfect now, than it was between the first Riot and the second, or between the second and the third? And why *"except the Indian Ravages,"* if a little Intermission is to be denominated "the most perfect Tranquility?" for the Indians too have been quiet lately. Almost as well might Ships in an Engagement talk of the most perfect Tranquility between two Broadsides. But "a Spirit of Riot and Violence is foreign to the general Temper of the Inhabitants."[9] I hope and believe

8. The attacks of the Paxton Boys on the Indians at Conestoga Manor and Lancaster and the march on Philadelphia.

9. The counter-petition declares that this "Spirit of Riot and Violence is so foreign to the general temper of its Inhabitants that there are as few instances

it is; the Assembly have said nothing to the contrary. And yet, is there not too much of it? Are there not Pamphlets continually written, and daily sold in our Streets, to justify and encourage it? Are not the mad armed Mob in those Writings instigated to imbrue their Hands in the Blood of their Fellow Citizens; by first applauding their Murder of the Indians, and then representing the Assembly and their Friends as worse than Indians, as having privately stirr'd up the Indians to murder the white People, and arm'd and rewarded them for that Purpose? LIES, Gentlemen, villainous as ever the Malice of Hell invented; and which to do you Justice, not one of you believes, tho' you would have the Mob believe them.

But your Petition proceeds to say, "That where such Disturbances have happened, they have been speedily quieted." By whom were they quieted? The two first, if they can be said to be quieted, were quieted only by the Rioters themselves going home quietly, (that is without any Interruption) and remaining there till their next Insurrection, without any Pursuit, or Attempt to apprehend any of them: And the third, was it quieted, or was the Mischief they intended prevented, or could it have been prevented, without the Aid of the King's Troops march'd into the Province for that Purpose? "The civil Powers have been supported." In some sort. We all know how they were supported. But have they been fully supported? Has the Government sufficient Strength, even with all its Supports, to venture on the apprehending and Punishment of those notorious Offenders? If it has not, why are you angry at those who would strengthen its Hands by a more immediate Royal Authority? If it has, why is not the Thing done? Why will the Government, by its Conduct, strengthen the Suspicions, (groundless no doubt) that it has come to a private Understanding with those Murderers, and that Impunity for their past Crimes is to be the Reward of their future *political* Services? O, but, says the Petition, "There are perhaps Cases in all Governments, where it may not be possible speedily to discover Offenders." Probably; but is there any Case in any Government where it is not possible to *endeavour* such a Discovery? There may be Cases where it is not

of any Disturbances of this kind to be met with among them since the first Settlement of the Colony, as perhaps among the like Number of People in any part of the world."

305

safe to do it: And perhaps the best Thing our Government can say for itself, is, That that is our Case. The only Objection to such an Apology must be, that it would justify that Part of the Assembly's Petition to the Crown which relates to the Weakness of our present Government.*

Still, if there is any Fault, it must be in the Assembly; for, says the Petition, "if the Executive Part of our Government should seem in any Case *too weak*, we conceive "it is the Duty of the Assembly, and in their Power to strengthen it." This *Weakness*, however, you have just deny'd; "Disturbances you say, have been speedily quieted, and the civil Powers supported," and thereby you have depriv'd your insinuated Charge against the Assembly of its only Support. But is it not a Fact known to you all, that the Assembly did endeavour to strengthen the Hands of the Government? That at his Honour's Instance they prepar'd and pass'd in a few Hours, a Bill for extending hither the Act of Parliament for dispersing Rioters?[2] That they also pass'd and presented to him a Militia Bill, which he refus'd, unless Powers were thereby given him, over the Lives and Properties of the Inhabitants, which the public Good did not require, and which their Duty to their Constituents would not permit them to trust in the Hands of any Proprietary Governor?[3] You know the Points, Gentlemen. They have been made public. Would you have had your Representatives give up those Points? Do you intend to give them up when at the next Election you are made Assemblymen? If so; tell it us honestly beforehand, that we may know what we are to expect, when we are about to chuse you?

I come now to the last Clause of your Petition, where, with the same wonderful Sagacity with which you in another Case dis-

---

*The Assembly being call'd upon by the Governor for their Advice on that Occasion; did in a Message, advise his sending for, and examining the Magistrates of Lancaster County and Borough, where the Murders were committed, in order to discover the Actors; but neither that, nor any of the other Measures recommended, were ever taken.[1] Proclamations indeed were published, but soon discontinu'd.

1. For the Assembly's recommendation on this point and the Council's rejection of it, see above, p. 30 and n.

2. See above, pp. 70–1.

3. See above, pp. 130–1, and below, pp. 360–5.

cover'd the Excellency of a Speech you never heard, you undertake to characterize a Petition you own you never saw; and venture to assure his Majesty that it is "exceeding grievous in its Nature; that it by no Means contains a proper Representation of the State of this Province; and is repugnant to the general Sense of his numerous and loyal Subjects in it."[4] Are then his Majesty's "numerous and loyal Subjects" in this Province all as great Wizards as yourselves, and capable of knowing without seeing it, that the Petition is repugnant to their general Sense? But the *Inconsistence* of your Petition, Gentlemen, is not so much to be wonder'd at; the Prayer of it is still more extraordinary, "We therefore most humbly pray, that your Majesty would be graciously pleased *wholly to disregard* the said Petition of the Assembly." What! without Enquiry! Without Examination! without a Hearing of what the Assembly might say in Support of it! *"wholly disregard"* the Petition of your Representatives in Assembly, accompany'd by other Petitions signed by Thousands of your Fellow-Subjects, as loyal, if not as *wise* and as *good* as yourselves! Would you wish to see your great and amiable Prince, act a Part that could not become a Dey of Algiers? Do you, who are Americans pray for a *Precedent* of such Contempt, in the treatment of an American Assembly! Such "total Disregard" of their humble Applications to the Throne? Surely your *Wisdoms* here have overshot yourselves. But as Wisdom shews itself, not only in doing what is right, but in confessing and amending what is wrong, I recommend the latter particularly to your present Attention; being persuaded of this Consequence, That tho' you have been mad enough to sign such a Petition, you never will be Fools enough to present it.

There is one Thing mention'd in the Preface, which I find I omitted to take Notice of as I came along, the Refusal of the House to enter Mr. Dickenson's Protest on their Minutes:[5] This is men-

4. The quotation is from the final paragraph of the counter-petition. The letter of those "principal Gentlemen" who had asked Dickinson for a copy of his speech (mentioned above) indicated to BF that they were not among the assemblymen who had heard it delivered. Both the preface to Dickinson's *Speech* (p. xii) and a statement earlier in the counter-petition made clear that no copy of the Assembly petition had been available to those persons who drafted the counter-petition.

5. See above, pp. 197–8. The Protest was printed in *Pa. Jour.*, July 19, 1764, and in *Pa. Gaz.*, July 26, 1764.

tion'd in such a Manner there, and in the News Papers, as to insinuate a Charge of some Partiality and Injustice in the Assembly. But the Reasons were merely these, That tho' Protesting may be a Practice with the Lords of Parliament, there is no Instance of it in the House of Commons, whose Proceedings are the Model follow'd by the Assemblies of America;[6] that there is no Precedent of it on our Votes, from the beginning of our present Constitution; and that the introducing such a Practice, would be attended with Inconveniences; as the Representatives in Assembly, are not, like the Lords in Parliament, unaccountable to any Constituents; and would therefore find it necessary for their own Justification, if the Reasons of the Minority for being *against* a Measure, were admitted in the Votes, to put there likewise the Reasons that induc'd the Majority to be *for* it. Whereby the Votes, which were intended only as a Register of Propositions and Determinations, would be fill'd with the Disputes of Members with Members; and the public Business be thereby greatly retarded, if ever brought to a period.

As that *Protest* was a mere Abstract of Mr. DICKENSON's Speech, every Particular of it will be found answer'd in the following Speech of Mr. GALLOWAY, from which it is fit that I should no longer detain the Reader.

Advertisement.

To introduce the following Speech to the Public, Some account of that to which it was an Answer, seems necessary.

During the Time of the several Debates respecting the Change of Government, Mr. Dickenson seldom attended, and was absent when the important one came on, which issued in the Resolve, to adjourn and consult the People.[7] At the next Meeting several Motions were made to bring this Resolution to an Issue, and after great Deliberation, it was resolved by a Majority of 27 to 3, that a Committee should be appointed to bring in the Petition to his Majesty to resume the Powers of Government.[8] But at none of these Debates and Resolutions, was Mr. Dickenson present, tho' he well *knew,* or at least had great Reason to *expect this Business was in continual Agitation.*

6. BF's statement of the differing procedures in the two houses of Parliament is correct, and his explanation is historically sound.

7. March 24, 1764; *Votes,* 1763–64, pp. 72–4; above, pp. 132–3.

8. May 18, 23, 1764; *Votes,* 1763–64, pp. 80–1, 82; above, p. 193.

During this Time, and the Recess of the Assembly, Mr. Dickenson employed himself in collecting his Sentiments in Opposition to the Measure, and in forming his Thoughts into the best Order, and dressing them in the best Language his Abilities were capable of. And upon the first reading of the Petition, and not till then, had he in all this Time, entered into the Debate, or publickly deliver'd his Opinion respecting the intended Change.[9]

After a Measure is resolved on in a House of Legislature, it is well known to be contrary to all Rule and Order, to object to the Measure; otherwise publick Business cou'd never be brought to an *Issue*. Members may speak to the Mode, but not object against the Thing resolved on. But this Rule, so necessary in public Transactions, was sacrificed either to Mr. Dickinson's Indolence in not attending, or to his Industry in forming his Speech. For he was permitted to object to the Design itself.

In the Debate on the first reading of the Petition, he attempted to deliver his Objections against the Measure, *ore tenus;* But finding every thing he offer'd judiciously and sensibly refuted by several Members, he was obliged to retreat to his Speech in writing, which after a short Introductory Apology, he read in his place, in a Manner not the most deliberate.[1]

This unparliamentary Mode of proceeding, and the Difficulty of Retaining in the Memory so long and elaborate a Performance, obliged, and indeed justified the Gentleman, the Author of the following Speech, in taking short Notes, from which, after Mr. Dickenson had concluded, he rose to answer the Objections offer'd

9. At the afternoon sitting of the House, May 23, 1764, the committee reported the draft of the petition; it was read and "was ordered to lie on the Table for the Perusal of the Members." On the afternoon of the 24th, "The House then resumed the Consideration" of the petition, "which was again read, and, after a considerable Debate thereon," the Assembly adjourned to the following morning. *Votes*, 1763–64, pp. 82, 83. It was on this occasion that Dickinson made his speech.

1. In his *Reply* to Galloway's speech, Dickinson defended himself strongly against the charges in this "Advertisement" of absenteeism when the petition was under consideration in the Assembly. "*Mr. Galloway must be conscious,*" he wrote, that on March 23 and 24 "I was confined to my chamber, and mostly to my bed, by a severe attack of the fever and ague." On May 23 he was likewise kept at home by a fever. He had appeared on the 24th, "tho' still extremely indisposed," and had delivered his speech "on the second reading of the petition." *Reply*, pp. 37–9.

against the Petition. But the Speaker being exceedingly indispos'd, the Debate was adjourn'd till next Day.

Before the Adjournment, Mr. Dickenson, was requested by several Members, and informed by the Speaker, that he ought to leave his Speech on the Table for the Perusal and Consideration of the House. But this he several Times evaded, alledging in Excuse, that it was too incorrect and indigested; altho' he was repeatedly informed, that none wou'd examine it with a View to make any critical Observations on the Stile or Method, but only to make themselves acquainted with the Substance. At length he was prevail'd on to promise in the most solemn Manner, that he would deliver it to Mr. Galloway that Evening. That Gentleman called on him at the Time appointed, but Mr. Dickenson continuing in the same Humour, declined delivering it. Nor did he give the Members an Opportunity of perusing it, until the Debate was over, and the Question called for, whether the Petition shou'd be transcribed for a third Reading. Which passed in the Affirmative by the Votes of all the Members who rose on the former Question. All that Mr. Dickenson had either said or read, not having the Success of altering the Opinion of a single Member.

Nor did the Speech then remain long upon the Table, for Mr. Dickenson immediately after, got it into his Hands again, and carried it out of the House.[2] What has been done with it since, to whose Care and Correction it has been committed, and by whom, and with what Views it has been published, the Preface attending it sufficiently demonstrates.

However, since, the Art and Dress in which it now appears to the Public, very different from that in which it appeared in the House,[3] renders it little less than necessary, that the Public shou'd

2. Dickinson replied that he had promised Galloway a copy of his speech for the evening of May 24, "*If I could get it ready*," but that proved impossible. He took the copy to the House the next morning and again in the afternoon, but no one called for it either time. *Reply*, p. 42.

3. Dickinson asserted that "The printed speech is exactly the same with that I pronounced, except the corrections, and additions I made to compleat the sense, the evening before it was to be delivered to the Members, as is above mentioned—and except some slight alterations in a few places." He insisted that he had received no help from anyone in composing or correcting it, and no one but his clerk had seen it until he delivered it in the House. *Reply*, p. 44.

know the Arguments and Reasons which prevailed on the Members to retain their former Resolution, of prosecuting the Petition to the Crown; the following Speech, in Substance the same that was offered by Mr. Galloway, in Answer to Mr. Dickenson, taken from his short Notes, and put into Order, is submitted to the Consideration of the Lovers and Supporters of public Liberty, Order, and good Government.

From Richard Jackson

Copy: American Philosophical Society; ALS (fragment): American Philosophical Society[4]

Copy
Dear Sir   Inner Temple, 11th. Augst. 1764
   I am just come to town, time enough before the Packet sails, or rather, I should say, before the Mail goes from London, to read your favours of the 25th together with the Dispatch brought from the Committee of Correspondence, by Mr. Hammet,[5] to return a short Answer; I shall send a longer by a ship that Sails tomorrow from the River,[6] by which too, I shall write to Mr. Coxe, to whom I have wrote several times, though I have reason to fear some of my Letters have miscarried.[7] I am sensible I ought to preserve the Dates of my own Letters, and transmit the dates of those I receive, but though I took a Clerk to assist chiefly in this part of my business; I am so frequently obliged [to] sit down to write Letters just before a Ship Sails or the Post goes out, that he has no time even to take the Dates, much less copy them, as I often wish he might,

4. One page of the original of this letter bearing Jackson's signature, together with the address page, has survived. It covers roughly one half of the penultimate and the whole of the last paragraph of the letter.
   5. For BF's letter of June 25, 1764, see above, pp. 234–40. The "Dispatch" sent by the Pa. Assembly's Committee of Correspondence has not been found, but a good idea of its contents can be formed from the Assembly's instructions to the committee of May 28, 1764; see above, p. 198. *London Chron.*, Aug. 2–4, 1764, reported the arrival of the *Dragon*, Capt. Francis Hammett, off Tor Bay.
   6. If Jackson sent such a letter, it has not been found.
   7. In his letter of June 25 BF urged Jackson to write "Messrs. Coxe" in the confirmation of whose claims to Carolana both men were interested.

and I have not an opportunity of looking for the Dates of my Bundles of Letters received though they lye by me.

I confess I am a little unwilling to be so explicit on the Question asked me respecting the delivery of the Petition, as I should be in conversing *ore tenus* on the subject.[8] I have already wrote several Letters from whence my Opinion may be pretty clearly known,[9] and I have opened my mind more fully to Mr. Allen[1] (whom I well know to be a friend of the Proprietarys) than I should have done, perhaps, had it been any thing but what it is.

Shortly, I think that the Assembly are clearly right in the late Controversy between them and the Governor.[2] I have more than once told the Proprietary and Mr. Allen, that the Assembly might well go further in loading his property without Injustice and the latter has frequently acknowledged it.[3]

I think too, that the present is not an unfavourable opportunity of presenting the Petition and pursuing the Application; I mean not substantially unfavourable because I think, the Delay of the Publick Service has palpably arose from the Conduct of the proprietary Government. And I think that the Application if made, will in the End meet with Success, I mean if kept up, perhaps for a Course of years, and this I have frequently I think convinced Mr. Allen of. On the other hand I think the Application will be

8. Apparently a reference to BF's request in his letter of June 1, 1764, for Jackson's sentiments on the "Seasonableness or Unseasonableness" of presenting the petition for royal government to the King. See above, p. 219.

9. Jackson is probably alluding to his letters to BF of June 4 and June 14, 1764, neither of which has been found, and possibly to other letters, not now extant, to the Assembly's Committee of Correspondence. See below, pp. 326–7.

1. Chief Justice William Allen (above, III, 296–7 n) returned to Pa. on Aug. 13, 1764, after spending close to a year in England. He exerted his influence there on behalf of the colonies and was credited in *Pa. Gaʒ.* with having had "considerable Influence in preventing" the passage of the Stamp Act in 1764. *Pa. Gaʒ.*, May 10, 1764.

2. The controversy over the assessment of the Proprietors' located, uncultivated lands.

3. Weeks before Jackson wrote, the Proprietors had instructed Governor Penn to yield to the Assembly's views on this matter, and Allen doubtless knew it. Yet he appears to have kept the information away from Jackson in England, just as he and the governor did from the Assembly leaders in the colony until after the election. See above, pp. 213–14 n.

Attended with a good deal of Expence[4] and perhaps may meet with some mortifying circumstances of Reception (not from his Majesty who is a Prince of the most boundless Grace) and at last end in a Burthen on the Province, that may be disagreable.

I think besides, that Good and Gracious as the King is, the Liberties of the Province, will be always safe in his Hands if it were possible for him always to manage and direct this part of the Administration himself, for what the Province has not a Strict Right to, (if such Privileges, there should be) he would probably indulge them in the Exercise of, of his Grace and favour. But new Ministers may arise, and we cannot flatter ourselves that even the King will live for ever. Power may come into the hands of Profligate Men who may prostitute their high Rank, their great Parts and Skill in the Law to the Infamous purposes of establishing the Doctrines that have by degrees enslav'd almost every part of Europe but this Island.

I think therefore that for the present, if the Proprietary is disposed to give way; it may be better, 'till future Misconduct on his part makes it necessary, to delay presenting the Petitions. If future Events should make such an Application necessary or if the Assembly still think it right to present them forthwith you may command my best Services.

I have not had time to peruse fully your thoughts on Paper Money.[5] You know mine, I did however endeavour as far as I could to postpone our Bill, I think the Government will not chose to meddle with the Mosquito Shore, but shall take an opportunity of mentioning this matter. We have hopes that Sugar will grow [to] the southward of St. Augustine and above Pensacola. My Compliments to Govr. Franklin and best respects to the Committee of Correspondence par[ticu]larly Mr. Galloway. I am very proud of their good Opinion and wish I could serve them more Effectually than I have done or fear can do.

I have seen Articles in the papers from America I do not like

4. In a letter of Sept. 1, 1764, Franklin informed Jackson that William Allen claimed that he (Jackson) had told him that the Crown would force the province to pay the Penns £100,000 to extinguish their rights to the government of Pennsylvania as well as £5000 per annum to support a royal governor. See below, pp. 327–8.

5. For many matters mentioned in this paragraph, see above, pp. 234–40.

respecting myself and which I do not pretend to be true in fact I have very little Weight or Influence here and perhaps the less for such Publications.[6] I am Dear Sir Very affectionately Yours

RD: JACKSON.

To Benjamin Franklin Esq

Endorsed: Copy of a Letter sent to Benjn Franklin Esqr
Address on the ALS: To / Benjamin Franklin Esq / at Philadelphia / by the Packet / a single sheet

Philadelphia Linen Manufactory: Stock Certificate for Charles Thomson

Printed form with MS insertions in blanks: American Philosophical Society

In July 1764 a group of Philadelphia citizens issued a two-page printed circular inviting subscriptions to the stock of a "Linen Manufactory" to be established in or near Philadelphia.[7] According to this announcement, benevolence furnished the principal motive. "Whereas the number of poor in and around this City, is at present great, and every Year increasing; and as for want of Employment, many of them, especially in the Winter, are reduced to great Straits, and rendered burthensome to their Neighbours; therefore, in order to alleviate their Wants" the promoters were launching this project. Obviously, they hoped their enterprise would be economically successful and that they and other stockholders would profit financially, and the Sugar Act of 1764 explains their optimism and their timing. This measure abolished the drawback on the exportation of foreign linens from Great Britain to the colonies, thereby assuring a rise in price to the colonial consumer. The promoters must have considered Pennsylvania

6. Examples of the publications of which Jackson was complaining appeared in *Pa. Jour.* in the spring of 1764. In the April 5 issue an extract of a letter from London, Feb. 7, 1764, praised Jackson as a man who had "great weight with all the Ministry, and whose honesty will prompt him to stand in our Interest: He has often been to the Board of Trade, and has succeeded so well, as to gain them over to our Interest." The May 10 issue stated that "it was chiefly owing to him [Jackson] that the stamp act did not take place."
7. Evans microprint edition, 9870. The circular is dated only "in July" 1764 and carries no names of promoters.

314

a natural place for producing such textiles because the province raised flax in sufficient quantity to carry on a brisk export trade to Ireland. Writing to Richard Jackson, June 25, 1764, Franklin boasted that "we have in the Nature of our Country every kind of Ability to provide ourselves with Linnen in Plenty, if Dearness should once compel us into the more general Practice and Habit of making it" (above, p. 235).

The articles of association printed in the circular called for subscriptions to stock at £100 per share, for which subscribers were to sign promissory notes. They were to pay £20 within ten days and the balance upon demand of a majority of the trustees. A treasurer, elected by ballot, was to issue certificates, and, as soon as £5000 had been subscribed, seven trustees were to be elected. These men were to complete the purchase of "Wilson Brown's Interest" on Penn Street, near Pine Street, for the use of the company and to appoint a manager. Distribution of profits and election of the treasurer and trustees were to take place annually on January 1, beginning in 1765.

Three stock certificates are known to the editors, all issued during the summer and autumn of 1764, all for subscriptions of £250, and all signed by Samuel Preston Moore, who was apparently the first treasurer.[8] The earliest of these three is printed here.

[August 13, 1764]

WHEREAS *Isaac Norris, Benjamin Franklin, Joseph Fox, Joseph Richardson, Abel James, William Brown, Peter Reeves, John Mifflin, Thomas Wharton, Charles Thomson Samuel Mifflin, Samuel Rhoads, William Plumsted John Meas two shares, for himself and William Allen, William Logan, Baynton & Wharton, William Fisher, Samuel Preston Moore, Isaac Greenleafe, Richard Wistar, Jacob Lewis,*

have entered into an Agreement of Copartnership, for erecting and carrying on a LINEN MANUFACTORY, in or near the City of Philadelphia; this is to certify that *Charles Thomson*[9] hath sub-

8. The other two certificates were issued Sept. 19, 1764, to Reuben Haines, printed in *PMHB*, XVIII (1894), 262–3; and Oct. 11, 1764, to Richard Wistar, John Carter Brown Lib. These two documents add the names of the following eight subscribers, making thirty in all: Daniel Roberdeau, John Redman, William Morris, Jr., Charles Coxe, Reuben Haines, Thomas Montgomery, John Hughes, and Philip Syng. In all three certificates the subscription figure of £250 is printed out, so the price of a share had probably been raised to that amount since the July circular was issued.
9. On Thomson, see above, VII, 266 n.

scribed, and by his Note of Hand engaged to pay Two Hundred and Fifty Pounds towards the joint Stock of the said Company, whereby he the said *Charles Thomson* is entitled to his Share of the Stock, and a Proportion of all the Profits arising from the said Manufactory. Witness my Hand, this *thirteenth* Day of *August* 176 *4*   SAML. PRESTON MOORE[1]

Endorsed: Charles Thomson Certificate for a Share in the Philada linen Manufactory[2]

To Henry Bouquet   ALS: British Museum

Dear Sir   Philada. Augt. 16. 1764
Returning just now from the Board of Commissioners, I found your agreable Favour of the 10th Instant.[3] We had a Meeting on Tuesday, when your Letter to the Governor was laid before us, his Honour not present, and the Board thin.[4] I think none but myself spoke then for the measure recommended; so, to prevent its being too hastily refus'd, I moved to refer it to this Day, when we might have a fuller Board. The principal Objection was, that the Act did not empower us to go farther. To day we got over that Objection and all others, and came to a Resolution which will be communicated to you, by the Governor I suppose, and the Money

1. On Moore, provincial treasurer, 1754–68, see above, IV, 295 n.
2. BF and the other promoters overlooked one thing: in spite of the alleged unemployment in the city, labor was not cheap. For this reason the factory had failed by 1767. Writing to the Board of Trade, Jan. 21, 1767, Governor John Penn reported the demise of the undertaking: a linen factory "was set up about three years ago in this City, by private Subscriptions, for the making of Sail Cloth, Ticking, and Linnens; but the Persons concerned have already sunk money by their Project, for the high Price of Labour will not allow any of the Articles to be made at so cheap a rate as those of the same Quality and Goodness, manufactured in England, are sold for by the Retailers here; they have, therefore, lately resolved to discontinue that undertaking." *Pa. Col. Recs.*, IX, 353–4.
3. See above, pp. 266–7.
4. Bouquet's letter to Penn, Aug. 10, 1764, 1 *Pa. Arch.*, IV, 199–200; Sylvester K. Stevens and Donald H. Kent, eds., *The Papers of Col. Henry Bouquet*, XVI (Harrisburg, 1943), 59. No minutes of the provincial commissioners for either Tuesday, Aug. 14, 1764, or Thursday, August 16, have been found.

sent by Capt. Young.[5] We have fully, as we understand it, comply'd with your Requisition. And 'tis a Pleasure to me to have done every thing you wish'd me to do in the Affair, before the Receipt of your Letter.

I recollect that I once, in Conversation, promised you some Papers I had by me, containing Hints for Conducting an Indian War. I have since found them, and on looking them over, am of Opinion you will meet with nothing new in them that is of any Importance; however, to keep my Promise, I now send them enclosed.[6]

The June Packet is arrived from England, as is also our Friend Mr. Allen; but we have no News by them that is material.[7] France and England are both diligently repairing their Marine; but I suppose 'tis a Matter of course, and not with Intention of any new Rupture. The Ministerial Party is said to be continually gaining Strength, and the Opposition diminishing.[8] Abroad the Poles are cutting one another's Throats a little, about their Election: But

5. For Capt. James Young, commissary general and paymaster of Pa. troops, see above, VII, 153 n. He wrote Bouquet, August 16, that the commissioners had directed him to supply funds sufficient to pay £3 to each man and 20s. per man to the recruiting officer for raising 200 enlistees to complete the Pa. regiment. He had already paid Captain Ourry (Bouquet's quartermaster and commissary) £300 and now authorized the colonel to draw on him for £500 more as needed. *Papers of Col. Henry Bouquet*, XVI, 67.

6. One of these papers may have been a copy of the postscript of BF's letter to James Read, Nov. 2, 1755, suggesting the use of dogs, the procedure to be followed by scouting parties so that they would not be surprised during night encampments, and the bringing together of remote settlers into stockades; above, VI, 235–6. See also above, pp. 225–6.

7. *Pa. Gaz.*, Aug. 16, 1764, reported the arrival of the *Philadelphia Packet*, Capt. R. Budden, on which were Chief Justice William Allen and his family. Allen, indeed, had certainly brought with him very important news: that the Proprietors were willing to accept the interpretation of the Privy Council's order of Sept. 2, 1760, for which BF and the Assembly had contended but which Governor Penn had so vigorously opposed. The governor and the chief justice, however, were very careful to keep this information secret until after the fall election. See above, pp. 213–14 n.

8. *Pa. Gaz.*, Aug. 16, 1764, printed an extract from a London letter dated June 5, which may have been one from Strahan to BF (not found). It reported political quiet in Great Britain, a relative balance between the factions, and "a Breathing Time" for the ministry. BF's comments on Polish affairs, which follow in this paragraph, were based on news printed in other columns of this issue of the *Gazette*.

317

'tis their Constitution, and I suppose reckon'd among their Privileges to sacrifice a few Thousand of the Subjects every Interregnum, either to the Manes of the deceas'd King, or to the Honour of his Successor. And if they are fond of this Privilege, I don't know that their Neighbours have any right to disturb them in the Enjoyment of it: And yet the Russians have enter'd their Country with an Army, to preserve Peace! and secure the *Freedom* of the Election!

It comes into my Mind that you may easily do me a Kindness; and I ought not, by omitting to acquaint you with the Occasion, deprive you of the Pleasure you take in serving your Friends. By this Ship I hear that my Enemies (for God has bless'd me with two or three, to keep me in order) are now representing me at home, as an Opposer and Obstructor of his Majesty's Service here.[9] If I know any thing of my own Heart, or can remember any thing of my own Actions, I think they might as justly have accus'd me of being a Blackamore. You cannot but have heard of the Zeal and Industry with which I promoted the Service in the Time of General Braddock, and the Douceurs I procur'd for the Officers that serv'd under him.[1] I spent a Summer in that Service without a

9. Thomas Penn wrote Benjamin Chew, June 8, 1764 (a letter probably carried on the *Philadelphia Packet*), that he had complained about BF to "some Persons in the Administration, and in particular to the Secretary of State," Lord Halifax. According to Penn, Halifax said he thought BF's behavior was "a kind of Rebellion against his Majesty's Government, and that Mr. Franklin must be turned out, if he does not alter his conduct." Lord Hyde, postmaster general, to whom Penn "gave a full account, as did Mr. Allen," was of the same opinion and "has promised to write him very closely upon this subject, and to tell him all the Officers of the Crown are expected to assist Government, whether in the hands of the Crown or of Proprietarys, and if he does not, he will be displaced." Penn Papers, Hist. Soc. Pa. Lord Hyde may have written BF such a warning, also by the *Philadelphia Packet*, but no letter of the sort from either of the postmasters general or from their secretary, Anthony Todd, has been found. BF may have received an intimation of Hyde's views from some personal friend in London.

1. On these and other services mentioned in this paragraph, see above, VI, 3–7, 13–28, 206–9, 390–2, 477–9; VII, 38–61, 63–5, 145–53, 181–2. It may be observed that in this recital BF confined himself strictly to his efforts on behalf of the British Army and said nothing of his activities in the defense of Northampton Co. during the winter of 1755–56, when only Pa. troops were involved. His support of forces operating directly under British commanders would be the most likely to impress members of the ministry at home.

Shilling Advantage to myself, in the Shape of Profit, Commissions, or any other way whatsoever. I projected a Method of supplying Gen. Shirley with £10,000's worth of Provisions, to be given at his Request by this Province, and carried the same thro' the House so as to render it effectual; together with a Gift of some Hundreds of warm Wastecoats, Stockings Mittens, &c. for the Troops in their first Winter Service at Albany. And at Lord Loudon's Request I so manag'd between the Governor and Assembly as to procure the Passage of the £60,000 Act then greatly wanted, and which met with great Difficulty. On your Arrival here, you know the Readiness with which I endeavour'd to serve the Officers in the Affair of their Quarters. And you have been a Witness of my Behaviour as a Commissioner, in the Execution of the present Act, and of my Forwardness to carry at the Board every Measure you proposed to promote the Service. What I would request is, that you would take Occasion in some Letter to me to express your Sentiments of my Conduct in these Respects, so far as has come to your Knowledge, or fallen under your Observation.[2] My having such a Letter to produce on Occasion, may possibly be of considerable Service to me. With the most perfect Esteem I am, Dear Sir, Your most obedient humble Servant   B FRANKLIN

Mrs. Franklin and Sally join me in Prayers for your Success and happy Return.

I send you enclos'd our last political Pamphlet, to amuse you on some rainy day.[3]

Col. Bouquet.

James Pearson and Benjamin Franklin:
Agreement for Sale   DS: Historical Society of Pennsylvania

This agreement provided for the sale by James Pearson to Franklin of a lot and two buildings on Pewter Platter Alley, Philadelphia. The

2. For two drafts of a similar request to General Shirley in 1756, see above, VI, 477–9. For Bouquet's prompt response to BF's appeal, see below, pp. 321–3.

3. Probably *The Speech of Joseph Galloway, Esq.*, with BF's preface, which had been published on August 11; see above, pp. 267–311.

actual deed seems never to have been recorded, and the parchment original has disappeared. Some additional details are found, however, in two other deeds: one from Israel and Mary Pemberton to Franklin, December 13, 1775, relating to the ground rent;[4] the other executed by the seven heirs of Franklin's daughter Sarah Bache, January 14, 1812, whereby they distributed among themselves the real estate she and her husband had inherited from her father.[5] The latter document establishes that the deed which fulfilled the present agreement was dated August 25, 1764.

These deeds show that the lot had a frontage on Pewter Platter (or Jones's) Alley, as measured in 1812, of 37 feet 9 inches and a depth of 60 feet. It was bounded on the east by a house and lot of Thomas Biles (or Ryles), deceased; on the south partly by a lot formerly belonging to Thomas Hine, sold to Franklin in 1761,[6] and partly by a lot formerly belonging to Sarah Read and later to John Lynn; and on the west by a house of Robert Grace.[7] The property had been sold to Pearson, June 6, 1760, by Israel and Mary Pemberton and was subject to an annual ground rent, payable to Pemberton quarterly, of "Fifteen Pistoles of fine Spanish Coined Gold each Pistole weighing four Penny weights and six grains or so much lawful money of Pennsylvania as will purchase fifteen such Pistoles."[8]

4. Department of Records, Recorder of Deeds, City of Philadelphia, Deed Book 1 16, pp. 175–7.

5. *Ibid.*, Deed Book 1 C, 19, p. 3. This property is there listed as the ninth parcel of Franklin-Bache real estate to be distributed; in the partition among the heirs it is designated as plot no. 35, allocated to BF's granddaughter Sarah Bache (D.3.8); *ibid.*, pp. 12, 19.

6. For BF's acquisition of the former Hine lot, July 11, 1761, see above, IX, 328–30.

7. For BF's lease in 1745 of the Grace property, which extended through from Pewter Platter Alley to Market Street, see above, III, 50–1. The Franklin & Hall printing office stood on the southern part of the Grace lot.

8. Earlier deeds of adjacent property mention that the Pearson lot had belonged to Griffith Jones in 1702 and to Sarah Read in 1750. 3 *Pa. Arch.*, IX, 556–60. Apparently BF became somewhat dilatory in paying the ground rent. On Oct. 10, 1770, Pemberton submitted a statement showing that in the five years from Sept. 25, 1765, to Sept. 25, 1770, a total of £101 5s. sterling had been due, of which BF had paid only two installments of £30 each, both in 1769. Hist. Soc. Pa. Again behind five years later, BF settled a new account, Nov. 23, 1775, by a payment of £105. Memorandum Book, 1757–1776, p. 24. On Dec. 13, 1775, Pemberton and his wife sold to BF all future rights to ground rent for £350 Pa. currency. BF paid this amount plus a final quarter's rent then due on March 5, 1776. *Ibid.*, p. 26.

Memorandum, August 18. 1764. That it is this Day agreed between James Pierson on the one Part, and Benjamin Franklin on the other, that the said James Pierson shall convey to the said Benjamin Franklin his Lot and Houses on Pewter Platter Alley, (the Workshop excepted which is to be removed); and that the said Benjamin Franklin shall pay the said James Pierson for the same Three Hundred and fifty Pounds, besides discharging the Groundrent of Fifteen Pistoles per Annum to Israel Pemberton. The said Lot is about 38 Feet front, and 60 feet deep, with one Brick and one wooden Tenement thereon. To compleat this Agreement as soon as possible, the Parties bind themselves hereby, and their Executors and Administrators. Having set hereto their Hands and Seals
Witness   B FRANKLIN
MARY PITT:S   JAMES PEARSON
JOHN FOXCROFT

Receiv'd the same Day, Ten Pounds in Part of the above Sum of £350 per me   JAS. PEARSON

Endorsed: Agreement Jas Pearson B Franklin Lot and Houses on Pewter Platter Alley Aug. 18. 1764

From Henry Bouquet (I)

ALS and copy:[9] American Philosophical Society

Colonel Bouquet wrote two letters to Franklin on August 22, 1764, in answer to the one Franklin had written him on August 16 (above, pp. 316–19). The first of the two was a direct response to Franklin's request that Bouquet "would take Occasion in some Letter to me to express your Sentiments of my Conduct" with regard to supporting and promoting the service of the British Army, "so far as has come to your Knowledge, or fallen under your Observation." Bouquet's letter, printed here, is somewhat formal in tone and was clearly intended to be, as Franklin hoped, such a letter as the deputy postmaster general might be able "to produce on Occasion" and which might "possibly be of considerable Service to me." The second of Bouquet's letters, printed as the document following this one, is more informal and personal, apparently intended for Franklin's eyes alone.

9. For an explanation of these two MSS, see the first footnote to Bouquet's letter of Aug. 10, 1764, above, p. 266.

Dear Sir   Fort Loudoun 22d. August 1764

I received yesterday your obliging Letter of the 16th. Instant with the welcome account that my Request to the Governor and Commissioners (to enable me to recruit the number of men wanted, to replace the Deserters of the Pennsylvania Troops) was granted.

An application of that Nature being unusual, I doubted of its Success, and nothing but the necessity of compleating those Two Battalions, could have induced me to make an attempt liable to so many objections, from the known Oeconomy of the Board of Commissioners in the disposal of Public money.

My Dependance was as usual upon you, and indeed had you not supported my Request in the warmest manner, It must have miscarried and lefft me exposed to many Inconveniencies.

Your conduct on this occasion does not surprise me, as I have not alone, experienced the favourable Effects of your Readiness to promote the Service:[1] I know that General Shirley owed to you the considerable Supply of Provisions, this Government voted for his Troops, besides Warm Cloathing &c.

That you alone could and did procure to General Braddock the Carriages without which, he could not have proceeded on his Expedition. That you had a Road opened through this Province to Supply more easily his Army with Provisions, and Spent a Summer in those different services, without any other Reward than the satisfaction of serving the Public.

And I am not unacquainted with the Share you had in conveying safely through the House, at a very difficult time the Bill for £60,-000 during Lord Loudoun's Command. But without recapitulating Instances in which I was not directly concerned, I remember gratefully that as early as 1756, when I was Sent by Lord Loudoun to obtain Quarters in Philadelphia for the first Battalion of the R.A. Regiment I could not have Surmounted the difficulties made by your People, who at that time unacquainted with Quartering of Troops, expressed the greatest Reluctancy to comply with my Request, till you was so good to take that affair in hand, and obtained all that was asked.

I have not been less obliged to you in the Execution of the present Act, having been an Eye Witness of your Forwardness to

1. For incidents referred to here, see the references to earlier volumes, above, p. 318 n.

carry at the Board as a Commissioner, every Measure I proposed for the Success of this Expedition. This acknowledgement being the only Return I can make for the repeated Services I have received from you in my Public Station: I beg you will excuse my Prolixity upon a subject so agreeable to myself as the Expression of my gratitude. I am with great Regard. Dear Sir Your most obedient, and obliged Humble Servant   HENRY BOUQUET

Benjamin Franklin Esqr.

Endorsed: Col. Bouquet Augt. 22. 64 His Acknowledgemts.[2]

From Henry Bouquet (II)   ALS: American Philosophical Society

Dear Sir   Fort Loudoun 22d. August 1764
    I return you my thanks for the continuation of your most friendly offices in the thorny affair you have so luckily carried for me. I flater myself you will not doubt that I shall chearfully embrace every opportunity to do you Justice, and convince you of my Sincere affection, having only to lament that it is not in my Power to do it effectualy. The Inclosed is far from expressing my Sentiments of the real obligations I lay under to you, but if I can add any thing to render it of any future use, I beg you will let me know it.[3]
    I am Sorry that your Sentiments concerning this Government have raised you some Enemies, as I am Sure you can have no others. I do not pretend to medle with Politicks, having no business with it. But being averse to all misunderstandings and Differences between men I love and Esteem, as they are the Bane of Society, and destroy that Confidence so necessary to Support it; I have long wished that the unhappy Disputes Subsisting in the Province could be adjusted in an amicable manner, and Harmony Succeed to these jarring Times. I aprehend that things are now carried too far to admit of Palliatives, and that Superior Powers, or Time still more Powerful, must Interfere to operate the miracle of a Reconciliation.

    2. The endorsement is in BF's hand.
    3. This sentence establishes that Bouquet had already written the more public letter printed immediately above before undertaking this one, in which he expresses his private views of the situation in Pa.

The Principle upon which your Government is calculated appears to me Erroneous in Supposing necessarily a close union of the Two Branches of Legislature, a notion which does more honor to the Heart of the Legislator, than to his Head; Where Power and Interest are concerned, Encroachments will be attempted or supposed; opposition ensue, and in that Case you want as in the System of Great Britain, the weight of a third Power to contain the other Two within their proper Limits, and act as Mediator, But that will be impracticable in America till Time has produced nobility and Wealth, whose intrinsic Influence will be Effective and not nominal, as that of a Counsel composed of Plebeyans, without personal preeminence:[4]

I don't expect to see any alteration in your present System, tho' the ministry appear averse to Proprietary Government: and The Board of Trade have just now overset the fine Super Structure raised by Lord Egmont, upon the Expectation of a Grant for the Island of St. John;[5] I send you his Plan, which I have not yet read:

4. Bouquet seems to have felt that the colonies lacked what he regarded as the essential third element in a balanced society and government: a cultivated and financially independent aristocracy, intermediate between the mass of the people and the Crown or its representatives. In Philadelphia he had mingled pleasantly with many of the wealthier families—the Allens, Shippens, and Willings, for example—but they hardly qualified as an aristocracy in the European sense. In a long letter to Miss Anne Willing of Jan. 15, 1761, he had explained his unwillingness to leave the army and settle in the province. The "Gentlemen" in America, he wrote, "are so much taken up with the narrow sphere of their Politicks or their private affairs that a Loiterer has no chance with them." Their wives "are commonly involved and buried in the details of their families" and can talk with a visitor over "a dish of tea" only of "anecdotes of their days work, and the pretty sayings of their children." If, on the other hand, he were to move in lesser circles, how could he "brook the supercilious look and the surly pride of the Humble Quaker? or the insulting rudeness of an Assembly-man, who, picked up from a dunghill, thinks himself raised to a Being of a Superior nature?" *PMHB*, III (1879), 141–3. As he comments above, only time could produce a true class of "nobility and Wealth" to serve as a "third Power" in politics. Without it, there was no prospect of true stability in the government of the province.

5. John Perceval, 2d Earl of Egmont (above, X, 286 n), petitioned the King in December 1763 for a grant of the island of St. John (now Prince Edward Island), over which he and his heirs—he had nine children—would be established as lords paramount with powers of subinfeudation and the erection of baronies on the island for a group of fellow petitioners. On May

It is said to be much aproved in England: when you and I settle our Colony upon the Scioto, we may make use of His Lordships Pamphlet:[6]

I have perused with Pleasure the Papers you have sent me; They are chiefly founded upon Circumstances which exist no longer, but in Mr. Bligh's Letter[7] I find several Ideas very well adapted to the present Times, and I wish the Plan of a Military Frontier could be put in Execution. I have taken the Liberty to keep Copies of some of them, and return you the originals:

We are perfectly quiet here, and I expect no disturbances till we cross the Ohio: I propose to leave this Camp on Wednesday next with a Second Convoy for Pittsburgh.[8] Be so good to present my Respects to the Ladies, and believe me with great truth Dear sir Your most obedient Humble Servant   HENRY BOUQUET

Benjamin Franklin Esqr.

9, 1764, following recommendations of the Board of Trade, the Privy Council rejected the scheme as proposed by Egmont but allowed him and the other applicants to receive smaller individual grants of land on the island on terms "consistent with those Principles of Settlement, Cultivation and Government which have been adopted for many Years past." *Acts Privy Coun., Col.,* IV, 654–8; *Board of Trade Journal,* 1764–67, pp. 6, 7, 31, 32, 33, 34; Andrew H. Clark, *Three Centuries and the Island. A Historical Geography of Settlement and Agriculture in Prince Edward Island, Canada* (Toronto, 1959), pp. 42, 231. Maryland and Pennsylvania remained as relics of a bygone system of colonial settlement, but the age of new proprietary grants, with rights of government and land tenure based on feudal privileges, was clearly over by 1764.

6. BF's "Plan for Settling Two Western Colonies" of 1754 (above, V, 456–63) called for one of the colonies to be planted on the Scioto River; he had written to George Whitefield in 1756, somewhat lightly perhaps, about their assuming the joint leadership of a colony on the Ohio (VI, 468–9); and his letters to Richard Jackson in 1763–64 show his real interest in various proposals for western settlement. Quite probably he had discussed some similar scheme with Bouquet while the colonel was in Philadelphia during the spring and early summer of 1764, but how serious such conversations may have been cannot now be determined. Lord Egmont had printed his plan for the settlement of St. John as *To the King's Most Excellent Majesty, the Memorial of John, Earl of Egmont* (London, [1763]).

7. Neither this document nor its author has been identified.

8. Bouquet did not leave Fort Loudoun until August 31; he arrived at Fort Pitt on September 18. *The Papers of Col. Henry Bouquet,* II, 314–15; XVI, 138, 139.

From Henry Bouquet

ALS: American Philosophical Society

Dear Sir   Fort Loudoun 27th. August 1764

I have the mortification to inform you *privately* that Bradstreet has granted Peace at Presqu'Isle to the Delaware and Shawanese without insisting on the least satisfaction for their Murders and Insults.

I flater myself that the General will not ratify Such a Scandalous Treaty;[9] for my part I take no Notice of it, and proceed to the Ohio, fully determined to treat as Enemies Every Vilain of those Nations (Deputies excepted) as shall come in my way, till I receive contrary Orders from the General.[1] I am Dear Sir Your most Humble Servant   H. B.

Addressed: To / Benjamin Franklin Esqr / At / Philadelphia

Endorsed: Col Bouquet Aug. 27.

To Richard Jackson

ALS American Philosophical Society

Dear Sir,   Philada. Sept. 1. 1764

I wrote a few Lines to you the 9th. of last Month,[2] expressing some Impatience that I had miss'd hearing from you by two Packets. But soon after I had the Pleasure of receiving yours of June 4,

9. Col. John Bradstreet commanded the northern force marching against the hostile Indians in the West. Leaving Niagara in early August, he landed near Presqu'Isle, where representatives of the Delaware and Shawnee met him to ask for peace. Something of an innocent in Indian negotiations and not realizing that others of these tribes were still on the warpath, Bradstreet accepted at face value these deputies' protestations of good intentions. Without any authority to do so, he concluded a treaty of peace with them, August 12. In this agreement he failed to require "satisfaction" for the Indians' prior depredations or adequate guarantees for the safe return of their white prisoners. General Gage was furious and, as Bouquet prophesied, refused to recognize the agreement. Howard H. Peckham, *Pontiac and the Indian Uprising* (2d edit., Chicago, [1961]), pp. 255–6.

1. Bouquet set out from Fort Pitt on October 1. He pursued the Indians as far as the Muskingum River, received the capitulations of several groups, and returned to Fort Pitt on November 28 with 200 restored captives and pledges (backed by the surrender of hostages) for the return of another hundred. *Ibid.*, pp. 262–3.

2. See above, pp. 263–4.

and 14.[3] the last by Mr. Allen. I am glad to learn that our Construction of the Article relating to the Proprietor's located uncultivated Lands is not like to be controverted in England.[4] As to the Prosecution of the Petition,[5] which you seem a little unwilling to engage in while more general American Affairs are on the Anvil, much will depend on the Complexion of the next Assembly. The Proprietary Party have taken true Pains, as it behov'd them, to represent the Change as dangerous to our Privileges, and made the Assembly odious for proposing it.[6] The Irish Presbyterians, too, piqu'd at the Reflections thrown on them by the Quakers for the late Riots and Murders, have join'd the Proprietary Party, by which they hope to acquire the Predominancy in the Assembly, and subdue the Quakers.[7] Hence the approaching Election will probably be a warm one, and the Event is uncertain: But if a Majority of the old Members continue, as I apprehend they may,[8] the Measure will, I believe be prosecuted, notwithstanding the Bugbears Mr. Allen endeavours to terrify us with about the Expence, which he says he had in charge from you to tell me would be £100,000 Sterling that the Parliament will oblige us to pay,[9] and saddle us

3. Neither letter has been found.
4. For the Proprietors' instructions to Governor Penn to yield to the Assembly's construction of the article in question, see above, p. 213 n. Although Jackson seems to have received no direct word of this capitulation, he had probably told BF in one of the missing letters that, as Thomas Penn later admitted, "no Person here" looked upon the disputed stipulation "in any other light than that the Assembly contended for." Penn to Smith, Oct. 12, 1764, Penn Papers, Hist. Soc. Pa.
5. The Assembly's petition to the King, praying him to assume the government of the province. When writing his June letters Jackson could only have seen BF's draft petition of March 29, 1764, not the petition adopted by the Assembly on May 26, 1764. See above, pp. 145–7, 199–200.
6. For example, Dickinson's *Speech* of May 24, 1764, printed in pamphlet form and published in late June; above, pp. 267–8 n.
7. William Allen reported to Thomas Penn, Sept. 25, 1764, that BF's opponents "are composed chiefly of Presbyterians, one half of the Church of England, and most of the other Societys, particularly the Lutherans, and Calvinist Germans." Of the last groups, many had signed the petition but now say "that they had been imposed on by his [BF's] and other's false storys." Penn Papers, Hist. Soc. Pa.
8. For the outcome of the election, see below, pp. 390–4.
9. On Nov. 18, 1764, Jackson denied that he had mentioned such a sum to Allen: see below, p. 464.

besides with a Salary to be paid by us to a King's Governor of £5000 Sterling per Annum more. I can scarcely conceive that you sent me such a Message, nor can I believe that so absurd a Thing would be propos'd by the Ministry, that we should pay the Purchase Money for the Government, unless we were to buy it for ourselves. It was not done in the Case of Carolinas, nor in any other Case of the kind that I have heard of. Mr. Allen adds, that Lord Halifax says our Resolves are *Rebellion!*[1] And that Lord Mansfield said to Mr. Penn, "Now is your Time to make a good Bargain for your self. Put these refractory People into our Hands, and we'll soon make them feel the Difference between a Proprietary and a Royal Government!"[2] Is it possible that so high an Officer of the Crown should speak in that Manner of Royal Government, to intimidate the King's Subjects from putting themselves more immediately under its Care and Protection? Telling us these Stories seems to be treating us like Children. You kindly wish a good Understanding could be obtain'd between Mr. Allen and me. I visited him upon Receipt of your Letter, to congratulate him on his Arrival, intending it as an Overture to that End; and then it was that he entertain'd me with the above Discourse, and deliver'd me the Message as from you before all the Company. I have not since seen him. You know I always spoke respectfully of him. Has he done the same by me? I respect even the Ashes of a departed Friendship. But he is at this time abusing me to the Quakers, as many as come in his Way, by a very unfair Account of some private Conversation that pass'd between us many Years ago, when we were great Friends.[3] With me therefore a second Confidence is impossible where the first has been betray'd. Our Assembly is to

1. For the Assembly's "Necklace of Resolves" of March 24, 1764, see above, pp. 126–33. Thomas Penn wrote Benjamin Chew on June 8, 1764, that Lord Halifax had said that the resolves were "a kind of Rebellion against his Majesty's Government, and that Mr. Franklin must be turned out, if he does not alter his conduct." Penn Papers, Hist. Soc. Pa.

2. In a postscript dated June 14 to a letter of June 8, 1764, Thomas Penn told the governor that he had just seen Lord Mansfield, who said "the resolutions are very mad ones" and BF ought to be displaced from his position in the Post Office. Penn Papers, Hist. Soc. Pa.

3. Probably a reference to the story of BF's earlier critical comments on the Quakers, which appeared in print during the election campaign; see below, pp. 375–6, 381.

sit the 10th. when I shall lay your Letter before them; and write by the next Opportunity what passes.[4] I suppose Mr. Dickinson's Speech against the Change has been sent you. With this you will receive Mr. Galloway's in Answer to it. I must own to you that the Preface was written by me.[5] It may possibly to cooler People seem too severe: But it was not without great Provocation. I bore the personal Abuse of five scurrilous Pamphlets, and three Copperplate Prints, from the Proprietary Party, before I made the smallest Return;[6] and they began to think they might continue to affront me with Impunity. You will, on the whole, I believe, be of my Opinion, that the Breach is now become irreparable, and the Difference between the Proprietaries and the Province irreconcileable, unless they can get an Assembly of a different Cast, which I think they will not.

To drop this disagreable Subject, let me tell you a little News. The Publick Papers will have inform'd you that Sir William Johnson had held a Treaty at Niagara, and made a Peace with all the Indians except the Delawares and Shawanese, who did not appear.[7] Yesterday came an Express from Col. Bradstreet, with Advice, that after that Treaty he had advanc'd with the Forces under his Command to Presqu'isle, where there met him Ten Deputies from the Shawnese, Delawares, Hurons of Sandusky, and those Indians of the 5 Nations that inhabit the Plains of Scioto, and other Rivers between Lake Erie and the Ohio.[8] These presented him, he says, first with a String and a long Compliment. 2dly. A String, with a Request that they might have Leave to speak, and might be favourably heard. 3dly. A Belt, desiring to know the Reason of his moving that way with so great a Force. To all which he answer'd. 1st. with Thanks for their Compliment. 2dly. Gave them

4. See below, pp. 339–40.
5. See above, pp. 267–311.
6. The five scurrilous pamphlets printed before BF's preface to Galloway's *Speech* appeared cannot be positively identified. One of them may have been Hugh Williamson's *An Answer to the Plot* (Evans 9581), and BF may also have had in mind Williamson's *Plain Dealer* series, the last of which was dated May 12, 1764 (nos. I and III reprinted in John R. Dunbar, ed., *The Paxton Papers*, The Hague, 1957, pp. 339–51, 365–86). Some may not be extant. For two of the copperplate prints during this year, see pp. 70, 374.
7. *Pa. Gaz.*, Aug. 23, 30, 1764, reported Johnson's peace negotiations.
8. See below, pp. 335–7, and *Votes*, 1763–64, pp. 97–9.

Leave to speak, and promis'd them a fair Hearing. 3dly. Told them that he was going to revenge on the Indians who had refus'd to treat of Peace, all the Injuries that had been done the English. They then said, that immediately on hearing a Peace was propos'd, they had call'd in all their Warriors. That they were very sensible they had injur'd the English, by making War on them without Cause, were very sorry for the same, and were come to beg for Mercy and Forgiveness, and that a Peace might be granted them. He told them that he was surpriz'd at their Begging for Peace so soon after the insolent Letter they had sent to the Treaty. But however, since they profess'd Sorrow for their past Conduct, he would grant them Peace on the following Conditions.

1st. That all the Prisoners they had among them should immediately be collected and brought to Sandusky (where he should directly proceed) and there be deliver'd up to him. This to be perform'd in 25 Days. None to remain on Pretence of Marriage Adoption, or otherwise. The Unwilling to be forc'd away among the rest.

2dly. That all the Posts the English now have in their Country, shall be ceded to us; that we shall be at Liberty to build as many more Forts and Trading Houses as we please wherever we shall think it necessary to protect the Trade; and that they shall yield to us forever as much Territory round each Fort as a Cannon Shot can fly over; that so the People of the Forts may have Lands to raise their own Provisions.

3dly. That if any of the Tribes renew the War, and kill or plunder any Englishman, the rest should join us to punish them. And if particular Murderers are delivered up to prevent a War, they shall be tried by the English Law, only that half the Jury shall be Indians of the same Nation with the Prisoner.

4thly. That Six of the Deputies should remain with him as Hostages, while the other four, with an English Officer and an Indian go to acquaint the Chiefs of the several Nations with these Terms, and return with their Ratifications of the Peace.

The Deputies accepted these Terms with Thanks. And he is gone on to Sandusky, and has wrote to Col. Bouquet, to stop his Army who are on their March from this Province against the same People, till he hears again from him. But Col. Bouquet will, I believe, continue his March till Orders come to him from the General; for he disapproves this hasty Peace, as it stipulates no Satisfaction for the Robberies committed on the Goods of our Merchants, and the bloody Injuries the Indians unprovok'd have done our Nation.[9]

To tell you my Opinion of this Transaction; I doubt the Indians mean no more than to parry our Blow, till they have got in and hid their Corn,* which they fear our two Armies may destroy; and that then they will renew their Hostilities. But I hope I am mistaken. Tho' I cannot but wish they had felt a little more from our just Resentment, before a Peace had been granted them. With sincere Esteem and Respect, I am, Dear Sir, Your most obedient humble Servant. B FRANKLIN

P.S. You speak of a Reconciliation between us and the Proprietaries on Terms that may be agreable to us.[1] Have any such been talk'd of? We hear nothing of them here.

R. Jackson Esqr.

Endorsed: 1 Sepr 64 B. Franklin Esqr

To William Strahan

ALS: Pierpont Morgan Library

Dear Straney   Philada. Sept. 1. 1764
I receiv'd your obliging Letter of June 5.[2] I find by my Letter Book, that I wrote to you May 1. and June 25.[3] I thought I had sent you one of my Narratives.[4] You cannot conceive the Number

*The Indian Corn is not ripe till October generally.

9. For Bouquet's "Mortification" with Bradstreet's peace terms, see the letter immediately above.

1. Jackson probably touched on this subject in his lost letter of June 14. BF's letter to Collinson, Sept. 24, 1764, indicates that rumors were circulating in England that the Proprietors had yielded on the taxation of their located, unimproved lands. See below, p. 352. This information, had it been officially announced when first received in Pennsylvania, might well have changed the course of political events.

2. Not found.

3. Above, pp. 188–90, 240–2. The May 1 letter commends Strahan's reports on British politics and the June 25 letter concerns Benjamin Mecom's bankruptcy, in which James Parker was acting as BF and Strahan's attorney; both matters are touched on in the present letter.

4. Above, pp. 42–69. Strahan had printed the substance of the *Narrative,* received through other friends in London, in *London Chron.*, April 10–12, 1764, and *Gent. Mag.*, XXXIV (April 1764), 173–8.

of bitter Enemies that little Piece has rais'd me among the Irish Presbyterians. I now send you a Pamphlet[5] that I have written since in favour of our projected Change of Government: and Mr. Galloway's Speech with a Preface of mine[6] against the Proprietary Party with whom I am still at War, and who will ere long either demolish me or I them. If the former happens, as possibly it may, Behold me a Londoner for the rest of my Days. At present I am here as much the Butt of Party Rage and Malice, express'd in Pamphlets and Prints, and have as many pelted at my Head in proportion, as if I had the Misfortune of being your Prime Minister.

I wrote to you that Mecom's Effects were in Parker's Hands. The following is a Copy of the Receipt he gave for them. Parker will write to you by the next Packet; at least I shall urge him to do it.

"New York, April 30. 1764

"Received of Benjamin Mecom, in Behalf of his Creditors, and as Attorney particularly appointed by Benjamin Franklin Esq of Philadelphia and Mr. William Strahan of London, Sundry Boxes of Books, a Printing Press, and Printing Materials, lately in the said B. Mecom's Possession, as particulariz'd in his Accounts with said Benjamin Franklin, William Strahan, Rivington & Fletcher, and Hamilton and Balfour; all which I am to account for to my Constituents: which said Ledger is received by me. As also the Cash of sundry of said Mecom's Effects sold at Auction, amounting to £28 10s. 7½d. an Account of which, and Receipt for it, is also render'd to him for the same Purpose, per me   JAMES PARKER"

You will consult the others what Steps to take for your common Benefit.

I thank you for your Intelligence concerning your Publick Affairs; accompanied with your judicious political Reflections. You

5. *Cool Thoughts on the Present Situation of Our Public Affairs;* above, pp. 153–73. *London Chron.,* June 17–20, 1764, commended the pamphlet and printed extracts from it.

6. Above, pp. 267–311. The pamphlet was reprinted in London by Richardson & Clark and sold by W. Nicoll in December (*London Chron.,* Dec. 6–8, 1764). *Critical Review,* XVIII (Nov. 1764), had reviewed it unfavorably, but *Monthly Review,* XXXII (Jan. 1765), 67, discussing both it and Dickinson's *Reply,* expressed surprise that Dickinson "should take no notice of the masterly Preface" to Galloway's speech, "supposed to be written by Mr. F——n."

can scarcely conceive how acceptable and satisfactory your Letters always are on that Topic to me and my Friends. For my Part, I rely entirely on your Accounts and Sentiments; only making a small Abatement where you forebode any Misfortune. But that is mere Temper in me, which always loves to view the bright Sides of things.

Will continues very happy in his Government and the Affections of the People. He and his Wife were well a few Days since, and desir'd their respectful Compliments to you and yours. Mrs. Franklin and Sally join me in every good Wish for you and Mrs. Strahan and your valuable Set of Children.[7] God bless 'em all, and my Peggy as mickle as any twa o' them. I want to hear Rachey upon the Armonica; but her Attention is probably withdrawn from that, by her new Plaything, the Baby, which furnishes more agreable Musick.[8] I am, my dear Friend, with sincere Esteem, Yours most affectionately   B FRANKLIN

P.S. News is just arriv'd of a Peace concluded at Presquisle with the Delawares and Shawanese by Col. Bradstreet.[9]

Please to send the Pamphlets to Mr. Small and Dr. Hawksworth as directed.[1]

I believe I complain'd to you before that Mr. Becket neglected me. The reason I cannot conceive, and wish you would tell me. I wrote to him last year for the following Books, and have never since heard a Word from him.[2] I now request you to send them to me. I know not what they will cost; but on your showing the Account and this Letter to Mr. Henton Brown, Banker, he will immediately pay it.[3]

7. For the Strahan children, see above, x, 169 n.

8. Rachel Strahan Johnston's first child, a daughter, was born in October 1762.

9. See the document immediately above.

1. For Alexander Small and Dr. John Hawkesworth, two of BF's closest British friends, see above, IX, 110 n, 265–6 n.

2. For BF's letter of Dec. 17, 1763, ordering the books listed below, see above, x, 393–5; the bibliographical problems presented by some of these books are discussed there. Becket answered BF on Aug. 10, 1764 (above, pp. 264–5), but of course his letter had not yet reached Philadelphia.

3. In a letter to Strahan of Sept. 24, 1764 (below, pp. 353–4), BF canceled his order for the books listed here, because he had received them in the meantime from Becket.

Debates of the House of Commons by Anchitel Gray, Esqr.
Print of the Earl of Bute by Ryland, if good 2 of them.
Astronomical Tables and Precepts for Calculating the Times of
the new and full Moons, projecting Eclipses, &c. to A.D.
7800 by James Ferguson.
Concise Account of the Rise of the Society of Arts. Hooper
Essay on Oeconomy. Richardson
Fielding's Universal Mentor.
Philosophical Transactions Part I. of Vol. 49. Part II of Vol. 50.
Also Vols. 52, 53, and 54, all in blue Covers.

Addressed: To / Mr. Wm. Strahan / New Street / Shoe Lane /
London / per Capt. / Caton[4]

To [Peter Templeman][5]

ALS: Royal Society of Arts

Sir   Philada. Sept. 2. 1764
Furman & Co. Merchants of this Place,[6] send by Capt. Caton,[7]
60 Keggs of Sturgeon, which they hope will be found so well cured
as to obtain the Society's Approbation, and a Premium. They have
desired me to introduce their Claim to you by a Line in its favour;
but I have told them the whole will depend on the Merits of their
Fish when it comes to London. I can only say, that what I have
tasted of it here, was excellent.[8] America can furnish any Quantity;

4. *Pa. Gaz.*, Sept. 6, 1764, reported the clearance of the *Myrtilla*, Capt. J.
Caton. Strahan acknowledged the receipt of BF's letter in one to David Hall
of Oct. 13, 1764. APS.

5. For Dr. Peter Templeman, secretary of the Society of Arts, see above,
IX, 322 n.

6. Moore Furman (d. 1808), former postmaster at Trenton, N.J., moved
to Philadelphia in 1762 and engaged in mercantile activities with various
partners. He returned to N.J. in the 1770s, served as deputy quartermaster
general of the state during the Revolution, and became the first mayor of
Trenton under its charter of 1792. 1 *N.J. Arch.*, XX, 148 n. In *Pa. Gaz.*, June
28, 1764, the firm of Coxe & Furman advertised "Choice Pickled Sturgeon,
cured in the best Manner for present Use or Exportation," for sale at the store
in Water Street or by Benjamin Yard and Jonathan Richmond in Trenton.

7. *Pa. Gaz.*, Sept. 6, 1764, reported the clearance for London of the *Myrtilla*, Capt. J. Caton.

8. Alexander Small wrote Dec. 1, 1764, that the sturgeon BF had recommended to Dr. Templeman "did not give Satisfaction" and explained its
defects. See below, p. 479.

but for our Encouragement methinks the foreign Duty should be taken off. With great Esteem for your self, and best Wishes for the Prosperity of the Society, I am, Sir, Your most obedient humble Servant   B FRANKLIN

Endorsed: Septr. 2d. 1764.

To Anthony Todd   ALS: Public Record Office

Sir   Philada. Sept. 2. 1764
   We have just receiv'd some important News from Presqu'isle on Lake Erie, which it is my Duty to take this first Opportunity of communicating thro' you to his Majesty's Postmaster General.
   The Public Papers, before this can come to hand, will have inform'd you, that Sir William Johnson had held a Treaty at Niagara, and concluded a Peace with all the Indian Nations or Tribes that were at War with us, the Delawares, Shawanese, and other Ohio Indians excepted, who had haughtily refused to send Deputies to the Congress.[9] We were much concern'd to hear of their standing out, as by their Situation they were most capable of injuring this and the neighbouring Provinces, and had actually committed all the late Ravages on the Frontiers of Pensilvania and Virginia.[1] But those People being inform'd, that Col. Bouquet from this Province with 1000 of our Provincials, besides Regulars, was on his March towards their Country;[2] and that Col. Bradstreet, with a considerable Force of Regulars, and New York and New Jersey Provincials was advancing along the Back of their Territories by Lake Erie, they suddenly chang'd their Resolution of continuing the War, and sent ten of their principal Men as Deputies, who met

9. *Pa. Gaz.*, Aug. 23, 30, 1764, carried accounts of Johnson's negotiations with the Indians.
   1. One of the ravages to which BF was referring was almost certainly an atrocity, committed by Indians on July 26, 1764, in Cumberland (now Franklin) County, Pa., which Francis Parkman called "an outrage unmatched in fiend-like atrocity through all the annals of the war"; the massacre of schoolmaster Enoch Brown and ten of his little pupils. *Pa. Gaz.*, Aug. 9, 1764, reported this gruesome incident. It is described in greater detail in C. Hale Sipe, *The Indian Wars of Pennsylvania* (Harrisburg, 1929), p. 473.
   2. For Col. Henry Bouquet's expedition against the Shawnee and Delaware, see above, pp. 266–7, 325, 326 n.

Col. Broadstreet at Presqu'isle, and in the most submissive Manner acknowledg'd their Fault in commencing this War on the English without the least Cause or Provocation, and humbly begg'd for Mercy and Forgiveness, and that a Peace might be granted them. The Colonel, after severely reproving them, granted them Peace on the following Terms,[3]

1. That all the Prisoners now in their Country should be immediately collected, and delivered up to him at Sandusky within 25 Days; none to remain among them under any Pretence of Marriage, Adoption or otherwise; and the Unwilling to be forc'd away.

2. That they should cede to the English, and renounce for ever all Claim to the Posts or Forts now or late in our Possession in their Country. And that we should be at Liberty to erect as many new Forts or Trading Houses as we pleased, wherever we thought them necessary for Security of our Trade: And that round each Fort now or hereafter to be built, they should cede to us forever as much Land as a Cannon could throw a Shot over, to be cultivated by our People for the more convenient furnishing Provisions to the Garrison.

3. That in Case any one of the Tribes should hereafter renew the War against the English, the others should join us in reducing them and bringing them to Reason. And that particular Murderers hereafter given up to preserve Peace, should be tried by the English Law, the Jury to be half Indians of the same Nation with the Criminal.

4. That Six of the Deputies should remain with him as Hostages, till the Prisoners were restor'd, and these Articles confirmed.

These Terms were thankfully accepted and signed by the Deputies with their Marks as usual; they declaring themselves fully authorized for that purpose by the Shawanese, Delawares, Hurons of Sandusky, and the other Tribes inhabiting the Plains of Scioto, and all the Countries between Lake Erie and the Ohio.

The other four Deputies with an English Officer and an Indian,

---

3. For Bradstreet's ill-considered peace treaty, repudiated by his superior, Gen. Thomas Gage, see above, p. 326 n. BF's account of the treaty is very close to that which he supplied Richard Jackson on Sept. 1, 1764 (see above, pp. 329–31) and also very close to the account which appeared in *Pa. Gaz.*, Sept. 6, 1764, which was copied in *London Chron.*, Oct. 23–25, 1764. It seems probable that BF composed the *Gazette* account.

were immediately dispatch'd to acquaint the Nations with what had pass'd, and inform them that the Colonel would not discontinue his March but proceed to Sandusky, where he expected their Chiefs would meet him and ratify the Treaty; otherwise they should find two Armies of Warriors in their Country, and no future Proposals of Peace would be hearkned to, but they should be cut off from the Face of the Earth.

If this Peace holds, it will be very happy for these Colonies. We only apprehend, that the Savages, obtaining a Peace so easily, without having suffered the Chastisement they deserved for their late Perfidy, and without being oblig'd to make any Restitution or Satisfaction for the Goods they robb'd our Merchants of, and the Barbarities they committed (except the Cession of those small Tracts round Forts) will more readily incline to renew the War on every little Occasion.[4]

Be pleased to present my Dutyful Respects to the Post-master General;[5] and believe me, with much Esteem, Sir, Your most obedient humble Servant   B FRANKLIN

Antho. Todd Esqr

Endorsed: Copy of a Letter from Deputy Post Master of North America to Mr Todd.
In Mr Todds of the 13 Octr 1764.

Benjamin Franklin and John Foxcroft: Power of Attorney to Tuthill Hubbart[6]

> Printed form with MS insertions in blanks: New Hampshire Historical Society

[September 17, 1764]

Know all Men by these Presents, That we *Benjamin Franklin and John Foxcroft Esquires his Majesty's Deputy Postmaster General for*

4. BF expressed similar apprehensions to Richard Jackson in his letter of Sept. 1, 1764.
5. The postmasters general of England at this time were Robert Hampden-Trevor and Thomas Villiers, 1st Baron Hyde; see above, X, 217 n, 411 n.
6. Tuthill Hubbart, stepson of BF's brother John (C.8), had been appointed postmaster of Boston in 1756 to succeed his stepfather. See above, VI, 286 n; VII, 223 n. He himself spelled his surname with a "t," though others often wrote it "Hubbard."

337

North America, have made, ordained and constituted, and by these Presents do make ordain and constitute, and in our Place and Stead put and depute our trusty and loving Friend *Tuthill Hubbard Esqr., Postmaster of Boston in New England to be* our true and lawful Attorney, for us, and in our Name, and for *his Majesty's* Use, to ask, demand, sue for, recover and receive all such Sum and Sums of Money, Debts, Goods, Wares, Dues, Accounts and other Demands whatsoever, which are or shall be due, owing, payable and belonging to us, *as Receivers for his Majesty of the Revenue of the Post Office in America* or detained from us by any Manner of Ways or Means whatsoever, by *John Sherburne Esquire, of Portsmouth in New hampshire Executor of the Testament of the late Ellis Huske, Esqr. Postmaster of Boston aforesaid;*[7] *hereby revoking and making null and void all former Powers for the same purpose by us given to any Person whatsoever, and* giving and granting unto our said Attorney, by these Presents, our full and whole Power, Strength and Authority in and about the Premises, to have, use and take all lawful Ways and Means, in our Name for the Recovery thereof. And upon the Receipt of any such Debts, Dues, or Sums of Money aforesaid, Acquittances, or other sufficient Discharges, for us and in our Name, to make, seal and deliver. And generally, All and every other Act or Acts, Thing and Things, Device and Devices in the Law whatsoever needful and necessary to be done in and about the Premises, for the Recovery of all or any such Debts or Sums of Money aforesaid, for us and in our Name to do, execute and perform, as fully, largely and amply, to all Intents and Purposes, as we ourselves might or could do, if we were personally present, or as if the Matter required more special Authority than is herein given. And attornies, one or more, under *him* for the Purpose aforesaid to make and constitute, and again at Pleasure to revoke.

7. Ellis Huske, former postmaster in Boston, had died bankrupt in 1755, leaving his post office accounts unsettled. BF had been trying ever since to get his debt settled, and as early as March 5, 1756, had sent directions to Hubbart to put Huske's bond in suit. Above, VI, 422; VII, 197. On Sept. 24, 1763, a Probate Court in New Hampshire, where Huske was residing at the time of his death, had granted a petition by Matthew Livermore, acting on behalf of the deputy postmasters general, for payment of a claim of £352 18s. 8d. on Huske's debt to the Crown. Otis G. Hammond, ed., *Probate Records of the Province of New Hampshire,* IV (n.p., 1933) [*The State Papers of New Hampshire,* XXXIV], 185–6.

Ratifying, allowing, and holding for firm and effectual all and whatsoever our said Attorney shall lawfully do in and about the Premises by Virtue hereof. In Witness whereof we have hereunto set our Hands and Seals, this *Seventeenth* Day of *September* Annoque Domini, 17 *64*
Signed, sealed and delivered in the Presence of   B FRANKLIN
                                                     J. FOXCROFT

The Words, as Receivers for his Majesty of the Revenues of the Post Office in America, being first interlined.[8] *As also the Words (his Majesty's)*[9]   MARY PITTS
                                                     JANE PARKER[1]

Philadia. Sept. 18. 1764. The within named Benjamin Franklin and John Foxcroft personally appearing, acknowledged the within Instrument to be their Act and Deed. Before me   I JONES[2]

To Richard Jackson   ALS: American Philosophical Society

Dear Sir   Philada. Sept. 20. 1764
     I receiv'd your Favour of June 30.[3] but no Line by this Pacquet. Things are here as they have been for some time past: Except that the Proprietary Party begin to doubt the Success they promis'd themselves at the next Election. Mr. Allen has exerted himself in the House to persuade a Recall of the Petition, but as far as I can

8. The fourth group of words italicized in this document was inserted above the printed line, with a caret at the point of insertion.
9. The third group of words italicized was similarly inserted above the line in place of the printed word "our," which was struck through.
1. The witnesses were probably: the former Molly Yeldhall, wife of one Pitts, who had owned property in Philadelphia, which was subject to a mortgage held by Joseph Grant of Boston (above, V, 16; X, 250–1); and Jenny Parker, daughter of James Parker, secretary and comptroller of the Post Office. She later married Gunning Bedford, Jr. (1747–1812), a delegate to the Federal Constitutional Convention of 1787. *DAB.*
2. The signature is nearly indecipherable but appears to be as given here. Isaac Jones was justice of the peace for Philadelphia Co. from 1757 until his death in 1773, and mayor, 1767–69. 2 *Pa. Arch.*, IX, 728–31, 748; *Pa. Gaz.*, Oct. 30, 1773.
3. Not found.

perceive, without the least Effect.[4] The Bugbears he would frighten us with, are rather laught at. No Concessions, however, on the Part of the Proprietaries have yet been propos'd to us.[5] This per Packet. I shall write you more fully by Budden, who sails on Sunday next.[6] With great Respect, I am, Dear Sir, Your most obedient humble Servant   B FRANKLIN

Addressed: To / Richard Jackson, Esqr / Inner Temple / London / via N. York / per Packet

Endorsed: from Phila: under Mr Franklin's Cover to Alexr. Colden 20 Sept 1764 Benjn. Franklin Esqr.

4. See above, pp. 327–8. At the short September session of the Assembly only one matter relating to the petition to the King appeared on the minutes. On August 10 some of the "principal Inhabitants" of Lancaster Co. had presented an address to their representative Isaac Saunders (one of the minority members) praising his "spirited and disinterested *Opposition*" to the petition and the loss of privileges it might entail. The address attacked the Assembly's proceedings as "the Offspring of Precipitation and Warmth, rather than of mature Deliberation and cool Judgment." Saunders had replied in similar language and expressed the hope that God would protect the people of Pa. "from their *domestick* as well as *foreign* Foes." *Pa. Jour.,* Aug. 16, 1764, printed both documents. On September 15 the Assembly appointed a committee to "draw up a Justification of the Conduct of this House against the Misrepresentations" in the address and reply. The day after BF wrote the present letter the committee reported, severely criticizing Saunders for failing "to inform his Constituents truly of the public Business and Resolutions of the past Sitting." The report quoted in full the resolution on instructions to Richard Jackson regarding the protection of the colony's privileges. The House took no further action on the matter. *Votes,* 1763–64, pp. 99, 102–3.

5. Governor Penn and his associates had kept secret the Proprietors' directions to accept the Assembly's interpretation of the conditions laid down in the order in council of Sept. 2, 1760. See above, pp. 213–14 n.

6. *Pa. Gaz.,* Sept. 27, 1764, reported from N.Y. that the *Harriot* packet boat had sailed on the 23d "with the Mail for Falmouth." The same issue recorded the clearance from Philadelphia of the *Philadelphia Packet,* Capt. R. Budden, for London. Presumably it carried BF's letter to Jackson of September 25.

Benjamin Franklin and John Foxcroft

to Anthony Todd

Draft:[7] American Philosophical Society

Sir   Philada. Sept. 21. 1764

We wrote you pretty fully of the 4th. Instant,[8] and sent our Letters to New York to be ready for the Packet[9] that has been some time expected. She did not arrive till the 17th. and we have now just receiv'd yours of July 14.[1] with Copies of your preceding Letters[2] and Duplicates of the Papers that accompanied them. Those that were proper for Publication we had before caused to be inserted in all the Newspapers on the Continent,[3] and given Directions to all our Officers strictly to observe and execute the several Acts of Parliament therein referr'd to.

We are concern'd that our Account of the State of the Office was delay'd so long beyond our Intentions. The Reasons will appear in our Letters.[4] Accidents, Sickness, and our Distance from each other contributed to that Delay. But we have now settled the Offices in so good a Way that we hope to have the Accounts rendred to us more regularly; and that such a long hazardous Journey will not be again necessary for some Years, and the latter Inconvenience will be removed by our living hereafter nearer together.

7. In BF's hand.

8. This letter has not been found, but it was probably the "Account of the State of the Office" mentioned in the next paragraph, which BF and Foxcroft had composed as a result of their long postal inspection journey to New England in the summer of 1763 (above, x, 276–9), and which Todd had been expecting since January 1764; see above, p. 38.

9. Probably the *Harriot. Pa. Jour.*, Sept. 27, 1764.

1. Not found.

2. The last letter from Todd that has been found is his of Aug. 13, 1763, to BF and Foxcroft; see above, x, 322–4.

3. *Pa. Gaz.*, July 26, 1764, published Todd's order of April 20, 1764, regulating the delivery of letters carried by ship in accordance with the Post Office Act of 1710, and his order of May 9, 1764, prohibiting "unlawful Collections and Conveyances" of mail. These were followed in the same issue by a notice dated July 10, 1764, signed by James Parker, Secretary, "by Command of the D. Post-Master General," requiring strict obedience to the law.

4. BF's letter to Todd of Jan. 16, 1764 (above, p. 20) suggests that one reason his and Foxcroft's report was delayed was that Foxcroft had to settle postal affairs in Virginia and Maryland before writing.

The Rule of Charging 2*d.* or 16 grains of Silver on every Letter coming from on Ship board, has been observ'd in America we believe from the first Establishment of the Office here. Mr. Franklin, who is now by much the oldest Officer in America, found it the Practice, [and remembers?] to have seen it in Tables of Rates printed long before his Time.[5] He knows not on what it was originally founded, (being sensible that the Act[6] mentions but a Penny) unless it were on the Considerations that have satisfied him in the Continuance of the Practice, viz.

In America most of the Letters received from on board a Ship, are delivered in the Capital Towns where the Ships arrive. The Law obliges the Office to give a Penny for every Letter coming from on board a Ship.

If the Office demands but a Penny for each such Letter, then the Attendance is given and the Business is transacted for nothing. Nay, for less than nothing; for all the Letters so paid for, not being taken up, the Dead Letters would be so much clear Loss to the Office.

Wherever a Law enjoins a Service, and appoints no Reward, for that Service, the Person who performs the Service in obedience to the Law has a Right to a *Quantum meruit* for the same, from the Person benefited by that Service.

What the Quantum meruit in this Case is, may be gathered from the same Law, which allows a Penny to be taken for the Service of putting a Letter on board a Ship. Now supposing that the Trouble of receiving a Letter and putting the same on board a Ship, is not greater than the Trouble of receiving a Letter from on board a Ship and delivering the same on shore, then the latter Service deserves a Penny as well as the former.

This Penny to the Office, added to the Penny paid the Captain, makes the Twopence to be paid for the Letter.

We knew not but that the same was practis'd in England. It seems now otherwise, by your requiring this Explanation. The Postmaster General will direct us how we are to proceed for the future. But should a Law more effectually enforce the Delivery of Ship Letters by all Captains to the Office hereafter, if we pay a

5. BF and Foxcroft had continued the charge in a table of rates which they published around the end of 1763; see above, X, 419.

6. The Post Office Act of 1710 (9 Anne, c. 10).

Penny for each, and deliver them for the same we conceive the Advantage to the Office will be much less than we think it ought to be, and than it may be here without occasioning any Complaint.[7] And this brings us to Amendments we would propose to the present Office Laws, on considering the Clauses you have sent us.[8]

We think, that for the Security of Correspondence, as well as for the Advantage of the Revenue, ALL Ship Letters should be delivered to the Deputy of the Post Master General in the Port where the Ship arrives, those belonging to Owners of the Vessel or of any Part of the Cargo, as well as others:[9] because the Exception of the former, makes it difficult to detect and hazardous to prosecute upon the Act; since, tho' we may prove the Captain or Passengers delivering Letters, it is not easy to prove that these Letters did not relate to the Cargo.

That for every Ship Letter or Packet of Letters, deliver'd in the Town or Port where the Ship arrives and not sent by Post, should be taken and receiv'd Two pence. The Addition of a Penny for every additional Letter in a Packet and 4 pence for every ounce after the first might perhaps appear too high in some Pacquets. And yet we think some such Addition should be made, to prevent Peoples Pacqueting their Letters to avoid Paying.[1]

That a Certificate from the Postmaster of his having receiv'd the Ship Letters should be produced by the Captain to the collector or Naval Officer, before he is permitted to break Bulk.

The Inland Postages directed by the Act, do not seem to be well proportioned. For Instance, A Letter from New York to any Place (generally) within Sixty English Miles is fourpence; and yet when particular Places are named, A Letter from New York to Perth Amboy (which is but 30 Miles) is Six pence. And so in other Instances. Then the added Postages practis'd here, which were ex-

7. BF and Foxcroft had proposed such a law to Todd on June 10, 1763, and the British postmasters general, apparently at Todd's instigation, supported it, with the result that the Post Office Act of 1765 (5 Geo. III, c. 25) contained clauses designed to improve the delivery of letters from ships. See above, x, 280–1, 322, and this volume, pp. 39–41.

8. Todd had apparently submitted to BF and Foxcroft's consideration clauses that were intended to be inserted in the Post Office Act of 1765.

9. The act of 1765 so stipulated.

1. This and the following suggestion were not accepted.

plain'd in Mr. Franklin's Letter of April 12.[2] and seem authoriz'd by the Act, do not appear equal or reasonable. For Instance, A Letter from Boston to New York (near 300 miles) is One Shilling; and if it is but One [hundred miles] further viz. to Philadelphia, it pays Nine pence more; which is out of Proportion. We would therefore propose, that instead of the many different Rates of Postage between different Places named in the Act, one general Rule should be made, in the new Act without naming any Places,[3] viz

All Letters and Packets carried by Post in America to any Place not exceeding Sixty English Miles	S[4]	4 pence
	D	8 pence
	T	12 pence
	Ounce	1s. 4d.
[To any Place exceeding] 60 Miles and not exceeding 100 Miles	S.	6 pence
	D.	12 pence
	T.	18 pence
	Ounce	2s.
And to any Place exceeding 100 Miles and not exceeding 200 Miles	S.	8 pence
	D	16
	T.	2s.
	O	2s. 8d.
And so the same Addition, of two pence, in every additional 100 Miles.		

This Rule would make the Postage from New York to Charlestown, much what it is now by the Act, viz. 18 Pence it being about 900 Miles. And it would moderate most of the other Postages, which are now generally deem'd too high and complain'd of; it would probably occasion more Letters to be sent per Post, so that the Revenue might gain in the Number of Letters more than is abated in the Price: And such an Abatement would be grateful to the People, and tend to lessen the Murmuring that might be occasion'd by the greater Strictness with regard to Ship Letters. And as some late Acts of Parliament restraining the Trade of the Colonies have seem'd severe to the Merchants here,[5] an Act that has the Appearance of Lenity and operates to the Ease of Commerce

2. Not found.

3. The act of 1765 incorporated BF and Foxcroft's mileage-rate rule. For a table showing the effect of this change on the rates between N.Y. and places named in the act of 1710, see below, p. 536.

4. Single letter; "D" meant double letter, and "T," triple letter.

5. BF is referring in particular to the Sugar Act.

and Correspondence, may be of use to conciliate Minds to those public Measures, and diminish Discontents.

Thus we have, with the Freedom requir'd of us, given our Sentiments; which we submit to our Superiors. And are, with great Esteem, Sir, Your most obedient humble Servants   B. F.

J. F.

[On additional pages in Franklin's hand:[6]]

For All Letters and Pacquets carried by Post in America any Distance not exceeding Sixty English Miles	Single	4 pence
	D	8
	T	12
	Ounce	1s. 4d.
For all &c. exceeding 60 Miles and not exceeding 100 Miles	Single	6 pence
	D.	12
	T.	1s. 6d.
	Ounce	2s.
For all &c. exceeding 100 Miles and not exceeding 200 Miles	Single	8 pence
	D.	1s. 4d.
	T.	2s.
	Ounce	2s. 8d.

With the like Addition of 2 pence in every additional 100 Miles

The Bulk of the Postage of N. America arises out of the 3 great trading Towns Philadelphia, New York and Boston.

By the above proposed Rates, the present Postage between those Places[7] will be abated as follows,

	Present Postage	future	Abated
Between Philadelphia and New York	9 pence	6 pence	3 pence
[*Struck through:* Between New York and Boston	1s. 0d.	10 pence	2
Between Philadelphia and Boston	1s. 9d.	1s. 0d.	9 pence

These Abatements are very considerable being between 30 and 40 per Cent. will be thought very favourable by the Trading People, and I fear that if the Rates are reduc'd so much lower as to be equal with the Rates in England, the Posts can hardly be supported in a Country where Labour and Service of all kinds is so much dearer; at least some of the new Stages, which at present do not

6. The repetitive character of what follows suggests that BF had prepared these pages in advance as memoranda for use in the letter he and Foxcroft were planning to write.

7. For a comprehensive table of postal rates between the post offices of North America, compiled about the end of 1763, see above, X, 417–20.

produce sufficient to defray themselves, but are supported by the old ones, must be dropt; for tho' the Number of Letters will undoubtedly encrease, yet I doubt their encreasing in so great a proportion, and I apprehend that 'tis more for the Advantage of the Trading People to keep those new Stages up, than it will be to make a farther Abatement in Postage.

The Offices in America have sometimes employ'd Letter Carriers to deliver Letters in the Towns and directed them to demand a penny for delivering each Letter; but the Right to demand such Penny above the Postage being frequently disputed and complain'd of as an Imposition and the Practice on that Account occasionally dropt, the Deputy Postmaster General some time since directed the Delivery of Letters in the several Towns gratis. This however is not generally comply'd with, being found very burthensome to the Office: but the Inconvenience may perhaps be remedied either in the Penny post Clause, or by a Clause for the purpose.

It is the Opinion of many People here that lowering the Rates of Postage would encrease the Revenue.

Suppose a General Rule, as the Distances are pretty well known.

All Letters and Packets carried by Post to any Place not exceeding Sixty English Miles	Single	4 pence
	Double	8 pence
	Treble	12 pence
	Ounce	1s. 4d.
All &c. exceeding 60 Miles and not exceeding 100 Miles	Single	6 pence
	D	12
	T	16
	O	2s.
And to any Place exceeding One Hundred Miles and not exceeding 200 Miles	S	8 pence
		16
		24
		32
And the same Addition of two Pence in every additional Hundred Miles		

Letters to be deliver'd to the Postmaster and his Certificate to be produced to the Custom House Officer before he be permitted to break Bulk.

Pennsylvania Assembly:
Instructions to Richard Jackson

Printed in *Votes and Proceedings of the House of Representatives,* 1763–1764 (Philadelphia, 1764), pp. 105–6.

A quorum of the Assembly gathered on September 11 to begin the short final session before its dissolution. The next day Speaker Franklin laid before the House an extract from the journal of the Massachusetts House of Representatives, June 13, 1764, together with the letter to himself from that body's committee, June 25, regarding the Sugar Act and the proposed Stamp Act (above, pp. 242–3). The Pennsylvania Assembly ordered these papers to "lie on the Table for the Perusal and Consideration of the Members." On the 18th the House took up the matter and, "after some Time spent therein," appointed a committee of nine members[8] to draw up instructions to Richard Jackson "to use his utmost Endeavours, in Conjunction with the Agents for the other Colonies," to secure a repeal of the Sugar Act, and to remonstrate against a stamp duty and any other intended taxes "repugnant to our Rights and Privileges as Freemen and British Subjects."[9] The committee reported its draft on September 22; "after some Alteration," the Assembly agreed to it, and Franklin signed it as speaker. On the 28th he wrote to the Massachusetts committee reporting on his Assembly's actions (below, pp. 365–6).

These instructions heavily emphasize the rights of the colonies to tax themselves. While not going quite so far as to deny explicitly the authority of Parliament to impose taxes upon them, the document comes very close to doing so. It points out that it would be "as great Injustice" to deprive the Pennsylvanians of rights conferred by their charter "as to disfranchise the People of England" of their rights under Magna Carta. It also insists that Parliament, in which the colonies were unrepresented, could not "lay such Taxes and Impositions with Justice and Equity" upon areas which differed greatly from one another. As events were to show, such an approach to the matter was futile. George Grenville seems to have "dismissed in advance all objections to the authority of Parliament," though he was willing "to listen to any other kind of objections from the colonies," and others in the House of Commons seem to have shared his sentiments.[1] It is doubtful

8. The committee was composed of one member from each of the counties and one from the city. It included the proprietary leader, William Allen, recently returned from England, who had taken his seat on September 11.

9. *Votes,* 1763–64, pp. 95–6, 100.

1. Edmund S. Morgan, "The Postponement of the Stamp Act," 3 *William*

347

whether the members of the Pennsylvania Assembly appreciated the strength of this sentiment, or, if they had, whether they would have modified to any significant degree their instructions to Jackson. One fact remains clear: in Pennsylvania as in several other colonies at about the same time, the issue of constitutional rights of British subjects residing in America was already being raised six months before the actual passage of the Stamp Act.

Sir,   September 22, 1764.

The Representatives of the Freemen of the Province of Pennsylvania, in General Assembly met, having received Information of the Resolutions of the House of Commons respecting the Stamp Duties, and other Taxes, proposed to be laid on the British Colonies, do most humbly conceive, that the Measures proposed as aforesaid, if carried into Execution, will have a Tendency to deprive the good People of this Province of their most essential Rights as British Subjects,[2] and of the Rights granted to them by the Royal Charter of King Charles the Second, and confirmed by Laws of this Province, which have received the Royal Approbation.

That by the said Charter, among other Privileges, the Right of assessing their own Taxes, and of being free from any Impositions but those that are made by their own Representatives, is fully granted to the People of this Province:[3] And, besides, we appre-

---

and Mary Quar., VII (1950), 356. Edward Montagu, agent for Virginia, quoted Grenville as telling the House of Commons that he "hoped that the power and sovereignty of Parliament, over every part of the British dominions, for the purpose of raising or collecting any tax, would never be disputed." He called for the sense of Parliament, and "The Members interested in the plantations expressed great surprise that a doubt of that nature could ever exist." *Ibid.*

2. These last words and some of those in the next paragraph are taken directly from the Massachusetts committee's letter to BF.

3. Only Pa., Md., Conn., R.I., and Mass. still operated in 1764 under royal charters, hence these were the only colonies that could claim possible exemption from parliamentary taxation on the basis of such charters. Actually, the charter to William Penn clearly reserved certain parliamentary rights to taxation of the inhabitants of the colony. Sect. 20 covenanted that no "Imposition, Custom or other Taxation, Rate or Contribution whatsoever" should be placed upon them "for their Lands, Tenements, Goods or Chattels within the said Province, or in and upon any Goods and Merchandizes within the Province, or to be laden or unladen within the Ports or Harbours of the

hend that this is the indubitable Right of all the Colonists as Englishmen.

That the said Charter and Laws are certainly of the same Validity, with respect to the Rights thereby granted to the People here, as the Laws and Statutes of England, with regard to the Privileges derived under them, to the People in England; and that it appears to us as great Injustice to divest the People of this Province of the Privileges held under the former, as to disfranchise the People of England of those Rights they claim under *Magna Charta* itself, or any other Law in Great-Britain.

That the Colonists here have paid a valuable Consideration to the Crown for the said Charter and Laws, by planting and improving a Wilderness, far distant from their Mother Country, at a vast Expence, and the Risque of many Lives from the savage Inhabitants, whereby they have greatly increased the Trade and Commerce of the Nation, and added a large Tract of improved Country to the Crown, without any Aid from, or Expence to Great-Britain in the said Settlement.[4]

These, with other Reasons, and in particular the Information we have received, that the Ministry are desirous of consulting the Ease, Interest and good Will of the Colonies,[5] prevail on us to

---

said Province, unless the same be with the Consent of the Proprietary, or chief Governor, or Assembly, or by Act of Parliament in England." *The Charters of the Province of Pensilvania and City of Philadelphia* (Phila., 1741), p. 12. How far this clause would affect such impositions as stamp duties would be a matter of legal definition.

4. BF developed this point in a letter signed "N.N.," printed in the *Gazetteer,* Jan. 11, 1766, where he pointed out that, with the exceptions of Georgia and Nova Scotia, none of the colonies "were settled at the expence of *any money* granted by parliament," that the settlers had established the colonies "at the expence of their own private treasure and blood:—That these territories thus became *new* dominions *of the crown,* settled under royal charters, that formed their several governments and constitutions, on which the parliament was *never consulted;* or had the *least participation.*" Verner W. Crane, ed., *Benjamin Franklin's Letters to the Press 1758–1775* (Chapel Hill, [1950]), p. 48. He said much the same thing again in 1770; *ibid.*, p. 177.

5. Quoted in the Mass. House of Representatives committee's letter to BF (cited in the headnote) from Jasper Mauduit's letter of March 13, 1764, to that House. Morgan, 3 *William and Mary Quar.*, VII, 357; Edmund S. and Helen M. Morgan, *The Stamp Act Crisis Prologue to Revolution* (Chapel Hill, [1953]), p. 55. Mauduit and the Mass. committee had written "the Ease, the Quiet, and the Goodwill."

hope, that an humble and dutiful Remonstrance to the Parliament, pointing out the Inconsistency of those Measures with the Rights and Privileges thus purchased, and solemnly granted and confirmed to the People of this Colony, may have its Use in prevailing on the Parliament to lay aside their Intention of imposing Stamp Duties, or laying any other Impositions or Taxes whatsoever on the Colonies, which may be destructive of their respective Rights.

The House of Assembly therefore most earnestly request you will exert your utmost Endeavours with the Ministry and Parliament to prevent any such Impositions and Taxes, or any other Impositions or Taxes on the Colonists from being laid by the Parliament, inasmuch as they neither are or can be represented, under their present Circumstances, in that Legislature: Nor can the Parliament, at the great Distance they are from the Colonies, be properly informed, so as to enable them to lay such Taxes and Impositions with Justice and Equity, the Circumstances of the Colonies being all different one from the other.

This we request you will do, either by an humble Address to the British Parliament, or in any other Manner, which to you shall appear to promise the most Success.

But as it may be contended, that there is a Necessity that some Plan should be formed to oblige the Colonies, in Time of Danger, to grant the necessary Aids to the Crown, and to contribute to their general Defence, and it may be expected that some Remedy should be proposed, on the Part of the Colonies, adequate to these Purposes, you will be pleased to take the proper Methods of informing the Ministry and Parliament, that we humbly are of Opinion such a Plan may be formed, without destroying or infringing the natural and legal Rights of the Colonies, or affecting those of the Mother Country; that such a Plan has been under the Consideration of this House, and will be transmitted with all Expedition for your Consideration, and which will, as we conceive, fully preserve the Rights of the Crown in America, and the Liberties of the Colonists: This Plan, if approved of, may be established by a temporary Act of Parliament.[6]

6. Nothing in the Mass. letter had suggested that the Ministry would welcome any such substitute plan; perhaps Jackson had hinted at such a possibility in his missing letter to BF of March 10, 1764. In any case, BF had told Jackson, June 25, that he thought he "could propose a better Mode

You will also be pleased to exert your Endeavours to obtain a Repeal, or at least an Amendment, of the Act for regulating the Sugar Trade, which we apprehend must prove extremely detrimental to the Trade of the Continental Colonies in America, particularly in the Prohibition of exporting Lumber to Ireland,[7] and other Parts of Europe, and deeply affect the Interest of the British Merchants and Manufacturers, as it will greatly disable us in making Returns to Britain.

After all in this Letter observed, the Assembly are well aware of the Impossibility, at this Distance, of giving all the proper and necessary Hints on this important Business; but this Difficulty is greatly alleviated by the high Opinion they entertain of your extensive Knowledge in the Affairs of America in general, and of this Province in particular; and of your Integrity and sincere Inclination to serve the Colonies, in which they have the fullest Confidence. Upon the whole, they submit these Affairs entirely to your Management and Discretion, and doubt not but you will conduct every Matter for the Interest of the Colonies in the best Manner possible, wherein perhaps it may not be amiss to unite with the Agents of the other Provinces.[8]

Signed by Order of the House,

BENJAMIN FRANKLIN, Speaker.

---

by far" than a stamp duty (above, p. 237), and it is possible that he had laid his scheme before other members of the Pa. Assembly during the summer. The reference here to the establishment of the Pa. plan by a *temporary* act of Parliament, however, would seem to preclude the theory that the plan under consideration was BF's proposal for a paper currency authorized by Parliament. On October 20, 1764, the new Assembly withdrew this part of the instructions to Jackson because a single legislature, acting alone, could not well draw up such a plan "from the disjointed State and separate Interests of the different Colonies." 8 *Pa. Arch.*, VII, 5678–9.

7. For BF's objections to this prohibition, see above, p. 235.

8. In the light of the Mass. committee's stress on the desirability of concerted action by the colonial agents and the Pa. Assembly's directions to its drafting committee on the point, the final clause here seems to be a rather hesitant and inadequate instruction to Jackson.

To Peter Collinson

ALS: Pierpont Morgan Library

Dear Friend,   Philada. Sept. 24. 1764

I received your kind Letter of June 29.[9] We hear nothing here of the Proprietary's relenting. If any have it in charge from him to offer Concessions for Peacesake (as we are told from your side the Water they have) they keep them back in hopes the next Election may put the Proprietaries in a Condition not to need the proposing them.[1] A few Days will settle this Point.

I receiv'd the Medal, and have sent it forward to Mr. Elliot.[2]

I shall endeavour to procure you some more of the Natural Buttons as soon as possible.[3] I am glad my Remarks that accompany'd them give you any Satisfaction.

Our Friend John Bartram has sent a very curious Collection of Specimens of all the uncommonly valuable Plants and Trees of North America, to the King. He was strongly persuaded by some to send them thro' the Hands of the Proprietary as the only proper Channel; but I advis'd him not to pass by his old Friend, to whom it must seem a Neglect. He readily concurr'd with my Opinion, and has sent the Box to you.[4] I am assur'd you have Means enough of introducing his Present properly; but as John seem'd willing to have as many Strings as possible to his Bow, for fear of Accidents, I mention'd Dr. Pringle to him, as a good Friend of the Arts, and one who would lend any Assistance in the Matter if necessary. He is Physician to the Queen; and I have, in my Letter hinted the Matter to him;[5] to prepare him if you should think fit to advise

9. Not found.

1. For the secrecy with which Governor Penn and his associates treated the Proprietors' instructions to yield to the Assembly on the principal point of contention concerning the Supply Act, see above, pp. 213–14 n.

2. The Society of Arts had awarded to Jared Eliot a gold medal for his method of extracting iron from black sea sand (above, VI, 176 n; X, 307 n); apparently it had been sent to BF for transmission and, because of Eliot's death in April 1763, BF had sent it to his son Aaron.

3. The pebbles from "Button-mold Bay," of which BF had sent samples to Collinson with a description, April 30, 1764; above, p. 182.

4. Bartram wrote Collinson, Sept. 23, 1764, explaining the shipment and expressing some jealousy of William Young's "sudden preferment," to which BF alludes later in this paragraph. William Darlington, ed., *Memorials of John Bartram and Humphry Marshall* (Phila., 1849), p. 266.

5. BF's letter to Pringle has not been found.

352

with him about it. I wish some Notice may be taken of John's Merit. It seems odd that a German Lad of his Neighbourhood, who has only got some Smatterings of Botany from him, should be so distinguish'd on that Account, as to be sent for by the Queen, and our old Friend, who has done so much, quite forgotten.[6] He might be made happy as well as more useful, by a moderate Pension that would enable him to travel thro' all the New Acquisitions, with Orders to the Governors, and Commanding Officers at the several Outposts, to forward and protect him in his Journeys.[7]

Please to acquaint Mr. Canton that I acknowledge the Receipt of his Letter, and shall write to him shortly.[8] I am, my dear Friend, Yours affectionately   B FRANKLIN

Addressed: To / Peter Collinson Esqr / Gracious Street / London

To William Strahan   ALS: Princeton University Library

Dear Mr. Strahan,   Philada. Sept. 24. 1764
    I wrote to you of the first Instant, and sent you a Bill for £13 and a little List of Books to be bought with it.[9] But as Mr. Becket

6. William Young, Jr. (*c.*1742–1785), born at Kingsessing, Pa., the son of a German immigrant, had gone to So. Car. (possibly accompanying Bartram in 1760) and had been recommended by Dr. Alexander Garden as nurseryman and gardener willing to collect specimens for the London market. He took several trips to England and received an appointment as botanist to the King and Queen in 1765. Later he gained notice in France, and a *Catalogue d'Arbes, Arbustes et Plantes Herbacées d'Amerique, Par M. Yong, Botaniste de Pensylvanie* was published in Paris, 1783. It is reproduced in Samuel N. Rhoads, ed., *Botanica Neglecta. William Young, Jr. (of Philadelphia) "Botaniste de Pensylvanie" and his Long-Forgotten Book* (privately printed, Phila., 1916).

7. Collinson set to work, and with the support of Lord Bute and the Earl (later Duke) of Northumberland, succeeded in April 1765 in having Bartram appointed King's botanist with a salary of £50 per annum. Darlington, *Memorials,* pp. 268–71, 424; Norman G. Brett-James, *The Life of Peter Collinson F.R.S., F.S.A.* (London, [1926]), pp. 135–6.

8. If BF wrote Canton again before his own departure for London in November, the letter has not been found.

9. For BF's letter, see above, pp. 331–4. Notations on a page at the end of Memorandum Book, 1757–1776 record a draft for Strahan for £13 sterling, Sept. 1, 1764, and an undated debit charged to Mrs. Stevenson for this draft, turned over to her as BF suggested later in this paragraph.

has since sent them to me, I hope this will come time enough to countermand that Order. The Money, if you have receiv'd it, may be paid to Mrs. Stevenson, to whom we have wrote for sundry Things.

I thank you for inserting the Messages and Resolutions intire.[1] I believe it has had a good Effect; for a Friend writes me, that "it is astonishing with what Success it was propagated in London by the Proprietaries, that the Resolutions were the most indecent and undutiful to the Crown, &c. so that when he saw them, having before heard those Reports, he could not believe they were the same."[2]

I was always unwilling to give a Copy of the Chapter,[3] for fear it should be printed, and by that means I should be depriv'd of the Pleasure I often had in amusing People with it. I could not however refuse it to two of the best Men in the World, Lord Kaims and Mr. Small,[4] and should not to the third, if he had not been a Printer. But you have overpaid me for the Loss of that Pleasure, by the kind things you have so handsomely said of your Friend in the Introduction.

You tell me, that the Value I set on your political Letters, is a strong Proof that my Judgment is on the Decline.[5] People seldom

1. As BF had asked, March 30, 1764 (above, p. 149), Strahan printed in *London Chron.*, June 12–14 and 14–16, 1764, the messages exchanged between Governor Penn and the Assembly, March 14–24, and the Assembly Resolves of March 24.

2. For "he" in this quotation one should probably read "I," referring to the writer BF is quoting. No letter containing this passage has been found; it may have been part of Peter Collinson's letter of June 29, now lost (see the document immediately above).

3. BF's "Parable against Persecution." For the history of one of BF's most successful hoaxes and its text, see above, VI, 114–24. Strahan had printed it in *London Chron.*, April 14–17, 1764, introducing it as by an (unnamed) friend from North America, who was "as well known throughout Europe for his ingenious discoveries in natural philosophy, as to his countrymen for his sagacity, his usefulness, and activity, in every public-spirited measure, and to his acquaintance for all the social virtues."

4. Henry Home, Lord Kames (above, IX, 5 n), and Alexander Small (above, IX, 110 n).

5. In his letters of May 1 and June 25, 1764, BF had commented enthusiastically on Strahan's "political Letters"; above, pp. 188–9, 242. The opening "You tell me" in this paragraph and the comments in the next suggest a letter from Strahan to BF not now to be found. The Scottish printer had written David Hall, June 30, 1764, "I think you and your Friends greatly overvalue" the political information in his letters. APS.

have Friends kind enough to tell them that disagreable Truth, however useful it might be to know it. And indeed I learn more from what you say than you intended I should; for it convinces me that you have observ'd that Decline for some time past in other Instances, as 'tis very unlikely you should see it first in my good Opinion of your Writings—but you have kept the Observation to yourself—till you had an Opportunity of hinting it to me kindly under the Guise of Modesty in regard to your own Performances. I will confess to you another Circumstance that must confirm your Judgment of me, which is, that I have of late fancy'd myself to write better than ever I did; and farther, that when any thing of mine is abridg'd in the Papers or Magazines, I conceit that the Abridger has left out the very best and brightest Parts. These, my Friend, are much stronger Proofs; and put me in Mind of Gil Blas's Patron, the Homily-maker.[6]

I rejoice to hear that Mrs. Strahan is recovering, that your Family in general is well, and that my little Woman in particular is so, and has not forgot our tender Connection.[7] The Enlarging of your House, and the Coach House and Stables you mention, make me think of living with you when I come; for I love Ease more than ever; and, by daily using your Horses, I can be of Service to you and them, by preventing their growing too fat, and becoming restif.

Mrs. Franklin, and Sally, join in best Wishes for you and all yours, with Your affectionate   B FRANKLIN

Dear Sir,[8]

I wrote a few Lines to you by this Opportunity,[9] but omitted desiring you to call on Mr. Jackson of the Temple, and pay him

6. BF could have read Lesage s *Les Aventures de Gil Blas de Santillane* in the original or in Tobias Smollett's translation, *The Adventures of Gil Blas* (London, 1749). The English edition, III, 30–3, narrates the episode in which the Archbishop of Granada asked Gil Blas to warn him of any signs of failing power. After a stroke of apoplexy the archbishop preached such a homily and Gil Blas dutifully told him it was an inferior discourse. The prelate replied that he had never composed a better, for his genius was as strong as ever. He thereupon dismissed his critic, wishing him prosperity and better taste.

7. Strahan had told Hall, June 30, of his wife's improvement in health at Bath. "My little Woman" was the Strahans' younger daughter Peggy, whom BF sometimes referred to affectionately as "my little Wife" (e.g., above, X, 162).

8. This addendum was written sideways in the margin in WF's hand.

9. WF had written the day before with a paragraph which he asked Strahan

for the Copying a Manuscript he sent me, which he paid the Stationer for doing on my Account.[1] Yours affectionately

WM: FRANKLIN

Addressed: To / Mr William Strahan / Printer / Newstreet, Shoe Lane / London.

From Thomas Moffatt[2]   ALS: American Philosophical Society

Sir   Newport Rhode Island Sept 24th 1764.

I return you thanks for sending me Dr. Heberdens method of inoculating the small pox of which perhaps to you it may not be necessary to say that it bears every mark of Jud[g]ment candour and benevolence.[3] The attention and regard shewn to this treatise in New England by the Authority and these in practise especially at Boston lately[4] will to some very well account for the use of mercury not being yet known or introducd into Britain in inoculation of the small pox.[5] At the Anniversary meeting of the university

---

to print in the *Chronicle* as "An extract of a letter from an officer at Philadelphia." The paragraph compared the "peace and tranquility" of the neighboring royal provinces with "the utmost anarchy and confusion" prevailing in proprietary Pennsylvania. Harmony would not be restored "unless a change of government should ensue." The "Officer" continued by reviewing the "iniquitous terms" upon which Governor Penn had insisted as the price for approving a bill granting "an Aid to his Magesty." The present was the ideal time for the Crown to take over the province. *PMHB,* XXXV (1911), 439–40. Strahan printed the paragraph, with the proposed caption, in *London Chron.,* Nov. 8–10, 1764.

1. The manuscript is unidentified, but WF wrote Strahan later that the charge had been about £27. *PMHB,* XXXV (1911), 444.

2. On Moffatt, see above, p. 191 n.

3. No letter from BF to Moffatt accompanying the Heberden pamphlet has been found. For BF's preface to William Heberden, *Some Account of the Success of Inoculation for the Small-Pox in England and America* (London, 1759), see above, VIII, 281–6.

4. BF had sent copies of the Heberden pamphlet to Jonathan Williams in February 1764 for distribution in the Boston area during a smallpox epidemic there; above, p. 88.

5. Dr. George Muirson of Long Island had developed in 1731 a method of inoculation for smallpox through the use of mercury. This had gained acceptance in N.Y. and N.J. Dr. Benjamin Gale of Killingworth, Conn., son-in-law of Jared Eliot, introduced it into his colony in 1761. He considered

here Our Governor was chosen Chancellor several other Great or Senatorial officers were also elected so that learning makes a great progress and figure here.[6] If I can serve or oblige you here it will be a great pleasure to Sir Your most Obedient Servant

THOMAS MOFFATT

Addressed: To / Benjamin Franklin Esqr / Philadelphia

To Richard Jackson

ALS: American Philosophical Society

Dear Sir   Philada. Sept. 25. 1764

I wrote to you the 1st Instant, and a few Lines last Week per the Packet.[7] Your Favour of June 30. is come to hand.[8] The Assembly rose on Saturday last.[9] Mr. Allen took a great deal of Pains to persuade the House to recall their Petition, but without the least Effect.[1] The Letter sent you by the Committee of Correspondence, with the Petition, being communicated to the House,[2]

---

going to Boston during the epidemic of 1764 to introduce this method there but met with no encouragement to do so. Franklin B. Dexter, ed., *The Literary Diary of Ezra Stiles, D.D., LL.D., President of Yale College* (N.Y., 1901), III, 177–80; Dexter, ed., *Extracts from the Itineraries and Other Miscellanies of Ezra Stiles, D.D., LL.D., 1755–1794, with a Selection from His Correspondence* (New Haven, 1916), p. 488. Mercuric inoculation seems not to have been practiced in Great Britain at this time.

6. The meeting to organize the College of Rhode Island (now Brown University) took place on Sept. 5, 1764. Governor Stephen Hopkins was elected chancellor. Hopkins (1707–1785), whom BF had first met as a fellow delegate to the Albany Congress in 1754 (above, v, 346), held many public offices in R.I. and was elected governor in most of the years between 1755 and 1768. He was a member of the First and Second Continental Congresses and, with BF, was a signer of the Declaration of Independence. His tastes were literary and scientific and he was active in several projects for the advancement of the cultural life of his community. *DAB.*

7. See above, pp. 326–31, 339–40.

8. Not found.

9. September 22.

1. BF had said the same thing in his letters of September 1 and 20, but because no formal vote relating to a recall took place, the minutes make no mention of Allen's efforts.

2. The Assembly had directed its Committee of Correspondence, May 28, to lay before the House at its next sitting "a minute Account of their Proceedings" in instructing Jackson on the petition to the King. *Votes, 1763–64,*

he fell into a violent Passion about that Part of it which says, that while the Judges are appointed by the Proprietor during his Pleasure, the People have no Security of an impartial Administration of Justice; this he took as a direct Attack upon his Character as a Judge, and would construe it so, tho' by no means intended, exposing himself not a little by the unreasonableness of his Anger. The new Election comes on in a few Days, in which, 'tis thought by those who speak to me, very little Change will be made.[3] But as at present only one Party comes about me, I can form no certain Judgment.

Before the House rose, they, in settling the Incidental Charges, order'd a Certificate for Seven Hundred Pounds Currency due to you for your Salary, being the Sum necessary to purchase Bills for £400 Sterling.[4] This Certificate is in my Hands, and I shall receive the Cash for you out of the first Money rais'd to discharge Publick Debts.

I think they make Terms of Granting Lands rather hard.[5] But however, if I am engag'd in the Grant you mention, I will do my

---

p. 87. Apparently the committee did so, but the *Votes* do not record any such report. Allen told Thomas Penn, Sept. 25, 1764, that on his motion the committee laid its letter to Jackson before the House "last night" (he must have meant the 22d, for the Assembly adjourned that day) and that it "contained pretty near the substance of their mad resolves." Penn Papers, Hist. Soc. Pa.

3. See below, pp. 390–4.

4. *Votes,* 1763–64, p. 113, lists the "incidental Charges" for which certificates were prepared, allowed by the Assembly, and signed by BF as speaker at the end of the session, including an entry: "To Richard Jackson, Esq; Agent for the Province in London, two Years Salary of £200 Sterling, *per Annum,* at 75 *per Cent* £750." The discrepancy of £50 in this arithmetic is not explained; if the exchange was 75 percent, BF's figure of £700 currency was correct.

5. In the spring of 1764 Jackson had expressed a hope of interesting BF in a grant of land in Nova Scotia and BF had been receptive to the idea; above, pp. 186–7. Jackson was one of 23 men in Great Britain who received large grants there in June and July 1764. Of these, 19, including Jackson, received 20,000 acres each; the others lesser amounts. General instructions of March 16, 1764, to Montagu Wilmot, the new governor of Nova Scotia, extended to that province new and more stringent requirements of occupation and improvement of land, which had been included the year before in instructions to the governors of Quebec and the Floridas. *Acts Privy Coun., Col.,* IV, 579–80, 815–16; Leonard W. Labaree, ed., *Royal Instructions to British Colonial Governors 1670–1776* (N.Y., [1935]), II, 528–32, 695.

Endeavour to forward the Settlement, by going to the Spot my self, examining all Advantages, and encouraging the People by Accounts of them, &c. I very much like the Partners.[6]

My Son happens to be with me, and desires his respectful Compliments to you. Mr. Galloway also desires his, and acknowledges the Receipt of your Letter per last Ship, and will write soon.

Nothing is now talk'd of all over America, but Frugality and Oeconomy, abating the Use of West-India and English Luxuries, particularly the former.[7] Our Papers are all full of these Discourses. I send you some Specimens of them. They will have some Effect, but not so much as the Writers expect from them. Habits are not easily changed. And as to Cloathing ourselves with our own Wool, 'tis impossible. Our Sheep have such small Fleeces, that the Wool of all the Mutton we eat will not supply us with Stockings. However, as we cannot, under the present Restrictions of our Trade make Pay for so much as we us'd to do, Necessity will enforce Frugality, and oblige us to use less of your Goods, or such as are coarser in kind. I am, dear Sir, with the greatest Respect Your most obedient humble Servant   B FRANKLIN

R. Jackson Esqr.

Endorsed: 25th Sept. 1764 Benjn. Franklin Esqr

6. This paragraph suggests that BF had no real expectation at this time that he would be leaving for England later in the fall to prosecute the Assembly's petition to the King. But as early as the previous spring WF seemed to think his father would be going to England soon. To William Strahan, May 1, June 18, 1764, *PMHB*, XXXV (1911), 436, 438. What individuals Jackson had mentioned to BF as prospective partners in the Nova Scotia grant has not been determined.

7. The passage of the Sugar Act of 1764, which laid burdensome restrictions on colonial trade, and the Currency Act of the same year, which seriously curtailed the colonial medium of exchange, aggravated the already noticeable post-war depression in America. Appeals for frugality and prophecies of a boycott of British goods were common in the newspapers in the summer and autumn of 1764, several of these probably intended, at least in part, as warnings to Great Britain of a sharp reduction in the colonial market which would follow if the unpopular acts were allowed to stand. Edmund S. and Helen M. Morgan, *The Stamp Act Crisis Prologue to Revolution* (Chapel Hill, [1953]), pp. 29–33. The preface to *Poor Richard Improved* for 1765 suggested some expedients the colonists might adopt to avoid ruinous importations from outside.

To the Freemen of Pennsylvania

Printed broadside: Library Company of Philadelphia; draft (fragment):
American Philosophical Society[8]

Governor Penn had asked the Assembly for a militia bill on Feb. 4,
1764, and the House sent him one on the 28th. After conferring with
his Council the governor returned the bill on March 12 with a series
of proposed amendments, but when the House considered the matter on
the 17th it took no formal action on his proposals. In the "Necklace
of Resolves" adopted on March 24, four resolutions (nos. 17–20) explained briefly the Assembly's objections to Penn's amendments, and
in Franklin's "Explanatory Remarks," March 29, he elaborated on the
first of these objections.[9]

Penn made his initial request at the time when the Paxton Boys
were beginning their march on Philadelphia, and he seems at the moment to have wanted the bill only as a means of dealing with civil
disorder.[1] The men who were creating that disorder came from the
frontier counties. After the Paxton Boys had gone home and the immediate threat was ended, however, it was easy for Penn and his supporters to cite the Assembly's failure to pass an acceptable militia bill
as another illustration of the Quaker party's refusal to adopt any con-
structive measure for the general protection of the colony. The most
vehement complaints of the Assembly's "do-nothing" attitude in matters of defense came from the frontier counties. In the election campaign
of 1764 the proprietary party was therefore able, paradoxically enough,
to use the failure of the militia bill as an argument for political support
from the very areas that had first provoked Penn into asking for the bill.

Franklin and his friends were obviously sensitive to the criticism.
What particular attack led him to produce this broadside as a defense

8. The surviving portion of the draft (in BF's hand) consists of the final
page only; it contains the second half of the next to last paragraph and the
whole of the final one. Someone used the blank part of this page to practice
fine penmanship; it was probably Sarah Franklin (aged 21 in 1764), for the
name "Sally" appears twice, and "Franklin" three times, along with other
words carefully written.

9. See above, pp. 74–5, 122, 130–1, 141–2.

1. His message to the Assembly of February 4 asked for a militia act because the security of the government was endangered, the British regulars
guarding the friendly Indians might be inadequate to protect them, and those
troops would soon be ordered away in any case. A militia act, he said, was
"the only natural and effectual Means of preserving the public Tranquility,
and enabling the civil Power to enforce the Laws, and vindicate the Honour
of the Government." *Votes*, 1763–64, p. 43.

of the Assembly's rejection of the governor's amendments is not certainly known. It is possible, as the opening lines suggest, that some deputation of citizens waited upon him with a specific request for a statement. More probably, he adopted this form as a convenient way of presenting his reply to one of the charges generally circulating among the voters during the final days of the campaign. He may have been moved to this last contribution to the debate by a note appended to an unsigned address "To the Freeholders and Electors Of the Province of Pennsylvania" printed in a Supplement to the *Pennsylvania Journal*, Sept. 27, 1764. Specifically charging Galloway and Franklin, "these pretended Sticklers for Liberty," with a desire to have regiments of British regulars stationed in the city and province, the writer declared that these men "would dragoon you into their Measures had they sufficient Power, tho' they are even now alarming you with groundless apprehensions of a Militia in order to promote their own purposes."

To the Freemen
of Pennsylvania

Gentlemen,   Philadelphia, September 28, 1764.

Your Desire of knowing how the Militia Bill came to fail in the last Assembly, shall immediately be comply'd with.

As the Governor press'd hard for a Militia Law, to secure the internal Peace of the Province, and the People of this Country had not been accustomed to Militia Service, the House, to make it more generally agreeable to the Freeholders, form'd the Bill so as that they might have some Share in the Election of the Officers, to secure them from having absolute Strangers set over them, or Persons generally disagreeable.

This was no more, than that every Company should chuse, and recommend to the Governor, three Persons for each Office of Captain, Lieutenant, and Ensign; out of which three, the Governor was to commission one that he thought most proper, or which he pleased, to be the Officer. And that the Captains, Lieutenants, and Ensigns, so commissioned by the Governor, should in their respective Regiments, chuse and recommend three Persons for each Office of Colonel, Lieutenant-Colonel, and Major; out of which three, the Governor was to commission one, which ever he pleased, to each of the said Offices.[2]

2. BF's Militia Act of 1755, the first ever passed in the province, had provided for the election of company officers by the men and their appointment

The Governor's Amendment to the Bill in this Particular, was, to strike out wholly this Privilege of the People, and take to himself the sole Appointment of all the Officers.

The next Amendment was to aggravate and enhance all the Fines. A Fine that the Assembly had made One Hundred Pounds, and thought heavy enough, the Governor required to be Three Hundred Pounds. What they had made Fifty Pounds, he required to be One Hundred and Fifty. These were Fines on the Commission'd Officers for Disobedience to his Commands; but the Non Commission'd Officers, or common Soldiers, who, for the same Offence, the Assembly propos'd to fine at Ten Pounds, the Governor insisted should be fin'd Fifty Pounds.[3]

These Fines, and some others to be mention'd hereafter, the Assembly thought ruinously high: But when, in a subsequent Amendment, the Governor would, for Offences among the Militia, take away the Trial by Jury in the common Courts, and required, that the Trial should be by a Court Martial, compos'd of Officers of his own sole appointing, who should have Power of sentencing even to *Death;* the House could by no Means consent thus to give up their Constituents Liberty, Estate, and Life itself, into the absolute Power of a Proprietary Governor; and so the Bill failed.[4]

That you may be assur'd, I do not misrepresent this Matter, I shall give you the last mention'd Amendment (so call'd) at full

---

by the governor, allowing him only the right of a choice of two substitute nominees in case he rejected the men's first candidate. The company officers were to elect regimental officers under a similar system. Above, VI, 270–1. The act had been disallowed in 1756 with this arrangement cited as one of its defects. *Pa. Col. Recs.*, VII, 274–5, 276–8. For BF's probable familiarity with the system of elected militia officers in some of the New England colonies and for his defense of the 1755 provisions, see above, VI, 268 n, 298–9.

3. The act of 1755 did not specify the amounts of fines which might be levied. After the governor and the regimental officers had drawn up articles of war and the men had voluntarily subscribed to them, courts-martial might impose such "Pains, Penalties, Punishments and Forfeitures" upon offenders as the articles prescribed. Above, VI, 271–2.

4. The act of 1755 made no provision for trial of militiamen by civil courts; the fact that the officers who would compose the courts-martial had been elected was presumably thought to be a sufficient safeguard against arbitrary sentences.

SEPTEMBER 28, 1764

Length; and for the Truth and Exactness of my Copy I dare appeal to Mr. Secretary Shippen.[5]

The Words of the Bill, P. 43. were, "Every such Person so offending, being *legally convicted* thereof," &c. By the Words *legally convicted*, was intended a Conviction after legal Trial, in the common Course of the Laws of the Land. But the Governor requir'd this Addition immediately to follow the Words [convicted thereof] *viz.* "by a Court Martial, shall suffer DEATH, or such other Punishment as *such Court,* by their *Sentence* or *Decree,* shall *think proper* to inflict and pronounce. And be it farther enacted by the Authority aforesaid, That when and so often as it may be necessary, the Governor and Commander in Chief for the Time being, shall appoint and commissionate, under the Great Seal of this Province, sixteen commissioned Officers in each Regiment, with Authority and Power to them or any thirteen of them to hold Courts Martial, of whom a Field Officer shall always be one, and President of the said Court; and such Courts Martial shall and are hereby impowered to administer an Oath to any Witness, in order to the Examination or Trial of any of the Offences which by this Act are made cognizable in such Courts, and shall come before them. Provided always, that in all Trials by a Court-Martial by Virtue of this Act, every Officer present at such Trial, before any Proceedings be had therein, shall take an Oath upon the holy Evangelists, before one Justice of the Peace in the County where such Court is held, who are hereby authorized to administer the same, in the following Words, that is to say; *I A. B. do swear, that I will duly administer Justice according to Evidence, and to the Directions of an Act, intituled,* An Act for forming and regulating the Militia of the Province of Pennsylvania, *without Partiality, Favour or Affection; and that I will not divulge the Sentence of the Court, until it shall be approved of by the Governor or Commander in Chief of this Province for the Time being; neither will I,* upon any Account, *at* any time whatsoever, *disclose or discover the Vote or Opinion of any particular Member of the Court Martial.* So help me God. And no Sentence of Death, or other Sentence, shall be given against any Offender, but by the Concurrence of Nine of the Officers so sworn. And no Sentence passed against any Offender by such

5. Joseph Shippen, Jr., son of Edward Shippen of Lancaster. His grandfather and an uncle were also named Joseph.

363

Court Martial shall be put in Execution, until Report be made of the whole Proceedings, to the Governor or Commander in Chief of this Province for the time being, and his Directions signified thereupon."

It is observable here, that by the common Course of Justice, a Man is to be tried by a Jury of his Neighbours and Fellows, impannelled by a Sheriff, in whose Appointment the People have a Choice; the Prisoner too has a Right to challenge twenty of the Pannel, without giving a Reason, and as many more as he can give Reasons for Challenging; and before he can be convicted, the Jury are to be *unanimous,* they are *all* to agree that he is guilty, and are therefore all accountable for their Verdict. But by this Amendment, the Jury (if they may be so called) are all Officers of the Governor's sole Appointing; and not one of them can be challenged; and tho' a common Militia Man is to be tried, no common Militia Men shall be of that Jury; and so far from requiring *all* to agree, a *bare Majority* shall be sufficient to condemn you. And lest that Majority should be under any Check or Restraint, from an Apprehension of what the World might think or say of the Severity or Injustice of their Sentence, an OATH is to be taken, *never to discover* the Vote or Opinion of any particular Member!

These are some of the Chains attempted to be forg'd for you by Proprietary Faction! Who advis'd the G-----r is not difficult to know. They are the very Men, who now clamour at the Assembly for a Proposal of bringing the Trial of a particular Murder to this County, from another where it was not thought safe for any Man to be either Juryman or Witness; and call it disfranchising the People![6] who are now bawling about the Constitution, and pretending vast Concern for your Liberties! In refusing you the least Means of recommending or expressing your Regard for Persons to be plac'd over you as Officers, and who were thus to be made your Judges in Life and Estate, they have not regarded the Example of the KING, our wise as well as kind Master, who in all his Requisitions made to the Colonies, of raising Troops for their Defence, directed that "the better to facilitate the important Service, the Commissions should be given to such as from their Weight and Credit with the People, may be best enabled to effectuate the

6. See above, pp. 27–8. BF had been a member of the assembly committee that had proposed this legislative change of venue.

Levies."* In establishing a Militia for the Defence of the Province, how could the "Weight and Credit" of Men with the People be better discovered, than by the Mode that Bill directed, *viz.* by a Majority of those that were to be commanded, nominating three for each Office to the Governor of which three he might take the one he lik'd best?

However, the Courts Martial being establish'd, and all of us thus put into his Honour's absolute Power, the Governor goes on to enhance the Fines and Penalties: Thus in Page 49 of the Bill, where the Assembly had propos'd the Fine to be Ten Shillings, the Governor requir'd it to be Ten Pounds: In Page 50, where a Fine of Five Pounds was mention'd, the Governor's Amendment required it to be made Fifty Pounds. And in Page 44, where the Assembly had said, "shall forfeit and pay any Sum, not exceeding Five Pounds," the Governor's Amendment says, "shall suffer DEATH, or such other Punishment, as shall, according to the Nature of the Offence, be inflicted by the *Sentence* of a Court Martial!"

The Assembly's refusing to admit of these Amendments in that Bill, is one of their Offences against the Lord Proprietary, for which that Faction are now abusing them in both the Languages of the Province, with all the Virulence that Reverend Malice can dictate, enforc'd by numberless barefac'd Falshoods, that only the most *dishonest* and *Base* would dare to invent, and none but the most *Weak* and *Credulous* can possibly believe.

To the Massachusetts House of Representatives Committee
Draft: Library of Congress

Gentlemen,   Philada. Sept. 28. 1764

I received duly your Letter of the 25th. of June, directed to the Speaker of our Assembly;[8] but the House not meeting till the tenth

*See Secretary of State's Letters in the printed Votes.[7]

7. The words within quotation marks in the text could serve as a close paraphrase of passages in virtually all letters from secretaries of state calling on the province to raise troops during the Seven Years' War; see for example, *Votes,* 1757–58, p. 50; 1758–59, p. 27.

8. See above, pp. 342–3.

Instant,⁹ I could not sooner acquaint you with their Sentiments on the Matters by you recommended to their Consideration. I have now the Pleasure of informing you, that they concur intirely with your Assembly in the Ends you have in View, and in the Means proposed to obtain them. They have accordingly wrote fully to their Agent on the Subject, and directed him to join with the Agent of your and the other Provinces in the Steps to be taken.¹

I heartily wish them Success, and have the honour of subscribing myself Gentlemen, Your most obedient &c.   B F.

Endorsed: Letter from Boston Assembly 1764²

To Henry Bouquet

Copy:³ British Museum; draft: American Philosophical Society

Dear Sir   Philada: Sept. 30. 1764

I have been so totally ocupied with the Sitting of the Assembly and other urgent Affairs,⁴ that I could not till now do my self the pleasure of writing to you, since the Receipt of your obliging Favours of Aug. 10. and 22. and a subsequent one relating to Broadstreet's Peace,⁵ of which I think as you do.

I thank you cordially for so readily complying with my Request.⁶ Your Letter was quite full and sufficient, and leaves me nothing to desire by way of Addition, except that if any Letter of yours relating to the present Expedition is like to be seen by the Secretary

9. The House was scheduled to meet on September 10, but there was no quorum until the next day.

1. See above, pp. 347–51.

2. On the same page with this endorsement is the beginning of an undated draft of a letter to William Dunlap regarding the Philadelphia postmastership. It reads in full: "Mr. Dunlap, / Sir / The Term of your Commission being expired,". On this subject, see below, pp. 418–22.

3. The entire copy, probably including the signature, appears to be in Sarah Franklin's hand, but the endorsement and the fact that these sheets are among Bouquet's papers, indicate that this is the document he actually received.

4. For the activities of the Assembly during its short September session, see above, pp. 339–40, 347–51, 357–8.

5. For all these letters, see above, pp. 266–7, 321–6.

6. That "in some Letter to me" Bouquet would "express your Sentiments of my Conduct" in supporting the military service. Above, p. 319.

of State,[7] you would take occasion just to mention me as one ready on that and every other Occasion to promote the Service of the Crown. The Malice and Industry of my Adversaries, have, I find, made these Precautions a little necessary.[8]

Your Sentiments of our Constitution are solid and just. I am not sure that the Change now attempted will immediately take place, nor am I very anxious about it. But sooner or later it will be effected. And till it is effected, we shall have little internal Quiet in the Administration of our Publick Affairs.

I have lately receiv'd a Number of new Pamphlets from England and France, among which is a Piece of Voltaire's on the Subject of Relegious Toleration.[9] I will give you a Passage of it, which being read here at a Time when we are torn to Pieces by Factions religious and civil, shows us that while we sit for our Picture to that able Painter, tis no small Advantage to us, that he views us at a favourable Distance.

"Mais que dirons-nous, dit il, de ces pacifiques *Primitifs* que l'on a nommés Quakres par dérision, et qui avec des usages peut-être ridicules, ont été si vertueux, et ont enseigné inutilement la paix aux reste des hommes? Ils sont en Pensilvanie au nombre de cent mille; la Discorde, la Controverse sont ignorees dans l'heureuse patrie qu'ils se sont faite: et le nom seul de leur ville de Philadelphie, qui leur

7. George Montagu Dunk, 2d Earl of Halifax; see above, VIII, 67 n.

8. Thomas Penn was trying to get BF removed as deputy postmaster general. He reported that the ministers were severely criticizing BF and that Lord Hyde would write a warning letter threatening loss of the office unless BF altered his conduct. T. Penn to Benjamin Chew, June 8, and to John Penn, June 8, 1764; J. Penn to T. Penn, Sept. 1, 1764; William Allen to T. Penn, Sept. 25, 1764; all in Penn Papers, Hist. Soc. Pa. No such letter from Hyde to BF has been found.

9. The bibliography of Voltaire's *Traité sur la Tolérance,* which is thought to have been first published in Geneva in late 1763 or early 1764, is, to say the least, complex. Contemporary editions differ in pagination and content, a circumstance that led Bigelow (*Works,* x, 307 n) to assert that "he did not find" the first of the two passages BF quotes here "precisely in any of Voltaire's writings." Both quoted passages are, however, precisely contained in three early editions of the pamphlet which are located in Yale Univ. Lib. None of them indicates a place of publication and one carries no date. With places of publication as suggested on the library catalogue cards, dates of publication (in two instances), total number of pages, and the page locations of the two quoted passages, they are as follows: I. [Amsterdam or La Haye?], n.d., 138 pp., pp. 25, 136–7; II. [Geneva?], MDCCLXIII, 183 pp., pp. 34, 180–1; III. [Paris?], MDCCLXIV, 191 pp., pp. 37, 188.

rapelle a tout moment que les hommes sont freres, est l'exemple et la honte des peuples qui ne connaissent pas encor la tolérance."[1]

The Occasion of his Writing this *Traité sur la Tolérance,* was what he calls "le *Meurtre* de Jean Calas, *commis* dans Toulouse *avec le glaire* [*glaive*] *de la Justice,* le 9me Mars 1762?" There is in it abundance of good Sense and sound Reasoning, mix'd with some of those Pleasantries that mark the Author as strongly as if he had affix'd his Name. Take one of them as a Sample.[2] "J'ai aprens que le Parlement de Toulouse et quelques autres tribunaux, ont une jurisprudence singuliere; ils admettent des quarts, des tiers des sixiémes de preuve. Ainsi, avec six ouindire[*sic*] d'un côte, trois de l'autre, et quatre quarti de présomption, ils forment trois preuves complétes; et sur cette belle demonstration ils vous rouent un homme sans misericorde. Une légère connoissance de l'art de raisonner sufirait pour leur faire prendre une autre méthode. Ce qu'on apelle une demipreuve ne peut être qu'un soupcon: Il n'y a point, à la rigueur, de demi preuve; ou une chose est prouvée, ou elle ne l'est pas; il n'y a point de milieu. Cent mille soupçons réunis ne peuvent pas plus etablir une preuve, que cent mille zéros ne peuvent composer un nombre. Il y a des quarts de ton dans la musique, encor ne les peut-on exécuter; mais, il n'y a ni quart de vérité, ni quart de raisonnement."

I send you one of the Pamphlets, *Jugement rendue dans l'affaire du Canady,*[3] supposing it may be the more agreable to you to see it, as during your War with that Colony you must have been made acquainted with some of the Character concern'd. With the truest Esteem and Affection, I am, Dear Sir, Your most obedient humble Servant   B FRANKLIN

Endorsed:[4] Mr. Franklin 30th Septr. 1764 Received in Janry 1765 Answered 14th March

1. Commenting on this panegyric on the Quakers, a writer in the *Critical Review,* XVIII (Dec. 1764), 413, said: "This assertion is equally ridiculous and false. Pennsylvania is, perhaps, the country in the world that is, at this time, the most torn by civil dissentions, and the strongest instance that exists to prove the impracticability and vanity of the principles of French theorists in government."

2. BF condensed into a single paragraph the following quotations which occupy three paragraphs in the original versions of the pamphlet.

3. This is probably *Jugement rendu souverainement et de dernier ressort, dans l'Affaire du Canada . . . du 10 Décembre 1763* (Paris, 1763).

4. In Bouquet's hand. The answer, mentioned here, has not been found.

Papers from the Election Campaign, 1764

I. Printed in *The Pennsylvania Journal; and Weekly Advertiser*, Sept. 27, 1764, Supplement. II. Broadside: Evans Microprint Edition, 9854, reproduced from an original in University of Pennsylvania Library. III. Photostat, from an original owned, 1929, by T. W. Schreiner, New York City: Yale University Library. IV. Pamphlet: Evans Microprint Edition, 9831, reproduced from an original in New York Public Library.

The election campaign of 1764 and the events and controversies that preceded it brought forth more political "literature" than had appeared in any previous year in Pennsylvania's history. Party lines became sharply drawn, candidates for election to the Assembly were aligned with one faction or another more distinctly than ever before, and supporters of each group rushed to the press with letters to the newspapers, pamphlets, and broadsides, intended to win over the voters to their side and to denounce the leaders of the other party.[5]

Some of the writers managed to stay clear of personalities and to discuss the central issue on its merits: should Pennsylvania at this time continue to seek a change in government to one directly under the Crown, or should it repudiate the petitions already sent to the King asking for the change? As matters stood, however, personalities became quite as important as policies: the seemingly grasping personality of Thomas Penn, for example; that of his nephew, the young Governor, John Penn; and the personalities and behavior of other proprietary officials and spokesmen, such as William Allen, William Smith, and some Presbyterian ministers; or, on the other hand, those of such Assembly leaders as Joseph Galloway and, above all, Benjamin Franklin.

During the last few weeks of the campaign, people, not principles, appear to have emerged as the most important consideration; predictably the writings, carried about from tavern to tavern and distributed from door to door of the householders, focused increasingly on men, individually or as groups. The anonymous writers seem to

---

5. The most extended treatment of this campaign and its partisan writings is J. Philip Gleason, "A Scurrilous Colonial Election and Franklin's Reputation," 3 *William and Mary Quar.*, XVIII (1961), 68–84. In addition to the numerous references cited there, titles of additional writings may be found by consulting the entries for 1764 in Charles Evans, *American Bibliography*, III (Chicago, 1905), and Charles R. Hildeburn, *A Century of Printing Issues of the Press in Pennsylvania 1685–1784* (Phila., 1886). For letters in the newspapers not separately reprinted, the files of *Pa. Gaz.* and *Pa. Jour.* should be examined, either in the originals or in microfilm reproductions. For some of the polemic writings earlier in the year, see John R. Dunbar, ed., *The Paxton Papers* (The Hague, 1957).

have vied with one another as to which could produce the most scurrilous attacks on the characters and the past behavior of their enemies. Sometimes the authors desisted from their attacks just long enough to defend their own leaders, but for the most part the scribblers were merely spurred on to more violent blasts against their opponents.

Writers on the proprietary side considered Franklin vulnerable on several counts, most of which had little or nothing to do with the issue of a change in government. He was, indeed, charged with wanting royal government because he hoped to be made the first governor under the King. But he was also accused of having secured a handsome income for himself while living at public expense as Assembly agent in England, 1757–62.[6] Contrary to the Assembly's orders, he had invested in British stocks the parliamentary grant for Pennsylvania's wartime expenses, and had thereby caused the province a substantial loss when he had to sell the stocks on a falling market.[7] To win over the German voters his opponents industriously circulated his unfortunate statement of 1751 in *Observations Concerning the Increase of Mankind* in which he had called these immigrants "Palatine Boors."[8] And then the fact that he had fathered an illegitimate son (a circumstance which had been no secret in Philadelphia) was sneeringly advanced as a reason for voting against him and his party. A maidservant named Barbara was said to have been William's mother, and Franklin was accused of cheating her of her wages and, when she died, of consigning her body to an unmarked grave.[9]

6. The expenses of £714 10s. 7d. sterling for which he was repaid were, in fact, only those directly connected with his official duties and did not include even the cost of his ocean passages. The Assembly voted him £3000 sterling as salary for his six years' service at the rate of £500 per year. Above, x, 194–7, 206–8.

7. This loss amounted to £3977 9s. 8d. sterling out of a total grant of a little less than £22,000. Above, x, 34–5 n.

8. Above, IV, 234; V, 205.

9. In earlier volumes (I, lxii; III, 474–5 n) the editors indicated their inability to identify the mother of William Franklin. Recently some information on the matter has come to light, but without an indication of the woman's name. Among the Charles Morton Smith Papers, Hist. Soc. Pa., is a MS letter to a London Quaker, Robert Crafton, dated Oct. 9, 1763, from George Roberts, son of BF's good friend Hugh Roberts. He says: "In answer to your hint relative to a Certain Gentleman now acting in a public Station—tis generally Known here his Birth is illegitimate and his Mother not in good Circumstances, but the report of her begging Bread in the Streets of this City is without the least foundation in Truth. I understand some small provision is made by him for her, but her being none of the most agreeable of Women prevents particular Notice being shown, or the Father and Son acknowledg-

To reprint in this volume all the writings on both sides that formed a part of this election campaign—or even only those that referred directly to Franklin—would require an amount of space far in excess of what the plan of this series would warrant. So far as firm evidence can be found, everything that Franklin himself wrote for the public from January through September of 1764 has been included in earlier pages of this volume.[1] It is possible that some of the other writings came from his pen, but careful investigation has established nothing more than a mere possibility in the case of any piece not heretofore reproduced.[2] None of these, therefore, can justifiably be called a real part of the Franklin papers.

Yet to pass over in complete silence this considerable body of material would result in failure to give a true picture of what may well be regarded as the most important election campaign of Franklin's entire career. For this reason a sampling of these writings is presented here—four pieces reproduced in full or in extract, equally divided between the two contending parties. They should convey at least the bitter flavor of the rest.

None of the authors of the documents has been certainly identified,

---

ing any Connection with her. The happy Qualities with which G[overno]r F--k--n is possessed and the Good he may do in his Sphere of Action, entitled him to an equal respect and regard with those of a more illustrious Extraction. His conduct has already overcome the Prejudices of the People so much that his Governorship probably will be easy and prosperous. The People's dislike arose partly from his Parentage, and the Veneration they entertained for the Predecessor made the Change not agreeable." Quoted in the bulletin of Hist. Soc. Pa. announcing the 140th annual meeting to be held March 31, 1965. If Roberts' statement is correct, WF's mother was still living less than a year before the scurrilous charge against BF.

1. With the exception of official documents of the Assembly which BF helped to compose or signed as speaker (all of which have been printed), these papers total seven: *A Narrative of the Late Massacres,* January 20; Petition of the Pennsylvania Freeholders and Inhabitants to the King, March 29; *Explanatory Remarks on the Assembly's Resolves,* March 29; *Cool Thoughts on the Present Situation of Our Political Affairs,* April 12; A Letter from a Gentleman in Crusoe's Island (draft fragment), April?; Preface to Joseph Galloway's *Speech,* August 11; and *To the Freeman of Pennsylvania,* September 28. All seven can be identified either by the survival of drafts or fragments of drafts in BF's hand, or by statements of authorship in his correspondence, or by both.

2. None of the other public writings of this period meets either of the tests of BF's authorship mentioned in the note immediately above. Occasional later attributions of one or another of them to him seem to be based solely on conjecture.

and only the first can be precisely dated. Probably the other three appeared at various times during the last six weeks before the election. Two, one from each side, are entirely in prose. The other two employ, wholly or in part, a literary form introduced into the contest by the prefaces to the printed speeches of Dickinson and Galloway. William Smith had composed an epitaph for William Penn, lauding his services and expressing the Pennsylvanians' gratitude and affection.[3] Franklin had responded in the same "Lapidary Stile" with an epitaph for Thomas Penn, but this one was a scathing denunciation of the man and his actions.[4] These effusions caught the fancy of other writers, and "Lapidary Characters" quickly attained what one of the authors called "a high Vogue." As the two examples reprinted here show, however, the imitators took their lead from Franklin, not from Smith, for they employed the device wholly to attack the men they were memorializing. All these epitaphs were originally printed in the manner in which they might have been carved on stone, with lines of varying lengths, each centered in the appropriate space. As reprinted below, however, they are set in solid lines with diagonals to show where the original line breaks came. It is hoped that this method of reproduction will not lessen unduly the impact of their often libelous words.

I

To the FREEHOLDERS and ELECTORS
Of the Province of PENNSYLVANIA.

FRIENDS and COUNTRYMEN,

The Day is now approaching, when your free Choice is to determine whether this Province is to continue the miserable Seat of Discord, and its admirable Constitution and Charter be at last sacrificed to private Ambition and personal Rancor; or whether, by delegating your Powers to Persons of known Independency, attached to our Constitution, and free from all Party-Animosity, we shall at length be restored to our wonted Peace and Prosperity.

Words would fail me to recount all the self-interested Views and wicked Purposes of a *few* Men who, having been chosen your *Servants,* now aspire to become your perpetual *Masters.* You have too long suffered and bled under their Misconduct to stand in Need of such a Recapitulation. [To provide a parallel the writer here quotes at considerable length from a speech by Memmius recorded

3. See above, p. 298 n.
4. See above, pp. 298–9.

372

by Sallust and indicates that he could apply it "(too closely, alas!) line by line, to our own State!"]

This last Attempt to change our Government and deliver up our *Charter,* had we no other Charge against them, is enough to make the Cup of their political Iniquity run over. It is so base in its Nature and Circumstances, that dropping the Multitude of other Matters against them, I shall confine the Remainder of my Arguments chiefly to this Point.

First then I would observe that it was by pretending a sovereign Regard to our Liberties and Privileges that these men first got themselves recommended to Power. With the Cry of our Constitution and *Charter*-Rights constantly in their Mouths, they fixed themselves in their Seats, and enriched themselves at our Expence. But when they thought they could enrich themselves yet farther, and were become too great for Opposition, their cry became—"down with the Charter and Constitution," as the useless Scaffolding and Lumber about a Building. The Detail of their Conduct in this Matter is worth observing.

By trifling Disputes, industriously and virulently worked up almost beyond a Possibility of Reconciliation, the chief Projector of this Scheme, got himself appointed on an Embassy to England. While he was employed *there,* his trusty Associates *here,* to keep them in humour, had the Management of our publick Treasure, to purchase unjust Laws of a corrupt Governor, each securing to himself a lucrative Post.* Nor did our Treasures suffer less from our

---

*Mr. G-----y is a provincial Commissioner and got a lucrative Office, torn from the grey Hairs of an old Man, by the re-emitting Act.[5]

Mr. F-----x got the Office of Barrack-Master, had the particular Patronage of Indians committed to him, and the Fingering their Presents, and is a Provincial Commissioner also. Some lesser Members got
[*Textual note continued on next page*]

5. Provincial commissioners received salaries of £100 each. Neither the Re-emitting Act of June 20, 1759, nor its supplement of Sept. 29, 1759 (*Statutes at Large, Pa.,* v, 427–43, 456–60), mentions Joseph Galloway by name, and the "lucrative Office" in which he replaced an "old Man" has not been identified. In each of the years 1757–64 the incidental charges reported to the Assembly listed payments to him of sums varying from £20 to £30 for unspecified "extraordinary Services." This charge against Galloway had been made earlier (but without directly naming him) in *Plain Dealer,* iii (Dunbar, ed., *Paxton Papers,* pp. 372, 375).

Ambassador in England; for after spending us immense Sums there, for several Years, he at last returned, leaving the Province in deeper Disgrace than he found it, as well with his Majesty and his Ministers, as with the Nation in general. And well were it for this poor injured Province, if these were the worst Effects of his Embassy. But if we may believe the dark Hints he has lately thrown out,

---

lesser Matters, some embezzled the public Money and died vast Sums in the Province Debt.[6]

Mr. H-----hs got a most profitable Office by the Act for reccording Warrants and Surveys; was made a Provincial Commissioner and a Judge; and from a poor B-----r, soon became a very great Man;[7] by the Possession of these old Papers, and the help of his Associate the Lawyer, trumping up Titles to immense Tracts of Land that has been long possessed and honestly paid for, by many poor industrious Men. When this Law was repealed by his Majesty, and the Transcripts which this Man had made of the old Warrants, were ordered by the Assembly to be put into sealed Chests and lodged in their Library Room, the Seals were soon after broken by some body, and such Papers taken out as were tho't necessary. These Papers and some others found in an old Chest belonging to Thoms Holmes, are like to be more fatal than Pandora's Box to many good Men.

And here I could unfold such a Tale, and lay open such a Combination——But I will wait a little, hoping these Men will be led by their own Conscience, if they have any, to fly from our public Affairs, and trouble their Country no longer. Besides the Time for making the right Use of these trumped up Titles is not yet quite come. Mr. H-----hs's Associates are not yet in full Power. Mr. G-----y is not yet *chief Justice,* nor Mr. F-----n *Governor* and *high Chancellor* of Pennsylvania.

6. By resolution of the Assembly, May 3, 1758, Joseph Fox was appointed barrack master of the newly erected barracks in Philadelphia. *Votes,* 1757–58, p. 94. For the provincial commissioners' orders for payments to him on account of expenditures for the friendly Indians lodged on Province Island and later in the barracks, see above, x, 364, and this volume, p. 224. The accusations in this paragraph against "lesser Members" are too vague to permit identification here.

7. John Hughes was a baker by trade. William Allen to Thomas Penn, Dec. 13, 1764, Penn Papers, Hist. Soc. Pa. The Act for Recording Warrants and Surveys of 1759 (*Statutes at Large, Pa.*, v, 448–55, and above, IX, 153–7) appointed him recorder. He served as judge of the Court of Common Pleas of Philadelphia, 1759–61, under appointment of Governor Denny. *PMHB,* XXXV (1911), 442 n.

374

Franklin

Quakers

both in Assembly and out of it, he entered (while eating our very Bread) into bargain for the Sale of our Charter, and received Encouragement in it from some great Men, whom he says he is not at Liberty to mention, but you may take *his Word* for the Truth of it. The Price of this Bargain on his Part, must no doubt have been the Government of the Province to himself, and a Security of high Offices to his Associates already mentioned. But they must have been some second or third rate great Men, who would enter into such a foolish bargain as this, and did not know that tho' our great Projector be Lord of the People of Pennsylvania, and could give away their Charter, yet there is another Charter in the Way, over which he has no power.[8] That they must have been great Men of this Stamp, we cannot doubt, since it is well known, (and shall be made appear before we conclude) that his Majesty's present Ministers look with the utmost indignation, as well upon this unwarrantable attempt to break thro' our Charter, as upon the scandalous *Resolves* that led to it.

[Here the writer devoted approximately 2000 words to a review of the controversy over the interpretation of the Privy Council stipulation on taxation of the Proprietors' located but unimproved lands, of the petition for a change in government, and of related events. He cited William Allen as having quoted Richard Jackson's opinion that to buy out the proprietary rights of government would cost at least £100,000 and that the colony would be expected to pay this sum since the change was to be made at its request.]

And who are these Men who have thus endeavoured to trample on our Charter Rights, and to scandalize the good People of this Province? They are all known sufficiently; and I doubt not but the same Pen, that dignified the poor Germans with the Appellation of "BOORS HERDING TOGETHER"* did likewise draw these shameful Instructions [to Jackson regarding the petition]. His old Friends and his *new Allies* have alike shared his abuse. He has before now held up his Hands in passing the *Quaker-Meeting,* and declared that more Mischief was hatched in that Place than in a meeting of

*See a Paper in an English Magazine Signed B---- F-----n.[9]

8. Probably an oblique reference to Magna Carta.

9. Extracts from *Observations Concerning the Increase of Mankind* were reprinted in *Gent. Mag.,* XXV (1755), 483–5. The slurring reference to the "Palatine Boors" was in the last sentence as reprinted.

JESUITS at St. Omers. And he made it his late Boast, that he has wholly destroyed the Quaker Principles, and got the Government of them, by setting the Sons against the Fathers, and the Fathers against the Sons.[1] And certainly he has Room to make this Boast, if it be true that he has brought any Number of them into a Party, to overset a Constitution which their Fathers built up with so much Care. We find the serious Part of them, at their late *Meeting* have openly disavowed the Attempt to change our Government;[2] and we shall know more of their Sentiments upon this matter, on the Day of Election.

[The paper concludes with an extended appeal to "crush this base faction" and elect the members of the opposing ticket. The names of the preferred candidates from Philadelphia County and City are listed and several of them singled out for praise and approbation.]

II

To the FREEHOLDERS and other ELECTORS for the City and County of Philadelphia, and Counties of Chester and Bucks.

GENTLEMEN,

The first of October, 1764, being the anniversary Day for electing Members of Assembly, &c. That great and important Day, big with the Fate of your Country. You will therefore deliberately determine, whether you will chuse for Representatives, those honest and firm Freemen who have faithfully served you a great Number of Years; whether you will refuse to be advised by your old Friends, and turn out those zealous Supporters of your Rights and Privileges, or whether you will adopt the Measures of P--------y Officers, and their Tools, and make an almost total Change of the late Members of Assembly; for it seems these Enemies to your

1. At least one of these remarks appears to have been made to William Allen; see above, p. 328. BF may have uttered his disparaging words about the Quaker Meetinghouse in 1747, when he was organizing a volunteer militia for the defense of the city and province.

2. The Quaker Meeting for Sufferings, Sept. 13, 1764, "decided not to take a stand on the issue inasmuch as Friends were so divided in Opinion." Theodore Thayer, "The Quaker Party of Pennsylvania, 1755–1765," *PMHB*, LXXI (1947), 35 n. *Pa. Jour.*, Sept. 27, 1764, reported approvingly its information on this meeting's "disapprobation" of the proposal for a change in government.

Welfare propose to have but *three of the old Members continued*.[3] As there are two Parties, we find that each of them, to gain your Votes and Interest, profess a zealous Concern for the preservation of the Rights and Privileges of the good People of this Province. It is therefore incumbent on us, as your faithful Friends, to give you an Account of the Conduct and present Views of the Party for *the new Ticket*, that you may judge for yourselves, and not be deceived. Let us then intreat you to review for a Moment, their former Transactions.

Among them you will find, almost to a Man, the People that opposed the Friends of the Constitution, when they in a peaceable Manner came to vote at the *Knock down Election*, in the year 1742, by encouraging an armed Mob, whom they afterwards, in the Face of the Inhabitants of this City, screen'd from Punishment, altho' they had *knock'd down* and wounded many of the worthiest Men of this Province, whose Lives were from thence in great Danger.[4]

3. Of the members of the outgoing Assembly who had represented Philadelphia Co., the "New Ticket" included only the names of Isaac Norris, Joseph Richardson, and John Dickinson. Both candidates for the seats from the city were new men. The composition of the "New Ticket" for the county and city is given in a part of document No. 1 (above) not reprinted here. For both tickets in the county and city of Philadelphia, see below, p. 390.

4. On Oct. 1, 1742, a group of sailors, said to number about 70, marched up from the wharves to the place of election, armed with clubs, and assaulted prospective voters. Several citizens appealed to Mayor Clement Plumstead, Recorder William Allen, and other city magistrates to stop the rioters, but most of the officials (according to later testimony) made little or no attempt to do so. The sheriff, constables, and some others who opposed the mob were beaten off. The proprietary leaders, among whom were several of the chief city officials, were said to have instigated the attack because of a failure of the two parties to agree in advance on the naming of election inspectors. During the next weeks the Assembly called in and took depositions from 49 witnesses (among them BF's friend Hugh Roberts) and addressed a long message to Governor George Thomas asking that he recommend to the judges of the Supreme Court an inquiry and prosecution. Thomas responded, arguing that the mayor, recorder, and aldermen, acting as a court, had exclusive jurisdiction in such matters within the city; the Assembly, led by Speaker John Kinsey, denied the assertion; and several city officials formally remonstrated with the Assembly for charging them with dereliction of duty. No formal prosecution took place. The major documents on the affair are printed in *Votes*, 1742–43, with an appendix (pp. 75–114) which includes the full texts of the depositions. In 1758 Roberts referred punningly to the affair in a letter to BF; above, VIII, 83 and n.

The same Men who encouraged the wantonly inlisting and robbing you of your Servants, in the two last Wars, and billeting Soldiers on private Houses,[5] *are all for the new Ticket.*

The same Men who have left no Stone unturned to blacken and abuse the former Assemblies, for the noble stand they made, in contending that the Proprietaries Estate should be tax'd in the same just and equal Manner with those of the Peoples, *are to a Man for the new Ticket.*

The same Men who to recommend themselves to the P--------rs, by screening their enormous Estates from being taxed by a Law, meanly offer'd to pay their Tax out of their own Pockets,[6] *these are all of them for the new Ticket.*

The same great Men, and their Creatures, who have been of late Years continually using their Interest and Arguments against our having Paper Money continued to us, and that you shou'd pay more of it to them for one Shilling Sterling Money, that to other People, *are all of them for the new Ticket.*

The same Men who supported the P--------s in the iniquitous Scheme of getting one Hundred Thousand Pounds of Paper Money, condemned by the King in Council, in your Hands, that you might be deprived of so much of your Property, and thereby be the more easily reduced to P--------y Slavery, which would have been done, had not your worthy Agent Benjamin Franklin, Esq; averted the fatal Blow, by pledging his own Fortune to indemnify the P--------s from an ill-grounded Suspicion of Injustice, said to be intended by you against them.[7]—*All these Men are for the new Ticket.*

The same Men who advocated and palliated the horrid Crimes of the Paxton Rioters, murdering in cool Blood, the Indians at Conestogo Manor, and at Lancaster, and in their marching to this City, *all are to a Man for the new Ticket.*

Those who contend that without any regard to their Numbers, or the Proportion of the public Tax they pay, each of the back Counties, should have as many Members to represent them as either of the three old populous and wealthy Counties of

5. See above, VII, 39–49, 53–65, for the controversy over quartering British troops in Philadelphia.
6. In 1755; see above, VI, 141.
7. Above, IX, 207–8.

Philadelphia, Bucks and Chester,[8]—*these are to a Man for the new Ticket.*

The People holding Commissions of all Sorts, depending on the mere Will and Pleasure of the P--------s, from the C— J— down to the Nine-penny Justice, a few upright worthy Souls excepted, whose Spirits cannot brook being the despicable Tools to the Party, some of whom have even by S----h and Al-ss-n[9] had Hints of the Loss of their Commissions, for refusing to do as they bid them, while those *irreverend* Gentlemen have behaved as if they had Commissions of the Peace at their Command, as much as they have Marriage Licenses;—*all these Men are for the new Ticket.*

Parson S----h, and his Supporters, who wrote the Brief State, and Brief View Pamphlets, published in London some Years ago,[1] blackening the Characters of you and your Representatives, in the most impudent and base Manner, in order to deprive you of your Privileges and aggrandize the Proprietaries on your Ruin, *all these are for the new Ticket.*

The Corporation of the City of Philadelphia, from the M-y-r down to the lowest Common Council Man (a few worthy Souls

8. The Remonstrance filed by Matthew Smith and James Gibson after the march of the Paxton Boys on Philadelphia presented as the first grievance of the frontier counties their underrepresentation in the Assembly. The paragraph closed with: "wherefore we humbly pray that we may be no longer deprived of an equal Number with the three aforesaid Counties to represent us in Assembly." *Votes,* 1763–64, p. 44. A literal reading of these words indicates a demand for the same number of representatives for each of the newer counties as the oldest three (each of which had eight), regardless of differences still existing in population and in taxes paid. Charles H. Lincoln has computed that on the basis of taxables (an approximation of population) only Philadelphia and Lancaster Cos. would be entitled to the maximum of eight members. The other constituencies would rank in order: Chester, 6½; York, 5; Bucks and Berks, 4½ each; Philadelphia City, 4; Northampton, 3; Cumberland, 2 plus. On the basis of taxes paid (reflecting wealth) the representation would be Philadelphia Co., 8; Philadelphia City and Lancaster Co., 7½ each; Chester, 6; Bucks, 4; York, 3 plus; Berks, 3; Northampton and Cumberland, 1½ each. *The Revolutionary Movement in Pennsylvania, 1760–1776* (Phila., 1901), p. 47 n. But Smith and Gibson had demanded "an equal Number," not "a proportionate number," as they might with greater justification have done.

9. William Smith and Francis Alison, respectively Anglican and Presbyterian clergymen, and provost and vice-provost of the College.

1. For these pamphlets by William Smith, see above, VI, 52 n, 213 n.

excepted) are none of them chose by the Freeholders of the City, but are generally by Directions of some great Man or Men, whom we have before pointed out.[2] They are elected chiefly to answer the Purpose of constantly opposing the Rights and Privileges of you and your Representatives; wherefore they are become so despicable and odious to their Fellow Citizens, to whom they never account for the large Sums they raise by Rent of the Market Stalls, Ferries, free Wharffs, Vendue Master's Place, &c.—a Revenue of at least three Thousand Pounds a Year—that they are convinced the Electors in this City, who know them, will not take their Tickets, and therefore 'tis on you that they expect to impose them. —Of these Men beware,—*as they are all Enemies to the old Assembly, and to a Man are for the new Ticket.*

The P--------y Officers have kept the Land-Office shut,[3] to the great Injury of the industrious Farmer, *while they, and certain great Men and their Dependents,* have taken up prodigious large Tracts of the *best Land;* some of which they have immediately sold, at very exhorbitant Rates, and by their baseness and Injustice, have prevented the quick Settlement of the Province, and compell'd Thousands of Families to settle in other Places.—*Beware therefore of these Engrossers, for they are all for the new Ticket.*

[The paper goes on, at almost the same length again, to list and describe some of the views of the supporters of the "new Ticket" and some of the measures they plan to get enacted if they win control of the next Assembly. The writer specifically mentions schemes of general injustice and others prejudicial to the people of the city and the three oldest counties.]

III

What is Sauce for a Goose is also Sauce for a Gander. BEING A *small Touch in the* LAPIDARY *Way.* OR TIT *for* TAT, *in your*

2. William Penn's charter for the city of Philadelphia empowered the mayor, recorder, aldermen, and common councilors to elect a mayor and recorder annually from among the aldermen and to fill vacancies among the aldermen and common councilors from among the freemen of the city. There was no form of popular election of these city officials.

3. It was apparently the practice of the officials of the proprietary Land Office to open and close it at their own pleasure, but in 1765 the Proprietors forbade the practice; although "that might be done in a private gentleman's affairs," they said, "it was not proper for the proprietors of a province." William R. Shepherd, *History of Proprietary Government in Pennsylvania* (N.Y., 1896), p. 65.

own Way. AN EPITAPH *On a certain great Man. Written by a departed Spirit and now Most humbly inscrib'd to all his dutiful Sons and Children, Who may hereafter chose to distinguish him by the Name of* A PATRIOT. Philadelphia, printed in Arch-Street 1764.[4]

AN EPITAPH &c.

TO the much esteem'd Memory of / B------F------Esq; L. L. D; / The only man of his day / In Pennsylvania, / Or perhaps of any age or in any country, / Whose *ingrate Disposition* and *Badness of Heart* / (These enormous Vices) / Ever introduced to / POPULARITY. / As he was the first *Philosopher* / Who, contrary to any known System, discovered / How to maltreat his / PATRONS / Without Cause, / And be angry without Reason, / He may be justly styl'd / A *stupenduously surprizing* / And a GREAT MAN. / By assuming the merit / Of other mens *discoveries,* / He obtain'd the name of / A PHILOSOPHER.[5] / By meanly *begging* and some Times *buying* / HONORARY DEGREES, / From several *Colleges* and *Universities,* / He obtain'd the Character of / A Man of LEARNING. / From an early Desire, that portended / GREATNESS, / Implanted in his original / Stamina. / To have *Power* lodged / *In his own Hands,* / He most tyranically opposed, / And even *insulted* / The highest order of Men. / And by an Address, peculiar to himself, / He found the Way to climb to Promotion / Upon the Shoulders of FRIENDS / Whom a few Years before / He *proposed* to, and even *boasted* that he would, *Ruin.*[6] / Thus, rising by degrees / From the meanest Circumstances / To a Politican of the first Magnitude, / He became perfectly acquainted / With every Zig Zag Machination, /

---

4. On the title page the author turned against BF his use in the preface to Galloway's *Speech* of the verses attributed to John Rogers from the *Primer* (above, p. 303), by quoting them as: "Dear CHILDREN, / I send you here a little Book / For you to look upon, / That you may see your *Pappy's* Face / When he is dead and gone." He then added: "*Thou hast taught us to speak Evil of Dignities.*" Compare Jude 8. As indicated above, x, 266 n, the author of this epitaph is generally believed to have been Hugh Williamson. There are, however, several indications in document No. IV (immediately following this one) that the "Scribbler" attributed this attack on BF to William Smith.

5. For the "Scribbler's" comment on this accusation, see below, p. 389.
6. See above, pp. 375–6.

And triming* Contrivance, / Peculiar to that Science. / Quick
as the Flashes of Lightning, / Darted from a Cloud, / He would
sometimes *level* / All DISTINCTIONS, / Pull down the very Walls
/ Of Power, / And fatally destroy the *Safeguards* / Of JUSTICE. /
Blasting with the same Breath, / Every *necessary Subordination;* /
And sitting [*sic*] at nought the Executors / Of LAW and ORDER.
/ But in finally aiming to overturn / The *best* of Governments, /
And dispossess the People of / Their CHARTER RIGHTS, / And
inestimable Privileges, / He fell beneath Himself, a lingering Martyr.

*Although we would not tire our Readers with a train of Circum-
stances, yet the following instances of the Great Doctor's *Triming* we
are oblig'd to mention, out of pure Respect to Truth, which some of
his Advocates, at Times, do not seem to Venerate sufficiently.

It can be made appear upon Oath, That when the Counties of York
and Berks were set off, and were contrary to Charter allow'd but one
or two Representatives a piece. Mr. F.------ said, in Vindication of the
Measure, "That a Majority of Dutch lived in those Counties, it was not
proper to allow them to sit in the Assembly in an English Government."[7]

At another Time, in a Piece that he published in the Gentleman's
Magazine, concerning peopling the Colonies, He loudly complains
"That so many *Palatine Boors* are suffered to swarm into our Settle-
ments, and by *herding* together, establish their Language and Manners,"
And yet he pretends to be the Friend and Patron of those people.

It is also well known, that he once proposed to a very considerable
Gentleman in this City, that they should Unite in Order to demolish
the Quakers entirely; and he never forgave that Gentleman for refusing
him. Even when he was last in *England,* tho' supported by the Influence
of those very People, He privately made a Merit of it, That he had
effectually put an End to their growth in this province.

7. York Co., erected by act of Assembly, Aug. 19, 1749, while BF was
clerk of the House, was allowed two representatives; Berks Co., erected
March 11, 1752, when BF had been an assemblyman just short of seven
months, was allowed one representative. *Statutes at Large, Pa.,* V, 70–77,
133–40. The royal charter said nothing about the composition of the Assembly. Penn's Charter of Privileges, 1701, in contemplation of a legislative
union of the province and the Delaware counties, specified that the Assembly
was "to consist of *Four* Persons out of each County," or more as the governor
and Assembly should agree. A later section provided that, in case the two
sections failed to consent to a common legislature within three years, the
three counties of Pa. then in being should each have eight assemblymen and
the city of Philadelphia, two. This charter was silent regarding representation
for later counties.

/ To the Loss of *popular Applause;* / Oh mortifying Consideration! / Yet studious and artfull, tho' conscious / of his Guilt, / He struggled hard, but in Vain, / To screen his Sins / From the Sight of the People; / While, with an Effrontery surprising, / He loudly *bellow'd* and vehemently *complain'd* / That MAGISTRACY, / Which he had trampled on and Wounded, / Was *impotent* and *feeble.* / Possessed of many lucrative / OFFICES; / Procured to him by the Interest of Men / Whom he infamously treated. / And receiving *enormous Sums* / from the *Province,* / For SERVICES / He never performed; / After *betraying* it to *Party* and *Contention,* / He lived, as to the Appearance of Wealth, / In moderate Circumstances. / His principal Estate, *seeming* to consist, / Till very lately, / In his Hand Maid BARBARA / A most valuable *Slave,* / The *Foster-Mother* / Of his last Offspring, / Who did his dirty Work,—— / And in two *Angelic* Females,[8] / Whom Barbara also served, / As Kitchen Wench and Gold Finder.*/ But alas the Loss! / Providence for wise, tho' secret Ends, / Lately depriv'd him of the Mother / Of EXCELLENCY.[2] / His Fortune was not however impair'd, / For he piously witheld from her / MANES, / The *pitiful* Stipend of *Ten Pounds per Annum,* / On which he had cruelly suffered her / To STARVE; / Then stole her to the Grave, in Silence, / Without a Pall, the

*We are sorry to give the Reader trouble, but if he will be pleased to consult Dyche's English Dictionary for his first Definition of Gold-Finder,[9] it will Convey that very Idea which we have of the *old Women* [*sic*] Barbara, the Drs. Hand Maid. Tho' we cannot help confessing that some Authors have positively asserted that Barbara is that Species of Animal which the Marylanders call a *Powne,* the Scots a *Gallowe:*[1] and the English by some other Name. However it be, Posterity are welcome to decide the Controversy.

8. Presumably Deborah and either her mother, Sarah Read, who had died in 1761, or the Franklins' daughter, Sarah, now aged 21.

9. "A genteel name for him whose business is to empty privies, vulgarly called a Tom-turd-man." Thomas Dyche, *A New General English Dictionary* (11th edit., London, 1760).

1. After consulting a considerable number of dictionaries, including the leading two on the Scottish language, and others on Americanisms and slang, the editors have been unable to find these two words defined. Presumably they are obsolete localisms meaning a prostitute.

2. The governor of a royal province such as New Jersey was addressed by the honorific "Your Excellency," while the proprietary lieutenant governor of Pennsylvania was only "Your Honour."

Covering due to her *Dignity,* | Without a *Groan,* a *Sigh* or a *Tear.* | Without a *Tomb,* or even | A *Monumental Inscription.* | Reader behold this striking Instance of | Human Depravity and Ingratitude; | An irrefragable Proof, | That neither the Capital Services | Of *Friends,* | Nor the attracting Favours of the Fair, | Can fix the Sincerity of a Man, | *Devoid of Principles* and | *Ineffably mean;* | Whose Ambition is | POWER; | And whose Intention is | TYRANY | Remember then O Friends and Freemen, | And be intreated to consider, | That in the howling Wilderness | When we would guard ourselves against | The covered Wolves of the Forest, or | The stinging Snakes of the Mountains, | Our Maxim should be | *Beware of taking them to our* | BOSOMS. | FINIS.

IV

THE SCRIBBLER, *Being a Letter From a Gentleman in Town To his Friend in the Country, concerning the present State of Public Affairs; with a Lapidary Character* (n.p., 1764).

A LETTER, &c.

Sir,

The pleasant laconic Manner, in which you have sometimes accounted for the many Divisions, that have rent this unhappy Province, has never struck me with so much Conviction as of late. The *Knavery* of *a few,* and the *Folly* of *many* are now so apparent, as not to escape the notice of the most common unprejudiced Understanding: And it is really amazing as well as affecting, to see what *iniquitous* and *silly* Arts, the designing Few, notwithstanding all their pretensions to *Wisdom* and *Goodness,* make use of to deceive and inflame the Crowd.

[The Proprietors have for many years been "wresting from the People their Charter-Rights and Privileges" and the people "have not only seen these practices, and designs in their proper Colours . . . but have likewise abhorred the Men, who pursued them." The only solution is to seek a change in government when the proper moment comes, and our representatives have concluded that that moment has arrived.] *Those* who hold Offices under a Proprietary Governor, *those* who have gathered Estates, and *those* who still *expect* to make their Fortunes under *Proprietary* favour *resolve* to think otherwise: . . . These State-Jobbers, fearing on a Change that the Posts of Honour, and Profit will be disposed of by a Royal Governor *only* to Men of Merit, seem prodigiously averse to it: and it is difficult for you, who are buried in the obscurity and quiet of a Country-Life, to conceive what a Racket they make to prevent it. [They have circulated a counter-petition; are trying "with might and main, to *force* out of the House" all the members who promoted the first petition; and have "*wrote*, and *lied*, and *swore* that the Assembly were all Quaker Politicians" and that they themselves were the "Champions of Liberty."]

. . . And such *innocent* Arrogance might be past over with a laugh, if they had stopt here [but the people would not believe them, so] their ill Success has transported them to personal Abuse. So long as the Characters of a Pliny and a Sejanus are not grossly misrepresented, there will be a striking contrast: while a F-------n continues to support the Rights of his Constituents, it will be impossible for servile Minions to destroy his popular and good Name. They must have recourse to the base Means of every sinking Cause, groundless Slander: this is an easier Task, and better suits their Genius; for those Polithicks [*sic*], which have their Foundations in Scurrility and Lies, require no great deal of Finess. Every *Parrot* is able to prate Rogue and Whore.

It happened *unluckily* for the Cause of *Liberty*, that Mr. F------n once wrote a small *Essay* on the increase of Mankind, and the peopling of Countries; which was published nine years since in the *Gentleman's Magazine*. In that Piece with great justice he observed, that the vast number of Germans who flocked into this Province settled together in particular Parts of it; and established their own Customs and Language to the exclusion of ours. For this and some other obvious Reasons, the P--y Faction have chosen to single him out, as the most proper Person to discharge their Artillery against, and without any regard to decency or Truth have they attacked him. In short, from the tall Knaves of Wealth and Power, to the sneaking Underlings of Corruption, they seem to a Man like Annibal jurati ad aras, sworn to load him with all the Filth,* and Virulence that the basest Heads and basest Hearts can suggest. . . .

See, much esteemed Sir, what it is to be conspicuous![4] Your

See an Epitaph called Tit *for* Tat.[3]

3. Document III, immediately above.
4. Here the author, dropping the pretension that he is writing to a "Friend in the Country," addresses BF directly.

noble Spirit, and the Truths which you have told, have drawn upon you much Malice, and many Lies. You cannot be answered, and therefore 'tis fit to abuse you. Your Slanderers are indeed for the most Part sufficiently contemptible: But it is worth considering who set them at work, and what palpable Falshoods, and gross Nonsense the poor Creatures are taught to utter.

To begin with those, who have no other Reason to say an unkind word of you, but envy of your superior Abilities. There are but few Men who are pleased with the Excellencies of others; vulgar Souls are provoked by them. Great Sir, you have galloped away so far before this Class of your Enemies to the Goal of Honour, that the poor Vermin conscious of their own Heaviness, can do nothing but crawl after you at a great Distance, and curse you.

But there are others who have more cause to complain. You have discharged all the Duties of a Parent to your Offspring; you and your Children may reciprocally delight in the Connection. The good Education of your only Son has made him worthy the notice of his Sovereign.[5] To his hands have been committed the Reins of——permit me to say, that I do not mean a Chariot——But an Honourable Government; which he directs with care to the Subject, and glory to his Royal Master. Here you shine and rejoice in the Character of a Father; while the illegitimate Progeny of your Adversaries are so *numerous* so *scandalous* and so *neglected,* that the *only* Concern of the Parents is least their *unhappy* By-Blows should commit Incest.

[Further encomiums on Franklin and his public services follow.] Lastly you have, as with an *electrical* Charge shock'd the Sensibility of those *profane* Blockheads, who dared to touch your *Lightning.* Hence, what do they say? faith I don't know, except that *"Powne* and *Gallowe"* are synonymous Terms. . . .

[The writer here went into the exploitation of the passage on the "Palatine Boors," declaring that Franklin's enemies have dispersed "carloads of pamphlets," but they fail to point out that William

---

5. When WF assumed the government of New Jersey in 1763, he and his father visited Princeton, where the president and tutors of the strongly Presbyterian college commended his "education under the Influence and Direction of the very eminent Doctor Franklin." Above, X, 201 n. Ironically, a year and a half later the Presbyterian clergy of the adjoining province were among BF's most vigorous critics.

Smith's *Brief State* (which had also attacked the Germans) "is still in being, an irrefragible proof of their Insincerity."[6] Smith had called the Germans disloyal subjects and "a *proud brutal Mob*." The writer then devoted five pages to an attack on the Presbyterian clergy essentially because of their opposition to the petition to the King and their support of the proprietary party.]

You have now Sir, the best Account of the Conduct of our P-----y Partisans, and their Auxiliaries that my present Circumstances permit me to give you. It is very imperfect; yet may serve to acquaint you that, altho' the Friends of *Liberty* struggle hard to throw off the galling Yoke of *Tyrrany;* there are some *selfish* Wretches, who for *private* Advantages wish to continue under it; and others who from base, *uncertain* Views, are ready to act as Understrappers to that venal Tribe. I remain, &c.

As Lapidary Characters are now in high Vogue, I send you one for your amusement: There were a great Number of Incidents at Hand, but I have selected only a few of the most striking.

*   *   *   *   *

In Memory / Of the ill-thought of, and much disesteem'd / W—— S——[7] / Who by an incessant perseverence / In all the grovling Arts / Of a consumate Sycophant, / By the dint of indefatigable *Lying,* / And *Back-biting* at one Party, and / A servile *fawning* and *cringing* to another, / Has brought himself to the *secret Scorn* of his Friends, / As well as the more open contempt of Others. / *This* IRREVERENT PARSON, / Work'd thro' many difficulties to arrive at / The *Pinnacle* of Publick *Odium.* / The perpetual Operations of a sinister cunning, / A *brazen* Effront'ry / And an *unparrellel'd* Impudence, / A *superior Uniformity in Knavery,* / And a *Tongue* bick'ring with *slander* / Join'd to a *Heart* bloated with *infernal Malice,* / Have been the *noxious* Clues / Which have con-

---

6. On William Smith's *Brief State of the Province of Pennsylvania* (London, 1755), and its proposals for abridging the privileges of the Germans as well as those of the Quakers, see above, VI, 52 n.

7. That this savage "Lapidary Character," obviously in reply to the one printed as No. III above, was directed against William Smith, is one of the evidences that "The Scribbler" believed Smith had written *What is Sauce for the Goose.* Several relationships between the two epitaphs are pointed out in later notes.

387

vey'd him thro' the Labyrinth / Of an obscure Birth, / Drain'd of his *primary penurious Blood,* / And enabl'd him to surmount his / Original *abject Circumstances.*[8] / The Unhappy Father / Of this / *Ordain'd Image* of *Insincerity,* / Was a poor, but as it is said, an honest *Blacksmith;* / He gave his Son *some Learning,* / (According to the custom, even of the poorest of his Country,) / And as it has unfortunately turn'd out, / Sent him abroad to be a *Ch at.*[9] / A few Years ago, he came a Raw-stripling / Into a neighbor'ing Government; / And was hous'd by a Gentleman there; / Who allow'd him a Stipend of / *Twenty Pounds, Currency per Annum,* / For taking care of his Children.[1] / He began presently after his Arrival to discover / That *promptitude* to *Party Feuds,* / *Which* seems to be inherent in his blood, / And *which* has so greatly *distinguish'd* him since. / When he first sojourn'd in this City, / He made his Court / To some of the Principle Gentlemen in it, / By assuring them a Portion in the skies, / Bepraising them in a lard of Poetry* / *One* of which Gentlemen, he has since perceiv'd, / To be *"ineffably mean"*[3] / Instead of a *Sky-Lark.* / And as a *suitable* Return for his / *Pristine* Civilities, / Has overwhelm'd him in a torrent of *infamous abuse.*[4] / The Gentleman who has been thus *grossly* treated / Being the original Promoter of / That INSTITUTION, / Which has been the *Creation* of this ungrateful / DEFAMER; / And enabl'd him to rise on / The *Stilts* of *Academical Dignity.* / He was early taken notice of / By the Ass-----bly of this Province, / They being under the necessity of ordering him / To *Goal,* / For his forward Impertinence

*When gentle H-lt-n shall grace our Skies,
And with A-ll-n, P-t-rs, F--kl--n rise.
A Poem on visiting the Academy[2]

8. No. III: "rising by degrees From the meanest Circumstance."

9. The omission of *"e"* in this word may have been a precaution against a charge of libel, or a mere printer's error.

1. Smith came to America in 1751 and became tutor to the sons of Col. Josiah Martin of Long Island, N.Y.

2. *A Poem on Visiting the Academy of Philadelphia, June 1753* (Phila., 1753), lines 205–6. The men mentioned are Governor James Hamilton, William Allen, Richard Peters, and BF. For the encouragement the last three gave to Smith in coming to Philadelphia, see above, IV, 475–6.

3. No. III: "a Man, *Devoid of Principles* and *Ineffably Mean.*"

4. No. III: "He found the Way to climb to Promotion Upon the Shoulders of FRIENDS Whom a few Years before He *proposed* to, and soon boasted he would, *Ruin.*"

to them. [5] / Besides a long and *regular series* of *blackening* Lies / In England as well as America, / (Venomous as from the Tooth of a Serpent.) / It is notorious that in / This City, he added P-------[6] to his Character. / He has also discovered the strange perturbations, / And strong Itchings to Illegal V----y.[7] / He once asserted in a Work* of his / Concernment, / Of a Gentleman of establish'd Reputation / In the literary World, / That he had usurp'd the Honour of some *discoveries* / In natural *Philosophy*, of which, he was not / The Author, but another Gentleman was. / *By which other* Gentleman the *falsity* of that Assertion / Was immediately afterwards publickly avow'd. / And he now again repeats / With a consummate Assurance, / That *Lye* which has been heretofore so *totally o'erthrown.*[8] / His depraved Example, / Has been instrumental, / In corrupting almost / The whole Body of P--sts[9] of another Community / In this Province. / Egg'd on by his *dual* Tricks, / Till they have expos'd Themselves to *Public Ridicule;* / By quitting their *Parsonic gravity,* / For the *preposterous* Employment / of State *Politicasters.* / Imperious as tho' he were a Sovereign, / Does this high-stomach'd *Pedagogue,* / Carry himself to his *Equals* and *Inferiors,* / But before his proud Superiors, opinionated as he is, / He sinks low! / And then / No sneaking Parasite can more pliantly / Buckle, flatter and fawn. / Oh! disdainful Reader! / If thou art mov'd with this, / Imagine not that no Service or Instruction / Is to be gain'd from such a Character. / It may convince Thee, that / Neither the *Surplice, Gown* nor *Band,* / Not the *composing* of *flatulent Preachments,* / Nor the Head devoted to Sanctity / By the venerable Hand

*American M--g--ne

5. Above, VII, 385 n.
6. Possibly, but not certainly, "Pederast."
7. "Venery." Compare the allusions in No. III to WF's illegitimacy and to "Barbara." The editors have seen no evidence to support these charges against Smith's personal life.
8. No. III: "By assuming the merit of other mens *discoveries*, He obtained the name of A PHILOSOPHER." For Ebenezer Kinnersley's open letter to Smith denying the allegations made in Smith's *American Magazine*, I, Supplement, 630–40, that BF had taken credit for Kinnersley's electrical experiments, see above, VIII, 188–90.
9. "Priests"; a reference to the Presbyterian clergymen who had opposed the petition to the King, although ministers of that denomination were not normally called "priests" except sometimes by enemies in other groups.

of a B---p, / Not the *pompous appellation* of / D.D.[1] / Can command our Love or Respect, / To a Man, that is / A Stranger to Godliness and devoid of Piety / And in whom no Vestige appears of / GRACE, TRUTH or HONESTY. / FINIS.

Election Results in Philadelphia County, 1764

AD: American Philosophical Society

The county elections for members of the Assembly and for local officers took place on Monday, Oct. 1, 1764, and those for representatives from the city on the following day. Both parties put up full tickets for election to the Assembly. The "Old Ticket" (representing what was often called the Quaker Party) supported for county representatives Isaac Norris, Joseph Richardson, Joseph Fox, John Hughes, Joseph Galloway, Rowland Evans, Plunket Fleeson, and Benjamin Franklin, and for city representatives Franklin and, apparently, Samuel Rhoads. Franklin was thus a candidate for election in both the county and the city, an arrangement permissible under the rules.[2] The "New Ticket" (drawn up by supporters of the Proprietors and other opponents of the petition to the King) was printed in full in the Supplement to the *Pennsylvania Journal*, Sept. 27, 1764. It included for representatives from the county, Isaac Norris, Joseph Richardson, John Dickinson, Amos Strettell, Henry Keppele, Frederick Antes, Henry Harrison, and Henry Pawling, and from the city, Thomas Willing (the outgoing mayor) and George Bryan.

Comparison of these lists shows that two men were nominated on both county slates: Norris, the respected speaker and long-time spokesman for the Quaker faction in the Assembly, who had nevertheless

1. No. III: "By meanly begging and some Times buying HONORARY DEGREES, From several Colleges and Universities, He Obtain'd the Character of a Man of LEARNING." On Smith's unsuccessful attempt to prevent BF from receiving a degree from Oxford (which had given Smith his D.D.), see above, X, 78 n.

2. The full slate of this party for both Philadelphia constituencies does not appear in any one place among contemporary documents; it must be deduced from a combination of evidences, including the paper printed here. The fact of BF's dual candidacy is confirmed in a letter from William Allen to Thomas Penn, Oct. 21, 1764; Penn Papers, Hist. Soc. Pa. BF's inclusion in the county list was clearly intended as a replacement of John Dickinson, since the latter was the only Philadelphia County member of the outgoing Assembly not renamed on the "Old Ticket." A letter from BF to Rhoads, July 8, 1765, strongly supports the deduction that Rhoads was BF's running mate in the city election of 1764, as he had been in previous years. Hist. Soc. Pa.

expressed grave misgivings over the proposal to change the form of government; and Richardson, who had likewise been hesitant about the petition but appears not to have stood by the minority opponents in the Assembly on the final votes.[3] Probably neither faction wished to insult Norris by leaving him off its list, while both hoped that Richardson would support them in the months to come. There was therefore a total of fourteen candidates for the eight seats.

Election day in Philadelphia was strenuous. The fullest surviving account of what occurred is in a letter from Charles Pettit, a merchant of Trenton and Philadelphia, to his brother-in-law, Joseph Reed, the later Revolutionary statesman, then a student at the Middle Temple in London. Under date of Nov. 3, 1764, Pettit wrote in part: "The poll was opened about 9 in the morning, the 1st of October, and the steps so crowded, till between 11 and 12 at night, that at no time a person could get up in less than a quarter of an hour from his entrance at the bottom, for they could go no faster than the whole column moved. About 3 in the morning, the advocates for the new ticket moved for a close, but (O! fatal mistake!) the old hands kept it open, as they had a reserve of the aged and lame, which could not come in the crowd, and were called up and brought out in chairs and litters, &c., and some who needed no help, between 3 and 6 o'clock, about 200 voters. As both sides took care to have spies all night, the alarm was given to the new ticket men; horsemen and footmen were immediately dispatched to Germantown, &c., and by 9 or 10 o'clock they began to pour in, so that after the move for a close, 7 or 800 votes were procured; about 500 or near it of which were for the new ticket, and they did not close till 3 in the afternoon, and it took them till 1 next day to count them off.

"The new ticket carried all but Harrison and Antis, and Fox and Hughes came in their room; but it is surprising that from upwards of 3900 votes, they shou'd be so near each other. Mr. Willing and Mr. Bryan were elected Burgesses by a majority of upwards of 100 votes, tho' the whole number was but about 1300. Mr. Franklin died like a philosopher. But Mr. Galloway *agonized in Death*, like a Mortal Deist, who has no Hopes of a Future Existence. . . . A number of squibs, quarters, and half sheets, were thrown among the populace on the day of election, some so copious as to aim at the general dispute, and others, more confined, to Mr. Dickinson and Mr. Galloway, with now and then a skit at the Doctor, but these had little or no effect."[4]

3. Above, p. 198 n.
4. William B. Reed, *Life and Correspondence of Joseph Reed* (Phila., 1847), I, 36–7.

No tabulation of the votes in the city election has been found, and Pettit's statement above of the plurality by which Willing and Bryan won the two city seats is the best approximation of the figures which has been located. For the Philadelphia County election, on the other hand, there survives among Franklin's papers a single sheet in his hand giving the totals for all candidates except those for county commissioner.[5] This paper is printed in full below.

Each elector was entitled to vote for eight representatives, though he might vote for fewer if he wished. Analysis of Franklin's tabulation shows that 30,911 votes were cast for the office of assemblyman from the county. Since Norris, running on both tickets, received 3874 votes, it is certain that the total number of those who went to the polls was not less than that figure. Probably he was a unanimous, or nearly unanimous, choice. If everyone who voted for him had also voted for seven other candidates, then at least 27,118 votes would have been divided among the remaining thirteen nominees. Their actual total, however, was 27,037, or 81 votes less. It becomes apparent, therefore, that a few scattered individuals failed to record choices of as many candidates as they might have done. The vote for Norris, whether or not it was unanimous, confirms Pettit's statement that "upwards of 3900" citizens of the county went to the polls in 1764—certainly a record-breaking figure.

The vote for Joseph Richardson, also running on both tickets, was 26 less than that for Norris. When his ballots are similarly deducted, there remain 23,189 to be divided among twelve other men, or an average of 1932 plus. The highest vote recorded among these twelve actively competing candidates was the 2030 cast for Dickinson; the lowest was the 1884 given to Fleeson. This difference of only 146 between high and low, when nearly 3900 voters were involved, attests to the general closeness of the election. It is clear, nevertheless, that the voters in Philadelphia County definitely favored the "New Ticket." Aside from the two uncontested candidates named on both slates, the party favorable to the Proprietors elected four candidates to the Quaker Party's two. And the "New Ticket" party added two more seats in the Assembly when both its candidates for the city seats won that election. Franklin himself suffered humiliation not only by having his arch-opponent Dickinson lead the list among all the real competitors in the county vote and by losing both elections himself, but by seeing his own name next to last on the entire county list.

Elsewhere the proprietary group was proportionately less successful.

5. *Pa. Gaz.* and *Pa. Jour.*, Oct. 4, 1764, report the election of Enoch Story for this office; he may have run unopposed.

It re-elected its two supporters in Cumberland County, two in York, and one in Lancaster. It gained one certain vote in Northampton and a somewhat uncertain one in Bucks, but it made no other inroads. It came nowhere near to winning a majority of the seats in the entire House. During the October sitting of the new Assembly seven motions arose on matters connected in one way or another with the petition for a change in government or with the appointment of Franklin as co-agent with Jackson, which were sufficiently controversial as to lead to the recording in the minutes of each member's vote.[6] Speaker Norris, of course, did not vote on any of the three occasions before he resigned from the chair, October 24, and he seems not to have attended thereafter. The choice of Joseph Fox as Norris' successor deprived the majority of one consistent vote. There were occasional absences or abstentions, and one member, Joseph Wright of Lancaster County, never appeared during this session. The total number of votes cast ranged between 30 and 32 and those cast by the proprietary supporters varied between 10 and 12. Richardson, elected without a contest, voted four times with the majority and three times with the minority.[7] Peter Shepherd, a new member from Bucks County, voted once with the Quaker Party, then twice with the proprietary supporters, then— perhaps discouraged—disappeared from the session.[8] Most curiously, Henry Pawling, one of the winning candidates on the "New Ticket," voted consistently all seven times with the old guard majority.[9] Proportionately the highest point the Proprietors' supporters reached in this series of votes was on the last one, when they were defeated 18 to 12 with 6 elected members not voting. In their best showing, therefore, they had 40 percent of the votes cast. They gained considerable strength in the House by this election, but they were unable to change the

6. *Votes*, 1764–65, pp. 11, 13–16.

7. Richardson voted with the majority on three motions relating to the petition to the King and on one to appoint an agent to assist Jackson. He voted with the minority on a motion to adjourn for a fortnight, on the appointment of BF as co-agent, and on provision for BF's expenses.

8. Shepherd opposed recall of the petition, but favored instructions to Jackson not to present it without further orders and, when that failed, he opposed instructions to proceed with "the utmost Caution" and to await further orders if the agent felt the change in government might jeopardize the colony's privileges.

9. Pawling had been a justice of the peace since 1752. Apparently in reprisal for his voting record, Governor Penn and the Council omitted his name from the new list of justices, Nov. 19, 1764. 2 *Pa. Arch.*, IX, 727–9; *Pa. Col. Recs.*, IX, 205. For later comments on this action, see below, pp. 484, 523.

official policy of the Assembly. Their major victory was a personal one: the elimination of Franklin and Galloway from the membership.

[October 1-3, 1764]

Assembly		County Assessors[6]	
Isaac Norris	3874	Barnaby Barnes	1212
Joseph Richardson	3848	Jacob Umsted	1190
John Dickinson	2030[1]	John Bowman	1043
Joseph Fox	1963	Andrew Bankson	1028
Henry Pawlin	1955	Josh Stamper	927
Henry Keppele	1932	Matthias Holston	557.
Amos Strettle	1930		
John Hughes	1925		
Henry Harrison	1921		
Joseph Galloway	1918[2]		
Frederick Antis	1914		
Rowland Evans	1911		
Benjn. Franklin	1906[3]	1955	
Plunkett Fleeson	1884	1884	
		71[7]	

Sheriffs

Wm Parr[4]	1822
John Biddle	1769

Cor[oner]s

Caleb Cash[5]	1822
John Luken	1800

1. The third digit in this figure is overwritten. On careful scrutiny it appears that BF first wrote "2040," then changed it to "2030," but it is possible that the correction was the other way around.

2. The third digit in this figure is badly blotted, but the position of Galloway's name and total in the ranking makes virtually certain that the figure was as printed here.

3. Writing to Jackson, Oct. 11, 1764, BF reported that the Proprietary Party had carried the county and city election "by about 26 Votes against me and Mr. Galloway." Below, p. 397. He may have meant that 26 additional votes, divided 7 to Galloway and 19 to BF, would have given each as large a

[Footnotes 3-7 continued on following page]

From Rhode Island Assembly Committee[8]

MS not found; printed in *Votes and Proceedings of the House of Representatives of Pennsylvania, Met at Philadelphia* [October 15, 1764] (Philadelphia, 1764), pp. 6–7.

Sir,   [October 8, 1764][9]

We being appointed a Committee by the General Assembly of the Colony of Rhode-Island, to correspond, confer and consult with any Committee or Committees that are or shall be appointed by any of the British Colonies on the Continent, and in Concert with them, to prepare and form such Representations of the Condition of the Colonies, the Rights of the Inhabitants, and the Interests of Great-Britain, as connected with them, as may be most likely to be effectual to remove or alleviate the Burthens which the Colonists at present labour under, and to prevent new Ones being added.[1]

The Impositions already laid on the Trade of these Colonies, must have very fatal Consequences. The Act in Embryo, for establishing Stamp Duties, if effected, will further drain the People, and strongly point out their Servitude: And the Resolution of the

---

total (1925) as the lowest of the candidates who actually won a seat in the county election.

4. On receiving the returns from this election, Governor Penn commissioned Parr as sheriff of Philadelphia County, Oct. 4, 1764. *Pa. Col. Recs.,* IX, 199.

5. Caleb Cash, Jr. (F.2.3), a Philadelphia merchant, was DF's first cousin once removed. See above, VIII, 140–1, 144 n. On receiving the returns of this election, Penn commissioned Cash as coroner of Philadelphia County. *Pa. Col. Recs.,* IX, 199.

6. All six were elected to office. *Pa. Col. Recs.,* IX, 241.

7. This calculation appears to have been made in order to determine, for an unknown reason, the difference between the votes for Pawling and Fleeson.

8. The Rhode Island Committee addressed this letter to BF in his capacity as speaker of the Pa. Assembly. They could not have known that he had lost his seat in the House in the election of October 1–2. When the new Assembly met on Oct. 15, 1764, Isaac Norris was unanimously chosen speaker. BF apparently gave this letter to Norris, who laid it before the House on Oct. 18, 1764. *Votes,* 1764, pp. 3, 6–7.

9. The letter is described as of this date in *ibid.,* p. 6.

1. The Rhode Island Assembly appointed this committee on July 30, 1764, and continued it in its fall session. J. R. Bartlett, *Records of the Colony of Rhode Island,* VI (Providence, 1861), 403, 406.

House of Commons (that they have a Right to tax the Colonies)[2] if carried into Execution, will leave us nothing to call our own. How far the united Endeavours of all the Colonies might tend to prevent those Evils, cannot be determined; but certain it is worth their While to try every Means in their Power, to preserve every Thing they have worth preserving.

Zealous to do all we can, in a Business of so much Importance, more especially as the Colony that employs us seems heartily disposed to exert its utmost Efforts to preserve its Privileges inviolate, looking on this as the critical Conjuncture when they must be effectually defended, or finally lost; we have given you the Trouble of this Address, desiring to be informed whether your Colony hath taken these Matters under Consideration; and if it hath, what Methods have been thought of, as most conducive to bring them to a happy Issue.

If all the Colonies were disposed to enter with Spirit into the Defence of their Liberties; if some Method could be hit upon for collecting the Sentiments of each Colony, and for uniting and forming the Substance of them all into one common Defence of the whole; and this sent to England, and the several Agents directed to join together in pushing and pursuing it there, in the properest and most effectual Manner, it might be the most probable Method to produce the End aimed at.[3]

2. The fifteenth resolution introduced into the House of Commons by George Grenville on March 9, 1764, which threatened a stamp act at some future date, was frequently spoken of in America "as an assertion of Parliament's right to tax the colonies." Edmund S. and Helen M. Morgan, *The Stamp Act Crisis Prologue to Revolution* (Chapel Hill, [1953]), pp. 55, 59–60, 62 n.

3. After considering this letter, as well as the instructions to Richard Jackson of Sept. 22, 1764 (above, pp. 347–51), the Assembly on Oct. 18, 1764, appointed a committee to draw up additional instructions to Jackson respecting "the present State of the Trade of this Province, the pernicious Effects of the Restrictions already imposed thereon by our Mother Country, and the Dangers apprehended to our Rights as Englishmen, from the internal Taxations proposed to be laid on the Colonies by future Acts of Parliament." Such instructions were brought in on October 19, debated by paragraphs, and agreed to on the 20th, and the same day the Committee of Correspondence was ordered to transmit a copy of them, together with the proceedings of the Assembly during its September session, "to the Committees of the Representatives for the colonies of Massachusetts-Bay, and Rhode-Island." These instructions expressed the House's continued willingness to contribute

However, as we do not pretend to prescribe Rules, but to receive Information, we hope to be excused for this Freedom, and that the Cause we are concerned in, and your Candour, will procure us your Pardon for this Trouble, given by, Sir, Your most obedient, and most humble Servants,   STEPHEN HOPKINS,
DANIEL JENIKES,
NICHOLAS BROWN.

To Richard Jackson   ALS: American Philosophical Society

Dear Sir   Philada. Oct. 11. 1764
    I have now only time to cover the enclos'd,[4] and acquaint you that I am no longer in the Assembly. The Proprietary Party by great Industry against great Security carried the Election of this County and City by about 26 Votes against me and Mr. Galloway; the Voters near 4000.[5] They carried (would you think it!) above 1000 Dutch from me, by printing part of my Paper sent to you 12 Years since on Peopling new Countries where I speak of the Palatine *Boors herding* together,[6] which they explain'd that I call'd them a *Herd* of *Hogs.*[7] This is quite a laughing Matter. But the Majority of the last Assembly remain, and will I believe still be for the Measure of Changing the Proprietary for a Royal Governor.[8] I am, with great Respect Dear Sir, Your most humble Servant
                                        B FRANKLIN

---

its full share to mutual defense when called upon, but insisted that the several assemblies "can alone know the state of their respective Provinces," and that any other method of taxation, "where the People are not represented, . . . would be unequal, oppressive and unjust." Jackson was further told of some of the economic burdens created by the Sugar Act and urged to procure legislation that would benefit the trade of the colonies. *Votes,* 1764, pp. 7–10, 12.
    4. Not identified; possibly the Assembly's instructions to Jackson of September 25, or bills of exchange for his salary.
    5. See above, pp. 390–4.
    6. For BF's *Observations concerning the Increase of Mankind,* written in 1751, see above, IV, 225–34, esp. p. 234.
    7. For a full discussion of the etymological disputes created by BF's description of the German farmers, see J. Philip Gleason, "A Scurrilous Colonial Election and Franklin's Reputation," 3 *William and Mary Quar.,* XVIII (1961), 78–81.
    8. On Oct. 20, 1764, the Assembly voted down, 22 to 10, a proposal to

I have received yours of July 18 and Aug 14. and shall write fully per next.

Addressed: To | Richard Jackson Esqr | Inner Temple | London | via N York | per Packet

Endorsed: 11 Octr 64 Benjn. Franklin Esqr.

Outgoing Philadelphia Mail, 1764-1767

Printed forms with MS insertions: American Philosophical Society

October 18, 1764

Benjamin Franklin's brother Peter was postmaster of Philadelphia from about the middle of October 1764 until his death on July 1, 1766.[9] He was succeeded by Thomas Foxcroft, brother of the other joint deputy postmaster general. Both the Foxcrofts became Loyalists upon the outbreak of the American Revolution and ended their service in 1775.

As early as 1753 instructions to the local postmasters had required them not only to maintain exact accounts of their financial transactions but to keep detailed records of letters received from or dispatched to other offices in the colonies. Printed forms were supplied for the purpose. Form "B" provided columns in which to list each outgoing shipment of mail, showing the date, the number of pieces of each kind (single, double, and triple letters, and packets) sent to every destination on that day under each of the three categories of unpaid, prepaid, and free mail, and (for each of the first two categories) the total charge for the group of letters, reckoned in pennyweights and grains of silver.[1]

A set of sixty-four of these completed forms, printed on both sides, survives from the Philadelphia Post Office among the Franklin papers. The entries are dated from Oct. 18, 1764, to Sept. 22, 1767, thus spanning the whole of Peter Franklin's postmastership and the beginning of Thomas Foxcroft's. There are several breaks in the series, four

---

recall the petition in Jackson's hands for a royal government. Later in the day the Committee of Correspondence was ordered to instruct Jackson to proceed with "the utmost Caution" in managing the petition and to refrain from presenting it if he saw any danger that the change to a royal government would endanger Pennsylvania's civil and religious privileges. *Votes,* 1764, p. 11.

9. *Pa. Gaz.,* Oct. 18, 1764; July 3, 1766.

1. The full instructions, issued by BF and Hunter, are printed above, v, 161–77, and their sample form "B" is reproduced at v, 171.

of them for periods of about a month apiece and one for six weeks; several sheets are badly torn, and, especially for the first part of the period, the ink was often so weak—or has faded so badly—that the writing is now virtually illegible. Nevertheless, the series is complete enough to permit one to form a reasonably clear idea of the amount and the destinations of the postal correspondence carried on by the people in the area served by the Philadelphia Post Office during the period.

To reprint in full the contents of these forms would serve little useful purpose. Instead, the records for four calendar months, distributed through the whole period, have been chosen and the total amount of mail of all categories sent from Philadelphia to every other post office has been tabulated for each of these months. Inadequacies in the records, as mentioned above, have necessarily played some part in the choice of months, but those selected are believed to be fairly representative of that time of year and of that year in general.[2]

Examination of the tabulations printed below reveals several aspects of the colonial postal system in general, as well as of the Philadelphia operations in particular, during the years which followed closely upon the considerable personal attention the deputy postmasters general, Franklin and Foxcroft, had been giving the service in 1763 and 1764. Several new post offices, especially in the South, appeared at this time, and expanded routes became available, notably the new one to Pennsylvania towns west of Philadelphia.[3] Perhaps most enlightening is the distribution of outgoing Philadelphia mail. It may come as something of a surprise to observe that almost half of all these letters and packets were going to New York City. Some of the New York total—it is impossible to say just how much—was sent there to be placed on board the monthly packet boats to England, but the correspondence between these two colonial cities themselves had become impressively heavy and clearly justified the increase in service to three times a week which had recently been provided.[4] Boston led all other single communities in the colonies, receiving a little over 8 percent of Philadelphia's mail.

2. It would have been desirable to include one tabulation from a January or February—the worst months for the post riders—but breaks in the series or the condition of some sheets prevented such a choice.

3. Comparison of the list of offices given below with that for 1763 (above, x, 418) shows the establishment of several new offices in Maryland and Virginia and changes in the names of a number of others there. On the new Pennsylvania route, see above, pp. 247–8.

4. Since Philadelphia was the junction between the northern and southern postal routes, some of the mail recorded as sent to New York undoubtedly originated further south.

Correspondence with offices in adjoining provinces, as might be expected, was substantial. The New Jersey post offices, taken as a group, accounted for approximately 6 percent of the total, and those in Maryland, on both sides of the Chesapeake, drew just over 16 percent, probably evidence of the close economic relations of Philadelphia with that province.

The number of letters sent to any one place fluctuated considerably from one mail to the next and, as this tabulation shows, sometimes from month to month. No single entry, therefore, should be regarded as particularly significant—for example other months in 1764 and 1765 than the ones selected show at least a sprinkling of letters to Connecticut towns—but the statistics as a whole indicate with considerable fidelity the nature and distribution of Philadelphia's outgoing mail during these years. While comparable records of mail arriving at the city in this period have not been found, it is reasonable to assume that the pattern was much the same.

Destination	Total Pieces of Mail			
	Dec. 1764	March 1765	Sept. 1766	May 1767
DISTRICT OF MAINE				
Falmouth	—	—	2	—
NEW HAMPSHIRE				
Portsmouth	—	6	9	6
MASSACHUSETTS				
Boston	120	128	120	105
Marblehead	—	3	7	1
Newbury	—	5	5	1
Salem	—	4	1	2
RHODE ISLAND				
Newport	33	57	25	20
Providence	4	3	1	5
CONNECTICUT				
Guilford	—	—	—	1
Hartford	—	—	—	3
Middletown	—	—	—	3
New Haven	—	—	2	8
New London	—	—	5	11
Norwalk	—	—	—	5
Stamford	—	—	—	1
Stratford	—	—	—	2
QUEBEC				
Montreal	3	—	8	6
Quebec	—	—	26	20

Destination	Total Pieces of Mail			
	Dec. 1764	March 1765	Sept. 1766	May 1767
NEW YORK				
Albany	—	7	17	11
New York	652	608	842	741
NEW JERSEY				
Brunswick	18	19	15	14
Burlington	12	10	15	5
Elizabethtown	12	10	17	12
Newark	—	—	1	3
Princeton	13	9	16	15
Trenton	17	13	17	21
Woodbridge	13	7	22	19
PENNSYLVANIA				
Bristol	—	—	—	3
Carlisle	22	4	—	—
Lancaster	73	37	140	65
Shippensburg	—	5	—	—
York	10	2	—	—
DELAWARE				
New Castle	28	1	31	9
Wilmington	4	—	9	2
MARYLAND				
Annapolis	47	48	61	29
Baltimore	54	68	71	61
Cambridge	—	—	—	3
Charlestown	—	—	—	13
Chester[town]	34	10	34	6
Fredericktown	16	8	41	33
Joppa	—	—	2	2
Marlboro	11	6	14	17
Newtown	21	—	69	58
Talbot	—	—	20	34
Queenstown	—	—	7	—
Vienna	—	—	22	10
VIRGINIA				
Alexandria	35	12	23	5
Dumfries	—	—	—	3
Fredericksburg	1	8	18	18
Hanover	—	—	—	1

[Continued on next page]

| | Total Pieces of Mail | | | |
| | Dec. | March | Sept. | May |
Destination	1764	1775	1766	1767
VIRGINIA—Continued				
Hobb's Hole	—	—	1	4
Norfolk	8	11	18	20
Richmond	—	—	—	3
Williamsburg	17	16	36	20
Yorktown	1	—	4	2
SOUTH CAROLINA				
Charleston	—	—	12	21
TOTALS	1279	1197[5]	1806	1483
TOTAL FOR THESE FOUR MONTHS				5765

Inhabitants of Philadelphia: Remonstrance against the Appointment of Benjamin Franklin as Agent

Printed in *Votes and Proceedings of the House of Representatives of the Province of Pennsylvania, Met at Philadelphia* [October 15, 1764] (Philadelphia, 1764), pp. 14–15.

The new Assembly met on Monday, October 15, and elected Isaac Norris speaker once more. On the following Saturday, after taking final action on the instructions to Richard Jackson concerning the Sugar Act and the impending Stamp Act (above, p. 396 n), the House took up the matter of the petitions to the King for a change in government.[6] On the question whether "further Directions respecting the said Petitions" should be sent to Jackson, "a considerable Debate ensued, in which a great Contrariety of Opinions" appeared among the members. At this point Speaker Norris received unanimous permission "to deliver his Sentiments on so interesting a Subject." After expressing his thanks for this courtesy, Norris told his fellow members "that he was

5. In a series of five consecutive entries for this month the place names are indecipherable. The 72 pieces of mail listed in these entries have been added to those recorded above in order to show a correct total of outgoing mail for March 1765.

6. Describing this session to Thomas Penn, Nov. 5, 1764, Benjamin Chew wrote that "Franklin Galloway and others tho excluded have had the entire direction of Matters within Doors. The measure and plan of each days proceedings being settled by them every Evening at private meetings and cabals held with their Friends in the house." Penn Papers, Hist. Soc. Pa.

not for immediately recalling the Petitions," but that, since he thought "the House had no Right to delegate their Powers to any Man, or Sett of Men whatever, to alter or change the Government, he was for putting an entire Prohibition on the Agent's presenting the said Petitions, without further and express Orders from the House for that Purpose."[7]

Thereupon the House voted on three successive motions, all regarded as being so important and so controversial that the names of those voting on each were entered on the minutes. The first question was whether the petitions sent to Jackson should be recalled. Thirty-two members voted, and the proposal for recall was defeated, 22 to 10. The House then took up the question of directing Jackson not to present the petitions "until he receives further Orders for that Purpose from this House." This proposal was defeated, 20 to 12, by the parliamentary device of moving the previous question.[8] What appears to have been intended as a compromise motion was then brought to vote: Should the Committee of Correspondence direct Jackson to proceed on the matter of a change of government "with the utmost Caution" for securing to the inhabitants "all those Privileges, civil and religious" which they enjoyed under the existing constitution; and should the committee tell him that, if he thought the proposed change would endanger those privileges, he was "positively enjoined and required" to suspend all proceedings until he had reported back and received further directions? With the proprietary faction voting against it, this lengthy motion carried in the affirmative, 20 to 12.[9]

The long and controversial Saturday sitting at which these votes took place again proved to be too much for Isaac Norris. On Monday he sent a message through the clerk that he was too ill to attend and asked the House to choose a new speaker. A bipartisan committee waited on him, but to no avail, and on Wednesday, October 24, the Assembly elected Joseph Fox to succeed Norris as speaker. As usual, a committee was directed to inform the governor, but it reported the next day that Penn had gone to Newcastle and was not expected back

7. *Votes*, 1764, p. 10.

8. On the eighteenth-century usage and effect of this maneuver, see above, v, 348–9 n.

9. *Votes*, 1764, pp. 10–11. Peter Shepherd of Bucks Co. and John Blackburn of York Co., who had voted with the majority on the first motion, switched to the proprietary side on the second and third. After the adoption of the third motion, the Committee of Correspondence was directed to send a certified copy of that order to Jackson and to lay "a minute Account" of its proceedings before the Assembly at the next meeting. For the committee's covering letter to Jackson, see below, pp. 423–6.

until the following week. The proprietary group thought it had an excuse to postpone all further action, and on the afternoon of the 25th moved that the Assembly adjourn for a fortnight. But the majority would have none of such a delay; by a vote of 19 to 12 the House declined to adjourn, even though the new speaker had not been confirmed.[1]

The House thereupon resumed its business. Taking into consideration "that Matters of the highest Concern to the Rights of the Colonies in general, and of this Province in particular" were depending in England and would probably be brought to an issue in the next session of Parliament, the Assembly debated at considerable length whether, "to prevent any ill Consequences from Indisposition, or other Accident," which might happen to Jackson, it ought to appoint "some proper Person" to join him as agent or, in case of Jackson's death, to replace him. When this question was put, it passed by a vote of 20 to 11.[2]

Everyone knew what "proper Person" the leaders of the majority had in mind,[3] but Franklin's name appears nowhere in the records of this series of debates and votes until the sitting of Friday morning, October 26, when the opponents of the proposal brought it into the open. Upon reassembling the House began consideration of the appointment of a second agent, "and, after some Time spent therein, a Remonstrance from a Number of the Inhabitants of the City of Philadelphia was presented to the House and read."[4] The original text of this "Remonstrance" has not been found, but its contents are so fully stated in the *Votes and Proceedings* that they are printed here from that source as being the earliest-known formal statement of some of the reasons for opposition to Franklin's appointment. Comparison of this Remonstrance with the Protest signed by ten members of the Assembly (below, pp. 408–12) shows that this paper is more temperate in general tone and deals less directly and emphatically with the alleged personal deficiencies of Franklin as a candidate for the appointment. It was obviously intended to win the support of a wide segment of the public.

1. *Votes*, 1764, pp. 12–13. Fox was formally approved on Jan. 10, 1765, when the Assembly reconvened after a long recess. 8 *Pa. Arch.*, VII, 5691–2; *Pa. Col. Recs.*, IX, 236.

2. *Votes*, 1764, pp. 13–14.

3. Commenting on rumors that BF was to be appointed to assist Jackson, William Allen wrote Thomas Penn, Oct. 21, 1764, that BF was going to England "under pretence that he may render his Country service, in opposing the Ministerial measure of taxing us internally, but the real Design is to promote those of his wicked faction; you may therefore expect him fully freighted with rancour and Malice, determined to use every measure to injure the proprietary family." Penn Papers, Hist. Soc. Pa.

4. *Votes*, 1764, p. 14.

[October 26, 1764]
[A Remonstrance was presented and read, setting forth] That the Remonstrants being deeply concerned about the uncertain State of our inestimable Privileges, civil and religious, and the Danger to which they may be exposed by a Change of Government, and being extreamly desirous that Peace and Harmony should again be restored among the different Denominations in the Province, humbly entreat that the honourable House would be pleased to take into their serious Consideration, what may be most proper to accommodate the Differences that have so unhappily subsisted between the honourable Proprietaries and the good People of this Province; this they hope may be easily effected, as they understand the Proprietaries are heartily disposed to comply with such reasonable Demands, as will fully satisfy the Desires of the greatest Part of the People who signed the Petition for a Change of Government: That they therefore humbly represent, if the honourable House cannot think it proper absolutely to recal the Petitions sent Home for a Change of Government, that they would at least put it out of the Power of our Agent to present them at this unseasonable Conjuncture; for the Remonstrants cannot but be very anxiously concerned, that our invaluable Privileges, which are committed to the Guardianship and Protection of the House only, and which our Charter has put it out of their Power to alter or give up, should be exposed to any Hazard, by being left, in a great Measure, at the Discretion of any Agent or Agents; and more especially at a Time when the House are very sensible, that the Measures now proposed in England must, if executed, terminate in Consequences fatal to the Rights and Privileges of all the American colonies;[5] and they humbly beg Leave to represent to the House, that their Fears are not a little excited by a Proposal which they understand is made to send Mr. Benjamin Franklin Home, as an Assistant Agent for this Province, as they are of Opinion that there are many weighty Reasons to determine the House to make Choice of some other Gentleman, if it is thought necessary and expedient to load this Province (already greatly burthened with public Debt) with the additional Expence of supporting another Agent: Because it is well known that Mr. Franklin has had a principal Hand in proposing and promoting the Petitions for a Change

5. The prospective Stamp Act.

of Government, which now appear contrary to the Sentiments of more than three Fourths of the Province, and he may be justly supposed to have a fond Partiality for his own Schemes: Because it appears highly necessary to engage the Influence of our honourable Proprietaries to assist in preventing, if possible, any unnecessary Burthens being laid upon the Province, against whom Mr. Franklin entertains such a rooted Enmity, that they cannot take joint Council for the public Good: Because, especially as both Mr. Franklin and his Son hold Offices of considerable Profit and Honour under the Crown, the Remonstrants cannot expect that a Gentleman of his moderate Fortune will sacrifice his Interest for the Sake of the Province, which he must necessarily do, if he but seems to oppose the Measures of the Ministry, and which our present Circumstances require an Agent to do, with unshaken Resolution and Fidelity: That if, upon the whole, it is still thought necessary to employ another Agent, in a Matter wherein we may promise ourselves the Assistance of the honourable Proprietaries, and wherein the joint Interest of all the other Colonies will necessarily secure to us the Concurrence of all their Agents, the Remonstrants suggest that it would, in their humble Opinions, be less expensive, and better answer the Proposed End, to engage some Gentleman in England, of an independant Fortune, and Weight both with the Ministry and House of Commons: That as this Remonstrance has been delayed till the last, in Hopes that the honourable House would have withdrawn their Petition for a Change of Government (upon their Knowledge that at least Fifteen Thousand of their Constituents have signified their Disapprobation of this Measure,[6] in Opposition to about Three Thousand Five Hundred who have appeared for it) the present Time will not allow many Hands to be got to this Representation; but if the House will give that Deliberation to this Affair, which its immense Importance requires, the Remonstrants are fully persuaded, that three Fourths of the whole Province will be found ready to petition the House not only against any Change of our present Government, but also against employing Mr. Franklin in particular as an Agent in our Affairs.

6. The editors have been unable to find any firm evidence as to the number of signers of the counter-petition to the King.

Pennsylvania Assembly: Resolutions on the Appointment of Benjamin Franklin as Agent

Printed in *Votes and Proceedings of the House of Representatives of the Province of Pennsylvania, Met at Philadelphia* [October 15, 1764] (Philadelphia, 1764), p. 15; also MS certified copy of the first resolution: American Philosophical Society.

After the reading of the Remonstrance against Franklin's possible appointment as agent (printed immediately above) on the morning of October 26, the Assembly adjourned for the mid-day recess. When it reconvened in the afternoon the Remonstrance was read again, and then the House spent "much Time" in debate over the appointment of a second agent. At length the question was put "Whether Benjamin Franklin, Esq; of this City, shall be appointed for that Service?" The question was carried in the affirmative by a vote of 19 to 11.[7]

The members who voted in the negative then asked to be allowed "to enter the Reasons of their Dissent on the Minutes of the House," but when "some Opposition" appeared in the following debate, "the said Members did not insist on the Vote." They did, however, publish their "Protest" in the next issue of the *Pennsylvania Journal;* it is reprinted as the document following this one. The Assembly then proceeded to adopt the two resolutions printed here. No formal record of the vote on the first of these is entered in the *Votes;* presumably it was the same as that taken on the basic question of Franklin's appointment. On the second resolution—that regarding the method of providing for his expenses—the vote was 18 to 12, one member, John Morton of Chester County, who up to now had voted consistently with the majority, switching his vote to the proprietary side. After transacting some minor business, the Assembly ordered that the votes and proceedings of this sitting be printed "with all convenient Dispatch," and then adjourned to January 7, 1765.[8] In this short session the majority party had carried as far forward as the Assembly alone could do the entire program for which its members had contended in the recent election.

7. *Votes,* 1764, p. 15. The negative votes were cast by Richardson, Dickinson, Strettell, and Keppele of Philadelphia Co., Willing and Bryan of the City, Saunders of Lancaster, McConaughy of York, Allen and Montgomery of Cumberland, and Taylor of Northampton.
8. *Votes,* 1764, pp. 15–16. Publication of the *Votes* for this sitting was announced in *Pa. Gaz.,* Dec. 27, 1764.

[October 26, 1764]

Resolved,[9]

That Benjamin Franklin, Esq; be, and he is hereby appointed to embark, with all convenient Dispatch, for Great-Britain, to join with and assist Richard Jackson, Esq; our present Agent, in representing, soliciting and transacting the Affairs of this Province for the ensuing Year.

Resolved,

That the Expence attending the Voyage of the said Benjamin Franklin, Esq; to Great-Britain, and the Execution of the Trust reposed in him, be provided for in the first Bill prepared by this House for raising Money to defray the public Debts, and in Case no such Bill shall be prepared by this House, that the said Provision be, and the same is hereby recommended to the Care of the succeeding Assembly.

John Dickinson and Others: Protest against the Appointment of Benjamin Franklin as Agent

Printed in *The Pennsylvania Journal and Weekly Advertiser*, November 1, 1764.

After the minority members of the Assembly had failed to get their reasons for opposing Franklin's appointment as agent entered on the minutes, October 26 (see above, p. 407), they sent their statement to William Bradford for publication in the *Pennsylvania Journal* with the following introductory note: "Mr. BRADFORD, The Subscribers, at the Close of the late Debate in Assembly, concerning the sending Mr. Franklin to England as an Assistant to our Agent there, having offered a PROTEST against that Measure; which was refused to be entered on the Minutes, it is now thought proper to take this Method, of laying before the Publick the Reasons on which their Dissent was founded." It is generally agreed that the author of this paper was John Dickinson.

The Protest as printed is signed by ten of the eleven assemblymen who voted against the appointment. Although Joseph Richardson of Philadelphia County had voted in the negative on both questions

9. The MS certified copy of this resolution carries an appropriate heading with the date and is attested: "A true Extract from the Journals CHAS MOORE, Clk. of Assembly." In this version the word "Expedition" replaces "Dispatch" in the second line of the text.

directly relating to Franklin's appointment, he did not sign this Protest. He had been nominated on both tickets in the election campaign, and during the October session he had sided with the majority on four of the seven critical votes; as a moderate he appears to have been unwilling to associate himself with this public attack on Franklin.[1]

For Franklin's reply to the Protest, written before he embarked for England, see below, pp. 429–41.

October 26, 1764.

We whose Names are hereunto subscribed, do object and *protest* against the Appointment of the Person proposed as an Agent of this Province, for the following Reasons.

First. Because we believe him to be the Chief Author of the Measures pursued by the late Assembly, which have occasioned such Uneasiness and Distraction among the good People of this Province.

Secondly. Because we believe his fixed enmity to the Proprietors will preclude all Accommodation of our Disputes with them, even on just and reasonable Terms; So that for these two Reasons, we are filled with the most affecting Apprehensions, that the Petitions lately transmitted to England, will be made use of to produce a Change of our Government, contrary to the Intention of the Petitioners; the greatest part of whom, we are persuaded, only designed thereby to obtain a Compliance with some equitable Demands—And thus, by such an Appointment, we, and a vast Number of our most worthy Constituents, are deprived of all hopes of ever seeing an End put to the fatal Dissentions of our Country; it being our firm Opinion, that any further Prosecution of the Measures for a Change of our Government at this Time, will lay the Foundations of unceasing Feuds, and all the Miseries of Confusion, among the People we represent, and their Posterity. This step gives us the more lively Affliction, as it is taken at the very Moment, when we are informed by a Member of this House, that the Governor has assured him of his having received Instructions

1. There is no certainty that the Protest as printed is in precisely the same language as the document the minority wished to have entered on the minutes, but the introductory note in *Pa. Jour.* and some of the phraseology in the body of the Protest as printed convey the impression that it was the same paper. If the printed text is sharper than what was offered in the Assembly, however, that would be a possible reason for Richardson's failure to sign it.

from the Proprietors, on their hearing of our late Dispute, to give his Assent to the Taxation of their Estates in the same manner that the Estates of other Persons are to be taxed, and also to confirm, for the Publick use, the several *Squares,* formerly claimed by the City;[2] On which Subjects, we make no doubt, the Governor would have sent a Message to the House, if this had been the usual Time of doing Business, and he had not been necessarily absent to meet the Assembly of the Lower Counties.[3] And therefore we cannot but anxiously regret that, at a Time when the Proprietors have shewn such a Disposition, this House should not endeavour to cultivate the same, and obtain from them every reasonable Demand that can be made on the part of the People; in vigorously insisting on which, we would most earnestly unite with the rest of this House.

Thirdly. Because the Gentleman proposed, as we are informed, is very unfavorably thought of by several of his Majesty's Ministers; and we are humbly of Opinion, that it will be disrespectful

2. It appears from this statement that during the course of the October debates in the Assembly William Allen had definitely revealed for the first time that the Proprietors had directed Governor Penn, more than four months before, to yield to the Assembly's interpretation of the 1760 stipulation on the taxation of located but unimproved proprietary lands; above, pp. 213–14 n. The Proprietors seem also to have conceded the claims of the city of Philadelphia to four public squares laid out as such on William Penn's original plan but eliminated from Scull and Heap's 1753 semiofficial map of the city; above, VIII, 369.

3. Governor Penn's failure to inform the previous Assembly officially of these concessions at its September session was clearly based on political considerations relating to the forthcoming election. John Penn to Thomas Penn, Sept. 1, 1764, Penn Papers, Hist. Soc. Pa. When the new Assembly met in October, however, still dominated by Penn's opponents, he knew of their intentions regarding the petition to the King and the prompt appointment of BF; he foretold the outcome on both matters in a letter to his uncle on October 20, written after the debates had begun and before he went to Newcastle; Penn Papers, Hist. Soc. Pa. His failure to inform the new House at once of the Proprietors' concessions, as a method of disarming the majority, or at least of neutralizing the moderates among the anti-proprietary assemblymen, must be regarded as a tactical blunder. Word-of-mouth information from William Allen, who had kept discreetly silent during the two months since his return to Philadelphia from England, was no substitute for an official message from the governor. The excuse offered here reflects little credit on the political astuteness of John Penn and his advisers.

to our most Gracious Sovereign, and disadvantageous to ourselves and our constituents, to employ such a person as our Agent.

Fourthly. Because the Proposal of the Person mentioned, is so extremely disagreeable to a very great Number of the most serious and reputable Inhabitants of this Province of all Denominations and Societies (one Proof of which is, his having been rejected, both by this City and County at the last Election, though he had represented the former in Assembly for 14 Years) that we are convinced no Measure this House can adopt, will tend so much to inflame the Resentments and imbitter the Divisions of the good People of this province, as his Appointment to be our Agent— And we cannot but sincerely lament, that the Peace and Happiness of Pennsylvania should be sacrificed for the Promotion of a Man, who cannot be advanced but by the Convulsions of his Country.

Fifthly. Because the unnecessary haste with which this House has acted in proceeding to this Appointment (without making a small Adjournment, tho' requested by many Members, to consult our Constituents on the Matters to be decided, and) even before their Speaker has been presented to the King's Representative, tho' we are informed that the Governor will be in Town the Beginning of next Week;[4] may subject us to the Censures and very heavy Displeasure of our most gracious Sovereign and his Ministers.

Sixthly. Because the Gentleman propos'd, has heretofore ventured, contrary to an Act of Assembly, to place the public Money* in the Stocks, whereby this Province suffered a loss of £6000; and that sum added to £5000 granted for his Expences,[6] makes the

*The Money here meant was a Sum granted by Parliament as an Indemnification for part of our Expences in the late War, which by Act of Assembly was ordered for its better Security to be placed in the Bank.[5]

4. See above, pp. 403–4.
5. The Agency Act of 1759; above, VIII, 442; IX, 164–7, 186 n.
6. It is not certain how this figure of £5000 Pa. currency was determined, and it seems too low if it includes all the costs to the province of BF's mission except the loss from the sale of stocks. BF's accounts, as rendered and approved after his return, show that these costs amounted to £3714 10s. 7d. sterling; above, X, 194–7, 206–8. Purchase of the necessary bills of exchange required the actual expenditure, first and last, of £6182 11s. 2d. Pa. currency; 8 *Pa. Arch.,* VI, 5154; VII, 5911. The £5000 figure, however, may relate

whole Cost of his former voyage to England, amount to ELEVEN THOUSAND POUNDS; which expensive kind of Agency we do not chuse to imitate, and burden the Public with unnecessary loads of Debt. For these and other Reasons we should think ourselves guilty of betraying the Rights of Pennsylvania, if we should presumptuously commit them to the Discretion of a Man, against whom so many and just Objections present themselves.

Lastly. We being extremely desirous to avert the Mischiefs apprehended from the intended Appointment, and as much as in us lies to promote Peace and Unanimity among us and our Constituents, do humbly propose to the House, that if they will agree regularly to appoint any Gentleman* of Integrity, Abilities, and Knowledge in England, to assist Mr. Jackson as our Agent, under a Restriction not to present the Petitions for a Change of our Government, or any of them, to the King or his Ministers, unless an express Order for that Purpose be hereafter given by the Assembly of this Province; we will not give it any Opposition: But if such an Appointment should be made, we must insist (as we cannot think it a necessary one) that our Constituents, already labouring under heavy Debts, be not burthened with fresh Impositions on that Account; and therefore, in Condescension to the Members, who think another Agent necessary, we will concur with them if they approve of this Proposal, in paying such Agent at our own Expence.

JOHN DICKINSON,	WILLIAM ALLEN,
DAVID McCANAUGHY,	THOMAS WILLING,
JOHN MONTGOMERY,	GEORGE BRYAN,
ISAAC SANDERS,	AMOS STRETTELL,
GEORGE TAYLOR,	HENRY KEPPELE.

*Dr. Fothergill was mentioned by the Subscribers as a proper Person.[7]

---

only to the salary of £3000 sterling (£500 per year for six years) voted on Feb. 19, 1763; above, x, 197. At the rate of exchange in effect on that date, the cost of the salary in Pa. currency would have been £5175. In his *Remarks* (below, p. 438) BF naturally did not question this £5000 figure, though he did challenge the £6000 said here to have been lost on the sale of stocks.

7. As a leading London Quaker, Dr. John Fothergill (above, IV, 126 n) was on good terms with both the Pa. Friends and Thomas Penn; during BF's first mission Fothergill had tried to smooth the relations between BF and the Proprietor; see, for example, VIII, 312–13.

From James Parker

ALS: American Philosophical Society

Honoured Sir   Woodbridge. Octob 27. 1764.

Both yours of the 20th and 25th I received late last Night:[8] I shall endeavour now to answer to both, as well as I can.

With Respect to Mr. Strahan: Tho' I wrote to him a while ago, that I would see he was paid, if he would wait a little longer;[9] I told him the Case and that I was in hopes to get it of Mr. Holt, but if he fail'd, I would at last see it paid:[1] Mr. Holt tells me he had sent him since only one £16 Sterling. I think there remains about £170 still due: Mr. Holt is returned from New Haven, says he has brought all the Accounts scattered, but he will exert himself to get them settled: He says there is above 6 or £700 Lawful Money due to us at New Haven, much of it in good Hands, of which the greater Part will belong to me, if ever got in: Green[2] having used all the ready Money, or otherways laid it out in purchasing his Materials: He Mr. Holt, has used great Part of his Dues, in purchasing that House,[3] and some other Matters whilst poor I have received for the four year Green had it about £12 Proc.[4] Things are in this Situation, Green sat up at Hartford, and the Debts uncollected in. I could sue Holt, but if I do, he is ruined: and perhaps I not a Farthing the better; He promises fair, and within this Year past, I continually am getting small Matter from

8. Neither letter has been found.

9. BF paid Parker's debt to Strahan, £163 13s. 7d. sterling, on Feb. 1, 1765, some weeks after he returned to England; see below, p. 520. Parker eventually repaid most of the money, although his heirs raised some controversy about the matter after his death. See above, x, 375 n, 406 n.

1. Parker was indebted to Strahan for a shipment of books which he had bought for John Holt (above, v, 441 n), his partner in the New Haven printing business from 1755 to 1760 and in a New York venture from 1760 to 1762. Beverly McAnear has explored the tangled relations between the two partners in "James Parker versus John Holt," N.J. Hist. Soc. Proc., LIX (April, July, 1941), 77–95, 198–212.

2. Thomas Green (above, x, 403 n), manager of Parker and Holt's New Haven paper, The Connecticut Gazette, from 1760 until 1764, when he set up for himself as a printer in Hartford.

3. In 1759 Holt bought a house and printing office in New Haven for £400. N.J. Hist. Soc. Proc., LIX, 82.

4. Proclamation money: the valuation prescribed for foreign coin in the colonies by a royal proclamation of 1704 and an act of 1707 (6 Anne, c. 57). In general, it was one-third higher than sterling valuation.

him, towards supporting my Family, that so what little Money I get may the better go towards paying my Debts: By these Means, the only safe ones I can think of, I hope to get all paid. Now, as I have almost brought all my Debts into the Compass of yours and Mr. Strahan's of which last the Allowance for the Office of Comptroller, I try chiefly to appropriate.[5] Would it be disagreable to you to pay Mr. Strahan, and take all my Debts upon yourself, as I would chuse to pay you Interest rather than any other; tho' Mr. Strahan has not yet demanded Interest, yet it is reasonable that he should either be paid or have Interest, which I had rather transfer to you. I fancy upon the Whole, what I shall have due from the Post-Office by the first of January next, will pay all Mr. Strahan's Debt, and then there will be only the Bond I owe you,[6] which going on Interest now, can remain till I can pay it, which I will exert all I can to do, when it may be wanted. If this Matter be practicable and agreeable to you, I shall be glad to have it carried into Execution as soon as possible. If you have any Money to spare in England: If not, I must try some other Method to get him paid: for I am as uneasy about it, as he can be.

You say you sent some of the Post-Office Instructions &c. There has none come to Hand yet.[7] I shall set about making up all the small Books, and send them now to the several small Offices as soon as possible.

The Law relating to the Division Line[8] I shall send you, but you will find but little in that to enlighten you: Mr. Alexander had

5. Parker had been appointed comptroller of the North American Post Office on April 22, 1757, with a remuneration of $7\frac{1}{2}$ percent of all the money he collected from local postmasters. In 1765, as a result of the Post Office Act of that year, he was granted a fixed salary of £80 per year. N.J. Hist. Soc. *Proc.*, LIX, 85 n; above, VII, 191–4.

6. This bond for £357 16s. 1d. (actually double the amount of Parker's debt to BF) was executed on Nov. 15, 1763; see above, X, 374.

7. These instructions have not been found. They may have been sent to BF and Foxcroft by Anthony Todd, perhaps in his lost letter of July 14, 1764 (above, p. 341), and forwarded by them to Parker.

8. On Feb. 23, 1764, the New Jersey Assembly passed an act submitting its boundary dispute with New York to the adjudication of commissioners appointed by the Crown. Thirteen commissioners were appointed in 1767 of whom BF was one. Being in England, he of course took no part in the actual work of the commission. For an account of this boundary dispute, see Edgar J. Fisher, *New Jersey as a Royal Province* (N.Y., 1911), pp. 210–39.

some Things printed when I lived in New-York, pretty large, that might probably enlighten you a little.[9] The opposite party also printed some Things, but I have not them, tho' I printed most of them.[1] Whether Lord Sterling[2] could not supply you with them especially of his side, I can't say: I believe, the Piece of the opposite side[3] can be found in my Store Room in New York. Among the Papers left there is the parting Division between Weyman and I, as that was printed by Weyman a little before we parted. If you get the other, and find that necessary, when I go to New York again I will endeavour to find it.

Now with Respect to the Virginia Affair.[4] If you should think it the best Method of securing that Matter to Mr. Hunter's Son for me to go there, which is the only Thing that would induce me to go, I shall be willing, if Mr. Royle dies, but he is not dead yet. Otherways, I should rather chuse not to venture into new Places: If it would suit as well, for any other, and you can rely on their Integrity, I shall be quite as willing: I know at the Death of Mr. Hunter, Mrs. Holt was there, and great Interest was making for Mr. Holt, who was mighty desirous of going but when the Contents and Conditions of the Will came to be known, that was knock'd in the Head: Mr. Holt would now be very fond of going

9. James Alexander was a prominent public official in both New York and New Jersey and a member of APS. One of the "Things" Parker had printed for him was *A Bill in the Chancery of New-Jersey* (N.Y., 1747) of the East Jersey Proprietors. BF had assisted in finding an engraver for the maps. Above, III, 32.

1. In 1752 Parker printed *An Answer to a Bill in Chancery.*

2. For William Alexander, Lord Stirling, son of James Alexander, see above, VI, 244 n.

3. *The Bill of Complaint in the Chancery of New Jersey,* printed in 1760 by Parker's former partner William Weyman; for the relations between Weyman and Parker see Beverly McAnear, "James Parker versus William Weyman," N.J. Hist. Soc. *Proc.,* LIX (Jan. 1941), 1–23.

4. This "Affair" was the disposition of the printing business of BF's deceased colleague, former Deputy Postmaster General William Hunter (above, V, 18 n). While he was still living, Hunter had been assisted in the publication of the *Virginia Gazette* by his brother-in-law, Joseph Royle. Hunter had instructed his executors to offer Royle the management of the paper until his own son Billy, whose education BF had undertaken to supervise (above, X, 317–8 n), came of age. Parker feared that his ex-partner, John Holt, whose wife, Elizabeth, was William Hunter's sister, might attempt to deprive young Billy Hunter of his inheritance by installing himself or his nephew in the Hunter family printing business.

thither again, and perhaps that would be the most natural: but when you consider, that Mr. Holt has taken his Brother's Son,[5] who is Mrs. Holt's Sister's Son also, and Brother to Miss Betsey,[6] and is bringing him up to the Trade, and he is a little older than Billy Hunter, whether he would not find Means to oust young Hunter, in Favour of his adopted Son: Besides, whether Mr. Holt's Incapacity, Neglect or Design in not settling true Accounts, and paying young Hunter his Share, might not greatly injure Hunter, even if he surrendered up the Business. I don't know One I would or could recommend prefereable to Mr. Holt; the present Race of young Printers seeming to me most of them, so abandoned to Liquor, as to deserve little Encouragement, besides their Honesty should be tried first. Another Objection against Holt, may be, your and others Opinion of his Honesty, or perhaps, his Incapacity to execute the Business well, for he does all now by the Help of other Hands, may not induce his Journeymen, to try to set up in Opposition, &c. Upon the Whole, with respect to myself, I could not form great Hopes of Advantage to myself, exclusive of doing Justice to Mr. Hunter. My own printing Business here, my Son could do very well with, as far as relates to the printing; but I could not even hope the Favour of your continuing him in my Office as Comptroller tho' since his Marriage he is somewhat more settld yet he wants that Thought and Solidity necessary to attend it:[7] In the Post-Office here only he might act: but the Profit of it, is very small, about 30s. per An. as Commissions, and it is in fact the worst Situation for one on the Continent, as 7 eighths of the Letters are for Amboy, to be sent thither, and perhaps twice going after for Pay before got once: I have many Times known it necessary to go to Amboy with 4 or 5 Shillings worth of Letters perhaps spend Six Hours Time, and get a Drink of 1s. 6d. and come home for the Profits of 1s. However, I never thought much of it, whilst I have the other Office, or whilst I had the Privilege of franking, &c.

5. John Hunter Holt, often called Holt's son, but in fact his nephew, although Holt adopted him as a son.

6. Betsey Holt, apparently John Holt's adopted daughter. In 1771 she married Eleazar Oswald (c.1755–1795), printer, editor, and officer in the Revolution.

7. Samuel Franklin Parker (c.1745–1779) married Sarah Ford (or Foord) of Woodbridge, N.J., in 1764; she died in October 1768, leaving a three-year-old daughter. In 1769 Samuel Parker married a Mary Moore, who survived him. James Parker to BF, Oct. 17, 1768, APS; 1 N.J. Arch., XXII, 297.

Nor can I suppose, if I went thither I could continue in the office. It is true it might suit tolerably better for those lower Offices, than to these: but it would be quite too very inconvenient for any this Way. Nor would I go, but upon some such Conditions as these, that I would not engage certainly for more than three years at first, in which Time, if it did not suit, by that Time another might be found out more to your Liking; and if I continued longer, to the Time Billy Hunter should be of Ability to carry it on himself, that I should return to my native Country, provided it pleased Heaven to spare me so long. Upon these Suppositions, if I can be of Service to Mr. Hunter's Estate, and to your Liking and Desire, it is all I should think well of. As I have always thought it my Duty and Interest to do any Pleasure of yours, so I am quite resigned either to stay or go, as it shall seem best to you if Mr. Royle dies,[8] upon these Principles you can proceed, according to your Pleasure: It is probable Mr. Royle may recover, and live long enough: if so, there is no Occasion.

I imagined Mr. Holt had wrote to you since he came home;[9] for he told me, and said he would write to you, (and in which I told him I had nothing to say,) that in those Accounts that Mr. Green settled with the Post-Office, there were a great Number of Letters, brought by his Bye-Posts, entirely different and off from the Post-Roads, which as you would not allow him any Thing towards his Rider's Pay, could not in Justice belong to the Post-Office; he said he had a List of the Letters, Places, and sums, where they came from &c. and I suppose he will yet write, tho' he has been much hurried in getting his Almanack Materials &c.

Thus I have, I believe almost tired your Patience, therefore 'tis Time to conclude, with all Respects Your most obliged Servant

JAMES PARKER.

PS. The Winds are so exceeding high, these two or three Days, and is so to-day That I fear the Posts cannot cross the Rivers, &c.

Addressed: For / Benjamin Franklin, Esqr / Philadelphia

Endorsed: Parker

8. Joseph Royle died in 1766.

9. If Holt wrote BF, his letter has not been found. On Dec. 19, 1763, BF had instructed Jared Ingersoll to sue Holt to recover £320 18s. 9d. which he owed the Post Office. See above, x, 402–3.

From Lewis Jones[1]   ALS: American Philosophical Society

Respected Sir   Woodbridge Oct. 30, 1764
   Being informed by Mr. Parker that you was going to England next Monday,[2] I take this Opportunity to beg the Favour of you to deliver the inclosed Letter to my Father or to Mr. Cummings,[3] who will deliver it to him, I have several Times wrote to my Father, and to several of my Relations, but have never received any Answer from any of them, which makes me the rather trouble you as being sure it will go safe, Dear Sir, that you may have a good Passage and safe return is the Earnest Prayers, of Sir Your's at Command   LEWIS JONES

Addressed: For / Benjamin Franklin, Esqr; / at / Philadelphia.
Endorsed: Lewis Jones

William Dunlap to Benjamin Franklin and John Foxcroft   ALS: American Philosophical Society

This letter and the two that follow directly concern the settlement of accounts between the deputy postmasters general, Franklin and Foxcroft, and William Dunlap,[4] postmaster at Philadelphia from 1757 until 1764, in which year he was replaced by Franklin's brother, Peter. Since it is not known precisely when Peter Franklin took over the post office in Philadelphia,[5] it is difficult to date the present series of letters, all of which appear to have been written after Dunlap left office. Dunlap's expression in this letter of a desire for a "Clearance in full

   1. For Lewis Jones, at this time an apprentice to James Parker, see above, x, 343 n, 344–5 n.
   2. BF sailed for London from Chester on Wednesday, Nov. 7, 1764, aboard the *King of Prussia*, Capt. Robinson.
   3. For Griffith Jones and Thomas Cumming, see above, x, 343 n, 345–6 n.
   4. For Dunlap, DF's nephew-in-law and a printer by trade, see above, v, 199 n. He was appointed Philadelphia postmaster on April 4, 1757; see above, vii, 168–9.
   5. Certainly he was in office by Oct. 17, 1764, on which day he signed a notice as "Peter Franklin, Deputy Post master," advising the citizens of Philadelphia that the post office had been removed to his house in Market Street. *Pa. Gaz.*, Oct. 18, 1764. The record of letters sent from Philadelphia, described above, pp. 398–402, begins with entries of October 18, 1764.

418

OCTOBER 1764

till July 6th." suggests that this was the termination date of his appointment and that the letters might have been written shortly thereafter. The records of the Philadelphia post office show, however, that Dunlap carefully recorded the receipt of letters until Oct. 5, 1764,[6] which appears to mean that he was serving as late as that day and makes an October dating likely. Supporting this conjecture is a reference in this first letter to the impatience to leave town of John Foxcroft, who can be placed in Philadelphia as late as Sept. 21, 1764.[7] In any case the letters cannot have been written later than Nov. 7, 1764, the date of Franklin's departure for England.

The state of Dunlap's account is as confusing as the dating of the letters. A rendering of it in Franklin's hand is published above, VII, 160–2, and it appears to show that by the summer of 1764 Dunlap owed the post office £1042 4s. 11½d., although in the letter below Dunlap indicates that he owes only about £300.

Gentlemen,   Monday Morning [October ? 1764]

As Mr. Foxcroft is impatient to leave Town, and I find a Discussion of my Accounts, from their Length and my extreme Indisposition, will take up a considerable Time, I have thought it might not be improper to make you an Offer, which, as it far exceeds any Thing you have any Right to expect or get from me, it is probable you may accept of: I am possessed of a certain Tract of Land of upwards of two hundred Acres, Situate in Chester County in this Province, which I value at, and am told is realy Worth £500:[8] This with Mr. Hunters Debt of £95.[9] I am ready to make over to you on your giving me a Clearance in full till July 6th. last. This is all the visible Estate I have in the World, and is full £300 more than I think I shall be able to make appear you

6. See above, VII, 158–60. A notice concerning Maryland and Virginia mails, dated September 13 and signed by Dunlap as postmaster, appeared in *Pa. Jour.* and *Pa. Gaz.*, Sept. 13, 1764.

7. See above, p. 341.

8. In *Pa. Jour.*, Sept. 20, 1764, and the next two weekly issues, Dunlap advertised this plantation in New London Township, Chester Co., for sale or long lease. Apparently the postal officials took over the property in partial satisfaction of Dunlap's debt, but a mortgage held by Amos Strettell and other complications created problems and led to extended correspondence among BF, DF, and James Parker, beginning almost at once; see below, p. 469 n.

9. Perhaps a debt owed to Dunlap by the estate of William Hunter, former deputy postmaster general; above, V, 18 n.

419

have any Pretence to, and is such as nothing but a Disire to get from under the Weight of your merciless Oppression, should induce me to make to the Injury of my Family and of my other Creditors: However if nothing will satiate your Resentment, but the Ruin of an helpless Family, I must apprize you that when it has had its full Swing, your Dividend of the Spoil, will fall vastly short of what I even am willing to allow you have any pretence to. I am Gentlemen, Your most humble Servant   W. DUNLAP

Addressed: To / Messrs. Franklin & Foxcroft / Present

From William Dunlap[1]   ALS: American Philosophical Society

Sir   Monday [October? 1764]

As I see nothing will satiate your unbounded, cruel and merciless Resentment but the entire Destruction of a poor helpless Family, no Branch of whom, I will dare to say, ever Injur'd you in Thought, Word or Deed, I have no Favor to ask at the Hands of a Man who thursts for nothing short of my Hearts Blood: Whet your Poynard Sir, and it is ready for you: Your Cruelty has brought on me a Disorder, (and to your Treatment alone my Orphan beggard Children will impute it,) viz. a depressed broken Heart, and its sure Consequence a deep Consumption, which I am well assur'd no Medicines can possibly conquer, so that even should your tender Mercy withold you from the former, the latter will soon effect to your Hands: Under these Circumstances, I have only to beg that you would spare the Appelations which you are disposed to bestow upon me of Rogue, Rascal, &c. because (let me whisper it in your Ear, and indeed it shall never go farther) had the same indirect, ungenerous, Mean Methods been taken, (which I will assert was never before practised upon any Officer) in sifting and twisting your own Son's Post-Office Accounts as there was with mine,[2] he would have deserved in the highest Degree, the Worst

1. Probably written following receipt of a reply, now missing, to Dunlap's letter immediately above. That he addressed this second letter to BF alone may be because he was particularly resentful that a relative, although one only by marriage, should have declined to accept his apparently inadequate proposal for settling the debt.

2. WF was Dunlap's predecessor as postmaster of Philadelphia. He re-

Appelation you have yet thought proper to bestow upon me: This Sir, I will prove whenever you may please to call upon me to do so: I am Sir, the unhappy wretched   W Dunlap

Addressed: To / Dr. B. Franklin / Postmaster General / In / Philadelphia

Benjamin Franklin and John Foxcroft
to William Dunlap   Draft: American Philosophical Society

Mr Dunlap,   [October? 1764]

We have read your extraordinary Letter[3] upon which we shall make no other Observation but this, That it is not in our Power to give a Discharge for your whole Debt to the Post Office on your Payment of a Part; the Debt not being to us but to the Crown: and that If you do not immediately come to a Settlement with us, in which we are willing to give you all the Assistance we can, our Duty will oblige us to commence Suit against you, whereby the Accounts will be examined and settled by indifferent Men; which indeed will be more agreable to us than a private Settlement, that might give Colour or Room for the abusive Reflections after[ward?] upon us, which you already seem forward to make them on us without the least Regard to Truth, as if we desired to oppress you, tho' we have really no Interest in getting a farthing more from you than you ought to pay.[4] Your Charge against your Predecessor

---

linquished the position when he accompanied his father to England in 1757. Among all the attacks on BF in 1764 and sneers at WF, there seems to have been no other suggestion that WF had mishandled post-office funds.

3. Possibly a reference to the first of Dunlap's letters immediately above, but more probably to the second, even though that was addressed to BF alone, because of the mention in the final sentence here of Dunlap's charge against WF's management of his post-office accounts.

4. Apparently the suggestion of a public settlement "by indifferent Men" cooled Dunlap off. The affair seems to have been handled quietly. Two years later, after Dunlap had gone to Barbados and then to England, where he was ordained by the Bishop of London, he returned to Philadelphia and combined his printing with preaching in St. Paul's Church. William Smith wrote the bishop, Dec. 18, 1766, complaining of Dunlap's inadequate education, but said nothing about any past legal or financial difficulties, calling him "a simple inoffensive man whom I never could have thought of recom-

you are hereby immediately called upon to make good; which if you can do, as it will be a Merit with Regard to the Office, may entitle you the more to favour from, Your humble Servants

F and F.

From Pennsylvania Assembly Committee of Correspondence[5]   Copy: Library Company of Philadelphia

Sir   Philada. Novemr. 1st. 1764

The General Assembly of this Province, having appointed Us to be the Committee of Correspondence; And in Pursuance of their Resolves from time to time during their late Sitting; We have Caused to be made out and furnished divers Certified Copys of Resolves and Instructions to Richd. Jackson Esqr. then Sole Agent of this Province to be sent by Us [to] Mr. Jackson.[6]

But as it appeared to the General Assembly, that matters of the highest Concern to the Colonies in General and to this Province in particular were depending in England &c: The House were pleased to Resolve that you should embark with all Convenient dispatch for Great Britain there to joyn with and assist the said Richd. Jackson Esqr. in the Agency of Representing, Soliciting and

---

mending for Orders tho' I know no harm of him only wish he had not come here." William S. Perry, ed., *Papers Relating to the History of the Church in Pennsylvania, A.D. 1680–1778* (n.p., 1871), p. 412.

5. On Oct. 17, 1764, two days after the Pa. Assembly convened for its annual fall session, it appointed a committee of correspondence to serve for "the ensuing Year." The members appointed to the committee were Speaker Isaac Norris (who resigned as speaker a week later), Joseph Fox (Norris' successor as speaker), Joseph Richardson, John Hughes, Isaac Pearson, and John Ross. The committee wrote the present letter to BF after the House had adjourned on Oct. 26, 1764. A copy of the letter was laid before the House and read on Jan. 12, 1765. *Votes*, 1764, p. 5; 8 *Pa. Arch.*, VII, 5700.

6. On Oct. 20, 1764, the House ordered the Committee of Correspondence to transmit to Jackson a copy of instructions adopted the same day detailing some of Pennsylvania's objections to the Sugar Act and the proposed Stamp Act and a copy of an order, also adopted the same day, advising Jackson to proceed with "the utmost Caution" in attempting to affect a change of government in the province. *Votes*, 1764, pp. 8–10, 11.

transacting the affairs of this Province for the Ensuing year; As will more fully Appear to you by a Certified Copy of the Resolves of the House for this purpose made out and signed by the Clark of the Assembly.[7]

Needless therefore will it be for Us to add more on this Occasion then to referr you to the Several Copys of Resolves and Instructions here with Delivered to you for Mr. Jackson[8] and to request that you will in every thing and measure Relative to the Colonies in General and this Province in particular, Aid Assist Joyn and Act in Concert with Mr. Jackson, and Strictly and attentively Observe the Directions of the House given him in every measure to be Prosecuted. We wish you a good Voiage &c.

To Benja. Franklin Esqr

Endorsed: Copy of the Committee of Correspondenc's Letter Dd. Benja. Franklin Esqr   Novr. 1st. 1764

Pennsylvania Assembly Committee of Correspondence to Richard Jackson[9]   LS: Library of Congress

Sir   Philada: November 1st. 1764.

The Present Assembly of this Province have been pleased to appoint us, together with the Speaker of the House to be the Committee of Correspondence for the ensuing Year.[1] The late Assembly transmitted to you certain Petitions from the House and Divers Freemen of this Province to His Majesty relative to a Change of Government to be presented only upon Certainty first had that we should Incur no Danger of the Loss of the Priviledges Enjoy'd by the Freemen of this Province under our present Constitution,[2] The present Assembly, hoping an Accommodation with our Proprietors may take place, and that he will in due Time make such Concessions as will fully satisfy the Assembly and Freemen of this Prov-

7. See above, pp. 407–8.
8. In addition to the documents mentioned in the second footnote to this letter, see the letter to Jackson immediately below.
9. The instructions to Jackson contained in this letter were binding also on BF, his newly appointed colleague in the agency.
1. *Votes,* 1764, p. 5.
2. Above, pp. 145–7, 193–200.

ince have determined not to withdraw those Petitions to His Majesty, but have order'd the same to remain with you, and to be proceeded in, or not, by you with the Utmost Caution for securing our Priviledges in Case the Change should happen.[3] We cannot add more Strength or Force of Words than are contained in the Resolve of the House,[4] (Copy whereof Signed by the Clerk We herewith transmit to you) for your Conduct in this Matter, it being clearly the Sense of every Member of the House, and We doubt not of every Freeman in the Province, that a Change is not to be attempted, if you apprehend the least Danger of the Loss of any one Priviledge Civil or Religious we now Enjoy, should you discover any such Danger, We rest assured You will conform Yourself most Stricktly to the latter part of the Resolve, Wherein you are positively Enjoined to suspend the presenting those Petitions, Untill you shall have acquainted the Assembly therewith and received their further Direction. For altho' we Reverence his Sacred Majesty, and his Government, And altho' we are of Opinion Our Proprietors have insisted on some and Contended for other Matters which we have thought Unreasonable and Unjust, Yet as under our Charter and Laws the Freemen of this Province Do Enjoy Priviledges peculiar to itself and unknown in any Royal Government We shou'd chuse to continue the Struggle for our Rights with our Proprietors rather than by getting rid of that Struggle loose our Inestimable Priviledges.

The late Assembly were pleas'd to send you some Instructions for your Conduct, Relative to the late Act of Parliament which greatly affects the Trade of the Northern Colonies, and the Danger

3. These words and those which follow, down to the sentence that speaks of the assemblymen's "Reverence" for the King, closely parallel the phraseology of the third resolution, which was adopted on Oct. 20, 1764, by a vote of 20 to 12. *Votes,* 1764, p. 11. Taken together with the remainder of this paragraph, the injunction is, if anything, somewhat more emphatic than the formal resolution. It seems probable that the information about proprietary concessions, which Governor Penn had transmitted indirectly through William Allen (above, pp. 409–10), though nowhere mentioned in the official minutes, had created some optimism among the members that a satisfactory "Accommodation" might be reached without royal intervention. Such optimism, however, was not strong enough to lead to the recall of the petition or to prevent the appointment of BF as co-agent.

4. The resolution referred to in the preceding note.

apprehended to our Rights as Englishmen, at the Approaching Sessions of Parliament.[5]

The present Assembly have taken that matter also into their Consideration and have prepared some further Instructions thereupon, which they have order'd us to Sign and transmit to you, and which you will herewith receive, and doubt not the Hints therein given with the Arguments your own Mind will furnish on this Important Matter, will prove sufficient to avert the Impending Blow.[6]

We have it further in Charge from the House to Request that all your Letters on Public Affairs may be addressed to the then Speaker Isaac Norris Esquire or to a Majority of the Committee of Correspondence in Order that the same may be laid before the House; which You'l please to observe.[7]

We are further to acquaint you that the House taking into Consideration the Matters of high Concern to the Colonies in General and to this Province in particular Expected in Parliament at their next Session, and to prevent any ill Consequences that might arise in Case of your Indisposition have thought proper to appoint Benjamin Franklin Esqr: to join with and assist you in Representing Soliciting and transacting the Affairs of this Province for the ensuing Year, and have directed him to embark with all convenient Dispatch for Great Britain.

Mr. Franklin will deliver this with the Resolves and Instructions of the House to you, and doubt not from your known Abilities and Joint Endeavours, You will render to the Colonies in General and to this Province in particular the most Acceptable Services. We have only to add, that Mr. Norris our late Worthy Speaker, thro' Indisposition, became unable to attend the Service of the House during their late sitting, and Joseph Fox Esqr was chosen in his stead and placed in the Chair Accordingly.[8] Inclosed you have a

5. Above, pp. 347–51.

6. The instructions referred to here were approved Oct. 20, 1764; they are printed in *Votes*, 1764, pp. 8–10, and reprinted in 8 *Pa. Arch.*, VII, 5678–82. They are summarized above, p. 396 n.

7. This order was voted Oct. 20, 1764, before Norris resigned as speaker. It may have been caused by complaints that Jackson had expressed many of his thoughts on Pennsylvania matters in conversations with Allen, when the latter was in England, or in letters to BF, rather than in official communications to Speaker Norris and the Committee of Correspondence.

8. Above, pp. 403–4.

Bill of Exchange for £106 6s. 4d. Sterling which we hope will meet with due Honour. We are Sir Your Real Friends and Very Humble Servants

Jos. Fox
Jos. Richardson
John Ross.
Jon Hughes

To Richard Jackson Esqr.

Endorsed: Philada 1st. Novr. 1764   Letter from the Committee of Correspondence

From John Smith[9]

ALS: American Philosophical Society

Esteemed Friend   Burlington, 11th mo: 2d. 1764

It is with great pleasure, I hear of thy undertaking a voyage to London, at a time, when not only the province which has deputed thee, but all North America, wants a friend there (and could have no other that I know of) so well qualifyed to serve both the particular and General Interest. May the Divine Blessing attend thy person and Benevolent designs, and Grant thee a safe return to thy family and country, is the fervent Wish of, Thy very Affectionate Friend   JOHN SMITH

Dr. Benja. Franklin

Endorsed: John Smith Esqr   Letter, Nov. 2. 1764

To Jonathan Williams

ALS: Yale University Library

Loving Kinsman,   Philada. Nov. 3. 1764

The Case of the Armonica came home to Night, and the Spindle with all the rest of the Work seems well done.[1] But on farther Con-

---

9. For John Smith, a son-in-law of James Logan, a merchant in Philadelphia and Burlington, N.J., an associate of BF's in the Pa. Hospital, the Assembly, and the Loganian Library, see above, III, 240–3 n; V, 290–330 *passim*, 423 n. See also Frederick B. Tolles, "A Literary Quaker: John Smith of Burlington and Philadelphia," *PMHB*, LXV (1941), 300–33.

1. BF had apparently undertaken to have an armonica made for Williams' son, Josiah, a blind young man with musical aspirations; see above, X, 156

sideration, I think it not worth while to take one of them to London to be fitted with Glasses as we intended. It will be better to send you one compleat from thence, made under my Direction, which I will take care shall be good.[2] The Glasses here will serve for these Cases when I come back, if it please God that I live to return, and some Friends will be glad of them.

Inclos'd I send you that Imposter's Letter. Perhaps he may be found by his Hand Writing.[3]

We sail on Wednesday.[4] The Merchants here in two Hours subscrib'd £1100 to be lent the Publick for the Charges of my Voyage, &c. I shall take with me but a Part of it, £500 Sterling; any Sum is to be had that I may want.[5] My love to all. Adieu. Yours affectionately   B FRANKLIN

Addressed: To / Mr Jonathan Williams / Mercht / Boston / Free / B FRANKLIN

Endorsed: Novr 5. 1764 F

From Baynton and Wharton[6]

LS: American Philosophical Society

Sir   Philadelphia, Novemr, 3d 1764.

The Tracts of Land, Which We mention'd to You, last Spring, are situated as follows.[7]

---

n, 295. For a bill from Benjamin Humphreys for "Two steel spendels For the Harmonica," see below, p. 446.

2. On April 28, 1766, BF wrote Williams that although he had tried "'till I am tir'd," he had been unable to have an armonica made in London. APS.

3. Neither the impostor nor his letter has been identified.

4. BF sailed from Chester, aboard the *King of Prussia,* Capt. Robinson.

5. BF carried the £500 to England in bills of exchange: one, D. Williams on John Strettel, for £300, and another, Reese Meredith on Samuel Bean, for £200. When he got to London he deposited the money with the banking firm of Brown and Collinson. Journal, 1764–1776, p. 1 (see below, pp. 518–20). On May 14, 1767, Speaker of the House Joseph Galloway signed an order for the repayment of the sum advanced for BF's mission (£870 in Pa. currency). 8 *Pa. Arch.,* VII, 6015.

6. On this firm of Philadelphia merchants (more properly by this time Baynton, Wharton & Morgan), see above, p. 187 n.

7. BF sent a "short Account" of these lands to Richard Jackson on May

One of Them, "is on the East side of Lake Champlaine and on the North side of the River Messesque,[8] including Twenty Thousand Acres."

The Other Tract "is situated on the North side of the Bay of Chaleur adjoining the Bay, including the same Quantity, as the above."

The Gentleman who gives us, the above Information, says, in his Letter of the 11th. of March Last[9] that "the first mention'd Tract, lies in a rich fine Country, is of a good Soil, full of excellent Timber, such as White Oak, Walnut, Chesnut, Pine &c. is Situated on the Lake (Champlaine) and convenient for transporting any thing, to Quebec."

With respect to the last described Tract, He writes us, That, "This is the best Cod Fishery in this Government. The Land is tolerably good, The Timber the same, But not comparable, to the former. The sooner You Petition their Lordships, the Better, as every Thing of this Kind, That is Valuable, will be taken up. Pray do not neglect the First Opportunity, in sending Your Petition Home, As you may depend, it will be of the greatest Importance."

The foregoing is the Description, We have of those two Parcels of Land; Wherefore, We apprehend if Mr. Jackson, has not apply'd For Them, You will think with us, That the sooner You do it, the more probable, it is, You will Succeed. With Sincere Respect We are Sir, Your very Obedient humble Servants

BAYNTON & WHARTON

To Benjamin Franklin Esqre.

1, 1764, and asked him to use his influence with the appropriate British officials to have the lands granted to Baynton, Wharton, and himself; BF offered his friend one half of his share of the lands for his trouble. See above, pp. 187–8. Apparently nothing ever came of this scheme.

8. The Missisquoi River rises in Vermont, flows northward into Province Quebec, then back into Vermont, and empties into Missisquoi Bay, an arm of Lake Champlain, near the Canadian border.

9. Baynton & Wharton's informant may have been either Samuel Eldridge or William Long, both of whom traveled from Crown Point to Montreal between March 7 and 12, 1764, and who wrote Baynton & Wharton a joint letter from Montreal on March 13, 1764. Pennsylvania State Library, Harrisburg.

To John Smith   ALS: Drayton M. Smith, Philadelphia (1959)

Dear Sir   Philada. Nov. 4. 1764
   I received your very obliging Letter.[1] I thank you cordially for
your kind good Wishes. I hope my Conduct in England will be
such as not to lessen the Esteem you honour me with; and that on
my Return I shall have the Pleasure of finding you and my other
Burlington Friends all well and happy. I am, with sincere Respect,
and Affection, Dear Sir, Your most obedient humble Servant
                                                      B FRANKLIN
John Smith Esqr
Endorsed: Novr: 4. 1764   Doct: B. Franklin

Remarks on a Late Protest

[Benjamin Franklin], *Remarks on a Late Protest Against the Appointment of Mr. Franklin an Agent for this Province* [Philadelphia, 1764]
(Historical Society of Pennsylvania; Yale University Library); also printed in *The Pennsylvania Journal and Weekly Advertiser,* November 22,
1764, Supplement; draft (incomplete): American Philosophical Society.[2]

Franklin's farewell to Pennsylvania took the form of a reply to the
Protest of the minority assemblymen against his appointment as an
agent (above, pp. 408–12). In these *Remarks* he undertook to defend
himself and the Assembly on the charges his opponents had made.
Since so much of what they had said and so much of his response
concerned himself personally, he followed the course, almost unprecedented in his writings for the general public, of using the first person
singular throughout and of signing his name at the end. The pamphlet
appears to have been published on November 7, 1764, the day he left
Philadelphia to take ship for England.[3] For William Smith's anonymous
answer to this paper, see below, pp. 486–516.[4]

   1. See above, p. 426.
   2. The printed pamphlet occupies the first seven pages of an eight-page
leaflet, the last page being blank. It has no title page. The copy in Hist.
Soc. Pa. is bound with a six-page copy in modern handwriting of the *Protest*
to which this piece replies. On the top of the first page of the printed text
appears the signature of Jeremiah Parker (d. 1827) of Philadelphia. The
surviving parts of the draft consist of pp. 1–2 and 5–8 of what must have
been about a twelve-page MS.
   3. Writing to Thomas Penn, Dec. 13, 1764, William Allen enclosed a copy
[*Notes continued on next page*]

Philadelphia, Nov. 5, 1764.
REMARKS on a Late PROTEST
Against the APPOINTMENT of Mr. FRANKLIN an Agent
for this PROVINCE.

I have generally passed over, with a silent Disregard, the nameless abusive Pieces that have been written against me; and tho' this Paper, called a PROTEST, is signed by some respectable Names, I was, nevertheless, inclined to treat it with the same Indifference; but as the Assembly is therein reflected on upon my Account, it is thought more my Duty to make some Remarks upon it.

I would first observe then, that this Mode of *Protesting* by the Minority, with a String of Reasons against the Proceedings of the Majority of the House of Assembly, is quite new among us; the present is the second we have had of the kind, and both within a few Months.[5] It is unknown to the Practice of the House of Commons, or of any House of Representatives in America, that I have heard of; and seems an affected Imitation of the Lords in Parliament, which can by no Means become Assembly-men of America. Hence appears the Absurdity of the Complaint, that the House refused the Protest an Entry on their Minutes. The Protesters know that they are not, by any Custom or Usage, intitled to such an Entry, and that the Practice here is not only useless in itself, but would be highly inconvenient to the House, since it would probably be thought necessary for the Majority also to enter their Reasons, to justify themselves to their Constituents, whereby the Minutes would be incumbered, and the Public Business obstructed. More especially will it be found inconvenient, if such Protests are made use of as a new Form of Libelling, as the Vehicles of personal Malice, and as Means of giving to private Abuse the Appearance

of the *Answer to Mr. Franklin's Remarks,* saying it would be "an Antidote to the poyson he published in a paper the day he went on ship board." Penn Papers, Hist. Soc. Pa.

4. John Dickinson also wrote some "Observations" on these *Remarks,* but did not publish them. They are printed from his MS in Paul L. Ford, ed., *The Writings of John Dickinson* (Phila., 1895), I, 157–67.

5. The first occasion was on May 28, 1764, following the vote to send the petition to the King for a change in government, above, p. 197. For BF's defense of the Assembly's refusal to enter that protest on the minutes, see above, pp. 307–8.

of a Sanction, as public Acts. Your Protest, Gentlemen, was therefore properly refused; and since it is no Part of the Proceedings of Assembly, one may with the more Freedom examine it.[6]

Your first Reason against my Appointment is, that you "believe me to the chief Author of the Measures pursued by the last Assembly, which have occasioned such Uneasiness and Distraction among the good People of this Province." I shall not dispute my Share in those Measures; I hope they are such as will in time do Honour to all that were concerned in them. But you seem mistaken in the Order of Time: It was the Uneasiness and Distraction among the good People of the Province that occasioned the Measures; the Province was in Confusion before they were taken, and they were pursued in order to prevent such Uneasiness and Distraction for the future. Make one Step farther back, and you will find Proprietary Injustice supported by Proprietary Minions and Creatures, the original Cause of all our Uneasiness and Distractions.

Another of your Reasons is, "that I am, as you are informed, very unfavourably thought of by several of His Majesty's Ministers." I apprehend, Gentlemen, that your Informer[7] is mistaken. He indeed has taken great Pains to give unfavourable Impressions of me, and perhaps may flatter himself, that it is impossible so much true Industry should be totally without Effect. His long Success in maiming or murdering all the Reputations that stand in his Way, which has been the dear Delight and constant Employment of his Life, may likewise have given him some just Ground for Confidence that he has, as they call it, *done for me*, among the rest. But, as I said before, I believe he is mistaken. For[8] what have I done

6. At the top of another sheet used later in his draft BF had written: "Your Protest being therefore no Part of the Proceedings of the House, but merely a new Form of writing private Libels that may carry some Appearance of being public Acts I shall with more freedom venture to examine it, and tho' you are dignify'd with the Honour of being Members of that House, which Honour I am depriv'd of, yet as the Man that injures me puts himself below me, you cannot take it amiss that I treat you at least on the foot of an Equality." BF apparently considered the passage as a possible substitute for the final sentence of the present paragraph, but he later struck out the longer version and did not use it.

7. Doubtless a reference to William Allen.

8. At this point in his draft BF had written: "as I hear, his Majesty has very lately been pleased to honour me with a Nomination to a small Em-

that they should think unfavourably of me? It cannot be my constantly and uniformly promoting the Measures of the Crown, ever since I had any Influence in the Province. It cannot, surely, be my promoting the Change from a Proprietary to a Royal Government. If indeed I had, by Speeches and Writings, endeavoured to make His Majesty's Government universally odious in the Province. If I had harangued by the Week, to all Comers and Goers, on the pretended Injustice and Oppressions of Royal Government, and the Slavery of the People under it. If I had written traiterous Papers to this Purpose, and got them translated into other Languages, to give His Majesty's foreign Subjects here those horrible Ideas of it. If I had declared, written and printed, that "the King's little Finger we should find heavier than the Proprietor's whole Loins," with regard to our Liberties; *then indeed* might the Ministers be supposed to think unfavourably of me.[9] But these are not Exploits for a Man who holds a profitable Office under the Crown,

---

ployment which however rather indicates a favourable Opinion of me among the Ministers. And indeed why should they think unfavourably of me." He then discreetly struck out the entire passage except the last four words and substituted: "what have I done that they should." BF may have learned from some letter of Richard Jackson's, or perhaps through WF, that on July 20 the Board of Trade had included him among the persons recommended to the Privy Council for appointment as commissioners to settle the disputed boundary between N.Y. and N.J. On Dec. 19, 1764, the Privy Council directed the Law officers to prepare a commission appointing 15 men, including BF and William Allen, but the document did not pass the seals until 1767. *Acts Privy Coun., Col.,* IV, 687; and above, p. 414 n.

9. The quoted words were brought up several times by the opponents of the Proprietors, and in William Allen's letter to Thomas Penn of Dec. 13, 1764, he admitted the essential correctness of the quotation while denying his disloyalty to the Crown. "In my Arguments in the Assembly," he wrote, "Though I spoke of his Majesty with the utmost reverence, yet, under a Kings Government, I said there were not so many priviledges injoyed which we possessd under our present charter that we might have bad men sent to rule us that our cries could not soon be laid before our Gracious Sovereign &c. This is dressed up to a story by that pragmatical Fool, Hughes and improved by that Crafty fellow Franklin." But Allen believed he had given many strong proofs of his fidelity and attachment to the government and could not be accused by anyone who knew him of want of loyalty. "I believe I said among other things that we should find the King's little finger heavier than the Proprietors Loyns, but if what was said before, and after, that Expression was also told, I should have with great readiness said it before one of his Majesty's Ministers." Penn Papers, Hist. Soc. Pa.

432

and can expect to hold it no longer than he behaves with the Fidelity and Duty that becomes every good Subject.[1] They are only for Officers of Proprietary Appointment, who hold their Commissions during his, and not the King's, Pleasure; and who, by dividing among themselves, and their Relations, Offices of many Thousands a Year, enjoyed by Proprietary Favour, *feel* where to place their Loyalty. I wish they were as good Subjects to His Majesty; and perhaps they may be so, when the Proprietary interferes no longer.

Another of your Reasons is, "that the Proposal of me for an Agent is extremely disagreeable to a very great Number of the most serious and reputable Inhabitants of the Province; and the Proof is, my having been rejected at the last Election, tho' I had represented the City in Assembly for 14 Years."

And do those of you, Gentlemen, reproach me with this, who among near Four Thousand Voters, had scarcely a Score more than I had? It seems then, that your *Elections* were very near being *Rejections,* and thereby furnishing the same Proof in your Case that you produce in mine, of your being likewise extremely disagreeable to a very great Number of the most serious and reputable People. Do you, honourable Sir, reproach me with this, who for almost twice 14 Years have been rejected (if *not being chosen* is *to be rejected*) by the same People, and unable, with all your Wealth and Connections, and the Influence they give you, to obtain an Election in the County where you reside, and the City where you were born, and are best known, have been obliged to accept a Seat from one of the out Counties, the remotest of the Province! It is known, Sir, to the Persons who proposed me, that I was first chosen against my Inclination, and against my Entreaties that I might be suffered to remain a private Man. In none of the 14 Elections you mention did I ever appear as a Candidate. I never did, directly or indirectly solicit any Man's Vote. For six of the Years in which I was annually chosen, I was absent, residing in England; during all which Time,

1. This sentence and the rest of this paragraph respond to a passage in the Philadelphia citizens' Remonstrance (presented to the Assembly October 26), which had pointed out that, since both BF and his son held offices "of considerable Profit and Honour under the Crown," BF could not be expected to "sacrifice his Interest for the Sake of the Province, which he must necessarily do, if he but seems to oppose the Measures of the Ministry." Above, p. 406.

your secret and open Attacks upon my Character and Reputation were incessant; and yet you gained no Ground. And can you really, Gentlemen, find Matter of Triumph in this *Rejection* as you call it? A Moment's Reflection on the Means by which it was obtained, must make you ashamed of it.

Not only my Duty to the Crown, in carrying the Post-Office Act more duly into Execution, was made use of to exasperate the Ignorant, as if I was encreasing my own Profits, by picking their Pockets; but my very Zeal in opposing the Murderers, and supporting the Authority of Government, and even my Humanity, with regard to the innocent Indians under our Protection, were mustered among my Offences, to stir up against me those religious Bigots, who are of all Savages the most brutish.[2] Add to this the numberless Falshoods propagated as Truths, and the many Perjuries procured among the wretched Rabble brought to swear themselves intitled to a Vote; and yet so *poor a Superiority* obtained at all this Expence of Honour and Conscience! Can this, Gentlemen, be Matter of Triumph! Enjoy it then. Your Exultation, however, was short. Your Artifices did not prevail every where; nor your double Tickets, and whole Boxes of forged Votes. A great Majority of the new chosen Assembly were of the old Members, and remain uncorrupted. They still stand firm for the People, and will obtain Justice from the Proprietaries. But what does that avail to you who are in the Proprietary Interest? And what Comfort can it afford you, when by the Assembly's Choice of an Agent, it appears that the same, to you obnoxious, Man, (notwithstanding all your venomous Invectives against him) still retains so great a Share of the public Confidence?

But "this Step, you say, gives you the more lively Affliction, as

2. At this point in the draft BF had written: "For Want of Actions to object against me, Recourse was had to my Words, Words spoken or rather written 12 Years ago. Words in themselves inoffensive, and only capable of an offensive Construction (very far fetch'd indeed) by which those who made it and those who receiv'd it, disgrac'd themselves more than the Words themselves could ever disgrace them." To the last "Words" in this sentence he appended a footnote: "Speaking of the German Peasants imported here, they were term'd Palatine Boors, which they were said [*illegible*] made to believe meant Hogs." BF later struck out both the text passage and the footnote. On the use in the recent election campaign of this quotation from *Observations concerning the Increase of Mankind*, see, for example, above, p. 375.

it is taken at the *very Moment* when you were informed by a Member of the House, that the Governor had assured him of his having received Instructions from the Proprietaries, to give his Assent to the Taxation of their Estates, in the *same Manner* that the Estates of other Persons are to be taxed; and also *to confirm,* for the public Use, the several Squares formerly *claimed* by the City." O the Force of Friendship! the Power of Interest! What Politeness they infuse into a Writer, and what *delicate* Expressions they produce! The Dispute between the Proprietaries and us was about the *Quantum,* the *Rate* of their Taxation, and not about the *Manner;* but now, when all the World condemns them for requiring a partial Exemption of their Estates, and they are forced to submit to an honest Equality, 'tis called *"assenting* to be taxed in the *same Manner* with the People:" Their *Restitution* of five public Squares in the Plan of the City, which they had near forty Years unjustly and dishonourably seized and detained from us, directing their Surveyor to map Streets over them (in order to turn them into Lots) and their Officers to sell a Part of them; this their *Disgorging* is softly called *confirming* them for the public Use; and instead of the plain Words *formerly given* to the City, by the first Proprietary their Father, we have the cautious pretty Expression of "formerly *claimed* by the City." Yes, not only *formerly* but *always* claimed, ever since they were *promised* and *given* to encourage the Settlers, and ever will be *claimed* till we are put in actual Possession of them. 'Tis pleasant, however, to see how lightly and tenderly you trip over these Matters, as if you trod upon Eggs. But that "VERY MOMENT," that precious Moment! why was it so long delayed? Why were those healing Instructions so long withheld and concealed from the People? They were, it seems, brought over by Mr. Allen.* Intelligence

*Extract from a Letter, dated London, August 6, 1764, from David Barclay and Sons, to Messieurs James and Drinker.[3]

"We very much wish for William Allen's happy Arrival on your Side, when we hope his Influence, added to the *Power* and *Commissions* the Proprietaries have invested him with, may prove effectual, in restoring Harmony and Tranquility among you, so much to be desired by every Well wisher to your Province. Pray be assured of our sincerest and best Wishes for the Success of this salutary Work, and that nothing in our Power, to contribute thereto, will ever be wanting."

3. On David Barclay and his sons, John and David, London Quakers,

was received by various Hands from London, that Orders were sent by the Proprietaries, from which great Hopes were entertained of an Accommodation. Why was the Bringing and the Delivery of such Orders so long *denied?* The Reason is easily understood. Messieurs Barclays, Friends to both Proprietaries and People, wished for that Gentleman's happy Arrival, hoping his *Influence,* added to the *Power* and *Commissions* the Proprietaries had vested him with, might prove effectual in restoring Harmony and Tranquility among us; but he, it seems, hoped his *Influence* might do the Business, without those Additions. There appeared on his Arrival some Prospect, from sundry Circumstances, of a Change to be made in the House by the approaching Election. The Proprietary Friends and Creatures knew the Heart of their Master, and how extreamly disagreeable to him that *equal Taxation,* that *Restitution,* and the other *Concessions* to be made for the Sake of a Reconciliation, must necessarily be. They hoped therefore to spare him all those Mortifications, and thereby secure a greater Portion of his Favour. Hence the Instructions were not produced to the last Assembly, though they arrived before the September Sitting, when the Governor was in Town, and actually did Business with the House.[4] Nor to the new Assembly were they mentioned, till the "*very Moment,*" the fatal Moment, when the House were on the Point of chusing that wicked Adversary of the Proprietary to be an Agent for the Province in England.

But I have, you say, a "fixed Enmity to the Proprietaries," and "you believe it will preclude all Accommodation of our Disputes with them, even on just and reasonable Terms." And why do you think I have a fixed Enmity to the Proprietaries? I have never had any personal Difference with them. I am no Land-Jobber, and therefore have never had any Thing to do with their Land-Office

---

see above, IX, 190–1 n. Abel James (*c.*1726–1790) and Henry Drinker (1734–1809), both Quakers, were partners in an important mercantile firm in Philadelphia. James was an ardent opponent of the Proprietors.

4. William Allen arrived in Philadelphia from London, Aug. 13, 1764; *Pa. Jour.,* Aug. 16, 1764. His letters to Thomas Penn of Sept. 25 and Oct. 21, 1764, indicate that after his return he worked actively but in private to persuade everyone he talked with to oppose BF and his party in the election. There is no suggestion in these letters that he discussed with anyone the nature and extent of the proprietary concessions with which he was certainly familiar. Penn Papers, Hist. Soc. Pa.

or Officers;[5] if I had, probably, like others, I might have been obliged to truckle to their Measures, or have had like Causes of Complaint. But our private Interests never clashed, and all their Resentment against me, and mine to them, has been on the public Account. Let them do Justice to the People of Pennsylvania, act honourably by the Citizens of Philadelphia, and become honest Men; my Enmity, if that's of any Consequence, ceases from the *"very Moment;"* and, as soon as I possibly can, I promise to love, honour and respect them. In the mean Time, why do you "believe it will preclude all Accommodation with them on just and reasonable Terms?" Do you not boast that their gracious Condescensions are in the Hands of the Governor, and that "if this had been the usual Time for Business, his Honour would have sent them down in a Message to the House." How then can my going to England prevent this Accommodation? The Governor can call the House when he pleases, and, one would think, that, at least in your Opinion my being out of the Way, would be a favourable Circumstance. For then, by "cultivating the Disposition shown by the Proprietaries, every *reasonable Demand* that can be made on the Part of the People might be obtained; in vigorously insisting on which, you promise to unite most earnestly with the rest of the House." It seems then we have *"reasonable Demands"* to make, and as you call them a little higher, *equitable Demands.* This is much for Proprietary Minions to own; but you are all growing better, in Imitation of your Master, which is indeed very commendable. And if the Accommodation here should fail, I hope that though you dislike the Person a Majority of two to one in the House have thought fit to appoint an Agent, you will nevertheless, in Duty to your Country, continue the noble Resolution of uniting with the rest of the House, in vigorously insisting on that *Equity* and *Justice,* which such an Union will undoubtedly obtain for us.

I pass over the trivial Charge against the Assembly, that they "acted with *unnecessary Haste* in proceeding to this Appointment, without making a small Adjournment," &c. and your affected Apprehensions of Danger from that Haste. The Necessity of Expedition on this Occasion is as obvious to every one out of Doors as it

5. Over the years BF had acquired a number of parcels of real estate in Philadelphia and the Northern Liberties, but always through purchase from private owners, never through the proprietary Land Office.

was to those within; and the Fears you mention are not, I fancy, considerable enough to break your Rest. I come then to your high Charge against me, "That I heretofore ventured, *contrary* to an Act of Assembly, to place the Public Money in the Stocks, whereby this Province suffered a Loss of £6000 and that Sum added to the £5000 granted for my Expences, makes the whole Cost of my former Voyage to England amount to ELEVEN THOUSAND POUNDS!" How wisely was that Form in our Laws contrived, which when a Man is arraigned for his Life, requires the Evidence to speak *the Truth*, the *whole Truth*, and *nothing but the Truth!* The Reason is manifest. A Falshood may destroy the Innocent; so may *Part of a Truth* without *the Whole;* and a Mixture of Truth and Falshood may be full as pernicious. You, Mr. Chief Justice, and the other Justices among the Protesters, and you, Sir, who are a Counsellor at Law,[6] must all of you be well acquainted with this excellent Form; and when you arraign'd my Reputation (dearer to me than Life) before the Assembly, and now at the respectable Tribunal of the Public, would it not have well become your Honours to have had some small Regard at least to the Spirit of that Form? You might have mentioned, that the Direction of the Act to lodge the Money in the Bank, subject to the Drafts of the Trustees of the Loan-Office here, was impracticable: that the Bank refused to receive it on those Terms, it being contrary to their settled Rules to take Charge of Money subject to the Orders of unknown People, living in distant Countries. You might have mentioned, that the House being informed of this, and having no immediate Call for the Money, did themselves adopt the Measure of placing it in the Stocks, which then were low; where it might on a Peace produce a considerable Profit, and in the mean time accumulate an Interest: That they even passed a Bill, directing the subsequent Sums granted by Parliament, to be placed with the former: That the Measure was prudent and safe; and that the Loss arose, not from *placing* the Money IN the Stocks, but from the imprudent and unnecessary DRAWING IT OUT at the very time when they were lowest, on some slight uncertain Rumours of a Peace concluded: That if the Assembly had let it remain another Year, instead of losing they would

6. Among the ten assemblymen who signed the *Protest*, William Allen was chief justice, and Isaac Saunders, George Taylor, and Thomas Willing were justices of the peace. The counselor at law was John Dickinson.

438

have gained Six Thousand Pounds; and that after all, since the Exchange at which they sold their Bills, was near Twenty per Cent. higher when they drew, than when the Stocks were purchased, the Loss was far from being so great as you represent it. All these Things you might have said, for they are, and you know them to be, Part of the *whole Truth;* but they would have spoiled your Accusation. The late Speaker of your honourable House, Mr. Norris, who has, I suppose, all my Letters to him, and Copies of his own to me, relating to that Transaction, can testify with how much Integrity and Clearness I managed the whole Affair.[7] All the House were sensible of it, being from time to time fully acquainted with the Facts. If I had gone to Gaming in the Stocks with the Public Money, and through my Fault a Sum was lost, as your Protest would insinuate, why was I not censured and punished for it when I returned? You, honourable Sir (my Enemy of seven Years Standing) was then in the House. You were appointed on the Committee for examining my Accounts; you reported that you found them just, and signed that Report.* I never solicited the Employ

*Report of the Committee on Benjamin Franklin's Accounts.[8]

"In Obedience to the Order of the House, we have examined the Account of Benjamin Franklin, Esq; with the Vouchers to us produced in Support thereof, and do find the same Account to be just, and that he has expended, in the immediate Service of this Province, the Sum of Seven Hundred and Fourteen Pounds, Ten Shillings and Sevenpence, out of the Sum of Fifteen Hundred Pounds Sterling, to him remitted and paid, exclusive of any Allowance or Charge for his Support and Services for the Province.

	JOHN MORTON,	JOSEPH FOX,
	WILLIAM ALLEN,	JOHN HUGHES,
February 19, 1763.	JOHN ROSS,	SAMUEL RHOADS,
	JOHN MOOR.	JOHN WILKINSON,
		ISAAC PEARSON.

"The House taking the foregoing Report of the Committee of Accounts into Considertion, and having spent some Time therein,
"*Resolved,*
"That the Sum of Five Hundred Pounds Sterling *per Annum* be

7. For BF's letters to Speaker Isaac Norris and to the trustees of the Loan Office, Charles Norris and Thomas Leech, on this complicated matter, see above, IX and X, *passim.*
8. These extracts from the *Votes* are also printed above, X, 196–7, 238.

of Agent: I made no Bargain for my future Service, when I was ordered to England by the Assembly; nor did they vote me any Salary. I lived there near six Years at my own Expence,[9] and I made no Charge or Demand when I came home. You, Sir, of all others, was the very Member that proposed (for the Honour and Justice of the House) a Compensation to be made me of the Five Thousand Pounds you mention.[1] Was it with an Intent to reproach me thus publicly for accepting it? I thanked the House for it then, and I thank you now for proposing it: Tho' you, who have lived in England, can easily conceive, that besides the Prejudice to my private Affairs by my Absence, a Thousand Pounds more would not have reimbursed me. The Money voted was immediately paid me. But, If I had occasioned the Loss of Six Thousand Pounds to the Province, here was a fair Opportunity of securing easily the greatest Part of it; why was not the Five Thousand Pounds de-

---

allowed and given to Benjamin Franklin, Esq; late Agent for the Province of Pennsylvania at the Court of Great Britain, during his Absence of six Years from his Business and Connections, in the Service of the Public; and that the Thanks of this House be also given to the said Gentleman by Mr. Speaker, from the Chair, as well for the faithful Discharge of his Duty to this Province in particular, as for the many and important Services done America in general, during his Residence in Great-Britain."

Thursday, March 31, 1763.

"Pursuant to a Resolve of the Nineteenth of last Month, that the Thanks of this House be given to Benjamin Franklin, Esq; for his many Services not only to the Province of Pennsylvania, but to America in general, during his late Agency at the Court of Great-Britain, the same were this Day accordingly given in Form from the Chair. To which Mr. Franklin, respectfully addressing himself to the Speaker, made Answer, That he was thankful to the House, for the very handsome and generous Allowance they had been pleased to make him for his Services; but that the Approbation of this House was, in his Estimation, far above every other kind of Recompence." *Votes*, 1763.

9. To be precise, BF was in England almost exactly five years and one month, though travel time added about six months to his total absence from Philadelphia.

1. This remark was addressed directly to William Allen. For William Smith's statement of Allen's part in this award of salary, differing markedly from what appears here, see below, pp. 501–2.

ducted, and the Remainder called for? The Reason is, This Accusation was not then invented. Permit me to add, that supposing the whole Eleven Thousand Pounds an Expence occasioned by my Voyage to England, yet the Taxation of the Proprietary Estate now established, will, when valued by Years Purchase, be found in time an Advantage to the Public, far exceeding that Expence. And if the Expence is at present a Burthen, the Odium of it ought to lie on those who, by their Injustice, made the Voyage necessary, and not on me, who only submitted to the Orders of the House, in undertaking it.

I am now to take Leave (perhaps a last Leave) of the Country I love, and in which I have spent the greatest Part of my Life. Esto perpetua. I wish every kind of Prosperity to my Friends, and I forgive my Enemies.[2]   B. Franklin.

Power of Attorney to James Parker

Copy: Bureau of Land Records, Department of Internal Affairs, Harrisburg[3]

[November 5, 1764]
Know all Men by these presents That I Benjamin Franklin of the City of Philadelphia Printer being now about to depart for England and the Time of my Return uncertain and there being long Accounts of Partnership unsettled between David Hall of the same place Printer and myself which partnership is now near expiring[4] and the Settlement of those Accounts, become for that Reason more immediately necessary. Therefore for the more expeditious and certain Settlement of the same I do hereby nominate and appoint my trusty and loving Friend James Parker Esqr. of Woodbridge in East New Jersey to be my lawful Attorney in my Behalf to examine all the Accounts kept of the said partnership by the

2. This farewell gains poignancy in retrospect when one recalls that BF never saw his wife Deborah again and that ten years and a half had passed and a revolution had begun before he returned to Pennsylvania.

3. Recorded in Letters of Attorney, D-2, No. 6, pp. 19–21.

4. For the articles of agreement between BF and Hall, establishing a partnership to commence on Jan. 21, 1748, and to run for eighteen years, see above, III, 263–7.

said David Hall, with the Books Receipts and other Vouchers and to make a State of the same with all such Allowances, as to him my said Attorney shall seem equitable where distinct Accounts cannot be obtained; And when such State is so far compleated as then it may be to transmit the same to me in London for my perusal six Months at least before the Expiration of the partnership[5] and also to value the Printing Presses Types and other Materials for printing belonging to me and now in the Use and Occupation of the said David Hall and which he has agreed to purchase of me at the Rate of such Valuation as shall be made by the said James Parker in my Behalf. And in Case I should not return to Philadelphia before the Expiration of the said partnership I do then hereby give and grant to my said Attorney full power to close the said Accounts, sell and deliver the said printing Materials to the said David Hall at the Valuation so as aforesaid by him to be made receive the Monies on the Whole to me arising for me and my Use, and make a final Ending of all Accounts between the said David Hall and myself, thereupon giving full Acquittances and Discharges in my Behalf which shall be of equal force and Validity as if made and given by me. IN WITNESS whereof I have hereunto set my Hand and Seal the fifth Day of November in the fifth Year of his Majesty's Reign Annoque Domini One thousand seven hundred and sixty four   B. FRANKLIN (Seal)
Sealed and Delivered in the presence of Sarah Franklin[6] Cha. Thomson[7]

I Acknowledge to have agreed to pay for the printing Materials such Sum as they shall be valued at by the above named Mr. James Parker
Witness CHA: THOMSON   DAVID HALL

Philadelphia ss. Be it Remembred that this fifth Day of November 1764 came Before me Thomas Lawrence Esqr.One of the Justices &ca. for the City of Philadelphia Charles Thomson of the said

5. Parker transmitted states of the account to BF in London at intervals throughout 1765 and 1766. These will be printed or fully described at their appropriate places in subsequent volumes. For earlier accounts between BF and Hall, 1748–1757, see above, III, 276.

6. BF's daughter.

7. For Thomson, one of BF's political associates and in later years secretary of the Continental Congress, see above, VII, 266 n.

City Merchant and on his solemn Oath declared that he was present and saw the within named Benjamin Franklin sign seal and as his Act and Deed deliver the within written Instrument or Power of Attorney. And that he the said Deponent subscribed his Name as Witness thereto and saw Sarah Franklin the other Witness do the like. IN TESTIMONY whereof I have hereunto set my Hand and Seal the Day and Year aforesaid

THO: LAWRENCE Mayr. (Seal)

Recorded the 12th. Novemr. 1764

From Samuel Eckerling[8]   ALS: American Philosophical Society

Esteemed Friend   Philadelphia, Novemr: 5th: 1764.

My Brethren Israel and Gabriel Eckerling were taken by the French and Indians from the Aligany Mountains in the Month of August 1757 and some Time after sent to Rochelle in France w[h]ere I am informed they died in the Hospital. I shall esteem it a particular Favour if you will enquire wether my Information be true or not.

Please to let me know by a few Lines directed to me to be left at Thomas Say's in Philadelphia[9] the Result of your Enquiry and

8. Samuel Eckerling (d. 1781), a leading Pa. Seventh-Day Baptist (Dunker), and his three brothers had once been members of Johann Conrad Beissel's Ephrata community, but left about 1745. Samuel, Israel, and Gabriel crossed the Alleghenies and settled on the Youghiogheny River, Samuel as a doctor and fur trader, the other two as hermits. The fourth brother, Emanuel, joined another group of sectaries elsewhere. In August 1757 a group of Ottawa Indians captured Israel and Gabriel; they were taken to Fort Duquesne and sent from there to Quebec and then to France, where they died of a distemper. BF had known Samuel since at least 1732, when he arranged for the publication of Beissel's hymnbook, *Vorspiel der Neuen-Welt*. Julius P. Sachse, *The German Sectarians of Pennsylvania 1742–1800* (Phila., 1900), esp. pp. 350–55; William A. Hunter, *Forts on the Pennsylvania Frontier, 1753–1758* (Harrisburg, 1960), pp. 126–7; Felix Reichmann, "Ezechiel Sangmeister's Diary," *PMHB*, LXVIII (1944), 306–8.

9. Thomas Say (1709–1796), Philadelphia apothecary and physician, a signer of the petition for the Pa. Hospital and a subscriber (above, V, 320, 329), was a mystic given to visions, of which his son Benjamin (1755–1813) published an account. A grandson, Thomas (1787–1834), was a well-known naturalist. *DAB* under "Benjamin Say."

all Charges that may accrue thereon shall be thankfully repaid by
Your Affectionate Friend   SAMUEL ECKERLING

To Benjamin Franklin

Addressed: To / Benjamin Franklin Esqr / in / Philadelphia

Endorsed: S. Eckerling concg. his Brothers

From Edmund Quincy, Junior[1]

ALS: American Philosophical Society

Worthy Sir   Boston Novr: 5th: 1764
I had not deferrd doing myself the Pleasure of writing you for
some time past on the Subject I mentiond to you when here, but
the Loss of my Wife,[2] besides several Avocations has prevented,
nor should I have troubled you now, but to inform you that I
publish'd in Edes & Gills paper[3] last Post Day a Letter from my
Bro' Huske to the Committee of Merchants here;[4] a Gentleman

1. Edmund Quincy, Jr. (1726–1782), son of BF's friend and correspondent
Edmund Quincy, Sr. (above, IX, 399 n), was a merchant who spent part
of his life in Portsmouth, New Hampshire.
2. Ann Huske Quincy, the daughter of Ellis Huske, formerly postmaster
of Boston and chief justice of New Hampshire (see above, IV, 318 n), died
on June 8, 1764.
3. Benjamin Edes (1732–1803) and John Gill (1732–1785), both leading
patriots during the American Revolution, were the publishers of the *Boston
Gazette*.
4. In 1748 Quincy's brother-in-law, John Huske (1724–1773), left Boston,
where he had been a merchant, to seek his fortune in England. There he
gained the reputation of being a "tough, unscrupulous adventurer" who
made and lost money fast. In 1763 he was elected to Parliament from Maldon
and served until his death. Americans conceived very unfavorable notions of
his role in the passage of the Sugar and Stamp Acts. Indeed, in Boston he
was held to be the author of the latter act and was burned in effigy. In the
Oct. 29, 1764, issue of the *Boston Gazette* Quincy published Huske's letter of
Aug. 14, 1764, to the committee of Boston merchants attempting to clear
himself of his countrymen's suspicions. In the course of the letter he contended that the necessity of a stamp duty "or other inland tax" seemed to
have arisen in Grenville's mind partly "from the indiscreet conversation of
some Americans, who deny the rights of Kings, Lords, and Commons, to
impose such a tax on America," and that when he proposed stamp duties
Grenville had told the Commons that such a "doctrine had been urg'd on

444

has in this days paper Remark'd upon it in which he insinuates that as a person of Figure he describes &c. as the principal Author and Abetter of this mushroom Policy is intended for One in Philadelphia; since which I hear some Persons not acquainted supposd Mr. Huske pointed at You, I know it can be only guess Work, and I beg you to be assured He means a person now Residing in London whose treatise on the Subject I hope soon to receive and shall forward it You. Interim I have the Honor to be with perfect Esteem and Regard Sir your most Obedient Humble Servant

EDM: QUINCY JR

The Honble: Benjamin Franklin Esq

To Anthony Todd

Extract: Public Record Office

Extract

Sir   Philadelphia Novr. 6. 1764

Col. Bouquet marched from Pittsburgh the 4th of October,[5] with 1500 Men, down the Ohio, to attack the Shawana Towns;

---

him." Huske continued with an involved passage in which he seems to have been saying that the person regarded by the colonists as the one to whom they were "indebted for the postponing of the Stamp duty" was also "the principal author and abettor of this mushroom policy" of denying Parliament's right to impose internal taxes on the colonies, and hence had been largely responsible for provoking Grenville into proposing stamp duties. When this fact came to be "truly known" in America, this person, not otherwise identified by Huske, "must be despis'd." In the Nov. 5, 1764, issue of the *Boston Gazette* a writer signing himself "Britannus Americanus" identified "the principal author and abettor of this *mushroom* policy" as probably "a person of figure in Philadelphia." It is not clear whom Huske had in mind; if Quincy was correct when he told BF in the present letter that it was "a person now Residing in London," he may have been thinking of Richard Jackson or Thomas Pownall. "Britannus Americanus," on the other hand, may have thought the reference was to BF, although his "person of figure in Philadelphia" was more probably Chief Justice William Allen, who had been in England when Grenville proposed a stamp duty to the Commons, while BF had left there more than a year and a half before. For Huske, see Namier and Brooke, *House of Commons*, II, 658–62.

5. Accounts vary as to when Bouquet left Fort Pitt, but the weight of the evidence favors October 3, not the 4th as BF gives it here, nor the 1st as stated in Howard Peckham, *Pontiac and the Indian Uprising* (Chicago, 1961), p. 262. Bouquet's journal, as read before the Pa. Council, Dec. 5, 1764, gives

the Peace made by Col. Bradstreet at Presqu'isle not being confirmed.[6] We have not since heard from either of those Armies. I am &c.   B FRANKLIN

Endorsed: Philadelphia Novr 6. 1764 Extract of a Letter from Mr Franklin Deputy Postmaster General of North America to Anth Todd Esqr R 10th Decr. from Mr. Todd.

From Benjamin Humphreys:[7] Bill and Receipt

ADS: American Philosophical Society

November the 6. 1764

Benjamin Franklen to Benja. Humphreys		Dr.	
	£	s	d
To Two steel spendels For the Harmonica[8]	4:	0:	0
Recevd the above in full		BENJAMIN HUMPHREYS	

To Richard Jackson

ALS: American Philosophical Society

Dear Sir   Philada. Nov. 7. 1764

The new Assembly at their first Sitting approv'd and resolv'd to prosecute the Measures of the last, relative to the Change of Government;[9] and supposing that my being in London during the in-

---

the date of departure as October 3 (*Pa. Col. Recs.*, IX, 212), as does William Smith's *An Historical Account of the Expedition . . . under the Command of Henry Bouquet, Esq.* (Phila., printed; London, reprinted, 1766), p. 9. An extract of a letter from Fort Pitt, dated October 3, in *Pa. Gaz.*, Oct. 25, 1764, says that the army "begins its March this Day," although *Pa. Jour.*, Oct. 25, 1764, quoting the same letter, dates it October 8. The last may have been a misprint. Bouquet penetrated to the upper Muskingum River, dictated terms to the Shawnee, Delaware, Mingo, and the Sandusky Hurons, received 200 captives, and returned to Pittsburgh by Nov. 28, 1764.

6. For Bradstreet's treaty of Aug. 12, 1764, with certain Shawnee and Delaware chieftains, which was repudiated by his superior, General Gage, see above, pp. 326 n, 335–6.

7. Humphreys was almost certainly a Philadelphia artisan, but nothing more is known about him.

8. See above, p. 426.

9. See above, pp. 402–8.

suing Sessions of Parliament may moreover be of some Use in our general American Affairs, have appointed me as an Assistant Agent with you for one Year, and directed me to proceed thither immediately. I accordingly embark this Day,[1] and hope to be with you nearly as soon as this Letter. It will be the greatest of Pleasures to me to find you well, I can now only add, that I am, with sincerest Esteem, Dear Sir, Your most obedient humble Servant

B FRANKLIN

Richd Jackson Esqr

Endorsed: 7 Novr. 64 Benjn. Franklin

To Sarah Franklin

Copy or transcript: American Philosophical Society[2]

Three hundred friends and admirers accompanied Franklin from Philadelphia to Chester, where he embarked on the *King of Prussia*, Capt. James Robinson, on Nov. 7, 1764. As he boarded the ship, he "was saluted by a Number of Cannon, and the Huzza's of the People; and an Anthem was sung . . . suitable to the Occasion." The text of the anthem is said to have been composed in Philadelphia; it was, however, an adaptation (with the stanzas rearranged) of "God Save the King," which had become popular during the Rebellion of 1745. A recent writer has called this version "the best literary expression of honor and respect for Franklin produced in the 1764 campaign."[3] It reads:

1. See the document immediately below.
2. While the ALS is lost, this MS remained in the possession of descendants until it passed to the APS with other family papers during the present century. Soon after 1900 its then owner, Miss Margaret H. Bache, gave it to her nephew Franklin Bache, who had it framed between sheets of glass and later sent a typed copy to George Simpson Eddy with the suggestion that Sarah Franklin Bache may have made this copy for one of her daughters. Franklin Bache to George Simpson Eddy, Jan. 3, 1933, Eddy Papers, Princeton Univ. Lib. The handwriting, however, does not appear to be that of BF's daughter.
3. J. Philip Gleason, "A Scurrilous Colonial Election and Franklin's Reputation," 3 *William and Mary Quar.*, XVIII (1961), 83–4. The anthem and the quoted description of BF's send-off are reprinted here from Gleason's article, which reproduces them from an anonymous letter from Philadelphia, Nov. 23, 1764, printed in *North Carolina Magazine . . . for 1764*, pp. 226–7. For the 1745 English version of these three stanzas of "God Save the King," see *Gent. Mag.*, XV (1745), 552, where some of the rhymes are little better than those in the Philadelphia adaptation.

O LORD our GOD arise,
Scatter our Enemies,
    And make them fall.
Confound their Politicks,
Frustrate such Hypocrites,
Franklin, on Thee we fix,
    GOD Save us all.
Thy Knowledge rich in Store,
On Pennsylvania pour,
    Thou [*sic*] great Blessing:
Long to defend our Laws,
Still give us greater Cause,
To sing with Heart and Voice,
    GEORGE and *FRANKLIN*
GOD Save Great GEORGE our King;
Prosper agent FRANKLIN:
    Grant him Success:
Hark how the Vallies ring;
GOD Save our Gracious King,
From whom all Blessings spring,
    Our Wrongs redress.

John Dickinson ridiculed the ceremonies attending Franklin's departure as a *"vainglorious Triumph* actually puff'd off at his Embarkation, for which silly Pageantry, ship Guns were borrow'd in Philadelphia, and sent down to Chester—the use there made of them, with other vain Exultations are unworthy repetition."[4] Whatever Dickinson and other opponents thought of the demonstration, however, the departing Franklin must have been gratified at this expression of regard from his friends and political supporters.[5]

Reedy Island[6] Nov. 8. 1764

My dear Sally,   7 at Night.
We got down here just at Sunset, having taken in more live Stock at Newcastle with some other things we wanted. Our good

4. "Observations on Mr. Franklin's Remarks," not published until 131 years after Dickinson wrote these words, in Paul L. Ford, ed., *The Writings of John Dickinson* (Phila., 1895), I, 163.
5. This was not the first time BF had been given a demonstrative send-off from Philadelphia which annoyed his opponents. See above, VII, 13–14.
6. A small island in the Delaware River, about ten miles below New Castle, Del.

Friends Mr. Galloway, Mr. Wharton,[7] and Mr. James[8] came with me in the Ship from Chester toNewcastle, and went ashore there. It was kind to favour me with their good Company as far as they could. The affectionate Leave taken of me by so many Friends at Chester was very endearing. God bless them, and all Pennsylvania.

My dear Child, the natural Prudence and goodness of heart that God has blessed you with, make it less necessary for me to be particular in giving you Advice; I shall therefore only say, that the more attentively dutiful and tender you are towards your good Mama, the more you will recommend your self to me; But why shou'd I mention *me,* when you have so much higher a Promise in the Commandment, that such a conduct will recommend you to the favour of God. You know I have many Enemies (all indeed on the Public Account, for I cannot recollect that I have in a private Capacity given just cause of offence to any one whatever) yet they are Enemies and very bitter ones, and you must expect their Enmity will extend in some degree to you, so that your slightest Indiscretions will be magnified into crimes, in order the more sensibly to wound and afflict me. It is therefore the more necessary for you to be extreamly circumspect in all your Behaviour that no Advantage may be given to their Malevolence. Go constantly to Church whoever preaches.[9] The Acts of Devotion in the common

7. Thomas Wharton (1731–1782), always called Senior to distinguish him from his cousin Thomas Wharton, Jr. (1735–1778), was a brother of Samuel Wharton (above, p. 187 n) and like his brother was a merchant and land speculator, although he was apparently not a partner in the firm of Baynton, Wharton & Morgan. In 1764 he was one of BF's most active political partisans, his services including carrying the petition for royal government from house to house in Philadelphia to collect signatures. Though a leader in the early resistance to British taxation of the colonies, he opposed taking up arms and in 1777–78 was banished to Va. and his property confiscated. John Penn to Thomas Penn, May 5, 1764, Penn Papers, Hist. Soc. Pa.

8. For Abel James, a prominent Philadelphia Quaker merchant, see above, p. 436 n, and *Autobiog.* (APS-Yale edit.), p. 287. On Nov. 3, 1764, a Philadelphian writing on local politics commented that the "most active or rather at the head of the active on the old side, appeared A. James and T. Wharton." William B. Reed, *Life and Correspondence of Joseph Reed* (Phila., 1847), I, 36.

9. In Elizabeth Montgomery's *Reminiscences of Wilmington* (Phila., 1851), pp. 288–9, it is said that the passage beginning with this sentence and ending with "very dirty Earth," further down in the paragraph, was presented by BF along with "his own prayer book" to James Parker's daughter Jenny. The editors have found no evidence to support this contention.

Prayer Book, are your principal Business there; and if properly attended to, will do more towards mending the Heart than Sermons generally can do. For they were composed by Men of much greater Piety and Wisdom, than our common Composers of Sermons can pretend to be. And therefore I wish you wou'd never miss the Prayer Days. Yet I do not mean that you shou'd despise Sermons even of the Preachers you dislike, for the Discourse is often much better than the Man, as sweet and clear Waters come to us thro' very dirty Earth. I am the more particular on this Head, as you seem'd to express a little before I came away some Inclination to leave our Church, which I wou'd not have you do.

For the rest I would only recommend to you in my Absence to acquire those useful Accomplishments Arithmetick, and Bookkeeping. This you might do with Ease, if you wou'd resolve not to see Company on the Hours you set apart for those Studies. I think you should and every Body should if they could, have certain days or hours to [*about six and a half lines missing*]¹ She cannot be spoke with: but will be glad to see you at such a time.

We expect to be at Sea to morrow if this Wind holds, after which I shall have no opportunity of Writing to you till I arrive (if it pleases God that I do arrive) in England.² I pray that *his* Blessing may attend you which is of more worth than a Thousand of mine, though they are never wanting. Give my Love to your Brother and Sister,³ as I cannot now write to them; and remember me affectionately to the young Ladies your Friends, and to our good Neighbours. I am, my dear Sally, Your ever Affectionate Father

B. FRANKLIN

1. The missing portion is the second quarter (from the top) of the second leaf of the folio MS. The last five words before the break are only just decipherable. When Sparks printed the letter in 1838 (*Works*, VII, 267–71) the loss had apparently already taken place. He omitted, without indication, not only the missing lines, but the surviving parts of the sentences before and after the break which are printed here; after printing "for those studies" he began a new paragraph with "We expect to be at sea tomorrow." Bigelow (*Works*, III, 256–9) and Smyth (*Writings*, IV, 286–7) followed Sparks, but when BF's great-granddaughter, Mrs. E. D. Gillespie, printed the letter in *A Book of Remembrance* (Phila. and London, 1901), pp. 18–19, she included the sentence before the break, reading it as "I think you should, and everybody should, have certain days or hours so set apart."

2. The *King of Prussia* arrived off the Isle of Wight on Dec. 9, 1764; see below, p. 516.

3. William Franklin and his wife, Elizabeth.

To Thomas Wharton[4]

ALS: Yale University Library

Cape Henlopen, Nov. 9. 1764

Dear Sir 2 aClock P M.

We are just putting to Sea, with a Wind fine and fair as can blow. My Love to my good old true Friend your Father,[5] and all his worthy Sons;[6] And my affectionate Regards to all enquiring Friends. I am Yours affectionately B FRANKLIN

Endorsed: Benja. Franklin Cape-Henlopen Novr. 9th. 1764

From James Bowdoin

Letterbook copy: Massachusetts Historical Society; ALS (fragment): American Philosophical Society[7]

Sir Boston Novr. 12. 1764

I observe by the last Papers that your Assembly have again appointed you one of their Agents in Great Britain:[8] which without doubt, is much to the mortification of the party, whose spleen has been lately gratified by your not being returned a member of the present assembly. I am very glad the Colonies are likely to have a Gentleman on t'other Side the water So well qualified to represent their Circumstances and State of Trade: a proper representation of which must make the ministry see (unless they dont choose to see) that they can expect nothing from the colonies by way of duties or

4. So identified on the basis of Wharton's reply of Nov. 13, 1764; see below, pp. 456–8.

5. Joseph Wharton (1707–1776), Philadelphia merchant, benefactor of the Pa. Hospital, and shareholder in Lib. Co. Phila. See above, V, 317, 320, 330.

6. Joseph Wharton had ten sons by his first wife, seven and possibly eight of whom were living in 1764. Of these Samuel (above, p. 187 n) and Thomas (above, p. 449 n) had been closely associated with BF in anti-proprietary politics in 1764. By a second wife Wharton had five sons, one of whom, a boy of seven, was living in 1764, and two more of whom had not yet been born.

7. Only the last few lines of the ALS survive.

8. *Pa. Gaz.*, Nov. 1, 1764, carried an account of BF's appointment, Oct. 26, 1764, "to embark immediately for Great Britain, to join with, and assist the present Agent in transacting the Affairs of this Province, for the ensuing Year."

tax whether internal or external; and that the duties already laid and those talked of, can have no other effect than to distress them, and injure Great Britain.

Whatever is forced from the Colonies in this way will at least so far disable them from paying their balances to Britain: it being demonstrably evident that all the remittances they can make, Gold and Silver included (the whole of which is gone and going) are not sufficient to pay those balances, and command the usual Supply of British manufactures. Much less will they be able to do either when their other trade (the Source of their ability to carry on the British) is so greatly embarrassed.

Our two houses have petitioned the house of Commons on this head.[9] Besides separate Petitions from the Colonies a joint Petition to Parliament from all the Colony-Agents on the Subject of their rights and Trade, and being heard by counsel thereon before the Lords as well as Commons Seem the most likely means to procure a redress of Grievances.

I wish you Success in this matter. I have not yet heard from Mr. Canton in relation to the telescope I sent him some time ago. I shall be much obliged if you'll speak to him about it, and desire the favor he would get it alter'd and sent as soon as his convenience will permit.[1] I have desired Messrs. Lane & Booth to pay the cost. You said when here you thought Dolland's Micrometer might be

9. At a special session of the Massachusetts legislature in October 1764 the House of Representatives approved a petition to the King vigorously denying the right of Parliament to lay a tax, in which category the Sugar Act was specifically put, on the colonies without their consent. The Council, with Bowdoin and Thomas Hutchinson taking the lead, persuaded the House to tone the petition down considerably—the privilege of taxing itself was requested by the Legislature, not the right—and to address it to both the King and House of Commons. The House rather reluctantly consented to the changes suggested by the Council, and the petition, dated Nov. 3, 1764, was sent to the province's agent in Britain for presentation. See Edmund S. and Helen M. Morgan, *The Stamp Act Crisis Prologue to Revolution* (Chapel Hill, [1953]), pp. 34–6. The petition, as sent to England, is printed in 6 Mass. Hist. Soc. *Colls.*, IX, 32–6.

1. For over a year BF had been attempting to assist Bowdoin in having a telescope fitted out in England with a micrometer and a "Pedistal of a new Construction"; BF was chiefly relying on the efforts of his friend and fellow electrician John Canton to see that the work was done properly. See above, x, 351 n, and this volume, pp. 21–2, 99, 244–5.

fixed to the telescope: if it can be conveniently done, I should be glad it might: in which case, if it would be in the way when not wanted, it may be best to have it fitted in such manner as to be put on and taken off at pleasure. Your Asistance in the contrivance of the Telescope, if your leisure will permit, I shall esteem a great favor. I heartily wish you a good voyage, success in your Embassy, and in due time a safe return, which I hope will be by the way of Boston. My best regards wait on you and your good Family. [?] yours[2]

Benjn. Franklin Esqr. at Phila.[3]

Samuel Rhoads, Junior: Account Book

 MS account book: Historical Society of Pennsylvania

On April 6, 1763, Franklin advanced to Robert Smith, carpenter, £96 towards purchasing materials for the house he was to build on the Franklins' lots on Market Street.[4] During the next nineteen months he paid at least £120 more to Smith and lesser sums to other workmen and suppliers, and on Feb. 9, 1764, he lent £200 to Smith, who probably lacked adequate working capital, and took back the carpenter's bond for the loan.[5] Franklin entrusted the general oversight of the building operation to his friend, the carpenter, builder, and merchant, Samuel Rhoads, who had been his fellow representative from the city of Philadelphia in recent assemblies. Before embarking for England in

2. The ALS fragment gives the full complimentary close: "I am with great respect Dear Sir Your most obedient humble Servant JAMES BOWDOIN." It adds a postscript: "I thank you for your last Pamphlet." There might have been just time for Bowdoin to have received a copy of BF's *Remarks on a Late Protest.*

3. The ALS fragment includes the address page: "Benjamin Franklin Esqr. / at / Philadelphia / per Post."

4. Memorandum Book, 1757–1776, p. 13; Receipt Book, 1742–1764, p. 85.

5. Memorandum Book, 1757–1776, pp. 14, 15, 18; Receipt Book, 1742–1764, pp. 86, 88. The exact amount he expended during this time cannot now be determined. On April 16, 1763, just before leaving on his trip to Virginia on post-office business, BF left in the hands of his friend Philip Syng £642 10s., to be drawn on by Samuel Rhoads "as Occasion requires to carry on my Building." On Jan. 11, 1764, Syng gave BF his account of disbursements and returned the unexpended balance (Memorandum Book, 1757 1776, pp. 14, 15), but Syng's account has not been found and the amount of the balance returned is not specified.

November 1764, Franklin turned over to Rhoads £350 in cash and Smith's bond for £200; Rhoads then gave Franklin his receipt for these advances "to be apply'd towards the Building of B. Franklin's House if wanted."[6]

Rhoads thereupon directed his son, Samuel Rhoads, Junior, aged twenty-four, to act as his disbursing agent in connection with the Franklin house, and the young man promptly set up a record of his transactions.[7] Seven pages of an account book designated "Account Benj: Franklin Esq. 1764" contain his receipt for £200 turned over by his father on Nov. 13, 1764, memoranda of various payments, and eight receipts signed by artisans and suppliers of materials. One may hope that the younger Rhoads and the men with whom he dealt were more skilled in their trades than they were in penmanship and that they kept their working tools in better condition than they did their quills, for in several places these records are almost indecipherable. They are printed here, however, as accurately as possible, to provide evidence of some of the operations involved and the slow progress achieved in completing the Franklin family's new house.

Receivd Novr. 13 1764 of my Father Samuel Rhoads two hundred pounds Money belonging to Benj. Franklin Esqr which sum I promise to Repay by Discharging Such Bills or payments of such Sums of Money from time to time as my said Father shall direct and order. Witness my Hand   SAMUEL RHOADS JUNR
£200

S R Junr. Receiv'd
£44 of Danl. Williams in april

No 1 Recd Philada. Novr. 13th. 1764 of Benjn. Franklin. By the hand of Saml. Rhoads the sum of fifty Pounds on Acco.
£50   Per ROBT: SMITH

No 2 Receiv'd Nov: the 20th: 1764 of Benj: Franklin by the Hands of Saml Rhoads the sum of six Pounds on Accot.
£6: 0   WILLIAM ANDERSON

6. BF's notation of the transaction and Rhoads's undated but signed receipt are the last two entries for 1764 in Memorandum Book, 1757–1776, p. 19.

7. Samuel Rhoads, Jr. (1740–1784), married in 1765 Sarah, daughter of Israel Pemberton; they had two daughters and a son, also named Samuel. Extracts from his first letterbook, 1762–72, suggest that his principal occupation at this time was that of a merchant. *PMHB*, XIV (1890), 421–6.

December the 4th: 1764

pd: Robert Erwin his Accot. in full for Carting	£ 7:	9
pd: Balti Clymer Do.	1:	18
	£ 9:	7

Dec 12th: pd. John & Joseph Ledru after the Accot. had been Examind and settled by John Palmer £39: 12: 9
pd: Jacob Graff his Accot. for Bricks now Deld. ⎫
per ordr of John Pa[?]er ⎭ 12: 7: 6

pd. Salter Brittain & Comp their Accot. for Boards &c.
pd: Receipt to S R Junr by Thos Forster £ 5: 17

No. 2 Receiv'd Feb: 8th: 1765 of Samuel Rhoads Six Pounds towards Work done for Benja Franklin at his new House
£6   WILLIAM ANDERSON

Receiv'd May the 13th: 1765 of Benjn: Franklin Esqr. by the Hands of Samuel Rhoads twenty Pounds which with several Sums formerly receiv'd Amts to fifty seven Pounds and is in full for Plaistering [No 2 *vertically in margin*] done for the sd: B: Franklin at his new House in this City and at his Plantation
£20: 0: 0   per WILLIAM ANDERSON

pd. Adam Achart £5 in part of his accot. Examd. to be pd. when ratifyd.

Receiv'd June the 1st: 1765 of Samuel Rhoads four Pounds and one Shilling in full for eighteen perches of Stone Deld: Robt. Erwin for use of Benj: Franklin Esqr. Sent from John Parishes [?] Quarry
£4: 1: 0   recd. per   GEORG KAFFART [?]
Note the English name is George Caphart [?]

Sundrys pd. per Sa Rhoads Junr. Vizt.

To David Rose	£ 9:	2	
Mich Weaver	13:	10	
David Rose Tyler	3:	12	
Conrad Bangon		12	
William Rush	68:	4:	11–

June 19th: pd. Michael Coon 27s. per note from John Ledru for Digging foundation 6 Days at 4s. 6d. per

Pd: James Davis 19s. 6d. being one half the Cost of Measuring the Plaistering done by Will. Henderson.

455

July the 23d Receiv'd of Deborah Franklin 50 Pounds which I paid the same Day to Robt: Smith   per loose [?] Rect:

Septr: 9th: pd: David Rose Brickmaker £10 in part of his Accot. for Bricks used in the Well.

£3 pd [*illegible*] £8: 5s. 3d. & Sammy in full of his Accot: in all £21. 5s. 3d. the 27th Day

Pd: John Elmsly 41s. 9d. for Turning Sundry
Pd. Do: 3s. 3d. for Drops for Stairs
Pd: Do. £3: pd £1: 14s: 7d. in full of his Acct. now brote in June 21st. [?]

No. 12 Receivd Feby: the 6th. 1766 of Benjamin Franklin Esqr. by the Hands of Samuel Rhoads twenty Pounds toward our Accots of Work done at his Well Little Hous &c.   JOHN LEDRU
£20   JOSEPH LEDRU

No. 13 Receiv'd July the 7th 1766 of Benj: Franklin Esqr. by the Hands of Samuel Rhoads two pound and ten shillings in full for takeing up all the Bricks in his well. Cleaning several large Stones from under the Curb, settling it deeper and finishing the same fit for use and we promise to sink the sd: Well one foot deeper at our own Expence, in Case the Water shall hereafter fail
Witness our Hands   DEANL BEARRD [?]
                                                    The true Accot

[*Cancelled:*] Pd: John Guy per S Rhoads Junr: 15s. for [?] Load Sand.
Receiv'd of Saml Rhoads five Pounds   per JOHN LEDRU

April 10 pd: Robert Smith £10 towards his Work &c. per Rect.

From Thomas Wharton   AL: American Philosophical Society

Philad[elphia, November 13, 1764][8]
Much Esteem'd Friend Benjamin Franklin
    Thy very kind Letter of the 9th. Instant[9] I [had the pleasure] of

8. The upper corner and right-hand edge of the sheet are badly torn. The endorsement on the address page apparently does not mean that the present letter was a double letter, begun on November 13 and continued on November 20, but that Wharton wrote separate letters on these two dates. The letter of November 20 has not been found.
9. See above, p. 451.

receiving yesterday the Contents whereof afforded Matter of real Satisf[action, and] on being shewn to my honoured Father gave Him that just Sensation, which [warms the] Breast of every true Friend.

I have done myself the pleasure of visiting [thy Wife] and Daughter[1] since thy departure; Who express'd their tender, and filial [Affection?] towards thee, sufficient to warm the coldest Heart: And be assured, if it Liys [in my] Power to contribute to their Ease and Pleasure, I shall be chearfull to do it.

The Party at present seem very [quiet, nor] can I, with any degree of Certainty learn, that They intend to give a formal A[nswer to] thy Remarks.[2] W A—— has been heared to say, that He was sorry to find [Mr. Frank]lin so warm, and did not know, He had given sufficient Cause therefor; We are [informed?] it sticks very close by Him, his Children and Friends being very uneasy about the Charge.[3] Many of the Pr——ns express their Surprise at their signing the protest,[4] when [such] Proofs could be brought in Opposition to it, And say that Had their Society been [left] unnoticed by thee—it might be well enough.[5] Some of Us, the last Evening determined to have thy Remarks translated into Dutch, and gave Orders for it's being distributed with Miller's Newspaper, and expect to have it published in Bradford's this Week.[6]

1. Alternatively, Wharton may have written "thy Son and Daughter," indicating a visit to WF and his wife in N.J., but the indicated rendering seems more probable.

2. For BF's *Remarks on a Late Protest Against the Appointment of Mr. Franklin an Agent for this Province,* Nov. 5, 1764, see above, pp. 429–41. For William Smith's *An Answer to Mr. Franklin's Remarks, on a Late Protest,* Dec. 7, 1764, see below, pp. 486–516.

3. BF attacked Allen on several accounts in his *Remarks;* the charge at which he was uneasy was probably that of acting traitorously by denigrating royal government.

4. For a "Protest against the Appointment of Benjamin Franklin as Agent," Oct. 26, 1764, see above, pp. 408–12.

5. In his *Remarks* BF had alluded to the Presbyterians who opposed him as "religious Bigots, who are of all Savages the most brutish."

6. BF's *Remarks* appear first to have been published on Nov. 7, 1764; they appeared as a supplement to the Nov. 22, 1764, issue of William Bradford's *Pa. Jour.* The *Remarks* and the "Protest" to which they were an answer were published as a pamphlet in German by Christopher Saur (above, II, 358 n). "Miller's Newspaper" was *Der Wöchentliche Staatsbote,* published in Philadelphia by John Henry Miller (above, VIII, 99 n).

On the 9th an Express passed through this City from Colo. Bouquet to General Gage—giving as I am informed, an Account of his being mett between the Tuscorora Hill, and the Shawanae's Town, by a considerable Number of the Delaware and Shawanae Indians. Who intreated Him for Peace, which He absolutely refused Unless They would first deliver up all the Captives, and their Offspring, which [They] have promised to do; They requested Him to stop his March down, and give them [Time to?] perfect this Matter. But He knowing their perfidy, told them, He should continue on if They did not comply in Twelve days, He would destroy everything in his Way. [It] appears that they were destitute of Ammunition, and every Necessary of Life, So that We hope a Peace is near at hand;[7] And as I am not able to give thee a circumsta[ntial] Account of this Matter, and being informed that [it is gone] home by the Packet shall refer [you th]ereto.

Captain Friend it's [said] will sail in a Week, but can not learn that [Governor] Hamilton has taken his Passage.[8] I am thy Sincere and Aff[ectionate]

Addressed: For / Benjamin Franklin Esqr. / Agent for the Province of / Pennsilvania / in / London

Endorsed: Tho. Wharton Nov. 13. and 20. 1764 answer'd Jan. 12[9]

7. A similar account of Bouquet's negotiations appeared in *Pa. Jour.*, Nov. 15, 1764. For the colonel's expedition and its successful issue, see above, pp. 445–6 n.

8. *Pa. Gaz.*, Nov. 29, 1764, reports the clearance of the *Carolina*, Capt. James Friend. In a letter of Dec. 4, 1764 (below, p. 483), Wharton wrote BF that Hamilton was a passenger aboard the *Carolina*; he was going to England on the advice of physicians, who feared that he might have cancer. William Allen to David Barclay & Sons, Nov. 20, 1764, in Lewis B. Walker, ed., *The Burd Papers Extracts from Chief Justice William Allen's Letter Book* ([Pottsville, Pa.], 1897), pp. 62–3.

9. In BF's hand. His letter of Jan. 12, 1765, has not been found.

From Martin Howard[1]

ALS: American Philosophical Society

Sir   Newport Rhode Island, 16 Nov: 1764

I learnt a few Days ago by the Pennsylvania Gazette that you was speedily to go for England,[2] and being Uncertain Whether a Letter would reach you before you embarked I determined to embrace the Oppertunity to write you by a Vessel bound from hence to London, and hope it may meet you safely arrived there, and making an auspicious beginning in the Matter of Colony Charters.

I had not the Pleasure to receive any Answer to what I wrote you some time ago, concerning the Motions making here by a few, to mend our Government;[3] I attribute this to the Attention you have been obliged to give, to the Affairs of your Province, which more nearly concerned you; I flatter myself however, that your Disposition to correct Abuses, is not confined to those of your own Province, And therefore I now trouble you, with this, to throw an Occasion in your Way, wherein, you may have an Oppertunity to extend your Benevolence further, and be instrumental in making this Colony too, something better, it is now Nothing but a Burlesque upon Order and Government, and will never get right without the Constitution is altered. I have not time to enlarge, and indeed your thorough Knowledge of the Subject would anticipate

<hr/>

1. Martin Howard, Jr. (d. 1781), was a lawyer, a delegate to the Albany Congress, and at this time a leading member of a small group of Rhode Island conservatives who were campaigning for a revocation of the charter of 1663 and the establishment of royal government in the colony. Either singly or with the assistance of Dr. Thomas Moffatt (above, p. 191 n), Howard had written extensively in the Rhode Island newspapers in 1764 in favor of his project, attracting a great deal of hostility and the epithet "Martinus Scriblerus." After his house was sacked by a Stamp Act mob in August 1765, Howard went to England and was appointed chief justice of North Carolina in 1766. He returned to England as a refugee in 1778. For Howard and the Rhode Island conservatives, see Edmund S. and Helen M. Morgan, *The Stamp Act Crisis Prologue to Revolution* (Chapel Hill, [1953]), pp. 47–52.

2. *Pa. Gaz.*, Nov. 8, 1764, reported BF's embarkation for London.

3. Howard's letter to BF has not been found, but he may have written in April 1764, enclosing the April 23 issue of the *Newport Mercury* which contained a letter signed Z.Y. (supposed to be written by either Howard or Moffatt) advocating royal government. BF sent the *Mercury* to Richard Jackson on May 1, 1764. See above, p. 186.

all and more than I could say. I would only mention to you, that a Petition to the King is now in the Hands of Joseph Harrison Esqr.[4] who sailed in the Mast Ship from New London above three Weeks ago, his Prudence, And the Secrecy enjoin'd him, will direct him, to be very circumspect in the Management of it,[5] is chiefly founded on an Act of our general Assembly, made directly in the face of an Act of Parliament; Nevertheless, if the Temper of the Ministry is not strong for resuming our Charter this Winter, Mr. Harrison will be entirely silent about it, because to make a Stir and miscarry, would bring a popular Odium on the few concerned in it here. If the times are favorable, it will be in your Power greatly to facilitate the wishd for Change, And I hope I am not mistaken, or too forward, in reckoning much upon your Intimacy with the *Great,* And the frequent Occasions you will have with them, of speaking upon American Affairs. But perhaps I have already wrote too much, and have presumed too far in addressing you on this Matter, if I am wrong, your Goodness will readily excuse it.

I have lost a Valuable and affectionate Wife,[6] she is gone to "that undiscovered Country, from whose Bourn, No Traveller returns." She died about seven Weeks ago, this is a very affecting Circumstance to me and therefore my mentioning of it, naturally

4. Joseph Harrison (1709–1787) was a Rhode Island merchant and a brother of the architect Peter Harrison. Harrison sailed to England with Jared Ingersoll and remained there throughout 1765, being much consulted on American affairs and being on friendly terms with Richard Jackson and Thomas Whately. In 1766 he served as an assistant to Edmund Burke, who was then secretary to Lord Rockingham. In this same year Harrison was appointed collector of the customs at Boston. He relinquished his post in 1769 after being severely injured in attempting to seize John Hancock's sloop *Liberty,* and he spent the rest of his life in England. See Carl Bridenbaugh, *Peter Harrison First American Architect* (Chapel Hill, 1949). 6 Mass. Hist. Soc. *Colls.,* IX, prints several of his letters from England in 1765 and 1766.

5. Word leaked out about the petition even before Harrison sailed. Governor Stephen Hopkins denounced it in a message to the Rhode Island Assembly on Nov. 4, 1764, and in his *Rights of Colonies Examined,* published shortly thereafter. In February 1765 Howard replied to Hopkins in *A Letter from a Gentleman at Halifax to his Friend in Rhode Island.* Both pamphlets are reprinted in Bernard Bailyn, ed., *Pamphlets of the American Revolution 1750–1776,* I (Cambridge, Mass., 1965), 499–544.

6. The former Ann Brenton Conklin, whom Howard married in 1749. In 1766 or possibly 1767 he married Abigail Greenleaf of Boston. Colonial Society of Mass. *Pubs.,* VI (1899–1900), 384–402.

enough accounted for. I have the Honour to be with the greatest Regard Sir your most faithful and obedient Servant

MAR HOWARD JUN.

Mr. Hall has not yet paid his Bond, but you may rely on my Care of it.[7]

Benja. Franklin Esqr.

Addressed: To / Benjamin Franklin, Esquire / at / London. / by the Pitt. / Capt Lyndsay

From Jonathan Williams   ALS: American Philosophical Society

Honoured Sir   Boston, Novr the 17: 1764
    Mr. Charles Russel[8] the Bearer hereof applies to me for a few Lines to Make him known to you. He is Son of the Honourable James Russel Esquire of Charlestown. Comes home to perfect His practice as a Physican, in one of the Hospotals, and being a Gentleman of good Character here I Beg Leave to recommend Him to your Civilities as a Stranger in the City of London in Doing Which you Will Oblige your Dutifull Nephew and Humble servant   JONA WILLIAMS

7. Samuel Hall, son-in-law and partner in the printing business of BF's sister-in-law, Ann Franklin, after her husband James's death. On his longstanding debt to BF, see above, X, 358 n.
8. Charles Russell (1738–1780), A.B., Harvard, 1757, took his medical degree at Marischal College, Aberdeen, in 1765. Returning to America, he practiced at Lincoln, Mass. In 1768 he married Elizabeth Vassall. A Loyalist whose property was confiscated by the Massachusetts Legislature, he settled in Antigua in 1775. Russell's father, James (1715–1798), was a respected public officeholder and judge who was appointed a mandamus councilor by Hutchinson, but refused to take the oath of office. The Charlestown bridge was built through his efforts. *New Eng. Hist. and Geneal. Reg.*, XVII (1863), 125–6; E. A. Jones, *The Loyalists of Massachusetts* (London, 1930), p. 253; Lorenzo Sabine, *Biographical Sketches of the Loyalists of the American Revolution* (Boston, 1864), II, 246–7.

From Richard Jackson[9]

ALS: American Philosophical Society

Dear Sir   18 Novr 1764

Nothing has given me or can [give] me more concern than the Disturbances, and Disputes in your Province, the Mischiefs and Dangers to Pennsylvania in particular and to all America in general are inconceivable to one who has not been, in England a good part of the past year;[1] the Effects that the foresight of their Mischief and Dangers had upon me and the firm Belief I entertained that Mr. Allen was affected by the Prospect as I was myself, made me open my Mind more fully to him than I should otherwise have done,[2] and which I was the more readily induced to do from the Warmth with which he entred into some of my Notions and the Candour with which he admitted others, at the same time that I was thoroughly convinced that the Interest of both Partys were the same, and have an 100 times heard him confess that one of them could not gain a Victory over the other without a Loss of much more than it was worth to themselves. By this I meant that if Government could go on under the Proprietary it was much better for all Partys than a Change of Government could well be expected to be in the long run, at the same time that a Triumph on the side of the Proprietary could it be hoped for; would infallibly in the End strip him of the Powers of Government; for that a Man must know little of America to suppose such a Superiority would last

9. So far as is known, this is Jackson's first letter to BF since the one of August 11 which discussed the petition for a change in government; above, pp. 311–14. Before he began to write, Jackson appears to have received BF's letters of July 12, August 9, September 1, September 20, and (probably) September 25; above, pp. 255–7, 263–4, 326–31, 339–40, and 357–9. Much of the first part of this letter is in response to BF's letter of September 1, in which he had reported on what William Allen had been saying publicly since reaching home on August 13.

1. On Jan. 26, 1764, Jackson had indicated his distress at "the most dangerous Errors in American Politicks" he was finding "in 100 Places" and was combating as vigorously as possible. Above, p. 34.

2. Jackson had written, Dec. 27, 1763, expressing his satisfaction with William Allen, "to whom I have opined my Sentiments fully on the *General Interests of America*, especially those that may be affected by expected Measures in Parliament." Above, x, 414–15. During the next months Allen's activity in opposing plans for colonial taxation were several times mentioned in colonial newspapers; e.g., *Pa. Gaz.*, May 10, June 7, 1764.

long, and little of England, to hope that all the Proprietarys friends could preserve to him a Possession, which he held by a Tenure so unlike that of every other Subject except Lord Baltimore and the Defence of which was no mans common Cause; when attacked and clogged by the Efforts of a respectable Party in Pennsylvania.[3]

I confess I had formed a very advantageous opinion of Mr. Allen's Honesty and good sense and therefore was disposed to talk with him frankly on a Subject, on which I thought all Honest Men of good Sense must think alike. I trusted him therefore with my Opinion on 2 or 3 Points which I was satisfied he could not use to the Mischief of any one without hurting himself and his friends, though he might make use of them for the Service of all Parties, to the good part of whom I sincerely wished Welfare and Happiness. But my Commission to him was to tell you my Apprehensions and not to make them publick, because I never thought that could do Service even to his own friends, in the End. I particularly gave him this Commission to you in order to open again that Corespondance which I was of opinion was of so much Consequence to the Province to bring about. I am sorry I was mistaken, but think that the Mischief will fall at last on those who have rejected Terms of Accomodation.

That I did not mean that Mr. Allen should make my Statement publick is evident that I did not even write them to any one else in the World but yourself, and that if I glanced at any such in my Letters to Mr. Galloway or the Committee it was at a distance; but I have to believe too that he has exaggerated my Expressions. I confess I have thought from the best Judgements I could form of the Opinions of People in Power, that it was probable they might be glad to take a favourable Opportunity of possessing the Crown of their Power of Government without giving the People of the Province any ground to triumph over those who have pre-

3. Jackson's view of the matter was well balanced. There is, however, no evidence in Allen's known writings or public statements that Jackson had convinced him that an ending of proprietary government could sooner or later become inevitable. From what follows in the next paragraphs it appears that Jackson's approval of Allen's position on the issues of *general* colonial policy had led him to underestimate Allen's partisanship in *local* Pennsylvania politics; hence Jackson may have been less discreet than an agent of the Assembly should have been in talking about strictly Pennsylvania affairs with a leader of the proprietary faction.

tended that they have been fighting the battle of the Crown; I had reason for this Opinion, and therefore wished, to defend the Province from the Dangers it threatened. I thought it my Duty to do so; and therefore hinted to you in more Letters than one what I apprehended. My Apprehensions were chiefly on the head of Purchase Money to be paid to the Proprietary and some Privileges of the People of Pennsylvania, but my Apprehensions never extended on the former head to £100000, nor on the latter did I think that the Crown, would by Violence and unconstitutionally strip the Province of its Privileges.[4]

I do not write you this for Publick Use, perhaps it might serve some purpose to make it publick, but I know you will make no Use of it, that I do not consent to, and my design is only to open to [sic] heart to you on the Subject; and that it should go no further.

Since I wrote the above I received your favour acquainting me with the Event of the Election.[5] I am heartily sorry for it, not for your sake, but for that of the Province. I now look on the hopes of Reconciliation as vanished for ever: and am Sure that the Event will be the vesting the Power of Government in the Crown. My Compliments to the Governor of New Jersey. I took all the Pains I could to get his Judge confirmed, but there was some want of form in his Appointment that rendered it impracticable.[6] Besides I have really little Interest with Ministers of any kind though I

4. When, after Allen's return in August, BF had visited him as an "Overture" towards re-establishing "a good Understanding," Allen had stated "before all the Company" that Jackson had sent a message to BF to say that it would cost the colony £100,000 if the Crown were to take over the government from the Penns and had added that Lord Mansfield had threatened severity if the "refractory People" of Pa. should come under direct royal government. Above, pp. 327–8.

5. Jackson apparently wrote this final paragraph after receiving BF's letter of October 11; above, pp. 396–7.

6. Following the death of Chief Justice Robert Hunter Morris and the disability, and later death, of Second Judge Samuel Nevill of N.J., Governor Franklin had appointed Charles Read and John Berrien to succeed them; above, pp. 96–7. Frederick Smyth (c.1732–1815), perhaps a recent arrival in the colony, had several friends high in British governmental circles, however, and in 1764 he received a royal appointment as chief justice, a position he held until 1776, when, as a Loyalist, he left the colony. N.J. Hist. Soc. Colls., x, 202–3; 1 N.J. Arch., IX, 475–6; x, 62–3, 145, 146–7, 220–1; XXIV, 426, 450–2.

keep a Post that gives me Access to them, perhaps it may be of Service and I may have more. Farewell Dear Friend and believe me to be with the greatest Sincerity your affectionate humble Servant   RD JACKSON

From Joseph Galloway

AL (incomplete): American Philosophical Society

Dear Sir   Philada. Novr. 23. 1764.
I wrote you from New Castle, the Substance of the Address of the Lower Counties' Assembly,[7] In which they inform the Crown, That altho they are Governed under the Same Charter with the People of Pennsylvania, yet that their Laws are different. Will it be amiss to inform the Crown, shoud our Intended Change meet with any Obstructions from this Address, That, by the Deed from the Duke of York to W. Penn, he was only Entitled to the Soil and not to the Powers of Government, the Soil being only granted—and that consequently Mr. Penn Exceeded his Power in extending the Charter to the Lower Counties.[8] And that therefore the Charter

7. Galloway's letter from New Castle has not been found. Benjamin Chew sent Thomas Penn a copy of the Delaware Assembly's address to the King with his letter of Nov. 23, 1764. Chew proposed the address and drafted it, and the Assembly adopted it without a dissenting vote after the members were satisfied that it could be worded in such a way as to avoid the appearance of meddling with the affairs of another government. Chew explained to Penn that its principal design "was First to manifest their Affection for you and your Family and to do justice to your Characters; Secondly by a Side wind to counteract the Petition from the Assembly of this province." Penn Papers, Hist. Soc. Pa.

8. Territorial and political rights in the Three Lower Counties (the present state of Delaware) were highly confused, and their status was never fully resolved during the colonial period. In 1682 the Duke of York leased the territory to William Penn by two deeds of enfeoffment, although his own claims were based purely on conquest, not on his charter of 1664. At no time, as duke or as king, did James, or his successors on the throne, formally confer rights of government on Penn, in spite of several applications by the Proprietor of Pennsylvania. In 1703, however, the Privy Council did allow him to appoint a common governor for Pennsylvania and the Lower Counties, subject to royal confirmation and an acknowledgment by Penn (to be repeated by his successors) that such approval did not diminish the Crown's right and claim to the Counties. After the establishment of separate assem-

being granted by a person not having the power of granting is void. And as to their Laws, The Ministry must certainly be surprized to find a Government carried on, and Laws made for upwards of 60 Years, without transmitting any of them for their Approbation. This conduct is not only treating the Crown with great disrespect, but is invading its prerogatives in a Dangerous Point. I apprehend the Reason of the Crowns reserving a Power to repeal or Confirm the Laws of the Colonies, is that it May by a Superintendant Power be able at all times to prevent the ill Consequences that [would] flow from Statutes made inconsistent with the Allegeance of the Subject, or contrary to the Royal Prerogative, But if a Colony should have it in its Power by a Juggle between the two Branches of the Legislature to pass Laws without ever presenting them to the Royal Eye or Ministerial Inspection, Sedition disloyalty, and Infringments of the Kings Prerogative may be promoted and sanctifyed by the solemnity of Laws, and all their attendant Mischiefs ensue, without the least Possibility of redress. I call it a Juggle, because you well know, That the Assembly of that Government have been indulged by the Proprietaries in many things which they have refused here; particularly the Loan Office Act which was passed about the Same Time in which the one in Pennsylvania was assented to by the Governor,[9] An Act Liable to the Same Objections, made by the Proprietaries to the one passed here. And yet they presented the latter for the Royal disapprobation and exerted all their Industry to obtain a repeal, while the former they permitted, with all the rest of the lower County-Laws to sleep unpresented. Nay more their present Governor, appointed by a new Act, a new Set of Trustees to carry the former Law into Execution. Does not a Conduct of this sort in a Proprietary Governor fully Justify the Assertion of the Lords of Trade, That his Majestys Prerogative is too weighty to be Entrusted to the Feeble Hands of private Individuals who from Attachments to their own private Interests, Views and

---

blies the laws passed for the Counties were never sent to the Privy Council for approval. There were few Quakers in the Counties, and jealousies and mistrust continued between the neighboring regions. For a summary account of this complicated matter, see Charles M. Andrews, *The Colonial Period of American History*, III (New Haven, 1937), 292–6, 321–6.

9. The Re-emitting Act of 1759; for the Board of Trade's adverse report on the Pa. act and its disallowance by the Privy Council, see above, IX, 146–53, 204–5, 210.

Schemes, are ever ready to Violate or Surrender it up to Serve their own purposes of a private nature.[1] Mr. Wharton has promised to send you the Act with the Supplement or I should do it by this Opportunity.

The Proprietary Party Still are industrous in endeavouring to prevent our Design to Change the Government; The Corporation of this City have been for several days engaged in Petitioning the Proprietaries not to Surrender the Government to the Crown. But in Case this cannot be avoided, to use his Interest to preserve their Charter Priviledges.[2] The Presbyterians likewise have been as Active in preparing and Signing a Petition, to the Same purpose, only differing in the Conclusion, that in Case the Change takes place to preserve their religious Priviledges.[3] These Petitions are to go over with Mr. Hamilton.[4]

The Confusion of the Government does not seem yet to be at an End, and I am convinced never will unless one more just, impartial and respectful than that of a Proprietary shoud Succeed. Every day furnishes further Proofs. At the last Election at Lancaster a Dutchman who Came into the Country young and is very capable of Executing the Office was Elected and appointed Sheriff of that County.[5] The Irish Presbyterians being disappointed in not having one of themselves elected to that Office, refused to Serve on either Grand or Petty Juries, Tho' regularly Summond by the Sheriff, because he was a Dutchman. So that there was a failure of Justice last Term in that County. The Sheriff, in endeavouring to serve a process on one of those people, was violently Assaulted,

1. In its report of June 24, 1760, the Board of Trade had severely criticized the Penns for failing to uphold the prerogative until "their Interests were affected, as Individuals." Above, IX, 171.

2. On Nov. 19, 1764, the Philadelphia Corporation resolved to petition the Proprietors expressing disapproval of the proposed change in government and asking, if the change could not be prevented, that the rights of the people and those of the Corporation under its charter be continued. *Minutes of the Common Council of the City of Philadelphia. 1704 to 1776* (Phila., 1847), pp. 703–5.

3. The record of this petition has not been found.

4. See above, p. 458 n.

5. John Barr received the highest number of votes in the election of 1764 and was appointed sheriff. 2 *Pa. Arch.*, IX, 787; [Thomas Balch, ed.], *Letters and Papers Relating Chiefly to the Provincial History of Pennsylvania, with Some Notice of the Writers* (Phila., 1855), pp. 206–7. No detailed account has been found of the subsequent disturbances reported in this paragraph.

had both Ears of his horse Cut off, and was Obliged to fly to save his Life. And here the Matter rests, For I cannot Learn there are any Measures taking to bring the Offenders to Justice, and were they taken, I much doubt their Success: such is the debility of this Proprietary Government!

I hear, The Governor, to show how little he regards the remonstrances from the Assembly respecting the Mal-Conduct of the Justiciary Officers, has reinstated Wm. Moore of Chester County as the President of Chester Court,[6] and has turnd out Mr. Hannums a very Worthy man for this only reason because he has supported the Measures prosecuted in favor of the Crown respecting a Change of Government.[7] And I am also well informed Mr. Pawling is to be left out in this County with several others for the Like reason[8] —and several Presbyterians are to fill their Places, Mr. Bryan of this City is one.[9] A Strange Government this in which Loyalty and Affection to the Sovereign is made Criminal, while a Servile Submission and Implicit Obedience to the unjust and Oppressive Measures of a private Subject is the only path to Promotion.[1]

6. On William Moore's alleged libel of the Assembly in 1755, in which William Smith became involved, and their imprisonment on orders of the House, see above, VI, 245–7; VII, 141 n, 385 n; VIII, 28–41. Moore had first been appointed presiding justice in Chester Co. in 1741 and had been regularly reappointed until 1761, when his name was omitted from the commission of the peace. He was again appointed, Nov. 19, 1764, and continued in office until the Revolution; 2 *Pa. Arch.*, IX, 697–700.

7. Galloway's statement is in error. John Hannum (1742–1799), who had first been appointed a justice of the peace in 1761, was reappointed in 1764 (*Pa. Col. Recs.*, VIII, 573; IX, 205; 2 *Pa. Arch.*, IX, 699), but declined to qualify. It was John Morton who was left out; see below, p. 485.

8. Henry Pawling had been a J.P. for Philadelphia Co. since 1752, but was left out of the new commission of Nov. 19, 1764; *Pa. Col. Recs.*, IX, 205; 2 *Pa. Arch.*, IX, 727–8. He had been elected to the Assembly in October 1764 on the proprietary ticket, but angered the leaders of that party by voting consistently with the majority party in the critical votes of the October session; see above, pp. 390, 393.

9. On George Bryan, see above, VI, 386–7. He and Thomas Willing had defeated BF and Samuel Rhoads in the city election in October.

1. This paragraph completes the fourth page of the only surviving folio of this letter, which up to this point is entirely in Galloway's hand. Someone else has added at the bottom in pencil "J. Galloway," as if it were a signature, but the usual complimentary close is lacking. Evidently the original letter continued on to a second folio now lost.

From James Parker

ALS: American Philosophical Society

Honoured Sir   Woodbridge, Nov. 23. 1764.

When you embarked at Chester, I purposed to return that Night, but I could not: However, I got to Philadelphia next Day before Noon: I immediately applied to Dunlap's Affair, as McCleave had arrived before me:[2] I found all the Security Dunlap had was Mc-Cleave's Bond, and McCleave could give no other Security. So I at last took his McCleave's Bond for £44 15s. 10d. payable next October, with Interest, as he affirmed he could not pay any sooner as he had nothing to support him but his Wages: Dunlap was willing to give a Deed for that Land, but not being willing to be at the sole Cost, I sat down, and wrote one myself on Parchment, from the other, with the same Reserves, for Dunlap could not grant

2. "Dunlap's Affair" refers to the land in Kemblesville, New London Township, Chester Co., which he had offered to turn over in settlement of his post-office account; above, pp. 419–20. This property originally belonged to a tavern keeper and post rider, George McCleave. In 1762 McCleave had given mortgages to two tracts, totaling about 216 acres, to Philotesia and Amos Strettell, executors of the estate of Robert Strettell, to secure debts amounting to £120. On May 3, 1763, he had given a second mortgage to the two tracts to William Dunlap as security for a debt of £110. The mortgages are entered in the Chester Co. records. This information has been generously supplied to the editors by Dr. Carl R. Woodward of Kingston, R.I. Apparently Parker, acting for BF and the Post Office, now took a deed to the tracts and, since McCleave appeared unable to make any further payments of principal or interest on his debt to the Strettell estate, and those mortgages still encumbered the title, the obligation to pay devolved on BF as deputy postmaster general. Unfortunately, Parker failed to leave the deed with DF, or even to inform her of the transaction, so she was completely surprised when in January 1766 Amos Strettell dunned her for £18 interest. DF to BF, Jan. 12, 1766, APS. That BF regarded the whole matter as a post-office transaction, not a personal one, is shown by entries in his Journal, 1764–1776, and Ledger, 1764–1776 (both described below, pp. 518–20). The final entry in the Journal, p. 61, dated October 1776, reads: "General Post-Office Dr. To sundry Sums paid Amos Strettell Interest on the Mortgages of Land £36 Pensils Currency is Sterling £21 12s. not settled." In the debit column of the General Post Office account in the Ledger, p. 11, is the following "Memorandum, Oct. 21. 1776 This day obtained from Mr. Amos Strettell an Account of Cash paid by Mrs. Franklin in my Absence in Discharge of Interest due on Mortgages of some Post-Office Land, amounting to £36 Pensilva. Currency which must be deducted from the above Ballance, being Sterling £21 12s. 0d. B.F."

more than he had, and as he could not redeem the Mortgage from Strettel. That was mentioned also, and Credit then was given for the Surplusage—the said Mortgage with its Interest to that Time amounted to £134 12s. so the Bond is credited for £215 8s. 6d. which makes the £350. and I told Dunlap if he would redeem those Mortgages, he should have Credit for them: but he was not then able: I got him and his Wife to acknowledge the Deed before the Mayor, but his Deed has not been recorded, nor have I got either of them recorded, as I had no Orders so to do, as I suppose that may be done any Time, and Dunlap gave up his Deed to me, so I have both of them in keeping. I left Philadelphia before your Letter from the Capes arrived,[3] with Advice of your leaving the Capes on Friday, tho' as we had the Wind Saturday Night and Sunday Morn at East, we were in pain for you, however as it cleared off at West Sunday Noon, and blew so a few Days after, we supposed you a good Way on your Voyage. Dunlap said Nothing to me about Col. McNott,[4] but I will write to him, Mrs. Franklin having sent to me that part of your Letter. I have not heard from Mr. Foxcroft since you departed, but have wrote to him the Transactions with Dunlap. Assoon as I got home, I sent off my Son to bring home Lady Jane.[5] Mrs. Franklin had some Thoughts of coming with her here, but she has declined it, as finding it would be inconvenient to her other Affairs.

I take the Freedom to inclose this to Mr. Strahan, to whom I also write, and send him a small Bill for £8 11s. 5d. which with a small Bill for £10 sent some Time ago, is all I can, or I fear able to get from Mr. Holt, and as I should be glad to close with Mr. Strahan in Conformity to your Promise, I trust you will pay him off the Ballance, and such Part thereof as shall remain unpaid to

---

3. Not found.

4. Col. Alexander McNutt, a Virginian, was promoting schemes for speculation in Nova Scotia lands and settlement there. Several Philadelphians, including BF, were interested in his projects, and later volumes in this edition will contain further references to the matter. See William O. Sawtelle, "Acadia: The Pre-Loyalist Migration and the Philadelphia Plantation," *PMHB*, LI (1927), 244–85, esp. 269–83. McNutt was in Philadelphia at the time BF left for England. Theodore G. Tappert and John W. Doberstein, eds., *The Journals of Henry Melchior Muhlenberg*, II (Phila., 1945), 143.

5. Parker's daughter Jane, most commonly called "Jenny." The son was Samuel Franklin Parker.

you at this Time, I shall freely pay you Interest for, and then I shall bring all my Debts into one Place.[6] Assoon as you have done it, wish you would send me Word of it. I purpose to go early in the Spring, if please God I live so long, to Philadelphia, and do all I can in your Affair,[7] and wish I may be able to do it to your Satisfaction.

I hope this will meet you safe arrived, and that you may have your desired Success. I heard yesterday from Philadelphia where they were all well, but you may possibly have later Letters than this of mine, as I send this to New York to go by a Merchant ship about to sail soon, and so may be full early, but I would not miss: I have had my Health since my Journey pretty well, and flatter myself with some Continuance. All Friends here remain much as they were—I do not recollect any Thing more material at this Time, so with all Respects remain Your most obliged Servant

JAMES PARKER

Addressed: For / Benjamin Franklin, Esqr / at / London

From Samuel Wharton[8]

AL (incomplete): American Philosophical Society

Dear Sir   Philada.Novr. 23d 1764
As some Matters have occur'd, since your Departure, Which it may not be disagreable to you, to know, I borrow an Hour, from Business, to communicate Them to you.

The Corporation of this City, met yesterday and agreed upon an Address to the Proprietors.[9] What the Particulars of it, are, I have not yet been able to Obtain, But I learn generaly; That it is expressive of *their* high Approbation of *their* Goverment and beseeches Them, to use their utmost Application and Interest, for the Continuance of it.

I have some Reason to apprehend, That They insinuated, in a part, of it, That if *unfortunately,* the Goverment should be changed,

6. See above, p. 414, and below, p. 520.
7. The settlement of BF's accounts with David Hall; see above, pp. 441–3.
8. On Samuel Wharton, one of Joseph Wharton's numerous sons, see above, p. 187 n.
9. See above, p. 467 n.

That Then, They flatter Themselves, The Proprietors will exert their Influence, In Order, to Mr. Hamilton's, being appointed Governor.[1]

At all Events They are determined, it would seem, That the Province should remain, under the Controul of that Gentleman and his Connexions.

The Presbyterians, met likewise yesterday, at their Meeting House and resolved also upon an *Address*.[2] But what its Contents are, I am not informed of.

As a Reward to this Sect, for the Services They have done, Mr. Geo. Bryan and Mr. Alexander Huston, two fiery Bigots, are appointed Justices, for this City and County.[3]

Another Prooff of the prudence of the proprietary Counsil, is the re-appointment of Mr. Moore, To the office of a Justice of Peace, for Chester County.[4]

If the Penn Family were determined, to exercise what little Abilities, They have, designedly, to confirm, The unfavorable Opinion, The *People* entertain of their Goverment They could not, more effectualy, do it, Than by commissioning Persons at this critical Juncture, Who are so obnoxious to Them.

It is indeed fortunate for Us, That They will thus foolishly affront, the sober and sensible part of the Inhabitants, By appointing Men, for Judges, during their Pleasure, Who are known to be *their* profess'd and thorough paced Creatures.

You will pardon Me Sir, for a Moment, Whilst I review, inpart, The Conduct of Those, who stile Themselves proprietary Friends.

When Mr. Hamilton arrived the last Time, as Governor, One of the first Acts, He did, was to disrobe that bad Man, Mr. Moore, (as They *then*, justly, called Him) of his Office.[5] This was intended,

1. James Hamilton, who had already served twice as proprietary lieutenant governor, 1748–54 and 1759–63, was about to sail for England to be treated for a suspected cancer on his nose. He remained until 1767, then returned, entirely cured of his disorder. Although he was never again appointed lieutenant governor, as senior councilor he served twice as acting governor for short periods in the absence of John Penn from the province.

2. Not found.

3. Bryan was appointed J.P., Nov. 19, 1764, but Huston was not. *Pa. Col. Recs.*, IX, 205; 2 *Pa. Arch.*, IX, 729.

4. See above, p. 468 n.

5. No evidence has been found that Hamilton "disrobed" Moore as one

as a recommendatory Introduction, to his Administration and had the happy Effect of generaly pleasing the Province.

Ever since, Mr. Moore, has remained in a private Character. But Now, Mr. Pen is told, It is a proper Period to restore Him, to his former Power and Dignity, But for What Reasons, is misterious, unless, because, He is inexpressibly disagreable, to the principal People, of the County, He dwells in. What must We infer, from such curious Conduct, as this? Except Either, That Our wise Counsellors, conceive it, The easiest Method, of conciliating the Affections of the Inhabitants—Or that, They are determined to plunge Mr. Penn into fresh Difficultys, That so, There may be the more Necessity, for his Uncle's calling Him, *home* and sending Out, Mr. Hamilton, In case, you should Not, be so successfull, as to perfect the Change.

The REMARKS[6] shock'd the Party, very much, as They so clearly and irresistibly develop'd, a variety of Truths, Which They had been long, basely perverting—Especialy that Part of Them, Which gave a History of the Money, That was put, into the Stocks. The Chief Justice was most sensibly affected, at the just Chastisement, you gave Him and his Friends murmured very much, That He should be so Weak, as *Now* to sign his Name to a *Protest,* Which his former *signing,* so flatly contradicted. In short, They became greatly ashamed of their Politician, and He to excuse Himself, was oblig'd to bellow Out, a Compliment to his Heart, at the Expence, of his poor Head. He said "to every Comer and Goer," That He was happy in knowing He had a good Heart, Though He had a bad Head and as a Prooff of the Latter, He declared He had forgot, That He had signed, the Report of the Committee, *Upon your Accounts.*[7]

An excellent Excuse this, for a Man who has the Effrontery to boast, of a good Heart, When He must be conscious That He has been incessantly, both secretly and publickly, disseminating his Poison, To the, almost, irreparable Injury of Another.

of his "first Acts" on assuming office in 1759; he was simply omitted from the commission of the peace of Chester Co., issued Feb. 23, 1761. *Pa. Col. Recs.,* VIII, 573; 2 *Pa. Arch.,* IX, 699.

6. BF's *Remarks on a Late Protest;* above, pp. 429–41.

7. This explanation (or excuse) by Allen may have been considered too weak, for it was not included in William Smith's *Answer to Mr. Franklin's Remarks,* which undertook instead to distinguish between BF's particular "account" of provincial money expended and his "accounts" in general.

He has long insolently domineer'd, in Sun Shine of Fortune and Power, But I am persuaded, you have done Him unutterable Service and That He will be very cautious in future, How He sports with Reputations; for He Now looks upon Himself, hung Up, as an Object, stript of its delusive Covering and exposed to the World, with all its practical [Suspicions?].

This I am told, gives Him exquisite Distress and particularly, Because, He is afraid, of a Publication in England.[8]

The party are very quiet—but dejected and do not Even talk, of an Answer to the *Remarks*.[9]

I expected to have sent you, The Re-emitting Act, pass'd by Mr. Denny, in the three Lower Countys, shortly after He had passed *Ours*, But I have lost Mine and Therefore must wait, Until I can get another, from New Castle.[1] I think nothing can more clearly prove, The suspicion of the Board of Trade, as express'd, at the close of their Animadversions, Upon the Laws transmitted from this Province, Then Mr. Penn's not presenting the lower County re-emitting Act and his Deputy, (To Wit Mr. John Penn) last Spring, passing another, for the appointing of New Trustees for the executing of this very Act. The part of their Lordships Report, which I allude to, is that, Where They say—"That the prerogative is not safe, In the feeble Hands of private Persons, Who too often, render it subservient to their Own Interests."[2]

Mr. Penn must certainly have his private Estate, in the 3 Lower Countys in View, or else He is wholy disregardfull of the Prerogative of the Crown otherwise He could not take so much pains to have Our Re-emitting Act, repealed and yet Never present *the One*—exactly similar, Almost totidem Verbis passed at New Castle

8. The *Remarks* were not reprinted in England, although Peter Collinson suggested the possibility; see below, p. 543.

9. But see the long *Answer*, below, pp. 486–516.

1. Galloway had expected Wharton to send BF a copy of this act; above, p. 467.

2. The words within quotation marks are at most a broad paraphrase of the concluding paragraphs of the Board of Trade report of June 24, 1760. Only the words "In the feeble Hands of private Persons," approximating the report's "in the feeble hands of Individuals," are taken directly from the Board of Trade. That body was criticizing the Proprietors for their laxity and self-interest, not arguing for assumption of the government by the Crown. See above, IX, 171–3.

and Even suffer his Deputy, To continue *that very Act,* By a law nominating New Trustees to execute it and this after, The Lords of Trade, had made the above pointed Insinuation, against proprietary Rulers.[3]

By King Charles's Charter to Mr. William Penn, it is positively enjoin'd, That all Laws shall be transmitted to the Privy Council, within five years and the same is directed, That so, the said Mr. Penn or his Heirs, or other the Planters &c. may not, at any Time, Thro' Inadvertency or Design, depart from their Faith and Allegiance.[4]

What can Mr. Thomas Penn then say, In Excuse for Himself, Why He has not taken Care to present, from Time to Time such Laws, As have been made in the three Lower Countys. He cannot alledge, That it was not his Duty, for I conceive it is as much his and more so, Than it is the Assembly's and with Respect, to this Province, He did, if I mistake not, gladly present Our Re-emitting Act &c.

You will doubtless see the Account of Colonel Bouquet's Expedition down the Ohio, As published in the *Papers,* I shall therefore only, add upon it. That We every Day expect to hear of his being returnd to Fort Pitt, with all the Prisoners delivered Up and Hostages, for the Accomplishment of such Terms, of Peace, as shall be granted to Them.[5]

3. On March 31, 1764, Governor John Penn, sitting in Council at New Castle, approved a group of bills including "An Act appointing new Trustees for the Several General Loan Offices of this Government." *Pa. Col. Recs.,* IX, 169. A copy of this bill, attested May 22, 1764, is among the Franklin Papers, APS.

4. Penn's charter applied to the province of Pennsylvania, the stated boundaries of which did not include the Three Lower Counties on Delaware. As mentioned above, p. 465 n, he never received formal powers of government over the Counties. Had such a document been issued to him, it would certainly have included a clause, similar to the one in the Pennsylvania charter, requiring the transmission of the Delaware laws.

5. On Monday, Dec. 3, 1764, an officer reached Philadelphia with dispatches from Bouquet for General Gage in N.Y. He reported that when he left the army at the forks of the Muskingum on November 18, the men were "in high Spirits," that more than two hundred prisoners had been surrendered, and that another hundred were "daily expected." *Pa. Gaz.,* Dec. 6, 1764. Bouquet reached Fort Pitt on his return march, November 28. [William Smith,] *An Historical Account of the Expedition against the Ohio Indians* (Phila., printed; London, reprinted, 1766), p. 29.

As soon as there is a certain Account of the Prisoners and Hostages being at Fort Pitt, Mr. Croghan will go from Hence thither, To hold a Treaty with The Delawars and Shawanese.[6] One of the Conditions, I have Reason to think, will be their assisting us, to obtain Possession of the Illinois. An Object of the highest Consequence to the Colonies; As it at present, gives an Opportunity to the Indians, To sell their Peltrys to the French and to receive Ammunition, in Return, from Them.

By conversing with Mr. Croghan, I am confirmd in my Suspicion, That He did Not urge the *last Losses,* Which were suffered by us and others in the Indian Trade. I have also from Him, That Our Friend Anthony Bacon Esquire has undertaken to introduce the former Losses, into Parliament.[7] Wherefor B. W & M [Baynton, Wharton & Morgan] have wrote to Him and informed Him, How They are circumstanc'd and beg'd the exertion of his Interest and Friendship, in their Behalf. I must Therefore request the Favor of you, to call upon Mr. Bacon and explain to Him, The Justice of our sharing equaly with the first Sufferers, in any Retaliation, That may be made by Parliament.

It may happen, That your earnest Endeavours may not be crown'd with success, in Obtaining a Restitution for Us, Either in Cash, or Lands. May We therefore be so free with you, As to hope, That in Case, Our Goverment should be changed, That you will be

6. George Croghan (above, v, 64 n), Indian trader, land speculator, and former deputy superintendent of Indian affairs, had recently returned from England with grandiose ideas of a settlement in Illinois and the re-establishment of the Indian trade. He bought a fine house on the outskirts of Philadelphia, entered into close business relations with the firm of Baynton, Wharton & Morgan, and infected Wharton with his enthusiasm. Nicholas B. Wainwright, *George Croghan Wilderness Diplomat* (Chapel Hill, [1959]), pp. 209–12.

7. Apparently, Croghan told Wharton what he had learned in London: that the only hope of recovering the traders' losses in the 1763 uprising was to get for them part of the western lands the Indians were expected to cede, and that the losses of 1754 could be recouped only by an act of Parliament. *Ibid.,* pp. 206–7. Anthony Bacon (*c.*1717–1786), M.P. for Aylesbury, was a former Marylander, now a prosperous London merchant. Namier and Brooke, *House of Commons,* II, 35–6; Lewis B. Namier, "Anthony Bacon, M.P., an Eighteenth-Century Merchant," *Jour. of Economic and Business History,* II (1929–30), 20–70. It is not known that Bacon took any parliamentary steps on behalf of the Pa. traders.

pleas'd to procure us a *Recompense* in another Way; That is, by having each of us appointed to some Office of Profit Even if the same, was in Reversion. This may be as easy a Way, as any, to the Ministry and will be satisfactory to Us.

Was I not convinc'd, That I am addressing myself, To a Gentleman, Who will I am persuaded, construe my [*remainder missing*].

From Samuel Johnson[8]

Letterbook copy: Columbia University Library

Most Worthy and Dear Sir   [November? 1764][9]

It was no small Mortification to me that you passed by last Fall without giving me the pleasure for a few moments of seeing you.[1] However I doubt not but your reasons were such as I should have allowed sufficient had I known them. It was with great [*word omitted*] that I read the Resolves of your house,[2] and Mr. Galloways Speech, with your excellent Preface,[3] and lastly that you are appointed immediately to go home to plead so good a Cause. Your way seems plain before you, and I heartily wish you a good voyage and happy Success. Would to God you were charged with pleading

8. For Johnson, Anglican clergyman, president of King's (Columbia) College, 1754–63, see above, III, 477–8 n.

9. So dated because of the reference to BF's trip through New England "last Fall" (his postal inspection tour with John Foxcroft in the summer and fall of 1763, above, X, 276–9, is meant) and because of Johnson's knowledge that BF had been "appointed immediately to go home" to England. BF's appointment as agent, Oct. 26, 1764, had been announced in *Pa. Gaz.*, Nov. 8, 1764, which Martin Howard had read in Newport, R.I., by November 16 (see above, p. 459), so that Johnson in Stratford, Conn., could have seen the news a day or two earlier. He probably wrote this letter soon thereafter.

1. On his way home from Boston in the fall of 1763 BF and his party passed through Stratford, Conn., sometime between October 28 and 31; see above, X, 279. Johnson had resigned as president of King's College in February 1763, after his wife had died in a smallpox epidemic in New York; he retired to Stratford to live with his son, William Samuel, and resumed the parish ministry. E. Edwards Beardsley, *Life and Correspondence of Samuel Johnson D. D.* (N.Y., 1874), pp. 286–92.

2. See above, pp. 126–33.

3. See above, pp. 267–311.

the same Cause in behalf of all the Governments, that they might all alike be taken into the Kings more immediate Protection. It would certainly [be] best for us all to be under one form of Goverment and I beg that your best Influence may be so directed, that the Goverment, at home when they take yours in hand may make but one work of it. I wish to Heaven, particularly in behalf of this, that that might be the happy Event for we greatly suffer for want of such a Change, particularly by our whole Assembly's being the Judges in all Cases of Equity, and our Constitutions being so monstrously popular, that all our Judges and other officers depend intirely on the people; so that they are under the strongest Temptation in many Cases to consider not so much what is Law or Equity, as what may please their Constituents.[4] I was quite tired with my College which was too Great a burthen for my years, and now I thank God I enjoy great Health and tranquility in this sweet Retirement with my dear and only Son, and remain &c.

To Mr. Franklin

From Thomas Osborne[5]   ALS: American Philosophical Society

Grays Inn, Novr. 1764

Mr. Osbornes Complyments to Dr. Franklyn and has taken the Liberty of sending him the 15th Vol. of Modern History,[6] with some of his Catalogues which Mr. O. does not doubt but the Dr. will order to be distributed to the best Advantage, and it wou'd

4. Since as early as 1732 Johnson had advocated royal government for the charter colonies of Connecticut and Rhode Island. In a piece sent to the Archbishop of Canterbury in 1760, "Questions Relating to the Union and Government of the Plantations," which he never published, Johnson attacked "two monstrous absurdities" in these two colonies: "they have vastly too numerous and unequal a representation, and . . . they make their general assemblies, courts of equity." Herbert W. and Carol Schneider, eds., *Samuel Johnson, President of King's College: His Career and Writings* (N.Y., 1929), I, 149–50, 293–301.

5. For Thomas Osborne, the foremost London bookseller of his day, see above, VII, 176 n.

6. For the complicated bibliography of this series, see above, III, 146 n. The fifteenth volume was advertised as "This Day" published in *London Chron.*, Sept. 29–Oct. 2, 1764.

give him infinite pleasure if that intricate Account with the Gentleman who had the Disposal of the books was Settled.[7]

Addressed: To / Dr Benjn. Franklyn / Speaker of the Assembly / in / Pensylvania

From Alexander Small[8] ALS: American Philosophical Society

Dear Sir   London Decr 1st 1764

Having called on our Friend in Craven Street[9] who informed me that my former Letter[1] was not yet gone I give you this second trouble to acquaint you that the sturgeon you recommended to Dr. Templeman was examined a few days ago, and did not give Satisfaction.[2] The Baltick Sturgeon has no Spices added to it. Capt. Blake[3] was of Opinion that the fish was boiled immediately after it was caught, which rendered it extremely hard. It was much too Salt, and of that red Colour which Salt Petre gives: and notwithstanding the quantity of Salt there was a putred taint. Should not sturgeon be preserved something on the Principle of the Berwick pickled Salmon, which you know has very little salt? How that is done I know not; tho' I dare say it is not a secret, being in so many hands. All the Sturgeon we have had sent from America has been much broken. I think it would be right to imitate the Berwick people in their small flat Kits. The Baltick Sturgeon is all bound round to prevent its breaking. Yours was not. I give these hints that the error may perhaps be amended.

7. A reference to Isaac Norris, who in 1761 wrote of the "very great Task" of settling his account with the bookseller; see above, IX, 336–7. Since Osborne sent this letter to Philadelphia, DF probably received it, and she may have passed on to Norris this reminder; but in writing BF, May 18, 1765, Norris made no mention of the Osborne account; APS.

8. For Alexander Small, Scots army surgeon living in London, see above, IX, 110 n.

9. Probably Margaret Stevenson, BF's London landlady.

1. Not found.

2. Above, pp. 334–5.

3. Probably Capt. John Blake, who proposed a scheme for bringing fish to the London market by land carriage from Channel ports. The project failed and later caused a quarrel between Blake and the Society of Arts. *Gent. Mag.*, XXXII (1762), 99–100; XXXIII (1763), 617, XXXVI (1766), 244.

We have since my last passed a severe Censure of Inefficacy on the Ingine for rooting up trees.[4] Indeed I think this pretended Improvement is not so good as the Original Berne Machine; I mean the 2d Edition of it, which seems much preferable to what we saw. My Namesake the Virginian Professor[5] is here; and desires to be most particularly remembered to you. I mentioned to him your Idea, of pulling them down by a force applied to a streight Rope. He says it will certainly do, and spoke of it as a new Mechanical Power not attended to by Mathematicians. I told him of your Clock weight.[6] The first thing that made him attend to it was, the practice of Sea Men, who when they have a very great weight to raise, or a great force to exert, do not pull the rope down, as in common, but pull it to them out of the right line, and thus keeping what they have got, convey the rope to others who secure it. This repeated, overcomes almost any resistance.

The News Papers have informed you that the Greenwich Observer Mr. Bliss is dead.[7] Mr. Mitchell[8] being much connected with Sir G: Saville,[9] and therefore with the Minority, has unsuccessfully

4. On Oct. 31, 1764, a demonstration took place before a committee of the Society of Arts of a "machine for pulling up trees by the roots." The results were disappointing and, after some modifications, a second demonstration was held on November 15. The machine proved "entirely ineffectual to answer the purposes proposed." Even with ten men working it, the device could "scarce bend a common planted elm, of two feet diameter, without damaging or breaking the greatest part of the apparatus, and rendering it (though so very unwieldy) entirely useless." *London Chron.*, Nov. 1–3, 17–20, 1764.

5. William Small (1734–1775), M.A. of Marischal College, Aberdeen, 1755; professor of natural history at William and Mary College, 1758–64. He went to England in 1764 to buy apparatus but remained there, settling in Birmingham, where he became one of the group from which the Lunar Society later sprang. H. L. Ganter, "William Small, Jefferson's Beloved Teacher," 3 *William and Mary Quar.*, IV (1947), 505–11; R. E. Schofield, *The Lunar Society of Birmingham* (Oxford, 1963), pp. 36–38, *et passim*.

6. What suggestion BF had made to Small, probably in conversation, for the operation of a clock weight is not known. From what follows here, it seems to have involved some scheme for a horizontal, rather than vertical, application of force.

7. Nathaniel Bliss (1700–1764), Savilian professor of geometry, Oxford, 1742; F.R.S., 1742; astronomer royal, 1762. He died Sept. 2, 1764. *DNB.*

8. For John Michell, astronomer, and geologist at Cambridge, see above, VII, 357 n. He resigned his fellowship in 1764.

9. Sir George Saville (1726–1784) was one of the leading independent Whigs; *DNB;* Namier and Brooke, *House of Commons*, III, 405–9.

offered himself a Candidate. From the same Motive, on his Attachment to the Minority, he opposed Lord Sandwich at Cambridge.[1] This our Friend Dr. Pringle took much amiss, because Mr. Mitchell had so lately lain under an Obligation to the Ministry. I endeavoured to plead the Character of the Man he opposed: but in vain. In the affair of the £5000 which was to have been given to Mr. Harrison, Mr. Mitchell seemed to sacrifice his own Opinion to that of the Lords joined with him in the Commission. The Dr. thought this rather mean, as it certainly was, if Mr. Mitchell could act so. There is however on the whole a shyness between them, so that I fear our C[l]ub has lost another excellent Member. Indeed now that he is married and left Cambridge, living retired near Newark, I suppose he would seldom visite us.

Rival geniuses are apt to be highly Jealous of one another. This is the Case between Cumming the Watch Maker; (a very ingenious Man, and excellent Mechanick) and Mr. Harrison.[2] They were formerly very intimate, and Mr. Harrison, who is frank and open, freely answered many questions that Cumming asked him. Whether from this Source, or from his own Noddle, I shall not determine, but Cumming thinks that he can make a Watch which shall answer the purpose of the Longitude, and therefore is become an Enemy to Harrison, or at least wants much to come in for an equal share of the glory, and therefore throws every rub in the way that he can. I do beleive that it was he who put the Commissioners of [off] the £5000 on demanding Conditions of Mr. Harrison, which the Act did not warrant them, in the Opinion of most people.[3] Mr. Short[4] was the only one who opposed these Lords, and stood firm to Harrison. Mr. Short is a Candidate for Greenwich but having

1. John Montagu, 4th Earl of Sandwich (above, X, 412 n), had recently been a candidate for the office of high steward of Cambridge University in a bitterly contested election which split the university voters, caused student riots, and wound up in the courts. D. A. Winstanley, *The University of Cambridge in the Eighteenth Century* (Cambridge, 1922), pp. 57–138.
2. Alexander Cumming (1733–1814), F.R.S., mathematician, mechanic, and watchmaker. *DNB*. John Harrison (1693–1776), inventor of the chronometer. *DNB;* and above, VII, 209.
3. For the delay in awarding John Harrison the full prize offered by Parliament for his chronometer (for determining longitude at sea), see above, VII, 209–10 n.
4. For James Short, optician, see above, V, 233; VII, 12 n; VIII, 158.

opposed Lord Morton[5] in the £5000 afair, Lord Morton now opposes him and gives it as a reason, that Mr. Short is a Scotch Man, though he acknowledges that he is the fittest for it of any Man. These two who would have done honour to the place, being thus laid aside, I beleive the Tory Interest, at present all powerful, will get it for an Oxonian, who never made an Observation.[6] What Candide Patrons we are of the Sciences!

The Persons to whom the Commissioners of Longitude gave the Observation made at Barbadoes and Portsmouth in order to ascertain the merit of Mr. Harrison's Watch have brought it so much within the Mark, that his Enemies are much at a loss how to act. The Gentlemen of the Law say that if there is Law in England, Mr. Harrison is sure of £20,000: and he is determined to adhere to the Law. There will not probably be a board of Longitude till the Parliament meets.

In our late Peace, we were guilty of the greatest Error in Politicks, in not restoring Canada to France, that so you might be a Check on one another.[7] We have left your western World almost independant, and are now more afraid of your shaking us off, than of any other object what ever. In order to preserve a Military Awe over you, we are likeways obliged to raise taxes. With our short Sighted Politicians, Smugling in general must be suppressed. They cannot distinguish where it may be beneficial. These are two Subjects which want much to be put in a proper light, both on your and our Account. Your Friends here wish you would once more take Pen in hand, and again give us the Information so much wanted of the Policy which ought to be followed in regard to your Continent.[8]

5. For James Douglas, 14th Earl of Morton, who became president of the Royal Society in this year, see above, IX, 272 n.

6. In spite of Small's prophecy that the post of astronomer royal would go to an Oxonian, the successful candidate, appointed Feb. 26, 1765, was Nevil Maskelyne (1732–1811), M.A., B.D., and D.D. of Cambridge. He was chaplain on the ship sent to Barbados (as mentioned in the next paragraph) to check on the testing of Harrison's fourth chronometer. *DNB*.

7. BF had vigorously refuted this argument in his Canada Pamphlet, 1760; above, IX, 90–5.

8. When he wrote this Small did not know, of course, that BF was then on his way to England, where within a few years he became the chief publicist in the British press for the American point of view on matters of colonial policy. See Verner W. Crane's invaluable *Benjamin Franklin's Letters to the Press 1758–1775* (Chapel Hill, [1950]).

Dr. Pringle will write to you by the Mail, and give all the literary News.⁹ I do not recollect any thing else worth troubling you with, and am Dear Sir Your affectionate humble Servant
ALEXR SMALL

From Thomas Wharton   ALS: American Philosophical Society

Philada. December 4th 1764
Much Esteemed friend Benjamin Franklin
I had the pleasure of writing thee on the 20th Ulto. (via Bristol) to which please to refer.¹
On the 28th Captn Friend left our Capes, with whom went Passengers—James Hamilton Esquire and his Nephew.²
Yesterday, We had the great satisfaction of receiving a Letter from Colo. Bouquet, by an Express sent forward for Gena. Gage³ —the substance of which is, that, He had made a Peace with the Shawaness and Delawares, that in conformity to the Conditions of the Peace, They had already delivered up Two hundred Prisoners, and that in a few days One hundred more would be surrendered; that He had received a Number of their best Warriours as Hostages, from whence it's hoped that the Peace will be lasting: the Army were returning, when the Express left them, from whence it's evident that the last £55000 granted to his Majesty, by this Province has been of singular Service, altho' obstructed by the the P——ry Governor in the manner it was.⁴

9. No letter from Pringle to BF at this time has been found.
1. Thomas Wharton's letter of November 20 not found; see above, p. 456 n.
2. Which nephew accompanied Hamilton is not certainly known; probably he was William Hamilton, son of the former governor's brother Andrew. Alternatively it could have been one of the sons of his sister Margaret and Chief Justice William Allen: John, Andrew, or James.
3. See above, p. 475 n. Bouquet's letter to Governor Penn, Nov. 15, 1764, and his journal and conferences with the Indians, read at the Pa. Council meeting of December 5, are printed in full in *Pa. Col. Recs.*, IX, 206–33. Penn thereupon issued a proclamation ordering a suspension of hostilities. *Ibid.*, p. 234.
4. The Supply Act passed May 30, 1764, after extended wrangling between Penn and the Assembly; above, pp. 206–13. In his letter of November 15 cited in the previous note, Bouquet wrote: "The Troops of your Government have carried on the Service with great Zeal and Chearfulness, and their Conduct does them Honour in every respect."

We have for some days past been advertiz'd of an Answer to thy Remarks, shortly to be published; But whither it will be signed by the Parties, or not, cannot by Us, be as yet known; tho' I am satisfied that J— D——[5] has been applied to for his Name, but his warmest Friends, insist He shall not place it there: I understand that the Cheif Points they answer to, are, first thy placing the Money in the Funds without an Act of Legislation; Secondly that as before last Election, thou never was sett up as a County Member of the Assembly so thou has not fairly stated the Matter; and therefore *They* Who to Us are well known both for want of Candour, and Common Honesty, will state it.[6]

I mentioned in my last that John Potts was left out of the Commission,[7] They have also left out Henry Pauling[8]—it's not unlikely that as his Actions as a Member of Assembly came to their Knowledge, so might his Story of the Black Snake, which doubt not thou recollect;[9] And both may have contributed to this Rejection. I also mentioned that George Bryan and Alexander Hueston were named for Magistrates in the new Commissions But find on it's being published yesterday, that A. Hueston is left out, and Wm. Humphreys placed in his stead,[1] which no doubt will afford thee proper Reflection; It's obvious to all here, which Way the stream is driving, And confirms to every thoughtfull Mind, the Necessity of thy Errand.

The more I have reflected on the State We are in, the clearer I am confirmed in my Judgement, of the absolute Necessity of the Measure; And for my own part, cannot help saying, that I think a Legislative Councill will one day or other be found, to be the great-

5. John Dickinson.

6. For this *Answer,* published anonymously, see the document immediately below.

7. John Potts (1710–1768), ironmaster, had been a J.P. for Philadelphia Co. since 1745, but was left out of the commission Governor Penn issued, Nov. 19, 1764. Mrs. Thomas Potts James, *Memorial of Thomas Potts, Junior, . . . with an Historic-Genealogical Account of His Descendants to the Eighth Generation* (Cambridge, Mass., 1874), pp. 91–116; 2 *Pa. Arch.,* IX, 726–8; *Pa. Col. Recs.,* IX, 205. Wharton had apparently mentioned this omission in his missing letter of November 20.

8. See above, pp. 393, 468 n.

9. Not known to the editors.

1. Samuel Wharton had also incorrectly reported that Alexander Huston had been named J.P.; above, p. 472.

est support of our Priviledges, as well as that of the Rights of the Crown.[2] For when I consider the natural Increase of the P——ns,[3] and the vast numbers yearly arriving among Us, I am induced to beleive, they will have the Rule and Direction of our Election's; If, that should prove the Circumstance, nothing can contribute to our Freedom so much as a Legislative Councill; Who would no doubt receive their Appointement from London, And every Avenue would be well guarded on that side of the Water, so that those People would not have it in their power to fill both the Legislative and Executive Branches of Government. In Chester County they plac'd Wm. Moore as President of [the] Court, John Hannum the last on the Commission, And have left John Moreton interely out; Hannum seeing their Views refused to qualify, and the Party were, as I am informed, much perplexed to make a Quorum the first Day.[4]

Since writing the above I have had the pleasure of seeing Colo. Bouquet's Letter to Governour Penn, which is dated at the Forks of Muskingham November 15th 1764 And mention's therein the following Circumstances—vizt.

First—that all the Prisoners should be delivered.

Secondly—That they should give him Fourteen Hostages, to remain in our hands as a security for the strict Performance of the first Article, And that They should committ no Hostilities against his Majestie's Subjects.

Thirdly That they should send Deputies to Sir William Johnson to confirm the Peace.

The Hostages deliver'd were—of the Mingoes - - - 2
Delawares - - - 6
Shawanesse - - - 6

2. In Pennsylvania (and the Lower Counties), alone among the British colonies, the Council served only as an advisory body to the governor and did not act as an upper house of the legislature. Councilors in the royal provinces were regularly appointed in Britain, frequently but not always on recommendation of the governor, and he was normally empowered to fill vacancies temporarily whenever the councilors available for service dropped below a fixed number, usually seven.

3. Presbyterians. The part they (notably the Scotch-Irish) had played in the recent election caused serious apprehensions among members of the political party to which Wharton and BF belonged.

4. See above, p. 468.

The Mingoes, and Delawares delivered their Captives, And even the Children born in their Nations of English Women.

The Letter mentions that the [Mingoes][5] Shawnese were extreamly obstinate, And that He expected to have had a Brush with them, before a Peace; But that they then appeared very humble.

That the Troops of this Government had carried on the Service with the greatest Zeal and Chearfullness.

David Hall informed me, that He expected a Declaration of the Cessation of Hostilities would be published here, to morrow:[6] And that He should have wrote thee hereof—But as I now undertook to do it.

Thy family are all Well, I have not to add but that I am with sincere respects thy Assurd Friend   THO WHARTON

Addressed: For / Benjamin Franklin / Esqr, / Agent for the Province of Pensilva: / In / London

William Smith: An Answer to Mr. Franklin's Remarks

[William Smith], *An Answer to Mr. Franklin's Remarks, on a Late Protest.* Philadelphia: Printed and Sold by William Bradford, at his Book-Store, in Market-street, adjoining the London Coffee-House. 1764. (Yale University Library)

On December 7, 1764, precisely one month after Franklin had left Philadelphia, the printer William Bradford published an anonymous pamphlet replying to Franklin's farewell *Remarks on a Late Protest.*[7] Though no author was indicated on the title page or elsewhere, Franklin's friends and supporters soon decided that Provost William Smith was at least primarily responsible, even if others might have had a hand in the composition. The attribution of authorship to Smith gained increasing credence and now is generally accepted by bibliographers and historians.[8]

5. Wharton first wrote "Mingoes" here, then crossed it out and substituted "Shawnese" above the line. Bouquet's letter, cited above, speaks particularly of the obstinacy of the Shawnee.

6. Penn's proclamation for the suspension of hostilities, cited above, was published in *Pa. Gaz.* and *Pa. Jour.,* Dec. 6, 1764.

7. *Pa. Jour.,* Dec. 6, 1764, announced that *An Answer to Mr. Franklin's Remarks* would be published "To-morrow in the Afternoon." For the *Remarks* and passages therein cited in this *Answer,* see above, pp. 429–41.

8. Twelve days after the publication Samuel Wharton wrote BF that

William Smith, D.D.

Still bitterly resentful, perhaps, of the "Lapidary Character" drawn of himself during the election campaign (above, pp. 387–90), Smith exercised little restraint in his choice of words to describe Franklin and Franklin's actions, or in the length of his *Answer*. Such pejorative expressions as "anarchical schemes," "shameful and scandalous manner," "ungrateful incendiary," and "ambitious and time-serving remarker" are scattered throughout the paper, and the adjectives "wicked" and "virulent" appear repeatedly. Franklin's *Remarks* on the Assembly minority's *Protest* had run to about 3,800 words; Smith's *Answer* took well over 10,000.

Almost as displeasing to Franklin's friends as the substance and tone of Smith's attack was the fact that the pamphlet was published anonymously. The minority assemblymen had openly signed their published *Protest*, and Franklin had done the same with his *Remarks*, but the *Answer* bore no acknowledgment of authorship. A group of Franklin's supporters, including his son William, got together and arranged for a communication to be published in both Philadelphia newspapers over the signature of John Hughes calling on the author of the *Answer* to disclose himself. Hughes challenged him to agree to pay £5 to the Hospital for every charge he could not prove, offering in turn to pay £10 to the Hospital for every one the writer might succeed in establishing. Each party was to choose one referee from a neighboring province and these two would name an umpire if they disagreed.[9] A reply, again unsigned, appeared in both newspapers a week later defending the practice of anonymity in political writings and ridiculing Hughes's proposal.[1]

On January 3, 1765, the *Gazette* printed a letter, signed by "Poplicola," which purported to be a defence of William Allen by a friend, but was actually a caustic criticism of the writer of the anonymous letter of the week before. On the same day both newspapers printed a

"Allison, Ewing, Smith and Edward Shippen junior, I have reason to think, were the Club of Geniuses, which composed that Compilation of Billingsgate and misrepresentation, called an *Answer*." Below, p. 526. WF told William Strahan, Feb. 18, 1765, that William Allen, "one of the principal Proprietary Tools in Pennsylvania, has employ'd that Miscreant Parson Smith, and two or three other Prostitute Writers to asperse his [BF's] Character, in which they have been very industrious." Pierpont Morgan Lib. In compiling a list of Smith's writings, his great-grandson, Horace W. Smith, included the pamphlet without question or the inclusion of names of any assisting authors. *Life and Correspondence of the Rev. William Smith, D.D.* (Phila., 1880), II, 536. Evans (9841, 9842) and Sabin (84586) both attribute the work to Smith without qualification.

9. Below, pp. 526–7; *Pa. Gaz.* and *Pa. Jour.*, Dec. 20, 1764.
1. *Pa. Gaz.* and *Pa. Jour.*, Dec. 27, 1764.

short piece signed by Hughes promising a full reply to the anonymous letter writer shortly.[2] This response appeared in both papers on January 10. Occupying about four columns, it again attacked the writer of the *Answer* at great length for his anonymity; it challenged him to furnish proofs of any one of his accusations against Franklin, and offered to produce full proofs in the Assembly of Franklin's charge that Allen had spoken derogatively there of royal government.[3] This letter brought the newspaper correspondence to a close, though some satirical verses, separately published, continued for a time to belabor the issue on both sides.[4]

The *Answer to Mr. Franklin's Remarks,* printed in full here, and its aftermath, summarized above, show forcefully that the bitter partisan feeling engendered by the election campaign of 1764 lingered on in Pennsylvania long after that contest was ended and after the most conspicuous person in it had left for England. As papers in the next volume will demonstrate, that bitterness and partisanship, carrying over into 1765, were significant factors in determining the attitude of Pennsylvanians towards Franklin at the time of the Stamp Act crisis.

An Answer to Mr. Franklin's
Remarks, on a Late Protest.

A day or two after Mr. Franklin's departure for England, having seen his remarks in the hands of a gentleman, I gave them a cursory perusal; but found them so replete with bitter calumnies and gross evasions, that I judged them unworthy of any further notice.

But being since told that his deluded partizans have begun to consider this neglect of his performance, as an argument of its unanswerable nature; I shall bestow a few hours (since no abler hand has thought it worth while) in order to convince them, if possible, that the real design of this their redoubted champion was not to elucidate, but to disguise and conceal the truth; which, it must be allowed, according to his usual custom, he has very artfully, but not honestly, done.

He sets out with telling us, that he has *generally* passed over with a silent disregard, the nameless pieces that have been written against him. The publick knows what sort of disregard he has shewn to the pieces written against him, and to their supposed authors. At present I pass on to the more material parts of his performance, which

2. *Pa. Gaz.* and *Pa. Jour.,* Jan. 3, 1765.
3. *Pa. Gaz.* and *Pa. Jour.,* Jan. 10, 1765.
4. WF to Strahan, Feb. 18, 1765, Pierpont Morgan Lib.

for my own sake I could have wished a little more methodical, and that the *calumny-part* had not been so indiscriminately blended with what he would have to pass as the *argumentative part*. I must, however, try to separate them as well as I can, for the greater clearness in writing; and shall begin with his remarks on the *Protest,* before I proceed to his shameful abuse of the *Protesters*.

His first remark is that "the mode of *protesting* by the minority, against the proceedings of the majority of the house of assembly, is quite *new* among us; is unknown to the practice of the house of commons, or of any house of representatives in America, and seems an affected imitation of the lords in parliament, &c."

It is acknowledged that *protesting* may not be an usual method in American assemblies, nor of late years practised in the house of commons in England, which is a very numerous body. But, in a constitution like ours, where there is no legislative council, it may not always be improper; and if the Remarker has nothing to urge against the *reason* or *necessity* of a thing, but its novelty, it will have but little weight. When cases and emergencies arise which are new and unprecedented in their nature, a new and unprecedented mode of proceeding against them, may become indispensably necessary.

If, for instance, contrary to the usage of the Commons in England, whose votes and transactions are regularly laid before their constituents from day to day, a house of assembly in America should keep their proceedings private for a whole year, and are, during that time, pursuing measures which are conceived fundamentally subversive of the constitution; and if those Members, who conscientiously oppose these measures, cannot even have so much as their *yeas* and *nays* made known to their constituents, to rescue them from odium which they have not merited—I say if such a case as this could possibly happen, then surely it becomes both a publick and private duty in those who are against such measures, not only to oppose them by every means in their power (by reasons both spoken and written) but likewise immediately, openly, and avowedly, to lay the whole before their constituents, from whom they derive their power, and to whom they are accountable for their conduct.

Had it not been for a publication of this kind made by three Members, (it matters not whether it was called a *Protest* or reasons of dissent offered in writing) I say, had it not been for a seasonable publication of this kind some time ago, and the papers that soon afterwards followed it,[5] the late Assembly might have made their measures for a change of government pass silently home to England as the sense of the People, without their constituents having any opportunity, upon their own certain knowledge of these measures, to represent dutifully to our most gracious sovereign, that they were unauthorized by the people, contrary to our Charter, and therefore, by the tenor of it, "void and of no effect." Such a silence as this would, no doubt, have very well suited the ambitious and destructive schemes of the Remarker, and would have saved him from some share, perhaps, of the general odium which he has the mortification to bear from the good people of this province, for his most wicked attempt to deprive them of their present excellent constitution, in the very face of their charter, and without their consent or authority.

It is no wonder then that this *mode of protesting* should not be agreeable to him, and that he should pour forth such abundance of abuse against all who think proper to follow that mode; tho', in fact, the *Protest* he has remarked on, was never offered by more than one of the signers to be entered on the Minutes, but was only read as the sum of the reasons that had been offered in the debate, and which, the House were told, would be laid before the publick. As the speaker of the House had not been presented to the governor, nor taken the usual qualifications to his majesty's person and government, most of the Members who signed the paper, printed in the nature of a *Protest,* did not think it necessary to press it on the House, which they judged, under these circumstances, could not regularly proceed to any business.

But the Remarker objects against this *mode* for another reason. He says "The Minutes would thereby be incumbered, &c." This may be of some weight with those who *pay* for the Minutes; but surely, you Mr. PRINTER* who *print* these Minutes and are *paid*

---

*The calling gentlemen by their professions and offices I find to be a favorite method of the Remarker, and I hope he will not be angry with me for adopting it as occasion offers. See page 5. "You, Mr. Chief Justice and other Justices among the Protesters, and you, Sir, who are a Counsellor at Law."

5. Dickinson's protest against the vote for a petition to the King, which he tried unsuccessfully to have entered on the Assembly minutes, May 28,

for them, cou'd not make this a serious objection. It is a pity, you had not learn'd this saving wisdom some years ago, when you *encumbred* the Minutes with such loads of scurrilous messages of your own drawing, and such long reports put together from law books, old histories and journals, that for *printing, copying,* and other services, you and your son shared between you near *two thousand pounds* of the publick money.[6] But you had not then got yourself saddled upon this province, with a large annual salary, as our ambassador extraordinary to England.

I shall now drop you, Sir, as Mr. Printer, and follow you in your higher characters of Mr. Ambassador, Mr. Post-master, (or by whatever other name you would be pleased to be called) while you go on modestly arguing your own cause, and proclaiming your own merits against the *Protesters.*

The first reason offered against you by these respectable gentle-men, is a very strong and clear one. They "believe you to be the chief author of the measures pursued by the late Assembly, which have occasioned such uneasiness and distraction among the good people of this province." With what a poor quibble do you pre-tend to answer this most grievous charge? Can any person but yourself, doubt what *measures* the Protesters mean? Do they not expressly specify them to be those identical "measures which oc-casioned such distractions among the people"—"measures like-wise pursued by the late Assembly." Now, is it not universally known that there was no uneasiness or distraction among the peo-ple on account of any measures pursued by the late Assembly, but their attempt to change the constitution of this province, of their own mere authority, and contrary to the very tenor of our charter.

The *Protesters* believed that you was "the chief author of these measures" and you yourself do "not dispute your share in them." The argument of the Protesters, then, against giving you any dis-cretionary powers over the liberties of the people, which they had

---

1764, and to which Isaac Saunders and John Montgomery adhered, was printed in *Pa. Jour.,* July 19, 1764, and *Pa. Gaz.,* July 26, 1764.

6. Smith seems to imply here that during BF's Assembly service before going to England in 1757 a motive for the many messages to governors and committee reports which he drafted was his expectation of receiving large payments as public printer for thus unnecessarily padding the *Votes and Proceedings.* WF would presumably also benefit from payments for increased labors as clerk of the Assembly.

reason to think you would make a willing sacrifice of to your own ambition, was a strong and conclusive one. And do you think to answer it by a ridiculous play upon words "saying that the distraction and uneasiness of the people were not occasioned by the measures, but the measures by the distraction, &c?" Such a subterfuge as this will not answer the charge brought against you by the Protesters. No, it will stick to you, and continue your name as odious to the next generation, perhaps, as it is to this.

You object to another reason of the Protesters against you, *viz.* "that you are, as they are informed, very unfavourably thought of by several of his majesty's ministers" You puzzle yourself to account for this dislike of some of the king's ministers to you, abuse your accusers, and proclaim your own services to the crown, which will yield you but little cause of boasting when they are fairly stated to you. But be that as it will, the fact is certain that your former anarchical schemes and virulent conduct, had rendered you very exceptionable to some of the king's ministers. You have met with severe rebukes from them,[7] and therefore were a very unfit person for this province to employ, even if another agent had been necessary.

Before I proceed to the next paragraph, I must beg leave to remind the reader, that you contend greatly for the justice of that form in our laws which requires *"the truth,* the *whole truth,* and *nothing but the truth,* to be spoken;" because, you say, "a falshood may destroy the innocent, and so may *part of the truth* without the whole." Will you now run contrary to a rule laid down by yourself? One would think not; but yet the next paragraph is one continued violation of it.

The Protesters had said, that "the proposal of you as an agent was extremely disagreeable to a very great number of the most serious and reputable inhabitants of this province, of all denomina-

7. Doubtless a reference to an admonitory letter Lord Hyde, postmaster general, was supposed to have written BF after Lords Hyde and Halifax had seen the Assembly Resolves of March 24, 1764. Thomas Penn to John Penn, June 8, 1764, and to Benjamin Chew, same date, Penn Papers, Hist. Soc. Pa. If Hyde did indeed write the letter Penn said he had promised, it has not been found; on Sept. 25, 1764, William Allen told Penn that BF seemed "very gloomy and thoughtful," though Allen was not sure whether the cause was the postmaster general's letter or BF's expectation of defeat in the coming election. Penn Papers, Hist. Soc. Pa.

tions and societies (ONE proof of which is, your having been re-jected both by this city and county at the last election, &c.)" Here the Protesters plainly mention this *rejection*, and that too in a paren-thesis, only as ONE proof. But you honestly alter the sentence as follows *viz.* "And THE Proof is my having been rejected, &c." making what they had suggested as only *one* proof to be the *whole* proof; whereas they had their own personal knowledge of your being disagreeable to the people, and petitions were then coming fast into the House to put the matter beyond all dispute, if there were any who doubted it.

Our Remarker goes on in the same manner transgressing his form laid down, and boasts, that in the county-election some who were chosen had scarce a score more votes than he; but does not say a word of the election for the city,[8] where he was rejected by a great majority, though he had "represented it in Assembly for fourteen years," which was the very argument of the Protesters; so that if what he says of the county election were the *truth*, it is only *part of the truth*, and not the *whole truth*.

In like manner when he says, "do you, honourable sir, reproach me with this, who for almost twice fourteen years have been re-jected *(if not being chosen is to be rejected)* by the same people, and unable with all your wealth and connections to obtain an election in the county where you reside, and the city where you were born?" Would not one think from this, that the gentleman here meant, had for near twenty-eight years been set up at every election, and pushed as a candidate both for the city and county of Philadelphia, with all the interest of his friends, as the Remarker was at the last election; and that old decrepit men had been carried out of their beds to vote for him; that his party had offered to the opposition to give up any, or all of the other nine Members to keep but this one man *in;* and that, after all, the gentleman had never once been chosen in the *county where he was born?* It would have required all this to make the cases similar, and all this the Remarker no doubt would have to be understood. And yet the truth is, that the gentle-man who he says has been thus rejected *"in the county where he was born"* was annually chosen to represent it for nine or ten years, by the almost unanimous voice of the people; that he then voluntarily

8. Actual figures on the votes in the city election, 1764, have not been found.

resigned his seat, and never was a candidate for that county since, but once during the late war, when his friends proposed him, as a person whose presence in the House they then thought necessary for the king's service, and the defence of their much distressed country. Another remarkable difference is, that when the gentleman consented at last to come a second time into the House, he was chosen at once by two counties of their own free motion;[9] whereas the Remarker has been rejected in two places at once, *viz.* both in this populous county and city, which pay half the taxes of the province. Nay farther; since the general election, when a resignation of some of his adherents was talked of, in order to give him a chance in two other counties, they were given to understand, that the principal inhabitants of these counties would oppose him to the utmost of their power; that they had good men within their own counties to represent them, and would not bear the reproach of taking in a man thrown out by the city and principal county of the province;[1] and indeed so justly obnoxious is this man's name, that there is no place in Pennsylvania, where at this day he could have the least chance of any election.

But to proceed, the Protesters had said further, that his proposed appointment as an assistant agent "gave them the more lively affliction as taken at the very moment when they were informed by a member of the House, that the governor had assured him, he had received instructions from the proprietaries, on their hearing of the late dispute (about the meaning of the royal decree) to give his assent to the taxation of their estates in the same manner as the estates of other persons are to be taxed, and to confirm for the

9. William Allen was born and lived in Philadelphia and was elected to the Assembly from Philadelphia Co. in each of the eight years 1731–38. The circumstances under which he "voluntarily resigned his seat" and ceased to represent his home county in 1739 have not been determined. In 1756 he was elected from both Cumberland and Northampton Cos. Being required to choose one of the two, he picked Cumberland and continued to be elected annually from that county through 1775. *Votes,* 1756–57, pp. 5, 14; 2 *Pa. Arch.,* IX, 739–40, 810. If we may judge by Smith's phraseology, the war year in which Allen's friends unsuccessfully proposed him for Philadelphia Co. must have been 1755 or 1756, but no additional information on this candidacy has been found.

1. The editors have found no other contemporary references to such proposals for finding a seat for BF from some other county.

public use, the several squares claimed by the city." Well! and if this was the ground of the dispute, was it not now high time to drop it, and to rescue the province from the vast expence and uneasiness attending it?[2] Our ambassador does not presume to say the contrary; but then his embassy would have been spoiled. He observes also that the Protesters used too delicate expressions on this subject. They should have made use of his choice language, and said, that "this step was taken at the moment, the *precious moment,* when the proprietaries (by virtue of some strong dose) were *disgorging five public squares,* which they had near forty years unjustly and dishonourably seized and detained, (swallowed and eat up it should be) from the city."

This language he would have liked better, but unhappily it could not be used on the occasion. The words inserted in the Protest were a report from the governor's mouth, and unless the Member who communicated the matter, had been possessed of the same dextrous turn for misrepresentation and falshood for which the Remarker is so distinguished, he could not report what the governor said in any other manner than that in which it was committed to him. Hence appears the absurdity of charging the terms of that paragraph, whatever their nature may be, either to the *politeness* or *unpoliteness* of the *Protesters,* who only stated a matter of fact as they had received it.

The truth is, as I have been credibly informed, that in the first draught of the Protest, the words "given to the city" stood in stead of the words "claimed by the city." But in reading it over afterwards, the gentleman who brought the report, desired the expression might be altered and put in the terms he had it from the governor; who said that he had instructions relative to the confirmation of the squares "claimed by the city." For if they had been sufficiently granted before, nothing more would have been now necessary. The whole matter stands as follows. The founder of this province, fond of the regular and beautiful plan of his city, and looking forward to its future extent and improvement, may no doubt have intended (and mentioned his intention) to have five public squares in it, two on the Delaware side, two on the Schuylkill side, and one in the centre. His suffering his Surveyor General

2. For editorial comments on Governor Penn's inept handling of this situation, see above, p. 410 n.

to publish a plan of the city, and all its proposed streets from river to river, leaving these squares open, is a sufficient presumption of this; and though they were never made a part of the original concessions to the people, nor formally granted to them, nor even publickly promised, by any evidence that appears, but seem only to be intended of his own free motion, both for ornament and use; nevertheless from the circumstances above mentioned, it is not denied but the city might have a right to claim and expect them. But still this amounted only to a *claim*, and the present proprietors have not disputed it. Far from *seizing* and *detaining* them for forty years; the city has all that time had the use of them, and now has it. One of them has long ago been applied by the city itself to the public use, as a *Potter's field*, and *negroe burying-ground*.[3] The other *four* (except some part of one of them*) remain open for the city; and the Proprietors, in pursuance of what appears to have been

*Even this part is granted to a publick and pious use, as a burying ground to a German congregation in this city. The warrant and survey are of an old date; and it may be fairly presumed that if the part so granted had been deemed at the time to be within any of the proposed squares, this congregation would neither have petitioned for it, nor accepted of it, unless burying grounds were understood to be one of the publick uses for which these squares were originally designed.[4]

3. On request of the Philadelphia Common Council the Commissioners of Property appropriated the Southeast Square (now Washington Square) in 1706 as "a common and public burying-ground, for all strangers or others who might not so convenient be laid in any of the particular enclosures appropriated by certain religious societies to that purpose." Burials continued in the square until 1794–95. The square occupies the land southwest of the intersection of Walnut and Sixth Streets, running 500 ft. along each. J. Thomas Scharf and Thompson Westcott, *History of Philadelphia. 1609–1884* (Phila., 1884), III, 1841, 1845, 2355–6.

4. In 1741 Thomas Penn directed his surveyor general to lay out a tract in the Northeast Square (now Franklin Square) in trust to the German Reformed Church. This burying ground ran 150 ft. along the south side of Vine St., midway east and west in the square as originally laid out west of Sixth St.; it extended 306 ft. south from Vine. The formal patent was issued only in 1763, and in 1797 the City Council concluded that Penn had made the grant without legal right to do so. The dispute between the city and the congregation continued for many years. Finally, after proceedings begun by the city in 1835, the Pa. Supreme Court agreed with the position taken by the Council (and indirectly with that taken earlier by BF) and voided the German Reformed Church's title. *Ibid.*, pp. 1841, 1846–8, 2357.

496

their father's intention, have now given certain orders relative to the confirmation of them; which it seems must not be received as a matter of favor, nor even the ratification of a just *claim,* but a *disgorging* and *spewing* up. With what a wicked and virulent spirit is this remarker possess'd? What calumny and misrepresentation will he stick at, in order to inflame and divide? If here on the spot, he will shamefully assert what every person who will walk a few hundred yards may see with his own eyes to be *false,* what wicked calumny may it not be expected he will propagate of the good people of this province as well as the proprietors, to carry his points in England, where he may not expect an immediate detection?

Much in the like manner does he argue about the taxation of the proprietors. He has, for many years, poured forth volumes of abuse against them for *not consenting* to have their estates taxed as other people's were: and now he abuses them as much *for consenting* to it. The truth is, that the proprietors had proposed, among the first land-tax bills we had, that their estates should be taxed in the same manner as those of the people by persons named in the body of the bill,[5] (as they had no voice in the choice of assessors and commissioners) which is strictly agreeable to the parliamentary mode of the land-tax, and was judged to be just and reasonable by the subsequent decree of the king in council. But when the Assembly would not even submit to this decree, but insisted on explaining one particular article in their own sense, the proprietors still willing to cultivate harmony, as soon as they heard of this new dispute, gave orders to admit the Assembly's own sense of the matter.[6] Yet after all these concessions, and whether they do right or wrong, they are alike to incur the obloquy of this inflammatory and virulent man, whose views are not those of peace and reconciliation. It is therefore a good reason, which the Protesters offered, against employing him as an agent in our affairs *viz.* "That they believed his fixed enmity to the proprietaries will preclude all accommodation of our disputes with them, even on equitable and reasonable terms." He does not deny this enmity, (tho' he asks the Protesters

---

5. The issue of taxation of proprietary estates arose in the summer of 1755, but the Proprietors' first public admission of willingness to allow any part of their estates to be taxed at all was in Ferdinand John Paris' "Answer to the Heads of Complaint," Nov. 27, 1758; above, VIII, 182.

6. See above, pp. 213–14 n.

497

the reason of their belief;) for he proposes the terms on which his *enmity* is to cease. I never doubted but his mouth, foul as it is, might be stopped; but I believe, (and if he asks the reasons, I will tell them) that it cannot be done on quite so *disinterested* terms as he mentions. But, be that as it may, certainly there was room to think that a professed enemy to the proprietors, was very unlike to accommodate disputes, which he hath long and industriously worked up with unexampled calumny, unless we believe he designedly worked them up, to have the merit of appeasing them again: and if this be the case, we have been too long deluded by this crafty ambitious man.

I come then, as he does, in the next place, to what he calls the high charge of the Protesters, *viz.* "That he heretofore ventured, *contrary* to an act of Assembly to place the publick money in the stocks whereby this province suffered a loss of £6000; and that sum added to the £5000 granted for his expences, makes the whole cost of his former voyage to England, amount to *eleven thousand pounds.*"

This is a very high charge indeed, and if the Protesters had been fond of magnifying, they might with truth have added to the account, *commissions* paid him for receiving the money at the treasury, and sundry other articles, which would have swelled the account of his expences to upwards of *twelve thousand pounds.*[7] This charge deserved something more like an answer than what he has given it.

It is a mean evasion to say, the *Bank* could not receive the money on the terms of the Act. And pray could it be placed in the *Stocks* on the terms of the act? He knows it could not. If then it had been

7. The Agency Act of 1759 authorized BF to take a commission of one half of one percent for receiving and handling the parliamentary grant to Pa. This commission, which BF duly entered on his accounts, amounted to £134 10s. sterling; above, IX, 242 n. The "sundry other articles" Smith had in mind are not identified; the most obvious possibility would be the brokerage fees for the purchase and later sale of the stocks. These totaled £75 sterling; above, IX, 313 n, 335, 392; X, 34. Combined commissions and fees, therefore, were £209 10s. sterling, or about £356 3s. Pa. currency, substantially less than the £1000 Pa. currency Smith indicated. Fees BF paid to officials at the Exchequer and Treasury upon receipt of the grant would have been unchanged, whatever disposition he made of the money later.

kept in the Bank, the spirit and design of the act would have been complied with, though the terms had not been strictly fulfilled. But by placing it in the Stocks, the terms of the act were not only violated, but the spirit of it likewise, added to a vast loss occasioned thereby to the province.

The partizans of the Remarker may pretend they do not see this clearly. I will therefore endeavour to explain it a little further. We all know that by the usage of the Bank, whoever deposits money there must subscribe their name, or write what is called their *Firm* at the Bank, for the greater security in drawing the money out; and we do not pretend that the trustees of the loan-office were to be transported to England to sign the books. No more did the trustees of the loan-office go to 'Change-Alley to receive a transfer of stock for the publick money. All this was to be done by agents or reputable merchants living in London, who were to answer the draughts of the trustees, which they could have done as well by placing the money in the Bank as in the Stocks. When money is placed in the Bank no loss can happen; and if it possibly could, the persons who placed it there are not accountable for it; and therefore the Bank is the place where all persons entrusted with the custody of any public cash chuse to deposit it; but if such persons, without authority, place it in the stocks, it is at their own risque, and as they may claim the profit of any rise of the Stocks, they are accountable for any loss that may happen by their falling.

Our Remarker tries to impose on the publick by saying "the House adopted the measure of placing the money in the Stocks, and even passed a bill directing the subsequent sums granted by Parliament to be placed with the former." Now who would not think by this that he had been indemnified by law for placing the first money in the Stocks, and had by law placed the subsequent sums along with it? Every person who reads what he has written, and entertains any opinion of his veracity, would believe this to be the case. And yet all he says is a wilful imposition. Had he chosen to tell the *truth,* and the *whole truth,* he would have added, that though the House did frame such a bill, it was never passed into a Law;[8] that none of the subsequent sums granted by Parliament

8. This was the bill the Assembly passed Sept. 24, 1760, which Governor Hamilton refused to approve because it allowed him no voice in naming the persons to receive the money in England, not because it provided for

were ever placed in the Stocks, but in the hands of some reputable merchants in London, the legislature of this province not chusing to entrust him with those sums, after having abused his trust with regard to the money he had already received;[9] which last sums were accordingly drawn out of the hands of these merchants, when the public service required, without the least loss to the province. He therefore remains alone accountable for the heavy loss on the first sums, which never would have happened if the law had been regarded; and no authority of any committee of the House, or even the whole Body, could dispense with a positive Law. And though I will not say, that he ought to *disgorge* a *loss,* as he makes the proprietors *disgorge five publick squares,* yet he ought to be made to refund this loss to the good people of this province, labouring under heavy debts on account of this and other parts of his conduct; it being of no consequence to them whether he brought this loss upon them by the spirit of gaming, or the spirit of pride, in figuring with the reputation of so much money placed by him in the publick funds.

If the exchange was higher at the time of drawing out the money than at the time of purchasing the Stock, it was an accident; and it might have happened to be lower, and so the loss would have been encreased. There was a necessity of drawing it out in aid of the supplies of this province. The money was granted by parliament for this very purpose, to ease us of part of our heavy burthens, and not to go a jobbing with, for the uncertain prospect of profit, which might never arise. The *drawing* the money out, which he seems very angry at, was not so *imprudent* a step as he is pleased to call it. It was a very prudent and necessary one. The people of this province could not very patiently bear the burthen of new taxes, to humour him in an illegal measure, nor remain easy while so

---

investing the money in stocks. See above, IX, 223, 225 n; 8 *Pa. Arch.,* VI, 5144, 5248.

9. See above, IX, 236–7 n; 8 *Pa. Arch.,* VI, 5166. Smith implies here that the Assembly resolutions of Oct. 18, 1760, excluded BF from the group of men named to receive and handle the second parliamentary grant, whereas he was alone specifically empowered to receive the money and was then directed to deposit it in the Bank of England in the names of himself, Robert Charles, and four London merchants, "or the Survivors or Survivor of them, their Heirs and Assigns." The trustees of the Loan Office were then to draw bills of exchange on these men for transfers to Pa.

much of their money lay in the name of any private man, however great their opinion of his integrity might be, when in case of his death, they could not have recovered the money, without the delay and expence of an act of parliament.

Having already shewn that he has violated the form he laid down, in concealing part of the truth; I would next observe that he has again transgressed it, by saying more than the truth. In hopes to alleviate this charge against him, on account of the heavy loss to the province, he says to the chief justice, "you, honourable Sir, (my enemy of seven years standing) were appointed on the committee for examining my ACCOUNTS; you reported that you found THEM *just*, and signed that report."

Now what can any one understand from this, but that the Chief Justice signed a report, approving all the accounts of this mans Agency, even including the money placed in the Stocks, with loss, &c. &c. And yet in the report there is no such word as ACCOUNTS in the plural number, or ACCOUNTS in general. It mentions only *one account* of particular expences compared with vouchers amounting to £714 10s. 7d.; which was the only *account* submitted to the committee. "In obedience to the order of the House we have examined the ACCOUNT of Benjamin Franklin, Esq; with the vouchers to us produced, and find that he has expended &c." These are the words of the report; and it requires a very uncommon force of logic to construe the signing of this report upon a particular account into a justification of all his conduct in his agency.

With the like truth a little afterwards, speaking of the gentleman above referred to, he says "you, Sir, of all others was the very Member that proposed, for the honor and justice of the House, a compensation to be made of the *five thousand pounds* you mention." If this were true, he has made the gentleman a very ungratful return for this, as well as many former favours. But it happens to be a gross falshood. The gentleman has publickly declared, that when the matter was first mentioned, it was only by some of the Members in occasional conversation at the committee, before whom it could not come as a matter of business; that those Members spoke of the reasonableness of making the *Remarker* some compensation for what they called his services in England, and mentioned an agent that had been allowed at the rate of *five hundred pounds sterling per annum,* by the colony of Virginia; which agent resided in

England and could attend to his other business, whereas Mr. Franklin was forced to leave his family, and quit valuable business here. To which the said gentleman, *viz.* the chief justice, replied, that he thought it a very great allowance, but at length acquiesced with what appeared to be the sentiments of a great majority of the committee, the matter not being then before them, as hath been observed. And when this business came into the House, it is notoriously known, that the motion was made, not by the chief justice, but by several of the *Remarker's* friends, and by a member of Chester county in particular, who further proposed that every expence of the Remarker during his whole absence, should be defrayed by the House. This was strenuously opposed by the chief justice, who said he had no fellowship with him nor his politicks, that he never had approved of sending the Member to England, nor saw any benefit the Province had received by it, that he had spent a great deal of time and money in parading about to different parts of England, and even into Scotland, and must necessarily be at a large expence in maintaining his son, which were matters this province had nothing to do with. But that notwithstanding, since the House had thought fit to employ him on an idle errand, he thought they were now obliged in *honour and justice* to make him a reasonable allowance; and *five hundred pounds sterling, per annum,* being the least sum mentioned by any body, he said that he would not object to it, tho' he thought the allowance rather too large.

This is a candid and circumstantial account of this matter, in which the Member acted as became an honest man; and the reader may judge how base a part the Remarker acts, in the false invidious turn he gives to the affair.[1]

Equally malicious and groundless is the accusation he brings against the gentleman for "concealing instructions which he was said to bring from the proprietors" for healing our differences; of which accusation a great handle has been made for party views. Whoever will suffer himself to reflect for a moment, will see the absurdity of thinking that ever instructions of this kind could be given to be communicated to the province, by a private gentleman,

1. The editors have found no official records or unbiased private accounts that would resolve the conflict between BF's and Smith's accounts of Allen's part in the fixing of BF's salary. Smith's statement is certainly the more circumstantial and detailed.

while the proprietors had a governor (one of their own family) on the spot. These instructions were not a moment *concealed,* nor was it necessary to communicate them in any other manner than they were.

If the words of the royal decree (which were inserted verbatim in the late act) were so clear, as the Assembly contest, that they could not be understood in any other sense but that which they contended for, there was nothing to hinder the act from being executed in that sense, if the proprietors had never given any instructions at all on that head. But to put the matter out of doubt, and to remove all cause of uneasiness, they were pleased to give instructions to the governor to acquaint the proper officers, that the law might be executed accordingly. This was all that was wanted; no new law was necessary.[2] Nothing remain'd but to let the Assembly know that such instructions were given; and this was done by a Member, from the governor's own mouth. Had the Assembly been willing or desirous to receive any further information, they might have obtained it by sending a very short message; for messages have often passed on matters of as little importance.

The chief justice, it is true, was in London when the instructions were sent. He was there made acquainted with them, and approved of them as just and tending to peace. It is not improbable but on his coming over he might be charged by the proprietors with letters to the governor on the subject, but he is known to have solemnly declared that he never was invested with any powers or commissions from the proprietors, to communicate their intentions to the House, or to settle any difference between them. But every

2. How incorrect this statement was, Governor Penn and his supporters were soon to learn. Penn sent a circular letter to the provincial commissioners of appeal, Jan. 17, 1765, directing that the Proprietors' located uncultivated lands were to be assessed in the manner the Assembly had wanted. The commissioners were to instruct the local assessors and county commissioners accordingly. On receiving this information, the officials of Philadelphia Co. wrote the governor, January 26, that these instructions directly contradicted the law and that "nothing can enable us to comply with the Governor's request, in that particular, but a Law to be made for that purpose." Thereupon the Council advised Penn to report the matter to the Assembly in a written message and ask for a supplemental act to amend the Supply Act of May 31, 1760, incorporating the very phraseology that the Assembly had fought so hard to retain in their several bills during the winter and spring of 1760. Penn sent the message on January 30. *Pa. Col. Recs.,* IX, 237, 240–1.

Member, nay every private man who conversed with him, can testify, that he did not keep the proprietors intentions secret. What is asserted in the extract of Mr. Barclay's letter, quoted by the Remarker, must therefore have been founded on some mistake.

Thus have I followed the *Remarker* through every thing that bears the least appearance of argument in his performance; and if the *Protesters* meet with no more formidable attack than this, their arguments will remain fully convincing to cool and deliberate minds. And though he exults in carrying with him the sanction of *two* to *one* in the House, which is a misrepresentation also;[3] yet let him take into the account, that he carries with him the bitter reproaches and indignation of at least *five* to *one* of an injured people.

Before I leave the *Protest*, let me observe that there is one part of it, which it did not suit him to mention.

The Protesters (after using their utmost endeavours against burthening this province with any more agents than one, and particularly against employing this man, who seems too ready to traffick our singular privileges away for gratifying his own ambition and resentment) frankly proposed, in condescension to their Brethren, who *thought* another *agent necessary,* to concur with them in the appointment of any person of weight and integrity in London; and in order to save the expence to the province, already burden'd with heavy taxes, they further proposed that it should be by subscription, to which they generously offered to contribute their quotas, if the other members would do the same.[4]

I now proceed to a more disagreeable part of my Task; *viz*, to take some notice of the gross slander and scurrility of this Remarker.

And first then, because he himself (the most unpopular and odious name in the province) lost his election, wherever it was attempted to set him up, he therefore abuses almost the whole body of the people.

"The *superiority*," he says, "was obtained over him at the expence of honour and conscience, by exasperating the ignorant, by falsehoods, by perjuries, &c." One set of men who opposed him

3. The critical votes in the Assembly during October 1764 had varied between 22 to 10 and 18 to 12. The vote specifically appointing BF as agent was 19 to 11. *Votes*, 1765, p. 15.

4. See above, p. 412.

meaning his majesty's faithful subjects the *Presbyterians,* (who have ever been among the foremost in defending their country, and promoting their sovereign's measures; while this virulent calumniator, and many of his present adherents, thought they did us a great favour in permitting us to spill our own blood, and spend our own money, in the publick cause) this numerous and loyal people are called *"religious* bigots, *of all savages the most brutish."*

The industrious GERMANS, to whom this province is so much indebted for its flourishing state, and who have suffered so much from this man's ill-timed disputes, that they thought him unworthy of further trust—they too are called by him *"a wretched rabble, brought to swear themselves intituled to a vote."* Much in the same manner he had treated them on a former occasion; calling them "a set of *boors herding together,"* as if he was speaking of *swine.* Yet this valuable body of men are true subjects to his majesty; have cultivated a great extent of our country under the faith of our *charter,* are possesed of large property, and entitled to the privileges of Englishmen and a vote by our laws; and have exercised these their rights, without interruption, for many years.

The members of the church of England have at present escaped his calumny. He considered, perhaps, the country to which he was going, and may hope to carry some future points by this complaisance. But he will probably be mistaken. For as he belongs to no religious society, and regards none, so he is alike detested by all, except one, and by many serious good men among that society also.[5]

These are some specimens of his shameful and scandalous manner of treating the People of this province in general. To bestow any answer on such odious scurrility, would be ridiculous. None but a very bad man, or one delirious with rage, disappointment and malice, would utter such language, even against a single antagonist, much less against whole bodies of people; unsupported, as it is, with any shadow of reason. In the same manner, he treats the respectable names, who, in execution of what they judged their duty in their place, opposed his appointment. They are called "proprietary minions, making use of a new form of libelling, as the

5. The Society of Friends. Among the many attacks on BF, public or private, during 1764, this is the only one the editors have found that suggests a criticism of his religious beliefs—or lack of them.

vehicle of personal malice &c." Yet the ten gentlemen who signed the Protest are known to be persons of the fairest character and men of fortune, absolutely independent of the proprietary family, holding no places under them, solliciting none, nor ever likely to accept of any. Out of this number, I should have excepted the Chief Justice, who has the trifling salary of about £120 sterling per annum, and that not depending on the proprietors, but on the yearly vote of the Assembly alone; which salary too, it is well known, he has constantly applied to publick or charitable uses. This office he accepted only thro' the earnest intreaties and persuasions of many good men, and after repeated refusals to serve in it. He has since often desired leave of the several governors to resign it, on account of his advanced age and bodily infirmities, and still wishes to do it as soon as his superiors can be prevailed on to fill it up with another.[6]

As the chief force of the Remarker's virulence seems directed against this gentleman, I shall take the liberty to state the account between them, a little more particularly.

The gentleman, I presume, does not pretend an exemption from human failings. His open and candid temper may have led him more than once, to rely too easily on the professions of false and insidious men; and he is, in no instance, more chargeable with this, than in what he has done for this ungrateful incendiary, who, probably, had never been of consideration enough to give the least disturbance to this province, but for the numerous favours so ill bestowed on him, by this gentleman and his friends. They were the persons who first raised him from his original obscurity, and got him appointed *Printer* to the province, and *Clerk* to the house of assembly. Not resting here, the gentleman whom he has so grossly villified, did likewise procure him the office of *joint-postmaster* of America, by means of his name-sake, the worthy RALPH ALLEN, Esq; of Bath, to whom this Remarker was utterly unknown.[7]

6. William Allen inherited a large fortune, added to it through commercial and industrial enterprises and the acquisition of land, and was generally regarded as the richest man in the colony. He contributed generously to many worthy causes. He finally retired as chief justice in 1775. Ruth M. Kistler, "William Allen," Lehigh Co. Hist. Soc. *Proc.*, XXIV (1962), 7–58.

7. William Allen was a member of the Assembly when BF was appointed printer in 1735 and clerk in 1736, but just what part he played in either appointment is uncertain. In 1751 he had recommended BF to his London

He seemed for a time to carry some appearance of gratitude for these favours; and this gentleman and his friends continued their regard to him, till, at length, upon some slight which he supposed the proprietors had put upon him, in not answering one of his letters, and on some personal difference with GOVERNOR MORRIS, they found him all at once renouncing every principle he had formerly professed; openly attacking government, fomenting division, and joining himself avowedly to those, whom before he had often spoke of with the greatest contempt and disapprobation.[8]

Then, indeed, the gentlemen dropped him; but they did it with a silent disregard; and he has not been without his moments of repentance for his conduct. He has made frequent overtures towards a reconciliation; and, within these two years, has passed the most lavish encomiums on the gentleman who is the present object of his resentment; declaring that *"he even revered the ashes of their former friendship."*[9]

But how strangely must he have forgot himself, when he says in his Remarks, that "the *dear delight* and *constant employment* of the

---

merchant correspondents, John and Thomas Simpson, for appointment as deputy postmaster general and had advanced £300 for payment of fees and charges. Above, IV, 134–6. No previous mention has been found of a recommendation to Ralph Allen of Bath, and it is not known how responsible that gentleman may have been for BF's becoming a deputy postmaster general. Ralph Allen (1694–1764) had entered the postal service at Bath as a youth and succeeded to the postmastership. He soon devised a major reform in the procedures for carrying those letters which did not involve the London office, and he received a contract in 1720 for managing this service. In spite of many obstacles he was so successful that his profits reached an average of £12,000 per annum. As an operator of quarries near Bath he added to his wealth and in time became one of its leading citizens. He does not appear to have had any blood relationship to William Allen. *DNB;* Herbert Joyce, *The History of the Post Office from Its Establishment down to 1836* (London, 1893), pp. 146–70, 185–6.

8. Until at least June 1755 BF had tried to act as a mediator between Governor Robert Hunter Morris and the Assembly; above, VI, 86. William Smith told Thomas Penn in September 1755 that BF was irritated over Penn's failure to answer a letter; *ibid.*, p. 211. By November BF had concluded that Morris was "half a Madman"; *ibid.*, p. 273. The breach soon extended to include some of Morris' political supporters.

9. The public occasion of this remark by BF about Allen has not been found; he did, however, use nearly the same words in a private letter to Jackson, Sept. 1, 1764; above, p. 328.

gentleman's life (the ashes of whose former *friendship* he reveres) has been the maiming or murdering all the reputations that stand in his way?" A poor compliment this, which the Remarker pays to his own choice of friends! Is it possible that *he* could have had so many years close friendship with a person, the *dear delight* and *constant employment* of whose whole life has been of so infernal a nature? Into what monstrous absurdities and contradictions will the frantic rage of virulent men transport them?

To take further notice of this infamous slander, would be perfectly needless. It stands self-refuted; and there is not a character, perhaps, in this province, to which it could less justly be applied. With regard to the chief justice of this province, his virtues are well known, and his character extended so greatly to his advantage through all parts of America, that it cannot receive the least injury from this vain and wicked attempt. The world is apt enough to fix blemishes and stains where there ought not to be any; nor will it suffer even a man's foibles to pass into oblivion; and surely, if the gentleman had been obnoxious to this heavy charge (and that through his whole life too) we could not but have heard of it before now. But the truth is, that "it was not invented before," as the Remarker says on another occasion;[1] and therefore the gentleman's character remained untouched, till, in the rage of disappointment, this furious attack was made upon it, by venturing to spread the most glaring falshoods; falshoods which have made the Remarker's friends blush for him, and his enemies triumph. He, no doubt, felt the weight of this gentleman's reputation against him, and therefore thought it necessary to attempt a breach in it; but the blow has recoiled upon himself, and has wounded the credit of every other part of his performance. Thus, like the hunted beast, while he bites the spear of his pursuer, he breaks his own fangs.

With the like slander he insinuates, that endeavours have been used in this province, "to render his majesty's government odious; that traiterous papers, to this purpose, had been written and translated into other languages; and that it had been declared, written and printed, that the king's little finger we should find heavier than

---

1. With reference to the charge that BF had caused the province a loss of £6000 through improper investment of the parliamentary grant; above, p. 441.

the proprietors whole loins, *with regard to our liberties;"*[2] and, by the whole reading of the paragraph, he seems to charge these "exploits" chiefly, if not solely, to the gentleman above-mentioned, as another mark of the "reverence he pays to the ashes of their former friendship."

But it is happy for the gentleman reflected upon, that wherever his character is known, this charge will meet with as little regard as the former. Thro' his whole life, he has been a constant friend to government and order; an enemy to every factious and anarchical scheme, and a strenuous promoter of the king's service. Every one of his majesty's officers, from the commanders in chief, to the lowest subaltern, will be ready to acknowledge the particular encouragement and assistance they have on all occasions received from him, in every part of their duty; while the public service has been almost constantly obstructed by the licentious spirit of this turbulent Remarker.

The two Characters afford a most striking contrast. The chief Justice, while in America, does his utmost to support government, and promote the king's service; and, when in England, he was equally zealous to support the Rights of America; with a firm and independant spirit, maintaining in behalf of the people here, "that they considered it to be their essential right as British subjects, *to assess their own taxes;* and that any *law* to subject them to *internal taxations,* otherwise than by their own representatives, would be *disfranchising* them of the rights of englishmen":[3] in which opinion,

2. For Allen's admission that he had used essentially this expression about "the king's little finger" in the Assembly, see above, p. 432 n. There seems to be no evidence, however, that he or his friends had circulated it in print.

3. Closing quotation marks, missing in the original, have been supplied here. The source of this quotation from Allen has not been identified. In a letter to Benjamin Chew, however, written from London, Dec. 9, 1763, he said he had been urging Thomas Penn, Richard Jackson, and the N.Y. agent, Robert Charles, to oppose British plans for colonial taxation by asserting, among other arguments, "That it is the right of Englishmen to be taxed by their representatives only, that In Ireland which is said to be a conquered country such a thing was never attempted. Our Agent Mr. Jackson who is a great favorite of the present cheif Minister Mr. Greenvile and is secretary to the Chancelor of the Exchequer is very industrious in indeavoring to ward of[f] the blow and has brought Mr. [James] Oswald who is much depended on by the ministry for American affairs to think that it is not right to lay any internal taxes on us but to confine it to dutys upon our

he has the concurring sentiments of, I believe, every representative body on this continent.

But very different is the conduct of our ambitious and time-serving remarker. Here in America, his delight is in contention, anarchy and opposition to government. And then, when he has created an embassy for himself, and gets on the other side of the Atlantic, he shifts with the scene; puts off the noisy demagogue, forgets the cause of his employers, truckles for preferment for himself and family, and boasts services he never performed.

As to any papers published at the late election, that could give the least colour to the charge he has brought, he or his adherents are called upon to shew them, and expressly to mention the passages, else to take the shame to themselves. I, for my part, have neither seen, or before heard of, any such; and as to the chief justice, who neither gave any vote, nor even stirr'd out of his house during the whole election, he has declared, that far from writing or publishing, he has not even read any thing written or published by either side, since his return from England, except the *Supplement to the Pennsylvania Journal*,[4] which he never saw, till a printed copy was put into his hands by a friend, desiring him to peruse it, as he was mentioned in it. There is but one paragraph in that paper that makes any comparison between the privileges enjoyed here, and those in royal governments; and that paragraph, far from making such governments odious, has these express words, *viz.* "That no government under his sacred Majesty can be an unhappy one; but that there are degrees of happiness, as well as privileges." This surely does not convey the least reflection against such governments.

The great founder of this province had the noble resolution, many years ago, to tell his superiors, in behalf of his people, that "they had not followed him so far, to lose a single tittle of the charter granted to them, or of the great charter to which all Englishmen were born." This he did without giving offence: and, I doubt not, if ever this Remarker should venture to push his daring attempts

imports." David A. Kimball and Miriam Quinn, "William Allen-Benjamin Chew Correspondence, 1763–1764," *PMHB*, XC (1966), 217. In Smith's quotation the distinction between internal and external taxation appears to have been made by Allen, while in the letter to Chew it is attributed to Jackson, who had convinced Oswald (an influential Scottish M.P. and member of the Privy Council) that the distinction was important.

4. Above, pp. 372–6.

farther against the liberties of Pennsylvania, there will be those found who will be ready to plead with unshaken firmness, and without giving the least offence to the wise, equitable and august judicature before whom only this matter can come "That when English colonies were first planted, and men were to quit their native country, and, for the extension of its commerce, to enter into what was then considered as a kind of voluntary banishment; it was thought proper to indulge and encourage them with particular grants and privileges, suitable to their circumstances.

"The first settlers of Pennsilvania, were highly favoured in this respect by their humane founder, who (under the ample authority of a royal charter) granted them many singular privileges and immunities; to which the rapid growth of this province is to be principally ascribed. By the very fame of these privileges, multitudes of people have been drawn from almost all quarters of the world; who have encreased the number of British subjects, cultivated a wilderness, and made it one of the fairest and most valuable parts of his Majesty's American dominions. Having thus amply fulfilled the considerations for which these privileges were granted, they now think themselves entituled to the perpetual enjoyment of them. They have not forfeited them by any act of disloyalty to their most gracious sovereign; nor are they pretended to be inconsistent with the nature of government, or such as could not have been legally conveyed to them. They do now, therefore, claim these previleges *entire;* and a majority of at least *five* to *one* of them have publickly avowed that claim, and say that their charter, which is their birth right, has expressly put it out of the power of their Representatives, by themselves, to do any matter, or thing, whereby their privileges may be affected. Under such circumstances as these, when they see a change (unsought for by our indulgent Sovereign, unwished for by the people, and even notoriously repugnant to their general sentiments) I say, when under such circumstances, they see a measure of such immense importance, hurried wickedly and vehemently on, by the ambition of a single man, it is impossible but indignation and resentment must rise to their utmost heighth."

All this, I say, may be asserted without the least offence. There is not a private corporation that would not stedfastly say as much as this, in behalf of their most inconsiderable immunities. And yet this is

511

the amount of all that is to be found in the papers which, for the credit of his country, the Remarker has been pleased to call treasonable.

There is no such expression to be found in them, as that "the king's little finger we shall find *heavier* than the proprietors whole loins, *in regard to our liberties.*" The Remarker, with his usual candor, has added words of his own to the sentence; for what is there said, is not spoken, *with regard to our liberties,* but with regard to instructions. The Remarker had made it a charge, against *proprietary instructions,* that our judges were thereby prevented from having their commissions *during good behaviour.* It is answered, that "we should find the king's little finger thicker than the proprietor's whole loins," with regard to the authority of instructions of this kind; and an instance is given of Mr. Hardy's case, who lost the government of New Jersey for appointing one judge during good behaviour.[5]

It is true, many papers have been publish'd in this province, which, by comparison, have a tendency to "render royal governments odious," as well with respect to the tenor of Judges commissions, as the tenor of militia-laws, the right of disposing the public money, and the appointment of the officers of the revenue, &c. But it is the Remarker's misfortune, that these publications have had him for their author, and are striking specimens of his boasted loyalty, and "constant endeavours to promote the measures of the Crown, ever since he had any influence in the province." Nothing but his own matchless assurance could make him hope that this assertion could obtain any more credit in England, than it can in America; when it is incontestably known, that, for many years past, he has taken every advantage of the distresses of his country, to retard the public supplies, to wrest the prerogatives of the crown out of the hands of the King's representative, to strip the executive part of government of its constitutional authority, and to affect even royalty himself.

I shall not, in imitation of his example, advance such charges, without proof.

During the last war, he drew up with his own hand, and afterwards defended in his news-paper, a militia bill (which the governor in the distress of the count[r]y, was obliged to pass into a law) by which the nomination of the officers, and consequently the command of the militia, were wrested out of the hands of the king's

5. Above, IX, 161 n.

representative;[6] by which, the Remarker himself got elected to the office of colonel, paraded his regiment about the streets to intimidate his opponents; and on setting out and returning from journies, was escorted with drawn swords, and received with rested arms, and other affectations of royal state; while the king's representative had nothing left, but to walk about, and look silently on.[7]

This law being repealed by his majesty, our Remarker, in the profusion of his loyalty had the assurance last spring, to get another presented to the governor, worse in many respects, than the former; still depriving the king's representative of the nomination of the officers, and even giving the provincial commissioners a *negative* on the direction of the operations of the militia. The governor having refused to pass this bill, he was charged (in a paper published under the Remarker's patronage at the last election) with being a tyrant, and being led by wicked proprietary instructions,* to subject the people to grievous fines and *death* by military courts; to refuse them the choice of their own officers, and the benefit of being tried for military offences in the civil courts, by a jury nominated by a sheriff of their own election; notwithstanding the governor, by his amendments, only desired the bill to be rendered conformable to the militia laws in all the governments around us, declaring that he would not pass it otherwise, as contrary to a known and positive determination of the king in council.

Surely, "these exploits of our Remarker, are not for a man that holds a profitable office under the crown; and, as he says, can expect to hold it no longer than he behaves with the fidelity and duty that becomes every good subject."† But yet these are not half of his loyal "exploits."

His majesty had repealed a law (pass'd by our infamous Governor Denny) appointing our judges *during good behaviour*.[9] The Remarker was then our agent and plenipotentiary at London, and either could not, or did not think it safe for him there to oppose

*See a paper call'd Reasons why the late Militia Bill miscarried. See also the resolves of March the 24th last.[8]
†See remarks, Page 2.

6. The act of 1755; above, VI, 266–73.
7. Above, VI, 409–12, 411 n, 425 n; VII, 13–14.
8. Above, pp. 360–5 and 130–1, respectively.
9. Above, IX, 160–2, 205.

that repeal; yet still this "faithful and dutiful subject," (as he calls himself) *resolves* it to be among the list of our grievances, and *unjust,* that the proprietors, in obedience to the king's determination, should "appoint judges during *their* pleasure." Again, though it be expressly subversive of the royal prerogative and unconstitutional, for an assembly to claim the appointment of officers in the *civil* and *executive* part of government, or the sole disposition of the public money, accountable, as they are, only to themselves; nay tho' his majesty has repealed a law, on this very account;[1] yet this man has constantly taken advantage of his country's distress, violently to repeat all these claims. By these means he has often endeavoured to deny the Governor even a voice in the disposition of the public money: and has got the nomination of the officers of the revenue, and even military officers, such as barrack-masters, &c. taken out of the hands of the King's representative.

These are some of the dutiful *exploits* which our Remarker has performed; and tho' he thought it his Interest to boast great loyalty, when he was setting out for England; yet his superiors there, to whom these things are well known, will be at no loss to form a right judgment concerning him. I could now proceed to give some striking Instances of his loyalty, extracted from his writing as a private man; in which he has treated his Majesty's *publick Boards, and royal Instructions,* much in the same bitter and licentious manner, as he treats the powers of government here. "It is not," says he,* "to be presumed that *such* as have been long accustomed to consider the colonies in general, as only so many dependencies on the Council-Board, the Board of Trade, and the Board of Customs; or as a hot-bed for causes, jobbs and other pecuniary emoluments, and bound as effectually by *instructions* as by *laws,* can be prevailed on to consider these *patriot-rustics* (of Pennsylvania) with any degree of respect."

*Historical review of Pensylvania.[2]

1. Among the subsidiary objections the Board of Trade had found to the Re-emitting Act of June 20, 1759, and its supplement of Sept. 29, 1759, were the two points mentioned here. Both measures were disallowed, Sept. 2, 1760; above, IX, 153, 204–5.

2. Smith was evidently among those who believed that BF, rather than Richard Jackson, had written *An Historical Review of the Constitution and Government of Pensylvania* (London, 1759). On the question of authorship, see above, VIII, 361. The quotation given here is from the Introduction, pp. 4–5.

But having already exceeded the length I intended, I shall not take further notice of this man as a writer. It is however to be hoped that some person of more leisure may, for the sake of an abused Province, give a compleat account of his conduct ever since it was the misfortune of this country that he had any influence in it. There is ample room to shew how diametrically opposite his principles have been at different times; how he has paid servile court to all sides, deceived all, calumniated all! How he has been endeavouring, first with one party, then with another, to pave the way to his present attempt! what misrepresentations he has spread, and what ferments he has worked up for this purpose!

It might likewise be shewn, by what means, after his schemes had rendered him odious to every other society in the province, he has formed a party in *one*, by sowing divisions among them; and tho' they have heretofore been thought remarkable for their sagacity and prudence, yet he has craftily drawn their young men into his measures; lessening the influence of the serious and considerate part of their body; and, under the mask of friendship, hurrying them on to that ruin, which he had before endeavoured to bring upon them, in open enmity.

This would furnish a character, not such as is given in the *lapidary* way, to which he has of late been accustomed; but such as will be preserved in the more lasting strokes of faithful history.

At present I shall conclude only with a *sketch;* and that he may not call it either "maiming or murdering"—I shall give part of it in his own *drawing;* and part of it in the drawing of a celebrated english poet. The reader may make the application where he pleases; for I cannot tell for whom the latter part was designed.

"Tho* soiled and disgraced, this Anti-Penn, this undertaker to subvert the building Penn had raised, is far from quiting the lists. On the contrary, he lies in wait with impatience for the verification of his own predictions[4]-----Factions he has found means to form,

*See the Remarker's historical review, page 274–5.[3]

3. The passage from the *Historical Review* from which this quotation was taken is an attack on Governor Robert Hunter Morris for his behavior in the autumn of 1755.

4. Here Smith omitted some 18 lines which charged Morris with hoping that Indian depredations on the frontier would so inflame its people that they would support him against the Assembly.

both in the city and in several counties. Tools and implements of all kinds he has------The prostitute writer, the whispering incendiary, the avowed desperado, surround him.[5] The press he has made an outrageous use of; a cry he has raised; and, in miniature, the whole game of faction has been here played by him, &c.

> "*Paleness,** not such as on his wings
> The messenger of sickness brings,
> But such as takes its coward rise,
> From conscious baseness, conscious vice,
> O'erspread his cheeks;—*disdain* and *pride,*
> To upstart fortunes ever tied,
> Scowl'd on his brow;—within his eye,
> Insidious, lurking like a spy
> To caution principled by fear,
> Not daring open to appear,
> Lodged covert *mischief; passion* hung
> On his lip quivering; on his tongue
> *Fraud* dwelt at large; within his breast
> All that makes villain found a nest."

To Deborah Franklin   ALS: American Philosophical Society

St. Helen's Road, Isle of Wight,
[My dear][7] Debby   Dec. 9. 1764 5 P.M.
    This Line is just to let you know that we have this moment come to an Anchor here, and that I am going ashore at Portsmouth, and

*CHURCHILL.[6]

5. The original passage, including the words omitted here, reads: "and Tools and Implements of all Kinds, from the officious Magistrate down to the Prostitute Writer, the whispering Incendiary, and avowed Desperado, he was surrounded with."
6. Charles Churchill, *The Ghost,* Book IV, lines 1879–92. The first two books were published in March 1762, the third in September 1762, but the fourth not until November 1763; *DNB.* Smith was therefore quoting a relatively recent work. The entire poem is conveniently reprinted in James Laver, ed., *Poems of Charles Churchill* ([London], 1933), where the quoted lines appear at I, 208, as part of a description of William Murray, Lord Mansfield.
7. The upper corner of the sheet is torn off.

hope to be in London on Tuesday Morning.[8] No Father could be tenderer to a Child, than Capt. Robinson[9] has been to me, for which I am greatly oblig'd to Messrs. James and Drinker's but we have had terrible Weather, and I have often been thankful that our dear Sally was not with me.[1] Tell our Friends that din'd with us on the Turtle that the kind Prayer they then put up for thirty Days fair Wind for me, was favourably heard and answered, we being just 30 Days from Land to Land. I am, Thanks to God, very well and hearty. John[2] has behav'd well to me, and so has every body on board. Thank all my Friends for their Favours which contributed so much to the Comfort of my Voyage.[3] I have not time to name Names: You know whom I love and honour. Say all the proper Things for me to every body. Love to our Children and to my dear Brother and Sister.[4] I am, dear Debby, Your ever loving Husband   B FRANKLIN

I write this in hopes of reaching the Packet.[5]

Addressed: To / Mrs. Franklin / Philadelphia / via New York / per Packet

8. *London Chron.*, Dec. 11–13, 1764, reported that "On Monday evening last [the 10th] the ingenious and much-esteemed Dr. Benjamin Franklin, arrived here from Philadelphia, in consequence of an appointment from the General Assembly there, to assist in transacting the affairs of that province for the ensuing year." BF's transatlantic voyage had been unusually fast, and his journey to London similarly exceeded his expected rate of travel.

9. Capt. James Robinson of the ship *King of Prussia*, belonging to the Philadelphia firm of James and Drinker, on which see above, pp. 435–6 n.

1. Apparently there had been some thought that the Franklins' daughter Sarah might accompany him to England. During the period before BF's arrival in England the *London Chronicle* had been reporting high winds in the eastern Atlantic and at the Channel ports.

2. BF's servant.

3. One of these was Thomas Wharton's woolen gown. BF returned it later in the winter with his "grateful Acknowledgements" and reported to DF that it had been "so comfortable a Companion in my Winter Passage." To DF, Feb. 14, 1765, APS.

4. Sally and William and his wife, Elizabeth; BF's brother Peter, now postmaster of Philadelphia, and his wife Mary.

5. DF reported the arrival of this letter, and two later ones, only on April 12, 1765, they having come "by the packit which was given up for loste."

Journal, 1764–1776; Ledger, 1764–1776

MS account books: American Philosophical Society

December 10, 1764

As Franklin had done when he went to England in 1757, he began a new record of his financial transactions when he started his second mission in 1764. Probably the new record consisted at first of a series of rather informal entries such as those in his "Account of Expences," 1757–1762, described above, VII, 164–5, and cited repeatedly in volumes VII–X of this series. When his grandnephew, Jonathan Williams, Jr., went to England in 1771 Franklin asked him, as he told the young man's mother, March 5, 1771, "to put my accounts in order, which had been much neglected. He undertook it with the utmost cheerfulness and readiness, and executed it with the greatest diligence, making me a complete new set of books, fairly written out and settled in a mercantile manner, which is a great satisfaction to me, and a very considerable service."[6] Williams completed the task on February 28, 1771, bringing all entries down to date, and then struck a trial balance. Thereafter Franklin seems to have maintained the books himself and was able to strike a second trial balance after his return to Philadelphia in 1775. A few entries of later date and some miscellaneous memoranda complete the volumes. The rough accounts Williams used to set up these records have not survived.

The two books Williams started and Franklin carried on take the familiar form of a Journal and a Ledger. The first is a folio volume inscribed on an otherwise blank initial page: "The Journal of Benjamin Franklin after his leaving Philadelphia Novr 7. 1764 and during his Residence in London." It consists of a series of chronological entries recording receipts and expenditures.[7] The first entries are dated Dec. 10, 1764, and the last May 31, 1775, except for about two pages of additions from October 1776 which relate, in one way or another, to earlier transactions. The 61 pages on which the entries appear are numbered consecutively.

The second of these account books, also a folio, is inscribed: "The Ledger of Benjamin Franklin containing Accounts of such Transactions only as have pass'd since his leaving Philadelphia Novr 7. 1764 and during his Residence in London." It consists of a series of facing-

6. [Jared Sparks, ed.], *A Collection of the Familiar Letters and Miscellaneous Papers of Benjamin Franklin* (Boston, 1833), p. 139.

7. The earlier entries in the Journal are all recorded by specific date, but after Williams had gone back to Boston BF usually entered his transactions only by the month in which they occurred.

page records of specific accounts. Although most of these are with individuals or business firms, including banking houses, there are also accounts with the General Post Office, each of the four colonies for which Franklin acted as agent during these years, and a few other bodies or institutions. On the left-hand page of each account, headed "Dr.," are entered by dates and brief descriptions the amounts which Franklin paid to the person or organization concerned. On the right-hand page, headed "Contra—Cr.," are similarly entered the amounts BF credited to himself in connection with that account, showing the nature and sources of such credits.

Jonathan Williams, who had been trained in accounting, set up these books to provide a full system of double-entry bookkeeping.[8] This system is based on the theory that every transaction involves simultaneously the receipt of a financial benefit by one person or organization and the conferring of a financial benefit by another. Hence for every transaction recorded in a double-entry ledger, two entries must be made—one debit and the other credit—in two different accounts. Realistically, however, there are numerous transactions for which an entry can be made in monetary terms in only one account, as, for example, when a person whose accounts are being recorded receives money for services rendered, or draws out currency from his bank, or pays cash for a purchase of clothing. To provide a second balancing entry it becomes necessary to create one or more "impersonal," or nominal, accounts in a ledger. Williams met this requirement for his uncle by establishing accounts, with both debit and credit pages, entitled conventionally "Profit and Loss" and "Cash." To provide for Franklin's special situation, where many transactions involved overseas transfers of monetary credit, he also set up a similar record headed "Account of Bills of Exchange." These three "impersonal" accounts, together with one or two others of minor importance, completed the categories required in the Ledger for a full recording of Franklin's financial transactions of every sort.

The first entries in the Ledger are again dated Dec. 10, 1764, and the last Oct. 21, 1776. There are 71 pairs of facing pages containing these ledger accounts, both pages of a pair identically numbered.

8. The surviving account books from BF's years in the printing business, Ledgers A & B, Shop Book, and Ledger D (above, I, 172–5; II, 127–8, 232–4), reflect a less sophisticated system of bookkeeping. "Account of Expences," 1757–1762, and Memorandum Book, 1757–1776 (above, VII, 164–5, 167–8), useful as they are, can hardly be said to reflect any system at all. It may be surmised that Williams had to teach BF the niceties of the system he set up in 1771.

Williams made no attempt at alphabetical arrangement; he simply opened an account under a new name on the next available pair of pages whenever it became necessary, and Franklin later followed suit.[9]

The entries in the two account books are closely related. For each entry in the Journal there must be two entries in the Ledger, one where it appears on the "Dr." page of one account, the other where it becomes a "Cr." entry in another account. Two ruled columns near the left margins in the Journal provide spaces where these page numbers in the Ledger are shown. Similarly, a column on each page of the Ledger contains a figure for each entry to indicate the page in the Journal where that transaction was first recorded. These columns thus provide a complete system of cross-reference between the books. There are, however, no alphabetical indexes.

Two simple examples will illustrate the system employed in these books. Under date of Feb. 1, 1765, there is an entry on page 2 of the Journal showing that Franklin paid William Strahan £163 13s. 7d. to assume James Parker's debt to Strahan, as Parker had asked before Franklin left Philadelphia.[1] Cross-references direct one to the Parker account in the Ledger, where the payment is recorded on the debit page as "To William Strahan," and to the Strahan account, where it appears on the credit page as "By James Parker." Both entries refer back to page 2 of the Journal. Again, the Journal records on page 3 that on June 11, 1765, BF received from the banking firm of Brown & Collinson a draft for £12 12s. in favor of Mason Chamberlain "for my portrait."[2] The credit page of the Brown & Collinson account in the Ledger records receipt of this draft on the same date, and the debit page of the Profit and Loss account records the transaction as an expenditure. While some of the financial operations shown in these books are more complicated than these two, the principles involved remain the same.

As occasion requires, these account books will be referred to in this edition as Journal, 1764–1776, and Ledger, 1764–1776, respectively.

9. When any of the more active accounts had filled all the space on its pair of facing pages, BF totaled the figures in each debit and credit column and carried these totals forward to an indicated pair of pages later in the book, where he continued the account. BF also pasted into the Ledger a number of bills received, promissory notes, and other papers he wished to preserve. Some of these are helpful in following his affairs, though they are not properly a part of the Ledger accounts.

1. See above, pp. 414, 470–1.

2. Above, x, xv, and frontispiece.

To Mary Stevenson

ALS: American Philosophical Society

[December 12–16, 1764][3]

I have once more the Pleasure of writing a Line to my dear Polly from Cravenstreet, where I arrived on Monday Evening in about 30 Days from Philadelphia. Your good Mama was not at home, and the Maid could not tell where to find her, so I sat me down and waited her Return, when she was a good deal surpriz'd to find me in her Parlour. She has this Afternoon receiv'd a Letter from you, and we rejoice to hear that you and our other Friends at Bromley are all well. My Love to good Doctor and Mrs. Hawkesworth, and to your amiable Friends the Miss Blounts.[4] Your Mama joins with me in every affectionate Sentiment, and bids me tell you that she is indeed but poorly, yet better than she was when you left her. I am, as ever, my dear Friend, Yours affectionately

B FRANKLIN

From Charles Thomson

ALS: American Philosophical Society

Dear Sir   Philada. 18th Decr. 1764

The Urgency of my business which called me another way deprived me of the pleasure of waiting on you to Chester.[5] However my best Prayers and wishes attend you, and I hope e'er now you are safe in London. The first Day of my Journey[6] I travelled about

3. Mention in the text of BF's arrival at his old lodgings in Craven Street, London, "on Monday Evening" places the letter during the six days that followed. Had he written as early as Tuesday, December 11, however, he probably would have said that he had arrived "last Evening," hence the suggested dating given here.

4. For the Hawkesworths and the Blunt sisters, see above, IX, 265–6 n, 327 n. A letter from BF to Polly on Jan. 9, 1765 (APS), indicates that she had been making a long Christmas visit to the Hawkesworths at Bromley, Kent.

5. Approximately 300 friends accompanied BF from Philadelphia to Chester to see him on board the *King of Prussia*, Capt. Robinson, on Nov. 7, 1764. See above, p. 447.

6. Thomson, a merchant, may have been traveling on business or possibly for his health, since in 1763 it was reported that he was suffering from a "powerful Consumption." *PMHB*, XVIII (1894), 38. In 1765 he and John Foxcroft were advertising land for sale or lease near Winchester, Va., and

32 Miles up the Lancaster Road and lodged at the 19th. Tavern. This Road tis true is much frequented and on that account the great Number of Inns might be in some measure excused, were it not that they are almost equally numerous on every other Road thro the Province; In consequence of this the Manners of the people are debauched, their bodies enervated, their time and Money uselessly dissipated and this I look on to be one great Reason of the want of Cash so much complained of and of the many failures that have and must happen among trading people thro the Province. I should therefore be exceeding glad to see this matter regulated, and instead of the perquisite arising from Tavern Licenses that our Governor had a handsome fixed annual Salary.[7] You remember the Story of Cyrus, the Way he took to break the Spirit and soften the War-like Disposition of the Lydians and render them more abject Slaves by erecting Bagnios and public Inns. I think 'tis Herodotus tells the Story.[8] I will not say that is the design of our great Ones. But certain it is that almost in every tavern keeper the Proprietors have a warm advocate and that the more effeminate and debauched a people are, the more they are fitted for an absolute and tyranical Government.

Since your Departure the Effects of Party Spirit has reached the Seats of Justice. In York County a Dedimus was sent up and an entire new set of Justices put into Commission.[9] In Chester County

---

seeking a sawmill operator and a blacksmith (*Pa. Jour.*, Sept. 12, 1765); his journey may have been connected with that project.

7. Tavern licenses were granted by the governor on the recommendation of the justices of the peace of the respective counties. The fees, according to a student of the subject, "remained stationary throughout the Colonial period. They were: £3 annually for the retailing of wine and other liquors; if wine were excepted, a forty-shilling rate applied to Philadelphia, Frankford, Germantown, Darby and Chichester; other localities paid thirty shillings. In addition to this, however, a fee of six shillings per license was paid to the governor's Secretary." Charles R. Barker, "Colonial Taverns of Lower Merion," *PMHB*, LII (1928), 208–9. For some years it had been a standing complaint of the Assembly that the governor issued an excessive number of licenses, solely for the purpose of augmenting his income.

8. Herodotus, *History*, Book I, chap. 155, although somewhat less luridly presented than Thomson suggests.

9. On Oct. 17, 1764, Governor Penn issued a commission appointing sixteen justices of the peace in York County. Their names are listed in *Pa. Col. Recs.*, IX, 201. No list of their predecessors has been found.

the change was not so great, some having voted right at the late Election and Mr. Chew it [is] said with much ado prevailing to have one or two Quakers continued.[1] However Morton, the chief Burgess of Chester and some others were left out, and Wm. Moore put at the head of the Commission. So ill had they concerted Matters and so eager was the president to resume his former seat that he published the Commission the morning before the Court, upon which some who were dissatisfyed with the Man and measure would not appear so that had not the Cheif Burgess of Chester been prevailed on to act in Consequence of the Charter granted to the Burrough the Court must have drop'd for want of a sufficient Number of Justices and all the Actions depending been discontinued. In Philadelphia County Pawlin (in whose favour they exerted themselves so much at the Election but who unluckily did not answer their purpose in the House), John Potts &c. are left out and others more pliant put in their Room. What Changes are made in the other Counties I have not heard. This however serves to shew the Spirit of the times and the necessity of a Change.

I am sorry to inform you there is Reason to fear the Indian War is not quite at an End. Colonel Boquet, as no doubt you have heard marched into their Country, at whose approach they were so alarmed that they begg'd for Peace, agreed to deliver up the prisoners and to give Hostages for their due observance of the Peace.[2] At the time appointed the Delawares and Senecas came in and brought with them near two hundred prisoners and gave the Delawares six and the Senecas two Hostages, the Shawanese kept back. However after some Days they also came and brought with them a few prisoners and gave six of their chief Men Hostages. With the prisoners and Hostages Colonel Boquet returned to Pitsburgh from which place in a few Days as we are just now informed the six Shawanese Hostages have made their Escape. So that it is to be feared it will require another Campaign to bring them to Reason. A Letter from the Army says the Indians have been supplied from the French on the Illionois. The Colonel is expectd [in] Town in a few Days.[3]

1. For other comments on the changes in Chester Co., and in Philadelphia Co., also mentioned here, see above, pp. 468, 484–5.
2. See above, pp. 475, 483.
3. Bouquet arrived in Philadelphia on Jan. 3, 1765. *Pa. Gaz.*, Jan. 10, 1765.

The Sunday before Mr. Hamilton sailed[4] Notice was given at the Presbyterian Meetings by the Ministers for the heads of the heads of the Congregations to meet next Day on Matters of the greatest Importance. The design was as I am informed to sign a Petition to the Proprietaries requesting them to exert their utmost Influence to prevent a Change of Government. As I did not see it I can say nothing certain but doubtless you will hear of it in London.[5] I am with sincerest Esteem Dear Sir Your hearty Welwisher and affectionate Friend   CHAS THOMSON

Addressed: To / Benjamin Franklin Esqr / in Craven Street / London

Endorsed: Mr Thomson. 19 Inns in 30 Miles

From Hannah Walker[6]   ALS: University of Pennsylvania Library

Honour'd Sir   Westbury, the 18th: Decr: 1764

I received yours on the 16th. Instant[7] with greater Joy then we Can Express to us all to think you are safe arrived in England in so short atime and were Extremely glad to hear that your good Family are all well when I read on the 10th: Instant in the Newse Paper as you was to Embark for England it was with the greatest Joy Imaginable to Read Over Such a paragraph but a great Deal more Agumented to hear of your Safe arival in so Short atine.[8]

---

4. James Hamilton sailed for England for the treatment of a suspected cancer on his nose aboard the *Carolina,* Capt. James Friend, which left the Capes of the Delaware on Nov. 28, 1764. See above, p. 483, and *Pa. Gaz.* and *Pa. Jour.,* Nov. 29, 1764.

5. For Joseph Galloway's brief description of the Presbyterian petition, see above, p. 467.

6. Hannah Farrow Walker (A.5.2.3.3.1) was the daughter of BF's first cousin, Anne Farrow (A.5.2.3.3) of Castlethorpe, Bucks, with whom he had corresponded during his first mission to England. He had divided his share of another cousin's small estate between Mrs. Farrow and one other, and he may have helped both Mrs. Farrow and Mrs. Walker financially. See above, VIII, 221–5, 237–9, 288, 325 n; X, 427.

7. BF's letter not found.

8. *London Chron.,* Dec. 8–11, carried an account of BF's embarkation from Philadelphia, while the next issue of the paper, December 11–13, reported his arrival in London.

Most Honour'd Sir I Return you Humble thanks for your kind Letter which is one of the greatest Comforts in this world to receive A Letter from you or any of your Dear Family. I hope Miss Franklin receiv'd my Letter as she was so kind to Desire me to write to her as I Did accordingly as She need not think I was so ungratefull not to return an answer to so kind an Invitation. I hope we may Live in hopes of seeing you in the Countrey. We all Joyn in Begging the Axeptance of our Dutys to you from your Ever Most Humble and Obedient Servant   HANNAH WALKER

Addressed: To / Benjamin Franklin Esqr / at / Mrs Stevensons Craven / Street Strand / London

From Samuel Wharton   ALS: American Philosophical Society[9]

Dear sir   Philada. Decr. 19 1764

When I wrote you last,[1] I must confess, I did not expect, That the *Protesters* would attempt to answer the *Remarks,* or Indeed? That they would [injure?] their Cause, so much, as to let an anonymous Reply appear, in their Behalf.[2]

The History of this Matter, as I am informed, is thus, The Protestors, at the Instigation of the Chief Justice, determined an Answer should appear and That They would sign it. But Dickenson, who heretofore was the most forward in publishing his Name, greatly disapointed Them, By refusing to do it, upon this Occasion.[3] He was induced thereto, By William Morris of Trenton,[4]

9. When the Franklin Papers in APS were arranged, the two folio sheets which comprise the MS of this letter were separated and so were bound in different volumes, the first folio in LVIII, 33, the second in I, 113. I. Minis Hays recognized their connection, however, and recorded them together, though in reverse order, in *Calendar of the Papers of Benjamin Franklin in the Library of the American Philosophical Society* (Phila., 1908), I, 36–7.

1. Above, pp. 471–7.

2. For *An Answer to Mr. Franklin's Remarks, on a Late Protest* and the matters discussed in the first part of this letter, see above, pp. 486–516.

3. Dickinson did draw up a reply, but he did not publish it. It is printed in Paul L. Ford, ed., *The Writings of John Dickinson* (Phila., 1895), I, 155–67.

4. William Morris (1695–1776), merchant and landowner in N.J., married as his second wife Dickinson's aunt, Rebecca Cadwalader. She had recently died, Oct. 9, 1764. Robert C. Moon, *The Morris Family of Philadelphia* (Phila., 1898), I, 181–97.

Mr. Joseph Richardson [the Member][5] and some Others of his Relations representing to Him, The Injury He was doing Himself; as the prop—y Party dare not, desert Chew and That almost, all the Quakers, were attached to Gallaway. Allison, Ewing, Smith and Edward Shippen junior,[6] I have Reason to think, were the Club of Geniuses, which composed that Compilation of Billingsgate and Misrepresentation, called an *Answer*. They will not, however, I dare say, fa[*torn*] Tho' They are so generously called upon, by your cordial Friend, Mr. Hughs, In this Days *Papers*. I went to Burlington on Saturday last, to confer with the Governor, On a Publication of this Sort. Which He approved of and immediately assayed a Draft of it and On Monday, He came to Town with Me to consult with Messrs. Gallaway, James, Hughs and Evans,[7] concerning it.

I flatter myself, the Plan will please you; As it is putting your Character, upon a fair Tryal, by your Country and in effect, silencing the insidious and poisonous Insinuations, of your rancorous and savage Enemies. The protesters expected, That their anonymous Answer, would be productive of *One* to Theirs and That Then, They should have a fair Opportunity, of adding to the Load of Lies and Malice, with which, They had so copiously abused your Reputation; But Mr. Hughs's calling upon Them, In the

5. Brackets in the original. Joseph Richardson (1706–1770) had married in 1745 Sarah Morris, daughter of William Morris by his first wife; she died about a year after their marriage and he never married again. There was therefore a family connection, but no blood relationship between him and Dickinson. *Ibid.*, I, 311–12. Richardson represented Philadelphia Co. in the Assembly, 1763–70. In the critical votes of October 1764 he sided with the majority four times and with the proprietary supporters three times, including the votes on the appointment of BF, but he did not sign the protest against the appointment. Wharton calls him "the Member" to distinguish him from the father and son of the same name, Philadelphia silversmiths.

6. Francis Alison (above, II, 392 n), vice provost of the College, and John Ewing (1732–1802), pastor of the First Presbyterian Church in Philadelphia, had signed the Presbyterians' address against the proposed change in government in March 1764. Edward Shippen, Jr. (1729–1806), was judge of the court of vice admiralty. William Smith, provost of the College, is now generally recognized as the author of the *Answer*, though he may have had help in writing it.

7. Joseph Galloway (above, VII, 29 n), Abel James (above, pp. 435–6 n), John Hughes (above, VI, 284 n), and Dr. Cadwalader Evans (above, VII, 287 n) were active members of the anti-proprietary faction.

Manner He has, Either to avow the Performance, Or take the Shame of it, To Themselves, must infallibly involve our peerless Chief Justice and his partizans, into great Distress; For He and [the other] Protesters, cannot adopt it, As it abounds with so much, fustian, bare faced Compliment to Themselves and neither Smith nor Allison, will be so fool Hardy, As to lend their religious and reverend Names, to patronize so infamously virulent and flagrant, a Libel. Therefore, if some person of Character, will not Own the Performance, It will undoubtedly reflect, the greatest Disreputation, upon the proprietary Party, both in England and America. But should Any One, join Issue and undertake to support those Assertions, which They have published as Facts, There will be the most happy Opportunity of proving the Contrary and delineating to the Publick, The many very important Services, You have, for a Series of Years, almost unceasingly, been doing, his Majesty and the Province.

Pardon Sir, This Intimation?

I am told, That Our Chief Justice declared last Week at Mr. Growdon's,[8] That He wished, He had [not][9] signed the Protest. If He did it, *then,* I am convinc'd, He will more sincerely wish it, When He comes to reflect On, the Conseque[nce of] his shamfull, nameless, Answer and Especialy, As He is now publickly, called upon, To Own it.

Dickenson appears likewise, To be in a penitent Mood. For a few Days ago, He told Mr. Rhoads,[1] That He would not serve as a Member of Assembly, any longer, then this year, for that, He had been used very ill, By Messrs. Norris and Pemberton.[2] The first, He alledges, earnestly press'd Him to publish *his Speech* and

8. Probably Lawrence Growdon (1694–1770), who became a member of the Council in 1747 and held a variety of judicial and other offices during his life. His daughter Grace married Joseph Galloway in 1753. Growdon's principal residence was Trevose in Bucks Co., but he also had a half-interest in a house on Arch St., Philadelphia. Charles P. Keith, *The Provincial Councillors of Pennsylvania* (Phila., 1883), pp. 223–4.

9. A small tear in the MS has obliterated this word, clearly required by the sense.

1. Samuel Rhoads, BF's former colleague in the Assembly, now supervising the building of his house.

2. In *Pa. Gaz.* and *Pa. Jour.*, Aug. 8, 1765, and some later issues, Dickinson published an announcement declining to serve again.

the Other, was constantly inflaming Him. The former, He says, He now perceives, prompted Him to serve his Purposes and as They did not succeed, He has retired pretty clear, of publick Clamor and The latter, He discovers, to be a vindictive Man, Who has lost his Interest, with both Quakers and Others.

Mr. Dickenson's Declaration and Conduct, I think, require no Comment As They are clearly expressive, of much Folly and great Want, of either, Principle or Firmness.

You will doubtless, before this reaches you, have heared of what Colonel Bouquet has done—which is certainly as much [as] any Person could, considering, That Bradstreet did not join Him.[3] I am sorry however to inform you, That The Shawanese Hostages have run off from Pittsburg.[4] That Tribe very reluctantly gave their Hostages, As I am well advised and The Reason assigned, is, That They were not in want of Necessarys, occasioned by French Traders going from the Illinois, into their Country, to supply Them.

It is as I mentioned in my last, of the highest Consequence, The taking Possession of that Country immediately; for Until, That is done—We cannot promise Ourselves any permanent Peace with the Indians, Either on the Ohio or in the Neighbourhood of Lakes Erie, Michigan &c.; as it is always, in the Power of the French, to infuse unfavorable Notions against Us and supply Them, with Cloathing and Ammunition; I therefore hope, General Gage will immediately, fall upon some probable Plan, to establish an English Garrison at the Illinois. What renders the Defection of the Shawanese, The more alarming, is, That Colonel Bouquet sent some Canada Indians, with One Owens, (The Person, Who appeared before the Commissioners and claimed the Reward for scalping so many Indians[5]) to invite the Hostages to return to Fort Pitt; When unfortunately some Difference arose between One of Them and this Owens, Who immediately took up his Riffle and shot Him dead, upon the Spott.[6]

3. On Bradstreet's failure to conduct an effective campaign, see above, p. 326.

4. Bouquet reported the escape of Mingo and Shawnee hostages from Fort Pitt in letters to Sir William Johnson of Nov. 30 and Dec. 3, 1764; *The Papers of Sir William Johnson*, IV (Albany, 1925), 606–7, 608–9.

5. See above, pp. 173–4.

6. Gen. Thomas Gage gave Sir William Johnson a different account of this affair, April 21, 1765. Two Delaware hostages had disappeared and were at first reported to have been killed, "but it's said from Fort-Pitt, that they

I hope however, my next Letter will afford you, a more pleasant Relation, in respect to the Shawanese; As Mr. Croghan, is now with the General, waiting his Orders to proceed to the Ohio, to hold a Treaty with the Indians. The Delawares and Mingos are in a very mild Disposition and desirous of a Confirmation of the Peace.

The first Division of the Pennsylvania Forces (and the Prisoners) are arrived at Lancaster and are to Morrow, To be paid off and disbanded and the Other, it is thought, is by this Time, got to Carlisle.[7]

Our Governor, I am told, says, He has Proposals to lay before the House; But He swears, He never will present Them—possibly, His Chief Justice, may prevail upon Him, To make Them known to the Assembly, At their next Meeting;[8] But the Faction is at present in high Spirits, As They give Out, since the October packet, is arrived, That there is not the least Fear, of a Change of Goverment &c. My Father begs to be remembered to you. He is in good Health, ardently praying, for that Change, which Only will restore Peace to a divided and most distracted Province. I am Dear Sir, with the sincerest Regard your faithfull and assured Friend

SAML WHARTON

Dr. Benjamin Franklin.

Endorsed: S. Wharton   Dec. 19. 1764

From David Hall

ALS: American Philosophical Society

Dear Sir,   Philada. Decr. 20. 1764.

Tho' I have nothing material to say, yet as I promised to write you by every Ship from this Port to yours, choose rather to put you to a small Expence of Postage, than be altogether silent.

---

went home, having been terrified by Owens the Interpreter, who is now with you. This Fellow it seems in a drunken Frolick, acquainted the Hostages that we intended to murther them." *Johnson Papers*, IV, 723.

7. Papers relating to the return of the Pa. troops and their payment are in I *Pa. Arch.*, IV, 208–13. In *Pa. Gaz.*, Jan. 17, 1765, is a list of 91 Virginian and 116 Pennsylvanian captives returned.

8. Probably his instructions to accede to the Assembly's interpretation of the stipulation on taxation of located but uncultivated lands belonging to the Proprietors. On Governor Penn's handling of this matter in January and February 1765, see above, pp. 213–14 n.

DECEMBER 20, 1764

I begin then with acquainting you, that Mrs. Franklin and Sally are well, as is your Son, who I saw the Day before Yesterday.[9] The Papers are sent you by this Vessel, and among them that of this Day, in which you will see a Paper in your Behalf, signed by John Hughes, desiring the Author or Authors of an Answer to your Remarks, to publish his or their Names, &c.[1] Mrs. Franklin tells me she has sent you the Answer, else I should have done it.

You will see a Proclamation in one of the Gazettes, in which there is a Cessation of Hostilities against the Indians,[2] and of Consequence the Troops will be discharged but the Six Shawanese Hostages have given Colonel Bouquet the Slip at Pittsburgh, which gives, I understand, some Uneasiness; the Reason of their going off not known, at least not made publick; but I have heard that one of them had a Quarrel with one David Owen, a white Man, but a worthless Fellow, in which the Indian was killed,[3] and that that was the Occasion of the others going off; however, as the Colonel is expected in Town in a Day or two, we shall probably hear further. If the Papers have come to your Hands, you will find the Shawanese were more backward than the other Indians in agreeing to the Peace, the Reason of which we have since heard was, that at the Time they were treating with the Colonel, there were a Number of French Traders in their Town, who, it is said, brought them Plenty of Goods and Ammunition, and that this is the third time they have been supplied by the French during the late War. I don't know any thing else in the News Way just now worth communicating; only that we have a very bad Gang about Town, who are every Night robbing Houses, or attacking People about the Skirts of the City, so that I suppose we shall have another Hanging Bout by and by. Our Roads as you will see by this Day's Paper, are also infested by Highwaymen.[4]

9. WF had come to Philadelphia with Samuel Wharton on December 17 to consult leaders of the party on what response to make to the *Answer to Mr. Franklin's Remarks;* see the letter immediately above.
1. See above, p. 487.
2. In *Pa. Gaz.*, Dec. 6, 1764.
3. See the letter immediately above.
4. Issues of the two Philadelphia papers during November and December 1764 carried accounts of several burglaries and robberies in the city. *Pa. Gaz.*, Dec. 20, 1764, reported that the week before two men had been found lying on the Lancaster Road, about fifteen miles from Philadelphia, in serious

Business goes on as usual; we are now printing the Votes of the New Assembly, there being an Order, it seems, to print the Minutes of every Sitting, as soon as conveniently they can be done.[5] Hope to have the Pleasure of hearing from you soon, with all your News; which will be most agreeable to Dear Sir, Yours most affectionately, DAVID HALL.

From John Ross[6]   LS: American Philosophical Society

Dear Sir.   Philadelphia, December 20th 1764.
Duty as well as Inclination ingage me to write you, tho' nothing very material occurs worth communicating since your leaving us; as I am certain Numbers of your Friends have given you Intelligence of all the Minutiae passing among us (for indeed there is nothing more.) I venture these few lines only for the pleasure arising, that I may not be accounted negligent or forgetful of an absent Friend.

Since your departure the most important matter that has happen'd has been the issuing new Commissions of the peace for this and the Countys of Chester and Bucks:[7] Mr. William Moore of Chester County is put at the head of the Commission there; and John Morton Esquire left out; for this Country Mr. Potts and Pawling are also omitted, to their great ease and quiet, but cer-

---

condition after having been beaten and robbed by two men on horseback. One of the victims was recovering but the other was expected to die.

5. In *Pa. Gaz.*, Dec. 27, 1764, Hall announced as "Just published" the *Votes and Proceedings* of the previous October session.

6. John Ross (1714–1776), Philadelphia lawyer, member of the Assembly, 1762–65, where he stood consistently with the majority on the critical votes of October 1764. He was the son of the Rev. George Ross, Anglican minister at New Castle, Del., and half-brother of George Ross (1730–1779), signer of the Declaration of Independence. In the controversies which rent Christ Church, Philadelphia in 1759–60 (above, IX, 182 n) he sided with the Rev. William McClanachan and left that church for St. Paul's. Later letters show that a warm personal friendship existed between Ross and BF. *PMHB*, L (1926), 94. He is not to be confused with John Ross (1729–1800), merchant, with whom BF corresponded on supplies for the Revolutionary Army, and who did not settle in Philadelphia until 1767. *Ibid.*, XXIII (1899), 77–85.

7. For earlier reports on changes among the justices of the peace, see above, pp. 468, 472–3, 484.

tainly to the great disquiet of the generality of the good People of those Countys. What Star governs or what Wisdom guides the present Councils, it is difficult to determine; but certain it is they are wild and confused, and tend to alienate some in their Affections, and rivet others in their prejudices against the present Administration.

Opinions here are various as our Faces concerning the grand Point, "Change or not"; but upon the whole, I beleive very few (save those immediately interested) wou'd disapprove our Dear Sovereign's Ruling over us, if he will do it, preserving to us our present Liberties granted by Charter, and what is much better, confirmed to us by positive Acts of Assembly, approved and ratify'd by his Majesty's Royal Predecessors which we think here equal to an Act of Parliament, and which we are confident his Majesty would never attempt to deprive us of, were it in his Power; for his Majesty's Goodness would rather give to, than take from his Subjects.

I am persuaded, good Sir, that you with our worthy Agent Mr. Jackson, will do every thing in your Joint powers to promote the happiness, prosperity and peace of the Colonys in general, and of this Province, in particular; permit me to say that I am with great Sincerity, Sir, Your Sincere Friend and Obedient Humble Servant

JOHN ROSS.

Benjan. Franklin Esqr:

Addressed: To / Benjamin Franklin Esquire / one of the Agents for the Province / of Pennsylvania / in / London / per favour / Mr. Footman

Endorsed: Ross

From [Springett Penn][8]   AL: American Philosophical Society

Dear Sir   Dublin Decemr. 22d 1764
Having this Day read in the paper of your Safe Arrival in London My Mother and myself Congratulate you on your safe Arrival

8. Identified by the contents of the letter. On Springett Penn (1739–1766), great-grandson of William Penn in the senior line, his mother Ann Penn

and hope you have left your Family and the rest of our Friends well. I the other day received a letter from Mr. Pennington[9] who informed me you were coming over in order to Petition his Majesty to take the Government on himself and that it would in such Case be adviseable for me to put in my Claim.[1] I should therefore be much Obliged to you if among the other marks of Friendship you have shewn me you would send to Mr. Life[2] who I hope will soon be able to wait on you (as he has been very ill of late) to consult what will be proper to be done. He can shew you an Opinion of Mr. Jacksons about this Matter.[3]

Mr. Pennington in a former Letter wrote me the Intail of Pennsbury[4] would be soon barred and in this last has not said whether it was or not but no Doubt you can inform me. My Mother joins in Compliments of the Season. I remain with great Regard [your] humble Servant   [SPRINGETT PENN][5]

(mentioned in this letter), and his Pennsylvania lands and claims to the proprietorship, see above, IX, 260–2, 315–17, 326; X, 6.

9. For Edward Penington, Philadelphia Quaker merchant, who was distantly related to Springett Penn and had represented him in connection with his Pa. estate, see above, IX, 315 n.

1. BF had suggested to Richard Jackson the previous March that if Springett could prove his right to the proprietorship he "no doubt would willingly surrender to the Crown" on reasonable terms; above, p. 151. William Allen wrote Thomas Penn, Dec. 19, 1764, that he had just learned that "the Party" had "sometime ago" urged Springett Penn to come over, asserting that the rights of government were properly his. Allen added that part of BF's errand to England was reported to be to persuade Springett to cross the ocean and take over the government, in the belief that the consequent disturbances in the colony would be an argument for the Crown to assume control. Penn Papers, Hist. Soc. Pa.

2. For Thomas Life, London solicitor, see above, X, 369 n.

3. What opinion of Jackson's was meant here is not known.

4. William Penn's country seat on the Delaware. Reconstruction of the main house and other buildings and restoration of the grounds were completed in 1946; the estate is now administered by the Pennsylvania Historical and Museum Commission.

5. The signature is lost because of a tear in the MS.

From Anthony Todd

AL: University of Pennsylvania Library

Monday the 24th: December 1764.

Mr. Todd presents his Compliments to Mr. Franklin, and would be glad to see him any Morning to shew him the proposed Clauses for the intended Act of Parliament.[6]

Addressed: To | Benjamin Franklin Esqr. | Cravenstreet

To Deborah Franklin

ALS: American Philosophical Society

My dear Child   London, Dec. 27. 1764

I have just heard that a Ship which left London before I arriv'd is still at Portsmouth and that a Letter may reach her. I can only write a Line or two, just to let you know that I am now almost well, tho' for 10 or 12 Days I have been severely handled by a most violent Cold, that has worried me extreamly.[7] Those of my old Friends who were in town, have given me a most cordial Welcome, but many are yet in the Country, the Parliament not meeting till the 10th. of next Month; so nothing has occur'd to be worth a Letter to my other Friends, but I shall however write to them per Packet. My Love to our Children, and to all that kindly enquire after Your affectionate Husband   B FRANKLIN

[Mrs.] Stevenson desires her Compliments.

Addressed: To | Mrs Franklin | Philadelphia | via New York | per Packet

---

6. The Postal Act of 1765 (5 Geo. III, c. 25) was passed May 10, 1765. Among other provisions, it changed the rates for mail between Great Britain and the colonies and between offices within the colonies, and it imposed stricter requirements for the handling of letters carried on merchant ships. See above, pp. 342–6, for the recommendations of BF and Foxcroft, several of which were adopted; and for a table showing the changes made in rates between N.Y. and the other places named in the act of 1710, see below, pp. 535–7.

7. BF had been similarly taken ill, but more seriously, after his arrival in England in 1757; see above, VII, 271, 272–4.

534

Table of Revised Postal Rates

Draft: American Philosophical Society

On Sept. 21, 1764, Franklin and Foxcroft recommended that the proposed new postal act change the schedule of rates between colonial offices from one based chiefly on a few specified places to one stated in general terms of mileage alone, thereby eliminating several inconsistencies resulting from the earlier method.[8] The postmasters general adopted this recommendation, and the clause in the new bill making the change was certainly one of those Todd showed to Franklin about December 24.[9] In brief, the bill (which was enacted without change in this particular on May 10, 1765, as 5 Geo. III, c. 25) specified that a single-sheet letter going not more than 60 miles should pay *4d.;* one going between 60 and 100 miles, *6d.;* between 100 and 200 miles, *8d.;* and any letter going more than 200 miles should pay another *2d.* for each additional 100 miles or fraction thereof.

Either in September, when Franklin and Foxcroft were drafting their recommendations, or in December, after Franklin's interview with Todd, Franklin prepared this table. Since the draft is undated, one cannot state with certainty which was the occasion; hence it is placed here with other undated documents of the year 1764.

The post offices listed here are the only ones specifically mentioned in the act of 1710, and the rates of postage prescribed in that act for letters between New York and each of the other offices are shown in one column in pence sterling.[1] The next column shows what the rates would be under the proposed bill when determined by the mileages given in an earlier column. Since the rates shown are only those between New York and the few offices mentioned in 1710, this is far from being a complete list of postal rates under the new law. For mail between any two places mentioned which would have to pass through New York, however, it is possible to determine the rate after adding together the two mileages. Thus, a letter between Boston and Philadelphia, said to travel a total of 366 miles,[2] which would pay *1s. 9d.* under the

8. Above, pp. 343–6.
9. Above, p. 534.
1. In general, the act of 1710 (9 Anne, c. 10) displays only a limited knowledge of colonial geography. It grouped together the places in both directions supposed to fall within the same 100-mile bracket of distance from New York, and prescribed a single rate for each group. Thus Newport, Boston, Portsmouth, and Annapolis all fell in the same group, although by 1764 their distances were believed to vary substantially.
2. This figure, combining the stated distances between each of these places

old act, would now pay only 1s. 4d. (6d. plus 10d.), a reduction of not quite one-fourth.

Table of the Distances of Places, and Rates of Postage in North America, showing the Changes propos'd to be made by the New Act.

Places	Distances in Statute Miles	Postage by the present Act	Postage propos'd by the New Act	Difference
From New York to Perth Amboy	30	6	4	abated 2d. which is 1/3
to Bridlington[3]	80	6	6	No Change
to New London	150	9	8	abated 1d. which is 1/9
to Philadelphia	96	9	6	abated 3d. 1/3
to Newport	196	12	8	abated 4d. 1/3
to Boston	270	12	10	abated 2d. 1/6
to Portsmouth	330	12	12	No Change
to Annapolis	240	12	10	abated 2d. 1/6
to Salem	290	15	10	abated 5d. 1/3
to Ipswich	300	15	10	abated 5d. 1/3
to Piscataqua	330	15	12	abated 3d. 1/5
to Williamsburgh	411	15	14	abated 1d. 1/15
to Charlestown	856	18	22	added 4d.

Note; That *Portsmouth* is at *Piscataqua* and the chief Office there and it was an Error in the old Act to give them different Postages; and a lower Postage from New York to Portsmouth, than to Salem and Ipswich, which are nearer the one by 40 and the other by 30 Miles.

1:0[4]

1:3

See Douglas[5]   1:6   1:10

and New York, considerably exceeds the total distance by any of the direct routes available today. The discrepancy may be explained in part by the fact that in the 1760s the postrider usually traveled by way of Newport, R.I.

3. Burlington, N.J., but spelled "Bridlington" in the act of 1710, as in the case of the Yorkshire town for which it was named.

4. The significance of these figures is unknown.

5. Probably intended to indicate that BF was using William Douglass, *A Summary, Historical and Political, . . . of the British Settlements in North-America,* as authority for the distances given in the table. A check with the then most recent edition, that of 1760, 1, 466–70, however, shows that none of the distances BF gives exactly matches that in Douglass, though most of those appearing in both places differ by less than ten miles. The distances in *Poor Richard improved* for 1764 are in most instances a little closer to BF's, although only that from New York to New London is precisely the same.

536

Endorsed: Post Office Changes of Rates

[*Also on this page:*] of the Kindness I met with in that Country and the happy Hours I spent in their Conversation.[6]

To [Grey Cooper][7]

ALS: Frank Glenn, Kansas City, Missouri (1955)

Sir,   [1764?–1775][8]

I used to put two Ounces of Bark finely powdered into a Bottle of Wine, and let it stand 24 Hours, in which time it will have given to the Wine a sufficient Quantity of its Virtue, and the Powder itself will be pretty well subsided.[9] When I had drank two or three Glasses out of the Bottle, I used to fill it up with fresh Wine, because the Bark will not give forth all its Virtue to the first Quantity of Wine, but continues communicating more as fresh Wine offers to receive it, so that on the whole I suppose I may have drank a Gallon of Wine off the first Quantity of Bark. Every time I pour'd out a Glass to drink, I us'd to shake the Bottle, generally not 'till I had fill'd my Glass; but sometimes before, when I felt any feverish Indisposition and chose to have some of the Substance of the Bark expecting thence greater or more speedy Effects. I am, Yours affectionately   B FRANKLIN[1]

6. BF probably was using some of the blank space on the sheet for the draft of a passage in some unidentified letter.

7. So identified because this letter was included in the sale of Sir Grey Cooper's books and MSS, Oct. 11, 1802, where it was bought by a Mr. Waight; information supplied by the present owner, Mr. Frank Glenn. For Grey Cooper (*c.* 1726–1801), barrister, M.P., and governmental officer, see above, X, 185 n.

8. This letter could have been written at almost any time during BF's years in England. The friendship between the two men, begun during the first mission, appears to have become much closer during the later period; hence, partly because of the word "affectionately" with which the letter closes, it is placed with the earliest documents of that period.

9. On BF's use of an infusion of "bark" (Peruvian bark, or cinchona, containing quinine) during his illness in the autumn of 1757, see above, VII, 273.

1. Accompanying this letter are two small slips of paper containing other prescriptions. One, in what appears to be Peter Collinson's hand, reads: "Receipt for the Piles [?] from Sir John Pringle two or three Leaves of Moth Mullein put in to a Pint of Milk and kept on the Fire till reduced to

To Peter Franklin

MS not found; reprinted from Benjamin Franklin, *Experiments and Observations on Electricity*, 1769 edition, pp. 473–8.[2]

In its surviving printed form this letter is headed "To Mr. P. F. Newport, New England," and since it begins "Dear Brother," the person addressed could only have been Franklin's brother, for many years a merchant and shipmaster in that town. Comparatively little is known of this member of the family, fourteen years older than Benjamin, and there is no other evidence than this letter that Peter wrote ballads or was interested in music. The verses he had written and asked Benjamin to have set to music have not survived in any identifiable form. Readers interested in eighteenth-century music, however, may be grateful to him, since he provided the occasion for the response printed here, which reveals a good deal of his more famous brother's views on that subject.

As printed in *Experiments and Observations*, the letter is undated and appears near the end of the volume close to and after another letter on a musical subject addressed to Lord Kames, dated June 2, 1765. This letter must have been written before that date, for it is known that Peter Franklin had moved from Newport to Philadelphia and had become postmaster of the latter city by October 1764, remaining there until his death in 1766. The suggestion in the first paragraph that "some country girl in the heart of the Massachusets" might have been more successful in setting the ballad to music "than any of our masters here" indicates that Benjamin was almost certainly writing from England, for there was no one whom he could have presumed to call a "master" of musical composition in Philadelphia in that period. The editors confess that in first assigning this letter a probable date they overlooked this passage and so failed to print it, as they probably should have done, no later than in volume x with other documents of 1762, the year Franklin left England at the close of his first mission. It is included here, however, at the end of 1764, the last year in which Peter Franklin spent any time in Newport.

---

half the Quantity which is to be taken at going to Bed." The other, in an unidentified hand, reads: "equal quantities of Camimile Flowers and Valerian Root put into a tea Pot that holds about a pint, about a quarter of an ounce of each and let it stand till it is Cold. Mr. Rusts Receipt for the Stomach." What connection, if any, these papers may have had with BF is not known.

2. Printed as Letter LVI, though it should have been numbered LVIII, as it was when it was reprinted in the 1774 edition, pp. 491–6.

Dear Brother,   [Before 1765]
***I like your ballad, and think it well adapted for your purpose of
discountenancing expensive foppery, and encouraging industry
and frugality. If you can get it generally sung in your country, it
may probably have a good deal of the effect you hope and expect
from it. But as you aimed at making it general, I wonder you chose
so uncommon a measure in poetry, that none of the tunes in common use will suit it. Had you fitted it to an old one, well known, it
must have spread much faster than I doubt it will do from the best
new tune we can get compos'd for it. I think too, that if you had
given it to some country girl in the heart of the Massachusets, who
has never heard any other than psalm tunes, or *Chevy Chace*, the
Children in the Wood, the *Spanish Lady*,[3] and such old simple ditties,
but has naturally a good ear, she might more probably have made a
pleasing popular tune for you, than any of our masters here, and
more proper for your purpose, which would best be answered, if
every word could as it is sung be understood by all that hear it,
and if the emphasis you intend for particular words could be given
by the singer as well as by the reader; much of the force and impression of the song depending on those circumstances. I will however get it as well done for you as I can.

Do not imagine that I mean to depreciate the skill of our composers of music here; they are admirable at pleasing *practised* ears,
and know how to delight *one another;* but, in composing for songs,
the reigning taste seems to be quite out of nature, or rather the
reverse of nature, and yet like a torrent, hurries them all away with
it; one or two perhaps only excepted.

You, in the spirit of some ancient legislators, would influence the
manners of your country by the united powers of poetry and music.
By what I can learn of *their* songs, the music was simple, con-
formed itself to the usual pronunciation of words, as to measure,
cadence or emphasis, &c. never disguised and confounded the language by making a long syllable short, or a short one long when

3. Both "Chevy Chace" and "The Spanish Lady" are contained in *The
Minstrelsy of England* (2 vols., Angener, London, 1905–1909), and V.
Jackson, *Melodies from the Thirteenth to the Eighteenth Century* (Dent, Lon-
don, 1910). No modern printing of "The Children in the Wood" has been
located. The editors are indebted to Brooks Shepard, Jr., librarian of the
Yale Music Library, for this information.

sung; their singing was only a more pleasing, because a melodious manner of speaking; it was capable of all the graces of prose oratory, while it added the pleasure of harmony. A modern song, on the contrary, neglects all the proprieties and beauties of common speech, and in their place introduces its *defects* and *absurdities* as so many graces. I am afraid you will hardly take my word for this, and therefore I must endeavour to support it by proof. Here is the first song I lay my hand on. It happens to be a composition of one of our greatest masters, the ever famous Handel. It is not one of his juvenile performances, before his taste could be improved and formed: It appeared when his reputation was at the highest, is greatly admired by all his admirers, and is really excellent in its kind. It is called, *The additional* FAVOURITE *Song in Judas Maccabeus.*[4] Now I reckon among the defects and improprieties of common speech, the following, viz.

    1. *Wrong placing the accent or emphasis,* by laying it on words of no importance, or on wrong syllables.

    2. *Drawling;* or extending the sound of words or syllables beyond their natural length.

    3. *Stuttering;* or making many syllables of one.

    4. *Unintelligibleness;* the result of the three foregoing united.

    5. *Tautology;* and

    6. *Screaming,* without cause.

For the *wrong placing of the accent, or emphasis,* see it on the word *their* instead of being on the word *vain.*

with   *their*   vain   My - ſte - rious   Art

And on the word *from,* and the wrong syllable *like.*

    4. The Israelitish Woman's aria, "Wise men flatt'ring may deceive us," in "Judas Maccabeus," Act II, *Georg Friedrich Händel's Werke,* XXII (Leipzig, [1866]), 152–7. In this authoritative edition the aria is set in the key of F; for the excerpts given below BF was probably using a popularized edition of the single aria, in which the music had been transposed to the key of G.

God-*like* Wisdom *from* a — bove.

For the *Drawling*, see the last syllable of the word *wounded*.

Nor can heal the wound*ed* Heart

And in the syllable *wis*, and the word *from*, and syllable *bove*

God-like *Wis*dom *from* a - *bove*

For the *Stuttering*, see the words *ne'er relieve*, in

Ma - gick Charms can *ne'er re - lieve* you

Here are four syllables made of one, and eight of three; but this is moderate. I have seen in another song that I cannot now find, seventeen syllables made of three, and sixteen of one; the latter I remember was the word *charms;* viz. *Cha, a, a, a, a, a, a, a, a, a, a, a, a, a, a, a, arms*. Stammering with a witness!

For the *Unintelligibleness;* given this whole song to any taught singer, and let her sing it to any company that have never heard it; you shall find they will not understand three words in ten. It is therefore that at the oratorio's and operas one sees with books in their hands all those who desire to understand what they hear sung by even our best performers.

For the *Tautology;* you have, *with their vain mysterious art,* twice repeated; *Magic charms can ne'er relieve you,* three times. *Nor can heal the wounded heart,* three times. *Godlike wisdom from above,* twice; and, *this alone can ne'er deceive you,* two or three times. But this is reasonable when compared with *the Monster Polypheme, the Monster Polypheme,* a hundred times over and over, in his admired *Acis and Galatea.*[5]

As to the *screaming;* perhaps I cannot find a fair instance in this song; but whoever has frequented our operas will remember many. And yet here methinks the words *no* and *e'er,* when sung to these notes, have a little of the air of *screaming,* and would actually be scream'd by some singers.

No magic charms can *e'er* re—lieve you.

I send you enclosed the song with its music at length. Read the words without the repetitions. Observe how few they are, and what a shower of notes attend them: You will then perhaps be inclined to think with me, that though the words might be the principal part of an ancient song, they are of small importance in a modern one; they are in short only *a pretence for singing.* I am, as ever, Your affectionate brother,   B.F.

P. S. I might have mentioned *Inarticulation* among the defects in common speech that are assumed as beauties in modern singing. But as that seems more the fault of the singer than of the composer, I omitted it in what related merely to the composition. The fine singer in the present mode, stifles all the hard consonants, and polishes away all the rougher parts of words that serve to distinguish them one from another; so that you hear nothing but an admirable pipe, and understand no more of the song, than you would from its tune played on any other instrument. If ever it was the ambition of musicians to make instruments that should imitate the human voice, that ambition seems now reversed, the voice

5. Chorus, "Wretched Lovers!," in "Acis and Galatea," Act II, *ibid.,* III (Leipzig, [1859]), 53–9.

aiming to be like an instrument. Thus wigs were first made to imitate a good natural head of hair; but when they became fashionable, though in unnatural forms, we have seen natural hair dressed to look like wigs.

From Peter Collinson   ALS: University of Pennsylvania Library

My Dear Friend.   Fryday [1764–1765][6]
   I think you[r] Vindication is admirably well drawn up You make Mee Smile now and then with a keen back Stroke and then with a Home Thrust. It must Mortifie Allen for it cuts Him to the Quick.[7] He has poisoned the Barclay Family.[8] I wish you had one to spare to send my penny post Directed to Mr. David Barclay Junior in Cheapside.
   If you have them not to spare I think they Should be reprinted Here you'l find them of great Service to remove prejudices.
   I am much yours   P COLLINSON

Addressed: To / Ben Franklin Esqr. / at / Mrs Stephensons / in Craven Street / Strand

6. So dated because of Collinson's discussion of BF's "Vindication," his *Remarks on a Late Protest,* Nov. 5, 1764 (above, pp. 429–41), which BF probably put in Collinson's hands soon after arriving in London on Dec. 10, 1764. See George S. Wykoff, "Peter Collinson's Letter Concerning Franklin's 'Vindication,' " *PMHB,* LXVI (1942), 99–105.
7. In his *Remarks* BF had attacked William Allen on a number of counts.
8. The Barclays, John and David, Jr. (above, IX, 190–1 n), were important London merchants who were on good terms with both the Assembly and the Proprietary party. They were grandsons of Robert Barclay, the famous apologist for the Quakers. In the fall of 1764 Allen had written them a stream of letters attacking BF with such epithets as the "Disturber of the Peace" (Sept. 25) and "the grand Incendiary" (Nov. 20) and had even asked David Barclay, Jr., to expose BF to his superior at the Post Office, Lord Hyde (Oct. 24). Lewis B. Walker, ed., *The Burd Papers Extracts from Chief Justice William Allen's Letter Book* ([Pottsville, Pa.], 1897), pp. 57, 62, 63. In his *Remarks* BF had printed a letter from the Barclays to James and Drinker expressing the hope that when Allen arrived in Philadelphia he would use his influence, "added to the *Power* and *Commissions* the Proprietaries have invested him with," to restore harmony and tranquillity. Allen had, however, joined the other proprietary leaders in concealing the news of the Penns' concession on the taxation of their located but uncultivated lands, the announcement of which was the one action by which he might have significantly reduced the animosities building up during the election campaign.

From John Greenwood[9]

Printed card with MS insertions: Historical Society of Pennsylvania

[1764–1775][1]

Mr. GREENWOOD,

TAKES the Liberty to inform *Dr. Franklin and friends* that he has THREE very large and CAPITAL PICTURES just arrived, and to be seen at an empty House, almost opposite the COCOA TREE, PALL MALL, from TEN in the Morning till THREE o'Clock.

From [Alexander Small][2]

MS not found; reprinted from Benjamin Franklin, *Experiments and Observations on Electricity*, 1769 edition, pp. 440–1.[3]

[*c.* 1764][4]

I have just recollected that in one of our great storms of lightning, I saw an appearance, which I never observed before, nor ever heard described. I am persuaded that I saw *the* flash which struck St. Bride's steeple. Sitting at my window, and looking to the north, I saw what appeared to me a solid streight rod of fire, moving at a very sharp angle with the horizon. It appeared to my eye as about

9. On John Greenwood, Boston-born painter and art dealer, who moved from Amsterdam to London in 1764, see above, IX, 357 n.

1. Greenwood might have sent this card at any time during BF's second mission to England; the "CAPITAL PICTURES" to which it refers have not been identified.

2. So identified because among BF's scientific friends, which the author of this letter obviously was, Small appears to be the only person whom the initials A.S. fit.

3. Printed as Letter XLVI, as it is also in the 1774 edit., where it appears on pp. 450–1. In both places it is headed "From Mr. A.S. to B.F."

4. This letter could not have been written any earlier than June 18, 1764, for it describes an event that took place on the afternoon of that day; at ten minutes before three, during a spectacular summer storm, lightning struck and "very greatly injured" the steeple of St. Bride's Church, Fleet Street. English electricians were fascinated by the catastrophe and two of them wrote papers about it which were read before the Royal Society. On Dec. 1, 1764 (above, p. 479), Small mentioned a "former Letter" to BF which the editors have not found. The present document may have been the whole or a part of that letter. For the letters on the destruction of the church steeple, see *Phil. Trans.*, LIV (1764), 201–27, 227–34.

two inches diameter, and had nothing of the zig-zag lighning motion. I instantly told a person sitting with me, that some place must be struck at that instant. I was so much surprized at the vivid distinct appearance of the fire, that I did not hear the clap of thunder, which stunned every one besides. Considering how low it moved, I could not have thought it had gone so far, having St. Martin's, the New Church, and St. Clement's steeples in its way.[5] It struck the steeple a good way from the top, and the first impression it made in the side is in the same direction I saw it move in. It was succeeded by two flashes, almost united, moving in a pointed direction. There were two distinct houses struck in Essex street. I should have thought the rod would have fallen in Covent Garden, it was so low. Perhaps the appearance is frequent, though never before seen by Yours,   A.S.

5. St. Martin's-in-the-Fields on the northeast side of Trafalgar Square, St. Mary-le-Strand in the Strand (the "New Church"), and St. Clement Danes, also in the Strand; thus the lightning came from west to east.

Index

Compiled by Margery Riddle

A.B., BF pseudonym, 173

Aberdeen, University of, Byles's degree from, 90 n

Account of the European Settlements in America, An: quoted in *Cool Thoughts,* 163–4; authorship, 164 n

Accounts: with J. Williams, 178; with Smith, Wright & Gray, 179–80; with Henton Brown & Son, 264 n; with Becket, 265; BF's Journal and Ledger, 518–20; for BF's house, 453–6

Achart, Adam. *See* Echert, Adam.

Address to the Freeholders and Inhabitants of Pennsylvania, An: attributed to Galloway, 154; supply bill disputes, 154; probably sent to Jackson, 186 n

Aepinus, Franz Ulrich Theodor: return of book by, 22, 230, 246, 254; theory of magnetism and electricity, 254

Africa, hospitality and honor of Negroes in, 61–2

Afterlife, BF's faith in, 79, 231–2, 241, 253

Agency Act of 1759: BF accused of violating, 370, 411, 498–9; BF's defense on, 438–41, 473; BF's commissions under, 498 n

Agents, colonial: confer with Grenville on stamp tax, 237 n, 242; joint efforts against parliamentary taxation recommended, 347, 351, 366, 395–6, 406, 452. *See also* Charles, Robert; Franklin, Benjamin; Jackson, Richard; Mauduit, Jasper.

Agents, Pa.: agree to Privy Council stipulations, 8, 18 n, 112, 203, 209, 220 n, 268, 278, 284; transmit parliamentary grant, 19 n; instructions on petitions, 198, 219, 229, 239, 255, 311, 357–8, 398 n, 402–3, 423–4; promise to amend supply acts, 204–5; to cooperate with other agents, 347, 351, 366; instructions on British legislation, 347–51, 366, 396–7 n, 424–5; should not be trusted with petition, 403, 405, 412; expense should be reduced, 406, 412, 504; BF to join Jackson as, 422–3 (*see also* Franklin, Benjamin); need for BF as, 426, 451; BF's hopes for, 429; will work for colonies, 532

Agriculture, Arts and Commerce, Society of. *See* Society of Arts.

Air, electrification of, Kinnersley experiment on, 98–9, 244

Albany, N.Y.: BF aid to troops at, 319; Phila. mail to, 401

Albany Congress: J. Penn at, 184 n; BF's plan for revenues at, 237 n

Alehouses: excessive number of, BF on, 139; licensing abuse, 139–40

Alexander, James: identified, 415 n; Parker prints for, 414–15

Alexander, William, Lord Stirling: recommends Read, 97 n; on N.Y.-N.J. dispute, 415

Alexandria, Va.: Bernard, Jr. stranded in, 6 n, 31; Bernard, Jr., leaves, 78 n; Phila. mail to, 401

Alison, Francis: identified, 526 n; helps stop Paxton Boys, 72; Bernard wishes son to board with, 153; BF to see for Bernard, 178; plan for association of colleges, 192 n; signs letter against royal government, 290 n; charged with intimidating voters, 379; part in Smith's *Answer,* 526, 527; signs Presbyterians' address, 526 n

Alleghenies, settlers not to go west of, 101 n

Allen, Andrew, James, or John, possible trip to England, 483 n

Allen, Ralph: biographical note, 507 n; BF recommended to, 506

Allen, William: knows of Jackson's efforts, 34; opposes colonial taxation, 34–5 n, 234 n, 312 n, 445 n, 462 n, 463 n, 509; angered by attack on judicial tenure, 130 n, 358; at hearing on paper money, 177 n; returns to Pa., 214 n, 263, 312 n, 317, 436; brings Penn supply bill instructions, 214 n; delivers Jackson's letter to BF, 264 n, 327; signs report on proprietary taxation, 285, 286; threatens to withdraw from politics, 288 n; admits justice of proprietary taxation, 312; Jackson discusses petition with, 312, 425 n; withholds Proprietors' decision on taxation dispute, 312 n, 317 n, 436 n, 543 n; cites Jackson on cost of change of government, 313 n, 327–8, 375, 463–4; subscribes to linen factory, 315; brings "no News," 317; complete breach with BF, 328; fails to get petition recalled, 339–40, 357; on Assembly committee on colonial tax, 347 n; on petitioning instructions, 358 n; as campaign issue, 369; inaction in 1742 election riots, 377 n; relations with W. Smith, 388 n; votes against BF appointment as agent, 407 n; reveals proprietary concessions, 410, 424 n, 434–6, 494, 495, 502–4; signs protest on BF appointment, 412, 438 n; attacks on BF's reputation, 431, 434, 438 n, 473–4, 543; remarks against royal government, 432, 457, defended, 488, 508–12; defends his loyalty, 432 n; as commissioner for boundary dispute, 432 n; Assembly seat, 433, 493–4; campaigns quietly, 436 n; signs report approving BF account, 439, 473, 501; enemy of BF, 439; part in fixing BF's agency salary, 440, 501–2; role in proposed stamp act, 445 n; BF's *Remarks* disturb, 457, 473–4, 543; Jackson's opinion of, 462, 463; Jackson too frank with, 462–4; "defense" of, 487; Smith answers BF's *Remarks* on, 493–4, 501–2, 506–12; BF's ingratitude to former friend, 501, 506–8; secured posts for BF, 506; wishes to resign as chief justice, 506; not dependent on Proprietors, 506; wealth, 506 n; on colonial taxation, 509–10 n; instigates *Answer* to BF's *Remarks*, 525; regrets signing Protest, 527; to influence J. Penn, 529; letters from, quoted or cited, 130 n, 327 n, 358 n, 404 n, 429–30 n, 432 n, 492 n, 509–10 n, 533 n

Allen family, Bouquet's relations with, 324 n

Amboy (Perth Amboy), N.J.: Indians escorted to, 28, 68 n; Dutch ship taken at, 91, 178; postal rates, 343, 536; post office unprofitable in, 416

America. *See* Colonies, North American

American Magazine, Smith's charges against BF in, 389

Amherst, Jeffery: requisition for troops, 7, 96, 212; Assembly to cooperate with, 7, 105, 113, 205; Gage succeeds, 7 n; excludes Pa. from 1761 return, 19 n, 108; Montgomery joins, 94 n; plan for Indian campaign, 96 n, 105 n, 217–18 n, 224 n; Pa. feels ill-used by, 108; cannot help Nantucket whalers, 187

Ammunition. *See* Arms and Ammunition

Anderson, William, paid for plastering BF's house, 454, 455

Anglicans. *See* Church of England

Annapolis, Md.: BF and Foxcroft to confer in, 20; Bernard charge at, 91; plans for postal route to, 248; Foxcroft trip to,

249; post-office receipts, 251; Phila. mail to, 401; postal rates, 536

Anne, Queen: repeals So. Car. acts against dissenters, 163; orders dissenters protected, 166–7; projected sale of Pa. to, 293 n

Answer to a Bill in Chancery, printed by Parker, 415 n

Antes, Frederick: on "New Ticket," 390; defeated, 391, 394

Anti-proprietary party: denounces Indian massacres, 44; frontiersmen oppose, 81, 125, 360; election platform, 123; elective power (1764), 124 n; alignment against, 125; pamphlets for royal government, 154, 157; control of Assembly by Quaker members, 161–2, 327, 385; militia-bill failure used against, 360; attacked in campaign paper, 372–6; change of government issue against, 372–6; BF's leadership of, 376, 515; slate, 390; loses ground in Phila. Co. elections, 392; keeps Assembly majority, 393–4, 434; passes program, 407; fear of Presbyterians, 485 n. *See also* Elections.

Appeals, in tax cases, 120–1, 282. *See also* Commissioners of appeal.

Apty, Thomas, pay order for, 223

Arabs, hospitality, 59–60

"Argument for Making the Bills of Credit Bear Interest," 7–18; Assembly rejects, 9–11, 238

Aristocracy, colonies lack, 324

Arithmetic, study recommended, 450

Armbrüster, Anthony (Anton): prints *Narrative,* 42 n; prints "Petition to Crown" in German, 145; prints Galloway pamphlet, 154 n

Armonica: glasses for, awaited, 179; BF has on Boston trip, 179 n; for Josiah Williams, 179 n; R. Strahan plays, 333; parts for, received, 426; to be made in London, 427; bill for spindles, 446

Arms and ammunition: bill to keep Indians from, 25 n; Moravian Indians charged with supplying hostiles with, 64 n; Quakers accused of giving Indians, 102; lent to Pa., to be used by Bouquet, 225; troops to have, 262; French supply Indians with, 476, 528, 530

Armstrong, John: with Paxton Boys, 73 n; frontiersmen's attitude toward, 83 n

Army, British: escorts and guards friendly Indians, 28–9, 47, 68–9, 70, 75, 360 n; troops to be maintained in colonies, 34 n, 35, 76, 169–70, 181; aid requested against Paxton rioters, 42; and Lancaster massacre, 43; troops moved to Lancaster, 70;

will replace militia, 78, 169; fails to protect settlers, 83; attack on Cherokee remembered, 94; Pa. must depend on, 122; 22d Regiment forced back, 217; number insufficient for Indian wars, 224; campaign under Bouquet, 224 n, 225 n (*see* Bouquet); prevents Pa. riots, 305; BF's aid to, 318–19, 322–3; dispute over quartering in Phila., 319, 322, 378; necessary to awe colonies, 482; Allen's support of, 509. *See also* Amherst, Jeffery; Barracks, Phila.; Bouquet, Henry; Bradstreet, John; Gage, Thomas; Montgomery's (77th) Regiment; Royal American (60th) Regiment.

Arts et Metiers, sent to BF, 265

Ashbridge, George: identified, 10 n; debates supply bill funding, 10; signs Assembly reports, 93, 286

Assemblies, colonial: asked to instruct agents on taxation, 243 n; do not record minority protests, 430, 489. *See also* under names of colonies.

Assembly, Pa.: J. Penn alienates, 7, 104, 106, 117, 148, 150, 210–11, 286–8; accedes to Amherst's requisition, 7, 96 n, 105, 113, 205, 218; passes £50,000 supply bill, 7–11, 95–6, 104–6, 111, 207; debates funding of supply bill, 7–10; dispute with Penn on supply bill, 7–8, 10–11, 18 n, 95–6, 105–6, 111–12, 142–3 n, 154, 181 n, 203–13, 207, 216–17, 220–1, 224 n, 286–7, 312; anxious to avoid dispute with Penn, 8; bill on overpayment of parliamentary grant, 19, 108; ineffective in frontier defense, 22–5, 27; advises governor on protecting friendly Indians, 22–30; accused of indifference to frontier settlers, 25, 27, 44, 81, 82 n, 125, 185 n, 360; to pay for Indian refugees' upkeep, 25, 27; proposal on site of trial of murderers, 27–8, 82, 364; messages printed, 133 n, 149, 354; advice on apprehending murderers refused, 30–1 n, 306; denounced for Indian support, 44, 67, 82, 102 n; passes Riot Act, 47, 70–1, 104, 306; agrees to pass militia bill, 69–75, 77–8, 104; frontier grievances to be heard by, 74, 86–7 n, 185 n, 291 n; dispute on militia bill, 76 n, 78, 130–1, 141–2, 306, 360–5, 513, 514; report on conference on frontier complaints, 80–6, 87 n; unequal representation in, 81–2, 86–7 n, 123–4, 126, 161–2, 185 n, 207, 378–9, 382; Penn rejects joint hearing with, 85–6, 104, 107; legislative rights, 85–6, 135–6, 274–7, 302; report on open doors, 91–3; Penn tries to maneuver, 103, 107, 121–2; BF's

support of J. Penn in, 103; present to J. Penn, 103 n, 104; accused of violating royal prerogatives, 104, 106–7, 302, 514; passes new supply bill (£55,000, 1764), 106, 111; conference on lighthouse collector, 107 n; feels ill-used by Amherst, 108; right to issue drafts and certificates, 111, 117–18; adjourns to consult people on petition, 121, 132, 145–6, 153–4, 289–92; not responsible for supply–bill failure, 121, 132, 154; elective, not to be overawed, 121–21; wants royal government, 122, 125–6, 132–3, 149, 213, 289; adopts Resolves, 123–33 (*see also* Resolves); denies Proprietors' legislative power, 126, 135–6; relations with Proprietors, 127–8, 150; money granted to governors by, 127, 139, 271–7, 304; protects Denny, 127 n; committee report on taxation, 127, 138, 206, quoted, 285–6; complaint of license abuses, 128, 139–40, 522 n; claims quitrents for support of government, 138–9 n, 210–11; misrepresented to Crown, 141, 210–11; receives inhabitants' petitions for royal government, 146, 193, 194, 204, 290; disputes with Proprietors, 146–7, 158–60, 378; right of adjournment, 158, 170–1; debates and votes petition for royal government, 161 n, 193–8, 218, 247, 267, 268, 291–2, 308–10, 393–4, 397, 402–3, 424 (*see also* Petition to King, Assembly); elections to, protected by acts, 170–1; petition to King, 193–200; order of listing committee members, 193 n; BF elected speaker, 196, 205, 218; privilege of electing speaker, 196 n; protests not placed in minutes, 197, 307–9, 407, 408, 430–1, 489–90; gives cautions on Pa. privileges, 198, 200, 220 n, 302, 398 n, 403, 423–4; Penn will disregard abuse by, 203, 211–12, 220 n; concedes to Penn on supply bill, 204, 206–13, 217; does not amend earlier Supply Acts, 204–7, 286; waives rights for supply bill, 206–7, 213; adjourns for summer, 208; Proprietors' concessions withheld from, 213–14 n, 312 n, 317 n, 340, 410 n, 435–7; meets at Norris' house, 218; members' lack of good breeding, 220, 324 n; alleged bribery of Denny, 268, 271–7; report quoted, 275; Privy Council action on laws, 277–85; past proposals for royal government, 288–9; tributes to W. Penn, 297–8; BF epitaph uses abuse of Proprietors by, 298–9; accused of stirring up Indians, 305; bills to aid government, 306; bill to provision Shirley, 319; refuses to recall petition, 339–40, 357, 397–8 n, 403, 424; Saunders accused of misrepresenting, 340 n; joins in Mass. proposal to protest taxes, 347, 351; orders agent to cooperate with other agents, 347, 351, 366; instructions to Jackson on taxation, 347–51, 396–7 n; considering self-taxation plan, 350; pays BF's agency expenses and salary, 370 n, 383, 411, 439–40, 498, 501–2; action on election riots (1742), 377 n; jails W. Smith, 388; program unchanged by election, 393–4, 397, 407, 410 n, 434; Fox succeeds Norris as speaker, 393, 403–4; appoints BF co-agent, 393, 446–7, 451, 504; acts on R.I. taxation proposal, 396–7 n; elects Norris speaker, 402; receives Remonstrance against BF appointment, 402–6, 407; does not await Fox confirmation, 404, 411, 437; conciliation with Penns hoped for, 405–6, 410, 423, 424 n, 436–7, 464, 497–8; BF's role in actions of, 409, 431, 491–2; Proprietors' concessions informally reported to, 409–10, 494–5, 502–4; repays BF's expenses, 427 n; handling of parliamentary grants, 438–9, 499, 500–1; accepts BF's account, 439, 501; BF charged with padding *Votes*, 490–1; Dickinson to retire from, 527; Penn refuses to present proposals to, 529; *Votes* printed, 531. *See also* Committee of Correspondence; Elections; Lighthouse Bill; Militia Bill; Riot Act; Supply bills and acts.

Assessment of proprietary estates. *See* Proprietary estates, taxation of.

Assessors, Phila. Co., election of, 394

Association, Phila.: formed to defend against Paxton Boys, 71–2, 77, 103; BF first to sign, 103

Astronomer royal, candidates for, 481–2

Astronomy, BF reorders book on, 334

Atkinson, Cornelius, wounded volunteer, 223

Atrocities: Paxton Boys massacre Indians, 42–3 (*see also* Massacres); Inidan, in Ohio Valley, 96 n; David Owens scalps Indians, 173–4; school massacred, 335 n

Augusta, Fort: troops not protecting settlers, 83; armorer at, 223; disbursements at, 223; to be garrisoned, 261

Augusta Co., Va., Indian uprising in, 229 n

Autenried (Autenrieth, Handenried) Friedrich Wilhelm, executed, 188 n

"Authentic Account of the Cause of the Indian War, An," attacks Quakers, 180 n

Axe, soldier should carry, 225

Azores, wines exempted from Staple Act, 216 n

Babcock, Joshua, BF print for, 231

Bache, Franklin, given BF letter, 447 n

Bache, Margaret H., passes on BF letter, 447 n

Bache, Richard, postmaster general, 4 n

Bache, Sarah: annotates BF letter, 179 n; inherited property, 320. *See also* Franklin, Sarah.

Bache, Sarah (D.3.8.), inherits BF property, 320 n

Bacon, Anthony: identified, 476 n; presents currency bill, 176 n; BF to explain Indian problem to, 476

Bahama Islands: in new postal district, 39 n; proprietary government in, 126 n; postal service, 260 n

Baltimore, Lord: appointment of Md. governors, 293 n; proprietorship of, 463

Baltimore, Md.: plans for postal route to, 248; Phila. mail to, 401

Bangon, Conrad, paid, 455

Bank, preferred to paper money, 177

Bank of England, refuses Pa. money, 438, 498–9

Bankson, Andrew, elected county assessor, 394

Baptists, disputes about R.I. College, 192 n

Barbara (maid): alleged to be WF's mother, 370; BF's alleged treatment of, 370, 383–4; scurrilous reference to, 383

Barclay, John and David, Jr.: identified, 543 n; Allen prejudices against BF, 543

Barclay, David & Sons, letters cited and quoted, 130 n, 435, 504

"Bark wine," recipe for, 537

Barker, Robert: Jackson interviews on N.J. estate, 33–4; returns to India, 34 n

Barnes, Barnaby, elected county assessor, 394

Barons, Benjamin, appointed deputy postmaster general, 39 n, 260 n

Barr, John, Irish reject as sheriff, 467–8

Barracks, Phila.: Indians placed in, 28, 70; raid planned against, 30, 70–1; troops defend Indians in, 68, 69–74, 360 n; reenforced for defense, 71–2; troops to leave, 75; Indians leave, 87 n; care of sick Indians in, 224; Fox in charge of, 224, 373

Barton, Thomas: identified, 52 n; *The Conduct of the Paxton-Men*, refutes BF's *Narrative*, 52–3 n, 64 n, 66 n, biblical analogies, 64 n

Bartram, John: identified, 180 n; Collinson letters to, delivered, 180; sends botanical specimens for King, 352; neglected, 353; appointed royal botanist, 353 n; letter to, cited, 181 n

Bath, Mrs. Strahan seeks relief at, 241
Bayle, Pierre, *Dictionary*, BF asks for, 89
Baynton, John: identified, 187 n; provincial commissioner, 261. *See also* Baynton & Wharton.
Baynton & Wharton (Baynton, Wharton & Morgan): Quebec land scheme, 187–8, 427–8; want compensation, 187 n, 476; reimbursed with Iroquois land, 187 n; pay order for, 223; subscribes to linen factory, 315; letter from, 427–8; mentioned, 449 n
Bayonet, axe used in lieu of, 225
Bealknap (Belknap), Sir Robert de: biographical note, 141 n; judicial decisions, 141
Bean, Samuel, bill of exchange on, 427 n
Bearrd, Deanl, paid for work on BF's well, 456
Beaver skins, annual acknowledgment for Pa. grant, 129 n
Becket, Thomas: identified, 228 n; delays BF book order, 228, 264 n, 333; BF's account with, 264, 265; apologizes, 264–5; sends order, 265, 353–4; letter from, 264–5
Bedford, Gunning, Jr., marries, 339 n
Beissel, Johann Conrad: BF aids publication of hymnbook by, 443 n; Ephrata Community, 443 n
Bell, John, *Travels*, BF quotes, 59–60
Bengals (fabric), duty on, 76 n, 235 n
Benson, John. *See* Brinckloe, John.
Berks Co.: grievances, 81–3; Assembly representation, 81–2, 379 n, 382; represented on petition committee, 193
Bernard, Francis (1712–79): thanks BF for aid to son, 31, 79; to start sturgeon fishery, 31; fish pickling recipes for, 31–2, 87; starts settlement on Penobscot R., 31–2 n; Mt. Desert granted to, 32 n; to reimburse BF, 79, 88; repays BF, 91, 153, 178; suggests WF due share in prize, 91; assists at Harvard fire, 255 n; letters from, 31–2, 78–9, 91, 153; letters to, 6, 87–8, 133–4, 178
Bernard, Francis (1743–70): BF arranges return of, 6, 31; on way home, 78–9, 87; returns BF's horse, 78; BF returns belongings of, 88; BF pays bill of, 133; letters of, forwarded, 133; greetings to, 134
Bernard, Mrs. Francis: BF aids son of, 6 n; greetings to, 134
Bernard, John Peter, translator of Bayle's *Dictionary*, 89 n
Bernard, Thomas, to attend College of Phila., 153
Berne machine, for uprooting trees, 480

Berrien, John: identified, 97 n; recommended as N.J. second justice, 97 n; appointment not confirmed, 464 n
Berwick-on-Tweed, European goods to be laden in, 91 n
Bethlehem, Pa., Indian relations of Moravians at, 25
Bethehemites. *See* Moravians.
Betty (Koweenasee; Conestoga Indian), massacre of, 49
Biblical analogy, BF's use of, 56, 64 n, 288
Biddle, John, shrieval election, 394
Biles (Ryles), Thomas, property of, 320
Bilious fever. *See* Yellow fever.
Bill in the Chancery of New-Jersey: printed by Parker, 415 n; BF assistance on, 415 n
Bill of Complaint in the Chancery of New Jersey, printed by Weyman, 415 n
Bills of credit: BF on, 7–18, 182–4; not legal tender for quitrents, 8, 10, 11, 18 n, 137, 142, 282–4; not to be legal tender for contracts, 12–13; depreciation of, 13–14; act restraining, 35 (*see* Currency Act); issue for Supply Act of 1759, 277, 279, 282–4; legal tender of, 282–3; BF protects, 378
Bills of exchange, for BF's traveling expenses, 427 n
Birch, Thomas, translator of Bayle's *Dictionary*, 89 n
Bishop of London: ordains Dunlap, 421 n; letter to, quoted, 421–2 n
Bishops, appointment for America, 150, 168
Blackburn, John: signs Assembly reports, 93, 286; voting on Assembly motions, 403 n
Blake, John: on sturgeon pickling, 479; scheme for getting fish to London, 479 n
Blankets, troops to have, 262
Bligh, Mr., letter on Indian warfare, 325
Bliss, Nathaniel: biographical note, 480 n; death, 480
Bloodhounds: to be used against Indians, 239; sent from England, 240 n; use of, 240 n
Blunt, Catherine, greetings to, 202, 521
Blunt, Dorothea (Dolly): greetings to, 110, 202, 521; health, 110, 202
Board of Longitude, to meet on Harrison prize, 482
Board of Trade: BF's post-office report read to, 20 n; hearings on colonial currency, 35 n, 176–7; N.J. justices, 97 n; criticizes Penns, 126 n, 466–7, 474–5; report on judicial tenure, 130 n; agreement on sale of Pa. to Crown, 148 n; report on N.J. petition for royal government, 165; has

approved acts on Pa. rights, 170–1; hearings on Pa. supply Act, 209; Jackson's influence at, 234 n, 314 n; report on linen factory to, quoted, 316 n; rejects Egmont scheme, 324; nominates BF as commissioner in boundary dispute, 432n; report on Re-emitting Act, 466 n, 514 n

Bolton, Mary, marriage, 259 n

Bolton, Robert: biographical note, 259 n; delivers letter, 259; wants southern postmastership, 259–60; commission for Ga., 260 n

Bookkeeping: study of, recommended to Sarah F., 450; double-entry, used in BF's Ledger, 519–20

Book of CommonPrayer, recommended to Sarah F., 449–50

Books: distribution of, in America, 189–90; sold from London, 190

Booksellers: negligence, 258; list of American, 258

Boors, German, as hogs, 397, 434 n, 505

Bordentown, N.J., pickled sturgeon advertised at, 32 n

Boston: siege of (1775), 7 n; mail service to N.Y. improved, 20–1; BF sends parcels to, 90–1 n; smallpox epidemic, 232 n, 254 n, 356; BF recovers from injuries in, 249 n; ban on inoculation, 254 n; post office, attorney for, 338; postal rates, 344, 345, 535–6; Phila. mail to, 399, 400; Harrison named customs officer for, 460 n

Boston Gazette, letter in, not aimed at BF, 444–5

Botany: Bartram sends collection for King, 352; Young, Bartram made King's botanists, 353 n

Boundary, N.Y.-N.J.: dispute over, 414 n; commissioners appointed for, 432 n

Bouquet, Henry: identified, 217 n; Price serves under, 93 n; Owens interpreter for, 174 n; campaign against Ohio Indians, 217, 224 n, 229, 256, 325, 326 n, 335, 445, 446 n, 528; in Phila. to organize campaign, 217 n, 248 n; borrows money, 223; request for dogs, 224–5, granted, 239 n; asks for men and supplies, 224–6; troops under, 225 n, 261 n; can recommend for Carlisle post office, 248; wants to replace deserters, 266–7; friendship with BF, 266 n; request for more troops granted, 316–17; papers on Indian warfare sent to, 317, returned, 325; BF asks for testimonial, 318–19; BF's aid to, 319; political pamphlet sent to, 319; praises BF services to Army, 322–3; thanks BF for aid, 322–3; on Pa. government, 323–4; on colonial society, 324 n; plans to settle

Scioto R. with BF, 325; will ignore Bradstreet treaty, 326, 330; BF thanks for testimonial letter, 366; asked to mention BF in reports, 366–7; Canadian campaign, 368; sent pamphlet on Canada, 368; makes peace with Indians, 446 n, 458, 483, 485–6, 523, 530; returns with hostages, 475; hostages escape from, 523, 528, 530; to come to Phila., 523, 530; letters of, cited and quoted, 317 n, 483, 485–6; letters from, 224–6, 266–7, 321–6; letters to, 316–19, 366–8

Bowdoin, James: attachments for telescope of, 21–2, 99, 244–5; BF print for, 90; BF to send Narrative to, 91 n; letter for Canton sent by BF, 246; likes BF print, 247; waiting for telescope, 452; effect on Mass. petition, 452 n; letters from, 21–2, 246–7, 451–3

Bowman, John, elected county assessor, 394

Braddock, Edward: BF's services to, 318–19, 322; mentioned, 7 n

Bradford, William: prints political writings, 267, 268, 408, 457, 486; note to, quoted, 408

Bradstreet, John: campaign against Indians, 217–18 n, 224 n, 326 n, 335; Detroit conference, 218 n; makes unauthorized Indian treaty, 218 n, 326, 329–31, 333, 335–7, 366; treaty repudiated, 326 n, 336 n, 446; BF's doubts on treaty of, 331, 337, 388; failure to join Bouquet, 528

Bravery, and mercy, 69

Bread, duty on, 179 n

Bribery, of Pa. governors, 271–7

Brinckloe, John (alias John Benson), reprieved, 188 n

Bristol, Eng., bloodhounds shipped from, 240 n

Bristol, Pa., Phila. mail to, 401

Britannus Americanus, piece in Boston Gazette by, 445 n

British Honduras. See Mosquito Shore.

Broadfield, Edward: pickled sturgeon recipe of, praised, requested, 32; Bernard will not compete with, 32

Brown, ——, mentioned as Paxton spokesman, 73 n

Brown, Enoch, massacred with children, 335 n

Brown, Henton: identified, 174 n; Pa. Gaz. sent to, 174

Brown, James, identified, 174 n

Brown, Nicholas, signs letter, 397

Brown, William, subscribes to linen factory, 315

Brown, Wilson, sells lot, 315

Brown, Henton, & Son: bills drawn on, 264, 333; BF's account with, 264

Brown & Collinson: BF deposits money with, 427 n; BF draft from, 520

Brown University. *See* Rhode Island, College of.

Brownrigg, William, *On the Art of Making Common Salt;* recommended by BF, 88

Brunswick, N.J., Phila. mail to, 401

Bryan, George: on "New Ticket," 390; elected, 391, 468 n; votes against BF appointment, 407 n; signs protest on BF appointment, 412; named justice, 468, 472, 484

Brycelius, Paul Daniel: identified, 73 n; helps stop Paxton Boys, 72

Buckmaster, George, BF print for, 231

Bucks Co.: Assembly representation, 81, 123, 379; bill for trial of Indian massacrers in, 82; petition for royal government from, 146; represented on petition committee, 193; election results, 393; new commission for justices, 531

Budden, Richard: carries mail, 263–4 n, 317 n, 340 n; commands *Phila. Packet,* 265 n

Bull, William: identified, 63 n; conducts Indians, 63

Burd, James, pay order for, 223

Burgesses, House of (Va.), refuses Amherst requisition, 96 n

Burgh, James: biographical note, 100 n; in Honest Whigs Club, 98 n; greetings to, 100; *Political Disquisitions,* 100 n

Burke, Edmund, Harrison assistant to, 460 n

Burke, William, book on colonies by, 164 n

Burlington, N.J.: Phila. mail to, 401; BF's friends in, 429; postal rates, 536

Burnet, seed sent, 258

Bushy Run, battle of, 217 n

Bute, Earl of: prints of, ordered, 334; aids Bartram, 353 n

Buttermilk, used to "correct" salt, 88

Button-mold Bay, discovery reported, 182

Buttons: BF's tale of natural, 182; sent to Collinson, 182, 352

Byles, Mather: biographical note, 90 n; BF print for, 90; letter from, cited, 90 n

Cadwalader, Rebecca, marriage and death, 525 n

Cadwalader, Thomas, provincial commissioner, 261 n

Calas, Jean, Voltaire on execution of, 368

Calicoes, duty on, 76 n, 235 n

Callender, Robert: identified, 261 n; pay order for, 223; to victual troops, 261

Calvinist German Church, Phila., needs money, 201

Calvinists, German: against BF, 327 n; reversal on petitioning King, 327 n

Cambridge, Md., Phila. mail to, 401

Cambridge University, election of high steward, 481

Camomile tea, recommended for stomach, 538 n

Campbell, Francis: identified, 248 n; recommended for post office, 248

Canada: postal service for, 41; pamphlet on, sent to Bouquet, 368; French, as check on colonial ambitions, 482. *See also* Nova Scotia; Quebec.

Canada Indians, accompany Owens, 528

Canada Pamphlet (1760): tone of, 45; refutes giving up French Canada, 482 n

Canton, John: and Bowdoin telescope, 21–2, 99, 244–5, 452; and Kinnersley experiment, 98 n, 99, 244; experiments on compressibility of liquids, 245–6; BF sends Bowdoin letter to, 246; BF to answer, 353; letter from, 244–6; letter to, 97–100

Captains: postal regulations for, 39–40 n, 40–1, 342–3; payment to, 40, 342

Cardigan, Earl of, claim to St. Lucia, St. Vincent, 175, 238

Carlisle, Pa.: British troops at, 42, 43; troops leave, 70, 226 n; Bouquet in, 224 n; needs postmaster, 248; Phila. mail to, 401; Pa. troops return to, 529

Carlisle, Treaty of, BF at, 64 n

Carns, Capt., Owens surrenders to, 174

Carolana: BF pessimistic about, 20; Coxes to clarify scheme for, 152; terms for sharing in, 185. *See also* Coxe grant.

Carolina, Hamilton sails on, 458 n, 524 n

Carpenter, Emanuel, signs Assembly tax report, 286

Carriages, to carry spare shoes for troops, 225

Cash, Caleb, Jr. (F. 2.3): identified, 395 n; elected coroner, 394

Catawba Indians, Iroquois protect delegates, 63

Caton, Capt. J., carries mail, pickled sturgeon, 334

Cavalry, *See* Horse, Light.

Cavendish, Lord Charles, greetings to, 99–100

Cavendish, Henry, greetings to, 100

Central America, British-Spanish dispute over, 236 n

Chaleur, Bay of: scheme for land grant at, 188, 428; suitable for Nantucket whalers, 188

Chamberlain, Mason: has prints made of BF portrait, 89n; BF distributes prints, 89–90, 90–1 n, 230 n; BF pays for portrait, 520

Champlain, Lake, scheme for land grant at, 428

Chapman, Abraham: on committee for petition to King, 193; position on petition, 193 n; signs Assembly tax report, 286

Charles, Robert: agrees to Supply Act amendments, 204, 220 n, 284; co-depositor for parliamentary grants, 500 n; urged to oppose colonial taxation, 509 n. See also Agency, Pa.

Charles II: first Navigation Act of, 35 n; grant to W. Penn, 129 n (see Charter, royal); revokes charters, 167, 168 n

Charleston, S.C.: postal service to, 3 n; to be southern central post office, 39; Timothy postmaster at, 93 n; Ga. post-office route suggested, 259; postal rates, 344, 536; Phila. mail to, 402

Charlestown, Md., Phila. mail to, 401

Charlotte, Queen, Pringle physician to, 352

Charter of Privileges (W. Penn): on Assembly representation, 82 n, 382 n; Proprietors' encroachments on, 127–8, 139, 159 n; Assembly rights, 159 n; guarantees liberty of conscience, 161 n, 162 n; provision for changing, 162 n, 405; on Assembly elections, 291; provision for uniting Pa. and Del. assemblies, 382 n

Charter rights and privileges. See Privileges.

Charter, royal, of Pa.: powers of absentee Proprietors in, 126 n; proprietary acknowledgments to Crown in, 129 n; assignment of powers, 135–6; proprietary instructions violate, 136–8; reserves legislative assent to Crown, 136; Penn's refusal to pass supply bill violates trust of, 277; Proprietors' rights under, 289; parliamentary taxes will violate, 347–50; parliamentary taxing power under, 348–9 n; Parliament had no part in, 349 n; BF accused of selling, 375; no provision for Assembly representation 382 n; extension to Del., 465–6; approval of Pa. laws under, 475; Pa. privileges under, 511. See also Privileges.

Chauncy, Charles: identified, 255 n; greetings to, 255

Cherokee (Indians), report on, 94–5

Cherokee War, Fort Prince George besieged during, 94 n

Chester, Md., Phila. mail to, 401

Chester, Pa., BF embarks from, 418 n, 427 n, 447–9, 521

Chester Co.: Assembly representation, 81,
123, 379; bill for trial of massacrers in, 82; petition for royal government from, 146; represented on petition committee, 193; Dickinson at court in, 268; Dunlap gives post office land in, for debt, 419, 469 n; Moore appointed chief justice for, 468, 472–3, 485, 523, 531; justices appointed for, 485, 522–3

Chestnut timber, in Lake Champlain area, 428

Chestnut Hill, Pa., Paxton Boys march through, 72

"Chevy Chase," BF recommends, 539

Chew, Benjamin: confers with Paxton leaders, 73; unpopular, 105; advises withholding Proprietors' concessions, 214 n; keeps silent on concessions, 280 n; advisor to J. Penn, 288 n; drafts Del. address, 465 n; urges Quaker appointments, 523; support of, 526; letters of, quoted, 280 n, 318 n, 328 n, 402 n, 465 n, 509–10 n

Chew, Joseph: biographical note, 109 n; BF recommends for customs post, 109

Chichester, Pa., liquor license fees, 522 n

"Children in the Wood, The," BF recommends, 539

Chillaway, Job, pay order for, 223

China, duty on fabrics from, 235 n

Chinese prints, sent to Stiles, 230

Chronometer: dispute over prize for, 481, 482; testing of, 482

Church of England, Anglicans: political alignment of, 125 n; prospects for bishops and church courts in colonies, 150, 168–9; Penns drawn to, 158, 279 n; laws favoring, 163 n, 168; in N.J. government, 167; members against BF, 327 n; no BF calumny on, 505

Churchill, Charles, The Ghost, quoted, 516

Cinchona. See Peruvian bark.

Civil liberties and privileges. See Privileges.

Clap, Thomas, plan for association of colleges, 192 n

Clayton, Asher, mentioned, 223

Climate, Pa., excessive heat, 256

Cloth, clothing: duty on, 76 n; British monopoly on, 183; colonial manufacture of, 183–4, 314–15; price of, 314–15; American wool insufficient for, 359. See also Linen; Wool.

Club of Thirteen: members of, 228 n

Clubs. See Club of Thirteen; Honest Whigs; Monday Club.

Clymer, Balti, paid for carting, 455

Coal, Louisburgh mines, 182

Cod, fisheries in Bay of Chaleur, 428

Coffeehouses, collect ship letters, 40 n

Cogly, James, pay order for, 224
Cold: effect on compressibility of liquids, 245; relation to electrical conductivity, 254
Colden, Alexander: inquires for E. Holland, 232; forwards BF mail, 340
Colden, Cadwallader: refuses Pa. Indians, 28-9; mentioned, 232 n
Coleman, William, Mifflin works for, 78 n
Colleges, colonial: union of, preferred, 192; proposed association of, 192 n. *See also* Harvard College; New Jersey, College of; Philadelphia, College of; Rhode Island, College of.
Collinson, Peter: gets Bartram appointed royal botanist, 353 n; recipe for piles, 537; letters of, cited, 181 n, 250 n; letter from, 543; letters to, 173-4, 180-4, 352-3
Colonies, North American: to be taxed for troops, 34 n, 35, 76, 169-70, 181 (*see also* Taxation, parliamentary); minerals, catalogue of, 97; plans for settling new, 97 (*see also* Settlement); Currency Act for, 176-7; little influence in England, 181; governors yield to assemblies, 207; lack of aristocracy, 324; botanical collection from, 352; need for BF in London, 426; royal government urged for, 478; British fear independence of, 482; BF becomes publicist for, 482 n. *See also* Agents, colonial; Economy, North American; Rights, colonial; Settlement; Trade, colonial.
Commission on N.Y.-N.J. boundary, BF appointed to, 414 n, 432 n
Commissioners of appeal, Pa.: expected to interpret disputed clause, 120-1; refuse to interpret, 214 n, 503 n; provision of, demanded, 282
Commissioners, provincial. *See* Provincial commissioners.
Committee of Correspondence, Pa.: directions to, 198, 398 n, 403; instructions to Jackson, 198, 219, 229, 239, 255, 311, 357-8, 375, 396-7, 423-5; postal charges, 257 n; greetings to, 313; members of, 422 n; instructs BF on agency, 422-3; Jackson's letters to mentioned, 473; letters from, 422-6
Commons, House of: expels Wilkes, 76 n; does not hold open debates, 92; Assembly examines journals of, 92 n; representation in, 124; passes colonial currency bill, 176 n; procedures imitated by colonies, 196 n, 308; Jackson's influence in, 234 n; BF reports Pa. population to, 290 n; does not record protests, 308, 430, 489; BF reorders debates of, 334; concurs in colonial taxation, 347; resolution on

stamp act, 396; Mass. petition on taxation to, 452 n
Composers, delight one another but not BF, 539
Comptroller, Post Office: salary paid, 250; receipts, 251; fixed salary for, 414 n. *See also* Parker, James.
Conestoga, Pa.: plans to try murders of Indians at, 27-8, 82; reports massacre, 42 n. *See also* Conestoga Manor Indians.
Conestoga Manor Indians: killed at Conestoga Manor, 9, 19, 26-7, 42, 50-1, 77, 102, 103, 160, 247, 304 n, 305, 378; killed at Lancaster, 42 (*see also* Lancaster); part of Iroquois, 47; welcomed first settlers, 48, 65; treaties with W. Penn, 48; numbers decrease, 48; welcome J. Penn, 50; charges against, 64-5. *See also* Massacre.
Congregational Church, Congregationalists: establishment in Mass., 168 n; disputes about R.I. college, 192 n
Connecticut: overpaid by parliamentary grant, 19 n; men granted for Indian campaign, 218 n; retains royal charter, 348 n; mercuric inoculation introduced in, 356 n; judicial role of assemblies criticized, 478; royal government urged for, 478 n
Connecticut Gazette: revived, 241 n; management of, 413 n
Conscience, liberty of. *See* Religion; Privileges.
Constitution, Pa.: legislative rights in, 86, 272, 274-7, 302; protects rights, 170; violated by forced supply-bill amendments, 207; Assembly will not endanger, 220 n; proprietary rights in, 274, 276, 292-5, 297; compels bribery of governors, 276, 293-4; proprietary encroachments on, 294, 295, 301-3; proprietary criticism of, 294-5, 301; proposed law to limit, 294-5 n; BF's party charged with wanting to destroy, 372-6; privileges of, unknown in royal governments, 424; lack of legislative council, 489. *See also* Charter of Privileges; Charter, royal; Privileges.
Continental Congress: elects BF postmaster general, 3 n; sets up postal service, 3 n; invites Price, 100 n
Contracts: BF on governmental control of, 12; currency not legal tender for, 12-13
Convicts from England, to be executed, 188
Cooke, Mr., takes notes at Privy Council hearings, 209 n
Cool Thoughts on the Present Situation of Our Public Affairs, 153-73; publication date of, 153 n; distribution of, 154, 157; answers to, 157 (*see also Plain Dealer*); sent to friends, 181 n, 185, 189, 190 n,

332; purpose, 185; Bowdoin comments on, 247
Coombe, Thomas (1721–1799), appointed collector, 107 n
Coombe, Thomas (1747–1822), mentioned, 107 n
Coon, Michael, paid for digging BF's foundation, 455
Cooper, Grey: identified, 537 n; greetings from, 246; BF sends medicinal recipe to, 537; friendship with BF, 537 n; letter to, 537
Cooper, Samuel: identified, 90 n; BF print for, 90; BF to send *Narrative* to, 91 n; greetings to, 255
Corn, Indian, harvest of, and treaty, 331
Cornbury, Lord, instructions on liberty of conscience to, 166–7
Coroner, Phila. Co., election of, 394
Council, Pa.: rejects Assembly advice on Paxton affair, 30–1 n, 83–6, 107, 306; advises on quartering Indians in Phila., 70; sends delegation to Paxton Boys, 73, 77; hears "Remonstrance," 81; minutes cited, 85 n; members for joint hearing, 85 n; at BF's house during Paxton crisis, 103; denies proprietary veto power, 136; J. Penn serves on, 184 n; advises new amendments to supply bill, 204; old advisors withdraw from, 287–8; not legislative, 485 n (*see also* Legislative council); recommends law to amend Supply Act, 503 n; criticized, 532
Counter-petition: Presbyterians urged to support, 256; circulation of, 264, 385; BF refutes, 271, 300–7; large majority said to support, 406
Counter-petition, Lancaster Co.: BF discounts, 218, 291; number of signers, 218, 291
Courts, Act for Establishing, protects appointment of judges, 170
Courts, Pa.: circuit sessions wanted, 87 n; judicial tenure in, 130, 140–1, 147, 301, 513–14; trials compared with courts martial, 364; proof in, 368; J. Penn ignores Assembly remonstrances on, 468; J. Penn's partisan appointments to, 468, 472–3, 484–5, 522–3, 531–2. *See also* Judges; Justices.
Courts martial: Penn wants provision for, 131; disagreement on, 362–4; in Militia Act of 1755, 362 n
Courts of Judicature, Supplementary Act for, disallowed, 513
Coxe, Charles, subscribes to linen factory, 315 n
Coxe, Dr. Daniel: heirs revive grant to, 108

n (*see* Coxe grant); memorial on Carolana claim found, 175
Coxe, Daniel, Jr.: explains settlement scheme, 152; Jackson to write, 238, 311, anxious about letters to, 311
Coxe, William: to confer on settlement scheme, 152; clarifies terms for sharing grant, 185
Coxe & Furman: sends pickled sturgeon for premium, 334, report on, 479; advertises pickled sturgeon, 334 n
Coxe grant: BF and heir to discuss, 108; Jackson advises on, 175–6; terms for sharing in, clarified, 185; Jackson to write on, 238
Crafton, Robert, letter to, quoted, 370–1 n
Creeks (Indians), report on, 94–5
Critical Review: reviews Galloway's *Speech*, 332 n; on Voltaire, quoted, 368 n
Croghan, George: identified, 476 n; returns to Phila., 476 n; on compensating traders, 476; to make Indian treaty, 476, 529
Cromwell, Oliver, Navigation Act of, 35 n
Crown: to receive Md. petition on government, 108; annual acknowledgment for Pa. grant to, 129 n; attitude toward Pa., 130, 141, 211–12; sale of Pa. to, started, 132–3, 151, 172, 289; right of legislative assent, 136; owed by Pa. Proprietors, 148, 151, 172; Mass. petition on taxation to, 452 n; Del. laws not sent for approval to, 466, 474–5. *See also* George III; Ministry; Petitions to the King; Royal government.
Crusoe, Robinson, BF pamphlet fragment uses, 184
Cudjoe (Negro), BF anecdote about, 61–2
Cumberland Co.: grievances, 81–3; representation, 81–2, 379; petitions Assembly on grievances, 86–7 n; proprietary complaint of taxes in, 127 n; represented on petition committee, 193; Indian atrocity in, 335 n; election results, 393; Allen elected from, 494 n
Cumberland Co. Rangers, pay and subsistence for, 223
Cumming, Alexander: identified, 481 n; rivalry with Harrison, 481
Cumming, Thomas, BF to take letter to, 418
Currency Act (Great Britain, 1764): in preparation, 35, 176–7; passed, 176 n, 238, 282; effects of, 238, 359 n; Jackson tried to postpone, 313
Currency, paper: maintaining value of, 13–18 (*see also* Depreciation); restraint on, in New England, 35, 282; bill to restrain, 35, 176–7, passed, 282 (*see* Currency Act); Board of Trade hearings on, 35 n, 176–7; not legal tender to Proprietors, 95, 283;

Jackson's views on, 176–7, 313; BF plan for revenue from, 238 n., 351 n; issuing of legal-tender, prohibited, 238 n, 282; legal tender of, 282–3; proprietary efforts against, 378. See also Bills of credit; Interest.

Cushing, Thomas, signs Mass. House appeal, 243

Cust, Sir John, greetings to, 152

Customs. See Duties.

Customs service, Navy used for, 215

Cyrus, anecdote about, 522

Daggestans, language and religion of, 59–60

Danforth, Samuel: identified, 255 n; greetings to, 255

Darby, Pa., liquor license fees, 522 n

Davenport, Ann Annis, health, 227

Davenport, Franklin, career, 227 n

Davenport, James, mentioned, 228 n

Davenport, Josiah, BF sends news of, 227

Davenport, Sarah Franklin, mentioned, 227 n

Davenport, William: biographical note, 228 n; greetings to, 228

David, King, mentioned, 299

Davis, James, paid for measuring plaster, 455

Death, BF condolence on, 79. See also Afterlife.

"Declaration" of Paxton Boys: delivered to Penn, 80; frontier grievances, quoted, 81; sent to Assembly, 83; charges Quakers with arousing Indians, 102

Defense, colonial, plan for financing, 350. See also Army, British; Frontier defense.

De Grey, Thomas, of Merton, election, 177

De Grey, William, mentioned, 177

Delaware, Three Lower Counties on: Assembly formed, 82 n; usefulness of Proprietors to, 125 n; quitrents owed Crown, 148, 151, 172; Penn's claim to, 172 n; troops not requested from, 212; Dickinson at court in, 268; charter provision for union with Pa., 382 n; Penn in, 410; Assembly address to King, 465; territorial and political rights in, 465–7; laws not sent for approval, 466, 474–5; indulged by Proprietors, 466–7, 474–5

Delaware Indians in Ohio River Valley: campaign to chastise, 96 n, 224 n, 248 n; boy recovered from, 174; party scalped by Owens, 174; Bradstreet's unauthorized treaty with, 326, 329–31, 333, 335–7, 446 n; Bouquet to continue campaign against, 326, 330; not in Niagara treaty, 329, 335;

Bouquet makes peace with, 446 n, 458, 483, 485–6, 523, 529; to sign treaty with Croghan, 476, 529; hostages terrified by Owens, 528–9 n

Delaware (Wyalusing) Indians: protection of, 19, 27, 67–9, 82, 87 n; charges against, 64 n; resettlement of, 87 n. See also Indians in Philadelphia.

Delaware River: blocked by ice, 87; troops stationed near, 261

Denny, William: Assembly protects, 127 n; alleged bribery of, 268, 271–7, 287, 373; disobeys proprietary instructions, 277; signs Re-emitting Act, 466; passes act on judicial tenure, 513

Density of fluids, not related to compressibility, 246

Depreciation: BF's scheme to avoid, 10–18, 238; Proprietors avoid, 142; problem in Va., No. Car., 176 n; of paper money, 282–3

Desertion, extensive in Bouquet's force, 266

Deshler, David, pay order for, 223

Detroit, Fort: Indian conference at, 218 n; Bradstreet to march to, 224 n

Dialogue between Andrew Trueman, and Thomas Zealot, cited, 56 n

Dickinson, John: biographical note, 10 n; supports BF currency scheme, 10; Letters from a Farmer, 10 n; votes against petition for royal government, 161 n, 198, 291 n; Assembly speech against petitioning king, 194, 308–10; publishes Assembly speech, 194 n, 195 n, 267, 311, 527, Preface to, 267 (see Smith, William); Reply to Galloway speech, 195 n, 268, quoted, 309 n, 310 n, ignores BF's Preface, 332 n; author of counter-petition, 256 n; position on bills of credit, 283 n; proprietary praise of, 296–7, 526–7; absent from Assembly debates on petitioning, 308–9; Speech sent to Jackson, 329; on "New Ticket," 377 n, 390; BF replaces on "Old Ticket," 390 n; elected, 394; votes against BF appointment, 407 n; and protest on BF appointment, 408, 412, 489–90; "Observations" on BF's Remarks, 430 n; as lawyer, 438 n; on BF's embarkation, 448; asked to sign reply to BF's Remarks, 484; refuses, 525–6; political relations of, 525 n, 526 n; disillusioned with proprietary leaders, 526–7; to retire from Assembly, 527

Disease, BF on purpose of, 101

Dissenters: rights protected in So. Car. and N.J., 162–7; privileges protected by royal government, 162–8; privileges in Mass. and New Hampshire, 167–8; laws favoring, 168; no tests imposed on, 168; T. Penn not considered, 279 n

Dods, George, pay order for, 223

Dogs: Bouquet asks for, 225–6; BF recommends for fighting Indians, 226 n, 239–40 n, 317 n; to be sent from England, 239–40

Dollond, John: biographical note, 22 n; micrometer of, 22, 245, 452–3

Dominion, "founded in opinion," 106

Donegal, Pa., raiders from, 42, 66. See also Paxton Boys.

Donnally, Felix, bill for Indians, 53 n

Douglass, John: signs Assembly reports, 86, 93; on committee for petition, 193; position on Assembly petition, 193 n

Douglass, William, *A Summary, Historical and Political*, BF's use of, 536

Dragon (ship), carries mail, 228 n, 229 n, 242 n, 255 n, 311 n

Dram-shops: licensing of, 128, 139–40; excess number of, 128, 139

Draper, Richard, BF to send books to, 91 n

Drinker, Henry: identified, 436 n. See also James and Drinker.

Duhamel du Monceau, H. L., *Art de Refiner le Sucre*, sent to BF, 265

Dumfries, Va., Phila. mail to, 401

Dunlap, William: identified, 418 n; announces improved postal service, 21 n, 248 n; letter in care of, 31; prints *Cool Thoughts*, 153 n; P. Franklin succeeds, 253 n; prints Galloway's *Speech*, 268; draft of letter to, 366 n; dispute over post-office debts, 418–22; made ill by BF's persecution, 420; charge against WF, 420–2; later career of, 421–2 n; gives land for post-office debt, 469–70; letters from, 418–21; letter to, 421–2

Dunwick, William, pay orders for, 223

Duties: Jackson prefers to internal tax, 35, 509–10 n; BF's views on, 76, 181–3, 215–16, 234–7; relation to balance of trade, 183–4, 235–6, 451–2; Mass. petitioning against, 452. See also Specific imports; Molasses, Stamp, Sugar acts; Trade, colonial.

Dysentery, kills Phila. Indians, 87 n

East India Company: Barker joins, 34 n; fleet, experience with lemons, 216

East Indies: new duties on goods of, 76, not objected to, 235

East Jersey, Proprietors *Bill*, 415 n

Easton Treaty: role of Pemberton in, 83 n; expenses at, 224

Echert (Achart), Adam, payment to, 455

Eckerling, Emanuel, joins sectarians, 443 n

Eckerling, Gabriel and Israel, captured in war, 443

Eckerling, Samuel: biographical note, 443; seeks confirmation of brothers' deaths, 443–4; letter from, 443–4

Eclipses, BF orders book on, 334

Economy, North American: BF views effect of trade restraints on, 76, 108, 181–3, 234–5, 344, 351; colonial manufactures, 183–4, 235, 314–15; sugar production, 236, 313; depression in, aggravated by Sugar and Currency Acts, 359 n. See also Currency, paper; Sugar Act; Trade, colonial.

Edes, Benjamin, publisher of *Boston Gazette*, 444

Education, plan for unity of colleges, 192 n. See also Colleges.

Edwards, Jonathan, mentioned, 32 n

Edwards, William, Spanish refuse to capture, 61

Egmont, John Percival, 2d Earl of: application for St. John, 175 n, 187, refused, 324; pamphlet on settling, sent to BF, 324

Elder, John, reports Conestoga Manor massacre, 42 n

Eldridge, Samuel, describes land, 428 n

Elections, Pa., 1764: militia bill issue in, 76 n, 360–1, 365; halt action on frontier report, 87 n; Resolves as platform for, 123; effect of Assembly representation on, 124 n; alignments for, 124 n, 125; effect on Assembly, 124 n, 393–4, 397, 407, 434; change-of-government issue in, 125, 264, 271, 327, 329, 369, 511; effect of frontier grievances on, 125; Presbyterians support proprietary party, 125 n, 327, 387, 389, 485 n; effect of governor-appointed officers on, 142; Proprietors' concessions withheld because of, 214 n, 312 n, 317 n, 331 n, 352, 410 n, 436; effect of supply bill dispute on, 214 n; criteria, 291; groups against BF in, 327 n, 504–5; proprietary party doubts success in, 339; BF's predictions on, 358; personalities as issues in, 369–70; campaign papers on, 369–90; candidates accused of inciting election riots of 1742, 377, slates, 377 n, 390; results in Phila. Co., 390–4, 397, 433, 468 n, 493–4; BF's defeat in, 391, 394, 397, 411, 433–4, 451, 468 n, 484, 492 n, 493–4, 504–5, BF on, 397, 433–4; Galloway's defeat in, 391, 394, 397; in Phila., 391–2, 397, 493–4; outside Phila. Co., 392–3; BF charges fraud in, 434; of Lancaster sheriff, 467; feeling aroused by, 488; Allen had no part in papers on, 510

Electricity: BF admired for work in, 33; in air, Kinnersley's experiment on, 98–9,

244; Aepinus theory of, 254; relation to magnetism, 254; impermeable fluid of, 254. *See also* Lightning.

Eliot, Aaron: identified, 257 n; accompanies Bernard to N.Y., 87; Mills book given to, 257–8; Society of Arts medal sent to, 352

Eliot, Andrew: identified, 255 n; greetings to, 255

Eliot, Jared: Gale protege of, 183 n; death, 257 n, 258, 352 n; medal awarded to, 352 n; mentioned, 356 n

Elizabeth (ship), protected by Spanish, 61

Elizabethtown, N.J., Phila. mail to, 401

Ellicott, John: identified, 232 n; search for E. Holland for, 232–3; greetings to family of, 233–4; letter to, 232–4

Elmsly, John, paid for work on BF's house, 456

Emigration, Pa.: price of land causes, 128–9, 140; considered, 181

Empson, Elizabeth, recommended to M. Stevenson, 190

Empson, Thomas, marriage, 190 n

England: Indians request ship to, 28; European goods to be laden in, 91 n; luxury exports, abatement of, 359. *See also* Great Britain; London.

English, proposed law for Pa. publications to be in, 295 n

Ennis, James (Jr. or Sr.): identified, 6 n; to escort Bernard, 6; pay order for, 223

Ephrate community, Eckerlings members of, 443 n

Episcopalians. *See* Church of England.

Epitaphs, political: BF's on Thomas and Richard Penn, 298–9; Smith's on William Penn, 298 n; BF starts vogue for, 372; on BF, 380–4; on W. Smith, 387–90

Erie, Lake: Bradstreet campaign to, 335; Indians aroused by French, 528

Erwin, Robert: paid for carting, 455; stones delivered to, 455

Eumaeus, BF's use of, 56–8

Europe: direct colonial trade forbidden with, 91 n, 216 n; drawback withdrawn on fabrics from, 235 n

Evans, Cadwalader, confers on reply to *Answer*, 526

Evans, John: reservation in commission to, 136; on quitrents, 138–9 n; dispute on adjournment, 159 n; acts passed by, 170–1

Evans, Lewis, map sent to British Post Office, 38 n

Evans, Rowland: on "Old Ticket," 390; defeat, 394

Ewing, John: identified, 526 n; signs letter against royal government, 290 n; part in

Smith's *Answer*, 526; signs Presbyterians' address, 526 n

Exchequer, Chancellor of. *See* Grenville, George.

Experience, relation to faith, 231–2, 241

Explanatory Remarks on the Assembly's Resolves, 133–44; dating of, 134–5; purpose, 135; start of pamphlet war, 154; on Militia Bill amendments, 360

Faith, BF's, based on experience, 231–2, 241

Falmouth, England, packets between N.Y. and, 38

Falmouth, Me.: postal service to, 3 n; Phila. mail to, 400

Farrow, Anne, correspondence with BF, 524 n

Fashions, in wigs, 543

Ferguson, James, *Astronomical Tables and Precepts*, BF orders, 334

Fetherstonhaugh, Sir Matthew: consulted on Coxe claim, 176; BF's dealings with, 176 n

Fevers: cause of, 191–2; James patents pill for, 202 n

Fielding, Sir John, *Universal Mentor*, BF reorders, 334

Fisher, Daniel, diary cited, 190 n

Fisher, Edward, BF distributes prints by, 89–90, 230–1

Fisher, John, land purchase, 140 n

Fisher, William, subscribes to linen factory, 315

Fisheries, fishing: sturgeon, Bernard plans for Penobscot, 31; duties on, should be light, 76; in Bay of St. Lawrence, 187; cod, in Bay of Chaleur, 428. *See also* Cod; Herring; Salmon; Sturgeon.

Flagg, Mr., must pay postage, 262

Flagg, Mary (Polly), death of, 253 n

Flagg, Sarah Mecom (C. 17.5), death of, 253, 262 n

Flagg, Sarah, death of, 253 n

Flagg, William, death of wife, 253 n

Flax, flaxseed, Pa. exports of, 235, 315

Fleeson, Plunket: on "Old Ticket," 390; defeated, 392, 394

Flora, North American, Bartram specimens sent to King, 352

Florida: in new postal district, 39 n, 260 n; sugar cultivation proposed in, 313; land-grant terms in, 358 n

Flour, Mass. duty on, 179 n

Fluids. *See* Liquids.

Footman, Mr., carries letter to BF, 532

Foppery, discountenanced by P. Franklin ballad, 539

Forbes, John, used horse troops, 225

Ford (Foord), Sarah, marriage and death, 416 n
Forster, Thomas, receipt by, 455
Fort Point, Me., settled, 31 n
Fort Pownall, Me., commander to start fishery, 31 n
Forts, English right to build, 330, 336. *See also* individual forts by name.
Fossils, American, catalogue of, 97
Fothergill, John: BF recommends retirement to, 101; BF sends *Narrative* to, 103; informs Thomas Penn of BF's letter, 103 n; recommended as Pa. agent, 412; political position, 412 n; smooths BF's way with Proprietor, 412 n; letter to, 101–5
Foulke, Hugh, mentioned, 9 n
Foulke, Samuel: biographical note, 9 n; journal quoted, 9–10, 28
Fox, Joseph: debates supply bill funding, 10; signs Assembly reports, 86, 286, 439; pay orders for, 223, 224; barrackmaster at Phila., 224, 373; provincial commissioner, 261; subscribes to linen factory, 315; elected on "Old Ticket," 390, 391, 394; elected speaker, 393, 403, 425; delay in confirmation of, 403–4, 411; on Committee of Correspondence, 422 n; signs Assembly instructions, 426
Foxcroft, John: gives post-office commissions, 3–5, 253, 260 n; improves postal service, 20–1, 37–9; inspection trip, 21, 249–50 n; greetings to, 22; and BF to report on survey, 36–8; inquires for E. Holland, 233; post-office account, 248–51; franking privilege, 253; gives power of attorney, 337–9; settles postal affairs in Va. and Md., 341 n; loyalism, 398; instructions sent to, 414; impatient to leave Phila., 419; denies abusing Dunlap, 421; informed on Dunlap affair, 470; and Thomson sell land, 521 n; letters from (with BF), 341–5, 421–2; letter to, 418–20. *See also* Post office, North American.
Foxcroft, Thomas: loyalism, 398; Phila. postmaster, 398; records of Phila. mail, 398–402
France, French: Indians protect British from, 64; colonies taken by British, 166 n; Coxe wants to press claim in, 175; neutrals, expenses for, 223; should be forced from Ill., 277, 528; repairing navy, 317; Eckerling brothers sent to, 443; supply and trade with Indians, 476, 523, 528, 530; argument for restoring Canada to, 482
Frankford, Pa., liquor license fees, 522 n
Franking of mail: BF asked to use, 32–3; new law restricts, 33 n, 39, 253–4, 262; abuses of, to be stopped, 39; granted to

M.P.s, 257 n; Parker previously entitled to, 416
Franklin, Abiah (C.11.1), mentioned, 231 n
Franklin, Benjamin: issues post-office commissions, 3–6, 253, 260 n; postmaster general of United Colonies, 3 n; facilitates return of Bernard, Jr., 6, 31, 79, 87, 133; scheme for interest-bearing currency, 7–18, 238; wants to avoid dispute with Proprietors, 18; views on British trade laws and duties, 19–20, 76–7, 181–3, 215–16, 234–7; views on colonial taxation, 19–20, 76, 169–70, 236–7; on Coxe grant, 20, 108, 152, 185; improves postal service, 20–1, 37–9; New England accident, 21, 95, 227, 250 n, 259; helps Bowdoin with telescope, 21–2, 99, 244–5; on Assembly committees, 27–9, 75, 86 n, 112–13, 117, 123, 204, 207, 274 n; praised for electrical work, 33; post-office accounts, 38 n, 248–51; pamphlet to influence opinion on Indian massacres, 42–69, 77, 434; tone of political pamphlets, 47; use of biblical analogy, 56, 64 n, 288; part played in Paxton crisis, 72, 73, 77, 103–4; said to aid in Paxton Remonstrance, 74 n; supports militia bill, 75–6 n; militia bills by, 76 n, 512–13; approves action against Wilkes, 76; faith in afterlife, 79, 231–2, 241, 253; signs Assembly documents, 86, 93, 200, 206, 213, 351; on pickled sturgeon, 87–8, 334–5; sends inoculation pamphlet, 88; distributes prints of portrait, 89–90, 90–1 n, 230–1; repaid by Bernard, 91, 153, 178; thanked for letters of introduction, 93; resumes scientific correspondence with Canton, 97–100; has made no new experiments, 98; relations with Penns, 103, 217–18, 247, 404 n, 406, 409, 412 n, 436–7, 497–8; supports change of government, 105, 153–73; 173 n, 185–6, 267–311, 409, 431, 432, 491–2, 511; on literal interpretation of council order, 106 n, 220–1; interest in Md. disputes, 108 n, 158 n; possible return to England, 110, 149, 189, 219, 256, 332, 355, 359 n; views on frontier representation, 125–6; explains Assembly's Resolves, 134–44; drafts popular petition for royal government, 145, 148 (*see* Petition to the King: inhabitants); weary with Pa. political disputes, 158 n; character described by J. Penn, 173 n; political leadership, 173 n, 376, 402 n, 515; land schemes, 175–6 n, 186–7, 187–8, 325, 359, 470 n (*see also* Coxe grant; Nova Scotia; Quebec; Scioto River; Settlement); to speak to Alison for Bernard, 178; account with Smith,

INDEX

Wright & Gray, 179–80; use of allegory, 184; petition for Nantucket whalers, 187; on the use of his popularity, 187; drafts Assembly petition to King, 193–4, 197, 199; elected Assembly speaker, 196, 205, 218; instructions to, on Assembly petition, 198, 422–3; praised for *Narrative*, 202 n; begged to move to England, 203; agrees to Privy Council stipulation, 204, 220, 284 n, 378; delivered transcript of Privy Council hearings, 209 n; asks Jackson's advice on going to England, 219, 229, 256, 263; love of England, 219; provincial commissioner, 222, 261, 266 n, 319, 322–3; suggested use of dogs against Indians, 226 n, 239–40 n, 317 n; delayed book order, 228, 264–5, 333, 353–4; forms Club of Thirteen, 228 n; search for Elizabeth Holland, 232–3; recommended Jackson, 234 n; on colonial textiles, 235; views on Stamp Act, 236–7; has alternative, 237, 350–1 n; considers withdrawal from politics, 237; financial transactions with Parker, 241 n, 251, 413 n, 414, 420–1, 520; on committee to verify Canton's experiments, 245 n; Bowdoin likes print of, 247; franking privilege, 253; comments on magnetism, 254; sends list of booksellers, 258; Mills sends book to, 258; men recommended to, 259–60, 461; forwards Bouquet's letters, 266 n; friendship with Bouquet, 266 n; asked to expedite troops, 267; subscribes to linen factory, 315; secures commissioners' consent for Bouquet, 316; sends Bouquet papers on Indian warfare, 317; on his political enemies, 318, 323, 449; tries to counterattacks, 318–19, 366–7; asks Bouquet for testimonial, 318–19; loss of postal office threatened, 318 n, 328 n, 367 n, 492 n; buys Phila. property, 319–21; buys ground rent, 320 n; Bouquet's testimonial for, 322–3; groups against, 327 n; relations with Allen, 328, 431, 432 n, 439, 501–2, 506–8, 543; critical comments on Quakers, 328 n, 375–6, 381, 382; opinion of Bradstreet's peace, 331, 337, 366; Mecom debt to, 332; Scotch-Irish angry at, 332; an optimist, 333; relies on Strahan's news, 333; gives power of attorney to Hubbart, 337–9; forwards medal, 352; aids Bartram, 352–3; satisfied with Strahan printing of "Parable against Persecution," 354; Strahan's praise of, quoted, 354 n; dislikes having his writings abridged, 355; thanked for inoculation pamphlet, 356; explains failure of militia bill, 360–5; attacked on military issue,

361; busy with politics, 366; scurrilous campaign against, 369–76, 380–4, 391, 434; political use of slur on Germans, 370, 375, 382, 385, 397, 434 n; investment of parliamentary grant in stocks, 370, 411, 438–41, 473, 484, 498–501; alleged ambition for governorship, 370, 375; alleged treatment of WF's mother, 370, 383–4; income as agent, 370 n, 373–4, 383, 411–12, 439–40 n, 498, 501–2; political writings (1764) listed, 371 n; political epitaph on, 380–4; honorary titles and degrees, 381; accused of trimming, 382, 510, 515; defended by *The Scribbler*, 385–7; praised as father, 386; relations with W. Smith, 388 n; Smith's charges against, refuted by Kinnersley, 389 n; Smith tries to prevent degree for, 390 n; election defeat, 390–4, 397, 411, 433–4, 451, 464, 468 n, 492 n, 493–4, 504–5; appointed co-agent, 393, 404–6, 407–8, 408–12, 422–3, 425, 446–7, 451, 477, 504; gives R.I. letter to Norris, 395 n; reports election results to Jackson, 397; Phila. remonstrance against appointment, 402–6; purpose of appointment, 404 n, 484; self-interest as bar to effective agency, 406, 432–3, 492, 504; holds crown appointment, 406, 432–3, 434, 513; to be paid for expenses as agent, 407; to protest against appointment, 408–12; appointment ill-timed, 409–10, 434–7, 494; minister's bad opinion of, 410, 431–3, 492; sends out post-office forms, 414; on N.Y.-N.J. boundary commission, 414 n, 431–2 n; education of Billy Hunter, 415 n; departs for England, 418, 426, 427, 429, 447–9, 450, 451, 453, 459, 470, 477, 521, 524; Dunlap calls "cruel and merciless," 420; denies abusing Dunlap, 421; Jackson communicates through, 425 n; to send armonica from England, 427; expenses for trip subscribed, 427; replies to protest on agency, 429–41; use of first person in public writings, 429; never campaigned, 433–4; real-estate purchases, 437 n; farewell to Pa., 441; gives power of attorney to Parker, 441–3; partnership with Hall to expire, 441–2, 471; to receive Franklin & Hall accounts, 442, 471; to inquire about Eckerling brothers, 443; and Grenville's taxation policy, 444–5; anthem on, 447–8; accounts for new house, 453–6; to further R.I. petition, 459–60; influence in England, 460; takes land for post office, 469–70; asked to help traders, 476; Johnson regrets not seeing, 477; asked to plead for royal government for all colonies, 477–8; Osborne sends

561

book, catalogues to, 478; horizontal clock weight, 480; idea for uprooting trees, 480; advice sought on taxation and smuggling, 482; becomes publicist for colonies, 482 n; Smith's *Answer* attacks, 484, 486–516; Pa. attitude toward, 488; charged with padding *Votes*, 490–1; attempt to find new seat for, 494; given parliamentary grants, 500 n; slander and scurrility by, 504–6; charged with agnosticism, 505; relations with proprietary leaders, 506–7; Allen's role in appointments of, 506; charged with obstructing government, 512; accused of affecting royalty, 512–13; loyalty attacked, 513–14; charged with *Historical Review*, 514; voyage and arrival, 516–17, 524, 532, 534; account books during second agency, 518–20; pays for portrait, 520; aid to cousins, 524 n; defended against Smith's *Answer*, 526–7; Smith's *Answer* and Hughes' reply sent to, 530; asked to confer on S. Penn claim, 533; to see Postal Act clauses, 534; getting over bad cold, 534; illness (1757), 534 n; friendship with Cooper, 537 n; recipe for "bark wine," 537; on setting words to music, 538–43; preference for old songs, 538–9; to get ballad set for P. Franklin, 539

Franklin, Deborah: greetings to, 22, 95, 227, 325; greetings from, 79–80, 89, 189, 232, 253, 319, 333, 355; Habersham calls on, 259; must pay postage, 262; does not send condolence, 262; death, 441 n; Sally to take care of, 449; gives Rhoads money for house, 456; Wharton reports on, 457; not told of Dunlap sale, 469 n; not to visit Parkers, 470; relays BF's letter, 470; receives BF's letters, 479 n; well, 486, 530; to relay BF's greetings, 517; letters to, 516–17, 534; mentioned, 383 n

Franklin, Elizabeth (mother of Elizabeth Hubbart), offers BF books, 89 n

Franklin, Elizabeth (wife of WF), greetings to and from, 36, 189, 333, 450, 517

Franklin, John (C.8): books of, offered to BF, 89 n; mentioned, 337 n

Franklin, Mary Harman: greetings to and from, 253, 517; inoculated, 253; pays postage, does not write J. Mecom, 262

Franklin, Peter: brings books to BF, 230; moves to Phila., becomes postmaster, 230 n, 253 n, 418–19, 538; greetings from, 253; inoculated, 253; does not write J. Mecom, 262; records of Phila. mail, 398–402; moves post office, 418 n; love to, 517; BF's advice on ballad of, 538–9; letter to, 538–43

Franklin, Sarah: greetings to, 22, 95, 227, 325; enjoyed New England trip, 79; greetings from, 89, 134, 189, 227, 253, 319, 333, 355; practices penmanship on BF's draft, 360 n; copies BF's letter, 366 n; witnesses power of attorney, 442; BF's farewell advice to, 449–50; Wharton reports on, 457; well, 486, 530; does not accompany BF, 517; BF sends love to, 517, 534; invites H. Walker to write, 525; letter to, 447–50; mentioned, 383 n. *See also* Bache, Sarah.

Franklin, William: permits Indian passage through N.J., 28; greetings to and from, 36, 189, 313, 333, 359, 450, 464, 517, 534; buys BF prints, 89 n; share of seized ship, 91, 178; appoints judges, 96–7; BF's "Remarks" sent to, 134–5; finds Pa. acts in England, 171 n; praises Strahan's letters, 189 n; aid to Crown, 218; prospers, 333; asks Strahan to pay Jackson, 355–6; sends Strahan extract against Pa. government, 356 n; thinks BF will go to England, 359 n; illegitimacy, as campaign issue, 370; information on mother of, 370–1 n; as governor, 371 n, 386, 406; education, 386; BF praised for, 386; office as issue in BF appointment, 406; post-office accounts questioned, 420–2; Jackson unable to confirm judges for, 464; defends BF, 487; on authorship of *Answer* to BF's *Remarks*, 487 n; money from Assembly clerkship, 491; BF supports in England, 502; drafts reply to Smith's *Answer*, 526; well, 530; letters cited and quoted, 38 n, 134; letter from, 355–6

Franklin & Hall: not BF's printer for *A Narrative*, 42 n; prints few political pamphlets, 42 n; prints Md. antiproprietary pamphlet, 108 n; prints "Assembly's Proceedings on the Supply Bill," 133 n; prints "Explanatory Remarks," 134; prints "a Petition to his Majesty," 145; edition of the *New England Primer*, 303 n; location, 320 n; accounts to be examined, 441–2, 471; to publish peace declaration, 486; prints *Votes*, 531

Franklin Square, Phila., dispute over, 496 n

Fredericksburg, Va., Phila. mail to, 401

Frederickstown, Md., Phila. mail to, 401

Freedom of conscience. *See* Privileges; Religion.

French Neutrals: coffins for, 223; support of, 223

Friedenshütten (Indian village), founded, 87 n

Friend, Capt.: commands *Carolina*, 458; Hamilton sails with, 483, 524 n

Friendship, BF on, 328
Friendship (ship), carries mail, 228 n
Frontier, Pa.: Indians attack, 22, 25, 44, 102, 125, 335; settlers abandon, 22, 25, 44; opinion on massacres of Indians, 44; rioting in, 77 (*see* Paxton Boys); supports proprietary party, 81, 125, 360; "Remonstrance" on behalf of, 81–3, 86 n; accuses Assembly of indifference in defense, 81, 185 n, 360; unequal Assembly representation, 81–2, 86–7 n, 123–4, 125–6, 161, 185 n, 207, 378–9; wants more representatives, 81–2, 86–7 n, 124 n, 125–6, 185 n, 207, 378–9; petitions to Assembly on grievances from, 86–7 n, 185 n, 207, 291 n; Quakers accused of provoking Indians on, 101–2; proprietary lands harm local defense of, 128–9, 140; distress during Indian war, 137, 138; position on petition for royal government, 161, 185 n; election results, 393. *See also* Berks; Cumberland; Frontier defense; Frontiersmen; Lancaster; Northampton; York.
Frontier defense: Assembly ineffective in, 22–5, 27; Assembly accused of neglecting, 25, 27, 44, 81, 82 n, 185 n, 360; troops for, 29, 68–9, 261–2, not paid, 150, 204; parliamentary duties for support, 76 (*see also* Army, British); supply-bill dispute delays, 116, 204, 224 n; responsibility for delays in, 116, 121–2, 132, 154, 158, 217, 312; and 1764 election, 125; proprietary instructions obstruct, 126–7, 132, 138; relation to proprietary estates, 128, 140; weakened by emigration, 129; amount voted for, 154; effect on supply-bill dispute, 206–7, 213; use of dogs for, 226; frontiersmen apathetic in, 267; procedures for, 317 n; Bouquet wants organized, 325. *See also* Army, British; Troops, Pa.
Frontiersmen, Pa.: flee Indian attacks, 22, 25, 44; criticize Assembly indifference, 25 (*see also* Assembly); want Indians removed, 25, 82; hostility toward Indians, 25, 27, 55, 82; march on Phila. rumored, 27, 30; Assembly partiality to Indians enrages, 44, 81, 82, 102 n; charges against friendly Indians, 64–5 n; lack protection, 81–3 (*see also* Frontier defense); want governmental medical care, 82; captured by Indians, 82 (*see also* Prisoners); blame Quakers, 82, 102; destitution, 82 n, 102 n; ally with proprietary party, 125, 360; return to Phila. rumored, 185; Bouquet scornful of, 267. *See also* Frontier, Pa.; Paxton Boys.

Frugality: urged in colonies, 108, 359; P. Franklin ballad encourages, 539
Fulton, Robert, reports Paxton Boys' plans, 70
Furman, Moore, biographical note, 334 n
Furman & Co. *See* Coxe & Furman.
Fusion, by electricity, experiment on, 98

Gage, Thomas: biographical note, 7 n; requests Pa. troops, 7; provides escort for friendly Indians, 28, 29, 47, 68–9, complains of Quebec postal service, 41; Penn requests military aid from, 42; to carry out Amherst's campaign, 105 n, 217–18 n, 224 n; desired not to ratify Bradstreet treaty, 326; refuses recognition of Bradstreet treaty, 326 n, 336 n, 446 n; Bouquet reports to, 458, 483; should establish Ill. garrison, 528; report quoted, 528–9 n; letter to, quoted, 44
Galbreath, John, pay order for, 222
Gale, Benjamin: biographical note, 183 n; introduces mercuric inoculation, 356 n; letter from, 183–4
Galloway, Joseph: debates supply bill funding, 10; confers with Paxton leaders, 73; signs Assembly report, 86; sends BF *Remarks* to WF, 134–5, letter on, quoted, 134; authorship of *Address to the Freeholders,* 154; pamphlet by, sent to Jackson, 186; on committee for petition to King, 193; supports Petition to King, 193 n; *Speech* in reply to Dickinson, 194, 267, 268, 309, 311, 319 n, 329, 332; Dickinson's *Reply* to *Speech,* 195 n; BF's Preface to *Speech,* 267–311 (see also Preface); English reviews of *Speech,* 332 n; provincial commissioner, 261; greetings to and from, 313, 359; election campaign against, 361, 369, 373, 391; on "Old Ticket," 390, defeated, 391, 394, 397; Assembly leadership after election, 402 n; signs Assembly order, 427 n; sees BF off, 449; Jackson letters to, mentioned, 463; Quaker support of, 526; confers on Smith's *Answer,* 526; marriage, 527 n; letter from, 465–8
Garden, Alexander, recommends Young, 353 n
Geerh, Balsar, pay order for, 223
Gentleman's Magazine: article attacking Quakers, 180; *Narrative* extracts in, 202 n, 331 n; BF's *Observations on the Increase of Mankind* in, 382, 385
Geology. *See* Mineralogy.
George (Wa-a-shens; Conestoga Indian), massacre of, 49

George and Vulture Tavern, Monday Club at, 234

George III: BF praises, 105, 144; pill used for mental illness of, 202 n; Jackson has confidence in, 313; Bartram sends botanical collection for, 352; Assembly reverence for, 424; goodness of, 532

Georgia: Bolton recommended for postmaster of, 259–60; postal service, 260 n; settlement of, at British expense, 349 n

German Reformed Church, Franklin Square burying ground, 496 n

Germans, Pa.: angry with Quakers and Moravians, 44 n; massacred on frontiers, 44 n; take sides on Paxton march, 72, 73 n; political alignment of, 125 n; have experienced oppression, 173; attempts to limit voting rights of, 294–5 n, 505; Calvinists, 327 n (see Calvinists); BF slur on, 370, 375, 382, 385, 397, 434 n, 505; Smith's slur on, 387; vote against BF, 391, 397, 505

Germantown, Pa.: Paxton Boys stop at, 72, 77; Paxton Boys confer with Phila. delegates, 72–4, 80–1; Lutherans persuaded not to aid Paxton Boys, 73 n; voters swing Phila. Co. elections, 391; liquor license fees, 522 n

Gibeonites, treatment compared to Indian massacres, 56

Gibson, James: expresses Paxton Boys' grievances, 73–4, 81–3 (see also "Remonstrance"); goes home, 86 n

Gil Blas, anecdote of, cited, 355

Gill, John, publisher of Boston Gazette, 444

Gilmor, Robert, Jr., acquires BF letter, 88 n

Glass, electrical conductivity of, 99, 244, 254

Glen, James, builds Fort Prince George, 93 n

God: BF's trust in, 231–2, 241; BF on afflictions under, 253

"God Save the King," adapted to honor BF, 447

Gold-finder, defined, 383 n

Goldthwaite, Col. Thomas, starts settlement on Penobscot, 31–2 n

Governors and lieutenant governors, Pa.: disputes on proprietary taxation, 7, 11, 113, 121, 137–8, 146–7, 161–2, 207, 302, 378; powers in relation to Proprietors, 126 n, 136–8; Assembly "gifts" to, 127, 139, 271–7, 304; income from perquisites, 127 n, 139–40, salary recommended instead of, 522; refuse to limit liquor licenses, 128, 139–40, 522 n; right to appoint militia officers, 130–1, 141–2, 361–4, 512–13; powers conferred by royal charter on, 135–6; discretionary power on legislation, 135 n; shackled by proprietary instructions, 136–7, 141–2, 171, 194, 287, 301; income from quitrents, 138–9; blamed for frontier problems, 154; proprietary, compared with royal, 171–2, 300–1; approval of assembly speaker, 196 n; control over disposition of money, 207, 281, 302; Proprietors' right to appoint, 293–4, 297, 300–1, 302; royal consent to, 300–1; salary for royal, 328; appointment for Pa. and Lower Counties, 465 n. See also Denny, William; Evans, John; Hamilton, James; Keith, William; Morris, Robert; Penn, John; Thomas, George.

Grace, Robert, property of, 320

Graff, Jacob, paid for bricks, 455

Grant, Joseph, mortgage, 339 n

Grass, seeds sent, 258

Gray, Anchitel, Debates, BF orders, 334

Gray, Henry, partner in banking firm, 179 n

Gray, Thomas, signs Mass. House letter, 243

Great Britain: political situation, 76, 317; colonial imports laden in, 91 n; civil dissensions in, 105; judicial tenure in, 140; relations with colonies, 169 n, 482; effect of colonial trade restrictions on, 181–2, 235–6, 351; desire to monopolize manufactures and trade, 183; Strahan's political letters on, 188–9, 242; Pa. privileges advantageous to, 197; dispute with Spain over Mosquito Coast, 236, 313; colonial taxation not in interest of, 243, 452; political system, 324; colonial settlements benefit, 349; mercury inoculation not yet used in, 356

Great Lakes, Indian campaign, 217, 224 n, 335. See also Bradstreet.

Green, Thomas: identified, 413 n; printing in Hartford, 413; post-office accounts unsettled, 417

Greene, Catharine: BF condoles, 79; greetings to children of, 80; BF print for, 231; letter to, 79–80

Greene, Rufus, post-office instructions for, 80

Greenleaf, Abigail, marriage, 460 n

Greenleaf, Isaac, subscribes to linen factory, 315

Greenwood, John: identified, 544 n; announces showing of pictures, 544

Grenville, George: Jackson appointed secretary to, 35 n, 186 n; Jackson's influence with, 35 n, 509 n; to get report on posts, 36; postponement of stamp tax, 236–7 n; decides against colonial self-tax, 237 n;

BF suggests revenue plan to, 238 n; confers with colonial agents, 242, 377 n; insists on parliamentary taxation, 347–8; resolution on stamp act, 396 n; provoked into imposing stamp duties, 444–5 n

Griffith, Abiah Davenport, BF print for, 90

Griffiths, Ralph (bookseller), BF will aid in America, 189

Growdon, Grace, marriage, 527 n

Growdon, Lawrence: biographical note, 527 n; mentioned, 527

Grube, Rev. Bernhard Adam, escorts Indians, 25–6

Guilford, Conn., Phila. mail to, 400

Guy, John, bill for sand, 456

Habersham, James: identified, 259 n; visits DF, 259; recommends Bolton to BF, 259–60; marriage, 259 n; letter from 259–60

Habersham, James, Jr. and Joseph, attend College of New Jersey, 259 n

Haines, Reuben: pay order for, 223; subscribes to linen factory, 315 n

Halifax, George Montagu Dunk, 2d Earl of: hears complaints about BF, 318 n; reaction to Assembly Resolves, 328, 492 n; BF wishes recommendation to, 367; letter to, cited and quoted, 38 n

Hall,——(of Madeira), Bernard letter sent to, 178

Hall, David: avoids printing political pamphlets, 42 n; warned against Rivington, 240 n; partnership with BF ending, 441–2; Parker to settle BF's accounts with, 471; letter from, 529–31, letter to, quoted, 354 n. See also Franklin & Hall.

Hall, Samuel: identified, 461 n; debt to BF, 461

Hamilton, Andrew, farewell speech, cited, 302

Hamilton, James: confers with Indians, 27; on proprietary-estate tax, 120, 210; removed from office, 120; advises withholding Proprietors' concessions, 214 n; relations with Assembly, 276, 302; messages to Assembly, quoted, 276, 278; believed to favor royal government, 276 n; use of Privy Council statement, 278 n; Assembly tax report sent to, 286; politically inactive, 288 n; relations with W. Smith, 388 n; sails for England, 458, 483, 524; suspected cancer, 458 n, 472 n, 524 n; to take proprietary petitions, 467; as future governor, 472, 473; political services, 472 n; removes W. Moore, 472–3; vetoes Assembly bill, 499–500 n

Hamilton, William, accompanies uncle, 483 n

Hamilton and Balfour: identified, 241 n; Mecom debt to, 240, 332

Hammett, Francis, carries mail, 228, 229, 242, 255, 311

Hampden-Trevor, Robert, greetings to, 337 n

Hancock, John, attempt to seize sloop of, 460 n

Handel, George Fredrick, BF criticizes arias by, 540–2

Hannum, John: reappointment of, 468; supports change of government, 468; refuses justice post, 485

Hanover, Va., Phila. mail to, 401

Happiness, temporal, BF on, 253

Hardy, Sir Charles: identified, 177 n; speaks for paper money, 177

Hardy, Josiah, violates tenure instruction, 512

Harman, Mary. See Franklin, Mary Harman.

Harriot (packet), carries mail, 19 n, 340 n, 341

Harrison, Henry: on "New Ticket," 390; defeated, 391, 394

Harrison, John: identified, 481 n; chronometer prize delayed, 481, 482; Cumming rivalry with, 481; chronometer tested, 482

Harrison, Joseph: biographical note, 460 n; has R.I. petition, 460

Harris's Ferry, stores carried to, 223

Harry (Tee-Kau-ley; Conestoga Indian), massacre of, 49

Hartford, Conn., Phila. mail to, 400

Harvard College, Bernard not to send son to, 153; BF will help replace library, 254–55; fire destroys library, 255 n

Hatchet, soldier should carry, 225

Haversacks, troops to have, 262

Hawkesworth, John: greetings to wife and, 110, 521; praises BF's Narrative, 202 n; pamphlets sent to, 333

Hay, John, reports on massacred Indians, 42 n, cited, 46 n, 49

Hazard, Samuel, mineralogy catalogue, 97

Heat: records for Newport, Phila., 191; and fusion by lightning, 244; effect on compressibility of liquids, 245; effect on electrical conductivity, 254; Pa. deaths from, 256

Heath, Sir Robert, grant to, 175

Heathens, hospitality of, 56–8, 65

Heberden, William, pamphlet on inoculation distributed, 88 n, 91 n, 356

Henlopen, Cape, BF sails from, 451

Herodotus, History, cited, 522

Herring, pickling of, 88

Highwaymen, Pa. roads infested with, 530

Hill, John, pay order for, 223
Hine, Thomas, property sold to BF, 320
Hines, John. *See* Williams, John.
Hobb's Hole, Va., Phila. mail to, 402
Hockley, Richard, requests supply bill changes, 204–5
Hoffman, Capt., entertainment of troops of, 224
Hogs, German boors defined as, 397, 434 n, 505
Holland, Agnes, daughter sought, 233 n
Holland, Elizabeth, BF continues search for, 232–3
Holland, Lucy, mentioned, 233
Holland, Richard and Rebecca, answer inquiry, 233
Holland, William, search for heir of, 232–3
Holland (Netherlands): pickled herrings, 88; ship seized, 91, 178
Holmes, Thomas, papers to be revealed, 374
Holofernes, murdered by Judith, 64 n
Holston, Matthias, elected county assessor, 394
Holt, Betsey: identified, 416 n; marriage, 416 n; mentioned, 416
Holt, Mrs. Elizabeth Hunter, interest in Hunter estate, 415–16
Holt, John: debt owed post office, 250 n, 417 n; debts of, 413–14; and Hunter's estate, 415–16; and Williamsburg printing office, 415–16; pays Parker, 470
Holyoke, Edward: identified, 255; greetings to, 255
Homer, *The Odyssey*, used by BF, 56–8
Honest Whigs, Club of: described, 98 n; BF to correspond with friends in, 98 n; greetings from, 246; loses Michell, 481
Hooper, Samuel, BF orders book printed by, 334
Hopkins, Stephen: biographical note, 357 n; political feud of, 192 n; chancellor, College of R.I., 357; signs R.I. Assembly letter, 397; denounces R.I. petition, 460 n
Hopkinson, Francis, music for poem of, 110 n
Horse, Light, troops of, Bouquet wants, 225
Hospitality, rights, and Pa. massacres, 58–66
Howard, Ann C., death, 460
Howard, John, pay order for, 223
Howard, Martin, Jr.: biographical note, 459 n; political writings, 186 n, 459 n, 460 n; wants royal government for R.I., 192 n; asks BF's help with R.I. petition, 459–60; death of wife, 460; letter from, 459–61

Howell, Isaac, pay order for, 223
Hubbart, Elizabeth: offers BF books, 89; BF print for, 90
Hubbart, Tuthill: identified, 337 n; executor of J. Franklin estate, 89 n; power of attorney for, 337–9
Hughes, John: identified, 374 n; speaks for supply bill, 7 n; attempt to buy Barker land, 34; signs Assembly reports, 86, 93, 439; pay order for, 224; provincial commissioner, 261 n; subscribes to linen factory, 315 n; alleged misuse of offices, 374; on "Old Ticket," 390; elected, 391, 394; on Committee of Correspondence, 422 n; signs Assembly instructions, 426; use of Allen's remarks, 432 n; reply to *Answer*, 487, 488, 526–7, sent to BF, 530
Hume, David, BF citation of, 144 n
Humphreys, Benjamin: identified, 446 n; bill for armonica spindles, 446
Humphreys, William, named justice, 484
Hunt, Abraham: biographical note, 3 n; commissioned deputy postmaster, 3–6
Hunter, John, inquires for E. Holland, 232
Hunter, William: death, 37 n; post-office accomplishments of, 37 n; estate pays post office, 251; commission to Parker, 251 n; management of business for son of, 251 n, 415–17; and BF devise postal forms, 398; debt to Dunlap, 419
Hunter, William, Jr.: Royle aids, 251 n; securing of father's business for, 415–17; education supervised by BF, 415 n
Hurons (Sandusky): treaty with Bradstreet, 329–31, 336; Bouquet makes peace with, 446 n
Huske, Ellis: identified, 338 n; bankruptcy, 338 n; estate to repay post office, 338; mentioned, 444 n
Huske, John: biographical note, 444 n; on passage of Stamp Act, 444–5; piece in *Boston Gazette* not aimed at BF, 444–5
Huston, Alexander, not named justice, 472, 484
Hutchinson, Thomas: Gage replaces, 7 n; moderates Mass. petition, 459 n
Hyde, Thomas Villiers, 1st Baron: to warn BF on political activity, 318 n, 367 n, 492 n; greeting to, 337 n; Allen attempts to turn against BF, 543 n

Illinois: Bouquet to take land and French posts in, 217; need to take, 476, 528; settlement scheme for, 476 n; French trade with Indians in, 523, 528
Immortality. *See* Afterlife.
India, Barker returns to, 34 n. *See also* East Indies.

Indians: campaigns against (1764), 7, 63, 105 n, 217, 224 n, 256, 326 n, 329–30, 335 (*see also* Bouquet; Bradstreet); massacre of friendly, 9 (*see also* Massacre); attacks on Pa. frontiers, 22, 25, 44, 82 n, 102; hostility toward, 25, 27, 77, 82; removal urged; 25, 82; Moravians' relations with, 25, 44; Quaker relations with, 25, 44, 82; bill on supplying arms to, 25 n; efforts to protect friendly, 29–30 (*see also* Delaware Indians; Moravian Indians; Indians in Phila.); decrease of, 48; English names of, 49; BF on injustice to, 55; honor and hospitality, 56, 62–5; Assembly's alleged favoritism toward, 81; bounty on scalps of, 82, 223; trade should be stopped with, 82; white captives of, 82 (*see also* Prisoners); campaigns halted against, 86 n, 475–6, 483, 486, 523, 528–9, 530; Ohio Valley uprising of, 96 n; Quakers accused of arousing, 101–2, 305; effect of uprising on Pa. politics, 125; land purchases from, 128; Owens scalps, 173–4; traders hope to be reimbursed with lands of, 187 n, 476; defeat 22d Regiment, 217 n; skill in evading pursuit, 225; dogs to be used against, 225–6, 239–40 n, 317 n; horses useful in fighting, 225; uprising in Va., 229 n; wars continue, 239; quiet, 304; Assembly accused of arousing, 305; papers on warfare against, 317; murderers to be tried by English law, 330, 336; massacre at school, 335 n; trade with French, 476, 523, 528, 530; to cede western lands, 476 n; to confirm peace with Johnson, 485; campaign against, may be renewed, 523; incited by French, 528. *See also* Catawba; Cherokee; Conestoga Manor; Creek; Delaware Indians; Huron; Iroquois; Mohawk; Moravian Indians; Ohio River Valley; Ottawa Indians; Seneca; Shawnee; Treaties, Indian.
Indians in Philadelphia: sent to N.J. and returned to Phila. barracks, 19, 28–30, 67, 68 n, 69–70; quartered on Province Island, 25–6; charges against, 25, 64 n, 74 n; Assembly support of, 25, 27, 44, 51–2, 67, 82, 102 n; massacre of, planned, 27, 42 n, 44, 70, 77, 102, 304; Army escorts and guards, 28–9, 47, 68–9, 70, 75, 360 n; Assembly advises Penn on, 29–30; defended against Paxton Boys, 69–75 (*see also* Paxton Boys); inspected by Paxton Boys, 74; expenses paid, 87 n, 222; deaths from disease, 87 n; moved to Wyalusing, 87 n; care of sick, 224; Fox in charge of, 373; BF's support of, contributed to his election defeat, 434

Industry: Sugar Act will stimulate in colonies, 108 (*see also* Economy); P. Franklin ballad encouraging, 539
Ingersoll, Jared: recommended Jackson, 234 n; legal work for post office, 250 n, 417 n; goes to England, 460 n
Inns, excessive number of, in Pa., 522. *See also* Licenses.
Inoculation, smallpox: Heberden pamphlets on, sent to Boston, 88, 91 n, 356; Gale introduces mercuric, 183 n, 356 n; successful on P. Franklins, 253; banned in Boston, 254 n; thought to spread smallpox, 254 n
Instructions, proprietary: given to Assembly, 8; on sterling payments, 8, 11, 142–3, 284; alternatives to, on taxation, 11–18; supply-bill dispute over, 95–6, 105–6, 127, 132, 142, 287; previous, disputes over, 126–7, 136–8; obstruct defense, Crown measures, 127, 138, 200, 287, 301; shackle governor, 136–7, 141–2, 171, 194, 287, 301, 513; violate colonial rights, 136–8; discontinuance of, asserted, 137; relation to emigration, 140; "inconvenience" of, 194; Assembly forced to yield to, 213; Denny disobeys, 277; hopes for withdrawal of, extinguished, 287; and judicial appointments, 512; compared with royal, 512
Interest, on bills of credit, BF advocates, 7–18, 238
Interests, conflict of, in proprietary government, 124–5, 199, 200, 301
Internal vs. external taxes. *See* Taxation, colonial.
Ipswich, Mass., postal rates, 536
Ireland: provisions from, exempted from Staple Act, 216 n; colonial exports forbidden to, 229, 235, 351; import restrictions repealed, 235 n; Pa. flax exports to, 315; not taxed by Parliament, 509 n
Irish, Pennsylvania. *See* Scotch-Irish.
Iron: experiment on electrical fusion of, 98; colonial, forbidden to Ireland, 235; extraction, medal for, 352 n
Iroquois (Six Nations): to be told of massacres, 43; Conestoga Indians members of, 45; honor, 62–3; reaction to massacres, 66–7; reaction to Indian scalping, 174 n

Jackson, Richard: sent copy of BF currency speech, 7–8, 10–11, 18 n; reports on Barker, 33–4; concern about Pa., colonies, 34, 462; assiduity as agent, 34–5, 36; opposes internal taxation of colonies,

34–5, 76, 186, 509–10 n; thinks colonial tax for troops inevitable, 34 n, 35, 169 n; on his influence, 35, 215, 313–14, 464–5; appointed secretary to Grenville, 35 n, 186 n, 509 n; greetings from, 35–6; to support WF's appointments, 97; asked to act for Md., 108, 152; to distribute Md. pamphlets, 109, 152; *Historical Review*, quoted, 139 n, 514–16; petitions and instructions sent to, 145, 148, 150, 151, 218, 229, 239, 255–6, 311, 423–5; asked to aid in changing Pa. government, 148, 151–2; earlier opinion on change, 151, 170 n; advises on Coxe grant, 175–6; on paper currency, 176–7; campaigns for de Grey, 177; informed on Coxe terms for grant, 185; urged to guard health, 188; settlement plans with BF, 188, 325 n, 358 n, 428; instructions on petition, 198, 219–20 n, 357–8, 398 n, 402–3, 423–4; credited with deferring Stamp Act, 215, 234 n, 314 n; denies influence in deferring, 215 n; intended work by, 216; sent messages on supply-bill dispute, 217, 220; BF allays doubts about, 219; asked to advise BF on going to England, 219, 229, 256, 263; asked to advise on presenting petition, 219; advice on, 219 n, 312–13, 327; asked to recall intent of Privy Council stipulation, 220; praised for service, 234; BF recommended, 234 n; to write Coxes, 238, 311; views on proprietary taxation, 239, 312; franking privilege, 257 n; apologizes for not dating letters, 311–12; too open with Allen, 312, 425 n, 462–4; not told of Proprietors' decision on tax dispute, 312 n; on change of government, 312–13, 327, 462–4; tried to postpone Currency Act, 313; Allen cites, on expenses of changing government, 313 n, 327–8, 375; report on supply-bill dispute, 327; reports rumors on Proprietors' conciliation of Assembly, 331; instructions on parliamentary taxation, 347–51, 366, 396–7 n, 424–5; Assembly has confidence in, 351; Strahan to pay money due from WF, 355–6; salary, 358; greetings to, 359; to correspond with committee, 425; role in proposed stamp act, 445 n; Harrison friendly with, 460 n; opinion of Allen, 462, 463; explains message sent through Allen, 462–4; unable to have WF's judges confirmed, 464; relations with Grenville, 509 n; opinion on S. Penn's claim, 533; letters from, 33–6, 175–7, 311–14, 462–5, cited or quoted, 19–20 n, 170 n; letters to, 19–20, 76–8, 95–7, 105–9, 148, 150–2, 185–8, 214–21, 229, 234–40, 255–7, 263–

4, 326–31, 339–40, 357–9, 397, 446–7, cited or quoted, 7, 18 n
Jael, murder of Sisera, 64 n
James, Abel: identified, 436 n; subscribes to linen factory, 315; accompanies BF to Newcastle, 449; political leadership, 449 n; confers on reply to *Answer*, 526
James, Robert: biographical note, 202 n; prescribes for Mrs. Stevenson, 202
James II or James, Duke of York: policies, 141; rights of Papists under, 166 n; lease of Delaware, 465
James and Drinker, BF sails on ship of, 517; letter to, quoted, 435
James River, Va., heir sought near, 233 n
Jeffreys, George, Baron Jeffreys of Wem: biographical note, 141 n; judicial decisions, 141
Jenikes, Daniel, signs R.I. Assembly letter, 397
Jenkinson, Charles: biographical note, 36 n; letter to, mentioned, 36
Jews, BF compares Paxton Boys with, 56
John (BF's servant), behaving well, 517
John (Kyunqueagoah; Conestoga Indian), massacre of, 49
Johnson, Joseph: identified, 258 n; advice on book distribution, 258
Johnson, Nathaniel, identified, 164 n
Johnson, Robert: identified, 164 n; on blessings of royal government, 164
Johnson, Samuel: identified, 477 n; retires to Stratford, 477 n, 478; retires from King's College, 478; letter from, 477–8
Johnson, Sir William: attempt to send Pa. Indians to, 28, 68 n, 69; to inform Iroquois of massacres, 42–3; confirms Owens' story, 174 n; makes Indian treaty, 329, 335; Indians to confirm peace with, 485; report to, quoted, 528–9 n
Johnson, William Samuel, father retires to, 477 n, 478
Johnston, George: identified, 6 n; repaid for Bernard, Jr., 6, 133; letters of, forwarded, 133
Johnston, Rachel: greetings to, 333; desertion of armonica for baby, 333
Jones, Ephraim, commands *William*, 88
Jones, Griffith: property of, 320 n; letter for, 418
Jones, Isaac: identified, 339 n; notarizes document, 339
Jones, Lewis: asks BF to deliver letter, 418; letter from, 418
Joppa, Md., Phila. mail to, 401
Joshua, analogy to, used by Paxton followers, 56

Journal and Ledger, 1764–1776, described, 518–20

Judas Maccabeus, BF criticizes, 540–2

Judges: appointment and tenure of, 130, 140–1, 147, 170, 301, 358, 512–14; Jackson unable to confirm for WF, 464; S. Johnson dislikes in Conn., 478. *See also* Courts.

Judith, murder of Holofernes, 64 n

Jugement rendu . . . dans l'affaire du Canada, sent to Bouquet, 368

Justice: relation to authority, 106; as principle of legal interpretation, 118–19, 203, 210–11

Justices of the peace: partisanship in appointments of, 468, 472–3, 484–5, 522–3; recommend tavern licenses, 522 n

Kaffart (Caphart), Georg, paid for stone for BF's house, 455

Kames, Henry Home, Lord, has copy of "Parable," 354

Keith, Sir William: stand on proprietary instructions, 137 n; removed from office, 137 n

Kembleville, Pa., post office deeded land in, 469 n

Kendall, Benjamin, reports Paxton Boys' plans, 70

Kent, Benjamin: biographical note, 80 n; compliment of, 80; BF print for, 90

Keowee (town), becomes Fort Prince George, 94

Keppele, Henry: on "New Ticket," 390; elected, 394; votes against BF appointment, 407 n; signs protest on BF appointment, 412

King of Prussia, BF sails on, 418 n, 427 n, 447–50, 517 n, 521 n

King's College, Johnson retires as president, 477 n, 478

Kinnersley, Ebenezer: experiments on fusion of iron and electrified air, 98–9, 244; in charge of student residence, 134 n; reply to Smith's charges against BF, 389 n

Kinsey, John, leads Assembly action on riots, 377 n

Labor, cost of, 316 n

Lancaster, James, anecdote on voyage of, 216 n

Lancaster, Pa.: Indians massacred in workhouse at, 9, 19, 26–7, 42–3, 52–5, 65, 77, 304 n, 305, 378 (*see also* Massacre); plans to try murderers of Indians, 27–8; officials' actions in massacre, 43, 50–1; troops moved to, 70; barracks at, 223; plans for

new postal route from, 248; Foxcroft's trip to, 249; Phila. mail to, 401; Pa. troops return to, 529

Lancaster County, Pa.: Indians massacred in, 9 (*see* Conestoga Manor; Lancaster; Massacre); proposal to remove trials from, 27–8, 82, 364; questioning of officials on massacre, 30, 306; fear of Paxton Boys, 55; unrest in, 71; Paxton Boys assemble in, 71; grievances, 81–3; Assembly representation, 81–2, 379 n; represented on Assembly committee, 83, 193; petitions on royal government from, 146, 218, 291; praises Saunders for opposing petition, 340 n; election results, 393, 467; German-Irish dissension in, 467–8

Land Office: injustices, 140; arbitrary closing of, 380; BF has not dealt with, 436, 437 n

Land schemes. *See* Settlement.

Lands, Pa.: purchased from Indians, 46; taxation of proprietors, 95 (*see also* Proprietary estates); reserved by Penns, 128, 140; price of, causes emigration, 128–9, 140; payment for, to be in sterling, 142–3 n, 284 n; disputes over purchase price of, 160; unfairly taken by proprietary leaders, 380. *See also* Taxation, Pa.; Town lots; Waste lands.

Lane & Booth, bill drawn on, 452

"Lapidary style," used in political writings, 298–9, 372, 380–4, 387–90. *See also* Epitaphs.

Lardner, Lynford, provincial commissioner, 261

Lawrence, Thomas, notarizes document, 442–3

Laws, ambiguous, "justice and equity" in interpreting, 118–19, 203, 210–11

Lebanon, Conn., library and school founded, 32 n

LeBoeuf, Fort, Price commander at, 93 n

Le Despencer, Lord, (Sir Francis Dashwood), Bouquet letters sent to, 266 n

Ledger, 1764–1776. *See* Journal and Ledger.

Ledru, John and Joseph, paid for work on BF's house, 455, 456

Leech, Thomas: confers with governor, 273; signs Assembly tax report, 286

Legislative council: possibility of, 170; Pa. needs aristocratic, 324; Pa. does not have, 301, 489; recommended for Pa., 484–5; in colonies, 485 n

Lemons: necessary for health, 215; should not come under Staple Act, 215–16; use against scurvy, 216

Lempriere, Clement: identified, 93 n; Price unable to see, 93–4

Letter from a Gentleman in Crusoe's Island, A (BF pamphlet fragment): source of form, 184; text, 184
Levers, Robert: identified, 261 n; pay orders for, 223, 224; to victual troops, 261
Lewis, Jacob, subscribes to linen factory, 315
Libel, protests as form of, 430
Liberty (sloop), attempt to seize, 460 n
Library Company of Phila., books on Eastern peoples, 58 n, 59 n
Licenses, liquor: abuses in, 128, 139–40, 522; governors refuse bills to limit, 128, 139–40; governor's perquisite, 272 n, 277, 522
Lieutenant governors, Pa. *See* Governors, Pa.
Life, Thomas: identified, 533 n; can locate S. Penn, 151; to confer with BF on S. Penn's claim, 533
Lighthouse Bill: Penn rejects, 104, 106–7, 302; enacted, 107 n
Lightning: experiment on, 98; in Southwark, 98; fusion by, 244; stroke on St. Bride's Church described, 544–5
Lightning rods, article published on, 98 n
Linens: effect of duties on imports, 184; drawback abolished, 235 n, 314; colonial production, 235, 314–15; rise in price of, 314–15; Phila. manufactory started, 314–15; colonial, unable to match English, 316 n
Liquids: Canton on compressibility of, 245–6
Liquor: licensing, 128 (*see* Licenses); needed in water during hot weather, 256 n
Little, John, pay order for, 224
Livermore, Matthew, gets judgment for post-office money, 338 n
Lloyd, David, pamphlet on proprietary rights, 126 n
Loan Office: accounts of, 222 n; and parliamentary grants, 500 n
Lockman, John, translator of Bayle's *Dictionary*, 89 n
Loftus, Arthur, forced to retreat from Mississippi R., 217 n
Logan, James, certified Pa. acts, 171 n
Logan, William: confers with Paxton leaders, 73; subscribes to linen factory, 315
London: charter revoked, 167; Americans buy books from, 190; BF may move to, 332 (*see also* Franklin, Benjamin); BF arrives in, 517
London Chronicle: reprints Pa. Assembly documents, 149, 354 n; advertises book on colonies, 216; reports bloodhounds sent to N.Y., 240 n; reprints BF pamphlets, 331 n, 332 n, 354 n; prints WF paragraph on Pa. government, 356 n; quoted on uprooting engine, 480 n; reports BF's embarkation and arrival, 517 n, 524 n
London Coffeehouse, Club of Honest Whigs meets at, 98 n
Long, Capt. P., carries mail, 240 n
Long, William, describes land, 428 n
Longitude, chronometer for, 481, 482
Lords, House of: So. Car. appeal to, 163 n; practice of recording protests, 308, 430, 489. *See also* Parliament
Lottery, post-office receipts, 251
Loudoun, John Campbell, 4th Earl of, BF's aid to, 319, 322
Loudoun, Fort: troops to assemble at, 226, 266; Bouquet expedition to leave, 325 n
Louisbourg, coal mines, status of, 182
Lowell, John: biographical note, 227–8 n; greetings to, 227
Lower Counties. *See* Delaware.
Ludwell, Philip, commissions BF portrait, 89 n
Luken, John, defeated for coroner, 394
Lumber, colonial, forbidden to Ireland, 235, 351
Lutherans: antagonism toward Quakers and Moravians, 44; opinion of Paxton Boys, 44; persuaded not to aid Paxton Boys, 73 n; against BF, 327 n
Luxuries, duties on, 76
Lydians, corruption of, 522
Lyndon, Josias: biographical note, 231 n; BF print for, 231
Lyndsay, Capt., commands *Pitt*, 461
Lynn, John, property of, 320

McClean, Capt., Owens deserted from, 174 n
McCleave, George: identified, 469; BF takes over bond of, 469
McConaughy, David: votes against BF appointment as agent, 407 n; signs protest on BF appointment, 412
Machine for uprooting trees: a failure, 480; BF's idea for, 480
Mack, James D., sends first BF photocopy, 228 n
McMurray, Thomas, wounded, 224
McNair, Andrew, pay order for, 223
McNutt, Alexander: Parker will write, 470; BF interested in Nova Scotia land schemes of, 470 n
Madeira, BF forwards letter to, 153, 178
Madeira wine: duty on, 76 n, 183 n; exempted from Staple Act, 216 n
Magna Carta: rights under Pa. charter equal those under, 347, 349; Pa. entitled to rights of, 510

Magnetism, observations on electricity and, 254. *See also* Aepinus.

Manchester, manufactures, duties on, 76

Manor lands, price of, 140

Mansfield, William Murray, Lord: quoted on Pa. change of government, 328; poem attacking, 516 n

Manufactures: British wish to monopolize, 183; colonies can produce, 183–4; relation to duties, imports, 183–4; of textiles, 314–16

Maps, of post roads to be sent, 38

Marblehead, Mass., Phila. mail to, 400

Marian persecution, victims of, 303 n

Marlboro, Md., Phila. mail to, 401

Marlborough, Mass., Kent dismissed from ministry at, 80 n

Martin, Josiah, W. Smith tutor for, 388 n

Martyn, Benjamin, authorship of pamphlet on So. Car., 163 n

Mary and Elizabeth (ship), carries books for BF, 265

Maryland: open Assembly debates in, 93; unhappy under proprietary government, 108, 158; Assembly has no agent, 108; Assembly, prorogations of, 109 n; usefulness of Proprietors to, 125 and n; proprietary government in, 126 n, 463; cheap land attracts immigration, 129; Assembly will petition for royal government, 152; pamphlets, supply bill, sent to Jackson, 152; Assembly dispute on supply bill, 152 n; BF's interest in disputes, 158 n; Catholics granted tolerance in, 166 n; does not receive military aid, 167; support of Episcopal clergy, 169; not requisitioned by Amherst, 212 n; proprietary appointment of governor, 293 n; proprietary system obsolete, 325 n; post-office affairs in, 341 n; retains royal charter, 348 n; new postal routes in, 399 n; percentage of Phila. mail to, 400

Massachusetts: Gage becomes governor of, 7 n; grants Bernard Mount Desert, 32 n; experience with royal government, 154; charters, dissenters privileges in, 167–8; established church in, 168 n; bounty on wheat, 179; duties on flour and bread, 179 n; General Court assists at Harvard fire, 255 n; retains royal charter, 348 n; petition on trade and rights, 452

Massachusetts House of Representatives Committee: proposes united remonstrance on colonial duties and taxes, 242–3; Pa. supports 347, 351 n, 366; stress on joint action, 351 n; Jackson's instructions sent to; 396 n; letter from, 242–3; letter to, 365–6

Massacres: of friendly Indians, 9, 19, 26–7, 42–55, 63, 77, 102, 103, 160, 247, 304 n, 305, 378; Penn's proclamations on, 26 n, 43 quoted, 51–5, unheeded, 160, discontinued, 306; Assembly proposal on site of trials for, 27–8, 82, 364; public opinion on, 27, 43–7, 77, 305; questioning of officials on, 30, 306; pamphlets on, 43 n, 52–3 n, 305; BF pamphlet on, see *Narrative of the Late Massacres;* reward offered, 53–4; possible effects of, 66–7; inquiry on, dropped, 104, 306; murderers unpunished, 160, 305–6; of Indian scouting party by Owens, 173–4; of school by Indians, 335 n

Maskelyne, Nevil, appointed astronomer royal, 482 n

Masterman, Thomas, pay order for, 223

Mather, Cotton, mentioned, 90 n

Mather, Increase, mentioned, 90 n

Mauduit, Jasper: on Grenville's postponement of Stamp Act, 242 n; instructed to oppose colonial taxation, 243; sent Mass. petition on taxation, 452 n; letters from, quoted, 242 n, 349 n

Mayhew, Jonathan: biographical note, 89–90 n; BF print for, 89; BF to send *Narrative* to, 91 n

Meas, John, subscribes to linen factory, 315

Mecom, Benjamin: bankruptcy, 240–1; Parker sets up in New Haven, 241; effects auctioned, 241, 332

Mecom, Jane: parcel sent to, 88; BF print for, 90; BF cannot frank letters of, 253, 262; condolences on daughter's death, 253, 262; letters to, 253–4, 262

Medicine: prescriptions sent Grey, 53; BF on practice of, 101; James patents for, 202 n; advice on dangers of water, 256 n; recipes, 537, 537–8 n. *See also* Fevers; Inoculation; Scurvy; Yellow fever.

Memmius, cited, 372

Mental illness, pill used to treat, 202 n

Mercury: in smallpox inoculation, 183 n, 356; compressibility of, 246

Mercy, and bravery, 69

Meredith, Reese, bill of exchange on, 427 n

Metals: hot fusion of, by lightning, 244; magnetism of, 254

Meteor, explosion reported, 263

Meteorology, Moffatt records on, 191

Methodists, buy Phila. church, 201 n

Mezzotint print, of BF, 89 n, 230 n, 247

Michell, John: identified, 480 n; not to be astronomer royal, 480–1; and Harrison chronometer prize, 481; marriage and retirement, 481; political subserviency, 481

Michigan, Lake, Indians aroused by French, 528

Micrometer, for Bowdoin's telescope, 22, 245, 452–3

Middletown, Conn., Phila. mail to, 400

Mifflin, John: subscribes to linen factory, 315; mentioned, 78 n

Mifflin, Samuel, subscribes to linen factory, 315

Mifflin, Thomas: biographical note, 78 n; introduced to Jackson, 78

Militia: to be superseded, 78; British troops may be preferable to, 169; criteria for officers of, 364–5. *See also* Officers; Troops, Pa.

Militia Act of 1755: BF author of, 76 n; naming of officers in, 362 n, 513; provisions for fines and trials, 362 n; charges against BF on, 512–13

Militia Bill of 1764: Penn requests, 69–75, 104, 360; passed, 75 n, 77–8; Penn demands amendments to, 76 n, 106, 122; dispute over, 76 n, 130–1, 141–2, 306, 360–5, 513, 514; as election issue, 76 n, 360–1, 365; Penn uses mob to get, 107; Assembly Resolves on, 130–1, 141–2, 513; paper on, 513

Miller, John Henry, publishes BF *Remarks*, 457

Mills, John: identified, 257 n; book on husbandry published, 258; thanks BF for list of booksellers, 258; letter from, 257–8

Minerals, American, catalogue of, 97

Mingo (Indians): Bouquet makes peace with, 446 n, 485–6; hostages escape, 528 n; want peace confirmed, 529

Ministry, British: proprietorships as buffer between colonies and, 124–5 n; Pa. in disfavor of, 130, 374; Jackson's influence on, 234 n, 314 n; wants colonial goodwill, 242; monetary principles, 282; control of Pa. under royal government, 313; party gains, 317; against proprietary government, 324; willing to consult colonies on taxes, 349; Pa. substitute plan for, 350; criticizes BF, 367 n; reaction to Pa. Resolves, 375; insistence on internal taxation, 404 n; agents to oppose, 406; unfavorable opinion of BF, 410, 431–3, 492; BF to influence, 451–2; attitude toward R.I. charter, 460; probable reaction to Pa. petition, 463. *See also* Grenville, George.

Mischief, BF inclined toward, 173 n

Missisquoi River: scheme for land grant at, 428; located, 428 n

Mississippi River: project for settling, 176; troops unable to ascend, 217

Modern History, vol. xv, sent to BF, 478

Moffatt, Thomas: biographical note, 191 n; authorship of letter on R.I. politics, 186 n; wants royal government in R.I., 192 n; writings on royal government, 459 n; letters from, 191–2, 356–7

Mohammed, on treatment of captives, 58–9, 65

Mohammedans, hospitality, 59–60, 66

Mohawks (Indians), honor, 63

Mohawk River, Indians to be sent to, 28

Molasses, duty on foreign: lowered by Sugar Act, 19 n, 34 n, 182 n, 215 n; BF's views on, 76, 235; still too high, 235

Molasses Act, stricter enforcement of, 108

Monckton, Robert: identified, 177 n; speaks for paper money, 177

Monday Club, greetings to members of, 234 n

Money. *See* Currency.

Money bills and acts. *See* Supply bills and acts.

Montagu, Edward, reports Grenville statement to Commons, 348 n

Montgomery, Archibald, action against Cherokee, 94

Montgomery, John: signs Assembly report, 93; votes against Assembly petition, 161 n, 193 n, 198, 291 n; on committee for petition to King, 193; pay order for, 224; votes against BF appointment as agent, 407 n; signs protest on BF appointment, 412; signs protest on petition, 491 n; letter by, 297 n

Montgomery, Thomas, subscribes to linen factory, 315 n

Montgomery's Regiment of Highlanders (77th): escorts friendly Indians, 28, 68; BF commends, 68; Cherokee remember, 94

Monthly Review, The: American circulation promoted, 189; criticizes Canton's experiments, 245 n; reviews Galloway and Dickinson pamphlets, 332 n

Montreal, Quebec: Gage military governor of, 7 n; gets regular postal service, 41; rates reduced to N.Y., 41 n; Phila. mail to, 400

Moon, BF orders book on, 334

Moor, John, signs report, 439

Moore, Charles: certifies £55,000 Supply Bill, 111; certifies Assembly resolves on appointing BF, 408 n

Moore, Mary, marriage, 416 n

Moore, Samuel Preston: subscribes to inen factory, 315; signs stock certificates, 315, 316

Moore, William: appointed chief justice,

468, 472–3, 485, 523, 531; alleged libel of Assembly, 468 n; Hamilton and removal of, 472–3

Moors, hospitality and honor, 56, 60, 66

Morals, public, corrupted by licensing abuse, 128, 139, 522

Moravian Indians: attempt to emigrate, 19, 28, 67, 69–70; charges against, 25, 64 n, 74 n; ask for safety, 25, 28; sent to Phila., 25–6. See also Indians in Phila.

Moravians: relations with Indians, 25, 44; Presbyterian and Lutheran animosity toward, 44; did not aid German settlers, 44 n

Morris, Robert Hunter: identified, 96 n; death, 96, 464 n; BF difference with, 507; unwilling assent to Militia Act, 512; attacked in Historical Review, 515 n

Morris, Sarah, marriage and death, 526 n

Morris, William; identified, 525 n; relation to Dickinson, 525 n; urges Dickinson not to answer BF, 525

Morris, William, Jr., subscribes to linen factory, 315 n

Morton, James Douglas, 14th Earl of, opposes Short, 482

Morton, John: signs Assembly reports, 86, 439; votes on appointing BF agent, 407; not reappointed justice, 468 n, 485, 523, 531

Mosquito Shore: dispute over, 236, 313; as source for sugar, 236

Moth Mullein, medicinal use of, 537 n

Mount Desert (island), granted to Bernard, 32 n

Muhlenberg, Henry Melchior, journals quoted and cited, 26 n, 44 n, 69 n, 72, 73 n, 74 n, 185 n

Muirson, Dr. George, method for inoculating, 356 n

Munsey Hill, soldier wounded at, 223

Murray, James: identified, 188 n; complains of Quebec postal service and rates, 41; may nullify Quebec plan, 188

Murray, William, 2d mate, protected in Africa, 61–2

Murray, William, Army captain, ordered to Lancaster, 70 Music, BF's views on, 538–43

Music, BF's views on, 538–43

Muskingum River: Indians capitulate at, 326 n, 485; Bouquet ascends, 446 n

Muslins, drawback on, 235 n

Myrtilla, carries mail, pickled sturgeon, 334 n

Nairne, Edward, work on Bowdoin's telescope, 22 n, 99, 244–5

Nantucket whalers: refused settlement on St. John, 187; Quebec tracts for, 187–8

Narrative of the Late Massacres, A: BF pamphlet, 42–69; publication date, 45; tone, 45; reply to, 52–3 n, 64 n, 66 n; purpose, 77, 103; sent to friends, 77, 91 n, 190 n, 331; praised, 202 n, 202–3; Bowdoin comments on, 246–7; printed in England, 331 n; Scotch-Irish bitter over, 332

Naturalization Bill (1743), passage of, 273

Navigation Act of 1663 (Staple Act): ship seized under, 91; provisions, 91 n, 216 n

Navigation Acts: control colonial trade, 25 n; enforcement of, 108, 215

Navy, British: in customs inspection, 108 n, 215; being built up, 317

Nazareth, Pa., Indians moved to, 25 n

Neate, William, to collect bloodhounds, 240

"Necklace of Resolves." See "Resolves upon the Present Circumstances."

Negroes, African: BF on justice and honor of, 56, 61–2, 66; BF wants duty on, 76; BF wants importation checked, 76; no duty on, in Sugar Act, 76 n

Nelson, John, pay order for, 223

Nevill, Samuel: biographical note, 96 n; disabled, 96, 464 n; death, 464 n

New and Accurate Account of the Provinces of South-Carolina and Georgia, A, quoted, 162–3

Newark, N.J., Phila. mail to, 401

Newbury, Mass., Phila. mail to, 400

New Castle, Del.: pickling salmon at, 32; Phila. mail to, 401; BF's friends leave ship at, 448, 449

New England: BF's accident in, 21 n; restraint on paper money in, 35, 282 (see also Currency Act); BF-Foxcroft postal trip to, 249 n; smallpox inoculations in, 356; militia system, 362 n

New England Primer, The, verses quoted from, 303, 381 n

New Hampshire: becomes royal colony, 168; dissenters privileges in, 168; BF postal trip to, 249

New Haven: press in, 241, 413–14; Mecom postmaster in, 241 n; Phila. mail to, 400

New Jersey: refuses Amherst requisition, 7; Indian refugees sent to, 19, 28; Barker land in, 34; map being prepared of, 38 n; right of governor to share of prize, 91; 178; Assembly doors closed in, 93; judges appointed in, 96–7, 464; Quakers flee to, 102; change to royal government, 165–7; religious liberty, 166–7; troops for Indian campaign, 217 n, 218, 335;

mercuric inoculation used in, 356 n; WF as governor of, 371 n, 386; percentage of mail to, 400; boundary dispute with N.Y., 414 n, 432 n; Hardy removed from government, 512

New Jersey, College of: Habersham sons at, 259; BF and WF commended at, 386 n

New London, Conn: customs post open, 109; Phila. mail to, 400; postal rates, 536

New London, Pa., Dunlap land in, 419 n

New News from Robinson Cruso's Island, BF's possible use of, 184

New Orleans, troops arrive at, 217 n

Newport, R.I.: Bernard, Jr. returns via, 31 n, 78–9; temperature extremes at, 191; P. Franklin moves from, 253 n; Phila. mail to, 400; postal rates, 536

Newport Mercury, letter in, 186 n, 459 n

Newspapers, Jackson displeased with praise in, 313–14

Newtown, Md., Phila. mail to, 401

New York (city): mail service to Boston and Phila., improved, 20–1, 399; Phila. mails, speed of, 21; Bernard, Jr. rides to, 31 n; packets to Falmouth, 38; report on post office in, 38; postal service to Canada, 41; E. Holland sought in, 232–3; BF trip to, 249 n; post-office receipts, 251; postal rates, 343–5, 536; percentage of mail to, 399; Phila. mail to, 401

New York (province): refuses Amherst requisition, 7; refuses Pa. Indians entry, 28, 68, 69; Assembly doors closed in, 93; troops in Indian war, 217–18 n, 335; bloodhounds to be kept by, 240 n; mercuric inoculation used in, 356 n; boundary dispute with N.J., 414 n, 432 n

N.-Y. Gazette, BF advertisement for E. Holland in, 232, quoted, 233 n

New-York Pacquet, fails, 240 n

Niagara, Fort: Bradstreet leaves, 218 n, 326 n; Indian treaty at, 329, 335

Nicaragua. *See* Mosquito Shore.

Nicoll, W., sells Galloway's *Speech,* 332 n

Norfolk, England, election campaign, 177

Norfolk, Va., post office in, 250 n; Phila. mail to, 402

Norris, Charles, Assembly meets at house of, 70, 218

Norris, Isaac: illnesses, 29, 70, 196, 218, 296, 310, 403; signs messages, 30, 116, 122; position on petition to King, 195–6, 218–19 n, 390–1; wants sentiments recorded, 195, 295 n; resigns as speaker, 196, 205, 218, 393, 403, 425; proprietary opinion of, reversed, 295–6; subscribes to linen factory, 315; on both tickets, 377 n, 390–1; elected, 392, 394; elected speak-er, 395 n, 402; on presenting petitions to King, 402–3; on Committee of Correspondence, 422 n; correspondence with BF, 439; account with Osborne, 479 n; use of Dickinson, 527; letter to, cited, 171 n

Northampton County, Pa.: Indians suspected of murders in, 25; Indian refugees from, 67; grievances, 81–3; Assembly representation, 81–2, 379 n; represented on committee on frontier grievances, 83; petition for royal government from, 146; atrocity in, 173–4; represented on petition committee, 193; election results, 393; Allen elected from, 494 n

North Carolina: in new postal district, 39 n, 260 n; cheap lands attract immigration, 129, 140; use of quitrents in, 139 n; settlement of, and Coxe grant, 175–6; currency depreciation in, 176 n; change to royal government, 328

Northumberland, Earl of, aids Bartram, 353 n

Norton, William, pay order for, 223

Norwalk, Conn., Phila. mail to, 400

Nova Scotia: BF and Jackson interested in grant in, 186–7, 358–9; BF will encourage settlement of, 187, 359; settlement of, at British expense, 349 n; terms for land grants in, 358; land grants issued, 358 n; McNutt land schemes in, 470 n

Oak, white, in Lake Champlain area, 428

Oaths, N.J. Quakers exempted from, 166–7

Observations Concerning the Increase of Mankind, slur on Germans in, 370, 375, 382, 385, 397, 434 n, 505

Odysseus, hospitality toward, 56–8

Officers, militia: dispute over right to appoint, 130–1, 141–2, 302, 361–2, 512–14; election of, 362 n, 512–13; instructions on criteria for, 364–5

Oglethorpe, James, authorship of pamphlet on So. Car., 163 n

Ohio River: Quakers accused of settling on, 101 n, 180 n; Bouquet to march down, 217; BF scheme for colony on, 325 n

Ohio River Valley Indians: uprising, 63; Amherst plans offensive against, 96 n; 105 n; campaign against, 217 n (*see also* Bouquet, Henry); refuse Johnson treaty, 329, 335; treaty with Bradstreet, 329–31, 333, 335–7; make peace with Bouquet, 446 n, 458, 483, 485–6, 523, 530; to sign treaty, 476, 529; hostilities may be renewed, 523; supplied by French, 523, 528, 530. *See also* Delaware Indians; Huron; Mingo; Shawnee.

Olive oil, compressibility of, 246

Oratorios, BF criticizes, 540–3
Order in council. *See* Privy Council, order of Sept. 2, 1760.
Ores, American, catalogue of, 97
Osborne, Thomas: identified, 478 n; sends catalogues, book to BF, 478; accounts with Norris, 479; letter from, 478–9
Oswald, Eleazer, marriage, 416 n
Oswald, James, opposes colonial taxation, 509–10 n
Otis, James, signs Mass. House appeal, 243
Ottawa (Indians), capture Eckerlings, 443 n
Ourry, Capt., given funds for Bouquet, 317 n
Owens, David: desertion, 173–4; scalps Indian party, 174; made interpreter for Bouquet, 174 n; incident with hostages, 528, 530
Oxford and Mortimer, Robert Harley, Earl of, Pa. left in trust to, 293 n
Oxford University: Smith tries to prevent BF's degree from, 390 n; Tory favoritism toward, 482

Packet boats: increase in use of, 21; to become self-sustaining, 38; new plan established for, 38 n; service to So. Car. planned, 39; postal charges for, 257
"Palatine Boors," BF remark used in election campaign, 370, 375, 382, 385, 397, 434 n, 505
Palmer, John, settles BF's accounts, 455
Paper currency. *See* Currency.
Papists. *See* Roman Catholics.
"Parable against Persecution": Kames and Small have copies of, 354; Strahan prints, 354
Parish, John, quarry, 455
Parker, James: identified, 240 n; post-office achievements, 37–8 n; handles Mecom bankruptcy, 240–1, 332; debt to Strahan, 241 n, 414, 470, 520; post-office salary paid, 250; post-office receipts, 251; debts to BF, 251, 414, 470–1; given additional post-office titles, 251–2 n; commission to, 251–3; franking privilege, 254; receipt from, quoted, 332; signs postal notice, 341 n; business relations with Holt, 413 n; income, 414; to distribute post-office books, 414; and Hunter estate, 415–17; power of attorney to, 441–3; to settle BF's accounts with Hall, 441–3; 471; acts on Dunlap's debt, 469–70; DF not to visit, 470; health, 471; letters from, 413–17, 469–71; mentioned, 418
Parker, Jane (Jenny): witnesses power of attorney, 339; marriage, 339 n; letter not written to, 449 n; returns home, 470

Parker, Jeremiah, signature on BF draft, 429 n
Parker, Samuel Franklin: uncertain future of, 416; character, 416; marriages, 416 n; escorts sister, 470
Parkman, Francis, quoted, 335 n
Parliament: will insist on colonial tax, 20 n, 34–5, 169–70, 181; bill on paper currency, 35; Long, establishes control of colonial trade, 35; passes act on franking, 39 n; treatment of proprietary colonies, 125 n; passes Currency Act, 176 n, 282; BF on taxation without representation in, 186; passes act using Navy for customs service, 215 n; Jackson praised for efforts in, 234; colonial taxation acts objected to, 242–3; members' franking privilege, 257 n; possible sale price of Pa., 327; right to tax colonies, 347, 348–9 n, 396 n, 425, 444–5 n, 452; colonies not represented in, 347, 350; Jackson to work against taxation by, 347–51; no role in colonial settlement, 349 n; remonstrance to, on taxation, 350–1; not able to tax colonies justly, 397 n; traders ask compensation from, 476. *See also* Commons; Lords; Molasses Act; Sugar Act; Taxation, parliamentary.
Parliamentary grant (for 1758): BF accused of mishandling, 370, 411, 484, 498–501; BF defense of charges on, 438–41, 473
Parliamentary grant (1760), Pa. passes bill to repay, 19, 108
Parliamentary grants: deposited in Bank, 499–500; BF directed to receive, 500 n
Parr, William, elected sheriff, 394
Pawling, Henry: elected on "New Ticket," 390, 394; Assembly voting record, 393, 468 n, 523; dropped as justice, 393 n, 468, 484, 523, 531
Paxton, Pa., raiders from, 66. *See also* Paxton Boys.
Paxton Boys: massacre Indians, 26–7, 42–3, 50–4, 102, 103, 199, 200, 304–5; public opinion on, 27, 43–5, 103; plan to kill Indians in Phila., 42 n, 44, 70, 304; pamphlets on, 43, 52–3 n, 305; march on Phila., 45, 69–75, 77, 102, 160–1, 199, 200, 287; BF pamphlet on, 45–69; defended, 52 n, 55–6, 305; reward for conviction of, 53–4; fear of, in Lancaster, 55; stop at Germantown, 72–4, 77; present grievances and disband, 73–4, 77, 80–1 (*see also* "Declaration"; "Remonstrance"); inspect Indian refugees, 74; Pemberton flees, 83 n; threaten Phila. Quakers, 102; allegedly used to "awe Assembly," 103, 107, 121; leaders confer

privately with Penn, 104, 107; alleged proprietary encouragement of, 107, 121, 305, 378; militia bill asked to curb, 107, 122 n, 360; unpunished, 160, 304–6; government unable to protect people against, 160–1; factor in supply-bill dispute, 207; public expenses caused by march, 222; Presbyterians justify, 239; new attack rumored, 304; Irish Presbyterians said to side with, 327; BF's opposition to, used against him, 434

Paxton volunteers, entertainment of, 224

Pearson, Isaac: on petition committee, 193; supports petition, 193 n; on Committee of Correspondence, 422 n; signs report, 439

Pearson, James, sells property to BF, 319–21

Peckstang, Pa. See Paxton.

Peggy (Chee-na-wan; Conestoga Indian): character, 49; massacred, 49; gives Hay list of names, 49 n

Pemberton, Israel: hated for supporting Indians, 83 n; flees Phila., 83 n, 102 n; and Mary, ground rent on BF property, 320, 321, sold to BF, 320 n; Dickinson feels ill-used by, 527–8; character, 528

Pemberton, Sarah, marriage, 454 n

Penelope's suitors, death of, 58

Penington, Edward: identified, 533 n; advises S. Penn, 533

Penn, Ann: greetings from, 532; mentioned, 151 n

Penn, Hannah, disputes with settlers, 158

Penn, John: alienates Assembly and people, 7, 11, 104–5, 106–7, 117, 148, 150, 220, 286–8; dispute with Assembly over supply bill, 7–8, 10–11, 18 n, 119–20, 181 n, 224 n, 286–7, 356 n, 483 (see also Assembly); transmits request for troops, 7; sends instructions on supply bills, 8; interpretation of 1760 agreement, 18 n, 106 n, 112, 116, 118–21, 131–2, 194, 280, 281 n, 286–7; sends Indian refugees to N.J., 19; delays approving Pa. bill on parliamentary grant (1760), 19 n; approves bill against arming Indians, 25 n; proclamations on massacres, 26 n, 43, 51–5, 160, 306; orders investigation of Indian murders, 27; reports on Indian safety and massacres, 27, 42, 50 n; messages to Assembly quoted, 29, 75, 112, 119, 121, 127, 203, 204, 205, 206, 209, 210, 211, 212, 278, 360 n; requests Assembly advice on Indian safety, 29; rejects proposal on questioning officials, 31 n, 306; asks for Riot Act, 47, 104; appointed governor, 50, 184; welcomed, 50, 103, 106, 184; will protect Indians on Province Island, 51–2; orders Indians

back to Phila., 70; orders Phila. defenses against Paxton Boys, 70–2; signs Riot Act, 71; relies on BF in Paxton crisis, 72, 77, 103–4; sends delegation to Paxton Boys, 73, 77; to consider rioters' grievances, 74; report to Proprietors on Paxton crisis, 74 n; requests militia law, 74–5, 104; unacceptable amendments for militia bill, 76 n, 78 n, 130–1, 141–2, 306, 360–5, 513, 514; receives Paxton grievances, 80–1; confers on frontier grievances, 83–6; rejects proposed joint hearing, 85–6, 104, 107; rejects supply bills, 95, 105–6, 111, 112, 117, 150, 203–4, 205, 206; position on taxation of town lots, 96 n, 280, 281 n, 286–7; accused of using Paxton Boys to awe Assembly, 103, 107, 121, 305; Assembly present to, 103 n, 104; rejects requested Assembly bills, 104, 106–7; says Assembly violates royal prerogatives, 104, 106–7, 302; drops Indian massacre inquiry, 104, 306; meets privately with Paxton leaders, 104, 107; on lighthouse bill, 104 n, 302; on BF's involvement in Md. politics, 108 n; says order in council is clear, 112, 115, 118, 211; wants order in council directly quoted in supply bill, 112–16, 118–19, 208–10, 287; refuses responsibility for delay in frontier defense, 116, 121; accused of self-interest, 119–20; instructions to, 142 (see also Instructions, proprietary); does not want payment stipulation quoted, 143 n; on opposition to proprietary government, 150 n; on BF's "black heart" and effect on Pa. politics, 173 n; sends Owens to Bouquet, 174 n; first visit to Pa., 184; confirms BF's election as speaker, 196, 205; "disregards" Assembly abuse, 203, 211–12, 220 n; adamant on supply bill, 203–4, 207, 217; Assembly yields to, 204, 206–13, 217; demands new supply bill amendments, 204–7; drops new demands, 205 n; enacts £55,000 Supply Bill, 207; instructed to use Assembly interpretation of disputed order, but keeps silence, 213–14 n, 312 n, 317 n, 327 n, 340 n, 352 n; asks for Supply Act amendment, 214 n, 503 n; refuses amendment, 214 n; voice in expenditures, 221–2, 514; grants dogs for Bouquet, 226 n; as commander-in-chief, 260–1; Bouquet requests more troops from, 266–7; use of Privy Council statement, 278 n; alienates Council, 287–8; youth of advisors, 288 n; reports linen-company failure, 316 n; grants Bouquet's request for more troops, 316–17, 322;

personality as campaign issue, 369; partisan judicial appointments, 393 n, 468, 472–3, 484–5, 522–3, 531–2; commissions election winners, 395 n; delayed confirmation of Fox as speaker, 403-4; informally reveals proprietary concessions, 409–10, 424 n, 435–7, 494, 495, 502–4; passes supplement to Del. Reemitting Act, 466, 474–5; recall possible, 473; proclaims end to Indian war, 483 n, 486, 530; refuses to present proposals to Assembly, 529; letters from or to, quoted or cited, 42 n, 44, 103 n, 123 n, 150 n, 173 n, 213 n, 214 n, 224–6, 266 n, 328 n, 483 n, 485–6

Penn, Lady Juliana Fermor, an Anglican, 279 n

Penn, Richard: relations with Thomas Penn, 165 n; directs J. Penn to yield to Assembly, 213 n; religion, 279 n; advisor to brother, 288 n; BF's epitaph on, 298–9; letter from, quoted, 213 n. See also Proprietors.

Penn, Springett: willingness to sell Pa. rights, 151; asks BF's advice on claim to Pa., 533; letter from, 532–3

Penn, Thomas: relations with BF, 103, 412 n, 507 n; asks about J. Penn's present, 103 n; on BF's aid to J. Penn, 103 n; claims family useful as "buffer," 124–5 n; on liquor licenses, 128 n; Anglicanism, 158, 279 n; relations with Quakers, 158; relations with R. Penn, 165 n; opinion on paper money bill, 177; at hearing on paper money, 177 n; directs J. Penn to yield to Assembly, 213–14 n, 280 n; BF's jibes at, 271; BF's epitaph on, 298–9; complains about BF to Hyde and Halifax, 318 n; wants BF removed from post office, 318 n, 367 n; on disputed stipulation, 327 n; self-interest as campaign issue, 369; relations with Fothergill, 412 n; gives Phila. square to German Church, 496 n; urged to oppose colonial taxation, 509 n; letters from or to, cited or quoted, 103 n, 108 n, 123 n, 150 n, 173 n, 213–14 n, 219 n, 280 n, 295 n, 318 n, 327 n, 328 n, 358 n, 402 n, 404 n, 429–30 n, 432 n, 465 n, 492 n, 533 n. See also Instructions, proprietary; Proprietors.

Penn, William: treaties with Conestoga Indians, 48; annual acknowledgment for Pa., 129 n; began sale of Pa. to Crown, 132–3, 148, 151, 172, 289, 293–4, 302; terms of royal grant to, 135–6 n (see also Charter, royal); claim to legislative assent, 136; personal uses of quitrents,

138–9; will, provisions for sale of Pa. government, 151 n, 293–4; disputes with settlers, 158; claim to Del., 172 n, 465; grandson becomes governor, 184; Assembly gratitude to, 268, 297–8; financial difficulties, 293 n; epitaph on, 298 n; gift of Phila. squares, 435, 495–7; grants Pa. privileges, 510–11 (see also Charter of Privileges).

Pennsbury, entail to be barred, 533

Pennsylvania: complies with Amherst requisition, 7, 96 n, 105, 113, 218, 295; expense of supporting Indians, 25, 27, 44, 51–2, 67, 82, 87 n, 102 n, 222; peaceful Indians massacred in, 42–3 (see also Massacres); conflict between old and new counties, 81–2; disturbed condition of, 105, 150, 160–1, 181, 185–6, 189, 199, 200, 239, 271, 304–6, 357 n, 367, 368 n, 431, 462, 467–8, 492; emigration talked of, 107, 181; proprietary system obsolete, 124, 325 n; weakened by emigration, 129; in disfavor of Crown, 130, 141, 211–2; harmed by disputes between Proprietors and Assembly, 146–7, 158, 161; does not receive military aid, 167; rights will not change under Crown, 170–1; wish for royal government, 172–3, 181; petitions for royal government being signed, 185 (see also Petitions to the King, inhabitants); effect of charter privileges on settlement of, 197, 200, 294, 301–2; charged for Jackson's postage, 257; population, 290, distribution, 124 n; textile industry started, 314–15; flax exports, 315; provisioning of Shirley, 319; lacks aristocracy, 324; right to self-taxation, 347–50; Voltaire on happiness of, 367; western postal route started, 399; loss of parliamentary grant for 1758, 411; debauchery in, 522; captives of Indians returned, 529 n (see also Prisoners); S. Penn's claim to, 533. See also Assembly; Charter of Privileges; Charter, royal; Council; Elections; Frontier counties; Frontier defense; Governors; Parliamentary grants; Privileges; Proprietors; Taxation; Troops.

Pennsylvania Gazette: silence on massacres of Indians, 26 n, 53 n; account of Paxton Boys' march, 69 n; prints political documents, 133 n, 134, 148 n, 149, 289 n, 487, 488; copies distributed, 148 n, 149, 150, 174, 181 n; report on St. John grant, 187 n; prints news of Sugar Act, 215 n; advice on drinking water quoted, 256 n; letter on meteor explosion, quoted, 263n; prints international news, 317 n; account of Indian treaty, 336 n; quoted on BF's appointment, 451 n; reports BF's embarkation, 459; publishes proclamation on Indian peace, 530

Pennsylvania Hospital, donations to, proposed, 487

Pennsylvania Journal: silence on massacre of Indians, 26 n, 53 n; account of Paxton Boys' march, 69 n; does not print Assembly documents, 133 n, 289 n; prints *Cool Thoughts,* 153 n; letters on Jackson, quoted, 234 n, 314 n; letter on meteor explosion, quoted, 263 n; attacks Galloway and BF on military issue, 361; prints protest against BF's appointment as agent, 407, 408; prints BF's *Remarks,* 457 n; announces publication of *Answer* to, 486 n; prints Hughes's challenges on, 487, 488; *Supplement,* remarks on royal government in, 510

Penobscot River: possible fishery in, 31; settled, 31–2 n

Pensacola, troops return to, 217 n

Perkins, John: identified, 90 n; BF print for, 90; BF to send *Narrative* to, 91 n

Persia, duty on fabrics from, 235 n

Perth Amboy. See Amboy.

Peruvian bark (cinchona): BF's recipe for preparing, 537; used by BF for illness, 537 n

Peter (Hy-ye-naes; Conestoga Indian boy), massacre of, 49

Peters, Richard: presents request for militia law, 75; politically inactive, 288 n; alluded to, 296; relations with W. Smith, 388 n

Peters, William: doubts Norris' sincerity, 295 n; letters from, cited, 219 n, 295 n

Petition of Right, Assembly petition compared to, 302

Petition to the King, Assembly: constituents consulted on, 132, 145–6, 153–4, 289–92; Assembly Resolves on, 132–3, 144, 358 n, 424; BF may be asked to present, 149; to be drafted, 149; votes on, 161 n, 196–7, 218, 291 n, 308, 310, 393–4, 403; move for change of government opposed, 185 n (see also Royal government); passage of, 193–8, 291–2; Norris' position on, 195–6, 295–6, 402–3; two versions compared, 197–8; claim to Pa. privileges in, 197, 198, 199, 200, 302; not printed in minutes, 197 n; Jackson to proceed with caution on, 198, 220 n, 398 n, 403, 422 n, 424; to be suspended if privileges are endangered, 198, 220 n, 398 n, 403, 423–4; financing of, 198 n; BF draft, 199; approved text, 199–200;

bitterness leading to, 207; general support for, 218, 290–2; and instructions for, sent to Jackson, 218–20 (see also Jackson, Richard); BF asks Jackson's advice on presenting, 219; Dickinson's speech against, 267, 308–10 (see also Dickinson, John; Smith, William); not published, 268, 300; BF's Preface supports, 271; compared to Petition of Right, 302; Allen and Jackson discuss, 312; Jackson optimistic about chances of, 312 advises delaying, 313; future depends on election, 327; attempts at recall fail, 339–40, 357, 397–8 n, 403, 424; Saunders' opposition to, criticized, 340 n; fear of loss of privileges from, 340 n (see also Privileges); Presbyterian clergy oppose, 387; effect of elections, 393; debate on further instructions to Jackson on, 402–3; agents should not present without Assembly orders, 403, 405, 412; large majority against asserted, 406; effect of BF appointment on, 409; resolution to prosecute, 446; address to counteract, 465; protest against, 489–90; and S. Penn's claim, 533

Petition to the King, inhabitants: BF drafts, 145, 148; German translation of, 145, 146; sent to Jackson, 145, 148, 150, 151, 218, 229, 239, 423–4; presented to Assembly, 146, 193, 194, 290; text, 146–7; sent to Collinson, 181 n; being circulated and signed, 185; read in Assembly, 193, 204; Assembly prepares petition to accompany, 193–8; number of signers, 218, 290, 406; character of signers, 290–1; German Calvinists regret signing, 327 n; conditions for presenting, 423–4

Petition to the King, Maryland, 108–9

Petition to the King, Quakers: printed and circulated, 145–6; stresses liberties, 145–6; presented to Assembly, 146; influence on wording of Assembly petition, 197; read in Assembly, 204

Petition to the King, Rhode Island conservatives, BF asked to aid, 459–60

Pettit, Charles: identified, 391; letter on elections, quoted, 391 n

Pewter Platter Alley, BF buys property on, 319–21

Philadelphia:—N.Y. mails, speed of, 21; Indians brought to, 25–6 (see also Province Island); newspapers fail to report attacks on Indians, 26 n, 53 n; Paxton Boys plan raid on, 27, 30, 42 n, 44; proposed site of trial of Indian murderers, 27–8; Indians returned to, 28–9, 67, 70 (see also Indians in Phila.); Lancaster officials not summoned to, 30–1 n; public opinion on massacre of Indians, 43–4; Paxton Boys march on, 47, 71–4, 77, 103, 304 n, 305, 360, 378 (*see also* Association); meeting at State House, 71–2; clergy meet Paxton Boys, 72–3; Assembly representation, 81, 123, 379 n; petitions for open Assembly debates from, 91–2; attitude toward Penn, 105; highest temperature in, 191 n; yellow fever in, 191–2; BF represents on petition committee, 193; Bouquet in, 217 n, 224 n; P. Franklin postmaster at, 230 n, 253 n, 398, 418–19; reputed unhealthiness of, 232; new post-office route to Shippensburg, 248 n; post-office receipts, 251; excessive heat in, 256; meteor explodes over, 263 n; taxes on lots in, 280 (*see also* Town lots); Presbyterian clergy in, oppose change of government, 290; unemployment in, 314, 316 n; linen manufactory started, 314–15, failure of, 316 n; high price of labor, 316 n; quartering of British troops in, 319, 322, 378 n; society described, 324 n; postal rates, 344, 345, 536; brotherly love in, Voltaire on, 367–8; election riots (1742), 377 n; city government not elected by or responsible to people, 379–80; account of election in, 391–2; election results, 397, 493–4; outgoing mail, 1764–67, 398–402; inhabitants' remonstrance against BF appointment, 402–6, 433 n; Proprietors concede squares to, 410, 435, 494–7; post-office accounts for, 418–22; Dunlap prints and preaches in, 421 n; squares used as burying grounds, 496; liquor license fees, 522 n; robbers abound in, 530. *See also* Barracks, Phila.

Philadelphia, College of: students' expenses and lodgings, 133–4; Bernard to send son to, 153; BF's promotion of, 388

Philadelphia Corporation: charter, preservation of, 467; asks Proprietors to keep Pa., 467, 471–2

Philadelphia County: representation, 81, 123, 379; bill to hold trial of Lancaster massacrers in, 82; petition for royal government from, 146; represented on petition committee, 193; assessors cannot comply with Penn, 214 n; Dickinson at court in, 268; election results, 390–4, 397, 433, 468 n, 493–4; election defeat of BF and Galloway in, 391, 394, 397 (*see also* Franklin, Benjamin); BF never elected from, 484, 493–4; Allen elected from, 493–4; commission for justices in, 523, 531–2

Philadelphia Linen Manufactory: stock certificate, 314–16; articles of association,

315; subscribers to, 315; failure of, 315 n

Philadelphia Packet: brings Allen, mail, 253–4 n, 317 n, 318 n; sailing date, 265 n; carries mail, 340 n

Philosophical Transactions, BF orders, 334

Physick, Edmund, requests supply-bill changes, 204–5

Piankeshaws (Indians), protection of strangers, 64

Pickling, salt for, 87–8. *See also* Salmon; Sturgeon.

Pictures, Greenwood announces exhibition, 544

Piles, medicine for, 537–8 n

Pine timber, in Lake Champlain area, 428

Piper, John: identified, 248 n; recommended for post office, 248

Piscataqua, N.H., postal rates, 536

Pitt, William, the younger, influence of R. Price on, 100 n

Pitt, Fort: G. Price retires to, 93 n; Bouquet starts campaign from, 224 n, 226 n, 325, 326 n, 445; Davenport has store in, 227; Bouquet returns to, 446 n, 475, 523; treaty to be held at, 476; Indian hostages escape from, 523, 528, 530

Pitt (ship), carries mail, 461

Pitts, Molly Yeldhall, witnesses power of attorney, 339

Pittsburgh. *See* Pitt, Fort.

Plain Dealer pamphlets: attack Quakers, 102, 154, 157; authorship, 154, 157; support proprietary government, 154; criticize *Cool Thoughts,* 157, 158 n, 159 n, 164–5 n, 167 n, 168 n, 171 n, 172 n; abuse of BF in, 329 n

Plain Truth (1747), tone of, 45

"Plan for Settling Two Western Colonies," colony on Scioto River in, 325 n

Plumsted, Clement, inaction in 1742 election riots, 377 n

Plumsted, William, subscribes to linen factory, 315

Poetry, BF on setting music for, 538–42

Poland: BF on elections, 317–18; Russians invade, 318

Polly (brig), carries mail, 240 n

Pontiac's Uprising: Quakers blamed for, 101 n, 180 n; traders' losses from, 187 n, 476

Poor Richard, uses Burgh's writings, 100 n; suggests ways to avoid imports, 359 n; distances between cities in, 536 n

Pope, Alexander: BF quotes *Odyssey* translation by, 57–8 n; *Essay on Criticism* quoted, 292

"Poplicola," letter on *Answer* by, 487

Population, Pa.: as basis for representation, 123–4, 378, 379 n; heads of households, 290; total, 290

Portraits: of BF by Chamberlain, prints of, distributed to friends, 89–90, 230; WF takes, 89 n, 100; Bowdoin likes, 247; paid for, 520; of Bute, BF orders print of, 334

Portsmouth, England, BF disembarks at, 516

Portsmouth, N.H.: BF's and Foxcroft's visit to, 249–50 n; Phila. mail to, 400; postal rates, 536

Portsmouth, Va., no post office in, 250 n

Portugal, wines, new duty on, 183 n

Postmaster general, deputy, office of: BF threatened with loss of, 318 n, 328 n, 367 n, 492 n; a bar to independence, 406, 432–3; Allen's role in BF appointment to, 506, 507 n. See also Foxcroft, John; Franklin, Benjamin; Hunter, William.

Postmasters general, memo on North American posts, 36–41

Post Office, Great Britain, creates Southern Postal District, 39 n, 260 n

Post Office, North American: commissions for postmasters, 3–6, 259–60; service to be increased, 20–1; franking privilege, 33 n, 39, 253–4, 257 n, 262, 416 (see also Franking); report on, 36–41; Foxcroft and BF report on, expected, 36–8, sent, 341; their achievements with, 37–9; goals of, 37; sends first remittance, 37; revenues improving, 37–8; effect of packets on, 38; maps of post roads to be sent, 38; packet service improved, 38; Southern District planned, 38–9, 260 n; ship letters to be regulated, 39–41, 341 n, proposed rules for, 40 n, 41 n, 343–4, 345, captains to deliver all letters to, 40; payment for ship letters, 40–1, 342; Quebec-N.Y. service, 41; new mileage-rate scheme, 41, 343–6, 535–7, instructions and orders, 80, 341 n, 414; Phila.-Shippensburg route set up, 248; western route to Annapolis proposed, 248; personnel suggested for new offices, 248; BF and Foxcroft accounts, 248–51; lawyers paid for, 250; accounts owed to, 251, 338, 417 n, 418–22, 469–70; commission to Parker, 251–3; comptroller's remuneration, 252–3, 414 n; officers to support proprietary government, 318 n; Hubbart made attorney for, 337–9; form for mail records, 398; record of Phila. outgoing mail, 398–402; colonial development, 399; Woodbridge-Amboy post unprofitable, 416; BF's table of revised rates for, 535–7. See also Comptroller; Packet boats; Cities by name; Post Office acts.

Post Office, United Colonies, commission to Hunt, 3–6

Post Office Act of 1710: ship letter rates and regulations, 39–40, 342; rates compared to 1765 act, 535–6

Post Office Act of 1764: restricts franking privileges, 33 n, 254, 262; gives M.P.'s franking privileges, 257 n; sets comptroller salary, 414 n; BF's execution of, used in election campaign, 434

Post Office Act of 1765: lowers postal rates, uses BF-Foxcroft mileage-rate scheme, 41 n, 344 n, 535; recommendations on ship's letters for, 41 n, 343, 534 n; BF to see clauses for, 534

Post roads: survey of, 37–8; maps to be sent, 38

Posts, to be ceded by Indians, 330, 336

Potts, John: identified, 484 n; displaced as justice, 484, 523, 531

Poulett, John Poulett, Earl, Pa. left in trust to, 293 n

Power, dangers of uniting wealth with, 132, 143–4

Pownall, John, BF report sent to, 20 n

Pownall, Thomas: Administration of the Colonies, to be published, 216, BF revenue scheme in, 238 n; role in proposed stamp act, 445 n

Preface to The Speech of Joseph Galloway: headnote and text, 267–311; sent to friends, 319 n, 329, 332; tone of, defended, 329; English reviews of, 332 n; use of epitaph copied, 372; use of Primer verses, copied, 381 n; praised, 477

Prerogative, royal: Assembly charged with encroaching on, 104, 106–7, 302, 514; not involved in taxation dispute, 119; Proprietors criticized for not upholding, 126 n, 466–7, 474–5; endangered by proprietary power and wealth, 132, 144; proprietary misuse of, 301–2; violated by not presenting Del. laws, 466, 474–5; legislative council would support, 485

Presbyterians: animosities against Quakers, 44, 107, 150, 327; antagonism toward Moravians, 44; support of Paxton Boys, 44, 239; support proprietary party, 125 n, 327, 485 n; fear loss of religious liberties under royal government, 150, 467; in N.J. government, 167; Boston, to be solicited for new Phila. church, 201; urged to sign counter-petition, 256; clergy, oppose change of government, 290, 387, 389, as campaign issue, 369; against BF, 327 n, 386 n, 505; Quakers condemn for riots, 327; bitter about Narrative, 332; BF alludes to, as "religious bigots," 434,

457, 505; petition Proprietors against changing government, 467, 472, 524, 526 n; to be made justices, 468, 472; growing political strength feared, 485

Presqu'isle, Indian treaty at: 218 n, 326, 333, 335; terms of, 329–31, 336–7; BF's doubts on, 331, 337; repudiated, 446

Price, George: biographical note, 93 n; letter from, 93–5

Price, Richard: biographical note, 100 n; in Honest Whigs Club, 98 n; greetings to, 100; revolutionary views, 100 n; greetings from, 246

Prince Edward Island. See St. John, Island of.

Prince George, Fort: located, 93 n; Price commander at, 93 n; report on, 94–5

Princeton, N.J., Phila. mail to, 401

Pringle, John: account of meteor, 262; to assist Bartram, 352; shocked by Michell's behavior, 481; to write BF, 483; remedy for piles from, 537–8 n

Printers, young, abandoned to liquor, 416

Printing equipment: Mecom's, given for debts, 241, 332; BF's, to be sold to Hall, 442

Prints: of BF, sent to friends, 89–90, 230–1, 247; Chinese, on silk culture, 230; of Bute, BF orders, 334

Prisoners of Indians: taken, 22; effect of Indian massacre on, 66; measures for forcing return of, 82; recovered by Owens, 174; Bradstreet's terms for return of, 326 n, 330, 336; Bouquet recovers, 326 n, 475, 476, 483, 485–6, 523; Bouquet demands, 458; arrive at Lancaster, 529

Privileges, Pa., civil and religious: proprietary encroachment on, 127–8, 139, 159 n, 294, 295, 301–3, 384; petitions to King stress keeping, 145–6, 147, 197, 198, 199, 200; loss under royal government feared, 150, 161 n, 194, 195, 264, 292, 327, 405, 432 n, 508–12; possible loss denied, 162–8, 293–5, 532; important in settlement, 197, 200, 294, 301–2, 511; Assembly instructions concerning, 198, 220 n, 398, 403, 423–4; Jackson's views on, 313, 464; proprietary campaign paper on, 372–6; BF accused of selling, 375; legislative council would support, 484–5

Privy Council: ruling on judicial tenure, 130 n; debate on Supply Act of 1759, 138; pleadings before, to be published, 141; petitions for royal government submitted to, 146; decision on Cardigan claim, 175; financing Assembly petition before, 198 n; refuses Egmont grant of St. John, 325 n; appoints boundary commissioners, 432 n; lets Penn appoint governor for Pa. and Del., 465 n; right to approve laws, 466, 475; Del. laws not sent to, 466, 474–5; disallows Re-emitting Act, 466 n, 474

Privy Council, order of Sept. 2, 1760: ratifies agreement on taxing proprietary estates, 8, 96 n; on payments to Proprietors, 8, 142; disputed stipulations on taxing Proprietors' located, uncultivated lands and town lots, 18 n, 95, 96 n, 105–6, 111–16, 118–21, 129–30, 131–2, 203–4, 207, 208–12, 217, 220–1, 279–81, 286–7 (see also Proprietary estates, taxation of); proprietary concession on disputed stipulations, 213–14 n, 280 n, 312 n, 317 n, 327 n, 340 n, 410 n, 424 n, 435–7, 494, 502–4; forbids taxing unlocated, unoccupied proprietary lands, 239 n; whole order reviewed, 268, 277–85; confirms principle of taxing proprietary lands, 277; disputed stipulations an election issue, 375

Proclamation money, explained, 413 n

Property: danger of uniting power with, 132, 143–4

Proprietary estates, taxation of: injustice in favoring, 11–12, 18, 106, 119–20; dispute over rate for located, uncultivated lands, 11, 18 n, 104 n, 105–6, 111–16, 118–21, 129–30, 131–2, 194, 203–4, 206–13, 217, 220–1, 239, 275, 277, 279–80, 286–7, 312, 327, 375; in supply bill, 95–6, 105; dispute over ungranted town lots assessment, 95–6, 105, 111, 116 n, 207; "unsurveyed waste land" exempted from, 114, 239 n, 278–9, 280; report on, under 1759 act, 127, 138, 206, 285–6; Proprietors' attempts to avoid, 129, 137, 278, 285; problems in reports for, 204–5; Proprietors instruct Penn to yield on, 213–14 n, 312 n, 317 n, 327 n, 331 n, 497, 529 n; right to, confirmed, 278, 284–5, 414; previous disputes over, 378, 497 n; friends offer to pay, 378; concession informally reported to House, 410, 424 n, 435–7, 494, 495, 502–4; BF established principle of, 441

Proprietary government, Pa.: Paxton Boys' massacres an attack on, 44; powers over militia, 78; unpopularity, 78, 106; weakness, lack of authority, 102, 104–5, 160–1, 199, 200, 305–6, 467–8; BF hopes for abolition, 105, 125, 148, 150, 189 (see also Franklin, Benjamin); extortionary tactics, 121; authority, Penn's attempts to expand, 122; Assembly grievances against, 123–33, 199–200, BF's Explanatory Remarks on, 134–44; conflict of interests in, 124–5, 199, 200; usefulness to Pa., 124; Assembly wants end of, 125, 132–3, 144, 193–200, 213 (see also Assembly; Petition to the King, Assembly); no hope for happiness under, 132, 144; royal charter provisions for, 135–6; use of quitrents for, 138, 272 n; abolished in other colonies, 147, 158, 162, 289; disputes inherent in, 147, 150, 158–60, 186, 189, 288, 293, 303–4; respect for, ended, 147; sentiment on abolishing, 148, 150 (see also Counter-petitions; Petitions to the King, inhabitants, Quakers; Royal government); in Md., efforts to abolish, 152; pamphlets supporting, 154, 157; blamed for delay in defense, 154, 312; effects of changing from, 154 (see also Royal government); loyalty of officials, 161–2, 433; responsibility for defense, 167; receives no military aid from Crown, 167; will not prevent tax for troops, 169–70; desirability debated in England, 175 n; attitude toward Quakers, 181; speech favoring retention, 194; nature and frequency of disputes in, 199, 200, 303–4; legislative-executive relations, 207; "bargain and sale" proceedings in legislation, 271–7, 304; revenues to support, 272 n; disadvantages of, 288–306; ministry against, 324; not likely to alter, 324, 529; dispute irreconcilable, 329; injustice in, 431; loyalty to Crown and, 468. See also Governors; Proprietary rights and powers; Proprietors.

Proprietary grants, end of, 325 n

Proprietary party: Dickinson's support of, 10 n, 296, 527–8; denounces Indian massacres, 44; rumored use of Paxton Boys, 107, 378; minority in Assembly, 124 n, 161–2; factions for, 125, 327, 360, 387, 389, 485 n (see also Frontiersmen; Presbyterians); BF papers deject, 134, 457, 473–4; Norris' opposition to, 195; circulates counter-petition, 264 (see also Counter-petition); criticism of Pa. constitution, 294–5, 301; opinion of Norris, 295–6; panegyrics on Dickinson, 296; use Assembly petition as campaign issue, 327; attacks on BF, 329, 332, 370, 372–6, 380–4, 397, 434; BF answers, 329; doubts election outcome, 339; and Proprietors' concessions to Assembly, 352; political use of militia-bill dispute, 360–1, 365; on civil rights in trials, 364; paper against ticket of, 376–80; charges against leaders, 377–80; support frontier demands, 378–9; election paper against, 384–90; alleged immorality among, 386; "New Ticket," 390; gain assemblymen in Phila. Co., 391–2, 397; election results elsewhere, 392–4, 434; mortified by BF's appointment as agent, 451; members made justices, 472; loyalty to Chew, 526; Answer will rebound on, 527; in high spirits, 529

Proprietary rights and powers: as absentee governors, 126, 135–8; in judicial tenure, 130, 140–1, 147, 170, 301, 358, 514; Assembly will not add to, 130–1, 141–2; dangers in, 132, 143–4; hereditary, 135 n; legislative assent excluded from, 136; instructions not part of, 136–8; consent to laws, 274–7; consent to money, 281; to govern Pa., 289; to appoint governors, 293–4, 297, 300–1, 302; additions to, 302; to taxation, 349 n; in Del., 465 n, 475 n. See also Governors; Instructions, proprietary.

Proprietors, Pa.: agreement with agents on bills of credit, 8, 18 n, 238; unrelenting about taxation, 11; BF anxious to avoid dispute with, 18; accused of cheating Indians, 102 n; relations with BF, 103, 217–18, 247, 404 n, 406, 409, 412 n, 436–7, 497–8; relations with people, 106, 147, 150, 160, 184, 207, 287; J. Penn's "duty" to, 119–20; as "buffer" between colonies and ministry, 124–5 n; criticized by Board of Trade, 126 n, 466–7, 474–5; charged with responsibility for supply-bill delay, 127, 132, 137–8, 172; Assembly regard for, abused, 127–8; infringing on Charter privileges, 127–8, 139, 384; secret agreement with Thomas, 127 n, 274; harmful land policies, 128–9, 140; exorbitant land prices, 129, 140; reduce land price, 129 n; efforts to avoid taxation, 129, 137, 278, 285; misuse of crises, 130, 138, 147; partiality in judicial tenure under, 130, 358; power dangerous to Crown and people, 132, 143–4; interest, conflict of, 137, 147, 160, 172, 199, 200, 285; share of taxes, 138 (see also Proprietary estates, taxation of); income from quitrents, 138–9; require sterling for all payments, 142–3, 282–4; disputes with Assembly harm Pa., 146–7; compensation for sale of Pa., 147, 172, 199, 200, 313 n, 327, 464; owe Crown rents, 148, 151, 172; right to Pa. government, 151, 289; message on Assembly adjournment, 158; constant disputes with, 158–62 (see also Proprietary government); wealth, 159, 175 n; compared to So. Car. proprietors, 165 n; duty to provide for defense, 167; should conclude W. Penn's sale agreement, 172; decide not to sell Pa., 172 n; and Coxe claim, 175–6 n; character not vindicated by J. Penn, 208, 212; concessions on taxation, 213–14 n, 220, 312 n, 327 n, 331, 340, 352, 405, 409–10, 424 n, 494–7, 502–4; relation to legislation, 274–5; refuse money for Indian expenses, 274 n, 275; Anglicanism, 278; opposition to Supply Act of 1759, 278–9, 378; equated with Rehoboam, 288 n, 299; tired of hearing about father, 297–8; relation to father, 297–8; BF mock epitaph on, 298–9; Bartram flora not channeled through, 352; propaganda against Assembly in England, 354; against paper currency, 378; forbid Land Office's arbitrary opening, 380 n; hopes for accommodation with, 405–6, 410, 423, 424 n, 436–7, 464, 497–8; aid needed on tax measures, 406; concede Phila. squares, 410, 435, 494–7; preferred to loss of privileges, 424 (see also Privileges); Del. supports, 465 n; preferential treatment of Del., 466–7, 474–5; petitions against royal government to, 467, 471–2. See also Penn, Richard; Penn, Thomas; Proprietary rights and powers.

Protest against appointment of BF as agent: not recorded in minutes, 407, 408, 430–1; published, 407, 408, 457 n; text, 408–12; BF's Remarks on, 429–41; Smith defends charges in, 486–504; signers offer to pay for agent, 504; signers defended, 505–6

Protest against petition to King: Assembly refuses to record, 197, 198 n, 307–8, 430; made public, 489–90

Providence: BF on disease and, 101; BF's ironic reference to, 183

Providence, R.I.: Phila. mail to, 400

Province Island: Indians quartered at, 26; massacre of Indians on, planned, 27, 42 n, 44; Indians on, to be protected and supported, 51–2; Indians escorted from, 68 n; guilty Indians alleged on, 74 n; rents to finance Assembly petition, 198 n

Provincial commissioners: report on Indians, 25; report Paxton Boys' plans, 71; pay orders listed, 221–4; duties, 260, 281–2; minutes on strategy and appointments, 260–2; named, 261; governor's control over, 281; grant Bouquet more troops, 316–17, 322; BF secures Bouquet's request to, 319, 322–3; salaries, 373 n; powers in militia bill, 513; letter to, 224–6

Publications: to be in English, proposed law for, 295 n; scurrilous pamphlets attacking BF, 329, 332, 372–6, 380–4; for election campaign, 369–90; BF's on politics, listed, 371 n. See also Newspapers by name.

Public houses: licensing of, 128, 139–40; increased number of, 128, 139

Purchas, Samuel, Hakluytus Posthumus, cited by BF, 216

Quaker Indians, in Phila., Paxton Boys plan to kill, 77. See also Indians in Phila.

Quaker meetinghouse, BF's disparagement of, 375–6

Quakers: relations with Indians, 25, 44, 82, 101–2, 305; German, Lutheran animosity toward, 44; dispute with Presbyterians, 44, 107, 150, 327; failure to aid settlers, 44 n, 66 n, 185 n; frontier sentiment against, 44 n, 66 n, 185 n; threatened by Paxton Boys, 70, 102; take arms against Paxton Boys, 72; accused of hiding Indians, 74 n; accused of arousing Indians, 101–2, 305; accused of causing Pontiac's Uprising, 101 n; flee Phila., 102; send defense to governor, 102 n; political party, 125 n (see also Anti-proprietary party); petition for royal government, 145–6 (see also Petition to the King, Quakers); fear loss of religious liberties, 150, 195; blamed for contentions, 154, 158; control of Assembly, 161–2, 327, 385; excused from swearing in N.J., 166–7; attacked in British and Pa. press, 180–1; Penns abandon faith of, 279; effort to bar from Pa. Assembly, 294 n; pride, 324 n; Allen "abuses" BF to, 328; Voltaire on, 367–8; BF leadership of, 376, 515; BF charged with trying to destroy, 376, 382; refuse to take official stand on changing government, 376; Fothergill's relations with, 412 n; few in Del., 466 n; attitude toward BF, 505; attached to Galloway, 526; Pemberton out of favor with, 528

Quebec (city): gets regular postal service, 41; postal rates to be reduced, 41; Phila. mail to, 400

Quebec (province): BF interest in land in, 187–8; as site for Nantucket whalers, 187–8; land grant terms in, 358 n; as check on colonial ambitions, 482

Queenstown, Md., Phila. mail to, 401

Quincy, Ann Huske, death, 444

Quincy, Edmund, Jr.: identified, 444 n; letter from, 444–5

Quinine, BF's recipe for bark containing, 527

Quitrents: bills of credit not legal tender for, 8, 10, 11, 18 n, 137, 142, 142–3 n, 282–4; dispute over payment of, 18 n; Proprietors do not pay to Crown, 128;

exemption from taxation claimed, 129; Pa. rates compared with southern colonies, 129 n, 140; Proprietors' not to be rated, 137; use of, 138–9; Assembly claims for government, 138–9 n, 272 n; Del., owed to Crown, 148, 151, 172; effect of disputes over, 160; reporting of, 204–5; Proprietors' income from, 272, 277

Quotas, as alternative to stamp tax, 237

Rall, Johann Gottlieb, accepts rebel hospitality, 3 n

Ralph, James, Rose friend of, 100 n

Ray, Deborah Greene, death of, 79

Read, Charles: biographical note, 97 n; recommended as chief justice, 97; reappointed second judge, 97 n, 464 n

Read, Sarah: property of, 320 n; mentioned, 383 n

Reading, Pa., stores carried to, 223

Receivers general, request supply-bill amendments, 204–5

Recipes: for pickling sturgeon, 31–2, 87, 133; for fever ("bark wine"), 537; for piles, 537–8 n; for stomach, 538 n

Recording warrants and surveys, act for: Hughes recorder under, 374; repealed, 374

Redman, John, subscribes to linen factory, 315 n

Reed, Joseph: identified, 391; letter to, quoted, 391

Reedy Island: BF's ship stops at, 448, 450

Re-emitting Acts of 1759: Galloway's alleged office under, 373; Proprietors object to Pa. but not Del., 466, 474–5; violate royal prerogative, 464, 474–5, 514; supplement passed to Del., 466, 474–5, BF to receive, 467, 474; objections to, 514; disallowed, 514 n

Reeves, Peter, subscribes to linen factory, 315

Rehoboam, King, Penns compared to, 288 n, 299

Religion: BF's beliefs, 79, 231–2, 241, 253; Pa. denominational strife, 107, 150, 327, 367, 405; and political alignments, 125 n, 161; effect of bishops on freedom of, 150, 168–9; safety of Pa. privileges for, 161 n (see Privileges); freedom of, guaranteed in Penn's Charter, 161 n; liberty of conscience preserved in Crown colonies, 162–8, royal instructions on, quoted, 166–7; Pa. privileges, important for immigration, 197, 200; Voltaire on Quaker tolerance in, 367–8; BF on bigots of, 434, 457, 505; advice to Sarah F. on, 449–50; BF charged with lacking, 505. See also Cal-

vinists; Church of England; Lutherans; Methodists; Moravians; Presbyterians; Quakers; Roman Catholics.

Remarks on a Late Protest: BF's self-defense, 429–41; sent to Bowdoin, 453 n; proprietary reaction to, 457, 473–4; published in German and Pa. Jour., 457; not reprinted in England, 474 n; answer to, forthcoming, 484; Smith's Answer to, 486–516, 525–7; Collinson praises, 543; reprinting advised, 543

Remarks upon a Message Sent by the Upper to the Lower House of Assembly of Maryland: sent to Jackson, 108, 152; authorship, 108 n

"Remonstrance," by Smith and Gibson: sent to Penn and Assembly, 81; grievances cited, 81–3, 102, 379; conference on, 83–6; Penn refuses joint hearing on, 83–6, 104, 107; Assembly report on, 86–7 n; Assembly inaction on, 87 n; public wants to hear debates on, 92 n

Remonstrance on BF's appointment. See Philadelphia.

Rennes, Brittany, grass seed sent to society in, 258

Rents, proprietary. See Quitrents.

Reparations: from Indians, 187 n, 331, 337, 476

Representation, political, in eighteenth century, 124. See also Assembly.

Reputation, BF on his, 438

Resolves upon the Present Circumstances: background and text, 123–33; published, 133 n, 289; BF's Remarks on, 134–44; unanimity on, 148, 151, 289; BF comments on, 149; pamphlets on, 153–4, 157; Collinson praises, 181 n; Halifax calls "rebellion," 328; Strahan (London Chron.) prints, 354; propaganda against, 354; instructions on petition similar to, 358 n; deal with militia bill, 360, 513; ministers' reaction to, 375; Jackson to heed, 424; mentioned, 247, 477

Retirement, BF on joys of, 101

Rhoads, Samuel: identified, 527; signs Assembly reports, 86, 286, 439; subscribes to linen factory, 315; on "Old Ticket," 390; to oversee building of BF's house, 453–4; election defeat, 468 n; mentioned, 527

Rhoads, Samuel, Jr.: account book for BF, 453–6; family, 454 n

Rhode Island: Bernard, Jr., goes by packet to, 87; royal government wanted in, 186, 192, 459–60, 478; politics, 192 n; retains royal charter, 348; suggests joint action on taxation, 395–6

Rhode Island, Assembly Committee: Jackson's instructions sent to, 396 n; letter from, 395–7
Rhode Island, College of: charter and act passed, 192; Hopkins elected chancellor, 357; organized, 357 n
Rice, So. Car. granted right of direct export, 164
Rich, O., sends BF letter to Gilmor, 88 n
Richard II, policies, 141
Richardson, Joseph: votes on Assembly petition, 198 n, 291 n, 391; subscribes to linen factory, 315; on both tickets, 377 n, 390–1, 409; elected, 392, 394; voting record, 393, 409, 526; votes against BF appointment as agent, 407 n, 408, 526; does not sign protest against BF, 408–9, 526 n; on Committee of Correspondence, 422 n; signs Assembly instructions, 426; urges Dickinson not to answer BF, 526; relation to Dickinson, 526 n
Richardson, Samuel or William, BF orders book printed by, 334
Richardson & Clark, reprint Galloway's speech, 332 n
Richmond, Jonathan, sells fish, 334 n
Richmond, Va., Phila. mail to, 402
Rifles, Paxton Boys armed with, 77
Right, Petition of. See Petition of Right.
Rights, colonial: violated by parliamentary taxes, 242, 347–50, 395–6, 405, 425, 444–5 n; Mass. urges joint remonstrance on, 242–3, 452; compared to British, 347, 349; assemblies', of self-taxation, 347–50, 509–10; settlers' "purchase" of, 349–50; R.I. anxious to protect, 395–6; internal taxes as violation of, 396, 405, 509–10; Mass. petitions on, 452
Ringgold, Thomas: Md. pamphlet attributed to, 108 n, to be edited and distributed, 108, 152
Riot Act (Great Britain): extended to Pa. by Assembly, 70–1; described, 71 n
Riot Act, Pa.: Penn asks Assembly for, 47, 104; Assembly passes, 70–1, 104, 306
Riots: Pa. to pass defense law against, 75; in Pa., 304; pamphlets encouraging, 305; Quakers accuse Irish Presbyterians of, 327. See also Paxton Boys.
Rivington, James, biographical note, 240 n
Rivington and Fletcher: Mecom debt to, 240, 332; bankruptcy, 240 n
Robbers, in Phila., 530
Roberdeau, Daniel: confers with Paxton leaders, 73; subscribes to linen factory, 315 n
Roberts, George: on WF's mother, 370–1 n; letter from, quoted, 370–1 n

Roberts, Hugh: testifies on election riots, 377 n; mentioned, 370 n
Robertson, James, BF commends for guarding Indians, 47, 68
Robinson, James: BF sails with, 418 n, 427 n, 447, 521 n; solicitous of BF, 517
Robinson, Thomas: in BF-Williams accounts, 178; pay order for, 222
Roche d'Avoin, Indian victory at, 217 n
Rochelle, France, Eckerlings taken to, 443
Rocque, Bartholomew, burnet seed of, 258
Rodman, William, signs Assembly report, 86
Rogers, John: Primer verses attributed to, 303, 381 n; martyrdom, 303 n
Rogers, Mary Davenport, BF print for, 90
Roman Catholics, liberty of conscience under royal government, 166 n
Rooke, Mrs.: identified, 110 n; health, 110, 202; greetings to and from, 110, 202
Rose, David, paid for bricks, 455, 456
Rose, William: identified, 100 n; in Club of Honest Whigs, 98 n; greetings to and from, 100, 246
Ross, George: biographical note, 248 n; letter to, answered, 248
Ross, John (1714–1776): biographical note, 531 n; on Assembly committees, 193, 422 n; supports petition to King, 193 n; signs Assembly instructions, 426; signs report, 439; letter from, 531–2
Ross, John (1729–1800), identified, 531 n
Rothenbuehler, Frederick: biographical note, 201 n; collecting money for church, recommended to Williams, 201
Royal American Regiment (60th): escorts and guards Indians, 28, 29, 68–9, 70; to be called from barracks guard, 75; Price commissioned in, 93; on Bouquet expedition, 224 n, 225 n; BF helped quarter, 319, 322, 378
Royal government, change to: Dickinson opposes, 10 n (see Dickinson, John); BF supports, 105, 153–73, 173 n, 185–6, 267–311, 409, 431, 432, 491–2, 511; wished for Pa., 107, 150, 181, 484, 523, 529; Assembly wants, 122, 125–6, 132–3, 144, 213, 289; of proprietary governments, 126 n; petitions for, 145–6, 153–4, 157, 213 n (see also Petitions to the King); Jackson's opinion on, 151, 170 n, 313, 462–4; ways of securing change, 151, 533 n (see also Penn, William); Md. to petition for, 152; BF on reasons for, advantage, 154, 164, 171–2, 303; BF answers objections to, 154, 162–71, 292–307; of So. Car., 162–4; of N.J., 165–7; of New Hamp., 168; will not change Pa. rights, 170–1; R.I.

conservatives want, 186 n, 192 n; Bowdoin approves of, 247; petition against, 256 (*see also* Counter-petition); recourse of proprietary colonies to, 289; expense of, 313, 327–8, 375, 464; major campaign issue, 327, 329, 369; Mansfield's alleged remarks on, 328; letter for, quoted, 356 n; BF on prospects for, 367; campaign papers on, 372–6, 384–5; Quaker position on, 376; feared loss of privileges from, 424 (*see also* Privileges); Allen's remarks against, 432, 457 n, 488, 508–12; addresses to Proprietors against, 467, 471–2, 524, 526 n; traders want offices after, 476–7; advocated for all colonies, 478; not thought likely, 529; Pa. opinion on, 532

Royal Highlanders. *See* Montgomery's Regiment.

Royal Society: committee to verify Canton experiments, 245 n; papers on lightning for, 544 n

Royal Society of Arts. *See* Society of Arts.

Royle, Joseph: identified, 251; publishes *Va. Gazette* for Hunters, 251 n; post-office accounts for, 251; manages Hunter's business for heir, 415, 417; illness, 415, 417; death, 417 n

Rum: possible tax on, 237; needed in water during hot spell, 256 n

Rush, William, paid, 455

Russell, Charles: biographical note, 461 n; recommended to BF, 461

Russell, James: identified, 461 n; mentioned, 461

Russia, invades Poland, 318

Ryland, William Wynne, print of Bute portrait, 334

Sailcloth, Phila., factory for, 316 n

Sailors: riot during 1742 elections, 377 n; rope-hauling method, 480

St. Bride's Church, London, observations on lightning striking, 544–5

St. Clement Danes, London, lightning misses, 545

St. George's Church, Phila., sold to Methodists, 201 n

St. John, Island of (Prince Edward Island): Egmont applies for grant of, 175 n, 187, refused, 324; Nantucket whalers refused, 187; grants given for, 325 n

St. Lawrence, Bay of, Nantucket whalers want to settle, 187

St. Lucia, decision on Cardigan claim to, 175, 238

St. Martin's, London, lightning misses, 545

St. Mary-le-Strand, London, lightning misses, 545

St. Paul's Church, Phila., Dunlap preaches at, 421 n

St. Paul's Coffeehouse, Club of Honest Whigs meets at, 98 n

St. Vincent, decision on Cardigan claim to, 175

Saladin, BF anecdote on, 59

Salem, Mass.: Phila. mail to, 400; postal rates, 536

Sally (Wyanjoy or Tea-wonsha-i-ong; Conestoga Indian): character, 49; massacre of, 49 n

Salmon, pickled: Bernard wants recipe for, 32, 87; Berwick process for, suggested for sturgeon, 479

Salt: type needed for pickling fish, 87–8; exempted from Staple Act, 216 n; amount for pickling fish, 479

Salter Brittain & Co., paid for boards, 455

Sand, black sea, iron extraction from, 352 n

Sandusky: Bradstreet at, 330, 337; prisoners to be brought to, 330, 336. *See also* Hurons (Sandusky).

Sandwich, John Montagu, 4th Earl of, Cambridge candidacy of, 481

Sandy Hook, Dutch ship taken at, 91, 178

Saracens, hospitality, BF's examples of, 56, 59–60, 66

Sargent, John: has BF money for Coxe grant, 20; consulted on Coxe grant, 176; BF's dealings with, 176 n

Saunders, Isaac: votes against petition for royal government, 161 n, 198, 291 n; criticized by Assembly, 340 n; votes against BF appointment, 407 n; signs protest on BF appointment, 412, 491 n; justice of peace, 438 n; letter by, 297 n

Saur, Christopher, prints "Protest" and BF's *Remarks*, 457 n

Savannah, Ga., postal service to, 3 n

Saville, Sir George: identified, 480 n; Michell connected with, 480

Say, Thomas (1709–1796): biographical note, 443 n; BF to write care of, 443

Say, Thomas (1787–1834), identified, 443 n

Scalps, Indian: rewards for, 82; premium for, 223; Owens takes, 174

Schlosser, Capt. J., escorts and guards Indian refugees, 69 n, 70, 71, 72

Schuylkill River, Paxton Boys cross, 72

Scioto River: BF-Bouquet talk about settling, 325; Indians sign treaty, 329–31, 336

Scotch-Irish in Pa.: political alignment of, 125 n, 327, 485 n; have experienced oppression, 173; animosities against Quakers, 327; bitter about BF's *Narrative*, 332; attack German Lancaster sheriff, 467–8. *See also* Presbyterians.

Scotland, provisions from, exempted from Staple Act, 216 n

Scott, David, pay order for, 223

Scouting party, procedures, 317 n

Scribbler, The, A Letter, anti-proprietary election pamphlet, 384–90

Scull and Heap, map of Phila., public squares omitted from, 410 n

Scurvy, lemon juice as preventative of, 215–16

Seagrave, Capt., account of voyage, 61–2

Seawater, compressibility of, 246

Seed, orchard grass and burnet, distributed, 258

Seneca (Indians), make peace with Bouquet, 523

Sermons, BF on value of, 450

Servants: exempted from Staple Act, 216 n; enlisted for Indian wars, 378

Settlement: on Penobscot River, 31–2 n; Friedenshütten (Indian village), founded, 87 n; schemes sent to Jackson, 97; not allowed west of Alleghenies, 101 n; effect of land price in Pa., 129, 140, 380; Coxe scheme for, 152 (*see also* Carolana; Coxe grant); of No. Car., and Coxe grant, 175–6; proposed for Island of St. John, 175 n, 187, 324–5; decision on Cardigan claims, 175, 238; desirability of proprietorships for, 175 n, 325 n; hopes for Coxes on Mississippi River, 176; of Nova Scotia, BF and Jackson interest in, 186–7, 358–9, 470 n; BF to use popularity to encourage, 187; for Nantucket whalers, 187–8; Quebec land scheme of BF and Baynton & Wharton, 187–8, 427–8; Wharton's schemes for, 187–8 n, 476 n; scheme for at Bay of Chaleur, 188, 428; Vandalia claim, 188 n; of Pa., effect of charter privileges, 197, 200, 294, 301–2, 511; of Mosquito Coast, 236; end of age of proprietary grants for, 325 n; BF-Bouquet plan for Scioto River, 325; BF's plans for Ohio River, 325 n; western, BF's interest in, 325 n; at colonial expense, 349; colonial rights earned by, 349; of Nova Scotia, Ga., at British expense, 349 n; stiffened terms for granting, 358; scheme for Lake Champlain-Missisquoi River tract, 428; McNutt land schemes for Nova Scotia, 470 n; Croghan's ideas for Ill., 476 n

Seven Years' War: bounty on Indian scalps during, 82 n; proprietary instructions during, 127 n, 137–8; qualification for officers during, 364–5

Shadwell, Richard: identified, 257 n; delivers mail, 257

Sharpe, Horatio: thinks BF had hand in Md. pamphlet, 108 n; Md. Assembly prorogations by, 109 n; prevents Md. petition to Crown, 152 n

Shawnee Indians: campaign to chastise, 96 n, 217, 224 n, 248 n; white boy recovered from, 174; party scalped by Owens, 174; Bradstreet makes unauthorized treaty with, 326, 329–31, 333, 335–7, 446 n; Bouquet to continue campaign against, 326, 445; not in Niagara treaty, 329, 335; Bouquet makes peace with, 446 n, 458, 483, 485–6; to sign treaty, 476; hostages taken, 483, 485; obstinacy, 486, 523, 528, 530; hostages escape, 523, 528, 530; supplied by French, 523, 528, 530

Sheaffe, Edward, signs Mass. House appeal, 243

Sheep, American, poorly fleeced, 359

Sheets, troops to have, 262

Shehaes (Sheehays; Indian): character, 48, 49; massacre of, 50, 65; on English protection, 53

Shepherd, Peter, voting record, 393, 403 n

Sherburne, John, executor of Huske will, 338

Sheriff: act protects election of, 170; election of Phila. Co., 394

Ship letters: to be regulated, 39–41; BF and Foxcroft propose rules for, 40 n, 343, 344; rules tightened, 341 n; existing customs, 342

Shippen, Edward (1703–1781): identified, 247 n; reports massacre, rumors of attack on Indians at Province Island, 42 n, 50 n; letter from, 247–8; mentioned, 363 n

Shippen, Edward, Jr. (1729–1806): identified, 526 n; advisor to Penn, 288 n; part in Smith's *Answer,* 526

Shippen, Joseph, Jr. or III: signs Penn proclamations, 52, 55; pay orders for, 223; premium for scalps paid to, 223; advisor to Penn, 288 n; provincial secretary, 363

Shippen family, Bouquet's relations with, 324 n

Shippensburg, Pa.: new post office at, 248; Phila. mail to, 401

Shipping, foreign, forbidden to colonies, 91 n

Shirley, William, BF aid to, 319, 322

Shoes, spare, to be provided for soldiers, 225

Short, James: supports Harrison, 481; candidate as astronomer royal, 481–2

Silk: duty on, 76 n, 235 n; Chinese prints on culture of, 230

Simpson, John and Thomas, Allen recommends BF to, 507 n
Singers, inarticulation of, 542–3
Sisera, murdered by Jael, 64 n
Six Nations. See Iroquois.
Small, Alexander: identified, 202 n; treats Mrs. Stevenson, 202; forwards letter and book, 258; pamphlets sent to, 333; has copy of "Parable," 354; reports on sturgeon, 479; observations on lightning, 544–5; letters from, 479–83, 544–5
Small, William: biographical note, 480 n; on tree uprooting, 480
Smallpox: kills Phila. Indians, 87 n; epidemic in Boston, 232 n, 254, 356; Winthrop family recovers from, 254. See also Inoculation.
Smibert, John, moves to Newport, 191 n
Smith, John (Saquies-hat-tah; Cayuga Indian), massacre of, 49
Smith, John: identified, 426 n; thanked for bon voyage, 429; letter from, 426; letter to, 429
Smith, Matthew: states Paxton Boys' grievances, 73–4; "Remonstrance" of, 81–3 (see Remonstrance); goes home, 86 n
Smith, Robert, Primer verses of, 303 n, 381 n
Smith, Robert, paid for carpentry on BF's house, 453–4, 456
Smith, Thomas, partner in banking firm, 179 n
Smith, William (Bucks Co.): opposes supply bill, 7 n; signs Assembly report, 93
Smith, William: procures funds for College of Phila., 134 n; Assembly "trial" of, 196 n, 468 n; Preface to Dickinson's Speech, 267–8, BF quotes and refutes, 271, 277–8, 284, 289–92, 294–6, 307–8, epitaph in, 297–8, 372; Brief State and Brief View pamphlets, 294–5 n, 379, 387; alluded to, 296; as campaign issue, 369; charged with intimidating voters, 379; authorship of epitaph on BF, 381 n, 387 n; attack on Germans, 387; political epitaph on, 387–90, 487; A Poem on Visiting the Academy praises BF, 388; charges against BF as scientist, refuted, 389; attempt to prevent BF's Oxford degree, 390 n; doctorate, 390; complains about Dunlap, 421–2 n; An Answer to Mr. Franklin's Remarks, 484, 486–516, 525–7, 530; letters to or from, quoted, 213–14 n, 327 n, 421–2 n
Smith, Wright & Gray: history of, 179 n; BF account with, 179–80
Smuggling: molasses duty reduced because of, 182 n; annoying aspects of control of, 215–16; BF advice on, sought, 482

Smyth, Frederick, appointed N.J. chief justice, 97 n, 464 n
Sneider, Hans, pay order for orphans of, 223
Society of Arts: gives premiums for N.J. sturgeon, 32 n; pickled sturgeon sent to, 334; medal for Eliot, 352; report on sturgeon, 479; rejects engine for uprooting trees, 480
Society for the Propagation of the Gospel, missionary activity, 169 n
Sock (Bill Sock or Sack), Will (Tenseedaagua; Conestoga Indian): massacre of, 49, 65; charges against, 49 n, 64–5; character, 65 n
Solomon, King, wisdom of, 299
Songs: BF prefers old to new, 538–9; BF on faults of eighteenth-century, 538–42
Sonmans, Peter, mentioned, 96 n
Soumaine, Elizabeth, marriage, 190 n. See also Empson, Elizabeth.
Soumaine, Samuel, BF recommends daughter of, 190 n
South Carolina: trouble with Creeks, 95 n; change to royal government, 126 n, 162–4, 328; cheap lands attract immigration, 129, 140; use of quitrents in, 139 n; religious liberty in, 163–4; postal service, 260 n
South Carolina Gazette, Timothy editor of, 93
Southwark, lightning in, 98
Spain, Spanish: hospitality and honor, 60–1, 66; wines, new duty on, 183 n; dispute on right to Mosquito Shore, 236
"Spanish Lady, The," BF recommends, 539
Spark, Capt., commands Mary and Elizabeth, 265
Speaker, delay in presenting for confirmation, 403–4, 411
Specific gravity of fluids, not related to compressibility, 246
Spinet, Josiah Williams studies, 179
Stamford, Conn., Phila. mail to, 400
Stamp Act: postponement, 34–5 n, 234 n, 236–7 n, 242 n; Allen tries to delay passage, 34–5 n, 234 n, 312 n, 445 n; effect on colonial relations, 169 n; applied to all colonies, 170 n; Jackson credited with deferring, 215, 234 n, 314 n; colonies will not agree on, 237; BF has alternative to, 237, 350–1 n; violates British colonial rights, 242, 347–50, 395–6, 405, 425, 444–5 n (see also Rights, colonial; Taxation, parliamentary); Mass. opposes, 242–3, 452; BF's views on, 243 n; Pa. Assembly opposes, 347–50; Jackson instructed to oppose, 347–50, 422 n, 424–5; R.I.

suggests joint action against, 395–6; Proprietors' aid needed on, 406; Grenville provoked into imposing, 444–5 n; and Pa. attitude toward BF, 488

Stamper, Mr., tax on lot of, 106

Stamper, Josh, elected county assessor, 394

Stanley, John, thanks to, for score, 110

Stanwix, Fort, Iroquois cede land at, 187 n

Staple Act. See Navigation Act (1663).

Staves, export to Ireland, forbidden, 229, 235

Steel, magnetizing of, 254

Steuart, Andrew, prints *Cool Thoughts*, 153 n

Stevens, William Bacon, copies letter to BF, 259 n

Stevenson, Margaret: dissuaded from trip to America, 110; packet for, 190; illness, 202, 521; paid for purchases for BF, 354; Small visits, 479 n; BF resumes lodgings with, 521; greetings from, 534

Stevenson, Mary: BF likes verses from, 190; begs BF to return, 203; visits Hawkesworths, 521 n; letter from, 201–3; letters to, 110–11, 190, 521

Stickney, Anthony: biographical note, 227 n; BF's visit to, 227 n; letter to, 227–8

Stickney, Dorcas Davenport (C.12.2): daughter born to, 227

Stickney, Dorcas (b. 1763), birth of, 227

Stiles, Ezra: returns books to BF, 22 n, 230, 246, 254; BF sends prints of silk culture and of self to, 90–1 n, 230; BF to send *Narrative* to, 91 n; given plan for association of colleges, 192 n; letter to, 230–1

Stirling, Lord. See Alexander, William.

Stomach, medicinal recipe for, 538 n

Stoneburner, Leonard, pay order for, 223

Story, Enoch, elected, 392 n

Strahan, Mrs. Margaret Penelope: greetings to, 149, 229, 333; health, 241, 355

Strahan, Margaret Penelope (Peggy): identified, 355 n; greetings to, 149, 333, 355

Strahan, Rachel, greetings to, 149

Strahan, William: prints Assembly dispute papers, 149, 355; political letters praised, 188–9, 242, 332–3, 354; BF pays Parker's debt to, 241 n, 520; BF sends pamphlets to, 331–2; Mecom debt to, 332; BF asks for books, 333–4, cancels order, 333 n, 353–4; to pay bill to Mrs. Stevenson, 354; prints "Parable against Persecution," 354; BF thinks of living with, 355; house enlarged, 355; Parker and Holt debts to, 413–14, 470; letters from, cited, 317 n, quoted, 354 n; letters to, 149, 188–90, 228–9, 240–2, 331–4, 353–6

Strahan, William, Jr., greetings to, 149

Strahan family, greetings to, 333, 355

Stratford, Conn., Phila. mail to, 400

Strettell, Amos: on "New Ticket," 390; elected, 394; votes against BF appointment as agent, 407 n; signs protest on BF appointment, 412; with wife mortgage on McCleave property, 419 n, 469; BF pays interest to, 469 n

Strettell, John, bill of exchange on, 427 n

Strettell, Robert, estate of, 469 n

Stuart, Gilbert (father of painter), brought to America, 191 n

Stuart, James: identified, 228 n; and Nicholas Revett, *Antiquities of Athens*, BF orders, 228

Stuart, John, dealings with Indians, 95 n

Sturgeon: fishery planned, 31; recipe for pickling, 31–2, 87, 133; pickled, submitted for premium, 334, 479; American supply unlimited, 334; duty on, 335; pickling process for, 479

Sugar: price raise will affect England, 182; foreign, complaint of duty on, 235–6; production in West Indies, 236; plantations for Mosquito Shore suggested, 236; BF sent book on refining, 265; cultivation to be tried in Florida, 313

Sugar Act of 1764: lowers molasses duty, 19 n, 76 n, 182 n, 235 n; debated, 34 n; duties, 76 n, 183, 235 n, 314, 351; effect on colonial economy, trade, 108, 182, 234–5, 344, 351, 359 n, 396–7 n, 424; passed to support British troops, 181 n; a blunder, 182; news of, reaches Phila., 215 n; BF discusses, 234–6; as denial of colonial rights, 242, 452 n; Mass. agent to work for repeal of, 243 n; encourages colonial textile manufacture, 314–15; postal reforms to offset, 344 n; Jackson instructed to work for repeal, 347, 351, 422 n, 424; Huske's role in, 444 n

Supply Act of 1757, BF's role in passing, 319, 322

Supply Act of 1759: agents agree to stipulations for, 8, 18 n, 112, 203, 220 n, 268, 278, 284; taxes paid under, 127, 138, 206, 285–6; Privy Council debate on, 204–7, 286; not amended, 204–7, 286; Privy Council ruling on, 239 n, 277–85; Denny's passage of, 268; Proprietors contest, 378

Supply Act of 1760: not amended, 204–7; references to, deleted from Supply Act of 1764, 206–7

Supply Act of 1763, commissioners reappointed, 222

Supply Act of 1764: provision for honest accounting, 143 n, 204–5; enacted, 207, 213; Proprietors' concessions on, 213–14 n (*see also* Proprietors, Pa.); bills to amend, 213–14 n, 503 n; copy sent to Jackson, 220; effect on 1764 election, 214 n; provincial commissioners named in, 221–2, 261 n, 266 n; Bouquet fumes at delay in, 224; bills of credit clause in, 283 n; useful in Indian campaign, 483. *See also* Assembly; Penn, John; Proprietary estates, taxation of; Supply Bills of 1764.

Supply Bill (1760), views on proprietary taxation in, 120

Supply Bill (£50,000; 1764): dispute on proprietary taxation in, 7–8, 10–11, 18 n, 104 n, 105–6, 111–12; instructions for, 8, 11; BF speech on funding, 7–18, 268; Assembly debates, 8–10; Assembly passes, 9, 111, 207; Penn rejects, 95, 105–6, 111–12, 150, 213; conforms partially to stipulations, 95–6, 105–6; defects, 95–6, 106, 111, 117–18; commissioners of appeals for, 111; Assembly agrees to revise, 111

Supply Bill (£55,000; 1764): disputed provision on proprietary taxation, 18 n, 112–15, 116 n, 129–30, 131–2, 203–4, 220–1; Penn rejects, 106 n, 112, 150, 213; Assembly defends, 111–22; Penn demands quotation of stipulation in, 112–16, 118–19, 208–10, 287; Penn gives his interpretation of disputed stipulation, 116, 119; role of assessors and board of appeals, 117, 120, 287; Assembly claims compliance with Privy Council order, 131–2, 143; instruction on sterling payments a cause of rejection, 142–3; provision for honest accounting in, 143, 204–5; *Pa. Gaz.* prints documents on, 148 n, 149 n; documents sent to English friends, 148, 149, 150, 181 n; documents printed in *London Chron.*, 149 n; Penn adamant on, 203–4, 217, 356 n; Assembly yields on, 204, 206–13, 217; new demands for, refused, 204–6; enacted, 207, 213. *See also* Assembly; Supply Act of 1764.

Supply bills and acts (in general): Pa. disputes over, 127 n, 137–8, 172, 301; proprietary instructions on, 126–7, 136–8; Md. dispute over, 152

Supreme Court, Pa., should send circuit riders, 87 n

Susquehanna River: friendly Indians of, ask for protection, 27 (*see also* Indians in Philadelphia); Indian uprising on, 63; Indians scalped at, 174; troops stationed between Delaware R. and, 261

Swan, Richard, pay order for, 224

Swede's Ford, Pa., Paxton Boys cross, 72

Syng, Philip: subscribes to linen factory, 315 n; accounts for BF's house, 453 n

Talbot, Md., Phila. mail to, 401

Taverns: number of, a scandal, 128, 139, 522; license abuses, 128, 139–40, 522; license fees, 522 n

Taxation, Pa.: BF's scheme for interest-bearing currency for, 7–18, 238; for supply bill, debated, 8–11; unequal, 11–12, 18; debates for Pa. supply bill (£50,000, 1764), 8–11, 96 n; rate for inhabitants' located, uncultivated lands, 96 n, 220–1; Hamilton's approval of equal assessment for, 120; role of assessors in, 120; appeals for, 120–1, 282; for Supply Act of 1759, amount paid, 138 n, 286; quitrents to substitute for, 139 n; proprietary lands increase, 140; provision for honest accounting for, 143, 204–5; annual rate for supply acts, 154; as basis for representation, 378, 379 n. *See also* Proprietary estates.

Taxation, parliamentary: BF's views on, 19–20, 76–7, 169–70, 186, 237; Jackson views as certain, 34 n, 35, 169 n; Jackson opposes internal, 35, 76, 186, 234 n; customs vs. internal taxes, 35, 76, 186, 509–10 n; internal without representation opposed, 186, 242–3, 396 n, 397 n, 452, 509–10; Allen opposes, 234 n, 462 n, 463 n, 509; decision against self-taxation for defense, 236–7 n; BF's alternative to, 237–8 n, 350–1 n; agents to remonstrate on, 242–3, 366, 395–7, 452; Jackson instructed on, 347–51; Assembly asserts rights of, 347–51; right of Parliament questioned, 347, 395–7, 444–5 n, 452 n; Pa. has substitute plan for, 350; BF to work against, 404 n; Grenville provoked into imposing, 444–5; will cause distress, 452; Mass. petition on, 452; necessary for colonial "awe," 482; BF's advice sought, 482. *See also* Rights, colonial; Stamp Act.

Taylor, George: votes against BF's appointment as agent, 407 n; signs protest on BF's appointment, 412; justice of peace, 438 n

Tea: BF suggests duty on, 76; not taxed in Sugar Act, 76 n; Camomile (herb), medicinal use of, 538 n

Telescope: Bowdoin wants attachments for, 22, 99, 244–5, 452–3; achromatic, invented, 22 n

Temperature, records for Newport, 191, Philadelphia, 191 n. *See also* Heat.

Templeman, Peter: sturgeon sent to, 334–5, 479; letter to, 334–5

Tennent, Gilbert: helps stop Paxton Boys, 72; death, 73 n; signs letter against royal government, 290 n

Textiles: rise in price of, 314–15; colonial manufacture of, 314–15
Thacher, Oxenbridge, signs Mass. House letter, 243
Thomas, George: secret agreement with Penns, 127 n, 274; Assembly transactions with, 272–4; messages to Assembly, quoted, 273–4; refuses to act on Phila. riots, 377 n
Thomson, Charles: identified, 442 n; stock certificate issued to, 314–16; witnesses power of attorney, 442; and Foxcroft sell land, 521 n; health, 521 n; letter from, 521–4
Three Lower Counties on Delaware. See Delaware.
Tickell, Mrs.: identified, 110 n; greetings to and from, 110, 202; health, 202
Ticking, Phila. factory for, 316 n
Tilghman, Edward and James, Md. pamphlet attributed to, 108 n
Timber: reports on Lake Champlain and Bay of Chaleur, 428
Timothy, Peter: identified, 93 n; receives Price, 93
Tissington, Anthony, to see mineralogy catalogue, 97
Tit for Tat epitaph. See What Is Sauce for a Goose.
Todd, Anthony: sends BF report to Board of Trade, 20 n; prepares post-office memorandum, 36; orders published, 341 n; possible instructions from, 414 n; to show BF clauses for postal act, 534; letters to, 20–21, 335–7, 341–6, 445–6; letter from, 534, mentioned, 36
Tomahawks: Paxton Boys armed with, 77; troops to have, 262
Tool, John: signs Assembly reports, 86, 93; on petition committee, 193; position on petition, 193 n
Tories, control astronomer appointment, 482
"To the Freeholders and Electors of the Province of Pennsylvania," proprietary election campaign paper, 372–6
To the Freeholders and other Electors for the City and County of Philadelphia and Counties of Chester and Bucks, anti-proprietary election paper, 376–80
To the Freemen of Pennsylvania, BF's defense of Assembly in Militia Bill dispute, 360–5
Toulouse, courts, 368
Tower Hill, R.I., post-office receipts, 251
Town lots: stipulation on taxation of, 96, 209 n, 280–1; dispute over taxation of,

105–6, 111, 116 n, 286; Assembly defeat on, 207
Townshend duties, applied to all colonies, 170 n
Trade, Board of. See Board of Trade.
Trade, colonial: prohibitions preferred to internal tax, 35 (see also Taxation, colonial); foundation for, 35 n; BF's views on British restraints, 76, 108, 181–3, 234–6; European ships forbidden, 91 n; effect of Sugar Act on, 108, 182, 234–6, 344, 351, 396–7 n, 424; restraints hurt Great Britain, 181–2, 351; relation to taxation, 181–2, 451–2; British desire to monopolize, 182–3; postage abatement to compensate for laws restraining, 344; benefit to mother country, 349; restrictions on, necessitate economy, 359; Mass. petitions on restrictions, 452; between Indians and French, 476, 523, 528, 530. See also Molasses Act; Navigation Acts; Smuggling; Sugar Act.
Traders, compensation for, 187 n, 476
Treasury, British, will not support paper money bill, 177
Treaties, Indian: Carlisle, 64 n; Easton, 83 n, 224; Quakers accused of violating, 101 n, 180 n; Proprietors refuse to pay for, 274 n, 275; Bradstreet's unauthorized, 326, 329–31, 333, 337, 446; 335–7, Bouquet's peace, 446 n (see also Bouquet, Henry); Croghan to make, 476, 529
Trees: mature, can be transplanted, 203; machine for uprooting, 480
Trenton, N.J.: postmaster commissioned for, 3–6; pickled sturgeon praised, 32; Pa. Indians arrive at, 70; Phila. mail to, 401
Trenton Academy, founded, 3 n
Trenton Banking Co., Hunt a founder, 3 n
Trevor, Robert: identified, 250 n; remittances to, 250
Tribunes, Roman, veto, 172
Troops, British. See Army, British.
Troops, Pa.: Assembly to provide, 7, 96 n, 105, 113, 212 n, 218, 295; defend frontier, 29, 68–9, 261–2; unpaid, 150, 204; governor's control of, 154; pay orders for, 223, 224; with Bouquet, 224, 229, 256, 261 n, 335; supplies for, 225–6; desertions in, 266; replacements for, 317 n, 322; Bouquet praises, 483 n, 486; to be paid and disbanded, 529, 530
Troops, provincial, instructions on criteria of officers, 364–5
Truth, Voltaire on fractions of, 368
Tunes, BF prefers simplicity in, 539–40

Turks, protection of captives, 56, 58–9, 65–6
Twightwees (Indians), protection of strangers, 64
Tyler, David Rose, paid, 455

Umsted, Jacob, elected county assessor, 394
United Colonies, BF postmaster general for, 3–6

Valerian root, medicinal use of, 538 n
Vandalia claim, Wharton sees BF on, 188 n
Van Doren, Carl, dates BF currency speech, 8 n
Vassall, Elizabeth, marriage, 461 n
Venue, issue in Indian massacre case, 27–8, 82, 364
Vergil, *Aeneid*, quoted, 296
Vienna, Md., Phila. mail to, 401
Virginia: refuses Amherst requisition, 7, 96; post-office affairs in, 37, 341 n, 399 n; open Assembly debates in, 93; Amherst requests troops from, 105 n, 212 n; cheap land attracts immigration, 129, 140; support of Episcopal clergy in, 169; hearings on currency in, 176 n; frontier horses requested, 225; frontiers attacked, 229, 335; E. Holland sought in, 232–3; BF paid for trip to, 249; Bouquet to recruit troops from, 266 n; agent's salary, 501; Indian captives from, returned, 529 n
Virginia Gazette: BF advertises for E. Holland in, 232; published by Royle for Hunter, 251 n, 415 n; possible successors to Royle, 415 n
Voght, Christian, pay order for, 223
Voltaire, *Traité sur la Tolérance:* bibliography of, 367 n; quoted on Pa. Quakers, 367–8; qualities of, 368

Waldron, Elizabeth Holland, answers inquiry, 233
Wales, European goods to be laden in, 91 n
Walker, Capt., carries mail, 228
Walker, Hannah Farrow: identified, 524 n; letter from, 524–5
Walnut, in Lake Champlain area, 428
Walpole Company, BF member of, 187 n
Ward, Samuel: political feud of, 192 n; BF print for, 230
Warner, Edward, confers with governor, 273
Washington, George, attacks Trenton, 3 n
Washington Square, Phila., as burying ground, 496 n
Waste lands: Proprietors', not taxed, 114, 239 n, 278–9, 285; price of, 140
Water: variable compressibility of rain and

sea compared, 245–6; cold, deaths attributed to drinking, 256; liquor should be added to, for drinking, 256 n
Watson, William, article on lightning rods, 98 n
Wealth, BF on dangers of uniting power and, 143–4
Weaver, Mich, paid, 455
Webb, James, pay order for, 223
Webster, Pelatiah: biographical note, 32–3 n; BF frank on letter to, 32–3
Wechquetank, Pa., Indians moved from, 25 n
Weiser, Conrad, report of Iroquois Council, 63 n
Weiss, Jacob, pay orders for, 223, 224
Welfare, linen company started for, 314
Western Settlement. *See* Settlement.
West Indies: to be taxed for troops, 35; postal service in, 40; trade with North America, 108, 181–2; influence in England, 181; luxury exports abated, 359
West Virginia, Iroquois give up tract in, 187 n
Weyman, William, Parker's ex-partner, 415
Whaling, in Bay of St. Lawrence, 187. *See also* Nantucket Whalers.
Wharton, Joseph: identified, 451 n; greetings to, 451; sees BF letter, 457; greetings from, 529
Wharton, Samuel: desires Quebec grant, 187; land speculations of, 187–8 n; relations with BF, 187–8 n, 451 n; to send Del. Re-emitting Act, 467, 474; confers on reply to *Answer*, 526; letters from, 471–7, 525–9; mentioned, 449 n. *See also* Baynton & Wharton.
Wharton, Thomas (1731–1782): biographical note, 449 n; subscribes to linen factory, 315; accompanies BF to Newcastle, 449; relations with BF, 449 n, 451 n; loans BF his woolen gown, 517 n; letters from, 456–8, 483–6; letter to, 451
Wharton, Thomas, Jr. (1735–1778), mentioned, 449 n
Wharton family, greetings to, 451
Whately, Thomas, Harrison friendly with, 460 n
What is Sauce for a Goose: campaign attack on BF, 380–4; use of *Primer* verses in, 381 n; authorship of, 381 n, 387 n
Wheat, Mass. bounty on, 179
Whitefield, George: travels, 232; health, 232; relations with Bolton, 259 n; letters to, 231–2, cited, 325 n; mentioned, 32 n
White oak, in Lake Champlain area, 428
Wighalousin. *See* Wyalusing.
Wigs, fashion for, 543

Wilkes, John: BF pleased with action against, 76; expelled from Commons, 76 n; *North Briton* no. 45 voted libel, 76 n; controversy over, 239 n
Wilkinson, John, signs report, 439
William (sloop), parcels sent on, 88
Williams, D., bill of exchange, 427 n
Williams, Daniel, payment by, 454
Williams, David, forms club with BF, 228 n
Williams, Mrs. Grace Harris, letter to, quoted, 518
Williams, John (alias John Hines), executed, 188 n
Williams, Jonathan: to deliver BF parcels, 88; Bernard remittances for BF to, 88, 91, 133, 153, 178; executor of J. Franklin estate, 89 n; sent BF prints to distribute, 89–90, 230 n, 247; BF print for, 90; BF's accounts with, 178; Roethenbuehler recommended to, 201; letter from, 461; letters to, 88–90, 178–9, 201, 426–7
Williams, Jonathan, Jr., sets up BF account books, 518–20
Williams, Josiah: studies spinet, 179; armonica for, 179 n, 426 n
Williams, Solomon: biographical note, 32 n; asks BF to frank letters, 32–3; letter from, 32–3
Williams, William, signs Declaration of Independence, 32 n
Williamsburg, Va.: inquiries made for E. Holland at, 233; BF trip to, 249 n; post-office receipts, 251; printing office run by Royle, 251 n (*see also* Hunter; *Virginia Gazette*); Phila. mail to, 402; postal rates, 536
Williamson, Hugh: authorship of *Plain Dealer* pamphlets, 154, 157; *An Answer to the Plot*, abuse of BF, 329 n; *Plain Dealers*, abuse of BF, 329 n; authorship of *Epitaph* on BF, 381 n
Willing, Anne, letter to, quoted, 324 n
Willing, Thomas: confers with Paxton leaders, 73; said to aid in Paxton "Remonstrance," 74 n; on "New Ticket," 390; elected, 391, 468 n; votes against BF appointment, 407 n; signs protest on BF appointment, 412; justice of peace, 438 n
Willing family, Bouquet's relations with, 324 n
Wilmington, Del., Phila. mail to, 401
Wilmot, Henry: advises yielding to Assembly, 213 n, 214 n; letter from, quoted and cited, 213
Wilmot, Montagu, instructed on land grants, 358 n
Wilson, Benjamin, BF portrait by, 230 n
Wines: duty on, 76, 183; exempted from

Staple Act, 216 n; compressibility of, 245–6; license fee for, 522 n
Winthrop, John: identified, 90 n; to deliver BF's book to Stiles, 22; BF print for, 90; sent book to Stiles, 246; family of, recovered from smallpox, 254; letter to, 254–5
Wistar, Richard, subscribes to linen factory, 315
Wochentliche Staatsbote, Der, prints BF's *Remarks*, 457 n
Wolfe Tavern (Davenport's Inn), opened, 228 n
Woodbridge, N.J.: Phila. mail to, 401; post office unprofitable, 416
Wool: British ability to export, 183; colonies forced into manufacture, 184; colonial imports unavoidable, 359
Wrangel, Dr. Carl Magnus: confers with Paxton leaders, 73; sends Brycelius to meet Paxton Boys, 73 n
Wright, James: friendship with Shehaes, 46 n; alluded to, 52–3 n
Wright, John (of Hemphill), alluded to, 52–3 n
Wright, John (of London): partner in banking firm, 179 n; friendship with BF, 180 n
Wright, Joseph, absent from Assembly, 393
Wright, Susanna, alluded to, 52–3 n
Wyalusing, Pa.: friendly Indians from, become refugees, 27–31 (*see also* Indians in Philadelphia); Indians found village at, 87 n

Yard, Benjamin, sells fish, 334 n
Yellow fever: outbreaks in Phila., 191; incidence and weather, 191–2
York, Pa.: plans for new postal route, 248; Foxcroft's trip to, 249; Phila. mail to, 401
York Co.: assembly representation, 81–2, 379 n, 382; grievances, 81–3; lacks assemblyman on petition to king, 193; election results, 393; commission for justices in, 522
York (Yorktown), Va.: Elizabeth Holland sought at, 232–3; post-office receipts, 251; Phila. mail to, 402
Young, James: identified, 317 n; pay orders for, 222, 223; sends Bouquet money, 317; letter from, cited, 317 n
Young, William, Jr.: biographical note, 353 n; preferment over Bartram, 352 n, 353

Zeisberger, David, leads Indians from Phila., 87 n